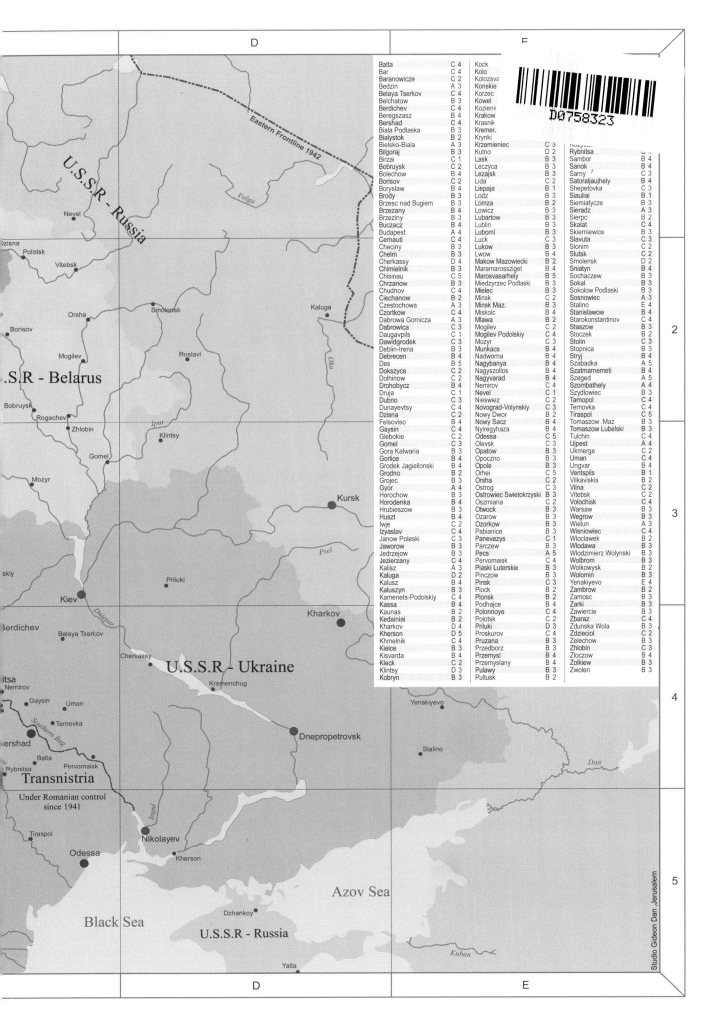

U.S.S.R - Russia

Eastern Frontline 1942

Volga

Nevel

Dzisna

Polotsk

Vitebsk

Smolensk

Kaluga

Orsha

Roslavl

Borisov

Mogilev

U.S.S.R - Belarus

Bobruysk

Rogachev

Zhlobin

Klintsy

Iput

Oka

Gomel

Mozyr

Gomel

Kursk

Psel

Priluki

Kiev

Dnieper

Berdichev

Belaya Tserkov

Cherkassy

U.S.S.R - Ukraine

Kharkov

Kremenchug

itsa

Nemirov

Gaysin

Uman

Yenakiyevo

Ternovka

Southern Bug

Dnepropetrovsk

Stalino

ershad

Balta

Pervomaisk

Don

Rybnitsa

Transnistria

Under Romanian control since 1941

Ingul

Tiraspol

Nikolayev

Kherson

Odessa

Dzhankoy

Azov Sea

Black Sea

U.S.S.R - Russia

Kuban

Yalta

Studio Gideon Dan ,Jerusalem

Balta	C 4	Kock				
Bar	C 4	Kolo				
Baranowicze	C 2	Kolozsva				
Bedzin	A 3	Konskie				
Belaya Tserkov	C 4	Korzec				
Belchatow	B 3	Kowel				
Berdichev	C 4	Kozieni				
Beregszasz	B 4	Krakow				
Bershad	C 4	Krasnik				
Biala Podlaska	B 3	Kremer.				
Bialystok	B 2	Krynki				
Bielsko-Biala	A 3	Krzemieniec	C 3	Rybnitsa	C 4	
Bilgoraj	B 3	Kutno	D 2	Sambor	B 4	
Birzai	C 1	Lask	B 3	Sanok	B 4	
Bobruysk	C 2	Leczyca	B 3	Sarny	C 3	
Bolechow	B 4	Lezajsk	B 3	Satoraljaujhely	B 4	
Borisov	C 2	Lida	C 2	Shepetovka	C 3	
Boryslaw	B 4	Liepaja	B 1	Siauliai	B 1	
Brody	B 3	Lodz	B 3	Siemiatycze	B 3	
Brzesc nad Bugiem	B 3	Lomza	B 2	Sieradz	A 3	
Brzezany	B 4	Lowicz	B 3	Sierpc	B 2	
Brzeziny	B 3	Lubartow	B 3	Skalat	C 4	
Buczacz	B 4	Lublin	B 3	Skierniewice	B 3	
Budapest	A 4	Luboml	B 3	Slavuta	C 3	
Cernauti	C 4	Luck	C 3	Slonim	C 2	
Checiny	B 3	Lukow	B 3	Slutsk	C 2	
Chelm	B 3	Lwow	C 3	Smolensk	D 2	
Cherkassy	D 4	Makow Mazowiecki	B 2	Sniatyn	B 4	
Chimielnik	B 3	Maramarossziget	B 4	Sochaczew	B 3	
Chisinau	C 5	Marosvasarhely	B 5	Sokal	B 3	
Chrzanow	B 3	Miedzyrzec Podlaski	B 3	Sokolow Podlaski	B 3	
Chudnov	C 4	Mielec	B 3	Sosnowiec	A 3	
Ciechanow	B 2	Minsk	C 2	Stalino	E 4	
Czestochowa	A 3	Minsk Maz.	B 3	Stanislawow	B 4	
Czortkow	C 4	Miskolc	B 4	Starokonstantinov	C 4	
Dabrowa Gornicza	A 3	Mlawa	B 2	Staszow	B 3	
Dabrowica	C 3	Mogilev	C 2	Stoczek	B 2	
Daugavpils	C 1	Mogilev Podolskiy	C 4	Stolin	C 3	
Dawidgrodek	C 3	Mozyr	C 3	Stopnica	B 3	
Deblin-Irena	B 3	Munkacs	B 4	Stryj	B 4	
Debrecen	B 4	Nadworna	B 4	Szabadka	A 5	
Des	B 5	Nagybanya	B 4	Szatmarnemeti	B 4	
Dokszyce	C 2	Nagyszollos	B 4	Szeged	A 5	
Dolhinow	C 2	Nagyvarad	B 4	Szombathely	A 4	
Drohobycz	B 4	Nemirov	C 4	Szydlowiec	B 3	
Druja	C 1	Nevel	C 1	Tarnopol	C 4	
Dubno	C 3	Nieswiez	C 2	Ternovka	C 4	
Dunayevtsy	C 4	Novograd-Volynskiy	C 3	Tiraspol	C 5	
Dzisna	C 2	Nowy Dwor	B 2	Tomaszow .Maz	B 3	
Felsoviso	B 4	Nowy Sacz	B 4	Tomaszow Lubelski	B 3	
Gaysin	C 4	Nyiregyhaza	B 4	Tulchin	C 4	
Glebokie	C 2	Odessa	C 5	Ujpest	A 4	
Gomel	C 3	Olevsk	C 3	Ukmerge	C 2	
Gora Kalwaria	B 3	Opatow	B 3	Uman	C 4	
Gorlice	B 4	Opoczno	B 3	Ungvar	B 4	
Grodek Jagiellonski	B 4	Opole	B 3	Ventspils	B 1	
Grodno	B 2	Orhei	C 5	Vilkaviskis	B 2	
Grojec	B 3	Orsha	B 2	Vilna	C 2	
Gyor	A 4	Ostrog	C 3	Vitebsk	C 2	
Horochow	B 3	Ostrowiec Swietokrzyski	B 3	Volochisk	C 4	
Horodenka	B 4	Oszmiana	C 2	Warsaw	B 3	
Hrubieszow	B 3	Otwock	B 3	Wegrow	B 3	
Huszt	B 4	Ozarow	B 3	Wielun	A 3	
Iwje	C 2	Ozorkow	B 3	Wisniowiec	C 4	
Izyaslav	C 4	Pabianice	B 3	Wloclawek	B 2	
Janow Poleski	C 3	Panevezys	C 1	Wlodawa	B 3	
Jaworow	B 3	Parczew	B 3	Wlodzimierz Wolynski	B 3	
Jedrzejow	B 3	Pecs	A 5	Wolbrom	B 3	
Jezierzany	C 4	Pervomaisk	C 4	Wolkowysk	B 2	
Kalisz	A 3	Piaski Luterskie	B 3	Wolomin	B 3	
Kaluga	D 2	Pinczow	B 3	Yenakiyevo	E 4	
Kalusz	B 4	Pinsk	C 3	Zambrow	B 2	
Kaluszyn	B 3	Plock	B 2	Zamosc	B 3	
Kamenets-Podolskiy	C 4	Plonsk	B 2	Zarki	B 3	
Kassa	B 4	Polonnoye	C 4	Zawiercie	C 4	
Kaunas	B 2	Polotsk	C 2	Zbaraz	C 4	
Kedainiai	B 2	Priluki	D 3	Zdunska Wola	B 3	
Kharkov	D 4	Proskurov	C 4	Zdzieciol	C 2	
Kherson	D 5	Pruzana	B 3	Zelechow	C 3	
Khmelnik	C 4	Przedborz	B 3	Zhlobin	C 3	
Kielce	B 3	Przemysl	B 4	Zloczow	B 4	
Kisvarda	B 4	Przemyslany	B 4	Zolkiew	B 3	
Kleck	C 2	Pulawy	B 3	Zwolen	B 3	
Klintsy	D 3	Pultusk	B 2			
Kobryn	B 3					

ENCYCLOPEDIA
OF THE GHETTOS
DURING THE HOLOCAUST

THE YAD VASHEM

ENCYCLOPEDIA
OF THE GHETTOS
DURING THE HOLOCAUST

Editor in Chief **Guy Miron**
Co-editor **Shlomit Shulhani**

VOLUME II
N-Z

Yad Vashem, Jerusalem

THIS PUBLICATION WAS MADE POSSIBLE THROUGH
THE GENEROUS SUPPORT OF:

Claims Conference ועידת התביעות
The Conference on Jewish Material Claims Against Germany

The Lisa and Norbert Schechter Fund

The Tema and Shlomo Kravitz (z"l) Fund
in memory of their family members and the martyrs of the Zhetl and Kowel
communities, who perished in the Holocaust

ISBN 978-965-308-345-5

Printed and bound by Keterpress, Jerusalem, Israel
Produced by Shlomo (Yosh) Gafni, Jerusalem, Israel

Nieśwież ghetto, Poland

"A single tree grows in the ghetto. The only one in the entire ghetto. Near our home. In the spring, it blossoms. I don't know if anyone in the ghetto notices it. More than anything else in the ghetto, it reminds me of life flowing in its channel, the people living all around us willing to accept our deaths, to pursue their happiness on our graves, as if nothing could be more natural than for them to have the right to live and for us—to be killed."

Shalom Cholawski, Beleaguered in Town and Forest *(Moreshet and Sifriat Poalim, 1974), p. 62 [Hebrew].*

NADWÓRNA

COUNTY SEAT, STANISŁAWÓW DISTRICT, POLAND

(After World War II in the USSR/Ukraine; Ukrainian: **Nadvirna**; Russian: **Nadvornaya**)

During the war: General Gouvernement, Galicia District

Coordinates: 48°38' | 24°34'

In the early 1930s, about 3,500 Jews lived in Nadworna, representing approximately half of the townlet's population. Most earned their livelihood from commerce and artisanship. Zionist parties and youth movements were active in Nadworna, as were the Bund and Agudath Israel (with many Hasidic members). Cultural activities in the community included Hebrew courses, a library, and drama circles.

In late September 1939, the Red Army entered Nadworna, and Jewish refugees thronged to the townlet. Under Soviet rule Jewish public life was suspended, private commerce was abolished, large factories were nationalized, and most of the artisans organized into cooperatives. Several Jewish families were murdered by the anti-Soviet Ukrainian underground.

On July 1, 1941, Nadworna was occupied by the Hungarians (allies of the Germans). A number of Jewish public leaders formed a council and called on the Hungarian military government to put an end the terrorization of Jews by Ukrainians, to no avail. In mid-July, the Ukrainians carried out a pogrom and murdered dozens of Jews. A few weeks later, about 1,000 Jewish deportees were transferred to Nadworna from Hungary (Carpatho-Ruthenia).

In September 1941, the townlet was handed over to the Germans. A Judenrat headed by Dr. Maximilian Schell and his deputy Yitzhak Shapira was established. Jews were ordered to wear a Star-of-David armband and a number were seized for forced labor. The terrorization and murders by Ukrainians continued all the while.

On October 6, 1941, a mass operation was carried out in Nadworna during which about 2,000 Jews, many of them children, women, and the elderly, were murdered in pits near Bukowinka. Among those murdered were Jews from surrounding localities and refugees from Hungary (Carpatho-Ruthenia). The Germans permitted the Jews to cover the pits, fence them in, and recite the *Kaddish* prayer for the murder victims. The apartments of the murder victims and their contents were turned over to the German authorities and to Ukrainian families. Following the murder operation, the Jews attempted to obtain work permits in places considered vital to the German economy. About 600 Jews worked in a sawmill daily.

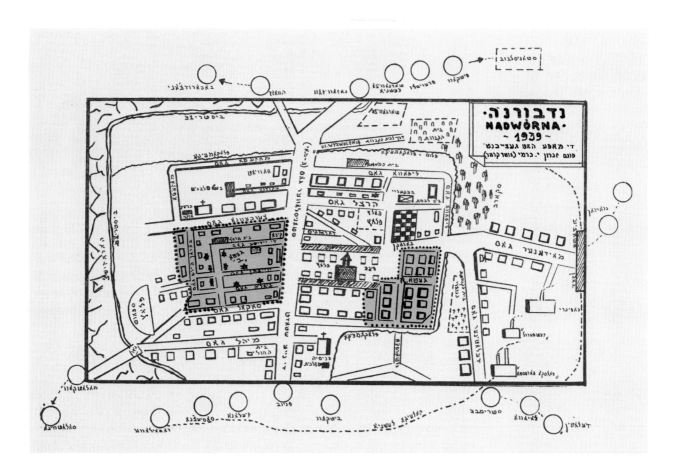

Nadworna scheme indicating ghettos boundaries, illustrated by Y. Karmi (Otto Kramer), based on his memory

(*Nadwórna Memorial and Records Book,* published by the Landsmanshaft of Nadwornian Jews in Israel and America, 1975)

In April 1942, about 3,600 Jews lived in Nadworna. On April 30, 1942, the Jews were confined in two sealed ghettos. Those considered fit for work and who were employed in vital factories were moved into Ghetto A, while those considered unfit for work were moved into Ghetto B. Soon thereafter, hunger and disease spread throughout the ghettos, taking many lives. In ghetto B, a hospital was established, most of whose patients were periodically removed by German and Ukrainian policemen and murdered, as well as an orphanage; many of the children starved to death due to a lack of rations. The Judenrat endeavored to organize help for the needy but were unable to effectively cope with the demand. In May–June 1942, yet more Jews from the area were concentrated in the ghettos. In August 1942, a number of Judenrat members, with Maximilian Schell at their head, were taken to Gestapo headquarters in Stanislawow*. They were interrogated while tortured for allowing groups of Jews to leave the ghetto for work in Stryj* without permission from the Gestapo. The interrogation was conducted against the backdrop of discord between the various German authorities. The Judenrat members were returned to the ghetto, which was required to pay a large ransom.

In the summer and fall of 1942, attempts by Jews to escape from the ghetto were stepped up. A number of people fled to nearby forests, but most were denounced or murdered by local citizens; several groups of Jews fled to Hungary. In the ghetto, the Milbauer brothers forged and sold false "Aryan" documents.

In September 1942, several hundred Jews were removed from Nadworna and sent to their deaths in operations in Stanislawow. The Nadworna ghetto was liquidated on October 24, 1942, when several of its inhabitants were murdered in it, while others were transferred to Stanislawow and killed. The few dozen artisans remaining in Ghetto A were executed in November 1942, in a nearby forest.

NAGYBÁNYA

TOWN IN SZATMÁR COUNTY, HUNGARY
(After World War II in Romania; Romanian: **Baia Mare**)

Coordinates:
47°40' | 23°35'

The last national census conducted in Hungary prior to the German occupation, taken in January 1941, recorded 3,623 Jewish inhabitants in Nagybanya, accounting for roughly 17 percent of the total population. Most were merchants and artisans and several were factory owners. The town's Jewish community was Orthodox and maintained a Talmud Torah, a Yeshiva, and other Jewish social and religious institutions.

After World War I, Nagybanya, which was formerly in Hungary, became part of Romania. On August 30, 1940, Nagybanya became once again an integral part of the Hungarian civil administration. The Hungarian anti-Jewish legislation that applied to the local Jews was enforced more harshly in North Transylvania, where the town was located, than in inner Hungary.

In 1940, a drafting center for forced labor service within the Hungarian army was established in Nagybanya, commanded by the militant antisemite Lieutenant Colonel Telek. Jewish men were required to report to the center. Many forced laborers were deployed to the Ukraine through to the spring of 1943. In May 1943, Lieutenant Colonel Imre Reviczky was appointed commander of the drafting center. He saved the lives of about 3,000 Jews, drafting Jews for forced labor service occasionally from the ghetto as well, to save them from deportation.

The German army occupied Hungary on March 19, 1944. A census conducted in the second week of April 1944 reported that 3,340 Jews belonged to the Orthodox Jewish community of Nagybanya.

On the night of April 4, 1944, fifty wealthy Jews from the town were arrested and, following a short period of local imprisonment, transferred to the internment camp in Kistarcsa. They were deported on to Auschwitz.

The Hungarian administration remained intact and in force after the occupation. The ghettoization and deportation of the Jews were implemented on the basis of the decrees and orders of the Hungarian national and local authorities. According to a local conference in late April or early May 1944, two ghettos were established in Nagybanya on May 3, 1944. The town ghetto was established in the Bernat iron and metal-ware factory. Dr. Jeno Nagy, the head of the central police station of Nagybanya, and Gyula Gergely, the North Transylvanian leader of the Arrow Cross Party, directed the process of the ghettoization of the Jews of Nagybanya with SS-Hauptsturmfuehrer Franz Abromeith serving as a consultant. Some 100 people had shelter, while the others lived in the open. Likewise on May 3, a ghetto was established for about 2,000 Jews from the vicinity, the county-districts of Nagybanya, Nagysomkut, and Kapolnokmonostor, in a stable and in the granary of the Molcsany estate near the town. About 200 inhabitants were lodged in the farm buildings. The men from the town ghetto were assigned to work on the Molcsany estate.

The great synagogue was turned into a hospital for the two ghettos. A Jewish Council operated in the ghettos. The Hungarian chief commander of the ghettos was gendarme commander Tibor Varhelyi. In both ghettos, policemen under the leadership of Jeno Nagy and Gyula Gergely tortured the Jews to ascertain the whereabouts of their hidden valuables. Several people committed suicide.

On May 20, 1944, the gendarmes brought about 400 forced laborers from among those working in Nagybanya into the ghetto, during the absence of Lieutenant Colonel Reviczky, the commander of the drafting center.

The inhabitants of the two ghettos were deported in two transports to Auschwitz on May 31 and June 5, 1944. It is possible that the patients in the hospital were killed by the Hungarian forces guarding the ghetto, prior to the deportations. Several local gentiles hid Jews from the time of the ghettoization until liberation.

NAGYKANIZSA

TOWN IN ZALA COUNTY, HUNGARY

Coordinates:
46°27' | 16°59'

The last national census conducted prior to the German occupation, taken in January 1941, recorded 2,091 Jewish inhabitants in Nagykanizsa, roughly 7 percent of the total population. Most of the Jews were merchants and artisans. Several Jewish landowners also lived in the town. The town's Jewish community was Neolog and maintained a Jewish elementary school and various Jewish social and religious associations. Nagykanizsa was the first Jewish community in Hungary to use an organ during synagogue services.

From 1938, the Hungarian government introduced a series of anti-Jewish laws as part of Hungary's anti-Jewish policy. In 1941, school students in Nagykanizsa were required to wear yellow armbands. That year, Jewish men were drafted into the Hungarian army for forced labor service. A number of them stayed in the country, others were transferred to the Ukraine, while still others were sent to the infamous copper mines of Bor in Serbia.

In 1942, an internment camp was established in the town that held many Jews from throughout Hungary accused of financial crimes. The Jewish community supplied the inmates with kosher food.

The German army occupied Hungary on March 19, 1944. Following the German occupation of Hungary, the SS, headed by local commander Hornicke, expropriated several Jewish houses, dissolved the Jewish community, and created a Jewish Council. A census conducted in the second week of April 1944 showed that 1,830 Jews belonged to the Neolog Jewish community of Nagykanizsa

The Hungarian administration remained intact and operational after the German occupation. The ghettoization and deportation of the Jews were carried out on the basis of the decrees and orders of the Hungarian national and local authorities. Nagykanizsa was located within the territory declared a zone of hostilities by the Hungarian authorities at the beginning of April 1944. As a consequence, the town underwent an earlier ghettoization process: at dawn on April 26, 1944, the Jews from Nagykanizsa and its vicinity, about 3,000 people, were concentrated in the synagogue and in other buildings of the Jewish community of Nagykanizsa. In addition, hundreds of Jews were brought to Nagykanizsa from elsewhere in the "zone of hostilities," including Nagyatad and the county-district of Nagyatad in Somogy County. The transfer of the Jews was carried out by the police under the command of chief of police Jeno Bukky. Hungarian gendarmes also brought the Jews to Nagykanizsa from the countryside. Three Jews committed suicide on the night of their transfer. The concentration of the Jews was completed by April 28, 1944. The local Jews were housed in the grand synagogue and nearby buildings. They were permitted to leave the ghetto accompanied by a police escort and solely for important reasons, for example to purchase food. The Jews who were brought to Nagykanizsa from the countryside were lodged in the school of agriculture, the school of commerce, the kindergarten, and the old-age home.

On April 29, 1944, about 800 men aged sixteen to sixty were selected for work and were later deported to Auschwitz. The rest of the Jews remained until mid-May 1944, starving and in severely overcrowded conditions. The local authorities supplied food to the ghetto once a day, but in quantities insufficient for a single daily meal per person.

The president of the Jewish Council of the ghetto was a lawyer, Dr. Jeno Halphen, the last serving president of the Jewish community. The ghetto had no hospital and suffered an acute shortage of medicine. A physician among the interned Jews, Dr. Bela Roth, cared for the sick.

On May 6, 1944, Jews from the Alsolendva and Csaktornya settlements were transferred to Nagykanizsa. The inhabitants of the ghetto of Muraszombat* (Vas County) were also brought to Nagykanizsa in May.

On May 17, 1944, the Jewish Council was ordered to submit to the authorities a list of the names of the ghetto inhabitants along with detailed descriptions of their possessions. On the following day, the Jews were deported to Auschwitz.

NAGYKÁROLY

TOWN IN SZATMÁR COUNTY, HUNGARY
(After World War II in Romania; Romanian: **Carei Mare**).

Coordinates:
47°41' | 22°28'

The last national census conducted in Hungary prior to the German occupation, taken in January 1941, recorded 2,255 Jewish inhabitants in Nagykaroly, accounting for approximately 14 percent of the total population. Most were merchants and artisans, but several were also owners of factories and farms. The town had Orthodox and Status Quo Ante Jewish communities; the latter became Orthodox in 1922. Jewish social and religious associations included two schools, a Talmud Torah, and a Yeshiva.

After World War I, Nagykaroly, which was formerly in Hungary, became part of Romania. On August 30, 1940, Nagykaroly became an integral part of the Hungarian civil administration again. The Hungarian anti-Jewish legislation that applied to the local Jews was enforced more harshly in North Transylvania, where the town was located, than in inner Hungary.

In the summer of 1941, the Hungarian authorities deported to German-occupied Ukraine two Jewish families whose members could not prove their Hungarian citizenship. They were murdered on August 27 or 28 at Kamenets-Podolsk*.

In 1942, about 150 Jewish men from Nagykaroly between the ages of twenty-one and forty-five were drafted into the Hungarian army for forced labor service. Most were deployed to the eastern front in the Ukraine, where the vast majority perished. Also in 1942, the local police raided the synagogues of the town on a Sabbath. Those who did not immediately produce their documents were beaten and tortured in the police station. In 1943, Hungarian soldiers billeted in the Jewish school broke into the synagogues, damaged the property and their contents, and desecrated the Torah scrolls.

The German army occupied Hungary on March 19, 1944. The Hungarian administration remained intact and in force after the occupation. The ghettoization and deportation of the Jews were implemented on the basis of the decrees and orders of the Hungarian national and local authorities. Following a conference held on April 26, 1944, regarding the process of ghettoization in North Transylvania, the local authorities planned the ghettoization of the Jews in Nagykaroly.

The ghetto for the approximately 2,000 Jews of the town and its vicinity was established by order of the mayor on May 3, 1944. The Jews were confined in the Barany house and in the storage buildings of a disused paper factory, where they lay on the bare floor of a warehouse with a roof full of holes. Jozsef Bujdoso was the official commander of the ghetto, but in practice, in charge were his subordinates: Istvan Marozsan and Ferenc Balintfi, the leaders of the youth organization of the Arrow Cross Party. The Barany house, meanwhile, was commanded by Istvan Torok, a member of the Arrow Cross Party. All of the Jews were subjected to a thorough body search upon arrival in the ghetto.

A Jewish Council operated in the ghetto; one of its members was Dr. Istvan Antal (a former president of the Status Quo Ante Jewish community). The ghetto existed for eleven days. Its inhabitants were transferred to the Szatmarnemeti* ghetto on May 13, 1944. The overwhelming majority of the Jews from the Nagykaroly ghetto were deported to Auschwitz in the first transport that left Szatmarnemeti on May 19, 1944.

NAGYKÁTA

TOWN IN PEST-PILIS-SOLT-KISKUN COUNTY, HUNGARY

Coordinates:
47°25' | 19°45'

The last national census conducted prior to the German occupation, taken in January 1941, recorded 214 Jewish inhabitants in Nagykata, accounting for roughly 2 percent of the total population. Most were merchants and vine-growers. The Neolog Jewish community in the town ran a Jewish school.

In 1940, Nagykata became a drafting center for forced labor service in the Hungarian army; Jewish men were called up to serve. Tens of thousands of forced laborers from Budapest* and the surrounding area were deployed from the Nagykata drafting center. At the beginning of 1944, the local authorities closed down the synagogue, claiming that the building was not safe.

The German army occupied Hungary on March 19, 1944. A census conducted in the second week of April 1944 reported that 203 Jews lived in Nagykata.

The Hungarian administration remained intact and operational after the German occupation. The ghettoization and deportation of the Jews occurred on the basis of decrees and orders issues by the Hungarian national and local authorities. On May 12, the Hungarian sub-prefect Dr. Laszlo Endre, a militant antisemite, ordered the establishment of ghettos in his county. The ghetto in Nagykata was established along two streets, accommodating altogether 628 Jews from Nagykata and from the county-districts of Gyomro and Nagykata. Rabbi Soma Breuer and Imre Szekely, the last serving president of the Jewish community, were among the five members of the Jewish Council.

On June 18, 1944, the inhabitants of the Nagykata ghetto were transferred to the copper factory in Kecskemet*, which served as an entrainment center. They were deported along with many other Jews to Auschwitz on June 25 and 27, 1944.

NAGYKŐRÖS

TOWN IN PEST-PILIS-SOLT-KISKUN COUNTY, HUNGARY

Coordinates:
47°02' | 19°47'

The last national census conducted prior to the German occupation, taken in January 1941, recorded 478 Jewish inhabitants in Nagykoros, accounting for approximately 2 percent of the total population. Most traded in agricultural produce. The town's Jewish community was Neolog and maintained a Jewish school, and various Jewish social and religious associations. During the White Terror following World War I, members of the "detachments"—semi-military units—murdered five local Jews.

The German army occupied Hungary on March 19, 1944. A census conducted in the second week of April 1944 showed that 375 Jews belonged to the Neolog Jewish community of Nagykoros.

After the German occupation, the Hungarian administration remained intact and operational. The ghettoization and deportation of the Jews occurred on the basis of decrees and orders issues by the Hungarian national and local authorities. On May 12, the Hungarian sub-prefect, Dr. Laszlo Endre, a militant antisemite, ordered the establishment of ghettos in his county. The move into the ghettos began at five o'clock in the morning on May 22, 1944. The 352 Jewish residents of Nagykoros were ordered to move into the local ghetto.

On approximately June 20, 1944, the inhabitants of the Nagykoros ghetto were transferred to the copper factory in Kecskemet*, which served as an entrainment center. They were deported along with many other Jews to Auschwitz on June 25 and 27, 1944.

NAGYMEGYER

TOWNLET IN KOMÁROM COUNTY, HUNGARY
(After World War II in Czechoslovakia/Slovakia; Slovak: **Velký Meder**)

Coordinates:
47°52' | 17°46'

The last national census conducted prior to the German occupation, taken in January 1941, recorded 522 Jewish inhabitants in Nagymegyer, accounting for approximately 12 percent of the total population. Most were merchants and artisans. The town's Jewish community was Orthodox and maintained a Jewish elementary school. After World War I, Nagymegyer (which was formerly in Hungary) became part of Czechoslovakia. In the interwar period, the Jewish Party had the widest support among the Jewish parties in the townlet. Agudath Israel established a local branch.

As a consequence of the First Vienna Award in November 1938, the townlet once again became part of Hungary. The Hungarian authorities expelled through the new Slovakian-Hungarian border several Jewish families whose members did not have Hungarian citizenship.

The German army occupied Hungary on March 19, 1944. A census conducted in the second week of April 1944 showed that 549 Jews belonged to the Orthodox Jewish community of Nagymegyer.

The Hungarian administration remained intact and operational after the German occupation. The ghettoization and deportation of the Jews occurred on the basis of the decrees and orders of the Hungarian national and local authorities. The Nagymegyer ghetto was established in early May 1944.

At the beginning of June 1944, all of the inhabitants of the ghetto, including local Jews as well as Jews from neighboring settlements, were transferred to an estate outside Nagymegyer. They were sent on to the entrainment center in Komarom* on June 5, 1944. On June 15, 1944, they were added to the second transport from Dunaszerdahely*, which left for Auschwitz.

NAGYSURÁNY

TOWNLET IN POZSONY-NYITRA COUNTY, HUNGARY
(After World War II in Czechoslovakia/Slovakia; Slovak: **Šurany**)

Coordinates:
48°05' | 18°11'

In 1941, 563 Jewish inhabitants lived in Nagysurany, accounting for approximately 9 percent of the total population. Most of the Jews were merchants and artisans. The town's Jewish community was Orthodox and maintained a Jewish elementary school and a Yeshiva. After World War I, Nagysurany (which was formerly in Hungary) became part of Czechoslovakia. In the interwar period, Agudath Israel was the most popular Jewish organization in Nagysurany. The Jewish Party was active as well.

As a result of the First Vienna Award in November 1938, Nagysurany became part of Hungary again. The Hungarian authorities expelled through the new Slovakian-Hungarian border several Jewish families whose members did not have Hungarian citizenship.

In 1941, Jewish men, including many of the local Yeshiva students, were drafted into the Hungarian army for forced labor service. The Yeshiva was reduced considerably in size, with only several dozen students remaining.

In 1942, when the Jews were deported from Slovakia, a Jewish group in Nagysurany helped Jews to escape from Slovakia to Hungary. A few members of this group were apprehended by the gendarmes and deported.

The German army occupied Hungary on March 19, 1944. A census conducted in the second week of April 1944 recorded that 524 Jews belonged to the Jewish community of Nagysurany.

The Hungarian administration remained intact and operational after the German occupation. The Nagysurany ghetto, which was established in late May 1944 according to national and local decrees of the Hungarian administration, was located in the vicinity of the great synagogue and the Jewish school. In addition to local Jews, Jewish inhabitants from the County-District of Ersekujvar were concentrated in the ghetto, which was very crowded, with five to six people to a room. A soup kitchen was established in the ghetto. A few people escaped from the ghetto and joined the partisans in Slovakia.

On June 10, 1944, the 1,115 Jews living in the ghetto were transferred to the Kurzweil brick factory in Ersekujvar*, which served as an entrainment center. On June 14, 1944, they were deported to Auschwitz.

NAGYSZŐLLŐS

TOWN IN UGOCSA COUNTY, HUNGARY
(After World War II in the USSR/Ukraine; Ukrainian: **Vinogradiv**; Russian: **Vinogradov**)

Coordinates:
48°09' | 23°02'

The last national census conducted in Hungary prior to the German occupation, taken in January 1941, recorded 4,264 Jewish inhabitants in Nagyszollos, accounting for roughly 32 percent of the total population. Most were merchants and artisans, but many were also clerks or members of the free professions. The town's Jewish community was Orthodox.

After World War I, Nagyszollos, which was formerly in Hungary, became part of Czechoslovakia. Once Nagyszollos became an integral part of the Hungarian civil administration in mid-March 1939, it was subject to the Hungarian anti-Jewish legislation that applied to the local Jews and that was implemented more harshly than in inner Hungary.

Beginning in 1940, many Jewish men were drafted into the Hungarian army for forced labor service. In 1940, they were assigned to work in Hungary, but from 1942, the majority of the forced laborers were deployed to the eastern front, in the Ukraine, where many perished.

In the summer of 1941, the Hungarian authorities declared dozens of Jewish families whose members could not prove their Hungarian citizenship to be stateless and deported them to German-occupied Ukraine. They were murdered on August 27 or 28 at Kamenets-Podolsk*.

The German army occupied Hungary on March 19, 1944. A census conducted in the second week of April 1944 reported that 4,607 Jews belonged to the Orthodox Jewish community of Nagyszollos.

The Hungarian administration remained intact and in force after the occupation. The ghettoization and deportation of the Jews were implemented on the basis of the decrees and orders of the Hungarian national and local authorities. Following an April 12, 1944, conference concerning ghettoization with Laszlo Endre, the undersecretary of state for internal affairs, held for the administrative leaders of Carpatho-Ruthenia, ghettoization in Nagyszollos was launched on April 16, 1944. The ghetto was established along five streets in the vicinity of the synagogue for the local Jews and the Jews of Ugocsa County. Altogether, 12,000 to 14,000 Jews lived in the ghetto.

A Jewish Council operated in the ghetto, one of whose members was Emil (Mendl) Wuerzberger, previously a mill owner and the last serving president of the Jewish community. A hospital was set up in Dr. Leszmann's house.

Baron Zsigmond Perenyi, the former governmental commissioner in Carpatho-Ruthenia and president of the Upper House of Parliament, along with his son, who had his estates in Ugocsa, assisted the Jews in the ghetto, for instance by supplying them with food.

The inhabitants of the ghetto of Nagyszollos, which also served as the entrainment center of Ugocsa County, were deported to Auschwitz in three transports between May 19 and the beginning of June 1944.

NAGYVÁRAD

(in Jewish sources: **Grosswardein**)

CITY IN BIHAR COUNTY, HUNGARY
(After World War II in Romania; Romanian: **Oradea**)

Coordinates:
47°04' | 21°56'

The last national census conducted in Hungary prior to the German occupation, taken in January 1941, recorded 21,333 Jewish inhabitants in Nagyvarad, accounting for approximately 23 percent of the total population. Most were merchants and artisans, but many were also clerks or practiced free professions. Active in the city were both Neolog and Orthodox Jewish communities (the latter included a Hasidic group). Each of the communities ran several schools and the Orthodox also had a Yeshiva. During World War I, Hasidic rabbis moved into the city along with their courts.

After World War I, Nagyvarad, which was formerly in Hungary, became part of Romania. On December 4–6, 1927, Romanian university students broke into Jewish shops, homes, and several synagogues causing great damage and also beat Jews in the streets. Zionism, not previously popular in the city, began to gain some ground.

Nagyvarad once again became an integral part of the Hungarian civil administration on August 30, 1940; the Hungarian anti-Jewish legislation was enforced more harshly in North Transylvania, where the city was located, than in inner Hungary. As of 1940, many Jewish men were drafted into the Hungarian army for forced labor service. From 1942, most of the laborers, about 500 Jews from Nagyvarad, were deployed to the Ukraine, where many perished.

In the summer of 1941, the Hungarian authorities deported to German-occupied Ukraine several Jewish families whose members could not prove their Hungarian citizenship. They were murdered on August 27 or 28 at Kamenets-Podolsk*.

The German army occupied Hungary on March 19, 1944. A census conducted in the second week of April 1944 showed that about 16,000 Jews belonged to the Orthodox Jewish community and about 4,500 Jews belonged to the Neolog Jewish community of Nagyvarad.

The SS units posted in Nagyvarad from the end of March 1944 inundated the Jews with demands, including the establishment of a Jewish Council. However, the ghettoization and deportation of the Jews in Nagyvarad were implemented on the basis of the decrees and orders of the Hungarian national and local authorities.

On April 30, 1944, the administrative leaders of the city held a meeting concerning the practical issues of ghettoization in the presence of Laszlo Endre, the undersecretary of state for internal affairs, and SS-Hauptsturmfuehrer Theodor Dannecker, the local representative of Eichmann. Dr. Istvan Soos, the mayor of Nagyvarad, resigned in protest and did not participate.

The decree ordering the ghettoization in Nagyvarad signed by the deputy mayor of the city, Dr. Laszlo Gyapay, was published on May 2, 1944. In Bihar County, the Hungarian sub-prefect, Dr. Janos Nadanyi, ordered the ghettoization of the Jews, and the Hungarian gendarme Lieutenant Colonel Jeno Peterffy directed the process.

On May 3, 1944, two ghettos were established in Nagyvarad, the "main ghetto" for the approximately 27,000 Jews of the city (the largest ghetto in Hungary after Budapest), and a smaller ghetto for the nearly 8,000 Jews from Bihar County. The main ghetto was established in the neighborhood most densely populated by Jews, in the vicinity of the Orthodox great synagogue. The Jews of Nagyvarad were required to move into the ghetto within five days. It was severely overcrowded, with fourteen to fifteen people to a room. Food supplies were insufficient and the city authorities frequently turned off the electricity and the water in the ghetto for extended periods. The smaller ghetto was established in the suburbs in a farmstead and in the Mezey lumberyard; its living conditions were dire. The inhabitants received seventy grams of bread daily, a ration of soup at midday, and coffee in the evening.

When the main ghetto was established, Gyapay appointed a new Jewish Council headed by Sandor Leitner, a merchant and the last serving president of the Orthodox Jewish community. A Jewish Order Service led by Izsak Pasztor and Jeno Pasztor also operated in the main ghetto. Jewish physicians attended to the medical needs of the ghetto inhabitants. A hospital was established in the synagogue of the Vizhnitzer rabbi.

The situation in the ghetto radically deteriorated from May 10 onward, when Jeno Peterffy and his gendarmes took over guarding the ghetto. On that same day, Peterffy published a notice entitled "Discipline in the Ghetto," in which he introduced numerous penal measures. A gendarme unit consisting of forty gendarmes tortured the Jews into revealing the whereabouts of their hidden valuables. The torture was conducted in the "mint" in the Dreher brewery. Many people committed suicide either to escape torture or as a consequence of it.

The Jews from the smaller ghetto, together with about 300 Jews from the main ghetto, were deported to Auschwitz on May 24, 1944. The Jews from the main ghetto were deported to Auschwitz on May 28, 29, 31, and June 1 and 3.

Several Jews escaped from the ghetto and crossed the border to Romania. Dr. Miksa Kupfer, a leading gynecologist at the Jewish hospital, attempted to save the last transport of about 3,000 Jews from deportation by simulating a typhoid epidemic that would necessitate immediate quarantine. While Kupfer's action did not thwart the last transport, it did bring about the establishment of the hospital for infectious diseases. As a consequence, nine former forced laborers faking typhoid fever, along with their families, about eighty people, were saved from deportation. Most of these families later managed to escape from the ghetto.

NARAJÓW

TOWN IN BRZEŻANY COUNTY, TARNOPOL DISTRICT, POLAND

(After World War II in the USSR/Ukraine; Ukrainian: **Narayiv**; Russian: **Naraev**)

During the war: General Gouvernement, Galicia District

Coordinates:
49°32' | 24°46'

In the 1930s, about 800 Jews lived in Narajow, representing approximately one-quarter of the townlet's population. They earned their livelihood from petty commerce, artisanship, and farming. Various Jewish political organizations, including Zionist parties, were active in Narajow, as were youth movements.

In mid-September 1939, the Soviets entered Narajow. Under their control, the Jewish parties and community institutions were disbanded, private commerce was abolished, large factories were nationalized, and most of the artisans were organized into cooperatives.

On July 1, 1941, Narajow was occupied by the Germans. Within a short time, Ukrainian police began to seize Jews from their homes for forced labor, amid humiliation and abuse. Their primary targets for attack were Jews who were considered sympathetic to the Soviet authorities. The Jews were ordered to wear an armband and were forbidden to engage in any commerce with non-Jews; young men started to be sent to labor camps. On German orders, a Judenrat headed by community figure Turno and a Jewish Order Service were established. From the fall of 1941 to the spring of 1942, additional Jews from surrounding localities arrived in Narajow as well as about 300 Jews from Brzezany*, who fled in fear of an impending operation. By April 1942, the Jewish population had grown to over 1,400.

On September 22, 1942, two trucks filled with policemen arrived from Tarnopol*, along with members of the Jewish Order Service from Brzezany. Narajow was encircled, and close to 1,000 Jews were rounded up and taken to Brzezany, where they were added to a deportation train leaving for the Belzec death camp.

Following the operation, the approximately 500 Jews who remained in the townlet were rounded up in a ghetto, which contained a few narrow alleyways. The ghetto was liquidated in late November or early December 1942, when its inhabitants were deported to the Brzezany ghetto, nearly all of whose inhabitants were murdered in an operation carried out in the early days of December. A few survivors returned to Brzezany, but they were hunted down by the Ukrainian police and shot by the Gestapo.

NEMIROV

(Ukrainian: **Nemyriv**)

COUNTY SEAT, VINNITSA DISTRICT, UKRAINE, USSR

During the war: Reichskommissariat Ukraine

Coordinates:
48°58' | 28°51'

In the mid-1920s, there were 4,000 Jews in Nemirov, roughly half of the townlet's population. As employment prospects changed under Soviet rule, many Jews took white- and blue-collar jobs. After private commerce was abolished in the early 1930s, Jewish artisans formed cooperatives or took up farming. The community's children were educated at a government school that taught in Yiddish. In 1936, Jewish youths continued to attend services in the local synagogue. Shortly before the German invasion of the Soviet Union, there were 3,000 Jews in Nemirov, more than one-third of the townlet's total population.

The Germans occupied Nemirov on July 22, 1941, and promptly assigned Jews to forced labor. One month later, they concentrated the Jews in a barbed-wire enclosed ghetto formed along three alleys. At ten to twelve people per room, the ghetto was densely crowded. Jews were required to wear a Star-of-David armband. Adult inhabitants were assigned to daily forced labor in the townlet. On August 7, 1941, the Germans ordered the community to remit a ransom in the form of money and jewelry.

On November 7 or 24, 1941 (sources vary on the date), 2,680 Jews (nearly all of the ghetto's inhabitants) were summoned to the great synagogue and brought to a brick factory, where they were murdered by an SS unit and buried in pits. The number of murders was only half of that planned, owing to the intervention of Willi Ahrem, a senior official with the Todt Organization, which was building bridges and roads in the area. Ahrem saved Jews by claiming that he required them for urgent work. He also concealed in his cellar members of a family that he had befriended, and later personally delivered to the west bank of the Bug River, to join relatives in the Romanian-controlled Dzhurin* ghetto.

After the first operation, the only Jews remaining in the townlet were skilled workers, their families, and several people who had hidden in the ghetto or with local Ukrainians. In the winter of 1941/42, a group of Jews was transferred from Nemirov to the Bratslav* ghetto, where they performed various services for the Wehrmacht until their murder.

In the second operation (June 26–27, 1942), the Jews were gathered in the great synagogue. Those unfit for labor were removed, trucked to a pit near the townlet, and murdered. On the grounds of the synagogue, the Germans established a labor camp for the 250 young men and women who had survived the operation. All Jews who were captured in the area of Nemirov, including children and the elderly, were sent to the camp, which was surrounded by barbed wire and guarded by Ukrainian and Lithuanian sentries. On August 19, 1942, some 360 Jews from Bessarabia and Bukovina were brought in as well. The prisoners were assigned to road construction. Epidemics and severe conditions claimed the lives of many of the camp residents.

On September 3, 1942, all 160 elderly people and children in the labor camp were murdered. An additional operation was conducted in December 1942, and on February 5, 1943, all camp inmates who were not working were killed. The last remaining Jewish prisoners, about 250 in number, were murdered on May 8, 1943.

NEVEL

COUNTY SEAT, KALININ DISTRICT, RUSSIAN FEDERATION, USSR

During the war: Military Administration Area

Coordinates:
56°00' | 29°59'

Nevel was an important Hasidic center prior to the Bolshevik Revolution. In the mid-1920s, altogether 6,000 Jews lived in the town, accounting for nearly half of the total population. The trend toward industrialization and urbanization in the Soviet Union, however, caused the Jewish population to dwindle to just over 3,000 people by the eve of World War II. Many worked in a local factory; others engaged in crafts and agriculture. Until 1939, the Jews of Nevel had a government school that taught in Yiddish.

In early July 1941, Nevel came under German aerial bombardment, setting in motion a concerted mass escape. By the time the Germans occupied Nevel on July 16, most Jews had evidently managed to flee from the town or had been evacuated to the east.

On August 7, 1941, the remaining Jews in Nevel were ordered to report to the town square. They were marched to Golubaya Dacha, a resort area on the outskirts of town that the Germans had earmarked for the establishment of a ghetto. A number of the inhabitants lived in shacks and mud huts in the ghetto area. That month, some 800 to 1000 Jewish townspeople and refugees from Vitebsk* and surrounding localities were concentrated in the area. Another approximately 200 Jews were interned on the Petino estate, where some may have lived before the war. The ghettoized Jews remained in contact with the local population when they left the ghetto to obtain food or to carry out various jobs outside its confines. Jewish girls, for example, were employed to clean the local prison.

On September 4, 1941, the Judenrat of Nevel, acting at the Germans' behest, prepared a list of all inhabitants of the ghetto. That day, the Germans murdered seventy-four Jewish men whom they accused of arson. The ghetto was liquidated several days later, evidently on September 6. (German sources confirm that the liquidation of the ghetto took place during September 1941.) First, the men were marched out of the ghetto and forced to dig pits, into which they were shot. Afterwards, the women and children were led out and shot to death. The Jews in Petino met the same fate. According to Soviet sources, some 2,000 people were murdered in Nevel.

NIEBYLEC

VILLAGE IN RZESZÓW COUNTY, LWÓW DISTRICT, POLAND

During the war: General Gouvernement, Cracow District

Coordinates:
49°52' | 21°54'

About 280 Jews lived in Niebylec, representing approximately half of the locality's population. The Jews largely engaged in farming and commerce and had access to support by the JDC and free-loan society aid. In 1919, over seventy Jews were injured and six were murdered in pogroms carried out by Polish peasants.

Niebylec was occupied by the Germans on September 12, 1939. In late 1939, a Judenrat was appointed and operated alongside a JSS chapter that assisted the needy. In February 1942, about 100 people were supported by this chapter.

In late 1941 or early 1942, the Jewish neighborhood of Niebylec was officially declared a ghetto, as with other localities throughout the Rzeszow County. The ghetto was not fenced in, but the Jews were forbidden to leave its grounds without permits from the German employment bureau or the police station in Strzyzow*. On April 14, 1942, seventeen Jews were shot by Gestapo men.

The Niebylec ghetto was liquidated in July 1942, and all its inhabitants were deported to the Rzeszow* ghetto, and from there to the Belzec death camp.

NIEŚWIEŻ

COUNTY SEAT, NOWOGRÓDEK DISTRICT, POLAND

(After World War II in the USSR/Belarus; Belarussian: **Nyasvizh**; Russian: **Nesvizh**)

During the war: Reichskommissariat Ostland

Coordinates:
53°13' | 26°40'

About 3,400 Jews were living in Nieswiez when World War II broke out, representing close to half of the townlet's population. Most earned their livelihood from small commerce and artisanship. Zionist parties and youth movements, Agudath Israel, and the Bund were active in the townlet, as was the Communist party. Children attended a Tarbut Hebrew school and a Yiddish school.

After Nieswiez was occupied by the Soviets in the second half of September 1939, the townlet's economy was nationalized and Jewish political life ceased.

By the time the Germans occupied Nieswiez on June 28, 1941, the Jewish population had grown to about 4,600 people, owing to the large number of refugees that inundated the townlet. Almost immediately, the Jews were ordered to wear a yellow badge, their freedom of movement was restricted, and they were seized for forced labor. Terrorization and abuse became daily occurrences. The Germans appointed a Judenrat headed by an attorney named Megalif, a refugee from Warsaw*.

On October 30, 1941, an operation was carried out in Nieswiez. Following a selection, some 600 people with required professions and their families were separated from the townlet's approximately 4,000 Jewish inhabitants, who were murdered.

The following day, the skilled workers were rounded up in the synagogue area under overcrowded conditions. The area was turned into a ghetto and surrounded with a barbed-wire fence. The workers were employed at hard labor outside the ghetto or in workshops within its grounds. The local Judenrat endeavored to regulate work and life in the ghetto and to distribute food in an organized manner. A Jewish Order Service was also established.

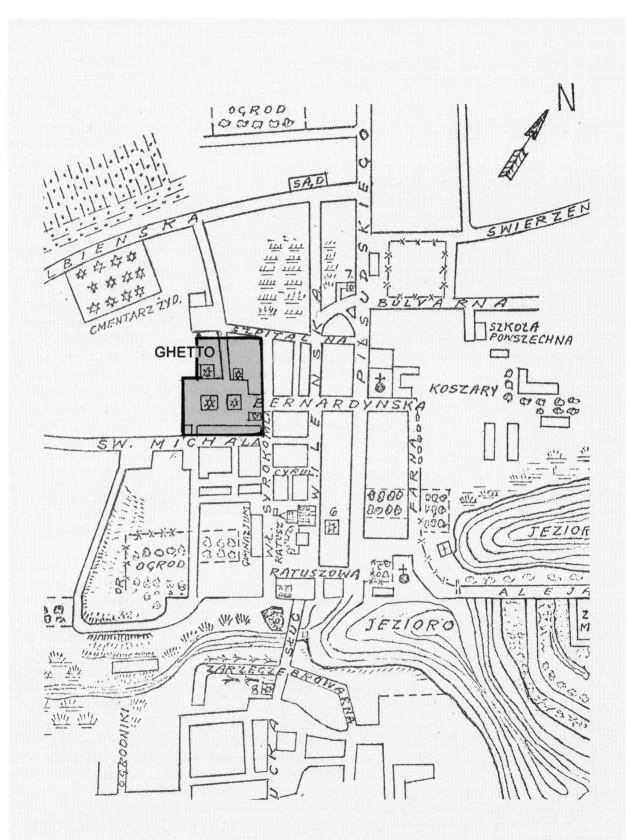

Nieswiez ghetto scheme. The ghetto boundaries were drawn by Gershon Gefen

(*Nieśwież Book*, published by Irgunei Yotzei Nieśwież in Israel and abroad, Israel 1976)

In December 1941, young Jews living in the ghetto met clandestinely and organized a fighting underground. They sought to undermine the Judenrat chairman, whom they considered unreliable. Judenrat members also belonged to the underground. They established a secret school in the ghetto, organized the ghetto workers into a labor union, manufactured various non-projectile hand weapons and fuel, and smuggled firearms into the ghetto.

On July 21, 1942, the Jews were ordered to assemble, but following news they received regarding the liquidation of the ghetto of Horodyszcze*, they refused to carry out the order. Instead, they mounted a resistance under the leadership of the members of the underground, including Shalom Cholawski. This was the first armed resistance of its kind in the ghettos. The Germans opened fire on the ghetto and a battle broke out, killing most of the ghetto's Jews and injuring or killing several dozen Germans and Lithuanians. The ghetto inhabitants set their homes ablaze, and the fire spread beyond the confines of the ghetto. About twenty-five Jewish fighters managed to escape to the forests, where they joined the partisans.

NOVAYA ODESSA

(Yiddish: **Nay Odese**;
Ukrainian: **Nova Odesa**)

COUNTY SEAT, NIKOLAEV DISTRICT, UKRAINE, USSR

During the war:
Reichskommissariat Ukraine

Coordinates:
47°19' | 31°47'

On the eve of the German invasion of the Soviet Union, there were approximately 200 Jews living in Novaya Odessa.

The Germans occupied the townlet on August 12, 1941. In September of that year, they established a ghetto that held local Jews along with Jewish inhabitants from the vicinity and refugees from Bessarabia. The duration of the ghetto's existence is not known.

The Germans subjected the ghetto population to abuse. They eventually led the Jews to the outskirts of the townlet and murdered them. The number of victims is estimated at between 125 and 250.

NOVAYA PRILUKA

(Yiddish: **Nay Priluke**;
Ukrainian: **Nova Pryluka**)

TOWNLET IN TURBOV COUNTY, VINNITSA DISTRICT, UKRAINE, USSR

During the war:
Reichskommissariat Ukraine

Coordinates:
49°28' | 28°40'

In the mid-1920s, there were 2,000 Jews in Novaya Priluka. The community suffered great losses in pogroms during the Russian Civil War (1918–20). After private commerce was abolished in the early 1930s, many Jews found work in state-owned enterprises, while artisans formed cooperatives.

When the Germans invaded the Soviet Union on June 22, 1941, a number of Jewish men were drafted by the Red Army. As the German forces advanced, many other Jews attempted to evacuate or escape to the east. Those who failed to reach the Russian interior were constrained to return to Novaya Priluka. The Germans occupied the townlet in the middle of July 1941. One week later, aided and abetted by local collaborators, they rounded up and brutally murdered approximately thirty Jewish men. Several weeks later, women and children were executed in an operation in Staraya Priluka. In September 1941, the remaining Jews of Novaya Priluka were packed into a ghetto on a single street. To stave off starvation, the Jews bartered their last possessions to Ukrainians for food, as Jewish youngsters watched for approaching Germans and Ukrainian police. In October 1941, a special ransom was demanded for every child in the ghetto.

The ghetto of Novaya Priluka was liquidated in November 1941, when its 350 inhabitants were murdered in pits in Staraya Priluka. In the ensuing months, Jews in hiding were hunted down and executed in the nearby Lisova Lisnivka forest.

NOVAYA USHITSA

(Yiddish: **Nay Ushitse**;
Ukrainian: **Nova Ushytsya**)

**COUNTY SEAT, KAMENETS-
PODOLSK DISTRICT,
UKRAINE, USSR**

During the war:
Reichskommissariat Ukraine

Coordinates:
48°50' | 27°17'

On the eve of World War II, there were 1,500 Jews in Novaya Ushitsa, more than half of the townlet's population. Under Soviet rule, a significant portion of the Jewish population was organized in cooperatives, and many were artisans. A number of Jews became farmers; a Jewish kolkhoz was established nearby.

The Germans occupied Novaya Ushitsa on July 14, 1941. In September 1941, they forced the Jews to move into a ghetto comprising several streets surrounded by barbed wire. Jews aged twelve and over were ordered to affix a yellow patch to their clothing. The Jews were allowed to visit the market to barter clothing and other items for food, and were removed for forced labor every morning. In the spring of 1942, Jews from nearby localities were concentrated in the ghetto.

On August 20, 1942, the ghetto population was rounded up for a selection. While expert skilled workers in high-demand occupations, along with their families, and youths were ordered to return to their homes, all others were murdered in the nearby forest at Trikhov. A total of 2,647 Jews were massacred. A number of those who returned to the ghetto were sent to a labor camp at Letichev to work in road construction; all perished. Most of the others were killed in Trikhov on October 16, 1942. The last thirty Jews, who had survived by hiding in the ghetto, were eventually captured, imprisoned, and executed by the Germans.

NOVOGRAD-
VOLYNSKIY

(Yiddish: **Zvil**; Polish: **Zviahel**;
Ukrainian: **Novograd
Volyns'kyi**)

**COUNTY SEAT, ZHITOMIR
DISTRICT, UKRAINE, USSR**

During the war:
Reichskommissariat Ukraine

Coordinates:
50°36' | 27°37'

In the early twentieth century, there were almost 10,000 Jews in Novograd-Volynskiy, more than half of the town's population. At the end of World War I and during the Russian Civil War (1918–20), the Jews were victims of pogroms that culminated in July–August 1919, with the murder of approximately 1,000 Jews by Ukrainian bands and Petliura's army. During the Soviet era, several factories opened in the town, and by the end of the 1930s, some 1,300 Jews had become factory workers. Artisans formed cooperatives. The community's children were educated at government schools and kindergartens that taught in Yiddish. In the late 1920s, Rabbi Chaim Shaul Bruk headed an unofficial Yeshiva with 130 students. On the eve of World War II, the number of Jews in the town had dropped to 6,840, roughly 30 percent of the population.

The Germans occupied Novograd-Volynskiy on July 10, 1941. During that month, Sonderkommando 4a conducted two operations in which about 100 Jewish inhabitants were murdered. Over 100 more Jews were murdered in August 1941. On September 23, 1941, an SS and police company under Army Group South murdered between 3,200 and 4,000 Jews in a forested area near the former Red Army headquarters and shooting range.

The Jews who survived the killings (most of them skilled workers in high-demand occupations) were rounded up and interned in the ghetto, which was composed of shacks belonging to a linen factory and surrounded by a barbed-wire fence. Jews from nearby towns and villages were also concentrated in the ghetto. Starvation was rampant, since only working adults received rations. The ghetto population declined steadily during the severe winter of 1941/42, as abominable living conditions, starvation, and exhaustion took their toll. Every week sick and enfeebled Jews were sent to the Sukhovlya forest and murdered. In early November 1942, many ghetto inhabitants fled to the forests of northern Zhitomir, where several joined Soviet partisan units, mainly in Saburov's division. Those who were captured were murdered, as were the remaining ghetto inhabitants.

NOVOMIRGOROD

(Ukrainian: **Novomyrhorod**)

**COUNTY SEAT,
KIROVOGRAD DISTRICT,
UKRAINE, USSR**

During the war:
Reichskommissariat Ukraine

Coordinates:
48°47' | 31°39'

In the early twentieth century, there were 1,600 Jews living in Novomirgorod, about one-sixth of the total population. On May 17, 1919, a Ukrainian gang murdered more than 100 Jews in a pogrom. Industrialization and urbanization under the Soviets led to a considerable decline in the townlet's Jewish population; by the eve of the German invasion of the Soviet Union in June 1941, only 300 Jews remained.

The Germans occupied Novomirgorod on August 1, 1941, and promptly ordered the Jews to wear what the Germans identified as a "badge of disgrace." A ghetto was established in a demolished schoolhouse for the Jews of Novomirgorod and the vicinity, holding 455 people in all. It was surrounded by barbed wire, and Ukrainian police diligently prevented inhabitants from obtaining food. In the winter of 1941/42, many of them died of starvation, cold, and disease. The Germans appointed one of the Jews to head a council in charge of preparing population lists.

On the night of February 6, 1942, local Ukrainian police conducted an operation in which they murdered sixty-nine Jews. The ghetto was liquidated in June 1942. In the adjacent village of Martonosha, the Germans murdered all the remaining Jews, as well as the children of mixed marriages—250 people in all.

NOVOMOSKOVSK

(Yiddish: **Nay Moskovsk**;
Ukrainian: **Novomoskovs'k**)

**COUNTY SEAT,
DNEPROPETROVSK
DISTRICT, UKRAINE, USSR**

During the war:
Reichskommissariat Ukraine

Coordinates:
48°37' | 35°12'

On the eve of the German invasion of the Soviet Union, there were 750 Jews in Novomoskovsk, less than 3 percent of the total population. As the Soviets had abolished private commerce, most Jewish inhabitants worked as artisans or held white-collar jobs.

The Germans occupied Novomoskovsk on September 27, 1941. Shortly afterwards, the Jews were ordered to register, to wear a Star-of-David armband, and to perform various forms of labor. In early December 1941, the townlet's Jews were concentrated in a compound near the synagogue that became a ghetto. They performed forced labor, including road building and street cleaning. In late December 1941, in a nearby forest, 136 Jews were murdered in reprisal for partisan action.

The ghetto was liquidated on March 2, 1942, when its 400 inhabitants were murdered in a sand quarry near the townlet.

NOVOVITEBSK

(Yiddish: **Nay Vitebsk**;
Russian: **Zheltaya**; Ukrainian:
Novi Vitebsk, Zhovta)

**JEWISH FARMING COLONY
IN STALINDORF COUNTY,
DNEPROPETROVSK
DISTRICT, UKRAINE, USSR**

During the war:
Reichskommissariat Ukraine

Coordinates:
47°58' | 33°54'

Novovitebsk was established in the 1820s by Jewish migrants from the Vitebsk area. During the interwar period, 550 Jews lived in the colony, accounting for roughly half of its population. Under the Soviets, Novovitebsk had a Jewish Ethnic Soviet and many Jews organized kolkhozes. The colony had a regular school and a Yiddish-language agricultural school.

After the German invasion of the Soviet Union, some of Novovitebsk's Jews managed to flee to the east. The Germans occupied the colony on August 18, 1941, and promptly forced the 300 remaining Jews to relocate to a single street that became a ghetto of sorts. The able-bodied were assigned to road construction work.

The ghetto was liquidated on May 29, 1942, when its inhabitants were led out and murdered in pits. The forced laborers were also murdered in 1942.

NOWA MYSZ

(Yiddish: **Mush**)

TOWNLET IN BARANOWICZE COUNTY, NOWOGRÓDEK DISTRICT, POLAND

(After World War II in the USSR/Belarus; Belarussian, Russian: **Novaya Mysh**)

During the war: Reichskommissariat Ostland

Coordinates: 53°08' | 25°54'

On the eve of World War II, about 630 Jews lived in Nowa Mysz, accounting for approximately one-third of the local population. Most earned their livelihood from small commerce and artisanship.

After Nowa Mysz was occupied by the Red Army in September 1939, a Soviet system was instituted in the townlet, and privately owned shops were nationalized.

On June 27, 1941, the Germans occupied Nowa Mysz. The townlet's Jews were immediately ordered to wear a yellow badge, their freedom of movement was restricted, their property was confiscated, and several were seized for forced labor.

The Jews were rounded up and relocated to a separate neighborhood that they were forbidden to leave, although it was not fenced in. In late summer 1942, the Jews of Nowa Mysz were assembled in the market square and subsequently shot to death outside the townlet.

NOWE MIASTO

(Yiddish: **Nayshtot**)

TOWNLET IN PŁOCK COUNTY, WARSAW DISTRICT, POLAND

During the war: Bezirk Zichenau

Coordinates: 52°39' | 20°38'

Either about 1,500 or 1,700 Jews (testimonies vary on the figure) lived in Nowe Miasto in the interwar period, representing nearly half of the townlet's population. They earned their livelihood from small commerce, peddling, and artisanship and were aided by a cooperative credit fund, a free-loan society, and trade unions. Most of the community's children attended traditional Hadarim. Nowe Miasto had a Beit Yaakov school for girls and a Jewish library. Zionist parties and youth movements, which had pioneer training facilities, were active in the townlet, as were Agudath Israel and the Bund.

When World War II broke out, young Jews and a number of families fled to Warsaw* and to surrounding townlets.

The Germans occupied Nowe Miasto on September 5, 1939, and immediately began to plunder Jewish property. After a few weeks, they began to seize Jews for forced labor. On the first day of work, seven Jewish men were murdered. Subsequently, the Jews were ordered to pay a ransom and to wear a yellow badge. The hours during which they were permitted to shop in the market were restricted.

In October 1939, Nowe Miasto was included in the Bezirk Zichenau, and the Germans began to drive out the Jews in the area to the General Gouvernement. As a result, from late November 1939, many of the townlet's Jews fled to Warsaw, and the Jews who remained in the townlet later received a Third Reich identity card.

In the spring of 1940, when the situation of the Jews in Warsaw deteriorated, most of Nowe Miasto's Jews returned home. However, lacking Third Reich documents, they were driven out of the townlet in July 1941, to the Pomiechowek camp. This group of between 250 and 300 Jews included both former residents of the townlet and refugees.

In November 1941, a fenced-in ghetto with a single gate was established in Nowe Miasto. At first, only 500 of the townlet's more than 2,000 Jews lived in the ghetto. The Judenrat, headed by Shlomo Fridman, opened a public soup kitchen and distributed food. The ghetto also had a bakery and a hospital. A ten-member Jewish Order Service was also established, headed by Shmuel Braunzweig, a refugee from Drobin*. The Jews were required to provide the townlet's administration with eighty male forced laborers every day. The Judenrat drew up work rosters, requiring every fit man to report for work two days each week. The affluent residents paid to be released from work. On the "Aryan" side, a cooperative of Jewish artisans was established, in which 100 Jewish artisans toiled for the Germans without pay. A number of the Jews were sent to labor camps in the area, such as Nosarzewo, Miechow, and Sierpc. The Jewish policemen were ordered to arrest Jews who attempted to smuggle food and other merchandise into the ghetto. Smugglers were constrained to pay a fine, which was transferred to the Judenrat.

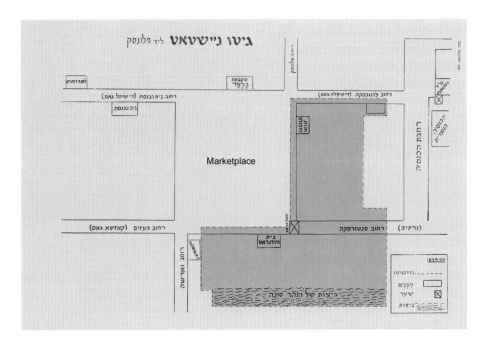

 גיטו ניישטאט ליד פלונסק

Marketplace

Nowe Miasto ghetto plan, as brought by Zvi Rozenberg in his testimony

(*Plonsk and Environment, Neishtadt and Sochocin, In Memory of the Jewish Communities*, published by Irgun Yotzei Plonsk in Israel, Tel Aviv 1963)

In the summer of 1941, the Judenrat shipped food packages to Jewish inmates imprisoned in the Pomiechowek camp.

In December 1941, between 1,200 and 1,500 Jews from Ciechanow* and 700 Jews from Drobin were brought to the ghetto. The population increase led to a further deterioration in the living conditions of the ghetto inhabitants, triggering starvation and an outbreak of epidemic typhus that caused the deaths of at least 170 and up to 300 people (sources vary on the data). The ghetto nevertheless sustained an active cultural life, which included secret prayer gatherings and study groups and the study of Hebrew.

Nowe Miasto had a German gendarmerie station. From February 1942 onward, its commander visited the ghetto daily, robbing and beating Jews. Members of the Gestapo from other towns also engaged in such activities, occasionally removing from the ghetto a group of Jews, who were never heard from again.

In early November 1942, all of the Jews toiling in the nearby labor camps were returned to the ghetto. On November 18, 1942, all of the inhabitants of the ghetto, between 1,800 and 2,400 people, were deported to the Plonsk* ghetto. Most were deported from there to Auschwitz in the third transport, on November 30, 1942.

Twenty-seven of Nowe Miasto's Jews survived the war.

NOWE MIASTO ON THE PILICĄ

TOWNLET IN RAWA MAZOWIECKA COUNTY, WARSAW DISTRICT, POLAND

During the war: General Gouvernement, Radom District

Coordinates:
51°38' | 20°35'

On the eve of World War II, about 1,300 Jews lived in Nowe Miasto on the Pilica, accounting for one-third of the townlet's population. Most were merchants and artisans; Jews also owned an edible-oil plant, bakeries, and a bus line to Warsaw*. Zionist parties, Agudath Israel, and the Bund were active in the townlet, as was a group of Jewish Communists. A Beit Yaakov girls' school and a Yavne school provided Jewish education. In the 1930s, the community endured antisemitic incidents and shop expropriations.

After the Germans occupied Nowe Miasto on the Pilica in September 1939, they deported some sixty Jewish men to Lublin* and interned them in a labor camp for several months. A nine- or ten-member Judenrat was established under Motel Tsylikh to collect and remit punitive taxes and organize groups of workers for the Germans. A Jewish Order Service was set up as well.

The Nowe Miasto on the Pilica ghetto was sealed in April 1941. Jews who had owned factories were briefly allowed to work as laborers in their former place of business; the rest of the ghetto inhabitants struggled to make a living illegally by performing random jobs for the local population. Children were sent to villages to buy food and were often harassed by German policemen. In 1940, one Jewish-owned bakery was still in operation.

By the summer of 1942, hundreds of Jewish refugees had been transferred to Nowe Miasto on the Pilica from various places, including 600 from Austria. The influx caused severe overcrowding and epidemic typhus in the ghetto. The Judenrat attempted to halt the epidemic by establishing an isolation room for the infected, but the lack of medication and the services of only one doctor in the ghetto hindered these efforts. In late 1941, the murders of Jews and raids on Jewish homes by German police became increasingly frequent.

The ghetto was liquidated on October 22, 1942. Its population of about 3,000 was deported to nearby Drzewica* and from there, along with the local inhabitants, to Treblinka. Twenty-five Jews were left behind to clean the ghetto and gather the deportees' belongings; they were later sent to Tomaszow Mazowiecki*. Fifty-five Jews from Nowe Miasto on the Pilica remained alive after the war.

NOWINY BRDOWSKIE

VILLAGE IN KOŁO COUNTY, ŁÓDŹ DISTRICT, POLAND

During the war: Wartheland

Coordinates:
52°20' | 18°45'

In October 1940, Jewish families from the town of Kolo*, 150 in number, as well as 50 Jewish families from Babiak were moved into Nowiny Brdowskie and to the village of Bugaj*. A rural ghetto was established within both localities. Its residents, who referred to the ghetto as a "Jewish colony", were allotted thirty acres of land to farm.

In January 1942, the Jews of both villages were deported to the Chelmno death camp.

NOWO ŚWIĘCIANY

TOWNLET IN ŚWIĘCIANY COUNTY, VILNA DISTRICT, POLAND
(After World War II in the USSR/Lithuania; Lithuanian: **Švenčionėliai**)

During the war:
Reichskommissariat Ostland

Coordinates:
55°09' | 26°10'

About 900 Jews lived in Nowo Swieciany in the interwar period, representing roughly one-quarter of the townlet's population. Most earned their livelihood from peddling, commerce, and shopkeeping. Nowo Swieciany had Jewish parties and youth movements, a Yiddish school, a Tarbut Hebrew school, a Jewish orphanage, a library, and religious institutions.

After Nowo Swieciany was occupied by the Soviets on September 18, 1939, privately owned shops were nationalized or closed and cooperatives were formed.

Following the German invasion of the Soviet Union, a number of Nowo Swieciany's Jews managed to escape to the east together with the retreating Soviets. The Germans occupied the townlet on June 24, 1941; Lithuanians murdered several Jews on the first day of the occupation. At German orders, Rabbi Kimkhi established a Judenrat, which was required to draw up a list of the townlet's Jewish inhabitants and recruit Jews for forced labor. One day, Lithuanian police arrested forty-three of the townlet's Jews and shot almost all to death for "conspiring with the Communist party".

In early September 1941, a ghetto was established in Nowo Swieciany. It was not fenced in, and on the weekly market day, Jews were permitted to leave for two hours to purchase food. These dispensations came in exchange for a bribe paid by the Judenrat to Korfis, the Lithuanian mayor of the townlet. Rabbi Kimkhi continued to live in his own home.

In late September 1941, Lithuanian policemen entered the ghetto and led its inhabitants to the Poligon camp, where they were joined in the coming days by Jews from other localities. A group of artisans from the Nowo Swieciany ghetto managed to escape during the deportation and join another approximately fifty Jewish artisans in the Swieciany* ghetto. On October 9, 1941, the men in the camp were shot to death; the following day, the women and children were executed as well.

NOWOGRÓDEK

(Yiddish: Novohorodok)

DISTRICT CAPITAL, POLAND
(Today: **Novogrudok**, Belarus)

During the war:
Reichskommissariat Ostland

Coordinates:
53°36' | 25°5'

About 6,500 Jews lived in Nowogrodek when World War II broke out, representing approximately half of the city's population. Most earned their livelihood from small commerce and artisanship. Nowogrodek boasted a Jewish-owned Folksbank and various Jewish aid institutions, including a hospital, an old-age home, and an orphanage. Jewish political organizations and youth movements were active locally, including Zionist parties, the Bund, the *Fareinikte Folks-Partei* (United People's Party), and the Communist party. Educational and cultural institutions that operated in the city included Hebrew and Yiddish schools, a Yeshiva, a Jewish theater, and two Yiddish weeklies. Jews held major positions in the life of the city. Avraham Ostashinsky, the chairman of the Zionist party in Nowogrodek, served as vice-mayor, and Jews were members of the city council.

When World War II broke out, about 1,000 refugees thronged to Nowogrodek from the areas of western Poland occupied by the Germans. The Soviets occupied the city on September 17, 1939, and nationalized private businesses.

On July 4, 1941, Nowogrodek was occupied by the Germans. During the battles, hundreds of Jews attempted to flee the city and about 200 succeeded. After the German occupation, men and women were seized for forced labor. On July 5, 1941, at least twenty-seven Jewish men were executed for arriving late to work. On July 17, 1941, seventy to eighty members of the Jewish intelligentsia and a few dozen members of the liberal professions were executed. On July 26, members of Einsatzgruppe B rounded up and tortured about 200 Jewish men in public in the city square; afterwards they executed fifty-two of the men. On August 8, 1941, many dozens of Nowogrodek's Jews were shot to death by the German police.

On September 1, 1941, the military government in the city was replaced by a civil administration, and Nowogrodek became part of the *Reichskommissariat Weissrusland* (White Russia), under the direct command of Johann Artmann. At German orders, on September 26, 1941, freedom of movement restrictions were imposed on the Jews, they were forbidden to trade in food and belongings, and Jewish residents were required to wear a yellow badge and mark their houses. A Judenrat was established in Nowogrodek, led by Zeldowicz, whose main job was to recruit Jews for forced labor. Several weeks later, a new Judenrat was established and attorney Henrik Ciechanowski was appointed to lead it.

On December 5, 1941, the Jews of Nowogrodek were rounded up in the court building, and on December 8, 1941, the SIPO unit from Baranowicze* headed by Waldemar Amelung carried out a selection. Most of Nowogrodek's Jews were shot to death together with Jews from nearby villages in pits dug in the forests near Skrydlewo. Some 4,000 to 5,000 Jews were murdered in the operation, which was carried out by Germans with the assistance of local police.

About 1,300 to 1,500 Jews remained in Nowogrodek, the vast majority holders of work permits and members of the Judenrat. They were concentrated in a ghetto located in the poor Peresieka suburb on the outskirts of the city. The ghetto was divided into twelve areas, and a member of the Judenrat was placed in charge of each. A small hospital was established in the ghetto by Dr. Berkman. The ghetto was very overcrowded, with about twenty people to a room.

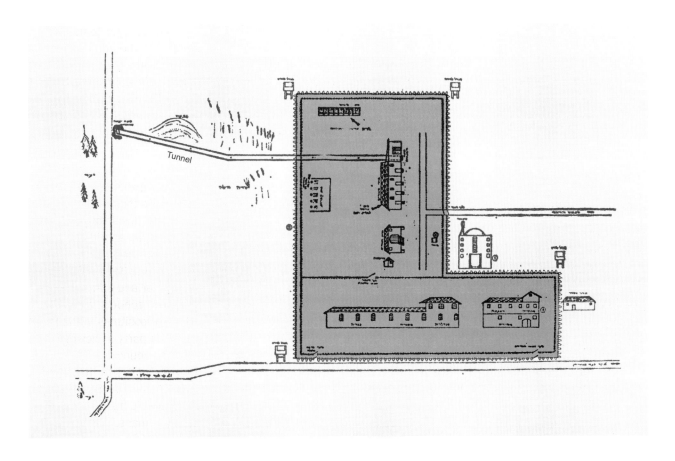

Nowogrodek, the "professionals" ghetto and the tunnel. Scheme illustrated by Yehoshua Yaffe (©Yehoshua Yaffe, *In Nowogrodek Ghetto and the Partisan Movement,* published by Irgun Yotzey Novogrodek Be'Israel, Tel Aviv 1988)

In the spring of 1942, the Germans murdered the members of the Judenrat and a new Judenrat was appointed, headed by Haim Isakovicz. During that period, the Germans transferred 3,000 to 4,500 Jews from surrounding localities to Nowogrodek, transforming it into a workshop center for the Jews working in the area. The severe overcrowding in the ghetto caused a deterioration in the situation of its residents, and the Jewish Order Service took harsh steps to halt the frequent escape attempts.

On August 7, 1942, another operation was carried out in which about 3,000 of the ghetto's residents were murdered, including children, outside the city near the village of Litovka, and another 500 were murdered next to the former barracks near the city.

At this stage, about 1,250 Jews remained in the ghetto. After a while the ghetto was divided into two parts: about 700 people with required professions and their families were moved into the buildings of the former courthouse and the remaining approximately 500 Jews stayed in the Peresieka ghetto. Attempts persisted by the ghetto residents to flee to the forests and find shelter among the partisan units and in the family camp established by the Bielski brothers, notwithstanding the opposition of the Judenrat and the Jewish Order Service.

On February 4, 1943, another murder operation was perpetrated in which about 500 Jews were killed. The survivors continued to toil in the workshops. On May 7, 1943, a selection was carried out among the professionals in the ghetto, which functioned as a labor camp. More than 300 Jews, mostly women and children, were murdered by the local police and a Lithuanian unit in Hardzilowka, near the courthouse. About 300 Jews, mostly artisans, remained in the ghetto.

After the operation, a Jewish underground formed in Nowogrodek in the spring and in September 1942. An underground council with forty-two members from various parties was established, headed by Yaakov Cohen. A number of ghetto inhabitants managed to escape, primarily with the assistance of Jewish emissaries sent from the partisan battalion of the Bielski brothers. The underground planned and organized an escape, and over a period of three months a 250-meter-long tunnel was dug, through which the 233 Jews remaining in the ghetto tried to escape on September 26, 1943. About 170 of them succeeded in reaching the forests, where they joined the partisans' brigade of the Bielski brothers. Others were shot and killed either during the escape or afterwards, when apprehended by the Germans in the forests.

NOWY DWÓR

TOWNLET IN WARSAW COUNTY, WARSAW DISTRICT, POLAND

During the war: Bezirk Zichenau

Coordinates:
52°26' | 20°43'

About 3,900 Jews lived in Nowy Dwor in the interwar period, representing roughly half of the townlet's population. They earned their livelihood from commerce, peddling, small industry, and artisanship; many were employed in the garment and food industries, and a number were factory workers. They were aided by trade and craft associations, a Jewish bank, and a free-loan association. Jewish children attended a Talmud Torah, a Yeshiva, a Yiddish CYSHO elementary school, and a school in which Hebrew was taught. Many of the community's girls studied in a Beit Yaakov school. The townlet also had a Szabasowka school that was attended mainly by girls. Jewish residents enjoyed two Jewish libraries as well as a drama group and a sports society. Nowy Dwor had Zionist parties and a Mizrachi pioneer training facility; Agudath Israel and the Bund were also active. A chapter of Agudath Israel maintained a free-loan society and an agricultural training facility. Groups of the Bund's youth organizations, Tsukunft and SKIF, were active as well. A number of Jews were members of the illegal Polish Communist Party.

On the eve of World War II, about 4,500 Jews lived in Nowy Dwor. When the war broke out, the townlet was bombed. Three-quarters of its houses were destroyed, and hundreds of Jews were killed. Most of the local Jews fled to Warsaw*.

The Germans occupied the townlet in September 1939. On September 29, they overran the nearby fortress, which Jews took part in defending. From the first day of the occupation, Jewish property was plundered and businesses were confiscated, and Jews were seized for forced labor. The Jewish institutions were closed. In the fall of 1939, Nowy Dwor was absorbed into in the Bezirk Zichenau, which was annexed to the Third Reich, and its name was changed to Neuhoff. As with all the other Jews of the Bezirk Zichenau, the Jews of Nowy Dwor were required to wear a yellow badge on their chest and back. In December 1939, the Jews were apparently forced to watch the burning of sacred books. During the period, the Germans also demanded ransom payments.

Towards the end of 1939, about 2,800 Jews lived in Nowy Dwor. The Germans announced the deportation of all the Jews to the General Gouvernement. Young men fled to the Soviet Union, while families headed mainly to Warsaw. It appears that in late 1939, no more than about 1,000 Jews lived in Nowy Dwor, on the whole residents from the poorer sectors. They received Third Reich identification cards and earned their livelihood working for the Germans. The group of Jewish workers was headed by Rothstein.

In 1940, when the situation in Warsaw worsened, many of Nowy Dwor's Jews returned home. Several were executed for illegally crossing the border, and in May 1940, fourteen of Nowy Dwor's Jews accused of the same crime were murdered in the Dzialdowo transit camp.

In early 1941, a sealed ghetto was established in the Piaski quarter. It was enclosed by a wooden fence and had two entry points. A Judenrat was likewise set up during the period, headed by Rothstein, and after he resigned, by Yosef Gershon. A Jewish Order Service was also appointed, headed by Yaakov Barank. The ghetto had a jail under the supervision of the Jewish Order Service, whose

Nowy Dwor, 1940
Jews wearing a round
yellow badge. *Photograph
taken with the personal
camera of a German soldier
who arrived in the town*
(Hans-Joachim Gerke,
courtesy of USHMM)

inmates were handed over to the Gestapo and apparently murdered, unless their families managed to free them by bribing members of the Jewish Order Service.

The ghetto was severely overcrowded and lacked rudimentary sanitary conditions. Only those with Third Reich identity cards received rations, compelling the Jews of the ghetto to risk their lives to smuggle food into the ghetto. Many of the Jews worked outside of it, and several received meager wages. Occasionally Jews were able to smuggle food into the ghetto. Epidemic typhus broke out, claiming the lives of many ghetto residents. An exceptionally small hospital was established there, with a staff of male and female nurses under a Polish paramedic. In May 1941, the Germans ordered the Jews of Nowy Dwor to remain in the river for hours on end while their belongings and clothing were disinfected. Many fell ill and died as a result. On May 14, 1941, of the ghetto's inhabitants 400 were deported to Ludwiszyn ghetto (see Jablonna-Legionowo*).

On June 17, 1941, the ghetto, which had a population of about 2,000, was officially sealed. On July 6 or 13, 1941 (sources vary regarding the date), SS and German and Polish police carried out a selection of the ghetto's population, leaving behind 600 to 750 youths. The rest were deported to the Pomiechowek concentration camp. Twenty-eight of the ghetto's Jews were murdered that day.

In mid-1941, the ghetto provided the Germans with between 300 and 400 Jewish forced laborers daily. German police and members of the Jewish Order Service seized people from their homes, sometimes violently, for forced labor.

It may be assumed that in early fall 1941, Jews from the surrounding localities were transferred to the ghetto. In November 1941, the Jews of Zakrocym, about 1,200 Jews from Wyszogrod*, and a few families from Plonsk* were also transferred to the ghetto. The ghetto population apparently approached 3,000. A "Small Ghetto" was established, inhabited by the Jews of Wyszogrod. Members of the Jewish Order Service guarded the passage from the main ghetto to the "Small Ghetto" and thwarted smuggling attempts.

In late 1941, three representatives of the Jews of Wyszogrod joined the Judenrat, and a public soup kitchen was established to help the refugees. In late 1941 or early 1942, epidemic typhus broke out in the ghetto, and at least 200 people died. The hospital continued to be active. In May 1942, seven young Jews aged sixteen to twenty-five were hanged in full view of the population of the ghetto for smuggling in food. These executions were repeated throughout the summer and included women.

On October 4, 1942, the nearby Ludwiszyn ghetto was liquidated. About 100 people who fled during the operation arrived in the Nowy Dwor ghetto and were arrested by the Jewish Order Service. Most were freed after their relatives bribed the Judenrat, but thirty-eight of them were handed over to the Germans and executed.

On October 26, 1942, the ghetto was encircled by the Gestapo, German gendarmes, and Volksdeutsche. The gates of the ghetto were closed and all work outside the ghetto was discontinued. Brought into the ghetto on October 28, 1942, were 2,800 Jews from Czerwinsk*. There were apparently more than 5,000 Jews in the ghetto at this time; overcrowding was severe. On November 16, 1942, the Germans demanded that all valuables be turned over.

On November 20, 1942, the first transport left Nowy Dwor for Auschwitz. All Jews over the age of forty together with the ill, handicapped, and women without husbands along with their children were on this transport. On December 9, 1942, the second transport left the townlet; it contained people fit for work. On December 12, 1942, the third and final transport left the townlet. The members of the Judenrat traveled in the hind car, which was disconnected from the train in Warsaw.

A number of Nowy Dwor's Jews fled from the ghetto and hid on the "Aryan" side of the townlet. Several were murdered by Poles or handed over to the Gestapo.

Some 400 to 450 of Nowy Dwor's Jews survived the war. Most had spent the war years in the Soviet Union. A few dozen survived the camps, and a number of individuals managed to save themselves by hiding on the "Aryan" side of the townlet.

NOWY KORCZYN

TOWNLET IN BUSKO COUNTY, KIELCE DISTRICT, POLAND

During the war: General Gouvernement, Radom District

Coordinates: 50°18' | 20°49'

After World War I, about 2,500 Jews lived in Nowy Korczyn, representing approximately 80 percent of the townlet's population. They earned their livelihood from commerce and artisanship, particularly in the various sectors of the leather, garment, and wood industries. Nowy Korczyn boasted a Beit Midrash and a home for the poor and elderly. The community also had pioneer movements and three Zionist libraries. Among the townlet's Jewish schools were a Yavne school established by the Mizrachi movement and a Beit Yaakov school established by Agudath Israel. In the late 1930s, the Jews of Nowy Korczyn received financial assistance from former members of the community who had immigrated to the United States.

The Germans occupied Nowy Korczyn on September 8, 1939. Jews were immediately subjected to abuse and seized for forced labor. Within several weeks of the occupation's onset, the Germans ordered the establishment of a Judenrat, which was placed in charge of collecting ransom payments and recruiting slave laborers.

At a later stage, the Jews of Nowy Korczyn were transferred to an open ghetto set up along a succession of the townlet's small streets. In the spring of 1941, Jews from western Poland and about 300 Jews from Radom* were brought to the Nowy Korczyn ghetto. In April 1941, the number of Jews living in it reached 3,700. During this period, the Judenrat established a public soup kitchen and a clinic for the victims of epidemic typhus, both supported by the JSS. A number of sewing, shoemaking, and carpentry "shops" were opened in the ghetto. The workers in the shops were persuaded that their contribution to the German war effort would forestall their deportation.

On October 2, 1942, contingents of SS guards along with German and Ukrainian policemen encircled the ghetto. The Jews were driven out on foot to the Szczuczyn train station; many people experiencing difficulty walking were murdered along the way. The Jews were transferred in freight cars to the Treblinka death camp. Some 270 Jews managed to escape to the forests during the deportation, but many were discovered and murdered.

About 300 Jews remained in the Nowy Korczyn ghetto, charged with collecting and sorting the belongings of the deportees. On November 24, 1942, these last inhabitants were taken to a labor camp in the area of Kielce.

NOWY SĄCZ
(Yiddish: **Tsanz, Sants**)

COUNTY SEAT, CRACOW DISTRICT, POLAND

During the war: General Gouvernement, Cracow District

Coordinates: 49°38' | 20°43'

When World War II broke out, about 10,500 Jews lived in Nowy Sacz, representing approximately one-third of the town's population. They earned their livelihood from artisanship and commerce, especially in the food, construction, and wood industries. Jewish artisans, trade employees, merchants, and industrialists were organized into various unions and were aided by a Jewish bank and a "credit organization." Nowy Sacz had numerous Jewish welfare institutions, including a hospital. Jewish schools in the townlet included Hebrew Tarbut and Yavne schools, a Talmud Torah, and a Beit Yaakov school for girls sponsored by Agudath Israel. The city had active Zionist parties and youth movements that ran a Zionist sports club called "Stern," as well as a Zionist pioneer training facility. The Agudath

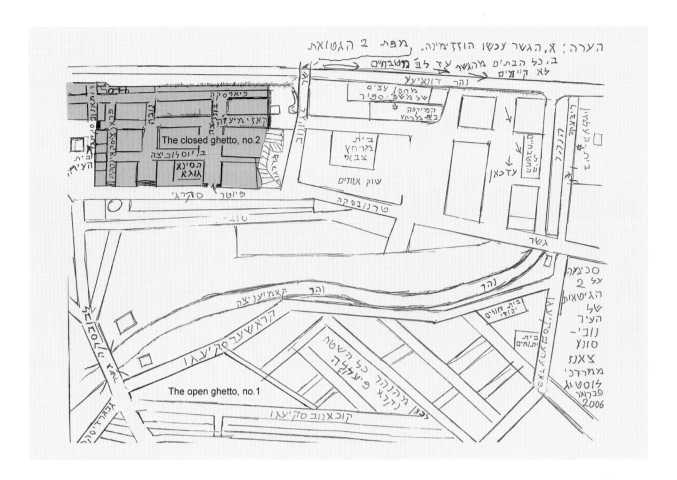

The closed ghetto, no.2

The open ghetto, no.1

Nowy Sacz ghettos scheme
hand-painted by Mordechaj (Markus) Lustig (Kanengiser), a ghetto survivor

Israel and Poalei Agudath Israel parties and their youth and women's movements were also active in the town, as was a chapter of the Bund. A number of Jews were members of underground Communist groups. Most of the Jewish parties and movements maintained libraries, choirs, and sports and drama circles.

Nowy Sacz was occupied by the Germans on September 6, 1939. The following day, the Germans began to plunder Jewish property, arrest Jews, and seize Jews for forced labor. The Germans also demanded ransom payments. A Judenrat was established, headed by Moshe Rindler, who was followed by Yaakov Marin and Joachim Bekerman. A Jewish Order Service was set up under the command of Y. Folkman. The Judenrat was ordered to turn over valuables, clothing, and furniture on demand as well as to provide the Germans with forced laborers. A series of decrees were imposed: Jewish-owned shops and workshops were marked with a Star-of-David and became the target of attacks and looting; Jewish businesses were confiscated and transferred to "trustees," largely from among the Volksdeutsche; and Jews were forbidden to buy provisions on market days.

In November 1939, the German police conducted searches for arms and foreign currency in Jewish homes, accompanied by looting and terrorization. In the same month, the first groups of Jewish refugees arrived from Lodz* and Sieradz*. The Jews suffered from increasing poverty. Deportation of Jews to labor camps in the area began in the summer of 1940: about 1,000 Jews were sent to the Roznow camp, and others to the Dabrowa, Kamionka, and Chelmiec camps. In the fall of 1940, about 600 young Jews were sent to the Lipie camp.

In October and November 1940, Jews deported from other localities in the area were transferred to Nowy Sacz. The Judenrat and a public council for the

Nowy Sacz, 1940
Jews on Kazimierza Street (YV)

refugees established a public soup kitchen and helped with funds. An orphanage and a Jewish hospital with an outpatient clinic were established. Beginning in November 1940, the local JSS chapter helped those in need of welfare.

In the fall of 1940, the Germans forbade the Jews of Nowy Sacz to reside in the area of the marketplace. A Jewish quarter was established in practice, before the establishment of a ghetto was officially declared. In December 1940, the number of Jewish refugees in Nowy Sacz grew to more than 2,500, including some 1,000 from Cracow*. The winter of 1940/41 brought epidemics, chiefly spotted fever and tuberculosis. The Jewish hospital strained to meet the demands for medical care and medications. In May 1941, deportees from Labowa and Chelmce were brought to Nowy Sacz. The Germans at that time likewise barred Jews from living outside the open Jewish quarter. In June 1941, eleven Jews were sent to the Auschwitz death camp, including a number of rabbis, and several Judenrat members were murdered in the local cemetery.

In July 1941, an injunction was published regarding the establishment of two ghettos in Nowy Sacz, which, once operational, had a population of about 12,000. At this stage, the boundaries of the ghettos were not marked out, but residents required a special permit to exit their grounds.

In the fall of 1941, the Germans murdered thirty Jews who returned to Nowy Sacz from the eastern side of the San River, the area that had been under Soviet control until the German invasion of the Soviet Union. In January 1942, about seventy young Jews involved in cigarette sales in the ghetto were murdered, and a short time later, a few dozen Jews accused of engaging in business speculation of ghetto apartments were killed. In April 1942, numerous young Jews were seized in the streets and sent to the Pustkow labor camp, where many perished. On April 29, 1942, about 150 Jewish men and women suspected of having belonged to leftist organizations before the war were executed. The members of the Jewish Order Service were ordered to help identify and arrest the suspects. Additionally, six members of the Judenrat who had been arrested earlier were murdered. During their execution, some of the victims denounced their murderers and called for revenge. That night, the Gestapo randomly murdered about 100 Jews in the ghetto streets.

Nowy Sacz, 1940
Jews wearing an armband on the right arm, on the corner of Kzimierza and Franciszkanska Streets. German soldiers are visible on the side. (YV)

In June 1942, it became public knowledge that the ghetto designated as Ghetto A (which had workshops, especially for the garment industry) was to become the premises of the Jews considered fit for work. The Jews of the second ghetto (Ghetto B) therefore sought to move over to Ghetto A in the hope of attaining immunity to deportations; a number of people resorted to bribery. A committee of the German employment bureau carried out a census and a selection of the workers designated for Ghetto A; following the transfer, only the handicapped, elderly, and children remained in Ghetto B. In July and August 1942, both ghettos were reduced in size, and dozens of Jews were murdered by German police who charged the areas. In the same month, high ransoms were levied on the Jews.

On August 16–20, 1942, the Jews of Sacz, Stary Sacz*, Limanowa*, Mszana Dolna*, and Grybow were transferred to the Nowy Sacz ghetto. Following the transfer, the population of the Nowy Sacz ghettos reached about 20,000.

On August 21, 1942, the members of the Jewish Order Service were summoned to Gestapo headquarters and were told that the evacuation of the Jews of Nowy Sacz would begin on August 23, ostensibly for farming work. A few inhabitants, once notified, attempted to escape from the ghetto to the nearby fields and forests.

On August 23, 1942, the Jews of the ghetto were rounded up in a square near the Dunajec River. They were ordered to remit a high ransom, which the Germans claimed was the cost of the evacuation to Ukraine. Following a selection, about 800 workers beneficial to the Germans economically were transferred into a few buildings in Ghetto A. The rest of the Jews were moved into Ghetto B, and from there were shipped in three transports, on August 25–28, 1942, to the Belzec death camp. During the deportations, dozens of Jews were killed when the Germans shot into a crowd in Ghetto B. After the deportation, the murder victims were buried in pits in the cemetery dug beforehand by Jews.

In early September 1942, about 150 of the 800 Jews remaining in Ghetto A were sent to labor camps in Roznow and Muszyna. The rest were employed collecting and sorting through the Jewish belongings. Thirty-eight Jews who were employed outside the ghetto were caught smuggling in food and were shot to death in the cemetery.

Nowy Sacz, 1940
Jews waiting near the Judenrat offices on Lwowska Street (YV)

Later in September and in October 1942, another several hundred Jews were evacuated from the ghetto. Most were sent to Tarnow* to work in workshops, principally in the garment industry, while others were transferred to Mielec*. The approximately 100 Jews who remained in the ghetto were deported in June and July 1943, to the labor camp in Szebnie near Jaslo*.

In 1940, a small underground group made up of Poles and Jews organized itself in Nowy Sacz. Its activities included monitoring radio broadcasts and gathering and disseminating information on the situation at the front. Group members included Dov Hirsheltal and attorney Bronislava Finder, both Jews. The group operated until the mass deportations in the summer of 1942. It held debates on the viability of taking action during operations, but no such activity on its part is known.

NOWY TARG
(Yiddish: **Neymarkt**)

COUNTY SEAT, CRACOW DISTRICT, POLAND

During the war: General Gouvernement, Cracow District

Coordinates:
49°29' | 20°02'

About 1,300 Jews lived in Nowy Targ, representing roughly 20 percent of the townlet's population. Most earned their livelihood from artisanship and commerce, and a few were members of the liberal professions. They were aided in their economic activities by unions of Jewish artisans and merchants, as well as by a Jewish loan cooperative, which established a free-loan fund. Nowy Targ had chapters of WIZO and CENTOS as well as a public soup kitchen and a dormitory for children. Community schools included a Talmud Torah, a supplementary Yavne Hebrew school, and, for some time, a Mizrachi school. Nowy Targ also boasted a Jewish student union that assisted Jewish secondary school students, a Jewish sports club, and a Jewish orchestra. Political activity included active Zionist parties and youth movements, and a *Dror-Frayhayt* pioneer training facility. These organizations maintained libraries and hosted cultural activities. Nowy Targ also had a chapter of Agudath Israel. A few young Jews were members of the outlawed Communist youth organization.

Many Jews fled to the east when the Germans invaded Poland, and several reached eastern Galicia, where they remained under the Soviet regime. In the summer of 1940, most of these refugees were exiled to remote areas of the Soviet Union.

The Germans occupied Nowy Targ in early September 1939, and immediately began to seize Jews for forced labor. The Jews' freedom of movement was restricted, they were forbidden to buy in the market during market hours, and either thirty-six or sixty (testimonies vary regarding the figure) Jews were imprisoned and never seen again. Within a short while, all the merchandise was stolen from Jewish shops, which were transferred to "Aryan trustees."

In late 1939 or early 1940, a Judenrat was established, headed by a man named Grinberger. The Judenrat was ordered to carry out a census of the Jews, collect ransom money and valuables for the Germans upon their demand, and provide forced laborers daily.

In 1940, abductions of Jews to labor camps got underway. In May 1940, about 100 young Jews were sent to work in a quarry in Zakopane. In early 1941, a public soup kitchen was opened in Nowy Targ with the help of JSS and food and medications were distributed.

In May 1941, a ghetto was established in the townlet that also held Jews from surrounding localities. In early 1942, about 2,500 Jews lived in the ghetto. In July and August 1942, Jews arrived in the ghetto from Kroscienko, Czorsztyn, Szczawnica, Czarny-Dunajec, and other localities.

On August 30, 1942, the approximately 3,000–4,000 Jews in the ghetto were rounded up, and a selection was carried out. About eighty elderly and ill Jews were led to the cemetery and murdered. Factory managers singled out their employees from among the crowd of Jews to insure that they remain temporarily in the townlet. Numerous families were divided up: parents were left behind and children were seized. When the selection was completed, those Jews not remaining in the townlet were ordered to turn over all valuables in their possession and were deported to the Belzec death camp. In searches carried out by the Germans, another approximately 150 Jews were found and summarily killed. Most of the Jews who fled during the operation were handed over to the Germans and murdered in the Jewish cemetery.

After the deportation, more than 100 Jews considered "fit for work" remained in Nowy Targ. A number of the survivors were sent to sawmills in Czarny-Dunajec, while others were concentrated in a labor camp established in Nowy Targ, which was liquidated on May 25, 1944.

NYÍREGYHÁZA

COUNTY SEAT IN SZABOLCS COUNTY, HUNGARY

Coordinates:
47°57' | 21°43'

The last national census conducted prior to the German occupation, taken in January 1941, recorded 4,993 Jewish inhabitants in Nyiregyhaza, accounting for roughly 8 percent of the total population. Most were merchants and artisans. The town had both Status Quo Ante and Orthodox Jewish communities, with various Jewish social and religious associations. The Status Quo Ante Jewish community operated a Jewish elementary school while the Orthodox ran a Talmud Torah.

In the summer of 1941, several Jewish families who could not prove their Hungarian citizenship were deported to a region in the Ukraine under German occupation. They were murdered on August 27 and 28 at Kamenets-Podolsk*. In 1942, young Jewish men were drafted into the Hungarian army for forced labor service; most were sent to the Ukraine, where many perished. Concurrently, numerous Jewish refugees arrived in Nyiregyhaza from Poland and Slovakia. Both Jewish communities supported the refugees despite their strained financial situation.

The German army occupied Hungary on March 19, 1944. A census conducted in the second week of April 1944 reported that 2,462 Jews belonged to the Status Quo Ante Jewish community and 2,054 to the Orthodox Jewish community in Nyiregyhaza.

The Hungarian administration remained intact and in force after the occupation. The ghettoization and deportation of the Jews were carried out on the basis of the decrees and orders of the Hungarian national and local authorities. On

April 13, 1944, the Hungarian sub-prefect of Szabolcs County, Dr. Sandor Bor-bely, distributed among the county officials the confidential decree issued by the minister of interior concerning the concentration of the Jews, with his own addition relating to his county. In Nyiregyhaza, the Eichmann-Sonderkommando was represented by SS-Hauptsturmfuehrer Dr. Siegfried Seidl.

On April 14, 1944, Hungarian gendarmes began moving the Jews into a ghetto established along a single block in a large Jewish neighborhood of the town; initially, Jews were brought in from other localities of the county, totaling 3,010 people.

A Jewish Council was established on April 15, headed by the last serving president of the Status Quo Ante Jewish community, retired bank manager Gabor Fischbein. On April 23, 1944, the Jewish population of the town began moving into the ghetto, which became extremely overcrowded: some 11,000 people lived in 123 houses. Jews from six county-districts of Szabolcs County were moved to the ghetto as well. While a number of the Jews were moved to the Varjulapos farmstead (*Varjulaposi puszta*) near Nyiregyhaza on the estate of the Counts Dessewffy, living conditions in the town ghetto were exceedingly poor. The town itself contained few public utilities, while the ghetto had no water mains or sewage system altogether. The ghetto had a makeshift hospital; patients requiring operations were taken to the town hospital. Dr. Kalman Breider was the ghetto's chief physician.

Zoltan Horvath was the Hungarian commander of the ghetto and Bela Farago was the commander of the Jewish Order Service that maintained internal order in the ghetto. The inhabitants of the ghetto were interrogated and tortured by gendarmes seeking hidden valuables.

The inhabitants of the Nyiregyhaza ghetto were starving, as the Jews arriving from the county-districts could not bring any food along. Water supplies were also insufficient. The Jewish Council informed the town authorities of the appalling conditions in the ghetto, particularly the danger of epidemics, in a letter. The town authorities thus decided to move the Jews out of the town, to three farmsteads: Simapuszta, Nyirjespuszta, and Harangodpuszta. On May 5, 1944, the Jewish Council petitioned the mayor not to relocate the ghetto, to no avail, and relocation was carried out as of the same day. On the farms, the Jews lived without shelter and were forced to sleep on the bare ground. A typhus epidemic broke out, claiming many victims.

On May 5, 1944, the local county governor reported 15,220 Jews living in the Nyiregyhaza ghetto. By May 10, this number had increased to 17,580. About 5,000 of the inhabitants were Nyiregyhaza Jews.

At the farmsteads, Jews were once more interrogated and tortured by gendarmes in search of any remaining hidden valuables. The viciousness of Jozsef Trencsenyi was exceptional even among the gendarmes notorious for their brutality.

The inhabitants of the ghetto were deported to Auschwitz on May 12, 18, and 26, and on June 4, 1944 (according to other sources in five transports on May 15, 23, 25, 29, and June 6, 1944).

Orsha, Belarus, USSR

"I saw the ghetto in Orsha. It was even more terrible than that of Minsk. Freezing old women rummaged among the corpses. Girls, bruised and swollen from hunger, asked: 'When will they come for us?' Death seemed a relief to them."

"The Story of Mrs. Pikman, an Engineer from Mozyr", The Black Book, *edited by Ilya Ehrenburg & Vasily Grossman, copyright © 1980 by Yad Vashem & Israel Research Institute of Contemporary Society, English Translation by John Glad and James S. Levine, p. 205.*

OBODOVKA

(Ukrainian: **Obodivka**)

COUNTY SEAT, VINNITSA DISTRICT, UKRAINE, USSR

During the war: Transnistria (under Romanian control)

Coordinates:
48°23' | 29°15'

In the early twentieth century, more than 1,500 Jews lived in Obodovka, representing roughly one-third of the townlet's population. During the civil war in Russia (1918–20), in May 1919, a Ukrainian gang murdered about 250 Jewish men in the townlet. The pogroms prompted many of Obodovka's Jews to leave, so that some 500 Jews lived in the townlet in the interwar period. Most engaged in artisanship, and, by the end of the 1920s, in commerce; a few were farmers. Under the Soviet regime, the townlet had a Yiddish-language school and a synagogue.

The Germans occupied Obodovka on July 28, 1941, but since most of the Jews had managed to flee when the Red Army retreated, only fifteen Jewish families remained in the townlet. On September 1, 1941, Obodovka was annexed to Transnistria, which was under Romanian control.

In November 1941, about 10,000 Jews deported from Bukovina and Bessarabia were transferred to Obodovka. The Jewish quarter, which was in the center of the townlet, was declared a ghetto and encircled by a barbed-wire fence. The Jews were ordered to work in construction and farming. Many Jews were assigned to forced labor in German labor camps, where most perished. The death rate in the ghetto was high, especially in the winter of 1941/42, when thousands of Jews perished owing to overcrowding, hunger, cold, and poor sanitary conditions, as well as from epidemic typhus.

At the initiative of the authorities, a Jewish council and Jewish Order Service were established in the ghetto. The council occasionally managed to add the names of Ukrainian Jews who had fled from the German occupation zone to the lists of deportees, thereby granting them legal status as residents of the ghetto. In the spring of 1942, the Jewish council established a public soup kitchen for the needy and later set up a twelve-bed hospital in the ghetto. In the fall of 1942, help in the form of food and medication began to arrive in Obodovka from the aid committee in Bucharest. According to the committee's figures, by March 1943, altogether 1,460 Jews remained in the Obodovka ghetto.

In 1943, a partisan unit active in the area maintained ties with the inhabitants of the ghetto, one of whom (Meir Pecherski) participated in its activities. In February 1944, the remaining Jews in the ghetto were robbed by retreating German and Ukrainian soldiers.

Obodovka was liberated by the Red Army on March 14, 1944.

OBOLTSY

(Belarussian: **Abol'tsy**)

VILLAGE IN TOLOCHIN COUNTY, VITEBSK DISTRICT, BELARUS, USSR

During the war: Military Administration Area

Coordinates:
54°36' | 29°50'

In the mid-1920s, there were about 300 Jews living in the village of Oboltsy. Many were farmers, who under Soviet rule were collectivized in a kolkhoz.

The Germans occupied Oboltsy on July 6–8, 1941. On August 26, 1941, about thirty Jewish families were concentrated in two school buildings, which became a ghetto guarded by Germans. The Jews were ordered to wear yellow Star-of-David armbands. Jews aged thirteen years and over were seized for forced labor. Boris Entin was named head of the Jews. In spring 1942, after the ghetto inhabitants learned that all Jews in the nearby Smolyany* ghetto had been murdered on April 5 of that year, about sixty Jews fled to the forests under the leadership of Semion Yofik, former head of the Jewish kolkhoz. Some crossed the front to the Soviet side; many joined the partisans. On June 4, 1942, the Germans murdered all remaining ghetto residents at a nearby location.

ODESSA

(Ukrainian: **Odesa**)

DISTRICT SEAT, UKRAINE, USSR

During the war: Transnistria (under Romanian control)

Coordinates:
46°28' | 30°44'

From the nineteenth century, Odessa was a port city with highly developed commerce and industry. Boasting one of the largest concentrations of Eastern European Jewry, Odessa was a major center of the Enlightenment, Hebrew literature, and the Hibat Zion movement, and stood as an exemplar of the modernization of Russia's Jews. In the early twentieth century, Odessa had a Jewish population of about 140,000, representing approximately one-third of the city's population.

During the period of Soviet rule, the city saw considerable development of its industry, and attracted many Jews who took up work as laborers and clerks. By the mid-1930s, more than 20,000 Jews worked in government factories and institutions. More than half of the members of the artisans' cooperatives were Jews. Throughout the entire Soviet period, Odessa was a magnet for Jews, and its Jewish population rose to about 200,000 in the 1930s.

In the 1920s, most of Odessa's Jewish children attended schools in which the language of instruction was Russian. Nevertheless, during this period, Yiddish-language schools and kindergartens continued to be active in Odessa, as were a department for the study of Yiddish language and literature in the Odessa Pedagogical Institute, the Mendele Mocher Sforim Museum of Jewish Culture, a Jewish academic library, and other Jewish institutions. From the mid-1920s onward, a Yiddish-language weekly was published in Odessa. Police departments and marriage registries whose working language was Yiddish also operated in the city. In the mid-1930s, the Soviet authorities began to reduce the number of schools and cultural institutions that operated in Yiddish.

Odessa was occupied by the Romanians (allies of the Germans) on October 16, 1941, following a weeks-long siege. About half of the Jewish population in the city managed to evacuate or flee to the east before the Romanians entered the city. Meanwhile, thousands of Jewish refugees arrived in Odessa from Bessarabia and southern Ukraine. Thousands of civilians were murdered in the city as early as the first night of the occupation (8,000 according to Soviet sources), many of them Jews.

On October 22, 1941, hundreds of Romanian soldiers were killed when a squad of Soviet sappers blew up the Romanian army headquarters in Odessa. In retaliation, the military and gendarmerie authorities launched a massacre and mass deportation, which was carried out over several months. Within a short time of the detonation, the Romanians began to drive out tens of thousands of Odessa's Jews on foot, while thousands of others were concentrated for short periods in areas designated as ghettos by the Romanians.

Odessa
With the occupation of the city on October 17, 1941, Jewish men were ordered to report for registration. (YV)

In late October 1941, at the orders of the Romanian governor of Transnistria, Gheorghe Alexianu, about 25,000 of Odessa's Jews were concentrated in a ghetto established in the Slobodka area of the city. The living conditions in the ghetto were extremely harsh, and hunger and bitter cold caused the death of hundreds, perhaps thousands of Jews. On November 3, 1941, ten days after they had been imprisoned in the Slobodka ghetto, children, women, and the elderly were permitted to return to their homes, whereas the men were transferred to the municipal jail. In mid-November, the Romanians once again concentrated the Jews in the Slobodka ghetto, as well as in the village of Dalnik and in other places in the city. Many Jews perished, committed suicide, or were murdered.

On December 28, 1941, the commander of the Romanian headquarters transmitted the orders handed down by Romanian ruler Marshal Ion Antonescu to deport the Jews from Odessa, claiming that it would be criminal to keep them in their present location in the event of a Soviet invasion of the city or its environs. The first stage of the deportation involved concentrating the Jews from Odessa in Slobodka. On January 10, 1942, the city commander issued a decree giving the Jews two days to move to Slobodka under the threat of severe punishment. The Romanian authorities designated Slobodka as a ghetto and forbade the Jews to leave its confines. It was encircled by a barbed-wire fence and guarded by special units. The Jews were compelled to pay to live in the houses belonging to the non-Jewish residents of the quarter. Hunger and epidemic typhus soon spread. The doctors organized a hospital that operated for a short time.

By January 12, 1942, the Romanians had begun to deport the Jews from the ghetto to villages in counties near Odessa, as well as to nearby districts, where most either perished or were murdered. The Slobodka ghetto existed until June 10, 1942, when its last 400 inhabitants were deported.

The Romanians murdered at least 25,000 of Odessa's Jews and deported another approximately 60,000, most of whom later perished in the places to which they were expelled. These actions were carried out by the Romanians without the collaboration of the Germans.

ODRZYWÓŁ

TOWNLET IN OPOCZNO COUNTY, KIELCE DISTRICT, POLAND

During the war: General Gouvernement, Radom District

Coordinates:
51°32' | 20°33'

During the interwar period, there were about 300 Jews living in Odrzywol, approximately one-quarter of the townlet's population. Most were merchants and artisans.

In the early stages of World War II, hundreds of Jewish refugees poured into Odrzywol. In the fall of 1941, German authorities created a ghetto in a small area on the edge of the townlet. Over 700 Jews were crammed into it, with twelve or thirteen people to a room. The Germans deported a number of the residents to labor camps.

The ghetto was liquidated on August 20, 1942, when its inhabitants were moved to the Nowe Miasto on the Pilica* ghetto. Two months later, they were sent to the Treblinka death camp.

OLEVSK

(Ukrainian: **Olevs'k**)

COUNTY SEAT, ZHITOMIR DISTRICT, UKRAINE, USSR

During the war: Reichskommissariat Ukraine

Coordinates:
51°13' | 27°39'

During the interwar years, there were 3,000 Jews in Olevsk, approximately 40 percent of the townlet's population. Under Soviet rule, Olevsk was a border townlet. As the last stop on the railroad to Sarny*–Brzesc on the Bug*, Poland, many Jews seeking to leave the USSR in the early 1920s passed through the townlet. In the first half of the 1920s, Hashomer Hatzair and Hehalutz sustained their illegal Zionist activities in Olevsk. The townlet had a government school that taught in Yiddish.

The Germans occupied Olevsk on August 8, 1941. Although many Jews managed to escape or evacuate from the townlet, more than 100 families remained. On August 20, 1941, the Ukrainian Poleskaya Sich Battalion under the command of Maxim Borovets (a.k.a. Taras Bulba) joined forces with the Germans. A ransom was imposed on the Jews, whose properties were also targeted by numerous break-ins and random acts of looting. Two Jewish workers at a porcelain factory were murdered. In late August, Ukrainian soldiers arrested thirty Jews and subjected them to various depredations.

In October 1941, on German orders, the Ukrainians concentrated the Jews in a ghetto that encompassed two streets, Oktyabrskaya and Komsomolskaya. The overcrowding was severe. A yellow-star and yellow-armband decree was instituted.

On November 19, 1941, the Jews were concentrated in a stable and garage. The elderly or ill who were unable to walk were shot there. On November 20, the others were taken to the nearby village of Varvarovka, and all 500 were murdered on the banks of the Ubort River. Ukrainian police played an active part in rounding up, escorting, and murdering the victims.

OLGOPOL

(Ukrainian: **Ol'hopil'**)

TOWN IN CHECHELNIK COUNTY, VINNITSA DISTRICT, UKRAINE, USSR

During the war: Transnistria (under Romanian control)

Coordinates:
48°12' | 29°30'

In the early twentieth century, about 2,500 Jews lived in Olgopol, representing approximately one-third of the town's population. During the civil war in Russia (1918–20), Ukrainian gangs murdered about twenty Jews in pogroms, prompting many Jews to leave the town. The town's Jewish population also decreased in the Soviet period as a consequence of industrialization and urbanization. In the 1930s, many of the town's Jews worked in a nearby Jewish kolkhoz. Olgopol had a Jewish Ethnic Soviet that produced documentation and ran meetings in Yiddish, and a Yiddish-language school. By the eve of the German invasion, 650 Jews remained in the town.

The Germans occupied Olgopol on July 26, 1941. By that time, many of the Jews had fled or been evacuated to the east. The approximately 100 to 150 Jews who remained were enclosed in a ghetto located in the town's Jewish quarter. On September 1, 1941, Olgopol was annexed to Transnistria, which was under Romanian control. In the course of September, several hundred Jews deported from Bessarabia were moved into the town and put up in the homes of Jews and in the synagogue building. Ghetto inhabitants were required to attach a yellow Star-of-David patch to their clothes and perform forced labor. A number of Jews worked for farmers or engaged in artisanship. Romanian gendarmes robbed and occasionally murdered Jews in the ghetto. Many of the Jews suffered from hunger, especially the refugees. In November–December 1941, many died of epidemic typhus.

In September 1942, assistance began to reach the ghetto from the aid committee in Bucharest, and in March 1943, a public soup kitchen for the needy was opened. Subsequent to the arrival in Olgopol of about 100 Romanian Jews from the camp for political prisoners in Vapnyarka in May 1943, the Jewish leadership in the ghetto was reorganized and a committee was established that operated with dual leadership: an official leader for outside purposes and an informal inside leader. The official leader, a Transylvanian Jew, convinced Romanian authorities to allow the ghetto to operate autonomously in matters related to order, discipline, and the division of labor. Jewish doctors determined the extent of the inhabitants' fitness for work, and the authorities in turn recruited Jews for work based on these medical decisions. The public soup kitchen was reorganized and expanded and a dental clinic was established as well. Further outbreaks of epidemic typhus were thwarted when the Jews received permission to use the bathhouse outside the ghetto and adopted rigorous hygiene practices. At the initiative of the youth counselors who had been transferred from Romania, cultural and social activities for the children were organized. According to the figures of the Bucharest help committee, 724 Jews lived in the Olgopol ghetto in March 1943.

The ghetto council also established contact with partisans as well as with the Jewish inmates from the concentration camp for political prisoners in Vapnyarka, who were distributed among the ghettos in the area. A number of soldiers of the Italian unit stationed near Olgopol assisted the ghetto with food supplies and helped the refugees in the Olgopol ghetto contact their relatives in Romania.

Olgopol was liberated by the Red Army on March 22, 1944.

OLKUSZ

COUNTY SEAT, KIELCE DISTRICT, POLAND

During the war: Upper Silesia

Coordinates:
50°17' | 19°34'

After World War I, there were about 2,500 living Jews in Olkusz, approximately one-quarter of the town's population. They worked in manufacturing, crafts, and commerce, and established large self-help enterprises. Vibrant Zionist and pioneering activities coexisted with political and educational activities sponsored by Agudath Israel. In the 1926 municipal elections, Jewish candidates won eight of twenty-four seats, and one candidate was elected deputy mayor.

The Germans occupied Olkusz in September 1939. A few Jews, chiefly youths, fled eastward to the Soviet-controlled zone of Poland. Immediately after taking the town, the Germans took to persecuting the Jews, looting their property, and conscripting workers for forced labor. Jews were not allowed to use the townlet's main streets. They were required to wear white armbands marked with a blue Star-of-David, later replaced by a yellow Star-of-David badge on the back and front of their clothing. The Germans expropriated Jewish-owned homes and businesses and forced the community to remit large sums in silver and gold.

A Judenrat was established in Olkusz in the autumn of 1939. In November, it set up a soup kitchen for the needy.

In 1940 a central Judenrat for the Jews of Central Upper Silesia, known as the Zentrale, was established in Sosnowiec*. The Olkusz Judenrat was subordinated to the Zentrale, and its members were evidently replaced. In early 1940, a Jew

Olkusz, July 31, 1940
"Bloody Wednesday." Rabbi Mosze Izak Hagerman is led to the marketplace, where the Jewish men were rounded up and ordered to lie face down. Following a day of humiliations and beatings, they were allowed to go home. (YV)

from Olkusz named Sobol was appointed as the Zentrale's representative in the town; he may have been appointed head of the Olkusz Judenrat at a later time. In March 1940, there were about 3,000 Jews in the town. More than one-third of this population required assistance from the Judenrat welfare department, which distributed food, supplied milk for children, provided meals at the soup kitchen, and absorbed preschool tuition costs.

On July 31, 1940, the Germans attacked several of Olkusz's Jews, killing two, as a reprisal for the murder of a German policeman (who was apparently murdered by members of the Polish resistance).

From the beginning of the occupation, the Germans conscripted Jews from Olkusz for forced labor in and around the town. Jews were initially abducted in the streets, but the responsibility for recruitment was eventually turned over to the Judenrat. As of October 1940, the Germans also sent Jews to distant labor camps, mainly in Silesia. The first group of young Jews from Olkusz whose names appeared on Judenrat lists departed in October 1940. A Jewish doctor examined the candidates and determined whether they were able-bodied. While their term of labor was set at three months, the youths never returned. In early November 1940, by order of the Zentrale, the Judenrat registered all Jewish men aged eighteen to forty-five. Thereafter, groups comprising dozens of Jewish men were sent to the labor camps every few months; from the end of 1941, women were sent as well. Although conscription was officially based on Judenrat lists, Jews were also seized in the streets and from their homes. Residents of Olkusz were distributed among numerous camps, including Annaberg (Gora Swiatyni), Neukirch (Nowy Kosciol), Brande (Prady), Hansdorf (Hanuszow), Klettendorf (Kielczyna), Markstadt (Laskowice Olawskie), Gross-Masselwitz, Gross-Rosen, Blechhammer, and Buchenwald.

Between January and May 1941, the Judenrat offered vocational courses of three- to five-months' duration. More than fifty young people studied electronics, tailoring, millinery, and other trades. In July 1941, a forty-bed hospital, staffed by a doctor and seven nurses, was established in the former high school. Most of the patients were laborers who had returned from labor camps around Opole*, Silesia.

In September 1941, with only several days' notice, the Jews of Olkusz were transferred to a ghetto on the outskirts of town. The Judenrat prepared living quarters in the designated area. The Germans allowed the Jews to bring along all of their remaining possessions, and the Judenrat hired horse-drawn carts to facilitate the move. Carried out over a ten-day period, the transfer was supervised by Germans from Bedzin* and Sosnowiec as well as members of the Jewish Order Service. The Olkusz ghetto was not fenced, but inhabitants were forbidden to leave unless accompanied by a member of the Order Service. Congestion was severe, rations were meager, and the purchase of food from Poles was forbidden. The Judenrat opened vegetable shops and helped the needy, but could not fully meet demand, and many families went hungry. Food smuggling ceased after March 2, 1942, when three Jews accused of the prohibited activity were executed in the ghetto streets.

In an operation that began in Olkusz on the morning of June 10, 1942, the Order Service removed the elderly and the ill from their homes and assembled them at the soup kitchen. The Germans announced that they intended to deport about one-tenth of the town's Jews, and the Judenrat accordingly prepared lists that only included the town's weakest inhabitants. The following morning, however, the Germans surrounded the ghetto and rounded up all of its residents. On June 12, 1942, a selection was performed in the ghetto assisted by Moshe Merin, chairman of the Zentrale. Several hundred able-bodied people were separated out from the rest and sent to labor camps. The weak, the elderly, and the ill were housed in one building, while the rest were held in the local high school.

The first transport of Jews from Olkusz and the vicinity left for Auschwitz on June 13, 1942. Two days later, the remaining Jews were deported to Auschwitz, except for some 200 to 300 who were transferred to the transit camp at Sosnowiec. These last were well-connected individuals, including members of the Judenrat and the Order Service and their families, staff of the Jewish hospital, and workers at "Rosner's workshop" (a branch of the large Rosner factory in Bedzin).

Fifteen Jews were sent back to Olkusz to gather the deportees' belongings; they were moved to Sosnowiec a few days later. Ten other Jews continued to work in the factory in Olkusz until they were deported to a labor camp in 1943.

OLSHANA
(Ukrainian: **Vil'shana**)

COUNTY SEAT, KIEV DISTRICT, UKRAINE, USSR

During the war: Military Administration Area

Coordinates:
49°13' | 31°13'

In the early twentieth century there were about 1,200 Jews in Olshana, approximately one-fifth of the population. During the Russian Civil War (1918–20), dozens of the townlet's Jewish inhabitants were murdered in a pogrom. The pogrom, together with the effects of the industrialization and urbanization of the 1920s and 1930s, depleted the number of Jewish townspeople to some 200 by the time of the German invasion of the Soviet Union. Under the Soviets, the townlet had a government school that taught in Yiddish.

The Germans occupied Olshana on July 25, 1941. On August 28, they established a ghetto composed of several houses along one street. The inhabitants were removed from the ghetto for forced labor.

In October 1941, about 100 male Jewish residents were led out of the townlet and murdered. In early May 1942, the remaining Jews in the ghetto were assembled at the school, where the children were separated from the adults. Both groups were escorted to the Zvenigorodka* ghetto, and shared the fate of local inhabitants.

OŁYKA

TOWNLET IN ŁUCK COUNTY, VOLHYNIA DISTRICT, POLAND

(After World War II in the USSR/Ukraine; Ukrainian, Russian: **Olyka**)

During the war: Reichskommissariat Ukraine

Coordinates: 50°43' | 25°49'

During the interwar years, there were about 2,100 Jews living in Olyka, accounting for approximately half of the townlet's population. Most Jews in Olyka were artisans or petty merchants. Jews owned flour mills, a brewery, and two savings-and-loan associations, one of which was subsidized by the JDC office in Warsaw*. Zionist parties and pioneering movements were active in the townlet, some of whose members moved to the Land of Israel. *Yeshivat Nowogrodek* had an Olyka branch for some time. The community also ran a kindergarten, a Hebrew-language Tarbut school, a Jewish library, and several Batei Midrash.

When the Soviet occupation began in September 1939, all Jewish organizations and institutions in Olyka were forced to disband. The Tarbut school became a Soviet state school that taught in Yiddish. The Soviets withdrew from Olyka on June 27, 1941, and the Wehrmacht entered on June 29. About 100 Jews perished in German air raids.

As of July 3, 1941, Jewish inhabitants of Olyka were ordered to wear a Star-of-David armband and were conscripted for forced labor. Jews were required to remit a ransom and their valuables were confiscated. Both a Judenrat and a Jewish Order Service were established.

In the middle of August 1941, Germans murdered about 100 men, including the *Admor* (Hasidic rebbe) of Olyka. In the fall of that year, fifty Jewish youths were sent for forced labor to Kiev, where they were murdered.

The Olyka ghetto was established in late March 1942. Many Jews were brought from surrounding villages, raising the ghetto population to about 3,500. In the spring of 1942, thirty young Jews were sent for forced labor to Rowne*, where they perished along with the Jews of Rowne in July 1942.

The Olyka ghetto was liquidated on August 27, 1942. Most of its inhabitants were taken to a nearby location where they were murdered and buried in trenches two days later. About 500 Jews attempted to hide or escape, but most were captured and murdered. About 130 Jewish artisans were kept alive in Olyka after the liquidation of the ghetto but in January 1944, shortly before the liberation, they, too, were murdered.

Some time before the ghetto was liquidated, a group of resistance fighters that included Shlomo Tsam conducted several operations; they planted mines, blew up railroad tracks and a bridge, ambushed German and Ukrainian soldiers and police, and killed Ukrainian policemen and a German civilian official. From the end of 1942, the group engaged in combat with units of the UPA and from December 1943, it cooperated with Soviet partisans against the UPA. Almost all members of the group perished.

OPALIN

TOWNLET IN LUBOML COUNTY, VOLHYNIA DISTRICT, POLAND

(After World War II in the USSR/Ukraine; Ukrainian: **Vyshnivka**; Russian: **Vishnevka**)

During the war: Reichskommissariat Ukraine

Coordinates: 51°17' | 23°42'

During the interwar years, there were about 500 Jews in Opalin, almost half of the townlet's population.

In September 1939, according to the Soviet-German pact, Opalin was located in a Soviet-controlled military frontier zone. There is no information concerning the local Jews during the Soviet occupation (September 1939–June 1941).

The Germans occupied Opalin on June 23 or 24, 1941, two or three days after they invaded the Soviet Union. There is no information about what transpired in the townlet during the German occupation, but the Jews of the townlet were most likely concentrated in an open ghetto and put to forced labor.

On October 2, 1942, five Germans and several dozen Ukrainian policemen came to Opalin from Luboml*, rounded up its 582 Jews, and murdered them near the Jewish cemetery.

OPATÓW

COUNTY SEAT, KIELCE DISTRICT, POLAND

During the war: General Gouvernement, Radom District

Coordinates:
50°48' | 21°26'

Opatow, 1942
Majer Sztajnman and his daughter Mania on a ghetto street (USHMM, courtesy of Marion Weinzweig)

When World War II broke out, about 5,500 Jews lived in Opatow, representing two-thirds of the townlet's population. Most earned their livelihood from small-scale commerce and industry, especially in the garment, food, and leather-tanning industries. A small number of the townlet's Jewish residents were wealthy, especially those that leased areas of forestland for timber or owned sizable factories. Opatow had two Jewish banks, in addition to a free-loan society, traditional charity societies, and a hospital. The townlet boasted a range of schools belonging to all the educational systems: a Talmud Torah and a Yeshiva, a state public elementary school for Jews and Poles, and a Tarbut school. Political institutions active in the townlet included chapters of Agudath Israel, Zionist and pioneer parties, and the Bund.

On a market day in 1936, thirty Jews were injured in a pogrom carried out by thugs from Opatow and farmers from the surrounding villages against Jewish shopkeepers and their families.

After the war broke out, many young Jews fled from Opatow to the areas of eastern Poland that had come under Soviet control. After they occupied the townlet, the Germans torched the marketplace and the surrounding homes, property primarily owned by Jews. The following day, they imprisoned between 1,000 and 1,500 of the townlet's inhabitants, Poles and Jews, in the local cinema and held them under guard for two days without food or water. The Jews were separated from the Poles and were targeted for abuse. After the Jews were released, German gendarmes seized about 200 young Jews and took them to an unknown destination, from which they never returned.

In late 1939, all Jews living in spacious homes were ordered to vacate their property and move into the Jewish quarter, one of the poorest areas of the townlet. The homes were used to house German officers.

In early 1940, the Germans ordered the Jews to wear white Star-of-David armbands. They were forbidden to use the sidewalks in the townlet or trade with non-Jews, and were required to submit exorbitant ransom payments. The Jews were ordered to establish a Judenrat, which was headed by M. Weisblum. The Germans often held Jews as hostages, and the Judenrat endeavored to pay ransoms to secure their freedom. By the beginning of 1941, the Germans had seized all Jewish-owned businesses.

In April 1941, an open ghetto was established in Opatow. Jews from villages and towns in the area were also concentrated in the ghetto, along with Jewish refugees from Warsaw*, Vienna, and Lodz*. The population of the ghetto reached about 7,000. Owing to severe overcrowding, epidemic typhus broke out in the ghetto, especially among the refugees.

The ghetto had a TOZ clinic, a hospital with thirty to forty beds, and two public kitchens. The children continue to receive an education, and professional training and social aid were sustained. The Judenrat established a workshop for brushes, with the intention of providing work—with its accompanying daily bread ration—for as many people as possible. On July 16, 1941, a school was opened in the ghetto that offered six classes, in which 220 children studied in Hebrew and Yiddish. A Torah study group convened in the *Ohev Torah* Beit Midrash. A pioneering training facility with some eighty to ninety members of the Dror (Frayhayt) youth movement, Hehalutz Hatzair, and Hashomer Hatzair was active in a farm near Opatow. Their leader was Kalman Cherniakovski.

The Judenrat initially supplied the Germans with between fifty and sixty forced laborers each day to perform various services; in exchange, the Germans refrained from seizing people in the streets. After the establishment of the ghetto, representatives of the Todt Organization periodically entered its grounds to seize hundreds of Jews for work in slave-labor camps. Many of the abducted died of hunger, disease, and abuse, and a number committed suicide. The Judenrat endeavored to help the slave laborers by sending them food packages. The Germans also sent many youths from the training farm, including their leader Cherniakovski, to the labor camp in Skarzysko-Kamienna.

In early 1942, a group of Jews deported from Silesia arrived in the ghetto. The young people who still remained in the ghetto organized in an underground, and obtained and hid weapons they received from their Polish counterparts in Ostrowiec*. Through their contacts in the underground, they reached additional arms merchants. The girls were primarily responsible for hiding the weapons. The members of the SD and the Gestapo stepped up the seizures of people for the labor camps at this time, while escapes to the forests and to the "Aryan" part of the townlet increased, as well. On a winter day in 1942, members of the SD and the Gestapo raided the weapons cache belonging to the ghetto underground (apparently after someone informed on the group), murdered the young women found on the site, and shot a number of passersby.

The Opatow ghetto was liquidated on October 20–22, 1942. Members of the German gendarmerie and Ukrainian policemen surrounded the ghetto, rounded up its inhabitants, and deported some 6,000 of the ghetto's Jews to the Treblinka death camp. About 500 people were sent to the Sandomierz labor camp. A few dozen Jews were returned to the ghetto to gather up the deportees' belongings; when they completed their task they were murdered in the Jewish cemetery.

OPATOWIEC

TOWNLET IN PIŃCZÓW COUNTY, KIELCE DISTRICT, POLAND

During the war: General Gouvernement, Cracow District

Coordinates:
50°15' | 20°44'

When World War II broke out, about 150 Jews, representing approximately 20 percent of the townlet's population, lived in Opatowiec, a port townlet on the banks of the Vistula. Most earned their livelihood from farming, and a few were small-scale merchants and shopkeepers, artisans, or stevedores.

When the Germans occupied Opatowiec on September 9, 1939, the townlet had a Jewish population of some 120 people. In the first few weeks following the occupation's onset, the Germans ordered the local Jews to pay a high ransom and seized Jewish property. The occupiers also evicted Jews from their homes, concentrating them in a single street that was turned into a ghetto. Public, cultural, and religious activities were outlawed, and the Jews were forbidden to leave the ghetto's grounds. The younger Jews were assigned to forced labor, mostly to regulate the water level of the Dunajec River.

By 1941, the Jewish population of the ghetto had doubled to about 240, owing to the arrival of refugees from surrounding localities.

On November 9, 1942, German police along with SS and Gestapo soldiers carried out an operation. Only a few Jews were in the ghetto at the time, mostly the elderly and ill, and all were murdered. Most of the others had escaped to villages in the area, but were caught within a few days and also murdered by the Germans.

On November 20, 1942, the Germans discovered a bunker containing thirty-six armed young men and women; all of the youths were killed following a battle.

OPOCZNO 549

OPOCHKA

COUNTY SEAT, KALININ DISTRICT, RUSSIAN FEDERATION, USSR

During the war: Military Administration Area

Coordinates:
56°39' | 28°38'

In the 1930s, Opochka had a Jewish population of 580 people, more than 10 percent of the total population. In the 1920s, the community had a Heder and a number of the local children attended a Yiddish government school in Pskov*. Modernization and Soviet policy drove down the Jewish population of the townlet to about 290 people by the eve of World War II, less than 1 percent of the municipal population.

The Germans occupied Opochka on July 8, 1941, and the looting of Jewish property began almost immediately. Within a few days, more than 100 Jews were imprisoned and at least four were murdered.

In August 1941, some 200 Jews in Opochka were concentrated in a ghetto that had been established in a half-burned barracks. They received a minimum ration of a bread substitute and a concoction of potato peels. Many were put to various forms of humiliating labor. Murders of ill ghetto inhabitants began in November 1941. On November 7, the Socialist Revolution Day, the Germans executed a Jewish woman named Basia Melk, a refugee from one of the Baltic republics and the wife of a Red Army officer. By March 1942, some 120 Jews had been murdered. The ghetto was liquidated on March 8, 1942, when its remaining inmates were led to a nearby forest and shot to death.

OPOCZNO

COUNTY SEAT, KIELCE DISTRICT, POLAND

During the war: General Gouvernement, Radom District

Coordinates:
51°22' | 20°17'

In the 1930s, Opoczno had a Jewish population of about 3,000. More than 90 percent of employed Jews earned their living as artisans or petty merchants. Zionist political parties and Agudath Israel were active in the townlet. The community had a library, a Talmud Torah, a Beit Yaakov girls' school, and a Tarbut school. In November 1935, anti-Jewish riots broke out fueled by incitement by the Endecja, which also engineered a boycott of Jewish merchants. The community responded to the escalating antisemitism by intensifying its self-help efforts.

The German occupation brought an influx of refugees that boosted the Jewish population of Opoczno to approximately 4,000. Two weeks into the occupation, the Germans imposed a large fine on the community and took three of its dignitaries hostage. Mordechai Rosenbaum, a Jew who was fluent in German, introduced himself to the military commander of the town as the Jews' representative and undertook to resolve the hostage case. Some time later, the Germans ordered Rosenbaum to establish a Judenrat. Adam Fridlewski, a glass factory manager, was appointed as its head.

The Opoczno ghetto was established in November 1940. As it was composed of only 115 small houses, the Judenrat accommodated some 1,000 homeless Jews and many refugees in a provisional hostel in the town's Beit Midrash.

The Opoczno ghetto was open and unfenced. German policemen were bribed to disregard the Jews who slipped out and Poles who sneaked in. This arrangement enabled Jews to work outside of the ghetto, smuggle in food, and generally to remain in touch with the outside world.

The Judenrat had to provide the authorities with 400 men daily for various forms of labor. The workers were mainly assigned to the peat mines, but they also removed snow, built roads, laid cobblestones, and quarried minerals. Several small factories, such as a soap plant, operated in the ghetto.

The ghetto was swept by epidemic typhus in the spring of 1941 and 1942; the Judenrat fought the contagion by setting up disinfection rooms and sending a mobile disinfection chamber from house to house. There was also a hospital.

Youth activities were organized in the ghetto. Most prominently, a Gordonia group educated and looked after refugee children. It also kept in contact with the

Opoczno
The members of a Jewish family are executed after they were discovered in hiding, in the nearby forests. (YV)

movement's headquarters in Warsaw*, whose members delivered underground newspapers and instructional material to the ghetto.

The German authorities organized two transports of Jews to labor camps: 500 men were sent to the Narol camp near Tomaszow Lubelski* in August 1940, while 400 were dispatched to the Hasag camp in Skarzysko-Kamienna* in July 1942.

In early 1942, the ghetto population stood at 4,231. A large wave of arrests began on April 27 of that year, culminating in the deaths of 250 people who were hanged in three mass public executions.

Rumors about an imminent deportation circulated the ghetto in the summer and fall of 1942. The Judenrat attempted to thwart the decree by bribing German authorities, to no avail. The liquidation began on October 27, 1942, as some 3,000 ghetto inhabitants were sent to Treblinka. Roughly 200 Jews were murdered during the operation. Several dozen fled to the forests and joined groups of Jewish partisans, including the "Lions", who perpetrated many acts of sabotage.

By the end of the operation, about 500 people remained in the ghetto to perform forced labor. They were housed in the Judenrat building.

In response to a late December 1942 German announcement that all those with relatives in the Land of Israel would be transferred to a neutral country and exchanged for German war prisoners, the Jews of Opoczno readily reported to German authorities. Those who did not have relatives in the Land of Israel presented forged papers. At the beginning of January 1943, the people who had supplied the requisite documents were moved to a newly established ghetto in Ujazd*, and from there were sent to Treblinka on January 6.

OPOLE

TOWNLET IN PUŁAWY COUNTY, LUBLIN DISTRICT, POLAND

During the war: General Gouvernement, Lublin District

Coordinates:
51°09' | 21°58'

During the interwar period, about 4,000 Jews lived in Opole, roughly two-thirds of the townlet's population. Most wage earners were artisans or petty merchants. The community benefited from the services of a Jewish savings-and-loan association, a free-loan fund, and traditional charitable associations. All Zionist parties, Agudath Israel, and the Bund were active in Opole, as were traditional and modern Jewish schools.

The Germans occupied Opole in mid-September 1939. During the first months of the occupation, many Jews in the townlet were conscripted for labor in neighboring villages. On December 29, 1939, some 2,500 refugees were brought to the townlet from Pulawy*, and another 300 refugees from Jozefow arrived the next day.

The Germans set up an eighteen-member Judenrat in Opole, headed by Yankel Hochman. The Judenrat offices were situated in the old synagogue. A thirty-member Jewish Order Service was established as well.

In mid-1940, the Judenrat was ordered to prepare a list of all Jewish men aged fourteen to sixty. The list was used to mobilize contingents of hundreds of ghetto inhabitants who were periodically assigned to forced labor duty in camps throughout the district. The Judenrat allowed individuals to evade forced labor at a cost, and used the money to pay the workers' daily wages. Judenrat employees and doctors at the small ghetto hospital were granted permits exempting them from service in the labor groups.

In February 1941, some 2,000 Jewish deportees from Vienna were brought to Opole in two large groups, including intellectuals, doctors, and members of other liberal professions. A number of these new arrivals were lodged in the synagogue as well as in various other public buildings. By September 1941, about 100 had been allowed to secretly return to Vienna, in exchange for a bribe paid to the German district governor, Horst Goede, and to others.

In March 1941, about 7,500 Jews in Opole were concentrated in a sealed ghetto.

In October 1941, the Judenrat established a welfare committee headed by two of its members, Naftali Rubinstein and Albert Adler. The committee was affiliated with the JSS in Cracow*, which provided financial aid. The Judenrat opened a soup kitchen for children, refugees, and others in need and was also placed in charge of assisting Jews in nearby towns.

Until the winter of 1941/42, Poles who entered the ghetto with special authorization occasionally smuggled in food. That winter, epidemic typhus broke out in the ghetto and claimed more than 500 lives. The dead were evacuated daily and buried in the Jewish cemetery at night by the undertakers' unit of the Judenrat.

In March 1942, the ghetto absorbed 2,000 refugees from Kazimierz Dolny*. The Germans dissolved the Judenrat and replaced it with a new twelve-member council.

On March 31, 1942, some 1,900 refugees from Wawolnica* passed through the townlet en route to the railroad station at Naleczow, where they were placed

Left: **Opole**
Sign posted near the ghetto wall: "Caution, Germans and Poles are absolutely forbidden to enter the Jewish quarters." (YV)

Right: **Opole, June 1941**
Wooden bunks in the living quarters of women deported from Vienna to Opole in February 1941 (USHMM, courtesy of Lilli Schischa Tauber)

Opole
Jewish refugees deported from Vienna to Opole in February 1941 (YV)

aboard trains for the Belzec death camp. Members of Opole's Order Service gathered up the deportees' belongings in wooden huts that had been built next to the ghetto.

On May 6, 1942, altogether 1,270 Jews were deported to Opole from Jozefow on the Vistula. The following day, they were taken to the Naleczow train station and from there on to Sobibor. On May 25, 1942, some 2,000 Jews from the Opole ghetto itself were also sent to Sobibor. On May 30, 1942, roughly 1,400 deportees were brought to the ghetto—most had been deported from Slovakia on May 26, although a few arrived from France as well.

On October 24, 1942, approximately 400 German policemen and Ukrainian auxiliaries performed a selection among the ghetto inhabitants. A small group of young workers skilled in high-demand occupations was sent to the labor camp at Poniatow; the rest were taken to the Naleczow railroad station and from there were transported to Sobibor.

Some 500 Jews were left behind in Opole to gather up the deportees' possessions. The Germans murdered most of the ghetto's remaining inhabitants in November 1942 and transferred the others to labor camps in the Lublin area.

OPSA

TOWNLET IN BRASŁAW COUNTY, VILNA DISTRICT, POLAND
(After World War II in the USSR/Belarus)

During the war:
Reichskommissariat Ostland

Coordinates:
55°32' | 26°50'

When World War II broke out, about 450 Jews lived in Opsa, representing approximately half of the townlet's population. They earned their livelihood mainly from commerce and artisanship and were supported by various welfare organizations. In the wake of the Soviet entry into the townlet on September 19, 1939, the shops were nationalized and the Jews took on work in cooperatives.

The Germans occupied Opsa in late June 1941, and the abuse and terrorization of Jews began within days. A group of young Jewish men and women was executed outside the townlet. The Germans ordered the establishment of a Judenrat, and David Levin was appointed as its head. In December 1941, most of Opsa's Jews were deported to the Braslaw* ghetto; on June 3, 1942, they were murdered together with the Jews of Braslaw.

About sixty Jewish professionals remained in Opsa together with their families. They were concentrated in a fenced-in ghetto, which was turned into a makeshift labor camp. Jews who survived murder operations in nearby towns secretly entered the camp. On July 1, 1941, there were about 300 Jews in the Opsa ghetto.

The ghetto was liquidated in late 1942, when the Germans transferred all of its inhabitants to the new one that they established in Braslaw.

ORHEI

COUNTY SEAT, BESSARABIA, ROMANIA

Coordinates:
47°22' | 28°49'

About 6,300 Jews lived in Orhei in the interwar period, representing roughly half of the town's population. They earned their livelihood from the wood trade and raising sheep, and through artisanship, while others were shop owners, estate owners, and landlords. Orhei's Jews were aided by charitable and welfare institutions, trade unions, and artisans' loan funds. The children of the Jewish community attended traditional Hadarim and a Talmud Torah that had the curriculum of a public elementary school, with lessons in Yiddish and Hebrew. They could also attend a Yeshiva and two private schools as well as a Tarbut Hebrew-language school and a general public high school. The ORT network supported three vocational schools. For a time, the town had a Hebrew-language kindergarten and high school. Orhei had a Zionist-oriented Jewish library and a Hebrew choir. The community also boasted active Zionist parties and youth movements, pioneer training facilities to prepare for immigration to the Land of Israel, as well as the Bund. A Jewish hospital operated in the town.

At midnight on June 27, 1940, the Romanians retreated from Orhei; the Red Army entered the town the following day. In the first week of Soviet rule, dozens of wealthy Jews were driven out of their homes, and on June 13, 1941, many were exiled to Siberia. Commerce was handed over to the authorities, and many Jewish businesses were confiscated.

In late June 1941, after the German invasion, convoys of refugees from the north began to arrive on their way to the Dniester River. Though numerous Jews joined the retreating Red Army, many of them were killed on July 7, 1941, when German planes bombed convoys of refugees on a bridge over the Dniester, near Criuleni. Many other Jews perished during the retreat, in bombings, and from epidemics. A number of Orhei's Jews who had fled before the entry of the Romanian army into the town, returned.

After the Romanian-German armies entered Orhei around July 20, 1941, a delegation of Jews reported to the new authorities, receiving them with bread and salt. All of the members of the delegation were murdered.

In late July 1941, the Romanian authorities concentrated the approximately 4,000 Jews who remained in the town in a closed ghetto. Dozens of Jews perished daily of hunger and disease. The Romanian Major Filip Bechi, who called himself Herod the Second, perpetrated horrific murders in the ghetto. He personally instigated and participated in the executions of babies and young children. Jewish men were assigned to forced labor, and several were executed on the pretext that they refused to work. Jewish hostages were seized. Freedom of movement was restricted and Jews were required to wear a yellow badge. On August 6, 1941, the members of the 23rd Regiment of the Romanian army murdered about 200 Jews, including babies and children, disposing of their bodies in the Dniester.

The Jews of the Orhei ghetto were among the first in the district to be deported to Transnistria. The deportation was carried out in transports of about 1,000 Jews each, starting in mid-October and lasting until early November 1941. On October 12, 1941, the first convoy of deportees from the Chisinau* ghetto passed through the ghetto on its way north to Rezina. In early November 1941, the final three transports from Chisinau, holding altogether about 2,100 Jews, passed by on the road to Rezina. The deportees' belongings were confiscated in Orhei by representatives of the Romanian authorities or robbed by the local population after the Romanian army entered the town. The authorities discovered 345 Jews near the town who had managed to evade the deportation. On November 5, 1941, they, too, were deported to Transnistria. Four Jewish women, converts to Christianity, remained in the town, as did three women and five children with "Jewish blood" (that is, one Jewish parent).

Several hundred Jews managed to cross the Dniester River and escape to Soviet territory before the Romanian army entered Orhei.

ORLA

TOWNLET IN BIELSK PODLASKI COUNTY, BIAŁYSTOK DISTRICT, POLAND

During the war: Bezirk Białystok

Coordinates: 52°42' | 23°20'

When World War II broke out, about 2,500 Jews lived in Orla, representing roughly three-quarters of the townlet's population. They earned their livelihood mainly from small commerce and artisanship.

On Rosh Hashanah eve in September 1939, Orla was occupied by the Germans, but a few days later control of the townlet was handed over to the Soviets. For close to two years, the townlet was part of the Soviet-controlled zone.

On June 26, 1941, the Germans reoccupied Orla and immediately began to terrorize and abuse the townlet's Jews. The Germans appointed a twelve-member Judenrat responsible for recruiting Jewish forced laborers. The Jews of Orla were ordered to wear a yellow badge, mark their homes, and cut off their beards and hair.

A ghetto was established in Orla in August 1942. In early November 1942, the Germans encircled the ghetto and deported all of its approximately 1,450 inhabitants to Bielsk Podlaski*. They were later sent to Bialystok*. Some 200 Jewish professionals and their families were separated out and transferred to the Bielsk Podlaski ghetto. The remaining Jews of Orla were deported together with the Jews of Bielsk Podlaski to the Treblinka death camp.

OROSHÁZA

TOWN IN BÉKÉS COUNTY, HUNGARY

Coordinates:
46°34' | 20°40'

The last national census conducted prior to the German occupation, taken in January 1941, recorded 579 Jewish inhabitants in Oroshaza, approximately 2 percent of the total population. Most were merchants and artisans. The town had a Neolog Jewish community, a Jewish elementary school, and various social associations. In 1941, many local Jews were deployed as forced laborers to the Ukraine, on the eastern front.

The German army occupied Hungary on March 19, 1944. In April 1944, an SS unit arrived in Oroshaza, seized forty Jewish men from their homes at night, and shot them near the town. According to a census conducted in the second week of April 1944, some 450 to 500 Jews belonged to the Neolog Jewish community of Oroshaza.

The Hungarian administration remained intact and in force after the occupation. The ghettoization and deportation of the Jews were carried out on the basis of the decrees and orders of the Hungarian national and local authorities. The Oroshaza ghetto was established on May 16, 1944, in the Der lumber yard, which consisted of one apartment and a storage building. Additional Jews from the county-district of Oroshaza were also confined in the ghetto, and the total number of its inhabitants came to about 600 Jews.

The ghetto had three physicians; the sick were placed in a private hospital in the town. Detectives who arrived from other parts of the country cruelly tortured the inhabitants of the ghetto into revealing the whereabouts of their hidden valuables. In the aftermath of the torture, several people committed suicide. A number of the ghetto men were drafted for forced labor service and therefore escaped deportation.

After more than five weeks in the ghetto, its inhabitants were marched on foot to the entrainment center of Bekescsaba* (twenty-two kilometers from Oroshaza). On June 25, 1944, most of the Jews were deported on to Strasshof, Austria, via the entrainment center of Szolnok*. Those who remained in Bekescsaba were deported to Auschwitz on June 26, 1944.

ORSHA

COUNTY SEAT, VITEBSK DISTRICT, BELARUS, USSR

During the war: Military Administration Area

Coordinates:
54°31' | 30°26'

In the early twentieth century there were about 7,300 Jews in Orsha, roughly half of the local population. Several important railway lines passed through the town, including a line that connected Moscow and the west.

During the Soviet era, many Jews took jobs in state-owned factories and institutions as well as in agriculture. A significant proportion, however, continued to work as artisans. Two Yiddish-language government schools functioned until the summer of 1938. Shortly before the German invasion of the Soviet Union, there were 7,992 Jews in Orsha, about one-fifth of the local population, and some 600 more lived near the railroad station.

When Germany invaded the USSR, the accessibility of train travel enabled many Jews in Orsha to flee to the Soviet interior. Several were inducted into the Red Army. The Germans occupied Orsha on July 16, 1941, and registered the entire population in the ensuing days. The Jews were required to wear a black armband with a yellow Star-of-David and to comply with various restrictions. In August 1941, a group of Jewish men was murdered near the town, and several individuals were killed shortly afterwards.

The Orsha ghetto was established in September 1941 on a largely "Jewish street" near a Jewish cemetery. During a three-day period, some 2,000 Jews were concentrated in the ghetto, and non-Jewish families were evacuated. Soon afterwards, the ghetto was fenced, sentries were posted, and relations between Jews and non-Jews were severed. Congestion, malnutrition, and poor sanitation led to a typhus epidemic. Forced labor was instituted. The Germans spread rumors among the Jews that they would shortly be sent to Palestine.

The Germans appointed a Jewish Council in the ghetto, chaired by an accountant named Kazhdan. A heavy ransom—half to be submitted in cash and half in valuables—was imposed on the ghetto.

On November 26 and 27, 1941, Germans under the command of Paul Karl Eick murdered most of the ghetto population, about 1,800 people, at the Jewish cemetery. Only about thirty skilled workers and their families remained in the ghetto; they were later also murdered. In January–February 1942, children of mixed marriages and women with Jewish husbands were arrested; most were murdered at the Jewish cemetery. April 1942 saw the murder of another fifty-three Jews, all of them skilled workers or individuals who had been hiding in the town. A few who had gone into hiding during the liquidation operation in November 1941 were also murdered at the cemetery.

OSIĘCINY

TOWNLET IN NIESZAWA COUNTY, WARSAW DISTRICT, POLAND

During the war: Bezirk Zichenau

Coordinates:
52°38' | 18°43'

In the early 1920s, about 435 Jews lived in Osieciny, representing more than half of the townlet's population. They earned their livelihood mainly from small commerce and artisanship. The community had mutual-aid organizations and chapters of Zionist parties as well as Agudath Israel, which dominated its leadership. Jewish children attended traditional Hadarim and a Talmud Torah. In the 1930s, antisemitic propaganda in Osieciny increased, and many Jews suffered from an economic boycott.

The German army occupied Osieciny on September 10, 1939. Murders and terrorization of Jews began immediately, growing worse with the annexation of the area to the Reich in October 1939. At that time a Judenrat (known as the Jewish labor bureau) was established, headed by the "leader of the Jews," Noah Leshchinski. The main function of the Jewish labor bureau was to provide the Germans with workers. All Jews of the townlet were ordered to wear a yellow badge on their clothing.

In 1940, a ghetto was established in one of the townlet's poorest neighborhoods (whose name in Polish meant "geese in the village"). Living conditions in the ghetto were very harsh. During that period, a number of young people were assigned to work in Bielsk and Mogilno as well as in camps inside the Third Reich. Jews from Osieciny were also sent to the Auschwitz death camp, where most perished.

In the ghetto, the plunder of Jewish property continued. In January 1942, all of the inhabitants of the Osieciny ghetto were ordered to bring their valuables and gather in a large hall. While the Jews were away from their residences, the Germans plundered their homes.

The liquidation of the Osieciny ghetto began on April 15, 1942. The Jews were rounded up in a church and transported on to the Chelmno death camp. Twelve members of Osieciny's Jewish community survived the war.

OSIEK
(Cracow District, Poland)

TOWNLET IN JASŁO COUNTY, CRACOW DISTRICT, POLAND

During the war: General Gouvernement, Warsaw District

Coordinates:
49°57' | 19°17'

When World War II broke out, about 250 Jews lived in Osiek, representing approximately one-quarter of the townlet's population. They earned their livelihood from small commerce, peddling, and artisanship.

The Germans occupied Osiek on September 8, 1939. Immediately after the occupation, they imposed anti-Jewish economic decrees and restricted the Jews' freedom of movement. Jewish inhabitants were required to wear white Star-of-David armbands, and men were seized for forced labor. The community had a chapter of the JSS and a public soup kitchen that distributed hot meals, and also received free medical care.

In May 1942, a ghetto was established in Osiek that also held Jews from surrounding localities. The number of ghetto inhabitants reached about 500. In the spring of 1942, the Germans levied fines on the Jewish community and demanded that the Jews turn over their valuables.

On October 17, 1942, the Jews of Osiek were deported to the Staszow* ghetto, where they shared the fate of its residents, most of whom were sent to the Treblinka death camp.

OSIEK
(Kielce District, Poland)

TOWNLET IN SANDOMIERZ COUNTY, KIELCE DISTRICT, POLAND

During the war: General Gouvernement, Warsaw District

Coordinates:
50°29' | 21°32'

During the interwar period, about 600 Jews lived in Osiek, nearly half of the townlet's population. They practiced petty trade, peddling, and skilled crafts. On the eve of World War II, the community had branches of the Zionist political parties as well as Zionist youth movements.

The Germans bombarded Osiek in early September 1939. The homes of dozens of Jewish inhabitants were destroyed or burned down. Several Jews fled to nearby localities. When the Germans occupied Osiek, they threatened to punish escapees who refused to return, and thus succeeded in luring many people back to the townlet. Jewish inhabitants were required to wear a yellow star and were forbidden to walk on sidewalks, the community was obliged to remit exorbitant ransoms, and a number of Jews were mobilized for forced labor.

In late October 1939, the Germans in Osiek appointed a Judenrat and immediately afterwards began to conscript workers for labor camps in the area.

The Osiek ghetto was established in April 1942.

On October 25, 1942, SS men, German gendarmes, and Polish policemen rounded up the ghetto population. The ill and the elderly were summarily murdered. About 500 others were taken to the nearby railroad station, loaded into railroad cars, and deported to Treblinka.

OSJAKÓW

TOWNLET IN WIELUŃ COUNTY, ŁÓDŹ DISTRICT, POLAND

During the war: Wartheland

Coordinates:
50°55' | 18°45'

After World War I, there were about 700 Jews living in Osjakow, one-half of the townlet's total population. The Jewish community boasted welfare and charitable societies, a library, and a sports association.

After the Germans occupied Osjakow in September 1939, a portion of the Jews left the townlet, while others were deported. By the end of October 1939, about 600 remained. A Judenrat was established. Over the course of 1940, the 600 Jews were evicted from their homes and concentrated in an area that became a ghetto, while a few were sent to labor camps.

In the summer of 1942, German authorities began to prepare for the liquidation of the Jews of Wielun County. In July, 500 Jews from nearby Kielczyglow were moved to Osjakow. In the second half of August, all Jews in Osjakow were deported to Wielun*, where the Germans conducted a selection. Those deemed fit for labor were sent to the Lodz* ghetto, while the remainder were murdered in Chelmno.

OSOWA WYSZKA

JEWISH FARMING VILLAGE IN KOSTOPOL COUNTY, VOLHYNIA DISTRICT, POLAND
(After World War II in the USSR/Ukraine; Ukrainian, Russian: **Osova**)

During the war:
Reichskommissariat Ukraine

Coordinates:
51°49' | 24°13'

During the interwar years, there were about 150 Jewish families in this farming community. Most made a living in trade, crafts, petty manufacturing, and small-scale farming. The village had three Batei Midrash and one Jewish school.

The Germans occupied Osowa Wyszka in early July 1941. Toward the end of that year, a number of the houses in the village were collectively fenced in with barbed wire, creating a ghetto which was guarded by Ukrainian police. The Jews of Osowa Wyszka continued to work their fields under police supervision, while the community's youths were sent to the Kostopol labor camp.

In October 1942, the Germans transported the Jews of Osowa Wyszka to Kostopol* and murdered them all. Before the liquidation, thirty young people fled to nearby forests under the command of Yitzhak Zakuska to carry out armed guerrilla acts. They were later joined by women and children. After the ghetto was liquidated, the members of the group torched the Jews' homes and confiscated weapons belonging to Ukrainian police officers.

OSTRÓG

(Yiddish: **Ostra**)

COUNTY SEAT, VOLHYNIA DISTRICT, POLAND
(After World War II in the USSR/Ukraine; Ukrainian: **Ostroh**; Russian: **Ostrog**)

During the war:
Reichskommissariat Ukraine

Coordinates:
50°20' | 26°31'

During the interwar years, there were about 8,500 Jews in Ostrog, more than half of the total population. They engaged in trade and crafts, exported agricultural produce, and manufactured haberdashery, fabrics, and iron. They received financial assistance from a number of sources: the JDC, an organization of Ostrog expatriates in the U.S., and four Jewish savings-and-loan associations. The closure of the nearby Soviet border in the mid-1920s dealt a severe blow to the livelihood of the Jews of Ostrog. The Jewish community nevertheless managed to sustain a hospital, a pharmacy, and an orphanage. A branch of TOZ in the town looked after schoolchildren's health and sponsored summer camps for youngsters from poor families. The town had a Hebrew-language religious school, a Talmud Torah, two Yeshivot, schools and kindergartens affiliated with the Hebrew-language Tarbut system and the Yiddish-language CYSHO system, and two Jewish libraries. From 1936, youths could also attend a Tarbut high school. Zionist political parties, the Bund, youth movements, and pioneering training communes were all active in Ostrog.

During the Soviet occupation from September 1939 to June 1941, the mayor of Ostrog was a former Bund activist named Motl Gorin. After the Germans invaded the Soviet Union, on June 22, 1941, about 1,000 of Ostrog's Jews fled to the east.

The Germans occupied the town on July 3, 1941. Some 500 Jews were killed in the fighting. The Germans placed the Jews under a nighttime curfew and ordered them to wear a Star-of-David armband. Several days into the occupation, the Germans appointed a Judenrat.

On August 4, 1941, SS men murdered anywhere between 957 and 2,000 Jews (sources vary in their estimates) from Ostrog outside of the town, principally the elderly, women, and the ill. The following day, the Germans confiscated all the Jews' valuables and imposed a steep ransom on the community. On September 1, 1941, the Germans murdered 2,100 Jewish men from Ostrog in the Nikitycze forest. After these two operations, in which most members of the Judenrat were murdered, a new Judenrat was appointed and a Jewish Order Service composed of five policemen was set up.

The remaining Jews in Ostrog, mostly women and children, were assigned forced labor in and near the town. Several Jews were executed for smuggling food. The town's Jewish population was concentrated in a sealed ghetto in June 1942.

The Judenrat of Ostrog cooperated with the Judenraete of Zdolbunow* and Mizocz* in an attempt to bribe the Germans into rescinding their decision to liquidate the Jews of the three localities. Their efforts failed. The Ostrog ghetto was liquidated on October 15, 1942. In this operation, some 3,000 Jews were led out of the town and between 1,000 and a majority (sources vary in their estimates) of the people were murdered. Of the 800 Jews who escaped, most were later captured and murdered.

Nearly thirty Jews from Ostrog, living in a forest near the village of Chorow, joined Soviet partisan units.

OSTROVNO

(Belarussian: **Astrouna**)

TOWNLET IN BESHENKOVICHI COUNTY, VITEBSK DISTRICT, BELARUS, USSR

During the war: Military Administration Area

Coordinates:
55°08' | 29°53'

In the mid-1920s, there were about 400 Jews in Ostrovno. They practiced various crafts; a few took up farming. The Jewish population of the townlet declined due to industrialization and urbanization in the Soviet Union.

The Germans occupied Ostrovno around July 9, 1941. On July 19, 1941, they concentrated the Jews in a ghetto composed of ten houses along a single street. Although the ghetto area was unfenced, Jews were not allowed to leave its quarters. One Jewish inhabitant who refused to move into the ghetto was murdered. The Germans instituted a yellow patch requirement.

The ghetto was liquidated on September 30, 1941, when its 163 inhabitants were murdered, beginning with the young men.

OSTRÓW

TOWNLET IN WŁODAWA COUNTY, LUBLIN DISTRICT, POLAND

During the war: General Gouvernement, Lublin District

Coordinates:
51°29' | 22°51'

During the interwar period, there were about 1,500 Jews in Ostrow, approximately one-third of the townlet's population. Most earned their living in the garment industry and through commerce; they also dominated the local baking industry. The community benefited from a number of mutual-aid associations: a free-loan fund, a savings-and-loan association, a medical service for the needy, and a soup kitchen. Most Jewish political streams were represented, including Zionist movements, Agudath Israel, and the Bund.

The Germans occupied Ostrow in the first week of September 1939. They withdrew several days later in the wake of the Red Army. The Soviets in turn retreated to the east in late September in accordance with the Molotov-Ribbentrop Pact, and the Germans returned to Ostrow. During the several weeks long Soviet occupation, young Jews from Ostrow fled to the Soviet-controlled zone in eastern Poland.

In the first days of the German occupation, the Jews were stripped of their rights, their businesses, and, owing to the imposition of a steep ransom, much of their wealth. They were forbidden to interact with non-Jews and were ordered to wear a white armband marked with the letter J, later replaced by a yellow Star-of-David. They were barred from using sidewalks, and were required to be in their homes as of six o'clock in the evening.

A Judenrat was established in late 1939; the ghetto was formed at a later date.

In May 1940, the deportation of Jews from neighboring villages boosted the Jewish population of Ostrow to more than 3,330. Five hundred deportees from Lubartow* arrived in 1941, and roughly another 1,200 Jews from Poznan, Lublin*, and the former Czechoslovakia arrived between December 1941 and May 1942. Severe overcrowding in the ghetto led to epidemics.

The ghetto was liquidated in October 1942. The elderly and the ill were shot in it; the remaining inhabitants were deported to the Sobibor and Belzec death camps by SS personnel, German gendarmes, and Ukrainian police.

Many Jewish youths succeeded in fleeing the ghetto before the deportation. Most joined partisan units of the Armia Ludowa while the others went into hiding in nearby villages.

Ostrowiec, 1941
Public soup kitchen established in the town with the help of the JSS, the Jewish self-help organization (YV)

OSTROWIEC

TOWNLET IN VILNA COUNTY, VILNA DISTRICT, POLAND
(After World War II in the USSR/Belarus; Belarussian: **Astravets**; Russian: **Ostrovets**)

During the war: Reichskommissariat Ostland

Coordinates:
54°36' | 25°57'

About thirty Jewish families lived in Ostrowiec during the interwar period. They earned their livelihood mainly from small commerce and peddling.

After the Soviets entered the townlet in the second half of September 1939, a Soviet-style system was applied to most spheres of life. Privately owned shops were nationalized or closed and cooperatives were formed. Jewish refugees thronged to the townlet from the areas of Poland occupied by the Germans.

After the Germans entered Ostrowiec in late June 1941, Jews from surrounding localities were transferred to the townlet and shot to death in a nearby forest.

In the fall of 1941, a ghetto was established in Ostrowiec that held the Jews of the townlet as well as Jewish refugees from other localities.

The Ostrowiec ghetto was liquidated in late 1941 when most of its inhabitants were executed. It was then reduced in size and transformed into a labor camp. The families of a few Jews with required professions were concentrated in the ghetto along with the survivors of other ghettos.

In April 1943, a rumor spread that the ghetto's liquidation was imminent. A number of Jews fled to the forests; some were saved. The others were taken on April 7, 1943, to the nearby village of Szumsk, where they were shot to death.

OSTROWIEC ŚWIĘTOKRZYSKI

CITY IN OPATÓW COUNTY, KIELCE DISTRICT, POLAND

During the war: General Gouvernement, Radom District

Coordinates:
50°56' | 21°24'

When World War II broke out, about 8,000 Jews lived in Ostrowiec Swietokrzyski, representing more than one-third of the town's population. Most earned their livelihood from commerce, peddling, and artisanship, especially in the garment and food industries. The community maintained traditional charity and mutual aid institutions, including a free-loan society. The town's Jewish inhabitants were also assisted by the JDC, which supplied credit, food, and medications and distributed firewood. The social life of the town's Jews revolved around the Beit Midrash and Hasidic shtiblech. The children of the community attended a Zionist Tarbut school, a Yiddish CYSHO school, and a Szabasowka school. Zionist parties and pioneer movements were active in the town, alongside the Bund and Agudath Israel.

Ostrowiec Swietokrzyski was occupied by the Germans on September 8, 1939. Upon their arrival, numerous Jews fled the town, especially the younger people and members of the intelligentsia. Many Jews were seized in the streets and in their homes for forced labor, and on September 8–10, the Germans murdered fifteen Jews in the streets. The Germans periodically ordered the Jews to pay a ransom in both cash and valuables.

In late September 1939, the Jews were ordered to establish a Judenrat. It was headed by an attorney named Zeisel, who was later replaced by a merchant, Rubinstein. A Jewish Order Service was also set up. The Judenrat was tasked with recruiting slave laborers for the Ostrowiec Swietokrzyski branch of the German employment bureau, which utilized thousands of Jews for the German war industries.

In December 1939, about 1,000 Jews who had been deported from the Poznan area were brought to Ostrowiec Swietokrzyski. In early 1940, all the Jewish businesses in the city were appropriated. As of January 8, 1940, the Jews were ordered to wear white Star-of-David armbands and were forbidden to use the town's sidewalks or to have any contact with non-Jews. As of February 1940, the Jews were prohibited from leaving their homes, save during two hours in the morning and one hour in the evening. In March 1940, some 1,000 Jews deported from Vienna were brought to Ostrowiec Swietokrzyski. Several remained in the town, and others were distributed among the localities in the area.

During the summer of 1940, hundreds of young Jews from Ostrowiec Swietokrzyski were sent to labor camps in the Lublin area and to Belzec, which also served as a labor camp at the time.

In April 1941, a ghetto was established in Ostrowiec Swietokrzyski. The Jewish Order Service was assigned the tasks of keeping order in it and recruiting Jews for forced labor in the Starachowice labor camp, among other places. Two Polish policemen also guarded the ghetto.

Thousands of refugees who arrived from Warsaw*, Lodz*, and other localities raised the number of Jews in the city in late 1941 to about 15,000. On December 20, 1941, the Judenrat was ordered to turn over furs to the Germans. A Jewish man caught hiding a fur was publicly executed in the square. On April 28, 1942, thirty-two Jews were shot to death in the ghetto by German policemen.

The Judenrat established workshops in the ghetto, whose workers were required to pay for their right to employment. Hundreds of additional Jews from among the ghetto's inhabitants toiled in factories near the town run by the German employment bureau. While searching for work, many Jews began to build bunkers, seek out hiding places outside the ghetto, or attempt to obtain "Aryan" papers.

On May 8, 1942, SS officers from Radom* entered the ghetto. Jews who were working in the Bodzechow labor camp near Ostrowiec Swietokrzyski left for work early hoping thereby to escape deportation.

A group of youths planned to escape from the ghetto. Frumke and Hanche Plotnitski, couriers of the Jewish Fighting Organization (ZOB) in Warsaw, furtively conveyed money and underground literature into the ghetto. Miriam David Sholman, the Gotman brothers, and other young people called upon the Jewish inhabitants to set the ghetto ablaze at the operation's onset in order to cause a commotion and enable youths to escape to the forest.

In May 1942, SS officers from Radom carried out an operation in which about 3,000 Jews from the Ostrowiec Swietokrzyski ghetto were deported to Auschwitz. Only a few young people managed to escape and reach Warsaw, where they joined the ZOB.

In the second operation, carried out on October 6, 1942, SS men, German gendarmes, and Polish and Lithuanian policemen encircled the ghetto and rounded up over 2,000 Jewish inhabitants along with some 800 Jews who worked in factories of the German employment bureau, shooting to death several hundred. The patients in the ghetto hospital were also murdered. The rest of the Jews were held for three days and nights without food or water, and finally deported to the Treblinka death camp. About 300 Jews were summarily shot. Another approximately 1,000 Jews who attempted to hide inside the ghetto were caught, and murdered in Ostrowiec Swietokrzyski's Jewish cemetery.

When these operations were completed, the area of the ghetto was reduced. The workers in the German factories and the members of the Judenrat and Jewish Order Service continued to reside in the ghetto together with their families. The remaining members of the Judenrat were added to the ranks of the Jewish Order Service, which assumed the functions of the Judenrat.

On January 10, 1943, another operation was carried out in the ghetto. Those in hiding were discovered and rounded up, along with the Jews of Ostrowiec Swietokrzyski who lived in the sub-ghetto in Sandomierz*. These formed a group of about 2,000 people who were all returned to Ostrowiec Swietokrzyski and then deported to Treblinka.

After the January operation, the Jews remaining in Ostrowiec Swietokrzyski included more than 1,000 Jews who worked in the German factories, 30 Jews employed collecting and sorting the deportees' belongings, the members of the Jewish Order Service and their families, a number of Jews who were still in hiding in the town, and others who had managed to escape from the train to Treblinka and return to the ghetto. In early March 1943, the Germans brought back the Jews from the labor camps in Bodzechow and Starachowice to Ostrowiec Swietokrzyski.

In March 1943, the Jews were recruited to build a labor camp on the outskirts of Ostrowiec Swietokrzyski. During this time, many Jews attempted to escape to join the partisans in the forests. A group of seventeen young Jewish men made contact with and managed to join a partisan unit of the Armia Krajowa in the Kunow forests; they were provided with food and weapons and were trained to fight. One day, however, the partisans abruptly turned on the Jews, killing twelve. The remaining Jews were injured but managed to escape and return to the ghetto. Two additional groups joined Polish partisan units, and their members participated in an attack on the SS headquarters in Ostrowiec Swietokrzyski, damaged a train transporting supplies to the front, and took part in additional operations. Another group of Jewish partisans from Ostrowiec Swietokrzyski and other towns in the area was also organized; its members lived in the Bukowicze forest near Ostrowiec Swietokrzyski.

The Ostrowiec Swietokrzyski ghetto was liquidated in April 1943. On April 1, most of the Jews were transported to the closed labor camp on the outskirts of the city; 150 of them were deported on to the Belzec death camp. On July 10, 1944, as the Red Army drew closer to the town, the labor camp was also liquidated, and its inhabitants were deported to Auschwitz. There were few survivors.

OSTROŻEC

TOWNLET IN DUBNO COUNTY, VOLHYNIA DISTRICT, POLAND
(After World War II in the USSR/Ukraine; Ukrainian: **Ostrozhets'**; Russian: **Ostrozhets**)

During the war: Reichskommissariat Ukraine

Coordinates: 50°40' | 25°33'

During the interwar years, about 650 Jews lived in Ostrozec, roughly one-third of the townlet's population. They engaged in petty trade and crafts. There is no information regarding the Jews of Ostrozec while under Soviet occupation (September 1939–June 1941).

The Germans occupied Ostrozec on June 26, 1941, and shortly afterwards conscripted the Jews for forced labor. Jews were required to wear armbands with a blue Star-of-David; in September 1941, the armband was replaced by a yellow badge.

In August and September 1941, the Germans abducted about 140 Jews and murdered them in a location outside of the townlet.

The ghetto of Ostrozec was established in April 1942. Jews were brought from villages in the vicinity as well as the town of Turowicze, raising its population to about 1,700.

The ghetto was liquidated on October 9, 1942, when its inhabitants were led toward Mirowicze and murdered. Many Jews who attempted escape were murdered, but a few survived with the assistance of a Ukrainian Baptist and peasants in surrounding villages.

OSTRYNA

TOWNLET IN SZCZUCZYN COUNTY, NOWOGRÓDEK DISTRICT, POLAND
(After World War II in the USSR/Belarus; Belarussian: **Astryna**)

During the war: Bezirk Białystok

Coordinates: 53°44' | 24°32'

When World War II broke out, more than 1,000 Jews lived in Ostryna, representing roughly two-thirds of the townlet's population. They earned their livelihood mainly from commerce and industry and were aided by former residents of the townlet living in the United States as well as by local welfare organizations. Zionist parties and youth movements were active in Ostryna, as was the Bund. The townlet also boasted a number of Jewish educational and cultural institutions, including a Yiddish school and a Tarbut Hebrew school.

In September 1939, the Soviets occupied Ostryna. On June 25, 1941, the townlet was occupied by the Germans. About one week later, the Jews were ordered to wear a yellow badge and were seized for forced labor. A Judenrat was appointed. In July 1941, a number of Ostryna's Jews were murdered, including community workers and teachers.

In October 1941, an unfenced ghetto was established in Ostryna, and approximately 500 Jews were brought in from surrounding localities and from Nowy Dwor*. The head of the Judenrat, who refused to cooperate with the Germans in recruiting forced laborers, was sent to a concentration camp, and a new chairman was appointed as a replacement. Two weeks later, the grounds of the ghetto were reduced in size, sealed, and encircled by a barbed-wire fence; it contained some 1,200 Jews. The Judenrat opened workshops for tailors and carpenters who filled orders for the Germans and the municipality in exchange for a small quantity of food.

In late December 1941, the inhabitants of Ostryna's ghetto were ordered to report to the marketplace. Any remaining valuables in their possession were taken, and several of the Jews were shot and killed.

On June 6, 1942, about 100 young Jews were sent from the ghetto to a labor camp near Bialystok*. Most were added to a transport that left Bialystok on November 2, 1942, for the Treblinka death camp. About 120 youths, however, managed to escape, and several joined a partisan unit in the forests near Oszmiana*.

In October 1942, in all 1,969 of the residents of the Ostryna ghetto were rounded up in the marketplace and marched to the Kielbasin transition camp, where they were guarded by armed Germans and farmers. Most of the people were deported on to Treblinka about one month later.

OSZMIANA

(Yiddish: **Oshmene**)

COUNTY SEAT, VILNA DISTRICT, POLAND
(After World War II in the USSR/Belarus; Belarussian: **Ashmyany**; Russian: **Oshmyany**)

During the war: Reichskommissariat Ostland

Coordinates: 54°25' | 25°56'

About 3,300 Jews lived in Oszmiana on the eve of World War II, representing roughly half of the townlet's population. Most were artisans, but a number of Jews also earned their livelihood from commerce and farming. The townlet enjoyed a lively Jewish political scene, which included the activities of various Zionist parties, Agudath Israel, and the Bund. The community also had Jewish educational, religious, and cultural institutions, including a Tarbut Hebrew school, a Yiddish school, Batei Midrash, and a Yeshiva.

After the Soviets occupied the townlet on September 18, 1939, a Soviet economic, social, and educational system was introduced into the townlet. Privately owned shops were nationalized or closed and cooperatives were formed.

The Germans occupied Oszmiana on June 25, 1941, and within a few days began to confiscate Jewish property and impose restrictions on the Jews' freedom of movement. The townlet rabbi, Rabbi Heller, was ordered to establish and head an eight-member Judenrat whose function was to supply the Germans with property and equipment. In July 1941, German soldiers raided the townlet's Jewish homes, bringing male residents to the marketplace, where a selection was performed. Several hundred young Jews were taken in the direction of Lida* and never heard from again. On July 25, 1941, SS men aided by locals arrested more than 700 Jewish men, boys, and elderly people, including Rabbi Heller. The men were brought to the village of Bartel and executed. Following this operation, only widows and orphans remained in Oszmiana, along with a few dozen men who had managed to escape or hide. At the authorities' demand, Hinda Deul, a local Jewish woman, volunteered to be in charge of arranging the supply of Jewish forced laborers.

On October 2, 1941, the Jews were ordered to move into a ghetto located on a single street, in which Jews from nearby areas were also concentrated. The ghetto was encircled by a barbed-wire fence and had one gate. After the establishment of the ghetto, Skszot, the commander of the local Polish police, decided to appoint a new Judenrat.

The Judenrat set up a Jewish Order Service and established contact with the local population with the goal of smuggling food into the ghetto. Overcrowding and hunger in the ghetto were severe, and death and disease were rampant. In December 1941, Jewish refugees fleeing from mass murders in Lithuania arrived in the ghetto, as did Jews from nearby localities, inflating the ghetto's population to some 1,800 people.

In November 1941, a Wehrmacht unit arrived in Oszmiana. After some time, the commandant of the local gendarmerie, Krause, was placed in charge of the ghetto. Krause was meticulous in his registration of the Jews, and ordered the execution of dozens of refugees who did not appear on his lists, among them Jews who had arrived from Holszany.

In the spring of 1942, the Germans revised the administrative division of the area and assigned Oszmiana to the administration of the Vilna District. At the orders of the new commander, in July 1942, altogether 130 Jewish professionals and their families were transferred from Oszmiana to Molodeczno, where Jewish professionals were concentrated. Three days after the Jewish workers left, Lithuanian police arrived in the townlet to replace the German gendarmes. On July 16, 1942, about 350 youths were sent from the Oszmiana ghetto to a labor camp.

Survivors of ghettos in Belarus who began to arrive in the Oszmiana ghetto towards the end of the summer of 1942 told of mass murders, which prompted the inhabitants of the ghetto to prepare hiding places or to escape. In August 1942, hundreds of Jews were deported to a Todt Organization labor camp. The population of the ghetto grew, however, with the arrival of Jews from Holszany, Smorgonie*, and Krewo*.

In October 1942, the Germans announced their plan to reduce the population of the Oszmiana ghetto by executing 1,500 people. The job of selecting the victims was assigned to the Jewish Order Service of Vilna*. On October 21, 1942, twenty members of the Jewish Order Service of Vilna, headed by Salek Dessler, entered the ghetto and handed the Germans a list of some 400 people, most of whom were elderly and ill. The people on the list were taken to nearby Ugliowo, where they were murdered by Lithuanians. The head of the Judenrat in Vilna, Yaakov Gens, took the responsibility for submitting the list, arguing that 4,000 Jews lived in the Oszmiana ghetto, and sacrificing the few would save many Jewish lives.

Following the massacre, the ghetto was calm for a period of five months, during which the Judenrat ran various workshops.

In the spring of 1943, the Germans decided to liquidate the Oszmiana ghetto as part of their plan to "purge" a fifty-kilometer-wide strip along the Lithuanian-Belarussian border of Jews. The governor, Horst Wulff, ordered the head of the Oszmiana Judenrat and the Jewish Order Service of Vilna to select Jews for transfer from the Oszmiana and various other ghettos, to the Vilna and Kaunas* ghettos. From March 26 to April 12, 1943, about 700 of Oszmiana's Jews were transferred to the Vilna ghetto (primarily the "privileged" Jews and those with required professions). About 1,500 Jews were sent to forced labor camps in the area of Wilejka, which very few survived. The last remaining Jews of the Oszmiana ghetto, some 700 people who were promised transfer to the Kaunas ghetto, were ultimately taken to Ponary and murdered.

An underground organization called the United Partisan Organization was established in the Oszmiana ghetto. When the ghetto was liquidated, about 100 of the organization's members escaped to the Narocz and Rudniki forests, where they continued to fight alongside the partisans.

OTWOCK

TOWNLET IN WARSAW COUNTY, WARSAW DISTRICT, POLAND

During the war: General Gouvernement, Warsaw District

Coordinates:
52°08' | 21°19'

In the early 1920s, about 5,400 Jews lived in Otwock, out of a total population of 8,500. Otwock was a major vacation site in the Warsaw area, and many local Jews earned their livelihood through providing medical services, musical entertainment, waiting tables, kosher food supply, and other professions related to the tourism and health resort industry. The Otwock Jewish community had a number of charitable societies, and its *Bikur Holim* society established a clinic for tuberculosis patients and a clinic for the poor. Zionist parties and Agudath Israel were active in Otwock, as was the Bund. The townlet boasted Jewish schools, cultural and sports institutions, as well as youth movements and organizations. During the interwar period, the Jewish inhabitants of Otwock were targeted by a number of antisemitic incidents, the most vicious of which were anti-Jewish pogroms that broke out in 1936.

At the onset of World War II, many Jewish youths fled the townlet for the east. Otwock was occupied by the Germans on September 29, 1939. At the time, out of a total population of 24,000, there were altogether 13,500 Jews in the townlet (primarily undergoing the cures in the various spas). The Germans immediately set about plundering Jewish property, abducting Jews for forced labor, and murdering Jewish inhabitants. In late 1939, the Jews of Otwock aged twelve and older were ordered to wear a yellow armband. Shop owners were required to display a Star-of-David on their store fronts.

In October 1939, a Judenrat headed by Y. Lasman was established in Otwock. The main role of the Judenrat was to remit ransom payments to the Germans and provide teams for forced labor. The Jews of the townlet were shipped to labor camps, starting in the summer of 1940. Most of the work groups were sent to camps in the Lublin area, and many laborers were involved in building the Treblinka death camp, while yet others were sent to Tyszowce*.

In early July 1940, the first orders were issued regarding the establishment of ghettos in Warsaw County. With Otwock's unique status as a health resort and the townlet's economic life resting on its medical institutions, Otwock's mayor, Jan Gademski, petitioned to postpone the establishment of a ghetto. The request was denied. The orders to establish a ghetto in the townlet were received on September 26, 1940. The approximately 1,500 Jews who had resided in the townlet for less than six months, primarily patients treated in sanatoriums, were ordered to leave it within two weeks. A number of the Jews were concentrated in the Jewish neighborhood prior to the official moving order, which was issued on November 4, 1940. The establishment of the ghetto was accompanied by the formation of a Jewish Order Service, headed by Bernard Kronenberg.

The ghetto was divided into two parts: a residential area and the sanatorium area. The two quarters were connected by a single street. Only those with a medical permit were allowed to live in the sanatorium area. The ghetto was not

Otwock
Jews waiting in line for food at one of the three public soup kitchens in the ghetto (YV)

completely closed, but the Jews were forbidden to leave their area of residence from seven in the evening to eight o'clock the following morning, and from Friday afternoon until Monday morning.

The ghetto was not fenced in until 1941, and Jewish smugglers managed to bring some food into the ghetto by bribing Polish guards. The Germans continued to demand forced laborers. A "work battalion" of some 4,000 people was established, with its members leaving the ghetto daily to perform forced labor in German army camps.

To assist the needy, the Judenrat established a number of welfare institutions, including three public soup kitchens, an orphanage with about 200 children, and a children's home in which some 100 displaced children resided. In addition, the Judenrat instituted a sanitation department to supervise the hospital. The ghetto had another hospital for the mentally ill with about 100 patients. The educational system also continued to function in the ghetto; a number of elementary schools and kindergartens were opened, and Torah classes and lectures on literature and history were offered. Despite the organization of help for the poor, the social disparities among the ghetto inhabitants continually widened. The wealthy could afford to purchase food and pay to be released from forced labor, whereas some 6,000 of the ghetto's inhabitants were in need of urgent assistance.

In early 1941, conditions in the ghetto worsened considerably. On January 10, 1941, the ghetto was encircled by a fence, and anyone who crossed its border was summarily shot. The plunder of Jewish property continued, and in the winter of 1941/42, all furs were confiscated. On July 7, 1941, the sanatorium quarter was reduced in size, and an order was issued restricting the patients and medical staff to three sanatoriums in the quarter.

In the winter of 1942, the Jews were ordered to report to a collection point, ostensibly for the registration of professionals. Few people obeyed the command. With the help of the Jewish Order Service, about 150 ghetto youths were transferred to the Treblinka death camp. The following transport to Treblinka took place in April 1942, when the Germans demanded 400 youths, once again on the false pretext that they were to be assigned to work. Another several hundred of Otwock's Jews were transported to Treblinka.

The Otwock ghetto was liquidated on August 19, 1942. About 12,000 Jews inhabited the ghetto at the time. The day prior to the liquidation, an SS company, several Ukrainians, and Brandt, the commander of the deportation unit, arrived in Otwock. Brandt appointed Bernard Kronenberg head of the Judenrat; Kronenberg's first job was to dismantle the ghetto's houses and use the bricks to build a wall around the ghetto. All patients in the ghetto hospitals were killed before the general deportation, as were the doctors and nurses in the mental hospital. On the day of the liquidation, some 8,000 Jews were transported to Treblinka and Auschwitz. Their property was plundered by the local Poles. Nearly all the Jews who managed to escape to the forest were soon caught and murdered. The members of the Jewish Order Service were sent to Wilanow and to the Tarchomin camp, where they too were shot and killed.

OŻARÓW

TOWNLET IN OPATÓW COUNTY, KIELCE DISTRICT, POLAND

During the war: General Gouvernement, Radom District

Coordinates:
50°53' | 21°40'

When World War II broke out, about 3,200 Jews lived in Ozarow, representing approximately two-thirds of the townlet's population. Among the Jewish-owned businesses in the townlet were a glass factory, a sawmill, a flour mill, and leather-tanning workshops. Jews were active both culturally and politically, and their community had chapters of the Zionist movements, the Bund, and Agudath Israel.

In early September 1939, Ozarow was occupied by the Germans, who almost immediately began to seize Jews in the streets for forced labor. In early October 1939, the Jews were ordered to establish a Judenrat, whose members were selected from among the community's most highly respected citizens. The Judenrat was ordered to provide the Germans with updated population lists of the Jews and with forced laborers on demand. The latter worked under the supervision of Polish policemen or German gendarmes.

In early 1940, the Germans appropriated all Jewish-owned businesses in Ozarow, all the while beating and abusing Jews. Some time later, the townlet's Jewish inhabitants were ordered to move into its Jewish quarter, which was neither fenced in nor sealed off. They were also instructed to wear a white armband marked with a Star-of-David, were forbidden to use the sidewalks or make contact with non-Jews, and were required to display a sign on the front door of their homes bearing the word *"Jude."*

In December 1940, altogether 706 impoverished Jews were brought to Ozarow from Wloclawek*. The Judenrat put them up in the Beit Midrash, and the Jews of Ozarow provided them with equipment, clothing, and food.

In March 1941, there arrived in Ozarow 100 Jews who had been deported from Vienna and 792 Jews who had been deported from Kielce* and other localities in the Radom District, and they too were put up in the Beit Midrash. Overcrowding in the Jewish quarter was severe and led to an epidemic typhus outbreak.

In April 1941, the Jews of Ozarow were ordered to pay a large fine, and then turn over all of their furs.

In early January 1942, the Jewish quarter was fenced in and turned into a sealed ghetto. It now had a population of about 4,500 people.

At the outset of the deportations to the death camps in the summer of 1942, the Germans selected Ozarow, which was located on a crossroads, as a site of concentration for the Jews of the district. Following the Germans' decision, 1,349 Jews were brought to the ghetto from the Radom District; the Germans concurrently reduced the number of ration cards for the ghetto workers to one-sixth of the previous number, as they likewise did in the other ghettos in the district. During the summer of 1942, large groups of youths were sent from the ghetto to labor camps, where they toiled in German factories for long hours in exchange for meager rations.

In late October 1942, the ghetto was liquidated. The Jews were ordered to gather in Warsaw Square and bring along their bedding, eating utensils, and clothing. SS men selected twenty-five men from among those congregated and brought them to the police station. The rest of the Jews were marched to the train station guarded by SS men and Ukrainian police. Along the way the guards shot many people, chiefly the elderly and children. The rest were deported to the Treblinka death camp.

The Jews who remained in Ozarow were put to work collecting the belongings left behind by the deportees and cleaning up the ghetto streets. When they completed their task, they were marched by foot in the direction of Sandomierz* and shot to death en route by Ukrainian guards. Their bodies were tossed into wells.

ÓZD

TOWN IN BORSOD COUNTY, HUNGARY

Coordinates:
48°13' | 20°18'

The last national census conducted prior to the German occupation, taken in January 1941, recorded 721 Jewish inhabitants in Ozd, approximately 3 percent of the total population. Most were merchants and artisans; several were factory owners and clerks. The town's Jewish community was Orthodox and maintained a Jewish elementary school.

In the summer of 1941, the Hungarian authorities deported to a region in the Ukraine under German occupation several Jewish families who could not prove their Hungarian citizenship. They were murdered on August 27 and 28, at Kamenets-Podolsk*.

The German army occupied Hungary on March 19, 1944. A census conducted in the second week of April 1944 reported that 677 Jews belonged to the Orthodox Jewish community of Ozd.

The Hungarian administration remained intact and in force after the occupation. The ghettoization and deportation of the Jews were carried out on the basis of the decrees and orders of the national and local authorities. The Hungarian sub-prefect of Borsod County, Dr. Gyula Mikuleczky, ordered the establishment of the ghettos in the county on May 13, 1944. In mid-May 1944, the chief administrative officer of the county-district of Ozd, Gyula Hubay, ordered the Jews of his county-district to move into the Ozd ghetto. Jozsef Fodor was nominated as the president of the local Jewish Council. Two physicians worked in the ghetto.

In early June 1944, the inhabitants of the ghetto were taken to an entrainment center in the brick factory on Tatar Street in Miskolc*. A number of the Jews were then transferred to the Diosgyor* ghetto and a few days later, on June 12, 1944, were deported to Auschwitz. Those who remained in the brick factory were deported to Auschwitz on June 13 and 15, 1944.

OZORKÓW

TOWN IN ŁĘCZYCA COUNTY, ŁÓDŹ DISTRICT, POLAND

During the war: Wartheland

Coordinates:
51°58' | 19°17'

During the interwar period, there were about 5,000 Jews living in Ozorkow, over one-third of the town's population. Most worked in the textile industry. The community participated in political life, and Jews were well represented on the town council. During the 1930s, antisemitism in Ozorkow escalated, and Jews were targeted in several violent incidents. They were also subject to an economic boycott manifest for example in boycott vigils that were set up outside Jewish-owned businesses on October 5, 1937.

The Germans occupied Ozorkow on September 7, 1939, and shot many townspeople, including twenty-four Jews. In the ensuing days, the synagogue was torched and Jews were assigned to forced labor. At German orders a Judenrat was established, headed by Shimon Barchynski and his deputy Shimon Liska, as well as a Jewish Order Service, under the command of Yehoshua Parechevski.

Ozorkow, April 10, 1942
Ten Jews are taken to the gallows. They were publicly hanged in front of all the ghetto's inhabitants for disobeying German orders. (YV)

The ghettoization of the Jews of Ozorkow began in late 1939 and occurred gradually; no official order to set up a ghetto was ever given. The Jewish quarter was surrounded by barbed wire but as no guards were posted, several Jews continued to live outside the ghetto. Most of the Jews in the ghetto worked in clothing and shoe factories that the Germans had built within its perimeter. Some people managed to find work in German factories outside the ghetto, which made it easier to smuggle in food. The Judenrat also established workshops in the belief that Jews working for the Germans might be spared deportation.

In 1941, the Germans began shipping workers from the ghetto to labor camps in the Poznan area. The deportations carried on until April 4, when 400 men were marched to Stadion Miejski near Poznan. The Judenrat offered support to the deportees' families and sent relief parcels to the camps. Ghetto inhabitants sustained their religious life surreptitiously, holding a regular underground prayer quorum and religious studies for children.

The first step in the liquidation of the Jews of Ozorkow was the execution of eight or ten Jews, as punishment for the escape of one ailing Jewish woman from isolation. The Judenrat was ordered to collect the condemned, while all the ghetto's inhabitants were brought to watch the public hangings, carried out by a unit commanded by SS Major Heinrich Butschkow. The bodies were left hanging for two days.

Transports from the ghetto began in March or April 1942, when 300 to 500 Jews, including children, were sent to the Chelmno death camp. In April 1942, German doctors examined all ghetto inhabitants, separating out the healthiest and strongest.

The deportation of the Jews of Ozorkow was carried out, following a selection, on May 21–23, 1942, with the participation of Company 2 of the Feldgendarmerie. About 2,000 frail men and women were sent to Chelmno, where they were murdered, while the remaining 1,387 people selected for labor were sent to the Lodz* ghetto. Nearly 1,000 Jews remained in the ghetto, crowded into a smaller area that was administered as a camp; these Jews left the ghetto to work every day. On August 20–21, 1942, they were evacuated to the Lodz ghetto.

Prużana, Poland

"On October 25 we were moved to the ghetto. Part of the ghetto was surrounded by barbed wire, and part had a solid wall [...] We were presented with a bill for equipping the ghetto which we ourselves had been forced to build [...] In March 1942, Jews began to arrive from Ivantsevichi, Stolbtsy, and other places. They were in terrible shape: they were half-naked, and their hands were frostbitten. In April more people than ever were packed into the ghetto. In May people began to be recruited for the camps, from which no one ever returned."

"The Story of Doctor Olga Goldfayn", The Black Book, *edited by Ilya Ehrenburg & Vasily Grossman, copyright © 1980 by Yad Vashem & Israel Research Institute of Contemporary Society, English Translation by John Glad and James S. Levine, page 207.*

PABIANICE

CITY IN ŁASK COUNTY, ŁÓDŹ DISTRICT, POLAND

During the war: Wartheland

Coordinates:
51°40' | 19°22'

Pabianice was an important textile center. Before World War II, there were almost 9,000 Jews living in the city, accounting for one-quarter of the population. Most of the Jews of Pabianice worked in the knitwear industry. During the interwar period, Jews ran a credit bank, a commercial cooperative, and a large number of factories. Zionist parties, Agudath Israel, the Bund, and the (illegal) Communist Party were all active in the community. The city had Hadarim and an Agudath Israel primary school, and for some time, a bilingual Polish-Hebrew high school as well. There were sports associations and local Jewish newspapers. The period saw the growth of Pabianice as an important Hasidic center where many rabbis based their courts.

From the moment they occupied Pabianice on September 7, 1939, the Germans persecuted its Jewish population. They destroyed the synagogue and turned it into a stable, expropriated Jewish businesses, and abducted Jews for forced labor. In the fall of 1939, they ordered the establishment of a Judenrat; representatives of Jewish parties and public institutions elected Yehoshua Alter, Wolf Yelinovich, and Yaakov Lubranetski as its members. The panel was only in force for a few weeks. In early November 1939, when the three officials attempted to dissuade the Germans from evicting Jews from one of the city's quarters, they were arrested and sent to a concentration camp. The Germans replaced the three men with a lawyer named Shapira, who was succeeded shortly thereafter by Yechiel Rubinstein, who appointed the other panel members. The Judenrat had departments for matters such as supplies, welfare, finance, labor, health, and justice, along with a secretariat, a general administration, and postal services. The Judenrat was also responsible for supplying the Germans with forced laborers and drawing up a list of 500 Jews for deportation. Equipped with cloth-

Pabianice, May 1942
Jews are brought to the train station, and transported either to the Lodz ghetto or to the Chelmno death camp. (YV)

ing, food, and a small sum of money, the deportees were sent to Kaluszyn*, a town in the Warsaw District. A Jewish Order Service was established in Pabianice under Aba Kuperwasser.

In February 1940, the Germans established a ghetto in the old town of Pabianice. Warszawska Street divided it into two parts: "south" and "north." At first, the ghetto was unsealed; the only indication that it was a ghetto were the yellow Stars of David posted at the street corners demarcating its limits. Since food could be smuggled in, prices remained reasonable. However, overcrowding in the ghetto was severe, with several families often having to share one room. It contained about 9,000 Jews.

The Judenrat ran textile workshops and factories in the ghetto (in mid-1941 there were as many as eleven), as well as a metals and electro-mechanics factory. Some 1,200 to 1,400 Jews were employed in ghetto enterprises. The Judenrat developed new manufacturing lines and cottage industries turned out work for "Aryan" customers. Between 450 and 550 Jews were employed outside the ghetto in various German institutions. Most laborers received meager wages, while others worked for nothing but the opportunity to smuggle food into the ghetto. Inside it, food was officially distributed according to prices that were set by the Judenrat and included community taxes.

Among the ghetto organizations were welfare and medical institutions as well as a soup kitchen that distributed 20,000 lunches per month, some free of charge. The welfare department established an old-age home and supported fifty to sixty elderly persons. There was a clothing society for the indigent and a teahouse that sold inexpensive bread. The youth department tended to 150 children and set up a residence that also provided them with primary schooling. Other children in the ghetto studied in groups of twelve to fifteen in private dwellings. There was a sanitation department, a clinic, a hospital, and a public bathhouse. There were no epidemics in the ghetto, as smallpox vaccination was compulsory and homes were disinfected. Dr. Shweider performed surgery with the help of a Polish surgeon, Dr. Majer, who visited the ghetto every day and brought in medication and money.

On May 23, 1941, the first deportation saw 231 Jews taken to the Lodz* ghetto, and on to a labor camp. A second deportation of 313 people left the ghetto on September 7, 1941. Additional deportations followed until January 1942.

A number of embittered ghetto inhabitants blamed their plight on the Judenrat and denounced Rubinstein to the Germans. The heads of the Judenrat were arrested in October 1941 and were executed in the summer of 1942, following a long trial.

Conditions in the ghetto steadily deteriorated. The ghetto was sealed, some of its factories closed, and many Jews lost their livelihood. As of September 1941, the use of telephones in the ghetto was prohibited. In the winter of 1941/42, the Germans removed fifteen cartloads of Jewish property for their "winter aid" program. The Judenrat was ordered to prepare a register of the entire ghetto population, to indicate whether each person listed was working, and to record children up to the age of six as well as anyone who was physically disabled or mentally ill.

In the first half of 1942, shortly after the Chelmno extermination center was activated, a central warehouse was established near Pabianice for the storage of the personal effects and clothing of Jews murdered in the camp. Forced laborers from the ghetto were employed at the warehouse to sort and mend the victims' property.

The Pabianice ghetto was liquidated on May 16–20, 1942. Two months earlier, all inhabitants had been marked: those considered able-bodied with an "A" and the rest with a "B." Several healthy people tried to obtain a "B" in order to avoid being sent to labor camps.

On May 16, the ghetto was surrounded by massive police forces headed by police commander Hans Mayer. The Jews were ordered to stand at their doorways without any of their belongings, ostensibly to be registered. The Germans combed the houses and shot anyone in hiding. Patients were thrown out of the hospital's windows, most to their deaths. That very day, the Germans led the Jews to an athletic field in the city center. Over the next two days, they carried out a selection. Anyone who resisted was immediately shot. Some 5,600 Jews who carried the "A" marking were sent to the Lodz ghetto; the rest were placed aboard trains bound for Chelmno, where they were murdered. After the liquidation, about 150 to 200 Jews, mostly tailors, were left behind in Pabianice. They were taken to Lodz on August 10, 1942

PACANÓW

TOWNLET IN BUSKO COUNTY, KIELCE DISTRICT, POLAND

During the war: General Gouvernement, Radom District

Coordinates:
50°24' | 21°03'

After World War I, about 1,700 Jews lived in Pacanow, representing approximately two-thirds of the local population. Most earned their livelihood from commerce and artisanship. Pacanow had a Zionist chapter, a public library, and a drama club; Hebrew classes were also held in the townlet. In 1919, several Jews were injured in a number of violent antisemitic incidents.

After the German occupation in September 1939, Pacanow's Jews were recruited for forced labor but not subject to any other German-imposed decrees. Consequently, in 1941, refugees from Cracow*, and in 1942, refugees from Kielce* and Radom* flocked to Pacanow.

In September 1942, a ghetto was established in Pacanow into which the Jews from the nearby villages were also concentrated. The Jewish population of the townlet rose to about 3,000. In late October 1942, hundreds of young Jews were taken to the Skarzysko-Kamienna labor camp. In either early or late October or early November 1942 (sources vary regarding the date), the remaining inhabitants of the ghetto were deported to the Treblinka death camp.

PAJĘCZNO

TOWNLET IN RADOMSKO COUNTY, ŁÓDŹ DISTRICT, POLAND

During the war: Wartheland

Coordinates:
51°09' | 19°00'

On the eve of World War II, there were about 800 Jews residing in Pajeczno, more than one-third of the townlet's population. Most were artisans and petty merchants. Zionist parties and Agudath Israel were active in the Jewish community. In the 1930s, Jews in Pajeczno endured deteriorating conditions owing to Poland's economic crisis; they were targets of an antisemitic economic boycott and assaults on their property.

The Germans entered Pajeczo on September 4, 1939. In the early days of the occupation they murdered several Jews, dispossessed others, and subjected many to severe abuse. In September and October 1939, a Judenrat was established under Yaakov Lieberman, a member of the pre-war community. Some time later, a Jewish Order Service was formed under David Kwart. The Germans ordered the Judenrat to collect a punitive tax, to deliver labor groups, and to take care of some 2,000 refugees (this last task was accomplished with the assistance of the JDC).

In late 1941, a ghetto was set up in the most squalid quarter of the townlet. It was surrounded with barbed wire, but as it was not hermetically sealed residents could sometimes obtain exit permits. Many ghetto inhabitants thus smuggled in food, and artisans continued to work secretly for "Aryan" customers. About thirty artisans worked in the ghetto officially, several Jews were employed in a German factory, and others worked for the German police. The Judenrat set up a food distribution shop in the ghetto. Jews were able to worship at a synagogue in the ghetto and children attended Heder and a kindergarten.

From the summer of 1941, the Germans periodically demanded labor groups for camps in the Poznan area. Sometimes the Judenrat was able to bribe German officials to cancel a given deportation. An organization named Bread for the Poznan People was set up in the ghetto to send parcels to the camps, despite express German prohibitions.

The ghetto was repeatedly charged punitive taxes. Dispossession of Jews reached a peak in the spring of 1942, two weeks before Passover, when German police surrounded the ghetto and went from house to house beating inhabitants, taking hostages, and looting property. In the spring and summer of 1942, the Judenrat was ordered to hand over specific Jews to the Gestapo. In June 1942, the chairman of the Judenrat and eleven other Jews were arrested; German police murdered them all. The Germans then named the ritual slaughterer Berl Mrovka as chair of the Judenrat.

The liquidation of the Pajeczno ghetto began on August 19, 1942. Some 1,800 Jews were led to a church, where they were held for several days under horrific conditions. During their confinement, they were joined by another 140 Jews who had been found in the ghetto area. On August 21, the Germans murdered all the elderly, including Mrovka, in the churchyard.

Most of the Jews of Pajeczno were deported to Chelmno on August 22. The small group of Jews that was allowed to remain was eventually sent to the Lodz* ghetto.

PAKS

TOWN IN TOLNA COUNTY, HUNGARY

Coordinates:
46°38' | 18°52'

The last national census conducted prior to the German occupation, taken in January 1941, recorded 730 Jewish inhabitants in Paks, approximately 6 percent of the total population. Many owned vineyards and worked in the wine trade. The townlet had an Orthodox and a Status Quo Ante Jewish community, a Jewish school, and a Heder. In 1942, Jewish men were drafted into the Hungarian army for forced labor service; they were deployed to the eastern front, in the Ukraine, where many perished.

The German army occupied Hungary on March 19, 1944. On March 22, 1944, SS-Obersturmführer Musslacher ordered the leaders of the Jewish communities to sign a document consisting of nine points, which severely restricted the daily life of the local Jews. They were, moreover, compelled to supply the German military commander with a list of the Jewish families in their communities. Musslacher also ordered the beards of the Jews to be cut off.

A census conducted in the second week of April 1944 reported that 573 Jews belonged to the Orthodox Jewish community and 122 to the Status Quo Ante Jewish community of Paks.

The Hungarian administration remained intact and operational after the German occupation. The ghettoization and deportation of the Jews were carried out on the basis of the decrees and orders of the Hungarian national and local authorities. On April 22, 1944, Hungarian gendarmes arrested nineteen Jewish residents of Paks who failed to prove their Hungarian citizenship.

On May 1, 1944, Edvin Szongott, the Hungarian sub-prefect of Tolna County, ordered the establishment of ghettos in his county. In addition to the local Jews, 125 Jews from the county-district of Dunafoldvar along with a number of Jews from Szekszard were concentrated in the Paks ghetto. It was established near the synagogue and the Jewish school. It consisted of twenty-seven houses marked with mandatory "canary-yellow" stars and was severely overcrowded. The gendarmes selected twenty-four women from the ghetto for agricultural labor in Ozsakpuszta, which belonged to the neighboring village of Ocseny. The Jews were interrogated and tortured into revealing the whereabouts of their hidden valuables.

On July 5, 1944, in a single transport, 1,082 Jews were deported from Paks to Auschwitz.

PANEVĖŽYS
(Yiddish: **Ponevezh**)

COUNTY SEAT, LITHUANIA

During the war:
Reichskommissariat Ostland

Coordinates:
55°44' | 24°21'

On the eve of World War II, about 6,000 Jews lived in Panevezys, representing over 20 percent of the town's population. Panevezys was an important center of ultra-Orthodox Judaism in Lithuania and was home to one of Lithuania's largest Yeshivot as well as various other Yeshivot. The Jews of Panevezys earned their livelihood from commerce, artisanship, and light industry, as well as from the liberal professions. The town had three systems of Jewish education: Hebrew Zionist, ultra-Orthodox, and Yiddishist. Chapters of Zionist parties and youth movements, Agudath Israel, and the Bund were active in the community.

After Lithuania was annexed to the Soviet Union in 1940, private businesses and large residences in Panevezys were nationalized, a number of the Jewish schools were closed while others changed their language of instruction to Yiddish, and the activities of the Jewish parties were discontinued.

On June 26, 1941, the Germans occupied Panevezys. Nationalist Lithuanians began to attack and abuse of the city's Jews, some of whom were arrested or seized for forced labor, even prior to the onset of the German occupation. Numerous Jews were murdered.

In early July 1941, the Jews were ordered to gather in a ghetto, and on July 11, 1941, the transfer of the Jews to the ghetto was completed. Jews from nearby townlets were likewise concentrated in its grounds, which occupied a number of streets. The ghetto was encircled by barbed wire, with Lithuanian guards posted to watch over it. While the Jews of the city were transferred to it, seventy of the community's most distinguished members were arrested as hostages and taken to Pajuoste, where they were executed.

Panevezys, August 1941 Jewish women from the ghetto forced to strip before their execution by Lithuanian collaborators in the Pajuoste forest (USHMM, courtesy of Saulius Berzinis)

The ghetto was headed by Avraham Rikels and Moshe Levit. Its inhabitants became targets of acts of robbery, abuse, and murder perpetrated by the Lithuanians.

In early August 1941, a Gestapo officer in charge of the ghetto suggested to the representatives of the Jews that they all move to barracks located near Pajuoste, with the promise of improved living conditions. The community representatives visited the barracks and determined that they were unfit for human habitation. Despite their objections, however, a large group of Jews was taken from the ghetto in mid-August, ostensibly to the new place of residence. In reality, these Jews were taken in groups to pits near Pajuoste that had been previously prepared, where they were murdered by armed Lithuanians.

The rest of the Jews of the ghetto were removed on August 24–26, 1941. They were taken in groups to the killing site and murdered. The last group of people driven out out the ghetto included the patients of the hospital and its entire white-coat–clad staff. Dr. T. Gutman, one of the doctors, addressed the patients and staff; to bolster their spirits he called upon them to die with heads held high. According to German and Soviet sources, over 8,000 people were murdered at this extermination site.

PÁPA

TOWN IN VESZPRÉM COUNTY, HUNGARY

Coordinates:
47°20' | 17°28'

The last national census conducted prior to the German occupation recorded, in January 1941, altogether 2,613 Jewish inhabitants in Papa, representing approximately 11 percent of the total population. Most were merchants and artisans. The town's Jewish community was Orthodox and maintained a Jewish elementary school, and various Jewish social and religious associations. In 1919, during the period of the revolutions following World War I, two Jews were killed together with several Communists. Several Zionist organizations operated in Papa in the 1930s.

In 1939, Papa became a local enlistment center for forced labor service within the Hungarian army. In 1941, a number of the forced laborers from Papa were deployed to various places within Hungary; few of the others sent to the Ukraine survived.

The German army occupied Hungary on March 19, 1944. Immediately after the occupation, several leaders of the Jewish community were arrested. They were transferred to the internment camps of Sarvar and Nagykanizsa and deported on to Auschwitz.

The Hungarian administration remained intact and operational after the German occupation. The ghettoization and deportation of the Jews were carried out on the basis of the decrees and orders of the Hungarian national and local authorities. The Hungarian sub-prefect, Dr. Istvan Buda, published the ghettoization decree of Veszprem County on May 17, 1944. The move into the ghetto took place between May 23 and 31, 1944. Seven streets in Papa were allocated for the establishment of the ghetto, in which 2,565 Jews lived, with four to five people on average sharing a room. Jews were permitted to bring along essential personal belongings and food. The infamously cruel police officer, Dr. Pal Lotz, was the ghetto's commander. Miksa Krausz headed the five-member Jewish Council. A Jewish Order Service was also established there. The maternity home was closed down by Buda. Men and women fit for work left the ghetto daily for agricultural labor. At the beginning of June 1944, men were seized for forced labor service, thus escaping deportation.

In addition to the city ghetto, another was established in Papa for the Jewish population of nearby localities. Altogether 992 Jews from the county-districts of

Devecser, Papa, and Zirc in Veszprem County were concentrated in the ghetto. They were held in an unused fertilizer factory in the Gypsy quarter. Gendarme captain Dr. Zoltan Pap commanded the ghetto. In mid-June 1944, the inhabitants of the town ghetto were moved into the second ghetto. Prior to their transfer, the Jews were interrogated and tortured into revealing the whereabouts of their hidden valuables.

Three thousand Jews were deported on July 5, 1944, from the fertilizer factory to Auschwitz. The remaining 537 Jews were transferred that same day to Sarvar* (Vas County) and were deported on to Auschwitz the following day. Fifty-one Jews from Papa boarded the Kasztner train and were saved.

PARAFJANOWO

TOWNLET IN GŁĘBOKIE COUNTY, VILNA DISTRICT, POLAND

(After World War II in the USSR/Belarus; Belarussian: **Paraf'yanava**; Russian: **Parafyanovo**)

During the war: Reichskommissariat Ostland

Coordinates: 54°53' | 27°36'

About 250 Jews lived in Parafjanowo during the interwar period. Jewish parties and youth movements were active in the townlet, where a Tarbut Hebrew school also operated.

The Soviets occupied Parafjanowo in the second half of September 1939, at which time private commerce in the townlet was abolished, artisans were compelled to work in the framework of cooperatives, and educational facilities were Sovietized.

The Germans occupied Parafjanowo in late June 1941 and began immediately to terrorize and abuse the townlet's Jews, seizing them for forced labor and murdering several inhabitants. Soon after entering the townlet, the Germans appointed a Judenrat headed by a man named Katz. The Judenrat's main functions were to collect ransom payments from the Jews and recruit forced laborers.

A ghetto was apparently established in Parafjanowo in October 1941, in a narrow alleyway. The Jews were forced to share the already overcrowded buildings with Jews from nearby localities. Throughout the ghetto's existence, all Jews aged twelve years and older were seized for forced labor. Women and girls were employed in knitting while the men worked as porters, chopped down trees in the forest, and performed road maintenance and snow removal.

On May 31, 1942, the approximately 500 inhabitants of the Parafjanowo ghetto were rounded up in the firehouse on the edge of the townlet. They were then taunted and humiliated as they were marched through the townlet to the heart of the forest, where they were shot to death. A number of young Jews escaped in the forest and joined the partisan units and the family camp run by the Bielski brothers.

PARCZEW

TOWNLET IN WŁODAWA COUNTY, LUBLIN DISTRICT, POLAND

During the war: General Gouvernement, Lublin District

Coordinates: 51°38' | 22°54'

About 4,000 Jews lived in Parczew in the interwar period, representing more than half of the townlet's population. Most earned their livelihood from artisanship, small-scale commerce, and peddling, although several Jewish inhabitants were factory owners. Parczew had Jewish trade unions and a credit bank in addition to traditional charity and welfare societies. Jews often received assistance from relatives who were former members of the community and had immigrated to the United States. Many of the townlet's children attended private Hadarim, a Talmud Torah, and a Beit Yaakov school for girls. Parczew had chapters of most of the Zionist parties, as well as a pioneer training facility, some of whose graduates immigrated to the Land of Israel. Also active were chapters of both Agudath Israel and the Bund. Jewish parties and youth movements played a major role in the townlet's cultural life, holding lectures, presenting plays and concerts, and hosting assorted cultural events.

In 1937/38, many Jews were injured in the course of a number of violent antisemitic incidents perpetrated in Parczew.

On October 5, 1939, units of the German army along with SS and Gestapo men entered Parczew and immediately began to seize Jews for forced labor. As of November 1939, the townlet's Jewish residents were ordered to wear a Star-of-David armband, were forbidden to use the sidewalks, and had their businesses confiscated. The Germans exacted large, extortionate "contributions" and evicted many Jews from their homes. Intermittent acts of abuse and murder of Jews took place.

In late 1939, the Germans established a Judenrat in Parczew. On February 4, 1940, the Judenrat was ordered to supply food for 607 Jewish prisoners of war who passed through the townlet on their way from Lublin* to Biala Podlaska*. In the spring of 1940, young Jewish women were seized for forced labor in nearby Jablonka, and additional Jews were periodically grabbed and assigned to forced labor near Parczew and in the Belzec labor camp. Many fell ill due to the harsh working conditions, and several people were murdered.

In April 1940, on Passover eve, soldiers belonging to a German unit stationed in Parczew looted Jewish homes, injuring numerous Jews and killing one. As of late 1940, the Jews were forbidden to purchase food from local farmers, and non-Jews were prohibited from selling to the Jews altogether. In the winter of 1940/41, deportees were brought to Parczew from Poznan, Suwalki, Cracow*, and Lublin. During 1941, deportees were brought to Parczew from different areas in Poland, raising the townlet's Jewish population to about 6,000.

On August 19, 1942, an operation involving the deportation of over 4,000 of Parczew's Jews to the Treblinka death camp was carried out by an SS company from Treblinka and the local gendarmerie. Shlomo Himelblau, an educator in Parczew's orphanage, accompanied the deported children, despite not appearing on the deportation list. Many were murdered on site. Another 400 people found in hiding were shot.

In September 1942, following the large-scale operation, a ghetto was established in Parczew, in which some 2,000 Jews from Czemierniki, Wohyn, and Kock* were concentrated. Due to serious overcrowding, many of the refugees were obliged to find accommodations outside the ghetto.

In October 1942, SS officers Fischer, Baunsemil, and Diekloff of the Radzyn county seat arrived in the townlet and oversaw the deportation of about 2,500 Jews to Treblinka.

The approximately 1,000 Jews remaining in Parczew were deported to the Miedzyrzec Podlaski* ghetto. Many escaped to nearby forests, and about 100 were apprehended and shot.

Parczew was one of the towns in which the Germans intended to reestablish a ghetto but ultimately opted against the plan, perhaps owing to the presence of partisan units in the surrounding forests that helped many of Parczew's Jews to escape. A number of Jews managed to escape from the ghetto; several joined the largest Jewish partisan unit in central Poland, headed by Yechiel Grinspan, while others joined the family camp that operated under the auspices of the partisan unit.

PÁRKÁNY

TOWNLET IN ESZTERGOM COUNTY, HUNGARY

(After World War II in Czechoslovakia/Slovakia; Slovak: **Parkan**)

Coordinates:
47°48' | 18°44'

The last national census conducted prior to the German occupation, taken in January 1941, recorded 291 Jewish inhabitants in Parkany, accounting for roughly 7 percent of the population. Most were merchants and artisans; several were factory owners. The townlet had a Neolog Jewish community. After World War I, Parkany became part of Czechoslovakia. During the interwar period, the townlet had a Hungarian-language school and various Zionist organizations. On November 2, 1938, Parkany reverted to Hungary.

The German army occupied Hungary on March 19, 1944. The Hungarian administration remained intact and in force after the occupation. The ghettoization and deportation of the Jews were carried out on the basis of the decrees and orders of the Hungarian national and local authorities. The Parkany ghetto was established in mid-May 1944, on the territory of a former internment camp for Poles. In addition to the Jews of the townlet itself (336 people), 260 Jews from the Parkany County-District (Esztergom County) were concentrated in the ghetto.

On June 6, 1944, the ghetto was liquidated and its residents were transferred to the entrainment center of Komarom*, and on to Auschwitz.

PARYSÓW

TOWNLET IN GARWOLIN COUNTY, LUBLIN DISTRICT, POLAND

During the war: General Gouvernement, Warsaw District

Coordinates:
51°58' | 21°41'

About 1,900 Jews lived in Parysow when World War II broke out, representing more than half of the townlet's population. Most were artisans, especially in the garment and shoe industries, and a number earned their livelihood as shopkeepers, petty merchants, and peddlers. The JDC, a free-loan society, and traditional charity and welfare societies assisted the Jews of Parysow. Most of the community's children studied in a traditional Heder and a Talmud Torah. Some of the girls attended a Beit Yaakov school. Parysow had chapters of the Zionist parties and youth movements with Zionist pioneering groups, as well as chapters of Agudath Israel and the Bund. The Zionist parties offered Hebrew classes and evening courses, and oversaw a range of activities, including an orchestra, sports teams, and drama groups. The townlet also had a Jewish public library.

In the first week of September 1939, refugees arrived in Parysow from Garwolin and other nearby localities. On September 17, 1939, the Germans entered Parysow and immediately began to seize Jews for forced labor. In the early days of the occupation, the Germans did not remain in the townlet continuously. In early October 1939, a twelve-member Judenrat was established in the townlet, headed by Aharon Geldstein, along with a twelve-member Jewish Order Service under the command of Chaim Moshe Poskolinski, a member of the Judenrat. In March 1940, more than 100 refugees arrived in Parysow from Garwolin, followed by large waves of refugees from Warsaw* and western Poland.

In November 1940, the Germans ordered the establishment of a ghetto in Parysow. During the winter of 1940/41, epidemic typhus broke out in the ghetto, and a hospital was established. In April 1941, Jewish forced laborers were sent to a labor camp in Wilga, near Garwolin. In the winter of 1941/42, the inhabitants of the ghetto were forced to pay a large ransom and to turn over all their furs.

In May and June 1942, the Germans murdered four members of the Judenrat, including Geldstein and Poskolinski. Yaakov Tsimlik, Geldstein's deputy, was appointed head of the Judenrat, and Tuvia Miller, the director of the hospital, was made head of the Jewish Order Service.

In August 1942, refugees arrived in Parysow from Minsk Mazowiecki*, Stoczek Lukowski*, and Otwock*, localities whose Jewish population had been sent to death camps. In early September 1942, in accordance with German demands and in anticipation of deportations, the Judenrat recruited about 600 young Jews for forced labor. On the eve of the deportation, Moshe Munk, a refugee who had arrived in Parysow in December 1939, replaced Tsimlik as head of the Judenrat.

The Parysow ghetto was liquidated on September 27, 1942, when SS men, along with Polish police and members of the Polish fire brigade, entered the ghetto. At the time, there were about 3,500 Jews residing there, including about 2,000 refugees. Thirty-nine Jews were murdered on site, and the rest were deported to the Treblinka death camp.

Parysow, September 27, 1942
The Jews of the ghetto are led to the train station in Pilawa and deported in cargo trains to the Treblinka death camp. (YV)

PASVALYS

(Yiddish: **Posvol/Poshvol**)

TOWNLET IN BIRŽAI COUNTY, LITHUANIA

During the war:
Reichskommissariat Ostland

Coordinates:
56°04' | 24°24'

On the eve of World War II, about 700 Jews lived in Pasvalys, representing approximately one-quarter of the townlet's population. Most earned their livelihood from commerce, especially in the food and garment businesses, and as artisans. They were aided by a Jewish bank and traditional Jewish charity and welfare societies. The townlet had a Hebrew-Zionist Tarbut school. A small proportion of the community's children studied in the local Lithuanian high school. The Jews maintained a library and two sports organizations, and were active members of Zionist parties and youth movements.

In late 1939, pioneers who had fled from occupied Poland moved into the townlet and established a kibbutz training camp.

In August 1940, after Lithuania was annexed to the Soviet Union, all Zionist organizations were dismantled, the Hebrew school was closed, many Jewish businesses were nationalized, and a great deal of Jewish property was confiscated.

Once Pasvalys was occupied by the Germans on June 26, 1941, the townlet was taken over by armed Lithuanians. They robbed Jews and murdered them in the nearby forest, specifically targeting people who had returned to the townlet following failed attempts to flee to Russia. A number of Jews from Pasvalys did manage to escape into Russia.

On July 4–10, 1941, the Lithuanians arrested at least 150 and, murdered more than 20 Jews. Most of those killed lost their lives in the forest near Kuziai following imprisonment in the Siauliai* jail.

A ghetto was established in the townlet in mid-July 1941. Pasvalys's townlet council provided its inhabitants with food. The distribution of provisions was supervised by the community's rabbi, Rabbi Yitzhak Agulnik.

In early August, the Jews of the nearby townlets were also brought to Pasvalys. The inhabitants of the ghetto were robbed and severely abused by Lithuanian nationalists; these attacks apparently did not occur in the presence of the Germans nor with their involvement.

On August 26, 1941, the Pasvalys townlet council ordered all Jews to gather in the Beit Midrash, which was situated outside of the ghetto boundaries. The Jews were then brought to the Zadeikiai grove outside of the townlet and murdered. En route to the murder site, some of the Jews attacked their guards with their bare hands, while dozens attempted to escape. Almost all of the Jews were murdered, including most of those who fled. A number of victims were thrown into pits while still alive. A few people did survive, along with the Jews who had taken flight to Russia in the summer of 1941. Pasvalys was liberated in September 1944.

PAVLOGRAD

COUNTY SEAT, DNEPROPETROVSK DISTRICT, UKRAINE, USSR

During the war:
Reichskommissariat Ukraine

Coordinates:
48°31' | 35°52'

At the beginning of the twentieth century, there were about 4,400 Jews in Pavlograd, nearly 30 percent of the population. On December 26, 1918, in the midst of the Russian Civil War (1918–20), a Ukrainian gang conducted a pogrom in the town and murdered a large number of Jews. The pogrom, coupled with the industrialization and urbanization of the USSR during the interwar years, reduced the Jewish population of Pavlograd to about 2,500 by the time of the German invasion. Many Jewish townspeople were artisans, a large number of whom had formed cooperatives. Others were farm workers, and a Jewish kolkhoz was established near the town. A Jewish school in Pavlograd taught in Russian and Yiddish.

The Germans occupied Pavlograd on October 11, 1941. An indeterminate number of Jews managed to escape or evacuate to the east before the occupation. Those who remained were registered and then concentrated in a ghetto on the grounds of a factory in the suburb of Gorodishche, along with Jews brought in from other localities. In November 1941, some 670 Jewish refugees from Poland were murdered in the factory. Jews in the ghetto performed grueling forced labor;

those whose strength failed were shot to death in pits near the village of Mavrino, where numerous children were also killed.

The ghetto was liquidated in June 1942, when all the 2,100 remaining Jews were murdered.

PÉCS

TOWN IN BARANYA COUNTY, HUNGARY

Coordinates:
46°05' | 18°14'

The last national census conducted prior to the German occupation, taken in January 1941, recorded 3,486 Jewish inhabitants in Pecs, roughly 5 percent of the total population. Between the two World Wars, most of the Jews were merchants, artisans, and clerks. In 1869, the Jewish community of Pecs became Status Quo Ante, but in 1923, it joined the Neolog trend. A local Jewish elementary school had 112 pupils in 1944. The community also ran a Talmud Torah, various social associations, and an old-age home.

During the time of the White Terror after World War I, self-defense units of local Jewish youths suppressed anti-Jewish riots.

In 1938, the Women's Association, together with the local WIZO group, assisted Jewish refugees arriving from Yugoslavia, Germany, and Austria.

The German army entered Pecs on March 19, 1944, as the Germans occupied Hungary. They immediately seized the Jewish old-age home, transforming it into the local headquarters of the Gestapo. The Germans arrested fifty-four affluent members of the Jewish community and three Jews who had converted to Christianity and deported them to Mauthausen. In the second week of April 1944 there were 3,060 Jews living in Pecs.

The Hungarian administration remained intact and in force after the occupation. The ghettoization and deportation of the Jews were carried out on the basis of the decrees and orders of the Hungarian national and local authorities. At the beginning of May 1944, the mayor of Pecs, Dr. Lajos Esztergar, marked out the territory of the ghetto on the basis of the ghetto-decree published by the Hungarian prime minister on April 28, 1944. It was established in the clerks' housing development near the train station.

The Jewish Council in Pecs was established on May 8, 1944. The following day, Deputy Chief of Police Jeno Borbola presented the ghetto regulations to members of the Jewish Council. The Jewish Council was made responsible for the move into the ghetto, which was launched on the same day. Dr. Jozsef Greiner (a lawyer and the last serving president of the Jewish community) headed the Jewish Council.

Thousands of Jews lived in the ghetto, which was established in 272 houses on the outskirts of the town. About 3,500 of the inhabitants were from Pecs. The balance was brought in from other localities in the county, such as the county-districts of Darda, Pecs, Szentlorinc, and Villany. The Jewish patients of the hospitals, as well as the mentally ill, were also brought to the ghetto, which was sealed on May 21, 1944. The Jewish Council established a Jewish Order Service armed with batons and set up thirty communal kitchens and an emergency hospital. Teachers looked after the children and kept them occupied. On Shavuot, the inhabitants of the ghetto held services in the courtyard of a house, with Torah scrolls they had brought with them from the synagogue.

Ghetto inhabitants were assigned to forced labor. The forestry used 120 men for logging, and 50 women worked in the market garden. The laborers left and returned to the ghetto every day.

Ferenc Virag, the Roman Catholic bishop of Pecs, approached Mihaly Nikolits, the prefect of Baranya County, with a view to improving the lives of the inhabitants of the ghetto. He also attempted to save a few Jews who had converted to Christianity, but they were eventually captured by the Gestapo.

On June 28 and 29, the inhabitants of the ghetto were transferred to the entrainment center in the Lakits garrison, following a body search by the police. In an apparent bid to prevent the smuggling of valuables, Deputy Chief of Police Borbola forbade inhabitants from bringing food from the ghetto of Pecs into the garrison.

The Jews were put up in the stable. About twenty people committed suicide in the Lakits garrison. On July 4 and 6, 1944, in two transports, 5,963 Jews (not all of them from the Pecs ghetto) were deported to Auschwitz.

After the liquidation of the ghetto, a unit of forced laborers arrived in Pecs, twenty-four of whom were killed on Yom Kippur, September 27, 1944, by order of the commander, Jozsef Revesz.

PERVOMAISK
(Olviopol, Bogopol, Golta)
COUNTY SEAT IN ODESSA DISTRICT, UKRAINE, USSR

During the war: Transnistria (under Romanian control)

Coordinates:
48°03' | 30°52'

In 1920, Pervomaisk encompassed the three towns of Olviopol, Bogopol, and Golta, which were divided by the Bug and Sinyukha rivers. In the early twentieth century, about 1,500 Jews lived in Olviopol, 5,900 in Bogopol, and 1,250 in Golta. In December 1919, during the civil war in Russia (1918–20), White Army soldiers carried out pogroms, murdering dozens of Jews living in the three towns. In 1920, during the early days of the Soviet regime, the three towns were united into a single town named Pervomaisk. A number of Jews continued to engage in artisanship; but many, however, took on work as clerks or laborers in government factories and institutions, while others were employed in flour mills. Jews also toiled as farmers in kolkhozes. Pervomaisk had a Jewish department of the court that conducted its affairs in Yiddish and a Yiddish-language school, both of which were closed in 1939. The rise of urbanization and industrialization in the Soviet Union caused a decline in the town's Jewish population to about 6,000 by the eve of the German invasion of the Soviet Union.

The Germans occupied Pervomaisk on August 2, 1941. An unknown number of the town's inhabitants had escaped, evacuated to the east, or joined the Red Army. Immediately after taking charge, the German commander of the town ordered the Jews to wear a Star-of-David armband and forbade them to leave their homes after six o'clock in the evening. By mid-September 1941, most of Pervomaisk's Jews had been concentrated in a part of the town located in Bogopol. On October 18, 1941, the Golta area was handed over to Romanian control and annexed to Transnistria. The Bogopol area remained under German control.

On September 17, 1941, the Germans carried out their first murder operation in the Bogopol ghetto, killing hundreds of Jews. In October 1941, executed near the brick factory were 120 Jews. On December 15, 1941, another large-scale operation was conducted in the ghetto. On January 9, 1942, the remaining Jews in the ghetto were shot and killed, with the exception of thirty professionals, who were murdered about one month later. In February–March 1942, the Germans murdered about 1,600 Jewish deportees who had been brought from the Romanian occupation zone.

Jews who had fled from the German-controlled area, especially professionals whose families had been murdered, lived in Golta (Transnistria). In June 1942, the Romanians concentrated them in a ghetto that was encircled by a barbed-wire fence. Until the fall of 1942, about 450 Jews were concentrated in Golta, including a group of deportees from Bessarabia and Bukovina. In late 1942, the local Jews from Golta were transferred to camps in Bogdanovka and Akmechetka, but two weeks later, several were returned to Golta. In December 1942, a group of 280 Jews from Bucharest and other localities in the Regat were sent to the town.

The Romanians concentrated the local Jews and the deportees from Romania in two separate areas, which were declared ghettos. The residents of ghettos elected a joint council.

The Jews performed forced labor, and doctors from among the deportees worked in Ukrainian and Romanian hospitals. Jews considered unfit for work were murdered or transferred to the Akmechetka camp. Conditions gradually improved for the deportees once most found work. The leaders of a new group of deportees that arrived in Golta, Avram Crestinu and Alfred Folender, were intent on taking over the leadership of all of the Jews in the ghetto. They collaborated with the Romanian gendarmes and were appointed leaders of the Jews in the entire Golta County. The help sent by the Bucharest aid committee was withheld from the ghetto inhabitants, and instead remained in the hands of the council heads, who obstructed the establishment of welfare institutions in Golta.

In October 1943, the Romanians allowed Jewish deportees from Bucharest and the Regat to return to their homes. According to the official statistics of the gendarmes, in late 1943, there remained in Golta 72 deportees from Bessarabia and Bukovina and 100 from the Ukraine.

PESTSZENTERZSÉBET

TOWN IN PEST-PILIS-SOLT-KISKUN COUNTY, HUNGARY

Coordinates:
47°26' | 19°07'

The last national census conducted prior to the German occupation, taken in January 1941, recorded 3,978 Jewish inhabitants in Pestszenterzsebet, approximately 5 percent of the total population. Between the two World Wars, the town had several Jewish-owned factories and workshops with many Jewish employees and numerous Jewish merchants. The town's Jewish community was Neolog and maintained a Jewish school, a Talmud Torah, and various Jewish social and religious associations.

In 1942, many of the town's Jewish men were drafted into the Hungarian army for forced labor service; most were deployed to the eastern front, in the Ukraine, where many perished.

The Germans arrested many prominent members of the Jewish community following their occupation of Hungary on March 19, 1944, according to a list readied in advance.

The Hungarian administration remained intact and operational after the German occupation. The ghettoization and deportation of the Jews occurred on the basis of decrees and orders issues by the Hungarian national and local authorities. On May 12, the Hungarian local governor, Dr. Laszlo Endre, a militant anti-semite, ordered the establishment of ghettos in his county. At the end of May 1944, the ghetto of Pestszenterzsebet was established along two streets. More than 3,000 Jews were forced to move into it.

At the end of June 1944, the inhabitants of the ghetto were relocated to the brick factory in Monor*, which served as the entrainment center for the ghettos of the county surrounding Budapest* from the south and east. They belonged to a group of approximately 8,000 Jews who were deported from the entrainment center to Auschwitz in three transports between July 6 and 8, 1944.

Prior to the deportation from Monor, a number of Pestszenterzsebet's Jews had been transferred to Budapest, and on to Guenskirchen, Austria.

PESTSZENTLŐRINC

TOWN IN PEST-PILIS-SOLT-KISKUN COUNTY, HUNGARY

Coordinates:
47°26' | 19°12'

The last national census conducted prior to the German occupation, taken in January 1941, recorded 1,101 Jewish inhabitants in Pestszentlorinc, accounting for roughly 3 percent of the total population. Most were clerks or laborers, while others were merchants and artisans. The town had a Neolog Jewish community with various Jewish social and religious associations. The Jewish school was closed down before World War II.

Jewish men from Pestszentlorinc were drafted into the Hungarian army for forced labor service from 1939 onward.

The German army occupied Hungary on March 19, 1944. A census conducted in the second week of April 1944 reported that 887 Jews belonged to the Neolog Jewish community of Pestszentlorinc.

The Hungarian administration remained intact and operational after the German occupation. The ghettoization and deportation of the Jews occurred on the basis of decrees and orders issues by the Hungarian national and local authorities. On May 12, the Hungarian sub-prefect, Dr. Laszlo Endre, a militant antisemite, ordered the establishment of ghettos in his county. The Pestszentlorinc ghetto had already been designated a day earlier and was established at the Lorinc state plant. By May 26, 1944, the local Jews and the Jews from the surrounding settlements, about 1,800 to 2,000 people in all, were concentrated into its grounds.

On June 30, 1944, the ghetto inhabitants were transferred to the brick factory in Monor*, which served as the entrainment center for the ghettos of the county surrounding Budapest* from the south and east. They belonged to a group of approximately 8,000 Jews who were deported from the brick factory to Auschwitz in three transports, between July 6 and 8, 1944.

PETRIKOV

(Belarussian: **Petrykau**)

COUNTY SEAT, POLESYE DISTRICT, BELARUS, USSR

During the war:
Reichskommissariat Ukraine

Coordinates:
52°08' | 28°30'

In the early twentieth century, about 2,500 Jews lived in Petrikov, roughly half of the population. In November 1920, during the Russian Civil War, Bulak-Balakhovich soldiers murdered eleven Jewish townspeople in a pogrom. During the era of Soviet rule, many Jews practiced artisan trades, some in cooperatives, while a few turned to farming in kolkhozes that had been set up in the area. The townlet had a government school that taught in Yiddish. Urbanization and industrialization induced many Jews to leave, so that by the late 1930s some 1,000 remained, about one-third of the population.

The Germans occupied Petrikov on July 29, 1941. Presumably, quite a few Jews managed to evacuate in advance of the occupation. On September 22, 1941, as those who remained in the townlet were performing the Rosh Hashanah ritual of *tashlikh* on the banks of the Pripyat River, Germans reached the townlet by boat and arrested 300 Jews, including women, the elderly, and children. Those detained were forced to march to the river, where they were shot dead. The following day, the Germans began shooting at Jews in the streets, murdering some 500 in all. In late February 1942, a special group of Germans, Finns, and Hungarians murdered between 150 and 200 Jews of Petrikov near the village of Balki. The fifty or sixty Jews who survived were concentrated under appalling conditions in a ghetto of sorts comprised of three buildings. Almost no food was allowed in. In late April 1942, all inhabitants of the ghetto were murdered near a former slaughterhouse a short distance from the townlet.

PETROVICHI

TOWNLET IN SHUMYACHI COUNTY, SMOLENSK DISTRICT, RUSSIAN FEDERATION, USSR

During the war: Military Administration Area

Coordinates:
53°58' | 32°10'

In the 1920s, about 930 Jews lived in Petrovichi.

When the Germans occupied Petrovichi on August 2, 1941, there were 300 to 600 Jews living in townlet, according to different estimations

A Judenrat was established, and charged with ensuring that the daily forced labor imposed by the Germans was carried out. That same month, all of Petrovichi's Jews were moved into one street, which became a ghetto. The word *Jude* was printed on signs placed on each home in it as well as on badges that the Jews were forced to wear.

The overcrowding in the ghetto was extreme: twenty to twenty-five people lived in a single house, and residents were forced to sleep in rows on the floor. Throughout the ghetto's existence, the plundering of Jewish property by both the Germans and local policemen persisted, and several young Jewish girls were raped. Despite prohibitions on contact between Jews and local inhabitants, Jews continued to work for and trade with local citizens; they also turned over valuables for safekeeping. A number of local inhabitants proffered assistance to the Jews.

In May 1942, between 100 and 170 Jews (sources differ on the figure) were taken from the Petrovichi ghetto to Roslavl*, where they were shot to death.

On July 22, 1942, the liquidation of the Petrovichi ghetto began, carried out by the Germans together with collaborators brought specially to the ghetto. During the march to the murder site, a girl named Sara Yasmin, who had an "Aryan" appearance, was given permission to leave the march, but she rebuffed the offer. When the Jews reached the murder pits, she screamed out, "Fascists! You will pay for everything in the end!" Many Jews then attempted to flee, but ultimately all were shot. Only a few of Petrovichi's Jews managed to survive with the help of locals.

On the eve of the liquidation of the ghetto, a group of thirty young Jews fled from the ghetto and made contact with partisans active in the nearby forests. They managed to obtain arms and join forces with a group of Soviet soldiers. The group was headed by eighteen-year-old Chaim Gurevich.

PIASECZNO

TOWNLET IN WARSAW COUNTY, WARSAW DISTRICT, POLAND

During the war: General Gouvernement, Warsaw District

Coordinates: 52°05' | 21°02'

About 2,200 Jews lived in Piaseczno in the interwar period, representing approximately one-third of the townlet's population. They earned their livelihood from small commerce and artisanship, and were aided by the JDC, a Folksbank, and trade and craft associations. Piaseczno had a Hebrew elementary school, a Beit Yaakov school, and a Yeshiva. Zionist parties and Agudath Israel took part in the local political activities.

In the early days of World War II, many of Piaseczno's Jews fled to Warsaw* and to eastern Poland. Meanwhile, hundreds of refugees arrived in the townlet from central Poland. The Germans occupied Piaseczno in early September 1939. During the siege on Warsaw, the German army concentrated forces there. After a short time, the Germans appointed a Judenrat in the townlet.

In the winter of 1940, the Jews were ordered to move into a ghetto, established near a forest, on a site with wooden cabins that had previously served as a vacation site. In late 1940, there were about 3,500 Jews in the townlet, of whom some 1,000 were refugees and deportees from other localities.

In early December 1940, the Germans declared the transfer of 1,000 of Piaseczno's Jews to Warsaw. On February 4, 1941, a deportation order for all of Piaseczno's Jews was issued, and over three days, about 2,500 Jews were transferred to Warsaw. They perished in the Treblinka death camp in the summer of 1942 and in January and the spring of 1943.

PIASKI
(Yiddish: **Piesk**)

TOWNLET IN WOŁKOWYSK COUNTY, BIAŁYSTOK DISTRICT, POLAND
(After World War II in the USSR/Belarus; Belarussian, Russian: **Peski**)

During the war: Bezirk Białystok

Coordinates: 53°21' | 24°38'

About 1,200 Jews lived in Piaski on the eve of World War II, representing roughly three-quarters of the townlet's population. Most earned their livelihood from commerce and peddling. Jewish political organizations were active in Piaski, including Zionist parties and the Bund, and the community had a Tarbut Hebrew school.

After the Soviets occupied Piaski in the second half of September 1939, economic activity in the townlet was restricted, privately owned businesses were closed, and cooperatives were formed.

The Germans occupied Piaski in late June 1941, and immediately plundered Jewish property, subjected Jews to humiliation, and murdered two Jewish inhabitants. Within a few days of the onset of the occupation, the Jews of Piaski were required to wear a yellow badge, their freedom of movement was restricted, and many were seized for forced labor.

Piaski, 1942
Members of the Judenrat in the ghetto (ŻIH)

In November 1941, a Judenrat was established in Piaski at German orders, headed by a German-speaking man named Mendel Brevin. A short time later, the Jews of Piaski were concentrated in a ghetto along with Jews from other localities. Living conditions in it were harsh, food rations were meager, and overcrowding was severe. The ghetto was fenced in and guarded by local policemen. Only the small number of Jews who worked for the Germans were permitted to leave the ghetto and were exempted from the requirement to wear a yellow badge. The Jews were periodically obliged to submit ransom payments to the Germans in the form of money and valuables.

On November 2, 1942, the Germans rounded up the Jews near the ghetto gate and carried out a selection. The elderly and ill were shot that day in the cemetery. The rest of the Jews, about 1,600 in all, were marched to the bunker camp near Wolkowysk*, and were deported a several days later to the Treblinka death camp. The few Jews found hiding during the operation were caught and shot.

PIASKI LUTERSKIE

TOWNLET IN LUBLIN COUNTY, LUBLIN DISTRICT, POLAND

During the war: General Gouvernement, Lublin District

Coordinates:
51°08' | 22°52'

During the interwar period, there were some 3,000 Jews in Piaski Luterskie, about three-quarters of the townlet's population. Their main sources of livelihood were trade and crafts. Most young people were members of Zionist parties. Some young Zionists joined pioneer training collectives and immigrated to the Land of Israel. Agudath Israel and the Bund were active, too. The community also had a Tarbut school, public libraries, and a drama group.

In early September 1939, many of the townlet's Jews fled eastward. Later that month, Red Army units entered Piaski Luterskie and set up a council of supporters headed by Yeheskel Koytser. The Soviets left within a short time and the townlet was included in the German occupation zone. Many young Jews accompanied the retreating Soviets eastward, although some returned a few months later. Before the Germans arrived, Poles murdered several Jews at the old cemetery.

In early 1940, the Germans set up an open ghetto in Piaski Luterskie, appointed a six-member Judenrat headed by Mendel Plisecki (or Polisecki), established a Jewish Order Service, made the Jews remit "ransoms," and conscripted hundreds for forced labor at the Cycow and Belzec labor camps.

In the winter and spring of 1940, large groups of refugees were brought to the townlet, bringing the ghetto population to around 5,000. In February 1940, arriving in Piaski Luterskie were 565 Jews from Szczecin, one of whom, named Biber, was appointed head of the Jewish Order Service. At around that time, the Judenrat opened a soup kitchen with the help of the JSS in Cracow*.

In June 1941, a second ghetto was established in Piaski Luterskie. In the first ghetto, the Judenrat attempted to set up a hospital and sanitation department to combat epidemic typhus.

In late March 1942, most Jews in the townlet—about 3,500—were deported to the Belzec death camp by units under the command of SS officer Dolew and a Volksdeutscher named Bartetchke. About 1,000 Jews remained in the townlet. In April 1942, some 4,200 Jews from Germany, about 1,000 from the Protectorate, and others from Kalisz* were brought into the ghettos. By June 1942, their population had climbed to about 6,500. In April–May 1942, deportees from Germany were still sending letters to their families.

Some ghetto inhabitants were deported to Belzec in September 1942, and the remaining some 4,000 were sent to Trawniki in October 1942 and thence to the Sobibor death camp. The operation was commanded by an SS officer from Trawniki named Karl Streibel.

The Piaski Luterskie ghetto was reestablished in late October or early November 1942, and some 6,000 Jews were concentrated there. This ghetto was liquidated in February or March 1943; the men were deported to Trawniki, and the fate of the women and children is not known.

Thirty-five Jews from Piaski Luterskie survived. Most were young people who escaped from the ghetto and joined partisan units in the area.

PIĄTEK

TOWNLET IN ŁĘCZYCA COUNTY, ŁÓDŹ DISTRICT, POLAND

During the war: Wartheland

Coordinates:
52°04' | 19°29'

On the eve of World War II, there were about 1,300 Jews in Piatek, more than one-third of the townlet's population. Most were artisans.

When the Germans entered the townlet on September 9, 1939, they seized fifty men, including seven Jews, for forced labor to repair the local bridge, and murdered the workers when the job was complete. Hundreds of Jews left the townlet during the first months of the occupation; on January 1, 1940, only 838 Jews remained. This was the approximate number of Jews who were confined in the local ghetto, which was established that same year.

Shortly before the liquidation, there was a series of executions of Jews in the townlet. The ghetto was liquidated in stages. Some inhabitants were transferred to the Chelmno death camp on April 22, 1942, and the ghetto was entirely emptied in July.

PIKOV

(Yiddish: **Pikev**; Ukrainian: **Pykiv**)

TOWNLET IN KALINOVKA COUNTY, VINNITSA DISTRICT, UKRAINE, USSR

(The townlet had two separate parts—Staryi Pikov and Novyi Pikov)

During the war:
Reichskommissariat Ukraine

Coordinates:
49°30' | 28°10'

In July 1919, a Ukrainian gang murdered some fifty Jewish Pikov townspeople in a pogrom.

During the Soviet period, a number of Jews in Pikov became farm hands while others took on white-collar jobs. Most, however, continued to work as artisans and, until the early 1930s, as merchants. The townlet had a Jewish Ethnic Soviet that operated in Yiddish and a government school that taught in Yiddish. Shortly before the German invasion of the Soviet Union on June 22, 1941, there were about 1,600 Jews in Pikov, accounting for roughly half of the population.

After the German invasion, a few Jews managed to evacuate to the east. The Germans occupied Pikov on July 16, 1941, and concentrated Jews from the vicinity together with the local population. Local Ukrainian police immediately set about pillaging Jewish property and abducting Jews for forced roadwork and farm labor. An eight- or ten-member Judenrat headed by Yankel Yosevich was appointed, mainly to supply forced laborers.

In September 1941, the Jews of Pikov were concentrated in a ghetto in Novyi Pikov. Although the ghetto was not fenced, anyone who attempted to leave its confines was severely punished. Its inhabitants were forced to wear a white armband with a yellow Star-of-David. In early 1942, when Pikov's Jews discovered that the Jewish population in the area was being liquidated, a group of youths organized in the ghetto for resistance. They revealed their plan to the Judenrat, which opposed it on the grounds that the Ukrainian authorities had vowed to leave the Jews of Pikov unharmed. Nevertheless, the resistance group remained active and attempted to establish contact with Soviet POWs who were working in the area as well as with partisans that had begun to operate nearby.

On May 30, 1942, altogether 960 inhabitants of the ghetto were murdered in an operation carried out at the cemetery. The ghetto was liquidated in two additional operations, on June 6 and 11, 1942, when 120 more people were murdered.

PILYAVA

(Yiddish: **Pilyave**; Ukrainian: **Pylyava**)

TOWNLET IN STARAYA SINYAVA COUNTY, KAMENETS-PODOLSK DISTRICT, UKRAINE, USSR

During the war: Reichskommissariat Ukraine

Coordinates: 49°36' | 27°27'

In the mid-1920s, there were about 600 Jews in Pilyava. Under Soviet rule, a number of artisans and merchants renounced their former occupations in favor of farm labor. A Jewish kolkhoz was established nearby. The townlet had a Jewish government school that offered instruction in Yiddish.

On July 11, 1941, the Germans occupied Pilyava and promptly established a ghetto.

In the fall of 1941, 180 Jews were removed from Pilyava to a quarry near the village of Alekseevka and shot to death. Others were murdered in Starokonstantinov*. The fate of the remaining Jews is unknown.

PILZNO

TOWNLET IN ROPCZYCE COUNTY, CRACOW DISTRICT, POLAND

During the war: General Gouvernement, Cracow District

Coordinates: 49°58' | 21°18'

About 800 Jews lived in Pilzno when World War II broke out, representing approximately 20 percent of the townlet's population. In the trying years following World War I, they were aided by the JSS and the JDC, which established a public soup kitchen and an association that provided care for orphans and needy children. Jewish inhabitants of the townlet earned their livelihood from commerce and artisanship. The community also had a free-loan society supported by former residents of Pilzno living in America. A Jewish cooperative bank supplied merchants with low-interest loans. Educational institutions included a Talmud Torah as well as *Ha-Shahar*, a study group for young women who pursued independent studies, which also ran a library. The townlet had chapters of Zionist parties and youth movements, as well as of Agudath Israel.

When the Germans occupied Pilzno in September 1939, they immediately began to seize Jews for forced labor. A Judenrat was established, and from mid-1940 onward, it arranged the recruitment of Jews for forced labor. In February 1941, the Judenrat ran a public soup kitchen. In late 1941, the JSS established a local chapter in Pilzno. On January 12, 1942, fourteen Jews were shot to death by German police.

On June 20, 1942, a ghetto was established in Pilzno, into which Jews from surrounding localities were also concentrated, raising its population to about 1,500. In late June or early July 1942, the ghetto was liquidated and all its inhabitants were deported to the Debica* ghetto, and on to the Belzec death camp. Another seventeen Jews were murdered in a liquidation operation in Pilzno.

PINCEHELY

(Today: **Görbőpincehely**)

TOWNLET IN TOLNA COUNTY, HUNGARY

Coordinates:
46°41' | 18°27'

The last national census conducted prior to the German occupation, taken in January 1941, recorded 147 Jewish inhabitants in Pincehely, accounting for roughly 4 percent of the total population. Most were merchants and artisans. The townlet's Jewish community was Orthodox. In 1942, Jewish men from Pincehely were drafted into the Hungarian army for forced labor service.

The German army occupied Hungary on March 19, 1944. A census conducted in the second week of April 1944 reported that 133 Jews belonged to the Orthodox Jewish community of Pincehely.

The Hungarian administration remained intact and operational after the German occupation. The ghettoization and deportation of the Jews were carried out on the basis of the decrees and orders of the Hungarian national and local authorities. On May 1, 1944, Edvin Szongott, the Hungarian sub-prefect of Tolna County, ordered the establishment of ghettos in his county. According to his decree, the local Jews were required to move into the ghetto of Pincehely along with 135 Jews from the county-district of Tamasi. It contained two blocks of houses; the Jewish residences were marked with mandatory "canary-yellow" stars.

At the end of June or beginning of July 1944, the inhabitants of the Pincehely ghetto were transferred to the artillery barracks in Kaposvar*, which served as an entrainment center. On July 4 and 5, 1944, the 5,159 Jews concentrated in the barracks were deported to Auschwitz.

PIŃCZÓW

COUNTY SEAT, KIELCE DISTRICT, POLAND

During the war: General Gouvernement, Radom District

Coordinates:
50°32' | 20°32'

After World War I, about 4,300 Jews lived in Pinczow, representing more than half of the townlet's population. Pinczow had three large synagogues and was a major rabbinical center in the region. Most of Pinczow's Jews earned their livelihood from small-scale commerce, peddling, and artisanship, but there were also several prominent businessmen, factory owners, and members of the liberal profession among the townlet's Jews. Pinczow had a Jewish bank supported by the JDC and a free loan society. The townlet boasted chapters of the Zionist parties, whose activities included the running of a large library and a drama class, as well as Zionist youth movements. A number of Pinczow's Jews were Communists who remained active even once the party was outlawed in 1926. The boys of Pinczow's Jewish community studied in a traditional Heder, a Mizrachi school, or an Orthodox *Yesodei Torah* school, while the girls attended a Beit Yaakov or a local public school.

On the eve of the war, many of Pinczow's Jews left for the United States, the Land of Israel, and various other countries.

About 3,500 Jews resided in Pinczow when it was occupied by the Germans on September 10, 1939. A number of young Jews managed to flee east, to the area under Soviet control.

The Germans imposed ransom payments on the Jews, confiscated their property, and placed restrictions on their freedom of movement. A Judenrat was established and ordered to recruit forced laborers and institute a Jewish Order Service. On February 15, 1941, a group of young Jews was sent from the townlet to labor camps.

In May 1941, a ghetto was established in a poor neighborhood in Pinczow. Though open, its inhabitants required exit permits to leave its confines. Epidemic typhus broke out in the ghetto and many people perished, predominantly the elderly and children. Jewish refugees from various localities were transferred into the Pinczow ghetto, but the high mortality rate and transports to remote work places kept the population of the ghetto from expanding.

In the summer of 1942, rumors began to circulate in the Pinczow ghetto of the impending liquidation of other ghettos in the region. Many people sought to prepare hiding places or to obtain false Polish papers.

One day between the dates October 2 and 6, 1942, members of the SS and the German gendarmerie surrounded the Pinczow ghetto. About 3,300 of the Pinczow ghetto's Jews were deported to Sandomierz*, and on to the Treblinka death camp.

Many were murdered along the way.

PINSK

COUNTY SEAT, POLESYE DISTRICT, POLAND
(After World War II in the USSR/Belarus)

During the war:
Reichskommissariat Ukraine

Coordinates:
52°07' | 26°07'

Before the War: According to a census taken in 1931, there were about 20,000 Jews living in Pinsk, approximately two-thirds of the city's population. They traded in lumber and wood products and engaged in artisanship and petty commerce. Pinsk's Jews were assisted in their economic activities by the JDC, mutual-aid societies, a Jewish savings-and-loan association, two free-loan funds, and Jewish trade unions as well as by relatives in America. The city had several traditional Jewish charitable and welfare institutions: an orphanage, a hospital, two old-age homes, a hostel, and a branch of TOZ.

Jewish educational institutions in Pinsk were varied, including a Yeshiva and vocational and technical schools. The community had Jewish libraries, drama groups, sports associations, and Yiddish-language weeklies.

All of the Jewish parties, apart from the outlawed Communists, were active in Pinsk, namely the Zionist and pioneering parties, the Bund, Agudath Israel, and their respective youth movements.

When the Poles and the Bulak-Balakhovich brigades occupied Pinsk in 1919 and again in 1920, a great deal of Jewish-owned property was plundered and about 1,000 Jews in and around the city were murdered.

Soviet occupation: The Soviets occupied Pinsk on September 20, 1939. Factories and large businesses were nationalized, while small-scale trade and manufacturing enterprises were closed. Jewish welfare institutions were shut down or removed from the control of the Jewish community administration. Hebrew-language instruction was forbidden, and Yiddish-speaking teachers were brought in from Russia. Local Zionist activists, Bundists, and a number of individuals accused of being Trotskyists were arrested and banished to Siberia. Wealthy individuals and "unproductive" elements (merchants and members of the bourgeoisie) were forced to relocate to nearby localities; a number were deported to Siberia. Some laborers enlisted for work in the east; others were drafted into the Red Army. A few Jews, mainly members of Zionist youth movements and Yeshiva students, fled to Vilna*.

German (Nazi) occupation: When Germany invaded the USSR on June 22, 1941, many young Jews were conscripted into the Red Army and ultimately survived by retreating to the east with the Soviet forces.

The Germans occupied Pinsk on July 4, 1941, and several days later murdered sixteen young Jews. Many sanctions were imposed on the Jews, including prohibitions against leaving the city or making contact with Christians, and a six o'clock evening curfew. Jews were required to wear a white armband bearing a yellow Star-of-David. The Germans demanded steep ransoms in property and clothing, confiscated Jewish-owned property, and abducted many men for forced labor, all with the assistance of the Polish auxiliary police, whose members also denounced Jews—subsequently murdered—who had held positions during the Soviet tenure.

The Jews of Pinsk secluded themselves in their homes. Few Jews received labor permits. On July 30–31, 1941, a twenty-seven-member Judenrat was established, under Benjamin Boksztanski. Between August 5 and 7, 1941, some 6,300 Pinsk Jews, including most of the local Jewish intelligentsia and eleven members of the Judenrat, were led to the nearby villages Posienicze and Kozlakowicze and murdered.

The Judenrat's main duties included the mobilization of forced laborers for the Germans. Eleven departments were established, among them a "general" department, a labor department, a burial association, a finance department, a welfare department (to which hundreds applied for aid), and a legal department. The Judenrat raised funds by charging for bread and selling off surplus gold.

The Judenrat's labor department was ordered to deliver 4,000 to 5,000 men and women for labor. The Judenrat also established a clinic, a hospital, a bathhouse, and a children's home.

More than 18,000 Jews remained in Pinsk after the August murder operations. The sanctions intensified: the armband was replaced with round patches, then later with two yellow stars, front and back, and Jews were repeatedly dunned for ransoms. The plunder of property resumed and included all furs and winter clothing—an especially severe decree in the harsh winter of 1941/42. Several Jews were hanged for concealing furs. The Germans gradually restricted the Judenrat's permission to purchase food in the market; eventually they did away with the privilege altogether. The Judenrat established a thirteen-member Jewish Order Service to prevent trade between Jews and Christians, but its members did not enforce the prohibition.

Ghetto setup, institutions, and internal life: In April 1942, Jews from nearby localities were brought to Pinsk. The Germans issued an order for the establishment of a ghetto, but the Judenrat postponed the implementation of the measure for a short time by offering bribes. The Pinsk ghetto was finally established on April 30, 1942. The Jews were constrained to move into it within one day, by May 1, and were allowed to bring only kitchen implements, bedding, and small quantities of clothing. The German and Polish policemen who guarded the ghetto gates confiscated contraband and beat the would-be smugglers. To maintain order, the Jewish Order Service was expanded to fifty members.

Starvation and epidemics became rampant in the ghetto. In September–October 1942, seventeen to twenty-five people died of hunger every day. Many were murdered for attempting to smuggle in food. The Judenrat opened a soup kitchen, several shops, and three bakeries. Vegetable gardens were planted. A hospital, an orphanage, and a pharmacy were opened, as were two large workshops, one for clothing and one for footwear. The Judenrat also purchased food from the Germans at exorbitant prices.

The Pinsk ghetto was considered a working ghetto. The Judenrat recruited forced laborers, mainly for artisan trades, agriculture, and office jobs, with hundreds of Jews leaving the ghetto to fill these positions as well as private jobs. The workers were paid in food for themselves and their families. A number of local non-Jews "hired" Jews ostensibly for work, when in fact they wished to feed them and to alleviate their suffering. Polish auxiliary police and German police escorted the ghetto inhabitants to and from work. The Germans and Polish inhabitants of Pinsk bought the output of the ghetto workshops for money and food. The Jews were forbidden to bring food into the ghetto. The policemen at the gates searched the belongings of Jews who returned from work, confiscated any food that they found, and beat the would-be smugglers, at times to death. Children slipped out of the ghetto to smuggle food; police shot many of them to death.

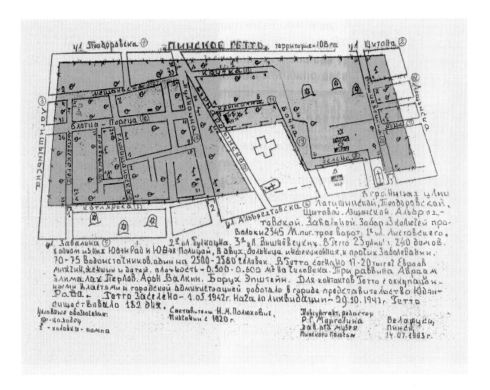

**Pinsk ghetto plan,
edited by N.M. Pluhovich,
illustrated by Nikolai
Polyvkhovich**
(YVA M41/226)

The ghetto had several synagogues but few other manifestations of religious or cultural life, as the greater part of the intelligentsia had been murdered in the August 1941 murder operations, and no one was left to organize studies or cultural activity.

Murder operations and the ghetto's liquidation: The first major murder operations in Pinsk took place in the summer of 1941. On August 5, 1941, approximately 3,000 Jewish men, including eleven members of the Judenrat, were led from Pinsk toward the village of Posienicze and shot to death. Several hundred skilled workers and a few unskilled workers were spared in the operation, and three Jews who fled from the massacre returned to Pinsk and reported what they had witnessed. Several dozen additional Jews managed to survive as well. The operation continued the following day, as 300 Jews were sent out to gather the corpses and place them in pits. When they completed their task, they too were shot dead, save two individuals who were ordered to cover the pits. On August 7, 1941, another 3,000 Jews were murdered near the village of Kozlakowicze. Most of the victims were men, including the elderly, a number of boys, and Jews who had been captured in hideouts. Both operations were perpetrated by soldiers from the mounted unit of the SS Second Cavalry Brigade, under Sturmbannfuehrer Franz Magill.

In July 1942, near Kozlakowicze, the Germans murdered forty mentally ill and severely sick Jews from the Pinsk ghetto.

The liquidation operation of the ghetto took place in late October 1942. On October 22, 1942, rumors that Christians were digging trenches near the village of Dobra Wola ran rampant in the ghetto. To quell the ensuing panic, Deputy Commissar Ebner called on several of the Judenrat's members and assured them that the installations being excavated were merely fuel dumps. The following day, word spread through the ghetto that the Germans were poised to remove 3,000 to 4,000 non-working Jews from the ghetto. However, the Germans' ruse worked; when it came time to liquidate the ghetto, they encountered barely any resistance.

On October 29, 1942, German forces including Gestapo men and members of a police battalion under Helmut Sauer surrounded the ghetto. Some 1,200 Jews were killed in the ghetto on the first day of the murder operation. SS men entered the ghetto, separated several hundred skilled workers from the rest of the population, and housed them in the hospital adjacent to the ghetto. The rest of the Jews were led to the pits near Dobra Wola in groups of 200 to 300, among them several members of the Judenrat, and were killed by gunfire. Several Judenrat members committed suicide by ingesting poison, while a few others were selected to join the skilled workers. Hundreds of young Jews attempted to escape by storming the fences, but they were struck by SS machine-gun fire.

On October 30 or 31, 1942, SS men assisted by dogs combed the ghetto in search of hiding Jews. Those they found were murdered at the pits near Dobra Wola.

About 18,000 Jews were murdered during the three-day operation. Approximately 150 escaped from the pits into the fields, but nearly all were caught by cavalrymen and murdered.

On November 1, 1942, about 200 of the skilled workers who had been separated from the rest of the Jews, a number of whom held labor permits, were murdered in the hospital near the ghetto. To house the 134 doctors, shoemakers, tailors, and print workers who remained after this operation, the Germans established a small ghetto in the Karlin neighborhood, which was fenced with barbed wire and guarded by Polish police. Jews who attempted to enter the ghetto were captured and murdered at Dobra Wola. Several inhabitants of the small ghetto, aware that their days were numbered, stockpiled provisions in an empty building outside the ghetto. Nearly all of the Jews in the small ghetto were murdered on December 23, 1942, in the Karlin cemetery. A few people managed to escape and go into hiding during the murder operation; several succeeded and joined the partisans.

Resistance: In mid-October, when the Jews of Pinsk became aware of the mass murders in nearby localities, many began to prepare hideouts in buildings and courtyards. Others proposed going to the forests and joining the partisans. A group of fifty Jews under Hershel Levin acquired and concealed several rifles, handguns, and two hand grenades. The Judenrat warned them that an escape might doom the entire ghetto to extermination, and they accordingly postponed and ultimately cancelled their departure.

There was also an attempt to organize clandestinely for forcible resistance against the Germans and their accomplices on the day of liquidation, to facilitate mass escape. Two members of the Judenrat and the commander of the Jewish Order Service were aware of the secret; the crux of the plan was to set the city ablaze, and for that purpose they provided the organizers with kerosene, rags, and matches for delivery to the Jews' workplaces. One person was assigned to each location, placed in charge of setting a fire when a signal was given. The scheme was scheduled for the final moments prior to the final murder operation. The Judenrat warned the activists that their strategy would endanger the Jewish residents of the ghetto, and thus before the liquidation operation on October 1942, most members of the resistance group abandoned their plan. One unarmed Jew attacked a German SS cavalryman and seized his rifle, but he was killed by SS men before he could fire the weapon. Otherwise, no organized resistance took place within the ghetto, and the plans of the underground had come to naught.

On November 1, 1942, while the murder operation was being carried out, a few groups left the ghetto in an attempt to reach the forests and join the partisans; a handful survived.

PIOTRKÓW KUJAWSKI

TOWNLET IN NIESZAWA COUNTY, WARSAW DISTRICT, POLAND

During the war: Wartheland

Coordinates:
52°34' | 18°30'

About 750 Jews lived in Piotrkow Kujawski, representing roughly 80 percent of the townlet's population. Most earned their livelihood from small commerce and artisanship. Piotrkow Kujawski had chapters of Zionist youth movements and a chapter of the Bund. The community had a well-stocked Jewish library with about 2,500 volumes in Hebrew, Yiddish, and Polish.

Piotrkow Kujawski was occupied by the Germans in early September 1939. A ghetto was established in the townlet in which Jews from the surrounding area were also concentrated.

The ghetto was liquidated in April 1942, when the Jews of the townlet were deported to the Chelmno death camp.

PIOTRKÓW TRYBUNALSKI

COUNTY SEAT IN ŁÓDŹ DISTRICT, POLAND

During the war: General Gouvernement

Coordinates:
51°24' | 19°41'

On the eve of World War II, about 10,300 Jews, representing approximately 20 percent of the local population, lived in Piotrkow Trybunalski, an ancient city that had been populated by Jews since the Middle Ages. Many of the city's Jews engaged in commerce and artisanship. Financial and related services in Piotrkow Trybunalski were provided by Jewish trade unions, a commercial bank, and an Agudath Israel cooperative bank. All of the Jewish parties and youth movements that operated at that time in Poland were active in Piotrkow Trybunalski. The community's children and youths attended a variety of Jewish schools, including private kindergartens and Bundist kindergartens, a CYSHO school, Yesodei Hatorah, Mizrachi and Agudath Israel schools, a Beit Yaakov school for girls, a secondary school for boys and girls, an ORT vocational school with a dormitory, and two Yeshivot. Cultural and sports institutions were highly developed, and three Jewish weeklies were published in the city. Care was provided by two orphanages, a Jewish hospital, and numerous charity institutions. The synagogue of Piotrkow Trybunalski was considered one of the most magnificent in all of Poland.

A number of antisemitic incidents occurred during the interwar period, including physical attacks, but most were publicly condemned by the city's Polish inhabitants and its leaders.

The Germans occupied Piotrkow Trybunalski on September 5, 1939. Many of the city's Jewish inhabitants fled to the nearby village of Sulejow, while more than 1,000 were killed in bombings. During the early days of the occupation, some 2,000 of the city's Jews managed to flee to areas under Soviet control, but once the battles ended, thousands of Jewish and Polish refugees thronged to Piotrkow Trybunalski. Dozens of Jews were killed on the first day of the occupation. The following day, German soldiers surrounded a neighborhood of the city largely inhabited by Jews, hurling hand grenades and shooting into windows; the quarter went up in flames, and many Jews were killed. The occupiers imposed numerous decrees against the Jews, involving property confiscations, heavy punitive fines, restrictions on freedom of movement, and forced labor seizures. Religious buildings and sacred objects were desecrated and stolen, prayer services were forbidden, and Jews caught worshipping were severely punished. The city's two Jewish cemeteries were destroyed and their tombstones were used to pave streets and roads. On December 12, 1939, the Jews were ordered to wear a white armband with a blue Star-of-David. All Jewish businesses and factories were "Aryanized."

In the wake of the German occupation, the structure of the Jewish community collapsed, and the local Jews soon felt the need to restore it. The chief rabbi of the city, Rabbi Moshe Khaim Lau, refused to serve as the "Jewish elder," but for one month did all he could to alleviate the Jews' suffering. On October 14, 1939, the Germans appointed Zalman Tannenberg, the former community leader, to serve as chairman of the Judenrat as well as president of the Piotrkow district Judenraete. Shimon Varshavski was appointed to serve as his deputy. The Judenrat initially

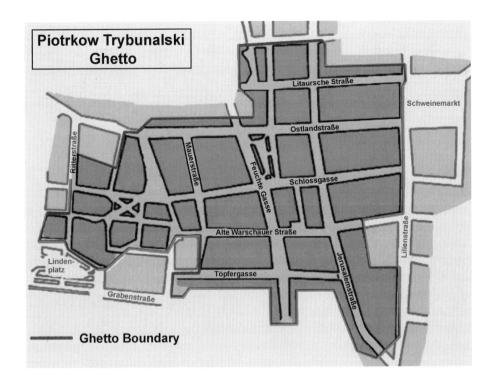

Piotrkow Trybunalski ghetto map, based on an original German map (Michael Peters, Germany)

had twelve members, but in time the number doubled. Most were members of the Bund. In the spring of 1940, a Jewish Order Service was established, headed by a man named Yitzhak. One of the Judenrat's main tasks was to provide the Germans with teams for forced labor; a system developed wherein Jews could be exempted from the labor requirement by paying fees that in turn provided a wage to the workers that labored in their stead. The members of the Judenrat did their best to ease the situation of Piotrkow Trybunalski's Jews and of the refugees, and most were also active in underground political work. The majority of the ghetto's residents regarded the Judenrat as an honorable leadership for the community.

In October 1939, the German commander (*oberburgermeister*) of the city informed Rabbi Lau of the intention to establish the Piotrkow Trybunalski ghetto. By late January 1940, the Jews were uprooted and transferred it. The Judenrat arranged, when possible, the exchange of apartments between Christian Poles who lived in the area of the ghetto and newly arrived Jewish inhabitants. Nevertheless, many Poles continued to live in the ghetto area until the spring of 1942. The ghetto comprised about 180 buildings distributed over a small area. Overcrowding was further exacerbated by the arrival of thousands of Jewish refugees. In April 1942, the official Jewish population of the ghetto reached 16,500, including about 8,000 displaced persons. However, the actual population was considerably greater owing to the approximately 2,000 unregistered Jews who lived there.

Signs marked "ghetto" with a drawing of a skull and crossbones were placed along the ghetto boundaries and its main gate. However, the ghetto was not fenced in or guarded. While subject to restrictions on freedom of movement, Jews could leave the ghetto without a permit for fixed periods of time; moreover, a number of ghetto residents were officially permitted to move freely throughout the county to engage in commerce for the Germans. Jews upheld existing commercial ties and fostered new ones with Warsaw*, Czestochowa*, and other cities. A leather-tanning factory was active in the ghetto. Flour, wood, and meat were smuggled into the ghetto, which also featured several cafés that served baked goods. A black market for the exchange of currency also operated, and many Jews visited the general market in the city, where people sold their belong-

Piotrkow Trybunalski, 1943
A group of Jews working in a glass factory near the ghetto (YV)

ings. Such illegal activities, along with smuggling, were known to the German and Polish authorities, who were bribed.

Most of the official workplaces were located outside the ghetto: several thousand Jews worked in glass, wood, and alcohol factories while hundreds of artisans were employed in various workshops run by the Judenrat. Many of the ghetto's inhabitants earned a living filling private orders from "Aryan" customers.

Groups of Jews were recruited for forced labor, such as construction, digging, and farming in the city and its environs; harsh conditions led to loss of life. Jews were also sent to labor camps: some 1,200 Jews worked in the Witow labor camp from April 1940 to December 1941, and in the spring and summer of 1940, hundreds of Jewish men were sent to camps in the Lublin area. The Judenrat, the community leaders in the ghetto, and Rabbi Lau organized projects to help and occasionally even free the laborers. Many Jews perished in the camps.

Many of the ghetto's inhabitants, particularly the refugees and members of the intelligentsia, were in need of support from the community, and a number of institutions were created in the ghetto for this purpose. The Judenrat initiated the establishment of an orphanage for 500 children, a club, small gardens, and playgrounds. The organization's welfare department dispensed modest grants to the needy and ran public soup kitchens, which eventually distributed more than 2,000 meals daily. A clinic headed by Leon Veintziher was set up, as were a pharmacy and a dental clinic. In mid-1941, the Piotrkow Trybunalski ghetto established contact with the JSS chapter in Warsaw, which supported the ghetto's existing welfare institutions and further opened a mother-and-child clinic, a clinic for children up to the age of fourteen, and a well-baby clinic.

In the winter of 1940/41, epidemic typhus broke out in the ghetto. All of the doctors in the ghetto were mobilized to fight the disease, temporary hospitals and a number of quarantine rooms were set up, and a sanitary police force was formed. The bathhouse was expanded and adapted for disinfection purposes. The epidemic was eradicated by April 1941, and when it broke out again in the winter of 1941/42, the Judenrat was better equipped, such as with trucks for removing waste.

Traditional Hadarim, Yeshivot, and Talmud Torah schools were active in the ghetto, but no secular schools were opened, despite the Germans allowing studies in the Hebrew language. There were also numerous private teaching groups and facilities: kindergartens, high school education, lending libraries, and drama circles. Religious Jews continued to worship in prayer quorums, they built booths on the Succot holiday, and on Passover of 1940 and 1941, the Jews of the Piotrkow Trybunalski ghetto received *matzot*.

Jewish parties and youth movements such as the Bund and Hashomer Hatzair continued their underground activities, maintaining ties with activists in Warsaw and other cities and with the Polish underground. On July 5, 1941, the German police arrested Zalman Tannenberg, the Judenrat chairman. The Germans discovered the underground activities of different Jewish groups in the ghetto, including the ties that the Bund maintained with the Polish Socialist Party (PPS). Several days later a large group of public activists and Bundists were arrested, including ten members of the Judenrat. Following their arrests, they were tortured, and their deaths were announced immediately after they were deported to Auschwitz in September 1941. This development severely undermined but did not entirely halt the Bund's activities in the ghetto. The Hashomer Hatzair movement also continued its activities. In 1940, an emissary from Warsaw arrived to rally the resistance in the Piotrkow Trybunalski ghetto: Mordechai Anielewicz (who would later become the commander of the Jewish resistance forces in the Warsaw ghetto).

The Germans appointed a second Judenrat headed by Shimon Varshavski. The commander of the Jewish Order Service was also replaced. Although some of the members of the previous Judenrat held their positions, the new Judenrat also included Jews not originally from Piotrkow Trybunalski. The revised Judenrat tended to be more obedient to the Germans and received less support from the population.

As of late 1941, the situation in the ghetto began to deteriorate. The ghetto boundaries were guarded more strictly and smugglers were executed. In early March 1942, the head of Piotrkow Trybunalski County ordered the ghetto completely sealed, and all Poles living within its boundaries were commanded to leave. Any Jews caught outside the ghetto were executed. On April 1, 1942, the ghetto was declared closed and was reduced in size.

In the spring of 1942, rumors seeped into the ghetto regarding large-scale deportations and the murder of Jews in the Chelmno death camp; at first, the rumors were not given much credence. In September 1942, the Judenrat learned of the plan to deport the Jews of the ghetto save some 2,000 laborers. Varshavski managed to increase the number of Jews who would be allowed to remain to 3,000, and a special barbed-wire-enclosed block was cleared for them.

In early October 1942, the Jews of the smaller localities around the city were driven into the Piotrkow Trybunalski ghetto. This influx, in view of the mounting rumors regarding the impending liquidation of the ghetto, was viewed by local inhabitants as a portent of bad news. They struggled to find employment and prepared hiding places, "Aryan" documents, and escape plans. The heads of the Judenrat, Rabbi Lau, and the leaders of the parties debated the predicament and concluded that collective resistance had no chance of success. They opted instead to strengthen the spirit of the Jews and encourage them to prepare hiding places.

On October 13, 1942, the ghetto was surrounded by SS units and German, Ukrainian, Lithuanian, and Latvian policemen, under the command of SS officer Willy Blum. The following day, under the command of SS Sturmbannfuehrer Freucht, the operation was launched as the approximately 25,000 ghetto inhabitants were ordered to gather in the square near the Franciscan Barracks. The Jewish Order Service and Jewish sanitary unit participated in the roundup. The factory workers had been ordered ahead of time to move their belongings into the factories and to remain there. Anyone found at home was murdered by the German police. A selection was carried out in the square, after which the first group of about 6,000 Jews was deported from the ghetto in cattle cars to the Treblinka death camp. The deportations lasted eight days, during which about 22,000 Jews (or 18,000 to 20,000 according to a different testimony) were deported to Treblinka. Some 300 members of the seemingly "safe" block were sent in the last transport, including some well-known Jewish dignitaries, the members of the Judenrat, and the ghetto's rabbis, Rabbi Lau among them.

Between 2,000 to 2,400 Jews remained in the block on Staro-Warszawska Street, known as the "small ghetto," officially called the "Jewish labor camp." Most were workers in the factories and workshops, including a number of Judenrat members and its chairman, Varshavski.

In the weeks following the large-scale operation, many Jews were discovered or came out of hiding. Hundreds of them, including women and children, were killed by the Germans in the nearby Las Rakowski forest. In one of these operations, on December 19, 1942, dozens of Jews attacked the Germans with their bare hands. Several were murdered and others managed to escape, but were later handed over to the Germans.

A number of the Jews who came out of their hiding places joined those living in the "small ghetto," whose population, approximately 4,000 by now, was employed in the factories and in collecting the belongings of the deportees. In February–March 1943, about 500 Jews were transferred from the "small ghetto" to a munitions factory in Skarzysko-Kamienna*.

Throughout the existence of the "small ghetto," the Germans continued to kill its inhabitants. On March 18, 1943, the Germans murdered in the cemetery ten Jews who had been promised passage to Palestine as part of a population exchange with Germans living in Sharon. Later in 1943, additional Jews living in the block were executed. The Jewish underground remained active. Its members received underground literature, and the Bund maintained contact with the movement's center in Warsaw.

In July (or May, according to a different source) 1943, most of the Jews of the "small ghetto" were deported. During the operation, all remaining children in the ghetto were murdered along with a number of women, about forty people in all. The altogether 1,720 surviving Jews were transferred to two camps located near the glass and wood factories. Some 500 to 600 Jews (1,500 according to another source) were sent to the Pionki, Blizyn, Starachowice, Radom, and Ostrowiec labor camps.

After the deportation, the German authorities posted a sign in the train station that read: "Piotrkow Trybunalski *Judenrein*." About one month later, a selection was carried out among the Jews working in the factories: 120 Jews were sent to the Pionki labor camp and another approximately 100 Jews to the factories in Troppau in the Sudetenland. The remaining Jews continued to work in the labor camps until November 25, 1944, when they were deported to concentration camps by the retreating German forces.

PIRYATIN

(Yiddish: **Piratin**; Ukrainian: **Pyryatyn**)

COUNTY SEAT, POLTAVA DISTRICT, UKRAINE, USSR

During the war:
Reichskommissariat Ukraine

Coordinates:
50°15' | 32°31'

In the early twentieth century, there were about 3,100 Jews in Piryatin, approximately 40 percent of the townlet's population. In February 1919, nineteen Jews were murdered in a pogrom perpetrated by the White Army. During the Soviet era, Jewish artisans formed cooperatives, took on white- or blue-collar jobs in state-owned factories, or took up farm labor. As part of the Soviet policy toward national minorities, the government established a Yiddish-language school. The industrialization and urbanization of the USSR caused the Jewish population of the town to dwindle to about 1,700 by the eve of the German invasion.

The Germans occupied Piryatin on September 18, 1941, and almost immediately concentrated the Jewish townspeople in a sealed ghetto made up of three streets. Jews were compelled to wear a Star-of-David armband. A census conducted by the Germans in late March 1942 tallied 1,530 Jews in the ghetto.

On April 6, 1942, the vast majority of the residents were removed to nearby Pirogovskaya Levada, where, over the next four days, they were murdered by Sonderkommando Platt with the help of local police. On May 18, 1942, scores of Jews from Piryatin were murdered along with Gypsies who had been captured in the townlet.

PISZCZAC

TOWNLET IN BIAŁA PODLASKA COUNTY, LUBLIN DISTRICT, POLAND

During the war: General Gouvernement, Lublin District

Coordinates: 51°58' | 23°23'

After World War I, about 400 Jews lived in Piszczac, representing approximately half of the townlet's population. They earned their livelihood from artisanship and small-scale commerce and were aided by a free-loan society that was established with the assistance of the JDC. The townlet boasted chapters of Zionist parties, Agudath Israel, and the Bund, and also had a Jewish library.

The Germans occupied Piszczac on September 8, 1939. A few days later, they retreated in the wake of the Soviet Army, but reoccupied the townlet a short time later in accordance with the Molotov-Ribbentrop Pact. When the Soviets withdrew from Piszczac, they were joined by some 500 Jews, both local residents and refugees who found themselves in Piszczac when the war broke out. Only about 200 Jews remained in the townlet.

On October 15, 1939, the Germans transferred dozens of Jewish families from surrounding villages to Piszczac. As of September 1940, the Jews of Piszczac were ordered to wear an armband with a Star-of-David. The Germans established a Judenrat in Piszczac charged with recruiting forced laborers.

In the spring of 1941, about 700 Jewish forced laborers were brought to the townlet. In late summer 1941, the Germans forbade the Jews to leave the village; four Jewish laborers were murdered for violating the prohibition. A ghetto was most likely established in the townlet during this time. In May 1942, the Judenrat was ordered to send a group of workers to Malaszewicze, near Biala Podlaska*.

In October 1942, the Jews of Piszczac were deported in freight trains to the Sobibor death camp. Polish police, under the command of German police, were placed in charge of their deportation. A small group of Jews was separated from the others and sent to work in Miedzyrzec Podlaski*, together with Jews from nearby villages.

PLESHCHANITSY/ PLESHCHENITSY

COUNTY SEAT, MINSK DISTRICT, BELARUS, USSR

During the war: Reichskommissariat Ostland

Coordinates: 54°25' | 27°50'

On the eve of the German invasion of the Soviet Union, there were about 800 Jews in Pleshchanitsy, approximately one-fifth of the population. During the era of Soviet rule, many Jews practiced artisan trades, and several turned to farming. There was a government school in the townlet that taught in Yiddish.

The Germans occupied Pleshchanitsy on June 28, 1941. In the early days of the occupation, the Germans murdered several residents who had been active Communists under the Soviets, including a few Jews. A short time later, all of the Jews in the townlet were concentrated in a ghetto and forced to wear a special yellow mark on their chests and backs. Some were sent to forced labor. In mid-October, skilled workers and the elderly were separated from the other inhabitants of the ghetto, who were murdered in a forest near the townlet. The ghetto was liquidated three weeks later when the skilled workers and the elderly were murdered.

PLISSA/PLISA

TOWNLET IN GŁĘBOKIE COUNTY, VILNA DISTRICT, POLAND
(After World War II in the USSR/Belarus)

During the war: Reichskommissariat Ostland

Coordinates: 55°13' | 27°57'

About 600 Jews lived in Plissa on the eve of World War II, representing approximately 40 percent of the townlet's population. Most earned their livelihood from small commerce, shopkeeping, peddling, and artisanship. The community boasted Jewish parties and youth movements as well as Jewish educational and cultural institutions, including a Tarbut Hebrew school.

After the Soviets occupied Plissa in the second half of September 1939, privately owned businesses in the townlet were closed and commercial activity was restricted.

In late June, the Germans occupied Plissa and placed restrictions on the Jews, seizing many for forced labor. A short time later, a Judenrat was established, and the Jews of Plissa were transferred to a ghetto. The Plissa ghetto was liquidated on June 2, 1942, when its approximately 420 inhabitants were shot to death outside the townlet by an SD unit under the command of Heinz Tangermann. A number of Jews who escaped during the operation were later caught and executed.

PŁOCK

COUNTY SEAT, WARSAW DISTRICT, POLAND

During the war: Bezirk Zichenau

Coordinates: 52°33' | 19°42'

When World War II broke out, about 6,500 Jews lived in Plock, representing approximately one-quarter of the town's population. They earned their livelihood from commerce and artisanship, mostly in the garment industry. Jews owned two large factories that manufactured farm machines. The Jews of Plock were aided by trade unions, and the town had at least three Jewish banks. The community boasted a ramified system of welfare and mutual-aid institutions, including a hospital. Plock had Zionist parties and youth movements, which ran a library, Hebrew courses, and a number of pioneer training facilities. The Bund and Agudath Israel were active in the town, as were secret cells of Communists that ran a library and sports club used to cover up illegal political activities. Plock boasted drama circles, orchestras, and numerous cultural events, as well as sports organizations belonging to the entire spectrum of political movements.

When World War II broke out, many of the town's Jews, especially the more affluent among them, fled to the east and to Warsaw*. During the same period, hundreds of Jews arrived in the town from small towns near the border with Germany, while many others were killed while fleeing.

Plock was occupied by the Germans on September 8, 1939. After a while, Jewish refugees began to return; they were robbed by the Germans when they entered the town. With the onset of the occupation, Jews were forbidden to maintain any form of religious life, so religious ritual was carried out in secret. On October 8, 1939, at Hitler's orders, Plock was annexed to the Reich as part of the Bezirk Zichenau, and its administrative control was handed over to the civil authorities and Gestapo in the district of East Prussia. The community was required to pay a ransom, and the Jews were robbed and beaten on a daily basis. In late October 1939, all Jewish businesses were seized and transferred to Germans and Poles. As of late November 1939, the Jews of Plock were required to wear a yellow badge on their lapel.

In late December 1939, a Judenrat was established in Plock, headed by Dr. Brumberger, along with a twenty-member Jewish Order Service. The Judenrat was ordered to supply 150 Jewish women daily for forced labor, along with varying quotas of men. Jews were also randomly seized for forced labor. The Judenrat organized work by artisans for the Germans for a meager salary.

During the early months of the occupation, many Jewish-owned apartments were appropriated for Germans and Poles, while Jews from surrounding localities flooded the town. The new arrivals were packed into a "Jewish quarter," located on a number of densely overcrowded streets.

Plock, February 1941
During the deportation from the ghetto, the Jews are rounded up on Szeroka Street, loaded onto trucks, and taken to the Dzialdowo camp. (GFH)

In September 1940, a ghetto was established in Plock with about 10,600 Jews, including some 3,000 refugees. During the establishment of the ghetto or a few days earlier, the Germans deported thirty old-age home residents to the Dzialdowo penal camp, where they were murdered. The Judenrat was ordered to draw up a list of the ill and handicapped, and they were taken away by the Germans, together with healthy people who were randomly seized, never to be seen again.

The Judenrat established a clinic, a bakery, a public soup kitchen, and shops where food was distributed in exchange for vouchers.

In January 1941, the Germans murdered a number of men and women and transferred others to Dzialdowo and to another labor camp. The number of those murdered and transported totaled about thirty-five Jews.

On February 20, 1941, SS Battalion 13 arrived in Plock. In February 1941, twenty-five Jewish men were arrested and shot to death near the border, between the villages of Imielnica and Podolszyce. The following day, on February 21, 1941, the SS murdered nearly half of the patients in the Jewish hospital in the ghetto. The Jews were concentrated on Szeroka Street and beaten, some of them until death; afterwards, about 4,000 Jews were deported from Plock to Dzialdowo. During the deportation, thirty-nine Jewish men who had been arrested by the Gestapo in January 1941 were shot and killed.

On February 28, 1941, the members of the Judenrat were arrested. On March 1, 1941, the second and last deportation of the Jews of Plock was carried out. The Jews were forced to wait for nearly twenty-four hours in the cold, in an exposed area, without food. Many were murdered on site, and dozens of others died on the way to Dzialdowo. During both deportations, a total of about 7,000 Jews arrived in Dzialdowo from Plock. Dozens or hundreds of Jews were murdered in the camp. After one or two weeks, the Jews of Plock were sent from Dzialdowo to other localities, mostly in the area of Kielce, and to the Radom District (in accordance with the German administrative division). A number of the deportees arrived in Warsaw.

PŁOŃSK

COUNTY SEAT, WARSAW DISTRICT, POLAND

During the war: Bezirk Zichenau

Coordinates:
52°38' | 20°23'

In the interwar period, about 4,900 Jews lived in Plonsk, David Ben-Gurion's birthplace, representing nearly half of the town's population. Most earned their livelihood from small-scale commerce and artisanship, especially in the garment industry, with a small proportion working in the construction, food, and chemical industries. They were aided by the JDC, relatives living abroad, trade and craft associations, a Jewish bank, a free-loan society, and assorted welfare and mutual-aid societies. Most of the community's children attended private traditional Hadarim and a Talmud Torah. Plonsk had a state elementary school for Jews, most of whose students were girls; a Tarbut Hebrew school; and a Beit Yaakov school. Plonsk had Zionist parties and youth movements, one of which, Tze'irei Hamizrachi, ran a pioneer training facility. The Bund and Agudath Israel were active in the town, as were their youth and women's movements. Many Jews were members of the illegal Polish Communist Party. Most of the parties and youth movements ran clubs, libraries, and sports and drama circles.

On the eve of World War II, more than 5,000 Jews lived in Plonsk. When the war broke out, many Jews fled to eastern Poland, later occupied by the Soviet Union, and to Warsaw*.

Plonsk was occupied by the Germans on September 5, 1939. A number of Jewish shops were looted. On September 19, 1939, the Germans began to seize Jews for forced labor, at first randomly and later in accordance with lists. In the fall of 1939, Jews who had been deported from towns annexed to the Third Reich arrived in Plonsk, as did Jews from places nearby. They all were required to wear a patch on their chest and back that was later replaced by a yellow patch with a Star-of-David. Eventually they were ordered to add the word *Jude* to the Star-of-David. At that time, a committee was established to provide assistance to needy Jews, especially the thousands of refugees. It was aided intermittently by the JDC in Warsaw until the end of 1940.

In late September or early October 1939, about 200 Jews were transported from Plonsk to the new border with the Soviet Union and were ordered to run in the direction of the border; several were shot and murdered.

In early October 1939, Plonsk was added to Bezirk Zichenau and subordinated to the civilian administration. Its name was changed to Plohnen. In November 1939, the Jews of Plonsk were ordered to pay a ransom. All Jewish businesses in the town were apparently confiscated in 1940.

On July 1, 1940, the Germans transformed the assistance committee into a Judenrat that was headed by Avraham Yaakov Ramek and given the task of recruiting Jews for forced labor. A six-member Jewish Order Service was also established. The Judenrat, complete with an employment bureau, was appointed by the Germans to serve as the regional Judenrat for the Plonsk County along with welfare and health committees. Jews were employed in cleaning and municipal maintenance, housework, peat mining, and earthwork. Skilled workers were employed in the factories that had been confiscated from Jews and Poles. Many of the forced laborers were sent to camps in Dalanowka, Nosarzewo, and Sierpc (a women's camp).

Ramek, the Judenrat head, strove to obtain food for Plonsk's Jews. He also managed to delay the establishment of a ghetto, free Jews from imprisonment, and bring about the elimination of Jews who were serving as Gestapo agents in Plonsk and Warsaw. Ramek's finances were drawn from the profits he earned in transactions carried out with the Germans and portions of forced laborers' wages. Wealthier members of the community paid the Judenrat in order to secure their release from forced labor. In 1941, apparently, twelve merchants established a cooperative to supply the Jews of Plonsk with food, with the knowledge of the Judenrat.

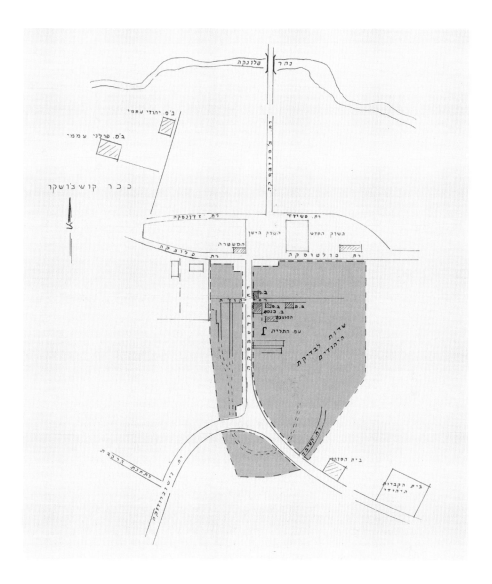

Plonsk ghetto plan, illustrated by Eng. Y. Aharoni. Ghetto boundaries given by David Kalmanowski

(*Plonsk and Environment, Neishtadt and Sochocin, In Memory of the Jewish Communities*, published by Irgun Yotzei Plonsk in Israel, Tel Aviv 1963)

In 1940/41, many Jews who had fled from Plonsk to Warsaw early in the war, returned, as did other Jews from towns near Plonsk who had been deported in the fall of 1939 and in 1940 to the area of the General Gouvernement. In September–December 1940, between 7,000 and 8,000 Jews lived in Plonsk, including about 3,800 refugees. In early 1941, the Judenrat established a public soup kitchen that distributed hundreds of hot meals each day, largely to refugees.

In May 1941, a sealed ghetto was established in Plonsk. It was separated into two parts that were located on either side of a main street and joined by a single street. About 8,000 Jews, half of whom were refugees, were concentrated in it. An epidemic of spotted fever soon broke out. A hospital with forty to fifty beds was set up and was managed by Dr. Eliyahu Fenigstein until late June 1941. In July 1941, Ramek recruited Dr. Arthur Ber of Warsaw, who established a clinic and pharmacy in the ghetto. The Plonsk ghetto served as a medical center for the Jews of Nowe Miasto*, Sochocin, and Czerwinsk*, with Dr. Ber traveling to these localities and returning with patients.

During the existence of the large ghetto, the Jewish Order Service had reached forty members. It was headed by Levin, who was from Dobrzyn, and his deputy, Chanan Ramek, the brother of the Judenrat head. The members of the Jewish

Order Service initially wore a cap with a blue ribbon, and after some time, they were supplied with dark blue uniforms. In 1941, a bathhouse was established in the ghetto, in which it was mandatory for all ghetto inhabitants to bathe.

On July 6 or 13, 1941, an operation was carried out, and about 1,200 Jews living in the Plonsk ghetto without permits or working without permits for Polish farmers in the area were driven out to the Pomiechowek camp, following a cruel selection. Many Jews who smuggled food into the ghetto were caught and murdered. In the fall of 1941, the remaining Jews of the Plonsk and Sierpc Counties were transferred into the ghetto.

In December 1941 and spring 1942, Yisraelovits and Shlomo Fukhs, the representatives of the Communists in the ghetto, held three meetings with Polish Communists. About thirty members of the Jewish Communist group joined the Polish workers party (PPR) founded in early 1942, established contact with Jewish Communists in the Czerwinsk ghetto, and smuggled out contributions to the Polish Communists for Soviet prisoners of war. An underground group of the Armia Ludowa, the military wing of the PPR, was formed in the ghetto, headed by Yaakov Pashigoda (Paul).

On October 28, 1942, another operation was carried out, and about 2,000 elderly and ill Jews were deported to Auschwitz, based on lists drawn up by the Judenrat. By November 30, 1942, another 4,000 Jews had been deported to Auschwitz in two additional transports. The Jews of the Nowe Miasto ghetto who had arrived in the Plonsk ghetto a few days earlier were also sent there in the transport of November 30, 1942. The last transport of Jews from Plonsk to Auschwitz left on December 16, 1942; it included young Jews, skilled workers, and those considered "privileged" by the Judenrat, including Ramek and his family. Also on the transport were 340 children from the children's house in the ghetto, along with their female teacher, Greenberg. All perished in Auschwitz. On the same day of that final transport, Schmidt, the assistant to Puk, the police commander in Plonsk, murdered the Jews Lazenski and Korman, who mediated between Puk and Schmidt and the Judenrat in the years 1940 through 1942. Schmidt then turned over the Jews' plundered property to the Germans.

During the liquidation of the ghetto, a few members of the underground escaped and joined units of the Armia Ludowa. They participated in battles against the Germans, and all fell in battle or were murdered by the Gestapo following their capture, along with their entire combat unit, in December 1943.

Dozens of Plonsk's Jews survived, some in the Soviet Union and others in camps or by hiding with Poles.

POCHINOK

COUNTY SEAT, SMOLENSK DISTRICT, RUSSIAN FEDERATION, USSR

During the war: Military Administration Area

Coordinates:
60°58' | 30°11'

On the eve of World War II, about 280 Jews lived in Pochinok, representing less than 10 percent of the townlet's population. They earned their livelihoods from artisanship or as farmers.

Pochinok was occupied by the Germans on July 17, 1941. Some of the townlet's Jews managed to flee to the east prior to the occupation. Under the occupation, the Jews of Pochinok were required to wear armbands. At an undetermined time, a ghetto was established in a single building, where all the Jews who remained in the townlet were concentrated.

The ghetto was liquidated on April 21, 1942, and all its inhabitants were murdered and buried in pits.

POCZAJÓW

TOWNLET IN KRZEMIENIEC COUNTY, VOLHYNIA DISTRICT, POLAND
(After World War II in the USSR/Ukraine; Ukrainian: **Pochaiv**; Russian: **Pochaev**)

During the war:
Reichskommissariat Ukraine

Coordinates:
50°01' | 25°29'

During the interwar years there were about 1,000 Jews in Poczajow, accounting for nearly half of the townlet's population. The Jews of Poczajow were merchants, chiefly in food and textiles, and petty manufacturers. The townlet had a Jewish-owned merchant bank and a mutual-aid society, instituted in part through the donations of local Jews who had emigrated to the United States and a subvention from the JDC. Poczajow had a Hebrew-language Tarbut school, a Yeshiva, a Jewish library, and chapters of Zionist youth movements.

The Soviets took control of the area in September 1939.

The Germans occupied Poczajow on June 30, 1941. In July, they confiscated a great deal of property, demanded a high ransom, and murdered 119 Jewish men. The local Ukrainian administration ordered the Jews to establish a twelve-member Judenrat and a Jewish Order Service composed of thirty policemen.

In January 1942, the Jews of Poczajow were concentrated into a ghetto, which was surrounded by a high fence crowned with barbed wire. The well was situated outside of it and inhabitants were allotted two hours a day to draw water. The already meager bread rations were gradually reduced until they were stopped altogether on the eve of the liquidation. Nineteen Jews were shot dead attempting to smuggle food into the ghetto.

The Poczajow ghetto was liquidated on September 7, 1942, when 794 Jews were murdered in pits outside the townlet. For eight days, those in hiding were hunted down and murdered. The thirty Jews who had been kept alive to sort the victims' possessions were murdered when they completed their task. Eleven Jews fled to Brody*, but all save two had died within ten weeks.

PODBRODZIE

(Yiddish: **Podbrodz**)

TOWNLET IN ŚWIĘCIANY COUNTY, VILNA DISTRICT, POLAND
(After World War II in the USSR/Lithuania; Lithuanian: **Pabradė**)

During the war:
Reichskommissariat Ostland

Coordinates:
55°00' | 25°47'

About 1,000 Jews lived in Podbrodzie during the interwar period, most of whom earned their livelihood from shopkeeping, small commerce, and artisanship. The community boasted several Jewish parties and youth movements, a Yiddish school, a Tarbut Hebrew school, and Jewish study circles and libraries.

After Podbrodzie was occupied by the Soviets in the second half of September 1939, a Soviet economic, social, and educational regime was introduced into the townlet. Privately owned shops were nationalized or closed and cooperatives were formed.

The Germans occupied Podbrodzie on June 29, 1941, and along with Lithuanians, began a short time later to abuse and terrorize the Jews. On July 15, 1941, about sixty Jews were murdered, including women and children. The Jews of Podbrodzie were required to wear a yellow badge and their freedom of movement was restricted. A Judenrat headed by Ben Zion Vilian was established and charged with recruiting forced laborers, including women and children aged twelve years and older.

After some time, the Jews of Podbrodzie were moved into a ghetto that was situated in two narrow alleyways. Harsh living conditions there led to extreme suffering. On September 23, 1941, the Jews were required to pay a high ransom in cash and jewelry. Two days later, the chief of the Lithuanian police, Virshnik, revealed to the head of the Judenrat that the Germans were planning to liquidate the ghetto. Within the following twenty-four hours, close to half of the Jewish inhabitants had fled, including the head of the Judenrat and his family.

On September 26, the remaining Jews were rounded up; following a selection, about 120 people were separated out and sent by the Germans to labor camps. The rest of the Jews were led to the Poligon regional transit camp, where they were murdered two days later, on September 28, 1941.

PODDĘBICE

TOWNLET IN ŁĘCZYCA COUNTY, ŁÓDŹ DISTRICT, POLAND

During the war: Wartheland

Coordinates:
51°53' | 18°57'

During the interwar period, about 1,400 Jews lived in Poddebice, more than one-third of the townlet's population. Most were cattle, grain, and flour merchants; some were wagoners. Agudath Israel and Zionist parties were active in Poddebice. The community had a reformed Heder, a Beit Yaakov girls' school, and libraries.

The Germans occupied Poddebice on September 7, 1939. An unfenced ghetto was established in November 1940 in the most rundown quarter of the townlet. It was crammed with about 1,500 Jews, including some 150 refugees. The ghetto population rose in the subsequent months with the transfer of approximately 600 Jews from Leczyca*. There were no sources of employment in the Poddebice ghetto, even for artisans, and its inhabitants suffered from starvation. The local Judenrat, headed by a man named Sosnovski, ran a public aid committee that provided the needy with heating fuel.

In the weeks preceding the liquidation of the ghetto, the Germans conducted a spate of public hangings to break the Jews' morale. On March 17, 1942, members of the Jewish Order Service were forced to hang five Jews in the ghetto. Following this incident, dozens of Jewish men volunteered for service in labor camps, including some ninety Jews who were sent to the labor camp at Konin, where they perished.

The deportation from the Poddebice ghetto was carried out in mid-April 1942 by substantial SS forces, some brought in especially from Lodz*. Approximately 1,800 ghetto Jews were crammed into the local church, where they were held for ten days under appalling conditions that caused the deaths of twenty-eight people. When removed from the church they were subjected to a selection, during which several children and elderly people were shot. The remaining Jews were deported to the Chelmno death camp, apart from a few men and women who were found fit for forced labor and were transferred to the Lodz ghetto. Two SS officers, Herman Werner and Bruno Uhle, directed the liquidation operation.

PODHAJCE

COUNTY SEAT, TARNOPOL DISTRICT, POLAND
(After World War II in the USSR/Ukraine; Ukrainian: **Pidhaytsi**; Russian: **Podgaytsy**)

During the war: General Gouvernement, Galicia District

Coordinates:
49°16' | 25°08'

In the early 1930s, about 3,100 Jews lived in Podhajce, representing approximately two-thirds of the townlet's population. They earned their livelihood from various types of commerce, artisanship, and the liberal professions. Podhajce had a commercial bank, various kinds of mutual-aid societies, and a Zionist academic union, *Kadima*. In 1927, the Zionist engineer David Lille was elected mayor of Podhajce. The townlet had various Zionist parties as well as Agudath Israel, and among the youth movements, the Hashomer Hatzair chapter was especially active. Jewish schools in the community included a Talmud Torah, a supplementary Hebrew school, and a kindergarten. In the early 1920s, a general secondary school was established at Jewish initiative.

In the second half of September 1939, the Soviets entered Podhajce. Jewish property was nationalized, and the various forms of Jewish public activity were discontinued, with the exception of the synagogues, which remained open and also served as mutual-aid centers. Private commerce was abolished, large factories were nationalized, and most of the artisans were organized into cooperatives. In the summer of 1940, Jewish refugees who had found asylum in Podhajce were exiled into the Soviet interior.

After the Germans invaded the Soviet Union, a few dozen young Jews managed to flee to the east. On July 4, 1941, Podhajce was occupied by the Germans. In the same month, a Judenrat was established, headed by L. Lilienfeld. A Jewish Order Service was also set up; one of its commanders was a lawyer, Herenfeld. On August 10, 1941, the Judenrat was required to pay the Germans a ransom of half a million rubles and valuables. The Jews were exploited for forced labor, repairing bridges and roads. From November 1941 onward, several hundred

Jews were transferred to labor camps in the area. The Judenrat succeeded in maintaining contact with the laborers, sending them food packages and attempting to secure the release of a number of ailing people.

In the spring and summer of 1942, Jews began to seek out permanent jobs in the townlet in the hope of gaining immunity from abduction to the labor camps. A number were employed in various workshops as well as at collecting scrap metal and arms left behind by the retreating Soviets. This work enabled them to leave the townlet legally and obtain food with which to stock their hiding places and bunkers.

On Yom Kippur, September 21, 1942, the Germans carried out the first mass operation, with the help of the Ukrainian police and Ukrainian civilians. Following a selection, about 1,000 Jews were deported to the Belzec death camp and a few dozen artisans returned to Podhajce. Several people jumped from the death train, and those who survived went back to Podhajce.

After the operation, the Jews of Podhajce were concentrated in a ghetto located along a few narrow streets. Many Jews deported from villages in the area were brought to it, as well, raising its population to more than 4,000. Artisans and workers considered vital to the German economy were housed outside the ghetto in a labor camp located in the building of the Grand Rabbi of Bursztyn, and afterwards in the home of a Jewish family in the heart of the townlet.

On October 30, 1942, the Germans carried out another operation, deporting about 1,000 more Jews to Belzec. In the winter of 1942/43, hunger and disease become more pervasive and epidemic typhus led to many fatalities. The Germans periodically murdered groups of Jews in the Jewish cemetery.

The ghetto and labor camp in the townlet were liquidated in operations carried out in June 1943. More than 1,000 Jews were murdered on June 6, 1943, in Stare Miasto, and another approximately 750 more were exterminated on June 16, in Zahajce. Hundreds of the ghetto's inhabitants fled to the forests, but many were discovered in bunkers and summarily murdered or handed over to the Germans. In the final months of 1943, a group of young Jews from Podhajce led by Yisrael Zilber had organized in the ghetto and obtained guns and rifles. They helped Jews in the forest, and a number of the youths managed to survive.

PODWOŁOCZYSKA

TOWNLET IN SKAŁAT COUNTY, TARNOPOL DISTRICT, POLAND
(After World War II in the USSR/Ukraine; Ukrainian: **Pidvolochys'k**; Russian: **Podvolochisk**)

During the war: General Gouvernement, Galicia District

Coordinates:
49°32' | 26°09'

In the 1930s, about 2,300 Jews lived in Podwoloczyska, representing the vast majority of the townlet's population. Most eked out a living as petty merchants and artisans, while a small number owned property or worked in the liberal professions. Podwoloczyska had chapters of various Jewish organizations, with the Zionist parties particularly dominant, and about 150 children attended a supplementary Hebrew school.

In the second half of September 1939, the Soviets entered Podwoloczyska. Under their rule, the Jewish parties and community institutions were disbanded, private commerce was abolished, large factories were nationalized, and most of the artisans were organized into cooperatives. A number of Jewish community leaders were exiled into the Soviet interior.

On July 7, 1941, Podwoloczyska was occupied by the Germans. A few days later, the Ukrainians began to terrorize Jews with the full consent of the German authorities. Houses of prayer were set ablaze, the community's rabbi and two ritual slaughterers were publicly humiliated, and a number of Jews were beaten to death with stones and sticks in the streets of the townlet. The Germans ordered the establishment of a Judenrat headed by attorney Schuller, whose main role was to collect fines levied on the community and recruit Jews for forced labor.

After some time, a ghetto encircled by a barbed-wire fence was established, and it operated until September 1942, when its inhabitants were transferred to the Zbaraz* ghetto, the fate of whose Jews they shared.

Podwoloczyska plan indicating ghetto boundaries, prepared by Shimon Neuman, based on his memory. Illustrated by Lily Shumski

(*The Book of Podwoloczyska and Environment,* published by Podwoloczyska Community in Israel, Haifa 1988)

A number of Jews remained in Podwoloczyska, in the Kamionka 3 labor camp established in the early months of 1942, as a branch of the Kamionka camp. The camp was active until its liquidation in June 1943.

POGREBISHCHE

(Ukrainian: **Pohrebyshche**)

COUNTY SEAT, VINNITSA DISTRICT, UKRAINE, USSR

During the war:
Reichskommissariat Ukraine

Coordinates:
49°29' | 29°16'

Red Army soldiers perpetrated a pogrom on May 18, 1919, during the Russian Civil War (1918–20), in which they murdered approximately 400 of Pogrebishche's Jews. In another pogrom carried out on August 18–21 of that year, Ukrainian gangs wounded about 100 and killed some 350 Jews. Although some Jewish merchants continued to run private businesses in the 1920s, during the early 1930s these were liquidated, and Jewish artisans gradually formed cooperatives. Pogrebishche's Jews were employed in various fields, such as in sugar factory work, farm labor, and white-collar jobs. The townlet boasted a Jewish Ethnic Soviet that operated in Yiddish and a Yiddish-language government school. Industrialization and urbanization under the Soviets halved the Jewish population to about 1,400 by the eve of the German invasion of the Soviet Union.

The Germans occupied Pogrebishche on July 21, 1941. Within a few days and with the assistance of Ukrainian police forces, they executed some forty townspeople, predominantly Jews. On October 17, 1941, news spread of the Gestapo's arrival in the townlet and of an imminent operation. Although people attempted to hide in the local forest or find asylum with farmer acquaintances in nearby villages, on October 18, Germans and Ukrainian police succeeded in assembling 1,300 Jews and murdering them in large pits in a nearby forest. In the ensuing days, another 400 Jews were caught in hiding and murdered in the same place, along with Jews from villages in the vicinity.

At a later date, some 200 Jews from Pogrebishche and nearby villages who had managed to escape during the operation were concentrated in a ghetto of sorts made up of several houses, where they suffered from hunger and cold. They were allowed out of the ghetto only for forced labor. A few artisans, such as tailors and shoemakers, worked in their homes for Germans and their Ukrainian assistants.

Eight months later, in June 1942, the ghetto was liquidated and all its inhabitants murdered, save sixteen to eighteen Jews who managed to escape.

POHOST ZAHORODNY

TOWNLET IN ŁUNINIEC COUNTY, POLESYE DISTRICT, POLAND
(After World War II in the USSR/Belarus; Belarussian: **Pahost-Zaharodski**; Russian: **Pogost-Zagorodskiy**)

During the war:
Reichskommissariat Ukraine

Coordinates:
52°19' | 26°21'

During the interwar period, 550 Jews lived in Pohost Zahorodny, accounting for about two-thirds of the townlet's population. The Jews of Pohost Zahorodny earned their living as artisans, petty merchants, and fishmongers who sold the harvests of Lake Pohost, as well as flour mill and sawmill operators. They were served by a free-loan society. Most were Stolin Hasidim. Pohost Zahorodny had a Hebrew-language school, a Talmud Torah, a library, and a drama group. Zionist parties and youth movements were active in the townlet.

During the Soviet occupation, which began in 1939, one Jewish family was exiled to the Russian interior.

The Germans occupied Pohost Zahorodny in late June 1941. They confiscated the Jews' valuables, required that Jewish inhabitants wear a Star-of-David armband, and imposed forced labor. On August 10, 1941, an SS unit murdered 120 Jewish men. At some time in the vicinity of November 1941, all males aged fourteen years and over who had not yet been recruited were sent to work at the Hancewicze labor camp. Nine months later, most of them escaped and returned to the townlet.

There was an unfenced ghetto in Pohost Zahorodny. It was liquidated, with most of its inhabitants murdered in pits, on August 15, 1942. Dozens fled to the forests. Eventually, twenty-one escapees formed a partisan group under the command of David Bobrov. They acquired weapons and sabotaged telephone lines and railway tracks. The unit later joined the Soviet partisans.

POHOST ZARZECZNY

TOWNLET IN PIŃSK COUNTY, POLESYE DISTRICT, POLAND
(After World War II in the USSR/Belarus; Belarussian: **Pahost-Zarechny**; Russian: **Pogost-Zarechnyy**)

During the war:
Reichskommissariat Ukraine

Coordinates:
51°49' | 26°08'

During the interwar period, about 260 Jews lived in Pohost Zarzeczny, comprising roughly one-third of the population of the townlet. They are believed to have been petty merchants, peddlers, and artisans.

There are no details about the fate of the Jewish residents of Pohost Zarzeczny during the Soviet rule (September 1939–June 1941). The Germans occupied the townlet on June 22, 1941. From the onset of the occupation until the Germans set up a local administration in August 1941, Pohost Zarzeczny was governed by local Ukrainians, who presumably dispossessed and murdered Jews during their tenure.

The Jews were apparently concentrated in an unfenced ghetto and murdered outside the townlet in early September 1942.

POŁANIEC

TOWNLET IN SANDOMIERZ COUNTY, KIELCE DISTRICT, POLAND

During the war: General Gouvernement, Radom District

Coordinates:
50°56' | 21°17'

After World War I, about 1,000 Jews lived in Polaniec, representing nearly half of the local population. They earned their livelihood from small-scale commerce and artisanship, especially in the clothing and carpentry trades, and via fruit groves and bakeries. The children of the community attended a traditional Heder, Talmud Torah schools, a CYSHO Yiddish school, and a public elementary school. By World War II, about 15 percent of Polaniec's Jews had left Poland in the wake of the economic depression.

The Germans occupied Polaniec in early September 1939. In the initial weeks of the occupation, the Jews were ordered to wear a yellow badge, forced to submit high ransom payments, forbidden to use the townlet's sidewalks, and recruited for forced labor. The Germans confiscated Jewish-owned shops and workshops. In October 1939, Polaniec's Jews were ordered to form a Judenrat.

In December 1940, altogether 336 Jewish refugees arrived from Radom*, and in March 1941, another 300 deportees came there from nearby localities.

In April 1942, a ghetto was established in Polaniec. On May 13, 1942, the townlet was declared one of seventeen localities in the Radom district (in accordance with the German administrative division) into which all of the county's Jews would be concentrated. Another 500 Jews were brought to Polaniec. In the summer of 1942, epidemic typhus broke out in the ghetto owing to food shortages and severe overcrowding.

In October 1942, about 2,000 Jews were transferred from the Polaniec ghetto to the Sandomierz* ghetto. Many Jews who had been hiding were discovered and summarily murdered. On October 29, 1942, the Jews of Polaniec were deported from the Sandomierz ghetto to the Belzec death camp.

POŁONKA

TOWNLET IN BARANOWICZE COUNTY, NOWOGRÓDEK DISTRICT, POLAND

(After World War II in the USSR/Belarus; Belarussian: **Palonka**; Russian: **Polonka**).

During the war:
Reichskommissariat Ostland

Coordinates:
53°09' | 25°43'

About 200 Jews lived in Polonka on the eve of World War II, representing approximately half of the townlet's population. Most earned their livelihood from small commerce and artisanship.

The Soviets occupied Polonka in the second half of September 1939. During the period of Soviet rule, Jewish refugees inundated the townlet from the areas of Poland occupied by the Germans, raising its population to some 300 people.

The Germans occupied Polonka on June 26, 1941, and immediately began to loot Jewish property and abuse the Jews, with the help of the local population. Several weeks later, a Judenrat was established in the townlet; its main functions were to collect ransom payments and to recruit forced laborers for the Germans. The Jews were required to wear a yellow badge and their freedom of movement was restricted. During the first few months of the occupation, the Germans murdered a number of Polonka's Jews, including several entire families.

A few months later, a ghetto was established in Polonka. On April 18, 1942, elderly Jews and children were murdered outside the townlet. In June 1942, local farmers were recruited to dig a deep pit. When news of this development reached the inhabitants of the ghetto, a group of Jewish youths called on the members of the community to flee, but they encountered adamant opposition. On August 12, 1942, the Jews of Polonka were shot to death outside the townlet. Only a few people managed to escape.

POLONNOYE

(Yiddish: **Polne**, Ukrainian: **Polonne**)

COUNTY SEAT, KAMENETS-PODOLSK DISTRICT, UKRAINE, USSR

During the war:
Reichskommissariat Ukraine

Coordinates:
50°07' | 27°31'

At the beginning of the twentieth century, there were about 8,000 Jews in Polonnoye, approximately half of the town's population. About twenty Jewish townspeople were murdered during the Russian Civil War (1918–20) in pogroms conducted by Ukrainian and Red Army soldiers. Under Soviet rule, many Jewish artisans took factory jobs, but a considerable number continued to practice their trades. In the early 1930s, a Jewish kolkhoz was established on the outskirts of town. Polonnoye had a government school that taught in Yiddish. Urbanization and industrialization in the Soviet Union prompted many Jews to leave the town; on the eve of World War II, 4,100 Jews remained there.

The Germans occupied Polonnoye on July 6, 1941. In early August 1941, they shot nineteen Jews whom they accused of being Communist agents. On August 23, a unit of the German gendarmerie murdered 113 Jews. On September 2, a penal unit that had been brought in from Shepetovka* murdered some 2,000 Jews in Polonnoye.

The approximately 1,300 surviving Jews in the town (chiefly skilled workers and their families) were locked in a ghetto. All inhabitants of the ghetto were murdered on June 25, 1942.

POLOTSK

(Yiddish: **Poltsk**; Belarussian: **Polatsk**)

COUNTY SEAT, VITEBSK DISTRICT, BELARUS, USSR

During the war: Military Administration Area

Coordinates: 55°29' | 28°47'

In the early twentieth century, there were about 12,500 Jews in Polotsk, roughly 60 percent of the population. While some Jews became white- or blue-collar workers during the Soviet era, most continued to practice artisan trades, some in cooperatives. Two government schools in the town taught in Yiddish. Urbanization and industrialization prompted many Jews to leave the town, so that by the late 1930s some 6,500 Jews remained, about 20 percent of the population.

After the German invasion of the Soviet Union on June 22, 1941, a number of Jews in Polotsk managed to escape or evacuate to the east, while others were forced to return to their homes. The Germans occupied the town on July 16, 1941. Several days later, two trucks laden with Jews departed for an unknown destination; none of the passengers returned. About two weeks after the onset of the occupation, the Jews were registered and then concentrated in a ghetto comprising four streets in the town center. The non-Jewish occupants were evicted and resettled in the Jews' homes. The ghetto was fenced in with barbed wire. Although no guards were deployed, Jews were not allowed to leave without a permit, and non-Jews were forbidden to enter. Jews were required to wear a yellow Star-of-David on the front and back of their clothing, and forced labor was instituted.

In September 1941, the Jews were moved to a new ghetto near the village of Lozovka on the outskirts of town, not far from Borovukha II, a former Soviet army camp. They were concentrated in ten barracks along with Jews from surrounding villages. The ghetto was surrounded with barbed wire and guarded by Belarussian police. A former carpenter, Abram Sherman, was appointed head of the Jews; his deputy was named Apkin. One of their duties was to send Jews to forced labor. After some time, the Germans shot Sherman dead. The Jews were periodically ordered to leave their barracks, whereupon their belongings were despoiled and gold and valuables taken. Starvation was rampant as the daily ration was 100 grams of bread per person. Malnutrition, the cold, and poor hygienic conditions were conducive to the spread of disease and led to high mortality rates.

The ghetto was liquidated on November 21, 1941, when Germans, aided by Belarussian police, murdered its inhabitants in a forest between Lozovka and Borovukha. On February 3, 1942, the Germans murdered the remaining 615 Jews of Polotsk in Lozovka, in a forest next to a railroad junction. Three Jewish artisans and their families survived for a time but were later murdered.

POROZÓW

TOWNLET IN WOŁKOWYSK COUNTY, BIAŁYSTOK DISTRICT, POLAND

(After World War II in the USSR/Belarus; Belarussian: **Porazava**; Russian: **Porozovo**)

During the war: Bezirk Białystok

Coordinates: 52°56' | 24°22'

About 600 Jews lived in Porozow on the eve of World War II, representing approximately one-third of the townlet's population. Most Jewish inhabitants of the townlet earned their livelihood from small commerce, farming, and artisanship.

Porozow was occupied by the Soviets in the second half of September 1939. Privately owned shops were nationalized or closed and cooperatives were formed.

The Germans occupied Porozow on June 26, 1941, and that very day murdered a number of the townlet's Jews. A short time after the onset of the occupation, the Jews were required to wear an armband, later replaced by a yellow badge, and many people were recruited for forced labor.

In July 1941, a Judenrat was established at German orders, headed by a baker named Lev. The Judenrat alleviated some of the pressure applied by the Germans on the Jews by paying ransoms and bribes. However, once the governor of the townlet was replaced by another SS officer, terrorization and abuse of the Jews were stepped up. About two weeks later, the Jews were rounded up, and for an entire night they were subjected to humiliation and torture; several people were also murdered.

In the fall of 1942, the Jews of Porozow were concentrated along with Jews from other localities in a ghetto established in two alleys. Living conditions were harsh. The Judenrat opened a small hospital headed by a local Jewish doctor.

On November 2, 1942, the head of the Judenrat together with the townlet rabbi and local doctor were ordered to round up the Jews in the marketplace within one hour. From there, the approximately 600 Jews of the Porozow ghetto were sent to the bunker camp near Wolkowysk*. Some 220 elderly and ill Jews were shot to death outside Porozow, while yet another approximately fifty elderly and ill Jews were transferred to the bunker camp several days later. On November 6, 1942, the Jews of Porozow were deported from the Wolkowysk camp to the Treblinka death camp. During the deportation to the bunker camp, a number of Jews managed to flee to the forests, where they joined the partisans.

PORYCK

TOWNLET IN WŁODZIMIERZ WOŁYŃSKI COUNTY, VOLHYNIA DISTRICT, POLAND
(After World War II in the USSR/Ukraine; Ukrainian: **Poryts'k**; Russian: **Poritsk**)

During the war: Reichskommissariat Ukraine

Coordinates: 53°19' | 27°55'

During the interwar years there were about 1,200 Jews in Poryck, more than half of the townlet's population. Most were petty merchants and artisans. The townlet boasted a Jewish mutual-aid society, a Tarbut school that taught in Hebrew, a private school that also taught in Hebrew, two libraries—Hebrew and Yiddish—and chapters of several youth movements, including Zionist movements.

The Soviets took control of the area in September 1939. On June 23, 1941, the Germans occupied Poryck, forcing the Jews to wear Star-of-David armbands and conscripting for forced labor, particularly in nearby farms. A Judenrat was appointed and an unfenced ghetto set up. Jews from neighboring villages were sent to the ghetto until its population climbed to about 3,000.

On September 1, 1942, the Poryck ghetto was liquidated and the Jews were marched to a nearby estate. The infirm and elderly were murdered before the march set out and stragglers were shot en route. For three days the Jews were held on the estate without shelter, food, or water, and were finally murdered in nearby pits. The murder operation was completed on September 5, 1942. Hundreds attempted to escape, but most were caught and murdered by members of the UPA. Only a few individuals survived.

PORZECZE

TOWNLET IN GRODNO COUNTY, BIAŁYSTOK DISTRICT, POLAND
(After World War II in the USSR/Belarus; Belarussian: **Parechcha**; Russian: **Porechye**)

During the war: Bezirk Białystok

Coordinates: 53°53' | 24°08'

About 400 Jews lived in Porzecze on the eve of World War II, representing less than one-third of the townlet's population. Most earned their livelihood from commerce and artisanship. The community had several active Jewish parties and youth movements.

After Porzecze was occupied by the Soviets in the second half of September 1939, privately owned shops were nationalized or closed and cooperatives were formed.

The Germans occupied Porzecze on June 23, 1941. In the following days, most of the townlet's Jewish men either disappeared or were executed. Others were seized for harsh forced labor, and the rest of the Jews were required to wear a yellow badge and had restrictions placed on their freedom of movement.

In late July 1941, a ghetto was established in Porzecze with a population of some 200 Jews. While initially open, the ghetto was later fenced in. At German orders, a six-member Judenrat was established, headed by Meir Shelkovich, the son of the townlet's rabbi. The Judenrat was required to periodically collect ransom payments for the Germans and to recruit Jewish forced laborers.

On November 1, 1942, the Jews of the Porzecze ghetto were rounded up. A number of inhabitants attempted to resist and stormed the gate of the ghetto, but the Germans opened fire and killed one woman. Altogether 234 of Porzecze's Jews were sent to the Kielbasin transit camp, and deported in early December 1942 on to Auschwitz-Birkenau. During the evacuation of the ghetto, several Jews managed to hide or escape.

POSTAWY

(Yiddish: **Postov**)

COUNTY SEAT, VILNA DISTRICT, POLAND
(After World War II in the USSR/Belarus; Russian: Belorussian: **Postavy**)

During the war:
Reichskommissariat Ostland

Coordinates:
55°07' | 26°05'

About 850 Jews lived in Postawy in the interwar period, representing approximately 55 percent of the local population. Most earned their livelihood from small-scale commerce and artisanship. Both a Tarbut Hebrew school and a Yiddish school operated in Postawy, while Zionist parties and youth movements held regular activities in the townlet.

The outbreak of World War II triggered antisemitic riots in Postawy, but these subsided after the Soviets occupied the townlet in the second half of September 1939. Under Soviet occupation, privately owned businesses in the townlet were nationalized and closed, and cooperatives were formed. Jewish refugees arrived in Postawy during that period from the areas occupied by the Germans, raising the townlet's Jewish population to about 2,500.

The Germans occupied Postawy in July 6, 1941; they immediately murdered nine local Jews, and six more a few days later. Within a few days of the occupation, the Jews of Postawy were required to wear a yellow badge and their freedom of movement was restricted. At German orders, a Judenrat and a Jewish Order Service were formed, headed by a dentist, Dr. Rubinstein.

In August 1941, a ghetto encircled by a barbed-wire fence was established on two streets in Postawy. Some 2,000 Jews, including local residents as well as refugees who had thronged to the townlet during the war, were crowded into the ghetto. The Jews were employed at forced labor outside the ghetto and in workshops organized within the ghetto.

In the summer or fall of 1942, an underground was formed in the Postawy ghetto, headed by Shmuel Zaslawski. The underground managed to procure arms. A number of its members escaped to the forests, and within a few days returned to Postawy with the authorization of Rachmanov, the partisan commander in the area, to collect other Jews from the ghetto to join their ranks. However, the Judenrat head objected to their initiative, arguing that it would endanger the inhabitants of the ghetto, and the young people returned to the forests alone.

The Postawy ghetto was liquidated on December 25, 1942. The Jews were rounded up in the market square and surrounded by members of Einsatzkommando 3, the German gendarmerie, and local police. A number of Jews attempted to flee, and in the melee that ensued, many of the Jews were murdered. The approximately 850 Jews who survived the shooting were led across the railroad tracks and shot to death in pits outside the townlet.

POWÓRSK

TOWNLET IN KOWEL COUNTY, VOLHYNIA DISTRICT, POLAND
(After World War II in the USSR/Ukraine; Ukrainian: **Povors'k**; Russian: **Povorsk**)

During the war:
Reichskommissariat Ukraine

Coordinates:
51°16' | 25°08'

During the interwar period, over 200 Jews lived in Poworsk, about one-sixth of the population. They were lumber merchants, shopkeepers, and artisans.

The Soviets took control of the area in September 1939.

The Germans occupied Poworsk on June 26, 1941. The Jews were conscripted to forced labor, and an unfenced ghetto was established. On August 29, 1942, Jews from villages in the vicinity were brought to the ghetto, which was guarded by Ukrainian policemen. By then, twelve young Jews had organized a resistance group. They prepared maps and weapons, including three homemade rifles and dummy weapons made of wood. As the ghetto was cordoned, members of the group slipped out of Poworsk and regrouped in the nearby woods.

The Poworsk ghetto was liquidated on September 4, 1942, and its Jewish inhabitants were sent to Mielnica, where they were murdered. The twelve members of the group that had assembled in the forest acquired weapons and promptly joined a Soviet partisan unit.

Praszka
German soldiers cutting off the beards of the town's community leaders (GFH)

PRASZKA

TOWNLET IN WIELUŃ COUNTY, ŁÓDŹ DISTRICT, POLAND

During the war: Wartheland

Coordinates:
51°03' | 18°28'

Shortly before World War II, about 1,000 Jews lived in Praszka. Most were artisans and merchants. Agudath Israel, the Bund, and Zionist parties were active in the townlet. The community's children attended a Talmud Torah, a reformed Heder, and a Beit Yaakov school, and members enjoyed the services of Jewish libraries, a Bund library, and a sports association.

During the 1930s, the number of antisemitic incidents in Praszka rose.

When the Germans occupied the townlet in early September 1939, they looted Jewish property, seized Jews for forced labor, and took hostages. The synagogue building was turned into a coal depot. The Germans set up a Judenrat and a Jewish Order Service.

The Praszka ghetto was established in the fall of 1940 along several alleyways around the synagogue. Some time later, the area was surrounded with barbed wire. Initially, 840 Jews lived in the ghetto, including 120 refugees. Another 700 arrived later. During the winter of 1941, approximately 500 Jews were transferred from the ghetto to the labor camp at Przedmoscie, where they built roads and worked in quarries under dreadful conditions.

The Praszka ghetto was liquidated in August 1942. In the course of the selection, several artisans were sent to the Lodz* ghetto, twenty-seven Jews were shot on site, and all the rest were deported to the Chelmno death camp.

PRILUKI
(Yiddish: **Priluk**; Ukrainian: **Pryluky**)

COUNTY SEAT, CHERNIGOV DISTRICT, UKRAINE, USSR

During the war:
Reichskommissariat Ukraine

Coordinates:
50°36' | 32°24'

In the late 1930s, there were about 6,000 Jews in Priluki, accounting for 17 percent of the local population. They endured pogroms during the Russian Civil War (1918–20) while Ukrainian soldiers murdered about 150 Jews in July 1919. During the interwar period, the Soviet-ruled city had a Jewish Ethnic Soviet and a Jewish department at the court of law that operated in Yiddish, as well as a Yiddish-language government school. By the late 1930s, an anti-religion campaign led to the closure of all synagogues save one.

In the weeks that followed the German invasion of the Soviet Union, many Jews from Priluki managed to flee or to be evacuated. The Germans occupied the town on September 18, 1941, and in the ensuing days registered the Jews and introduced an armband requirement. Ghettoization was instituted either by the end of that month or on January 1, 1942 (sources vary on the date). The ghettoized

Jews of Priluki were taken out daily for forced labor under punishing conditions that claimed many lives.

Thirteen hundred Jews were removed on May 20, 1942, and murdered in a location near the village of Pliskunovka. The ghetto was liquidated in two additional operations on July 10 and September 10, 1942.

PROPOYSK

(Belarussian: **Prapoisk**; from 1945: **Slavgorod**)

COUNTY SEAT, MOGILEV DISTRICT, BELARUS, USSR

During the war: Military Administration Area

Coordinates: 53°27' | 31°00'

At the beginning of the twentieth century, there were about 2,300 Jews in Propoysk, accounting for approximately half of the population. During the era of Soviet rule, many Jews practiced artisan trades, several turned to farming, and others took white- or blue-collar jobs at government institutions. Many Jews left Propoysk as a result of industrialization and urbanization in the Soviet Union; by the late 1930s about 1,000 remained, roughly one-third of the population. The townlet had a government school that taught in Yiddish.

In the weeks after the German invasion of the Soviet Union, many Jews in Propoysk managed to evacuate or escape to the Soviet interior. Some townsmen, Jews among them, were inducted into the Red Army. The Germans occupied Propoysk on August 15, 1941. In October, the Jews were concentrated in a ghetto consisting of a single street that was guarded by German police. They were required to wear a yellow mark on their backs.

The ghetto was gradually liquidated in November 1941. On November 5, about forty Jewish males, including elderly people and teenagers, were murdered in an anti-tank trench. On November 14, about fifty women were killed at the same location, and on November 28, fifteen children who remained in the ghetto were drowned in the lake.

PROSKUROV

(Ukrainian: **Proskuriv**; since 1954, **Khmelnitskiy**)

COUNTY SEAT, KAMENETS-PODOLSK DISTRICT, UKRAINE, USSR

During the war: Reichskommissariat Ukraine

Coordinates: 49°25' | 27°00'

In the early twentieth century, there were about 11,000 Jews in Proskurov, accounting for approximately half of the city's population. During the Russian Civil War (1918–20), the Jews suffered acute losses in pogroms. In one pogrom alone conducted by Petliura's army on December 15, 1919, there were 1,600 Jews murdered. Proskurov's Jewish inhabitants adopted new occupations under Soviet rule. Several people took white- and blue-collar jobs in state-owned factories and institutions, while many artisans organized into cooperatives. The local court of law opened a Jewish department and heard cases in Yiddish. Government schools that taught in Yiddish were also opened, but a large proportion of Jewish children attended Ukrainian schools. On the eve of the German invasion of the Soviet Union, there were 14,500 Jews residing in Proskurov.

When the invasion began, many of the city's Jews were conscripted into the Red Army, while others fled east to the Soviet interior. The Germans occupied Proskurov on July 7, 1941, and murdered 146 Communists—some of whom were Jewish—in the middle of the month. In September 1941, Ukrainian police and members of German Order Police Battalion 320 killed some 800 Jews in the city. Resistance during the operation resulted in the deaths of three German soldiers and five Ukrainian policemen.

In August 1941, the Jews were ordered to move into two ghettos, a large one surrounded by a barbed-wire fence and a smaller one, unfenced and reserved for skilled workers in high-demand occupations ("specialists"). It is estimated that between 10,000 and 12,000 Jews were concentrated in the ghettos, including a number of people who were brought in from neighboring locales. A representative of the Jews (the Judenrat chairperson) was appointed in each ghetto. In the skilled workers' ghetto, the position was held by Lisa Lindenboim, a known collaborator with the Germans who treated the population cruelly. Jews performed unpaid forced labor and survived by bartering possessions for food in the market every week.

In addition to the ghettos, there was a labor camp in Proskurov in which Jews from various nearby localities were concentrated, including 2,000 in the fall of 1942. Another labor camp in the nearby village of Leznevo held many POWs and young Jews from the area.

In October 1941, the large ghetto was liquidated and either 5,300 or roughly 8,000 Jews (sources vary regarding the figure) were murdered along with another 2,500 Jews who had been sent to Proskurov from Chernyi Ostrov*, Nikolaev, and Gvardeiskoye. Several Jews who had been hiding in the large ghetto managed to slip into the skilled workers' ghetto and register as "specialists." On November 12 or November 30, 1942 (sources vary regarding the date), a further 2,500–3,000 or 7,000 Jews (sources vary regarding the figure) were murdered. This group was composed of the "specialists" in the small ghetto, prisoners from the Proskurov camp, and others. According to another source, the Leznevo camp prisoners were shot to death on January 1, 1943. Youths made several attempts at resistance during the killings. A number of Jews from the ghettos joined partisan units.

PRUSZKÓW

COUNTY SEAT, WARSAW DISTRICT, POLAND

During the war: General Gouvernement, Warsaw District

Coordinates:
52°10' | 20°50'

About 1,300 Jews lived in Pruszkow in the interwar period, representing approximately 5 percent of the town's population. Most earned their livelihood from small-scale commerce and artisanship. A small proportion were merchants or wealthy factory owners, and several worked in nearby Warsaw*. An association of artisans and mutual-aid societies such as a free-loan society and a Jewish popular bank provided financial aid. Jewish schools included a Hebrew school founded by the Zionists and a modern Mizrachi Heder. Active political organizations were the Bund and Zionist parties and youth movements that established a pioneer training facility. The community also boasted a library, classes, and sports and drama circles.

When World War II broke out, many Jews fled from Pruszkow to Warsaw. Numerous Communist youths fled to the areas that were handed over to Soviet control in accordance with the Molotov-Ribbentrop Pact. The Germans occupied Pruszkow between September 6 and 7. During the siege of Warsaw, Pruszkow was flooded with thousands of Jewish refugees.

Three weeks later, after Warsaw surrendered, many Jews returned to Pruszkow. A number of the young Communists who had fled to the USSR and were disillusioned by Soviet living conditions also came back to the city.

In October 1939, a Judenrat was established in Pruszkow, headed by Yitzhak Koenigstein, a Jew from Lodz*. Jews were forbidden to appear in the streets after dark and to ride on the train. They were ordered to wear a white Star-of-David armband, and men up to the age of sixty were required to perform forced labor. In late 1939, the Jewish patients in the mental hospital were murdered. In the fall of 1940, the Germans imposed a collective fine on the Jews of Pruszkow.

On November 11, 1940, a ghetto was established in Pruszkow in a small, fenced-in area. It was packed with 1,300 to 1,600 Jews under conditions of extreme overcrowding, with several families occupying the same apartment. Jews were initially permitted to leave the ghetto up to the time of curfew. At night, the German police guarded the ghetto. The Jews earned their living from small trade and smuggling. Young Jews set up an underground school in the ghetto along with a library and drama circle. A chapter of Dror continued to be active.

On February 1, 1941, the Pruszkow ghetto was liquidated and its inhabitants were transferred to Warsaw. They shared the fate of the Warsaw Jews. They were permitted to take along their belongings in exchange for a ransom payment. A total of 180 workers remained in Pruszkow, in detention camps encircled by a high wall. Others managed to flee. In the summer of 1942, most of the remaining workers were deported to the Treblinka death camp, and dozens of others were shot to death near Pruszkow.

Dozens of the city's Jews survived the Holocaust.

PRUŻANA

COUNTY SEAT, POLESYE DISTRICT, POLAND
(After World War II in the USSR/Belarus; Belarussian, Russian: **Pruzhany**)

During the war:
Reichskommissariat Ukraine

Coordinates:
52°13' | 24°21'

During the interwar period, about 4,200 Jews lived in Pruzana, more than half of the townlet's population. Most were petty merchants, artisans, sawmill workers, and lumber merchants. A number of the Jewish inhabitants also owned flour mills or small food factories, while several were farmers. Their economic endeavors were supported by a free-loan society, a Jewish savings-and-loan association, the JDC, and Jewish trade unions. The townlet's traditional welfare institutions included the CENTOS and TOZ health and welfare organizations. Among the Jewish educational establishments operating in Pruzana were three Jewish primary schools (one of which was a CYSHO school with an affiliated kindergarten), two post-primary schools, a Hebrew-language kindergarten and a Hebrew-language school both belonging to the Tarbut system, a Hebrew-language high school, as well as a Talmud Torah, Hadarim, and a Yeshiva. Pruzana boasted two Jewish libraries (Hebrew and Yiddish), two Yiddish weekly publications (one of which was Zionist), culture clubs, and drama groups. Zionist parties and youth movements and the Bund were all active in the townlet.

The Soviet occupation of Pruzana began in September 1939. Private commerce was abolished, Jewish schools were Sovietized, the hospital and orphanage were nationalized, and five families of Bund and Zionist activists were exiled to the Russian interior.

The Germans occupied Pruzana on June 23, 1941. A five-member Judenrat was appointed on July 5; ten days later its membership was expanded to twenty-four. A Jewish Order Service was established. On July 10, 1941, eighteen Jews accused of being Communists were murdered outside the townlet. On July 20, 1941, the Jews were charged a ransom of gold, silver, property, clothing, and grain.

On August 10, 1941, the Jews of Pruzana were ordered to establish a ghetto. On September 18, 1941, thousands of Jews from Bialystok* and the vicinity were brought to Pruzana, and all were sent to the ghetto on September 25. A few weeks later, additional Jews from surrounding localities were brought to Pruzana, bringing the population of the ghetto to about 18,000 people. In the ensuing months, many Jews returned to their hometowns clandestinely.

The Jews of Pruzana were conscripted for forced labor in town and in the surrounding forests. Skilled workers practiced their trades. The Judenrat smuggled food and medicine into the ghetto, where a hospital had been established. On January 3, 1942, the Germans confiscated all furs and woolens and imposed another ransom on the community.

In March 1942, Jews from additional localities were brought to the ghetto. By the spring of 1942, an anti-Fascist organization had been established under Yitzhak Sharshevski, Josef Rosen, Aharon Goldstein, and Ruth Shekh. A group of resistance members headed by Yitzhak Fridberg, working at barracks on the road to Linowo*, pilfered weapons and ammunition and smuggled the arsenal into the ghetto. Fridberg was sent to the labor camp in Bialowieza, where he organized resistance groups and established contact with Soviet partisans in the forests. When members of the Judenrat heard that the partisans were willing to accept Jews, they agreed to install a clandestine radio and to disseminate the news it transmitted. Later, several members of the Judenrat helped to procure weapons and equipment for the fighting groups. While the Judenrat opposed flight to the forests for fear that the entire Jewish population would be held accountable, in practice they agreed that individuals should flee. On November 1, 1942, the ghetto was blockaded for a census in which 9,976 heads were counted. In response to the siege, forty-seven Jews committed suicide by poison, while others prepared for uprising and escape. A group of eighteen people fled to the forests, remained in contact with the ghetto, and removed people, weapons, and food. On January 2, 1943, members of the anti-Fascist group managed to smuggle out a group of twelve Jews who were armed and equipped with a radio.

On January 27, 1943, messengers of the resistance who had come from the forest for a meeting fell into a gun battle with the local SD command staff. The treasurer of the Judenrat was killed and another member wounded; the messengers escaped to the forest.

On January 28, 1943, the Pruzana ghetto was surrounded and besieged. The Judenrat alerted the public to the ghetto's liquidation and advised that each person act as he or she saw fit. By February 2, 1943, the Jews in the ghetto had been deported to Auschwitz in four transports from the Linowo station. Two hundred people survived until liberation, including two members of the Judenrat.

Several days after the deportation, a group of Jewish fighters blew up the SD building in Pruzana, killing all of its occupants.

Out of approximately 2,700 Jews from Pruzana who attempted to escape or to hide in bunkers, about twenty survived until liberation. Many of those who reached the forests and joined the fighting groups fell in combat while serving in Soviet partisan units.

PRZEDBÓRZ

TOWNLET IN KOŃSKIE COUNTY, KIELCE DISTRICT, POLAND

During the war: General Gouvernement, Radom District

Coordinates:
51°05' | 19°53'

On the eve of World War II, about 4,500 Jews lived in Przedborz, comprising a majority of the townlet's population. Most were merchants and artisans. Almost all Jewish political parties apart from the Bund were active in the Przedborz community. In the 1930s, the Jews' economic circumstances worsened, and several antisemitic attacks took place.

When the Germans occupied Przedborz, they murdered all the Jews in their path. During the ensuing days, Jewish men were seized for forced labor and for labor camps. Jews found trading in food were peremptorily killed. Many Jews fled to nearby villages. By early 1940, only 2,800 Jews remained in the townlet.

A Judenrat was established in Przedborz, chaired by Avigdor Tenenbaum, the leader of the local Revisionist Party before the war. A Jewish Order Service was also set up in the townlet.

In early 1940, the Przedborz ghetto was established in Widoma, a quarter whose central area had a large Jewish population. Signs warning Jews not to leave the ghetto were posted at the its boundaries, but the absence of a fence allowed people to purchase food in surrounding villages and enabled Poles to come and go freely.

When the ghetto was sealed at the end of 1941, the inhabitants' living conditions deteriorated, and they were forced to subsist on official food rations. An influx of Jewish refugees from nearby localities boosted the ghetto population to 4,300 in the spring of 1942.

The Przedborz ghetto was liquidated on October 9, 1942. Its inhabitants were moved to the ghetto in nearby Radomsko*, and from there were deported two days later to the Treblinka extermination camp. Some were murdered while trying to escape. Nine Jews from Przedborz who survived the war in hiding were murdered after the war by members of the right-wing Polish resistance.

PRZEMYŚL

(Yiddish: **Premislo**)

COUNTY SEAT, LWÓW DISTRICT, POLAND

During the war: General Gouvernement, Galicia District

Coordinates: 49°47' | 22°47'

Before the War: In the early 1930s, about 17,300 Jews lived in Przemysl, representing approximately one-third of the city's population. Most earned their livelihood from commerce, artisanship, and small-scale industry, and a considerable proportion were salaried workers. A few hundred Jews engaged in the liberal professions, such as law, medicine, and teaching, and a few families owned factories. The Jewish community of Przemysl had chapters of various Zionist parties, the Bund, and Agudath Israel as well as the entire political range of Jewish youth movements. The parties also engaged in assorted cultural activities. Particularly notable was the active participation of Jews in the city's outlawed Polish Communist Party.

Przemysl's Jewish community operated a ramified health and welfare system that included an old-age home, an orphanage, and a modern hospital with outpatient clinics. Its stratified system of Jewish schools included elementary schools, vocational schools for boys and girls, a kindergarten, and a supplementary Tarbut Hebrew school, as well as a coeducational Jewish secondary school with hundreds of students. Children from ultra-Orthodox families attended a Talmud Torah, the *Etz Chaim* Yeshiva, and a Beit Yaakov school for girls. Przemysl also had a Yeshiva that ordained rabbis. In 1938, sixteen of Przemysl's Jews were injured in antisemitic attacks.

Soviet occupation: On September 15, 1939, Przemysl was occupied by the Germans, and the humiliation, abuse, and murder of Jews began almost immediately. In less than two weeks, the Germans killed hundreds of Jews and burned a number of synagogues to the ground.

On September 28, 1939, Przemysl was handed over to Soviet control. Under the Soviets, the Jewish parties and community institutions were dismantled and handed over to the control of the city; private commerce was almost completely abolished and large factories were nationalized; most of the artisans were organized into cooperatives; and a number of Jewish community leaders were exiled to remote areas of the Soviet Union. The language of instruction in the Jewish secondary school was changed to Yiddish. The synagogues remained open, also serving as mutual-aid centers for the city's needy as well as for the thousands of refugees who thronged to Przemysl.

In April–May 1940, some 7,000 Jews were exiled into the Soviet Union. Most were refugees from western Poland. A few hundred Jews managed to evacuate with the Soviets as they withdrew, although many were unable to find entry into the Soviet interior and fell into the hands of the advancing German army.

German (Nazi) occupation, ghetto setup and internal life: On June 28, 1941, Przemysl was occupied by the Germans. At this stage, about 16,500 Jews lived in the city. The Jews were ordered to report for a roll call and the men were seized for forced labor, accompanied by humiliation and abuse. In July 1941, at their own initiative, the Jews of Przemysl organized a Jewish Council headed by Dr. Ignatz Duldig. A short time later, the council was turned into a Judenrat complete with departments of finance, economics, health, and housing as well as an employment bureau responsible for registering the Jews and recruiting workers for forced labor. A Jewish Order Service under the command of Mark Trau and his deputy Goldberg was also established.

In the summer of 1941, groups of Jews were periodically imprisoned in the central prison and then executed. Beginning in March 1942, the Germans brought groups of Jews to the local cemetery and shot them to death.

The Germans plundered Jewish property in Przemysl from the first days of the occupation. They levied fines on the Jews and confiscated property. In late 1941, they demanded that the Jews turn over all furs in their possession for the German army. The official food rations allocated to the Jews were meager, insufficient to maintain a minimal existence. The Jews were restricted to shopping in the market in the early morning or late evening hours, when the market was empty of produce and merchandise. The Jews became increasingly impoverished, and the members of the poorer families suffered from starvation. In the winter of 1941/42, many Jews died of starvation and disease. At the beginning of its term, the Judenrat organized public soup kitchens.

The situation of the Jews working in factories and Wehrmacht camps in the city and its environs was relatively tolerable. The people who were deported to labor camps, however, were subjected to an especially brutal regime and dire living conditions that led to a high death rate. In November 1941, following German demands, about 1,000 young Jews were sent from Przemysl to various labor camps throughout eastern Galicia.

In the spring of 1942, the Judenrat, aiming to prevent further deportations, founded factories and workshops to provide work for unemployed Jews. Despite this tactic, however, in June 1942, the local Gestapo commander, Adolf Benthin, demanded that the Judenrat provide 1,000 Jews for the Janowska labor camp on the outskirts of Lwow*. After much indecision and amid great reservations, the Judenrat finally decided to accede to the request. An internal committee drew up the list of people designated for the camp based on the files in the work bureau, and on June 18, 1942, all 1,000 young men were sent to the Janowska camp. The Gestapo shot a number of deportees' family members who came to bid the laborers farewell, accusing them of interfering with the implementation of the deportation.

In early July 1942, a ghetto was established. Jews previously evicted from their homes in non-Jewish neighborhoods had been placed, from the earliest days of the German occupation, in the area designated for the ghetto. By mid-July 1942, all of Przemysl's Jews were concentrated in the narrow territory allotted for the ghetto, and they were soon joined by Jews from surrounding localities, including Bircza, Krzywcza, Nizankowice, and Dynow. The population of the ghetto ranged from 22,000 to 24,000, and every square meter was densely inhabited. It was forbidden on pain of death to leave the ghetto without a permit. Rumors circulated there regarding the destruction of Jewish communities in the area, and many people sought immunity by obtaining "good" jobs in the Wehrmacht camps, a number paying sizeable bribes for the posts.

Murder operations: About ten days after the ghetto was closed, the first stage of its liquidation was launched. As a preliminary step, the Gestapo examined all of the Jews' labor cards on July 24–26, 1942, revoking some and authorizing only about 5,000 others. Notices were published indicating that the "deportation eastward" would not include those people bearing labor cards newly authorized by the Gestapo, members of the Judenrat and its employees, or hospital staff. On the night of July 26–27, 1942, the ghetto was encircled and blockaded by contingents of German, Ukrainian, and Estonian police. The following day, a murder operation was carried out under the command of SS officer Martin Fellenz. On July 27, 1942, about 6,500 Jews were arrested and deported to the Belzec death camp. Another approximately 2,500 Jews, including the elderly, ill, and children, were brought to the nearby Grochowce forest and shot to death. Duldig and his deputy Rechter were murdered that day, after attempting, through their connections with Wehrmach officers, to thwart the deportation of Jews who worked in the army camps. For their part, meanwhile, the German local military commander, Major Max Liedtke and his adjutant lieutenant Albert Battel, did succeed in preventing the deportation of Jewish workers, following a confrontation with the Gestapo. Both were later honored as Righteous Among the Nations by Yad Vashem.

The following day, the area of the ghetto was reduced, and its inhabitants were ordered to move into the smaller area and leave their belongings behind. On July 31, 1942, approximately 3,000 more Jews were deported from the ghetto to Belzec, and on August 3, 1942, yet another 3,000 were deported, including a few people who held authorized labor permits, along with the hospital staff. The hospital patients were murdered in their beds. On August 4, 1942, the Germans delivered the Judenrat a bill for the expenses incurred in the "deportation eastward" along with orders to build a new fence around the reduced area of the ghetto. Another approximately 100 Jews were murdered in the ghetto from then until the end of August 1942.

Those who remained in the ghetto after the July–August 1942 killing operations tried to save themselves by obtaining false Aryan papers, fleeing to Romania and Hungary, or preparing sophisticated bunkers stocked with supplies sufficient for a long stay. Jews also attempted to obtain jobs considered vital to the German economy and army. The Judenrat, whose newly appointed head was Yaakov Ravhan (a former chairman of the community council), bribed the owners and managers of German factories to create jobs for the inhabitants of the ghetto. The Gestapo did not always honor these labor permits.

On October 18, 1942, the Germans carried out another killing operation in the ghetto. About 3,500 Jews arrived at the gathering point, while the rest remained concealed in the various hiding places they had prepared. The Germans managed to locate about 500 people in hiding, and the number of Jews in the deportation train to Belzec reached 4,000, including hundreds of workers with authorized labor permits as well as the eighty children from the orphanage.

After the October killing operation, artisans and professionals who worked in Wehrmacht camps were removed from the ghetto and transferred to camps contiguous to the factories. In late November 1942, the ghetto was divided into Ghetto A and Ghetto B. Ghetto A included about 800 workers (with another 300 "illegal" children and elderly, most of whom were the workers' family members). Sewing shops, precision mechanics factories, a mechanical workshop for the cleaning of feathers, and laundries and warehouses to clean and sort the clothing of the murder victims were set up in the ghetto. In February 1943, Ghetto A was officially turned into a labor camp under the command of SS officer Josef Schwammberger. The approximately 4,000 Jews who were considered unfit for work were concentrated in Ghetto B, along with survivors who periodically arrived from other communities that had been destroyed. Jews from Ghetto B attempted to move to Ghetto A, which was considered safer.

On September 2, 1943, the Germans began to liquidate Ghetto B. Most of the Jews hid in their bunkers while the Germans carefully combed through the ghetto, using heavy machinery to uncover the Jews' hiding places. About 3,500 Jews were rounded up and deported to Auschwitz. Approximately 600 additional Jews were transferred to the Szebnie labor camp and were later deported to Auschwitz.

About one week after the September murder operation, the German commander Rudolf Heinrich Bennewitz proclaimed that Jews in hiding who agreed to turn themselves in would be transferred to a labor camp; following the announcement, 1,580 Jews gave themselves up. Nearly all were taken in groups to the Judenrat building in the old ghetto and shot to death.

During this period, the Germans began to distribute the Jews of the Ghetto A labor camp among various other labor camps, until Ghetto A was finally closed in February 1944. Several hundred Jews continued to take cover in bunkers and other hiding places in the area. Many of them were discovered and executed, but a number managed to survive until the liberation.

Resistance: In mid-April 1943, a group of young people under the leadership of Green and Bruno Kastner organized in Ghetto A, and its members escaped to the forest to join forces with the partisans. Most were killed in confrontations with Ukrainians. The underground commander, Green, returned to the ghetto and was arrested while carrying a weapon. On May 10, 1943, a young man named Meir Krebs grabbed a gun from a drunk German who entered the ghetto. In retaliation, the Germans murdered dozens of Jews.

PRZEMYŚLANY

COUNTY SEAT, TARNOPOL DISTRICT, POLAND

(After World War II in the USSR/Ukraine; Ukrainian, Russian: **Peremyshlyany**)

During the war: General Gouvernement, Galicia District

Coordinates:
49°40' | 24°33'

In the 1930s, about 3,300 Jews lived in Przemyslany, representing more than half of the townlet's population. They earned their livelihood from commerce, artisanship, and a number of brandy and oil factories and sawmills. Credit unions were designed to assist the merchants and artisans. Religious (in particular Hasidic) activists competed with the Zionist party activists over the administration of the Jewish community. Children and youths attended a vocational school and a Tarbut Hebrew school, both of which offered instruction free of charge.

In the second half of September 1939, Przemyslany was occupied by the Red Army and handed over to Soviet control. After the Soviet withdrawal in late June 1941, a number of the Jews who had been active in Soviet institutions during the period of Soviet control evacuated together with the retreating soldiers.

On July 1, 1941, Przemyslany was occupied by the German army. On July 8, a series of restrictions were imposed on Jews. Jewish inhabitants were required to wear a Star-of-David armband, their freedom of movement was curtailed, their property was plundered, and they were required to perform forced labor. The Jews were ordered to supply the Germans with valuables, furniture, and household items. On July 15, 1941, the Germans and Ukrainians torched the town's synagogue, and about ten Jews were thrown alive into the flames. The fire spread and destroyed dozens of Jewish houses. Also in July, a Judenrat was established, headed by Dr. Rotfeld, who was later replaced by David Mandel. A Jewish Order Service under the command of the Kahana brothers was likewise instituted. In October 1941, the Jews were required to pay a high ransom, and in December 1941, they were ordered to turn over all furs in their possession to the German Army.

On November 5, 1941, the Germans carried out the first operation against the Jews of Przemyslany. All men aged eighteen to sixty were ordered to report to the yard of the city Gymnasium to register for work, and underwent a selection. Several of the professionals were released, and about 450 Jewish men were marched to the Kroscienko forest and murdered.

In late 1941 and early 1942, groups of Jews were sent from Przemyslany to various labor camps. The Judenrat and their families shipped them food and clothing, but over time, they lost contact, and most of those imprisoned in the camps perished. In the winter of 1941/42, many Jews died in Przemyslany of hunger and typhus (*rickettsia*). The Judenrat established a public soup kitchen and hospital, but these were unable to meet all of the community's needs. The ill opted to refrain from seeking out treatment in the hospital after the Germans murdered about 100 patients in May 1942. In the summer and early fall of 1942, the Germans carried out a number of operations in which hundreds of Jews were murdered.

In October 1942, the surviving Jews of Przemyslany were concentrated in a ghetto. In November, numerous Jews from Gliniany and other localities in the area were also crowded into the ghetto. The thousands of Jews living in the ghetto had access to two wells that supplied vastly insufficient quantities of water. On

December 5, 1942, about 3,000 Jews were deported to the Belzec death camp. After the operation, a selection was carried out among the ghetto inhabitants. Dozens of Jewish workers whose occupations were in demand were transferred to a labor camp outside the ghetto and the rest remained within its confines, whose dimensions were also reduced. Frantic efforts were made to prepare places to hide in the ghetto and the forests. A number of the hiding places were intended for large groups and were stocked with food and water sufficient for a long stay.

On May 22, 1943, the Germans launched a week-long operation to liquidate the ghetto. During the operation, the Germans and their Ukrainian helpers combed through the ghetto and the surrounding forest in search of Jews in hiding. The victims of the operation, put by one estimate at about 2,000, were murdered inside the ghetto or shot in a nearby forest. About seventy Jews were left in the ghetto to collect and sort through the Jews' belongings; when they finished their assigned task, they were executed. On June 28, 1943, the labor camp was also liquidated, and its imprisoned Jews were murdered.

Groups of Jews that managed to escape the operations wandered throughout the surrounding forests. A number of the escapees bore arms to protect themselves and obtain food. Only a few managed to survive the hunts carried out by Germans and Ukrainian ultra-nationalists and live to see the day of liberation.

PRZYSUCHA
(Yiddish: **Pshiskha**)

TOWNLET IN OPOCZNO COUNTY, KIELCE DISTRICT, POLAND

During the war: General Gouvernement, Radom District

Coordinates:
51°22' | 20°37'

Once a famous center of Polish Hasidism, Przysucha had a Jewish population of about 2,500 on the eve of World War II, making up a majority of the townlet's population. Most were petty merchants and artisans. Zionist parties, Agudath Israel, and the Bund were active in Przysucha and the Zionists ran a training commune. For a short while, the community had a Beit Yaakov school for girls.

When the Germans occupied Przysucha in September 1939, they implemented anti-Jewish sanctions such as punitive taxes and forced labor. A group of Jewish men was sent to work in Odrzywol*. A Judenrat was established under Moshe First, a secretary in the pre-war community. A Jewish Order Service was set up with members largely conscripted from the refugee population.

The number of Jews in Przysucha increased gradually with the arrival of refugees from nearby villages, along with 400 Jews from Plock*. By 1942, there were some 4,000 Jews in the townlet. The Przysucha ghetto was established on the relatively late date of August 15, 1942. It was surrounded by a barbed-wire fence, and German and Polish guards were posted at its two gates. Nevertheless, relations between Jews and the outside world were not severed, and many Jews made a living through smuggling and trade. In several incidents, Jews caught trading outside the ghetto were murdered.

The Judenrat opened a soup kitchen for refugees and supplied the Germans with laborers. Every able-bodied man had to work three days a week, and the poor earned their living by replacing those who could afford to pay to release themselves from the labor requirement. There were no workshops in the ghetto itself, and the Germans seldom sought out skilled Jews for odd jobs. In the winter of 1941/42, epidemic typhus broke out and a provisional hospital was set up. Dr. Krongold was on staff, and women volunteers tended the ill.

In the summer of 1942, the Germans executed all members of the Judenrat and the Jewish Order Service. According to one testimony, only the chairman, Moshe First, survived.

The Przysucha ghetto was liquidated on October 27–31, 1942. A selection was conducted among the inhabitants. The elderly and ill were summarily murdered and most others were sent to Treblinka. About 100 people were left behind to sort through their fellow Jews' belongings. Several others survived by hiding on the "Aryan" side.

A few months after the liquidation of the ghetto, the last Jews in Przysucha were moved to the Ujazd* ghetto, where the remnants of nearby communities were concentrated before deportation to the Treblinka death camp.

Between ten and thirty Jews from Przysucha survived the Holocaust.

PSKOV

COUNTY SEAT, LENINGRAD DISTRICT, RUSSIAN FEDERATION, USSR

During the war: Military Administration Area

Coordinates:
57°50' | 28°20'

On the eve of World War II, about 1,100 Jews lived in Pskov, accounting for 2 percent of the city's total population. In 1929, a Jewish boy was killed by two laborers in an antisemitic attack. The community had a Yiddish-language Jewish elementary school and high school.

Pskov was occupied by the Germans on July 9, 1941. Apparently, about half of the city's Jewish population managed to flee or was evacuated to the east. The approximately 500 Jews who remained in the town were required to wear a Star-of-David patch on their chest and back.

In August 1941, a ghetto was established in Pskov, into which over 1,000 Jews from the town and its environs were moved. It was liquidated in January–February 1942, when its inhabitants were shot to death near the town. The last Jews of Pskov—doctors employed in a hospital for prisoners of war—were murdered in June 1942.

PUŁAWY

COUNTY SEAT, LUBLIN DISTRICT, POLAND

During the war: General Gouvernement, Lublin District

Coordinates:
51°25' | 21°58'

After World War I, there were some 3,200 Jews in Pulawy, almost half the townlet's population. Most were merchants and artisans, mainly shoemakers. Many were supported by emigrant relatives, the JDC, and local Jewish welfare societies. The Jews of Pulawy had a merchants' association, a savings-and-loan association, a free-loan fund, a society for care of the ill, a group that provided lodging for the indigent, an orphanage, and a chapter of TOZ. Pulawy was an important Hasidic center. Many Zionist parties, the Bund, and Agudath Israel had chapters there. They ran their own youth movements, offered cultural and sports activities, set up a drama group, and maintained their own libraries. A Yiddish weekly was published in the townlet. Most children attended a Talmud Torah or Szabasowka state schools. About 100 girls attended a Beit Yaakov school, and dozens of children attended Tarbut and Yavne schools.

The Germans occupied Pulawy in mid-September 1939 and began abducting Jews for forced labor. In October 1939, a Judenrat was set up under Henrik Adler, a community activist and school secretary before the war. The Judenrat was ordered to conscript forced laborers and to collect occasional ransoms for the Germans.

An open ghetto was established in late October 1939, and 2,000 Jewish townspeople had been moved into it by November 4. Jews were forbidden to leave the ghetto between 5:00 p.m. and 7:00 a.m.

On December 28, 1939, some 2,500 Jews in Pulawy were deported to the Opole* ghetto by German gendarmes from Kazimierz Dolny*. They remained in the Opole ghetto until 1942, a year of mass deportations from Lublin District, and shared the fate of their local brethren.

In 1942, a labor camp was set up at Pulawy that employed about 200 forced laborers from the area. Most were Jewish. In mid-1943, the camp was closed, and the laborers were moved to other camps in the district.

PULTUSK

COUNTY SEAT, WARSAW DISTRICT, POLAND

During the war: Bezirk Zichenau

Coordinates: 52°43' | 21°06'

About 6,000 Jews lived in Pultusk in the interwar period, representing roughly half of the town's population. Most earned their livelihood from commerce and artisanship. Several food, garment, wood, and construction factories were owned by Jews. During the economic depression after World War I, the JDC assisted and supported two Jewish banks and the free-loan society in the town. Pultusk had trade unions as well as traditional welfare and charity associations. Educational institutions included a Talmud Torah, traditional Hadarim, a Beit Yaakov school for girls, a Zionist Hebrew kindergarten, and Szabasowka school with a student body in which girls accounted for 90 percent. A number of Jewish teenagers attended a state high school. In the 1920s, a Tarbut Hebrew school was active for a few years, as was a Jewish-Zionist high school in which the languages of instruction were Hebrew and Polish. Among the political institutions were Zionist parties and youth movements, Agudath Israel and its youth and labor movements, as well as the Bund. Quite a few Jews belonged to the illegal Communist Party in the town. The parties established libraries. Pultusk had a chapter of the Maccabi sports union and published a Yiddish periodical, *Unzer Vort*.

When World War II broke out, many Jews who lived near the Polish-German border arrived in Pultusk. The Germans occupied Pultusk on September 7, 1939. Immediately afterward, the Germans demanded ransom payments, confiscated money deposited by Jews in the banks, forbade the Jews to use the sidewalks, and began to seize Jews for forced labor.

On September 11, 1939, the Germans murdered fifteen or seventeen Jews and ostensibly sent away a number of Jews in trucks to perform forced labor; they were never heard from again. On that day, SS and German soldiers deported about 300 Jews eastward out of the town to localities within the boundaries of the General Gouvernement or the Soviet occupation zone. As early as the beginning of November 1939, dozens of these deportees were murdered in Ostrow Mazowiecka, in the Bialystok District, in a massacre that claimed the lives of more than 500 Jews. The homes of Jews in Pultusk were looted by Germans and Poles and transferred to "Aryans". Most of Pultusk's Jews settled in the Soviet Union and were murdered following the German invasion, as of June 1941.

In October 1939, Pultusk was annexed to the Generalbezirk Zichenau in the Third Reich. It appears that in 1943, when there were no longer any Jewish communities in the area, the Germans set up a ghetto in the large synagogue in Pultusk for the hundreds of Jews caught in the Generalbezirk Zichenau. These Jews were assigned to forced labor outside the town; several months later, they were deported to Auschwitz.

PUMPĖNAI/ PAMPENAI

(Yiddish: **Pumpian**)

TOWNLET IN BIRŽAI COUNTY, LITHUANIA

During the war: Reichskommissariat Ostland

Coordinates: 55°56' | 24°21'

On the eve of the German occupation, about 300 Jews lived in Pumpenai. They earned their livelihood from commerce, artisanship, peddling, and farming. The community boasted traditional Jewish religious and educational institutions as well as Zionist activity.

In June 1940, after Lithuania was annexed to the Soviet Union, the livelihood of Pumpenai's Jews was severely undermined, and all Zionist activity in the townlet was outlawed.

The townlet was occupied by the Germans on June 27, 1941. A few days later, Lithuanian policemen began to remove Jewish inhabitants for forced labor; they also abused Jews and stole their property. On July 15, 1941, all of Pumpenai's Jews were concentrated in six Jewish-owned houses that had been encircled by barbed wire and turned into a ghetto of sorts. For six weeks, the Jews were held in overcrowded conditions and with insufficient food supplies.

On August 26, 1941, Lithuanian rioters tortured Rabbi Yitzhak Meir Chait to death; the same day, the ghetto's Jews were marched to pits in the Pajuoste forest and murdered. A few families were taken to the village of Zadeikiai, where they were annihilated a short time later.

PÜSPÖKLADÁNY

TOWN IN HAJDÚ COUNTY, HUNGARY

Coordinates:
47°19' | 21°07'

The last national census conducted in Hungary prior to the German occupation, taken in January 1941, recorded 552 Jewish inhabitants in Puspokladany, representing roughly 4 percent of the total population. Most were merchants and a number were artisans. The town's Jewish community was Orthodox and maintained a Jewish elementary school and a separate Hasidic prayer house.

In the summer of 1941, the Hungarian authorities deported a number of Jewish families that had arrived from Maramaros and could not prove their Hungarian citizenship. They were expelled to the Ukraine, where most of them were murdered by the Germans.

After the occupation of Hungary on March 19, 1944, the Germans arrested three prominent members of the Jewish community and five other Jewish merchants. All were transferred to the internment camp in Hajduszentgyorgypuszta, near Debrecen*. According to a census conducted in the second week of April 1944, about 554 Jews belonged to the Orthodox Jewish community of Puspokladany.

The Hungarian administration remained intact and operational after the occupation. The ghettoization and deportation of the Jews were carried out on the basis of the decrees and orders of the Hungarian national and local authorities. In May 1944, Laszlo Szilassy, the sub-prefect of Hajdu County, ordered the establishment of ghettos in his county. The ghetto of Puspokladany was established in the synagogue and its vicinity in the second half of May 1944. In addition to the local Jews, about 200 Jews from two neighboring settlements, Foldes and Tetetlen, were confined there. A Jewish Council operated in the ghetto.

In mid-June 1944, the inhabitants of the ghetto were transferred to an entrainment center in the Serly brick factory in Debrecen. The Jews were deported between June 25 and 28, 1944, a number of them to Strasshof, Austria, and the balance, to Auschwitz.

PUSTELNIK

TOWNLET IN MINSK MAZOWIECKI COUNTY, WARSAW DISTRICT, POLAND

During the war: General Gouvernement, Warsaw District

Coordinates:
52°17' | 21°28'

Prior to World War II, about 200 families—some 850 Jews—lived in Pustelnik, a small townlet located near Radzymin*. As with the other residents of the area, the Jews earned their livelihood mainly by manufacturing bricks, although several engaged in commerce. Most of the Jews belonged to Zionist parties.

When war broke out, Pustelnik was not damaged by bombings. Consequently, the Germans used the townlet as a frontline base during the siege of Warsaw*. Retreating Polish units also reached the area of the townlet. Exchanges of fire between the Polish and German armies led to the imprisonment of the Jewish and Polish men in Pustelnik. The German army did not harm the civilian population, but the homes of Jews who had fled in the early weeks of the war were plundered by the local population (the property was later returned, owing to the good relations the Jewish community had forged with the Polish police prior to the war). Following the battles, normal life was restored and the brick factories resumed activities. Gendarmes paid occasional visits from Warsaw and Radzymin, but the Jews managed to reach an arrangement with them through bribes.

In early fall 1940, a decree was issued to establish a ghetto. Attempts to intervene with the authorities in Warsaw to thwart the order were unsuccessful;

three separate ghettos were established in three groups of demolished buildings located between half a kilometer to one kilometer apart. Inhabitants were permitted to move from one group of buildings to another.

About 1,200 Jews lived in the ghettos and continued to work in the brick factory; several earned a good living. A manual flour mill operated, as did bakeries that, owing to their low prices, supplied bread not only for local consumption, but to the Polish population of Pustelnik and Warsaw as well. The ghetto also provided the Warsaw ghetto with kosher meat. Living conditions were dire, epidemic typhus raged, and the mortality rate rose, mainly among poorer people. Medical care rested solely in the hands of Polish doctors. Young German soldiers occasionally entered the ghetto to terrorize its inhabitants, shaving off Jews' beards and beating them. In the winter of 1942, changes were introduced in the factory's production setup: work tools were sold and the level of production fell.

On Tuesday morning, March 24, 1942, wagons were brought to the Pustelnik ghetto. An evacuation was carried out with great violence and brutality, including acts of looting and shooting. All of the ghetto's Jews were deported to the Warsaw ghetto.

PUSTOSHKA

COUNTY SEAT, KALININ DISTRICT, RUSSIAN FEDERATION, USSR

During the war: Military Administration Area

Coordinates:
59°13' | 29°00'

In the mid-1920s, there were about 930 Jews in Pustoshka. Modernization and urbanization, coupled with Soviet policy, caused a drop in the Jewish population to about 200 people by the eve of World War II. Most of the townlet's Jews engaged in crafts. Until the mid-1930s, the community had a Yiddish government school.

About half of the Jews in Pustoshka fled the townlet when the German-Soviet war broke out. The Germans occupied Pustoshka on July 16, 1941, and ordered all Jews to wear a yellow patch.

In February 1942, a ghetto was established in Pustoshka to house the townlet's seventy remaining Jews. Although it was enclosed in barbed wire, the inmates maintained contact with their surroundings and in the following weeks performed various kinds of forced labor.

On the night of March 3–4, 1942, the ghetto was liquidated, and all its inhabitants were shot to death.

PUTNOK

TOWNLET IN GÖMÖR AND KISHONT COUNTY, HUNGARY

Coordinates:
48°18' | 20°26'

The last national census conducted in Hungary prior to the German occupation, taken in January 1941, recorded 519 Jewish inhabitants in Putnok, approximately 11 percent of the total population. Most were merchants and artisans. The town's Jewish community was Orthodox and maintained a Jewish elementary school, and a Talmud Torah.

In 1942, many Jewish men were drafted into the Hungarian army for forced labor service. They were deployed to the eastern front, in the Ukraine, where about sixty of them died.

The German army occupied Hungary on March 19, 1944. The Gestapo arrested about sixty Jews in Putnok, and on April 5, 1944, they were taken first to Budapest* and from there on to the internment camp in Garany. They were deported to Auschwitz in mid-May 1944.

A census conducted in the second week of April 1944 reported that 468 Jews belonged to the Orthodox Jewish community of Putnok.

The Hungarian administration remained intact and operational after the occupation. Hungarian national and local authorities decreed the ghettoization and deportation of the Jews. On May 2, 1944, a ghetto was established in Putnok for 588 Jews from the townlet and from the county-district of Putnok. The ghetto included the synagogue, the Jewish school, and other buildings of the Jewish community. Its inhabitants were tortured into revealing the whereabouts of their hidden valuables.

On June 3, 1944, the inhabitants of the ghetto were transferred to the entrainment center in the brick factory in Miskolc*. They were deported on to Auschwitz in several transports between June 12 and 15, 1944.

PYATKA
(Yiddish: **Pyatke**)

TOWNLET IN CHUDNOV COUNTY, ZHITOMIR DISTRICT, UKRAINE, USSR

During the war:
Reichskommissariat Ostland

Coordinates:
50°01' | 28°22'

About 800 Jews lived in Pyatka in the mid-1920s, representing approximately one-quarter of the local population. At a later stage, the Jewish population dwindled owing to the deteriorating economic situation in the townlet and as a result of the mounting urbanization and industrialization during the Soviet regime. In 1929, about 100 pupils attended the local school, in which Yiddish was the language of instruction.

The Germans occupied Pyatka on July 7, 1941, and immediately arrested eleven Jews, including the manager of the factory, the chairman of the cooperative, and the school principal; they were taken to Chudnov* and murdered.

The approximately 200 Jews who remained in the townlet were concentrated in the synagogue compound in a ghetto of sorts and removed every day to harvest sugar beets in the fields. On Yom Kippur 1941, many of the townlet's Jews fasted, including the children.

On October 24, 1941, all of the Jews were gathered in the synagogue building. Seventy-four people were taken outside the townlet to a site near the ruins of a flour mill on the banks of the river and murdered by Germans with the help of Ukrainians. Their property was stolen. Individual Jews found in hiding places were executed.

Riga, Latvia

"In the Moscow Vorstadt they are beginning to fence in several blocks—they are building a ghetto. The Middle Ages have come to life before our eyes. Jews are forbidden to shop in the stores, to read newspapers, and even [...] to smoke.

[...] Men are almost nowhere to be seen—only old women and children. But one never sees even one child playing; all of them, like beasts at bay, cling timidly close to their mothers or sit in the gateways.

Jews come from all sides pulling carts containing various junk. A large former school yard is overcrowded with people. Even here there are very few men. The majority are women; they have sad faces and eyes red from weeping. Along the fence there are huge piles of furniture and junk which they were permitted to take with them after they were moved out. Some of the furniture has come unglued from being out in the rain."

"Diary of the Sculptor Rivosh (Riga)", The Black Book, *edited by Ilya Ehrenburg & Vasily Grossman, copyright © 1980 by Yad Vashem & Israel Research Institute of Contemporary Society, English Translation by John Glad and James S. Levine, page 324.*

RABKA

TOWNLET IN MYŚLENICE COUNTY, CRACOW DISTRICT, POLAND

During the war: General Gouvernement, Cracow District

Coordinates: 49°37' | 19°57'

When World War II broke out, about 170 Jews lived in Rabka, representing approximately 10 percent of the townlet's population. They earned their living mainly through providing services to vacationers in the townlet's spas. Rabka had a sanitarium for Jewish children. A *Bikur Holim* society in the townlet was supported by the JDC. The few Jewish merchants and artisans in the townlet maintained trade unions. The community provided Hebrew lessons, and the townlet had an active chapter of Zionist parties and youth movements.

In September 1939, the Germans occupied the townlet and required the Jews to pay periodic ransoms and perform forced labor. The Jews' freedom of movement was restricted, and they were compelled to wear a Star-of-David armband. German soldiers plundered Jewish shops and apartments; Poles occasionally participated in the looting, as well. After several weeks, the Germans seized thirteen Jews, whose fate is unknown.

In late 1939, a Judenrat was established in Rabka, headed by Sigmunt Buksbaum and charged with providing the Germans with forced laborers.

In 1941, all of Rabka's Jews were concentrated in a separate neighborhood. A special school operated in Rabka that instructed trainees of the German SIPO and SD on methods of oppression and murder. Ukrainian ultranationalists also studied at the school and targeted the Jews of the townlet as well as Jews who were brought in from surrounding localities. Jews were housed in the school under concentration camp conditions for the trainees to practice their abuse and murder skills. After a short time, most the Jews were murdered, including a number of Jewish artisans from Rabka.

In February 1942, the Jews were ordered to turn over all furs and ski equipment in their possession. By May 1942, about fifteen Jews had been murdered in the townlet on various pretexts.

On May 20, 1942, an operation was carried out resulting in the shooting deaths of forty of the townlet's Jewish inhabitants. On June 26, 1942, another approximately 160 Jews were murdered, including Jews brought in from Nowy Sacz*. In July 1942, hundreds of Jews (800 according to one testimony) were murdered and buried in mass graves.

From August 28 to 31, 1942, a final operation was carried out in Rabka that nearly liquidated its entire Jewish community. Following a selection, about 200 Jews were left behind in Rabka; they were held in a labor camp composed of three buildings in the townlet. The rest were deported to the Belzec death camp, via Nowy Targ*.

RĂDĂUȚI

(Yiddish: **Rodevits**)

COUNTY SEAT, BUKOVINA DISTRICT, ROMANIA

Coordinates:
48°14' | 26°48'

About 5,600 Jews lived in Radauti in the interwar period, representing approximately one-third of the town's population. They earned their livelihood from the many industrial factories they had established as well as from commerce, banking, hotels, and restaurants. Jews also owned sawmills, flour mills, and other enterprises. Most of the members of the liberal professions in the town were Jewish. The Jewish community had the traditional Jewish welfare institutions as well as an old-age home and a public soup kitchen that served meals to about 100 needy people daily. The community's children studied in traditional private Hadarim and at a Talmud Torah. Other educational facilities in the community were two Beit Yaakov schools for girls, a Jewish elementary school, a Jewish high school, a Hebrew-language kindergarten, and next to it, a *Safah Brurah* school in which classes were conducted in Hebrew. Until 1940, the curriculum in the public schools also featured religious studies for Jewish students. Zionist parties and youth movements were active in the town and established pioneer training facilities, hundreds of whose graduates immigrated to the Land of Israel. The Bund party organized cultural and sports activities. Radauti had a Jewish sports association.

In June 1940, a number of Jewish townspeople were murdered, along with more than twenty Jews in nearby villages.

When the Romanian Iron Guard rose to power in September 1940, the situation of the Jews deteriorated: their homes were confiscated, their children ejected from schools, Jewish officials were dismissed from their jobs, and Jewish doctors were forbidden to treat non-Jewish patients. Jews were deported to Radauti from the villages in the Radauti, Suceava, and Campulung counties. On December 8, 1940, seventy families of Jewish refugees were driven out of Radauti, and on January 24, 1941, twelve Jews, including two community leaders, were murdered in the town in an orchestrated pogrom.

On June 22, 1941, when Germany invaded the Soviet Union with Romania fighting at Germany's side, the Jews were forbidden to leave their homes for the greater part of the day. The town's Jewish neighborhood was turned into a ghetto of sorts, which the Jews were forbidden to leave, although it was not fenced in. The Jewish community was forced to hand over hostages to the military administration. Jews were seized for forced labor for the German and Romanian armies. The Jews of Radauti were also required to wear a yellow badge.

In early July 1941, about 1,000 deportees were brought to Radauti from northern Bukovina, Seletin, Storojineti*, and the surrounding localities, en route to Transnistria. The Jewish community lodged the deportees in homes and in the synagogue, and supplied them with food and clothing for the journey. Wealthy Jews donated money for the purchase of wagons to transport the Jews who had difficulty walking. Most deportees were transferred on foot to the Edineti camp in Bessarabia. In August 1941, all the Jews of Siret, about 1,600 people, were transferred to Radauti, where they awaited their deportation to Transnistria.

On October 11, 1941, all of Radauti's Jews, together with the refugees, altogether 9,169 people, were given two days to leave the town and set out for Transnistria. A number of Jews committed suicide. On October 14–15, 1941, the Jews were deported by train to the Marculesti camp in Bessarabia and to Atachi. Their belongings were stolen by the gendarmes who escorted the trains and by the gendarmes in the camps.

About one-quarter of the Jews transferred to Atachi perished due to the hardship on the way and in the camps. Approximately 90 percent of those sent to Marculesti perished as well, either en route to the ghettos in Transnistria, or in the Bershad*, Obodovka*, Balta*, and other ghettos. Of a transport containing 1,500 Jews that left Radauti for Marculesti and continued on to the Tsibulevka* ghetto, 210 people were still alive in February 1942. The rest perished from disease, hunger, and cold, or were shot to death during the deportations.

In 1942, sixty-two Jews remained in Radauti.

RADOM

COUNTY SEAT, KIELCE DISTRICT, POLAND

During the war: General Gouvernement, Radom District

Coordinates:
51°25' | 21°09'

Before the War: About 30,000 Jews were living in Radom when World War II broke out, representing approximately one-third of the city's population. Most earned their livelihood from artisanship, small-scale industry, and commerce, especially in the garment, food, construction, and metal industries. They were aided by Jewish trade unions, most of which were dominated by the Bund and Po'alei Zion; Jewish workers also received assistance from a savings-and-loan fund supported by the JDC and from a number of Jewish banks that were active in the city. Radom had traditional welfare and charity institutions, and the community supplied the unemployed with financial aid. A TOZ chapter in Radom provided Jewish children with medical treatment, held summer camps for about 100 children, and supported Radom's Jewish hospital.

The city's Jewish schools included a Yavne and a *Horev* school, as well as an ORT vocational training school. Hasidism was very influential in Radom, and a number of shtiblech were active.

Radom had Zionist parties and youth movements, which established pioneer training facilities, as well as Agudath Israel and the Bund. Many Jewish workers were members of the illegal Polish Communist Party. Each party maintained a few libraries. From time to time, periodicals were published.

During the 1920s and 1930s, a number of Jews were murdered in a series of antisemitic incidents that took place in Radom.

German (Nazi) occupation: After the Germans invaded Poland in September 1939, many of the city's Jews, including leaders and public figures, attempted to flee to the east. On September 8, 1939, the German army occupied Radom, and a few days later, SS forces also entered the city. They soon began to seize Jews for forced labor and abuse them. In late September 1939, the military governor appointed fifty community leaders to serve on a temporary Jewish Council (Judenrat), headed by Yaakov Goldenberg. Yosef Diamant, a long-time Jewish community activist, was appointed his deputy. On October 4, 1939, the council

Radom ghetto, November 1941

Sign at one of the ghetto entrances: "Danger of epidemic, Jewish living area. Those entering without written permission from the police chief will be severely punished. Non-Germans will be punished by the city commander; Germans will be punished by the governor. Jews from other areas entering this area will be punished by death. Signed: City commander." (LStAM)

was ordered to collect a ransom payment and provide the Germans with clothing and bedding. The Germans meanwhile appropriated Jewish property; Jewish businesses were confiscated for the Reich and placed in the charge of German custodians. Many Jewish business owners continued to work in their own businesses for paltry wages. Jews who lived in certain areas of the city were forcibly evicted from their apartments, which were taken over and inhabited by Germans.

In December 1939, a twenty-four-member Judenrat was established that also served as the district Judenrat (Oberjudenrat), with Yosef Diamant appointed to head the organization. The Judenrat employed about 500 people and set up numerous departments, including a housing department, which was in charge of devising housing solutions for the Jews evicted from their homes. The department also found accommodations for refugees who had arrived in Radom from nearby Przytyk as well as from Warsaw*, Lodz*, and Kalisz*. The employment bureau was responsible for arranging the recruitment of forced laborers. In the first few months of occupation, the Germans demanded 80 to 100 workers each day; later, the number rose to 500 to 600, and in 1940, the number grew as high as 1,000 to 1,400 workers daily. The health committee strove to prevent the spread of epidemic typhus. In April 1940, the Jewish hospital was expanded and placed under the direction of Dr. Kleinberger, and a dental clinic, a sterilization room, and x-ray clinic were opened. The Germans had all of the patients hospitalized in the general hospital in Radom transferred to the Jewish hospital, which was turned into a center to fight the spread of contagious diseases in the city. In the spring of 1940, the JSS established a chapter in Radom to help with welfare and opened three public soup kitchens in the city, which distributed more than 3,700 meals a day for a token sum or for free. In July 1940, the JSS established three additional public soup kitchens that distributed free meals to children.

In April 1940, the Germans carried out a "political operation" against public figures in Radom, during which eighteen Jews, most of whom had been members of Po'alei Zion Left, were also executed. In July 1940, the Germans completed the confiscation of all Jewish property and its transfer to German administration. In the summer of 1940, the Judenrat began to recruit Jews for forced-labor camps in the Lublin area. On August 20, the first group, which had some 2,000 workers, was dispatched to the camps and employed digging fortifications and anti-tank trenches. The Judenrat shipped food and clothing to the workers, but nearly all of them perished. During the coming months, two additional groups were sent to the labor camps near Radom, including Kruszyna and Jedlinsk. The majority of the workers did not survive; those who returned to Radom were in serious condition, and many were admitted into the Jewish hospital for treatment.

In December 1940, Hans Frank, the governor-general of the General Gouvernement, ordered the deportation of 10,000 Jews from Radom to other locations in the district. The members of the Judenrat made every effort to reduce the number and to find locations for the deportees. On December 18, 1940, there were 1,840 Jews deported from Radom. During this period, Jews who were expelled from other places were brought to Radom. In early December 1940, about 2,000 Jews who had been deported from Cracow* were brought to Radom, and in the spring of 1941, numerous deportees were brought to Radom from Przytyk and other localities in the area. On the eve of the establishment of the ghettos there, the city had a Jewish population of about 32,000.

Ghetto setup and internal life: In March 1941, the Germans issued an order to concentrate the Jews of Radom into two ghettos several kilometers apart. Some 27,000 Jews were moved into one of the ghettos, located in the center of the city, while about 5,000 Jews were concentrated in the second ghetto in the poor neighborhood of Glinice. On April 1, 1941, the Judenrat was ordered to establish a Jewish Order Service. Joachim Geiger was appointed to head it, and young men over the age of twenty-one who had served in the Polish army were urged to join. On April 7, 1941, the concentration of the Jews in both ghettos was completed and the ghettos were sealed, its borders marked by the buildings located on the ghetto's perimeter. The large ghetto had thirteen gates with large signs posted that read: "Danger—Contagious diseases—No entry." Although the small ghetto was less crowded, most Jews preferred to live in the large ghetto, which contained the Judenrat and the help and welfare institutions.

Clandestine educational activities were organized in the ghetto. Teachers and young graduates of the Jewish high school organized activities for the kindergarten-aged children. In November 1941, engineers and technicians in the ghetto organized courses for vocational training in metalwork, mechanics, and other subjects, to enable Jewish teenagers to find work in and outside the ghetto. Most of the courses were held in the small ghetto.

The Jewish hospital was located in the large ghetto, while the old-age home and orphanage remained outside the ghettos. A Christian old-age home and a shelter for the mentally ill operated inside the large ghetto. The most serious health problem faced by ghetto inhabitants was epidemic typhus. By the fall of 1942, 3,000 to 4,000 people had been hospitalized; many more were treated in their homes, owing to the shortage of beds.

Murder operations and the ghetto's liquidation: On February 19, 1942, the Germans invaded the ghetto and murdered several dozen people. They also carried out a "political murder operation," arresting and deporting to Auschwitz about forty community leaders, most of whom had been activists in leftist parties. The arrests were based on lists prepared beforehand.

On April 28, 1942, a day that came to be known as "Bloody Wednesday," the SS carried out another operation intended to undermine the Jewish leadership in Radom and prevent any future resistance during the liquidation of the ghetto. Members of the Gestapo led by Richard Schoeggl and Paul Fuchs entered the ghetto and seized a large number of Jews in their homes. A few people were murdered directly in front of their homes, while others were taken to the local prison and deported on to Auschwitz. That day, between 58 and 70 Jews were murdered in the ghetto, and another 150 Jews were deported to Auschwitz, including Judenrat head Diamant and three of his assistants. In the wake of the operation, a new Judenrat was formed, headed by Ludwig Fasman.

After the murder operation of April 1942, rumors spread in the ghetto regarding the impending deportation of Radom's Jews, prompted in part when the Jews of Radom learned the news of what had happened in Lublin*. During this period, the demand for jobs rose, as ghetto inhabitants believed that people who held a worker's permit would be saved.

In early summer 1942, SS officer Wilhelm Blum was sent to Radom to plan and prepare the deportation of Jews from the city, in coordination with SS and police leader Herbert Boettcher, who was responsible for the area. On the night of August 5, 1942, the SS encircled the small ghetto and a brutal selection was carried out at a site near the railroad tracks by SS officers, including Boettcher, Blum, Franz Schippers, and Adolf Feucht, together with Ukrainian policemen under the command of Erich Kapke. Following the selection, the SS officers and Ukrainian policemen transferred about 800 Jews with work permits to the large ghetto. About 600 children and elderly Jews were murdered during the selection, and the rest were deported to the Treblinka death camp, together with about 2,000 Jews from the large ghetto. Approximately 100 young Jews with work permits were given the task of burying the murder victims near the Lenz factory and collecting their belongings.

On August 16, 1942, all of the gates of the large ghetto were blocked, and the ghetto was encircled by German and Ukrainian police. On the night of August 16, another murder operation was carried out under the command of Boettcher and Blum, and about 1,000 Jews were killed in the ghetto. Jews who resisted or were found in hiding were summarily shot. A group of children was murdered with hand grenades in a slaughterhouse. The rest of the ghetto's inhabitants were rounded up in the old city square and put through a selection by SS officers under Feucht's command. About 4,000 people with work permits were assigned to forced labor. Nearly all of the balance of the ghetto's inhabitants, close to 18,000 people, were deported on August 17 to the Treblinka death camp. Fifty patients in the Jewish hospital were murdered in pits prepared near the ghetto. Hundreds of Jews managed to find places to hide in the area.

Following the operation, about 200 Jewish workers were given the job of collecting and sorting the Jews' belongings, some of which were sold or distributed, gratis, among the Polish residents of Radom. The belongings of Jews from nearby localities who had also been deported to Treblinka were later shipped to the warehouse for Jewish property in Radom.

The ghetto population gradually increased as Jews who had been in hiding slipped back inside. About 5,000 Jewish workers and their families, along with 300 members of the Jewish Order Service and their families, were transferred to the area of the small ghetto. Three members of the Judenrat, including Dr. Ludwig Fasman, who stayed on as Judenrat head, were also transferred into the small ghetto. The Jews were now concentrated in two labor camps, one in the large ghetto and the other in the small ghetto.

On December 3, 1942, a Ukrainian guard unit and a group of SS soldiers deported about 800 Jews from the large ghetto to the ghetto that had been reestablished in Szydlowiec*. A number were murdered along the way by the Ukrainians. Most of the rest perished.

On January 13, 1943, about 1,600 Jews whose names appeared on a list of people who had requested visas to Palestine or who had received permits to emigrate, were deported to Treblinka in an operation that was known as the "Palestine murder operation." On January 20, 1943, the Germans murdered a group of Jews accused of sabotage at their jobs.

In January 1943, Fasman was arrested and deported to Auschwitz and Nachum Shenderovich was appointed his successor. On May 1, 1943, the Gestapo arrested the last remaining members of the Judenrat and its officials and sent them to a labor camp near Wolanow*. Most were murdered, and the rest, including Shenderovich, were deported to Auschwitz.

The small ghetto was turned into a labor camp under the supervision of the SS. The workers were registered and received worker numbers. They lived in the camp together with a few hundred Jews who had survived in hiding during the murder operations and had later slipped back into the ghetto.

On November 8, 1943, the Germans liquidated the small ghetto. About 100 women, children, and elderly people were shot, and the rest were transferred to a shack camp on Szkolna Street. Two hundred Jewish workers were transferred to Skarzysko-Kamienna* and Pionki to work in arms factories.

About 2,450 Jewish men, some 500 women, and approximately fifty children, survivors of the Radom ghetto and nearby localities, were held in the Szkolna camp. The shack compound functioned as a concentration camp under the supervision of the SS. Yechiel Friedman was appointed head of the camp. It was liquidated on July 26, 1944.

Resistance: A number of inhabitants of the Radom ghetto attempted to join partisan groups in the area. In early December 1942, a group of seventy-six Jews, including women and children, fled from the ghetto and established contact with the Armia Ludowa in the Radom District. The escapees reached the Polish partisan group that was active in the area, but the Germans surrounded them. After a prolonged battle, a number of the group's members managed to get away, but their fate is unknown.

Immediately after the first large-scale deportation in August 1942, an underground group with thirty members was formed under the command of the Bornstein brothers (Zalman, Leib, and Yonah). Its members made contact with representatives of the Polish underground and managed to obtain a few firearms. Their goal was to join the partisans rather than organize armed resistance inside the ghetto. In late October 1942, part of the group apparently left the ghetto and headed for the forested area of Swietokrzyska in search of groups of Polish partisans, but encountered obstacles. A number of them were killed during a German manhunt and the hostile local population drove the survivors back to the ghetto. Aside from this group, a number of other loosely organized underground youth groups sought ways to resist, but the details of their activities remain unknown.

RADOMSKO

COUNTY SEAT, ŁÓDŹ DISTRICT, POLAND

During the war: General Gouvernement, Radom District

Coordinates:
51°04' | 19°27'

On the eve of World War II, 6,500 Jews lived in Radomsko, comprising one-third of the town's total population. Most were manufacturers, merchants, or artisans; several practiced liberal professions. All Jewish parties and youth movements in interwar Poland had chapters in the town. The community boasted Jewish professional organizations as well as two savings-and-loan associations. Youngsters attended two Jewish primary schools, a Jewish high school, and schools run by the Mizrachi organization and Agudath Israel.

The Germans occupied Radomsko on September 3, 1939, looting Jewish property at once. In a pogrom on September 12, 1939, known by the Jews as

Black Tuesday, the Germans seized several hundred Jewish men, beat them, and photographed staged scenes for propaganda purposes. The Germans also struck Jewish religious life by desecrating the synagogue and cemetery, forbidding public worship, and tormenting the town's rabbis.

From the beginning of the occupation, Jews were put to forced labor under harsh conditions. The Judenrat, headed by the chairman of the community, Moshe Berger, drew up a list of work groups and raised donations from wealthy Jews to pay wages to some of the forced laborers. The Judenrat also took care of the many refugees who reached Radomsko, including Polish refugees from the Poznan area. The organization was responsible for paying punitive taxes to the Germans; the pressure that the Judenrat brought against the Jews of Radomsko to submit the required funds fostered ill feeling, which led to several demonstrations and, in 1940, an aborted uprising. A Jewish Order Service was also set up in the town, commanded by Dr. Markovich.

In late 1939, the Jews of Radomsko discovered that their town was shortly to be declared *Judenrein*. On December 20, 1939, a small area in the town was designated as a ghetto, one of the first to be established in Poland. The ghettoization policy was implemented brutally and swiftly. A sign in German and Polish posted at the ghetto's gate prohibited Jews from leaving and "Aryans" from entering. Many Jews in the Radomsko ghetto engaged in smuggling despite the penalty of death incurred by the activity. Hundreds of Jewish refugees continued to pour into Radomsko, bringing the ghetto population to about 7,000 by May 1940, with inhabitants living in severely crowded conditions.

The Jews supported themselves mainly by selling their few residual belongings. Artisans continued to work for "Aryan" customers, despite prohibitions. Other Jews retained their factory jobs even once the plants had been transferred to the Germans. To combat starvation, the Judenrat set up a soup kitchen in January 1940.

The Judenrat had several departments including a postal service, a Jewish Order Service, and a court of law that adjudicated petty disputes. It likewise ran a health department. When epidemic typhus broke out in the winter of 1939–40, however, attempts by the Judenrat and the municipal authorities to contain the outbreak failed owing to the ghetto's appalling housing conditions. Only in April 1940 were the Jews given preventive medication. Another epidemic erupted in the winter of 1940–41. This time, the Judenrat was able to bring another doctor to the ghetto from Warsaw*, Dr. Mieczyslaw Sachs. He was joined by a doctor originally from Radomsko, Dr. Hirsh Aba Rozevich, who returned to the town. A 100-bed hospital was set up with donations from Czestochowa* and Radomsko. A crash course was given to hospital staff.

The Germans sent Jews from the ghetto to labor camps and to perform forced labor. On July 13, 1940, German police rounded up forty Jews whom they alleged were Communists and sent them to Auschwitz. Some 400 Jews were transferred from the ghetto to labor camps in the Lublin area. In August 1941, 200 Jews were sent to Plaszow. Another approximately 400 local Jews were sent to the Gidle labor camp in the Radomsko area.

In May 1941, the chairman of the Judenrat, Moshe Berger, was replaced by Viktor Gutstadt. In June 1941, the Jews' plight worsened as the ghetto was downsized. The Judenrat strove to solve the critical housing problem but desperate ghetto inhabitants were again dissatisfied and attempted its overthrow.

In response to the high mortality rate among Jews in the ghetto caused by dire living conditions and wanton murders, an orphanage was established in Janu-

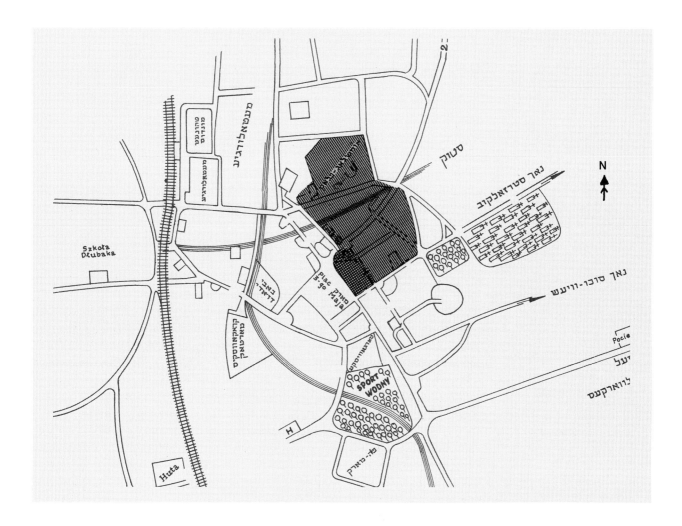

Radomsko plan indicating ghetto boundaries

(Shimon Kanc, ed., *Yizkor Book for the Community of Radomsko and Kartshev*, published by Irgun Yotz'e Otvozk – Kartshev and its Vicinity, Tel-Aviv 1968)

ary 1942. A drama group produced two plays and donated the proceeds to the orphanage. Ghetto inhabitants were involved in surreptitious political activity. Members of Dror and Po'alei Zion–Right met periodically and maintained contact with Warsaw through the assistance of women who acted as liaisons. Members of Hano'ar Hatziyyoni youth movement ran a training commune. In 1942 and 1943, members of Jewish organizations in the ghetto were in contact with Polish partisan groups and devised plans that never materialized for the mass escape of youths to the forests.

When reports about the deportation of Jews from Warsaw reached the ghetto, the inhabitants of the Radomsko ghetto sensed that their lives were imperiled. As circulating rumors suggested that only working Jews were spared deportation, the unemployed frantically searched for work, sometimes resorting to paying for jobs. Fears grew in September 1942, when a large contingent of displaced Jews arrived at the ghetto. On October 8, 1942, Jews from the Gidle labor camp were shipped back to the ghetto. That night, the ghetto was surrounded by patrols of German, Polish, Ukrainian, and Lithuanian police. The following day, the Judenrat was advised by telephone of an impending operation. Its purpose, as was soon revealed, was the liquidation of the ghetto. That day, more than 4,000 Jews from Przedborz* arrived in the Radomsko ghetto after their own ghetto had been liquidated. All the Jews were ordered to assemble in front of the Judenrat building. Elderly and ill people who were unable to leave their home were summarily murdered. Hospital patients were murdered in their beds. Members of the

Jewish Order Service were forced to dig a mass grave in the cemetery. A selection was carried out among all those assembled. A small group of 350 Jews, including members of the Judenrat and the Jewish Order Service, doctors, and a few artisans were permitted to stay in the ghetto and were imprisoned in the Judenrat building. Some 5,000 of those assembled were deported to Treblinka. The remaining 9,000 were held for four days in various synagogues, and then also deported to Treblinka. The 350 Jews held in the ghetto were put through an additional selection: 29 were added to the transport and 321 were lodged in a block of buildings surrounded by barbed wire. Two weeks after the ghetto was liquidated, another selection took place and 175 Jews were deported to the Hasag labor camp at Skarzysko-Kamienna. The others cleaned out the Jews' homes and gathered up their belongings.

On November 14, 1942, another ghetto was established in Radomsko for all remaining Jews in the area. The ghetto was initially unfenced; warning notices were the only evidence of its boundaries. Gradually, about 4,500 Jews arrived, some from nearby towns and others after coming out of hiding. Living conditions were atrocious, with an average of fifteen to twenty people quartered per room. Diseases spread, but not a single doctor was available. The Jews were given various jobs at the factory and in carpentry and were bidden to sort out the deportees' belongings. The Judenrat distributed meager rations.

In late 1942, the German authorities announced that they were registering all ghetto inhabitants, ostensibly to exchange them for German prisoners of war. The Jews hastened to register, but there was no exchange. Upon learning that the German police had ordered fifty railroad cars, several of the Jews fled, including the chairman of the Judenrat, Gutstadt.

The ghetto was liquidated on January 6, 1943. Two hundred and fifty youths were sent to the Hasag labor camp; 260 were shot dead, and nearly all the others were deported to Treblinka. A few were left behind and housed together in what became a camp.

RADOMYSHL
(Yiddish: **Radomisl**;
Ukrainian: **Radomyshl'**)

COUNTY SEAT, ZHITOMIR DISTRICT, UKRAINE, USSR

During the war:
Reichskommissariat Ukraine

Coordinates:
50°30' | 29°14'

In the early twentieth century, there were about 7,500 Jews in Radomyshl, constituting a majority of the town's population. The community suffered acute losses in pogroms during the Russian Civil War (1918–20), culminating in March–June 1919, with the murder of 1,400 people (including the Hasidic Rabbi Avraham Yehoshua Heshel Tverski and his son, Mordekhai) by Sokolovski's gang. The ravages of the pogroms, the urbanization and industrialization that followed, and Soviet policies in the 1920s and 1930s collectively reduced the Jewish population, which stood at 2,350—roughly one-fifth of the total population—in 1939. By the early 1930s, private enterprise had been abolished in Radomyshl and many Jewish merchants became artisans and formed cooperatives. In the 1920s, the government opened a school that taught in Yiddish. The local synagogue was closed in conformity with the Soviets' anti-religion policy.

The Germans occupied Radomyshl on July 20, 1941, and at once set about abusing Jewish inhabitants. Jews were evicted from their homes and concentrated in an open ghetto that was periodically relocated from one street to another. Almost as soon as the ghetto was established, Jews were forbidden to remove belongings from their homes. A unit of Sonderkommando 4a murdered 110 Jews on August 7, 1941, and another 160 Jews on August 12. The Germans concentrated Jews from the entire county in the Radomyshl ghetto, creating conditions of congestion and starvation that claimed many lives.

The Radomyshl ghetto was liquidated on September 6, 1941. Members of Sonderkommando 4a rounded up the population, separated the men from the women and children, led everyone to nearby Chernyi Yar, and murdered 1,100 adults while Ukrainian police murdered some 550 children.

RADOMYŚL ON THE SAN

TOWNLET IN TARNOBRZEG COUNTY, LWÓW DISTRICT, POLAND

During the war: General Gouvernement, Cracow District

Coordinates:
50°41' | 21°57'

About 800 Jews lived in Radomysl on the San when World War II broke out, representing approximately one-third of the local population. Most earned their livelihood from small commerce and artisanship. Radomysl on the San had a Beit Midrash and two traditional Hadarim as well as chapters of Zionist parties and Agudath Israel.

The Germans occupied Radomysl on the San in September 1939. Before the occupation, many young Jews fled east, to eastern Galicia; several returned to the townlet a short time later. After the Germans entered the townlet, a number of Jewish families were deported to the area under Soviet control, east of the San River. The Jews who remained in the townlet were required to pay a ransom, their freedom of movement was restricted, and they were recruited for forced labor, especially in building fortifications on the border with the Soviet Union.

In 1941, a ghetto was established in the townlet in which about 400 Jewish refugees from Cracow* and Krasnik* were concentrated. In 1942, many of the ghetto's Jews died of epidemic typhus.

In the fall of 1942, the Radomysl on the San ghetto was liquidated and its inhabitants were deported to the Belzec death camp.

RADOSZKOWICE

TOWNLET IN MOŁODECZNO COUNTY, VILNA DISTRICT, POLAND

(After World War II in the USSR/Belarus; Belarussian: **Radashkovichy**; Russian: **Radoshkovichi**)

During the war: Reichskommissariat Ostland

Coordinates:
54°09' | 27°14'

About 1,200 Jews lived in Radoszkowice on the eve of World War II, representing roughly half of the townlet's population. Most earned their livelihood from artisanship, commerce, and farming. The community had a Tarbut Hebrew school and a religious Hebrew school. Chapters of Zionist movements held social and cultural activities in the townlet.

After Radoszkowice was occupied by the Soviets on September 18, 1939, a Soviet economic, social, and educational system was introduced into the townlet. Privately owned shops were nationalized or closed and cooperatives were formed.

The Germans occupied Radoszkowice on June 25, 1941. Jewish residents were ordered to register, and at German orders, a Judenrat was established, headed by a man named Klaczkowski. The Jewish residents of the townlet were compelled to wear a special badge, their freedom of movement was restricted, and they were required to make ransom payments. All Jews aged thirteen years and older were seized for forced labor.

On March 11, 1942, the Germans rounded up the majority of the townlet's Jewish inhabitants. The elderly and ill were shot to death in their homes. The rest of the Jews were led outside of the townlet, and once they were joined by the Jews from the village of Udranka, a selection was carried out. Most people were shot to death, save 110 Jews and their families who were identified as fit for work. More than fifty Jews who fled to the forest were caught and murdered, but about 200 others managed to escape. Some 860 of Radoszkowice's Jews were murdered that day.

The Jews considered eligible for work and their families were put up in two buildings that were encircled by a barbed-wire fence and turned into a ghetto of sorts. These Jews were compelled to share their meager rations of 250 grams of bread per day with another approximately 100 Jews who remained in hiding. In September 1942, the Germans brought in another ten survivors of the Grodek* ghetto.

In response to local partisan activity, on October 10, 1942, the Germans concentrated the inhabitants of the ghetto in one area. After shooting into the ghetto, they rounded up its inhabitants, issued numbered panels to be worn, and threatened that if even one person went missing all would be executed. Despite the warning about thirty-five young Jews escaped from the ghetto in the coming months. On March 7, 1943, following these escapes, the Germans rounded up most of the ghetto's remaining inhabitants into a barn, which they set ablaze.

Twenty-two Jews who continued to work remained in the ghetto. The day after the March 7 operation, the Germans discovered three Jewish women and four children among the ruins of the ghetto and shot them to death. Five additional Jews from among the ghetto workers were shot to death a few days later. The last seventeen Jews managed to escape in the spring of 1943 and join the partisans.

RADUŃ

(Yiddish: **Radin**)

TOWNLET IN LIDA COUNTY, NOWOGRÓDEK DISTRICT, POLAND

(After World War II in the USSR/Belarus; Belarussian, Russian: **Radun**)

During the war: Reichskommissariat Ostland

Coordinates: 54°04' | 24°55'

About 900 Jews lived in Radun on the eve of World War II, representing approximately two-thirds of the townlet's population. Most earned their livelihood from small commerce, peddling, and various types of artisanship. Radun was home to the celebrated *Chafetz Chaim* Yeshiva, established by and named for Rabbi Yisrael Meir Hacohen, who was known as the *Chafetz Chaim*. The Yeshiva had 300 students. The townlet also had a Tarbut Hebrew school.

Following the Soviet occupation of Radun in the second half of September 1939, a Soviet economic, social, and educational system was introduced into the townlet. Privately owned shops were nationalized or closed and cooperatives were formed. The Yeshiva buildings were converted into granaries, and the Yeshiva's students moved to Vilna* in early 1940.

On June 30, 1941, the Germans occupied Radun and immediately demanded ransom payments, ordered the Jewish inhabitants to wear a yellow badge, and seized Jews for forced labor. At German orders, a four-member Jewish Order Service was established as well as a six-member Judenrat, headed by Noach Dolinski.

In late September 1941, Jewish refugees arrived in Radun from Ejszyszki (after World War II Eisisok, Lithuania), and were provided with resident permits by the Judenrat.

In October 1941, the Jews of Radun were concentrated in a ghetto along with Jews from the surrounding localities, and the collective population reached 1,700 people. In January 1942, the Germans executed about forty refugees from Lida* who had come to the Radun ghetto, as well as the head of the Jewish Order Service and his family. In the spring of 1942, a group of Jews was transferred from Radun to the labor camp in Krasne*.

On May 8, 1942, the ghetto was encircled and its exits blocked. On May 10, 1942, about 100 Jewish men were seized to dig pits outside of the townlet. While they were digging, at a signal given by the blacksmith Meir Stoler, the Jews attacked their guards with their shovels and began to flee. Seventeen men managed to escape, while the others were shot to death. Once the pits were dug, a selection was carried out. Some 1,000 of the ghetto's inhabitants were led to the pits and shot, leaving about 300 artisans and their families in the ghetto. Another 300 Jews managed to escape or hide during the operation.

On June 7 or 8, 1942, the inhabitants of the ghetto, including a number of Jews in hiding, were transferred to the Szczuczyn* ghetto.

RADVILIŠKIS

(Yiddish: **Radvilishok**)

TOWNLET IN ŠIAULIAI COUNTY, LITHUANIA

During the war:
Reichskommissariat Ostland

Coordinates:
55°49' | 23°32'

On the eve of the German occupation, there were about 250 Jewish families living in Radviliskis. They earned their livelihood from artisanship, small-scale commerce, and light industry. Radviliskis had a Jewish Folksbank, chapters of Zionist parties and youth movements, and a Tarbut school.

After Lithuania was annexed to the Soviet Union in 1940, private businesses in Radviliskis were nationalized and Jewish national activities were discontinued.

Radviliskis was occupied by the Germans on June 26, 1941. The Jews of the townlet were forced to perform slave labor. Many suffered abuse and humiliation, and their homes were marked with the word "Jude."

On July 8, 1941, all of Radviliskis' Jews were moved into a ghetto of sorts established in a number of abandoned Lithuanian army shacks and fenced in with barbed wire. The ghetto was guarded by one German and one Lithuanian policeman. Jewish inhabitants were forbidden to maintain contact with the local population and were required to wear a yellow badge on their chest and back. The Jews continued to leave the ghetto every day to execute various forms of forced labor. On July 12, 1941, almost all of the ghetto's men were removed and murdered in a grove near the Jewish cemetery. Women and children now formed the larger part of the ghetto population, along with a handful of men. From time to time, Jewish refugees from Russia were brought to the camp.

Several weeks later, about 500 inhabitants of the ghetto were taken to a site that had previously served as a camp for Soviet prisoners of war. The inhabitants of the new ghetto worked outside its grounds at various jobs, while a communal kitchen was set up in the ghetto itself. On August 26, 1941, about 400 of the ghetto's inhabitants were transferred to the Zagare* ghetto, and on October 2, 1941, they were murdered together with Jews similarly brought from villages and townlets in the area. On August 26, several dozen residents of the Radviliskis ghetto were taken to the Siauliai* ghetto. A number of people were killed along the way, while the rest were murdered together with the inhabitants of the Siauliai ghetto.

RADZIECHÓW

COUNTY SEAT, TARNOPOL DISTRICT, POLAND
(After World War II in the USSR/Ukraine; Ukrainian: **Radekhiv**; Russian: **Radekhov**)

During the war: General Gouvernement, Galicia District

Coordinates:
50°17' | 24°39'

In the 1930s, about 2,000 Jews lived in Radziechow, representing nearly half of the townlet's population. Most were merchants, peddlers, and artisans, and they used the services of a Jewish Folksbank and a free-loan society. Several of the Jewish inhabitants of Radziechow were affluent, including a dozen owners of estates in the surrounding villages. Belz Hasidim and Zionist parties and youth movements were very influential in Radziechow. The townlet had a complimentary Tarbut Hebrew school, a *Ha-Poel* sports union, and a pioneer training facility of the *Achva* youth movement.

On September 20, 1939, the Soviets entered Radziechow. During this period, numerous Jewish refugees from western Poland arrived in the townlet, and the community provided them with food, clothing, and housing. The refugees who refused to take on Soviet citizenship were exiled into the Soviet Union interior in June 1940. Under the Soviets, the Jewish parties and community institutions were disbanded, private commerce was discontinued, large factories were nationalized, most of the artisans were organized into cooperatives, and a number of Jewish public leaders were exiled into the USSR interior. Synagogue activity was permitted.

Radziechow was occupied by the Germans in the last week of June 1941. On the first day of the occupation, a number of Jews who had been active in Soviet institutions were murdered. The Ukrainian militia seized Jewish men daily for forced labor in the townlet and its environs. In the summer of 1941, additional Jews were brought to Radziechow from surrounding localities as well as some

500 Jews from Cholojow whose homes had been destroyed in a fire. In early August 1941, a Judenrat headed by Adolf Kranz was established. Decrees involving the requirement of Jews to carry out forced labor were issued in the early days of the occupation. Artisans were employed in the army camps and factories, and other Jewish men were sent to labor camps, where the living conditions were considerably worse and the mortality rate high. Hunger and disease spread among the Jews, and their situation further deteriorated when additional Jews were brought to the townlet in June and September 1942.

On September 15, 1942, an operation was carried out in which about 1,400 Jews were deported from Radziechow to the Belzec death camp. On September 21, 1942, another 500 Jewish men were sent to the camp in Kamionka Strumilowa, where they perished within a few months. Only a group of skilled artisans, whose occupations were in demand, remained in Radziechow.

In the weeks following the operation, the Germans concentrated Jews from the surrounding localities in Radziechow into the houses vacated by the murdered Jews. In early October 1942, a ghetto was established in the townlet that served as a point of concentration for Jews of the area headed to their extermination. Most of the ghetto's approximately 1,000 inhabitants were deported as early as October 7, 1942, and sent to their deaths in Belzec. A few weeks later, Jews from Witkow Nowy were brought to the ghetto and on December 1, 1942, all of the inhabitants of the Radziechow ghetto were relocated to the Sokal* ghetto. The Germans left about 100 Jews in the townlet to tend to the residual Jewish property, and on March 15, 1943, they were executed in the nearby forest.

Of the many Jews who escaped the operations and fled to the forests, most were caught by local citizens or in hunts carried out by the Germans and murdered.

RADZIWIŁŁÓW

TOWNLET IN KRZEMIENIEC COUNTY, VOLHYNIA DISTRICT, POLAND
(After World War II in the USSR/Ukraine; Ukrainian: **Radyvyliv**; Russian: **Radivilov**)

During the war: Reichskommissariat Ukraine

Coordinates: 50°08' | 25°15'

During the interwar years, about 3,000 Jews lived in Radziwillow, roughly one-half of the townlet's population. Most made a living from commerce and artisanship; some owned factories, chiefly for grain and food processing. They availed themselves of a savings-and-loan association and a mutual-aid society. Most of the 300 children in the community attended a Hebrew-language school. For a period of time, a Talmud Torah and Hebrew-language kindergarten operated in the townlet. A Jewish public library organized cultural activities. Zionist youth movements and parties were active as well.

In September 1939, when Radziwillow was annexed to the Soviet Union, the Jewish organizations and institutions were disbanded, the Hebrew-language school became a Russian school, and twelve wealthy Jewish families were exiled to the Soviet interior. When the Germans invaded, many Jews fled Radziwillow, also heading for the Soviet interior.

The Germans occupied Radziwillow on June 27, 1941. From time to time, local Ukrainians and German soldiers appropriated Jewish property. The Jews were made to wear Star-of-David armbands and were conscripted for forced labor.

On July 15, 1941, twenty-eight Jews who appeared on a list prepared by members of the local Ukrainian administration were murdered.

On August 15, 1941, the Jewish committee became a Judenrat. The committee head, Weiderhorn, resigned. In late February 1942, the Judenrat was ordered to dispatch a group of young people for labor. All members of the group were murdered, apart from two who escaped.

The ghetto of Radziwillow was established on April 9, 1942. It was a sealed compound, encircled by a fence crowned with barbed wire. The ghetto and its population of about 2,600 Jews were divided into two parts: one for those deemed "useful" (skilled and other workers and their families), and another for the "useless" (all the rest). Since the Judenrat issued "useful" certificates to the highest bidders, few workers received them.

On May 29, 1942, the ghetto for the "useless" was liquidated and its 1,500 inhabitants were murdered by SS and Ukrainian auxiliary police in pits outside the townlet. Forty people who had survived in hiding moved into the "useful" ghetto. On June 6, 1942, forty youths were sent to work in Rowne*, where most were murdered.

In the fall of 1942, the names of both those who had perished and those still alive were inscribed on scrolls that were buried near the synagogue. On October 6 of that year, the ghetto for the "useful" was liquidated and the Jews were murdered in pits. Eleven Jews committed suicide and about 300 tried to escape. Most of the escapees perished. A few went into hiding, mostly among Ukrainian Baptists.

RADZYMIN

COUNTY SEAT, WARSAW DISTRICT, POLAND

During the war: General Gouvernement, Warsaw District

Coordinates: 52°25' | 21°11'

About 2,200 Jews lived in Radzymin in the interwar period, representing roughly half of the townlet's population. They earned their livelihood from commerce, peddling, and artisanship, especially in the garment industry. A number of Jews living near the townlet were farmers. The Jews of Radzymin were assisted by relatives abroad and by a Jewish bank and free-loan society, which were supported by the JDC. Radzymin also had trade unions that maintained their own free-loan funds as well as traditional welfare and charity societies. The townlet had a Beit Yaakov school. Zionist parties and youth movements were very active in the community, and those who trained in their pioneer training facilities later immigrated to the Land of Israel. The youth movements established libraries and art and sports circles. Radzymin also had chapters of Agudath Israel and the Bund and its youth movement, *Tsukunft*. The Bund ran a club, drama circle, and library.

When World War II broke out, many of Radzymin's Jews fled east, to the area under Soviet control.

The Germans occupied Radzymin in September 1939, and immediately began to plunder Jewish property and seize Jews for forced labor. In October 1939, the Germans ordered the Jews to pay a ransom in money and furs, and in November 1939, they murdered fourteen distinguished members of the community. In December 1939, the Jews of Radzymin aged twelve and older were required to wear a yellow armband.

On December 25, 1940, an open ghetto was established. The head of the Judenrat was David Izraelski, followed by Meir Winterman. A Jewish Order Service was founded under the command of Bunim Radzyminski. Hundreds of Jews were removed from the ghetto every day for forced labor.

Early 1941 saw the arrival in Radzymin of Jewish refugees who had fled or been driven out of surrounding localities and areas annexed to the Third Reich, such as Pultusk*, Serock, and Konstantynow*. Overcrowding was severe, and refugees were put up in the Beit Midrash and the synagogue as well as in the building used to prepare bodies for burial. A special committee aided by the JDC in Warsaw* set up a public soup kitchen for the needy that served hundreds of meals every day. Most of the Jews supported themselves by selling their belongings, bartering with the local population, and smuggling food into the ghetto.

In mid-April 1941, spotted fever broke out in the ghetto, which was consequently sealed off, causing a severe food shortage that led to starvation. The hunger spurred the spread of the epidemic and raised mortality. In November 1941, the Jews were ordered to fence in the ghetto; the smuggling of food from the Aryan side became a very dangerous undertaking.

In the spring of 1942, additional deportees arrived in the ghetto from Tluszcz* and Jadow*, swelling the ghetto's population to some 2,800. In the spring of

1942, about 100 young people were removed from the ghetto for forced labor digging peat in the Izabelin camp, some ten kilometers from the townlet.

On October 2, 1942, the liquidation of the ghetto was launched. German gendarmes encircled the ghetto, rounding up Jews and forcing them to hand over anything of value in their possession. Many Jews resisted and were murdered on site. About 200 young Jews managed to flee to the forests. Approximately seventy people were sent to the Izabelin camp, where they were murdered a short time later. On October 3, 1942, the last surviving Jews of the Radzymin ghetto were deported to the Treblinka death camp. Those who fled during the liquidation of the ghetto were captured by the Germans, usually after being denounced by Poles. A small number of Radzymin's Jews survived the war.

RADZYŃ

COUNTY SEAT, LUBLIN DISTRICT, POLAND

During the war: General Gouvernement, Lublin District

Coordinates:
51°47' | 22°37'

Radzyn
Hasidic Rabbi (*Admor*) Shmuel Shlomo Leiner with his followers. The rabbi called upon the Jews to flee to the forests and act against the Germans. In May 1942, the rabbi was executed in the synagogue courtyard in Wlodawa. (GFH)

During the interwar period, there were some 2,900 Jews in Radzyn, more than half the townlet's population. Most engaged in petty manufacturing and petty trade. Jews in Radzyn established metal factories, a sawmill, and a flour mill. The great Hasidic center in Radzyn, founded by the Radzyner Rebbe, aided the local economy by using the townlet's hotels, eateries, and shops, and by buying the products of its workshops. The townlet boasted a large chapter of Agudath Israel, a chapter of the Bund and its youth movements, and Zionist parties and youth movements. Cultural life was rich. Quite a few children attended a traditional Talmud Torah, a Beit Yaakov school, and a Tarbut school, but many others, especially girls, attended the local Szabasowka school.

The Germans occupied Radzyn in the middle of September 1939. The townlet spent two weeks under Soviet control, and when the Soviets retreated to the east under the terms of the Molotov-Ribbentrop Pact, many young Jews followed them.

In the first days of the re-occupation, SS men subjected the Jewish townspeople to abuse, abducted Jews for forced labor, and demanded a ransom from the community.

On December 3, 1939, Jews who had been expelled from Lubartow* reached Radzyn. After hearing their reports, many young Jews and some entire families in Radzyn fled to the Soviet occupation zone.

On December 6, 1939, most Jews in Radzyn were expelled to nearby Slawatycze. At the Germans' orders, D. Lichtenstein, the last chairman of the pre-war Jewish community, established a nine-member Judenrat for the few who were left behind. The Judenrat, aided by a Jewish Order Service, regulated the departure of Jews for forced labor. In early 1940, the Jews' property was seized "for the benefit of the Reich."

In April 1940, most of those who had been expelled to Slawatycze were brought back to Radzyn. They were joined by Jews from Slawatycze and Miedzyrzec Podlaski*, bringing the Jewish population of Radzyn to about 2,000. In July 1940, 300 Jewish men were taken to labor camps.

An open ghetto was established in Radzyn in late 1940. On January 1, 1941, the Judenrat was ordered to surrender to the Gestapo all furs owned by members of the community. Although the Judenrat obeyed, several hostages were murdered. The ghetto was sealed in the autumn of 1941. In May 1942, its population was 2,071.

A resistance group whose members came from Hashomer Hatza'ir and other Zionist movements operated in the ghetto. The group engaged in cultural endeavors and planned an escape to the forests and the establishment of a fighting unit. The Hasidic rebbe Shmuel Shlomo Leiner, founder of the Yeshiva *Sod Yesharim* in Radzyn, urged his followers to flee to the forests and not to cooperate with the

Germans. The Germans murdered him in Wlodawa*, in May 1942 after a denunciation. Escorted by his sobbing Hasidim, wrapped in his prayer shawl, praying, the rebbe was led by Gestapo agents to the plaza in front of the synagogue and shot to death. The poet Itzhak Katzenelson commemorated this event in a poem.

On September 22, 1942, Gestapo men arrested 200 Jews and murdered them in a location outside the townlet.

The ghetto was liquidated from October 1 to 16, 1942, when SS forces, German gendarmes, and Polish police deported 1,800–2,000 of its inhabitants to Treblinka via the Miedzyrzec Podlaski ghetto in several operations. About 1,000 deportees attempted to hide before they could be placed aboard the transport. After the transport set out, many tried to escape by leaping from the train; some were killed in this attempt, and most of the others were captured by Poles and turned over to the Germans. The few who did escape joined partisan units, where they later formed into several groups or found refuge with peasants. The Gestapo employed a small group of Jews from Radzyn in labor camps.

RAFAŁÓWKA

TOWNLET IN SARNY COUNTY, VOLHYNIA DISTRICT, POLAND
(After World War II in the USSR/Ukraine; Ukrainian: **Rafalivka**; Russian: **Rafalovka**)

During the war: Reichskommissariat Ukraine

Coordinates:
51°22' | 25°52'

During the interwar period, about 600 Jews lived in Rafalowka, accounting for approximately one-third of the townlet's population. Some were petty merchants and artisans, a number owned a sawmill, and still others were wholesalers. The community boasted a savings-and-loan association, a Tarbut school that taught in Hebrew, a cultural center, and chapters of Zionist parties.

During the era of Soviet rule that began in September 1939, many Jewish refugees from central and western Poland settled in Rafalowka.

The Soviets retreated from the area on July 4, 1941. A Ukrainian administration and police force were established in the townlet. Its agents looted Jewish property and drafted Jews for forced labor.

The Germans entered Rafalowka in late July 1941. They forced the Jews to remit ransoms and set up a Judenrat, which included representatives from two nearby Jewish farming hamlets, Olizarka and Zoludzk.

The Rafalowka ghetto was established on May 1, 1942. Jews from Olizarka, Zoludzk, and villages in the vicinity were brought in, raising its population to approximately 2,500.

In July 1942, sixty Jewish forced laborers were murdered outside of the townlet.

On August 29, 1942, the Rafalowka ghetto was liquidated, and 2,250 Jews were taken to pits on the road to Suchowola*, where they were murdered. Dozens escaped to forests and villages, where Polish peasants and Ukrainian Baptists assisted them. Some young people formed fighting units and later joined the Soviet partisans. A group of Jews from Rafalowka attacked the townlet and took revenge on Ukrainian collaborators.

About thirty of Rafalowka's Jews survived.

RAJGRÓD

COUNTY SEAT, BIAŁYSTOK DISTRICT, POLAND

During the war: Bezirk Białystok

Coordinates:
53°44' | 22°42'

About 750 Jews lived in Rajgrod in the interwar period, representing approximately one-third of the townlet's population. Most earned their livelihood from commerce and artisanship; several were factory owners and wood merchants. The Jews were aided by a free-loan society that was supported by the JDC. Rajgrod had a Beit Yaakov school for girls. Zionist parties and youth movements were active in the townlet, as were Agudath Israel and the Bund. Zionist youth organizations held evening Hebrew classes, and the clubs of most of the political organizations in the townlet had libraries. Rajgrod also had a *Bar Kochva* sports association, a drama circle, and an orchestra.

The Germans occupied Rajgrod during the second week of World War II, in September 1939, but in accordance with the Molotov-Ribbentrop Pact, Rajgrod was handed over to Soviet control.

The Germans apparently reoccupied Rajgrod on June 22, 1941. A few days later, two Gestapo men arrived in Rajgrod, and, with the help of a number of Poles, rounded up about 100 Jews, among them entire families. They led the Jews to the Chojniki forest outside the townlet, where they murdered and buried them.

In July or August 1941, a ghetto encircled by a barbed-wire fence was established in the townlet, and a Judenrat was appointed, headed by Yieshaya Grodzhinski, a driver by profession. The inhabitants of the ghetto were seized for forced labor and were compelled to smuggle food supplies into the ghetto, as the meager food rations provided to its inhabitants were insufficient for survival. Farmers in the area were permitted to employ Jews on their farms, and several of the Jewish artisans worked in workshops outside the ghetto. The Germans periodically entered the ghetto to loot property and abuse and murder Jews.

In late October 1942, German and Polish policemen deported the approximately 600 Jews of Rajgrod to Grajewo*. Four brothers of the Zukerbraun family, all butchers, resisted the deportation and were murdered in the ensuing struggle.

After spending six days in Grajewo, the Jews of Rajgrod were transferred to the Bogusza transit camp, together with Grajewo's Jews. They were subsequently deported to the Treblinka and Auschwitz death camps.

A number of Jews managed to flee during the deportation, but most were caught by Poles and handed over to the Germans or murdered. Few of Rajgrod's Jews survived.

RÁKOSCSABA

TOWN IN PEST-PILIS-SOLT-KISKUN COUNTY, HUNGARY

Coordinates:
47°29' | 19°17'

The last national census conducted prior to the German occupation, taken in January 1941, recorded 406 Jewish inhabitants in Rakoscsaba, accounting for roughly 3 percent of the total population, and most were merchants and artisans. The Jews in Rakoscsaba were organized in a Status Quo Ante community.

In 1942, twelve Jewish men were drafted into the Hungarian army for forced labor service. A few of the men were later seized as war prisoners by the Soviets during the retreat of the Hungarian forces.

The German army occupied Hungary on March 19, 1944. A census conducted in the second week of April 1944 showed that 246 Jews belonged to the Status Quo Ante Jewish community of Rakoscsaba.

The Hungarian administration remained intact and operational after the German occupation. The ghettoization and deportation of the Jews occurred on the basis of decrees and orders issued by the Hungarian national and local authorities. On May 12, Hungarian sub-prefect Dr. Laszlo Endre, a militant antisemite, ordered the establishment of ghettos in his county, and a ghetto was established in Rakoscsaba in May 1944. Altogether, about 500 people, including local Jews and Jews from nearby settlements, were concentrated in several houses designated for the ghetto. On the morning of June 9, 1944, they were moved by the gendarmes to the local school building.

At the end of June 1944, inhabitants of the ghetto were transferred to the brick factory in Monor*, which served as the entrainment center for the ghettos of the county surrounding Budapest* from the south and east. They belonged to a group of approximately 8,000 Jews who were deported from the brick factory to Auschwitz in three transports, between July 6 and 8, 1944.

RÁKOSPALOTA

TOWN IN PEST-PILIS-SOLT-KISKUN COUNTY, HUNGARY

Coordinates:
47°34' | 19°08'

The last national census conducted prior to the German occupation, taken in January 1941, recorded 2,240 Jewish inhabitants in Rakospalota, representing approximately 5 percent of the total population. Most were merchants and artisans, but many were clerks. The town had an Orthodox Jewish community that maintained a Jewish school, a Talmud Torah, and an old-age home. During the 1930s, the Zionist movement gained popularity in the town, and the Mizrachi movement established a local branch.

In 1942, all Jewish men between the ages of eighteen and forty-eight, including the sick, were drafted into the Hungarian army for forced labor service. A number of them were sent to various places in Hungary and Transylvania, while others were assigned to the eastern front, in the Ukraine.

The German army occupied Hungary on March 19, 1944. The Hungarian administration remained intact and operational after the German occupation. The ghettoization and deportation of the Jews occurred on the basis of decrees and orders issued by the Hungarian national and local authorities. On May 12, Hungarian sub-prefect Dr. Laszlo Endre, a militant antisemite, ordered the establishment of ghettos in his county. The houses into which the Jews were ordered to move were marked out on May 15, 1944. In addition to the local Jews, the Jews of Pestujhely were concentrated in the ghetto.

Many of the Jewish men who had not previously been drafted for forced labor were called up on May 1, 1944, while young women were assigned to work in war factories in the vicinity of Budapest*. They were thus saved from moving into the ghetto and subsequent deportation. At the end of June or beginning of July 1944, the inhabitants of the Rakospalota ghetto were transferred to the brick factory in Budakalasz, which became one of the entrainment centers for the ghettos of Pest-Pilis-Solt-Kiskun County surrounding Budapest from the north. They were deported from the brick factory to Auschwitz between July 6 and 8, 1944.

RAKÓW
(Kielce District, Poland)

TOWNLET IN OPATÓW COUNTY, KIELCE DISTRICT, POLAND

During the war: General Gouvernement, Radom District

Coordinates:
50°41' | 21°03'

When World War II broke out, about 1,500 Jews lived in Rakow, representing more than half of the townlet's population. Most earned their livelihood from commerce, peddling, and artisanship, especially in the garment industry, as well as from transporting goods and providing recreational services to vacationers. Assistance could be obtained from a range of institutions, including traditional charity and welfare societies, a Jewish bank, and a free-loan society. Most of the community's children attended a Heder and a Talmud Torah, a Beit Yaakov school for girls, and for a certain period a Hebrew Tarbut school. Chapters of the Zionist parties, the Bund, and Agudath Israel held political activities. The Zionists had active youth movements and operated pioneer training facilities.

Rakow was occupied by the Germans toward the beginning of the war. In early 1940, a ghetto was established in the townlet, one of the first in the district (in accordance with the German administrative division). In April 1942, Rakow was one of seventeen sites in which the Radom governor concentrated Jews from the area.

On August 28, 1942, the inhabitants of the ghetto were transferred to the Jedrzejow* ghetto. On September 16, 1942, they were deported to the Treblinka death camp, together with the Jews of Jedrzejow.

RAKÓW

(**Vilna District, Poland**)

(Yiddish: **Rakavey**)

TOWNLET IN MOŁODECZNO COUNTY, VILNA DISTRICT, POLAND

(After World War II in the USSR/Belarus; Belarussian: **Rakau**; Russian: **Rakov**)

During the war: Reichskommissariat Ostland

Coordinates: 53°58' | 27°03'

When World War II broke out, about 2,400 Jews were living in Rakow, representing roughly two-thirds of the townlet's population. Most earned their livelihood from small commerce and artisanship. Zionist parties and Agudath Israel were active in Rakow, and the townlet had a Yiddish school and a Tarbut Hebrew school.

After Rakow was occupied by the Soviets in the second half of September 1939, a Soviet economic, social, and educational system was introduced into the townlet. Privately owned shops were nationalized or closed and cooperatives were formed.

On June 26, 1941, Rakow was occupied by the Germans. A short time later, forty-nine young Jews were accused of Communist activity and shot to death outside of the townlet. The three members of the burial society who buried the victims were also killed in the Jewish cemetery. Two weeks later, the Germans killed another fourteen Jewish youths outside Rakow. The Germans appointed a Judenrat with four members.

In October 1941, the Germans rounded up the Jews of Rakow in the marketplace. They then searched their homes and shot anyone who failed to appear in the marketplace, including the elderly and ill. During that day, 112 Jewish men were murdered in the local cemetery.

Following the operation, the Germans concentrated the approximately 2,000 Jews remaining in Rakow in a ghetto established in the synagogue compound. The Jews left its confines daily to perform forced labor. SS men repeatedly demanded gold, winter coats, and various types of merchandise, leaving the Jews penniless. During this period, young Jews from Rakow began to escape from the ghetto to the forests, where several joined the partisan units in the area.

Most of the Jews of Rakow were murdered on February 4, 1942, in the vicinity of the ghetto synagogue. The few surviving Jews were employed in sorting the belongings of the victims. A number of them managed to flee with the help of local farmers to the Lebiedziew* ghetto, and were sent together with other Jews on to the labor camp in Krasne*.

RASEINIAI

(Yiddish: **Raseyn**)

COUNTY SEAT, LITHUANIA

During the war: Reichskommissariat Ostland

Coordinates: 55°22' | 23°07'

On the eve of the German occupation, about 2,000 Jews lived in Raseiniai, representing approximately one-third of the townlet's population. Most earned their livelihood from artisanship and commerce. Raseiniai had a Yavne elementary school as well as a Tarbut high school; chapters of the Zionist parties, the Bund, Agudath Israel, and youth movements were active and the townlet boasted various welfare and charity institutions.

After Lithuania was annexed to the Soviet Union in 1940, private businesses in Raseiniai were nationalized. The Hebrew schools were closed and the activities of the Jewish parties were discontinued. Some twenty families were exiled to the Soviet Union.

By the time the Germans occupied Raseiniai on June 24, 1941, most of the local Jews had already fled the townlet in the wake of the heavy bombardment that preceded the occupation. After the Germans took control of the townlet, however, the Jews returned, only to find that most of their homes had been burned and their property stolen. They were forced to crowd together in the homes that emerged intact from the bombings.

The Lithuanians removed the Jewish inhabitants daily for various forms of forced labor. The Jews of Raseiniai underwent a terrible series of humiliations, and a number of women were abducted and raped. As of three weeks after the occupation, the townlet's Jews were forced to wear a white badge and to abide by various other decrees.

One week later, Jewish men and women aged fifteen to forty five years were ordered to gather in a ghetto of sorts that was established in the yards and stables of a monastery located about one and a half kilometers from the townlet. The ghetto was encircled by a barbed-wire fence and forty Lithuanian guards. Family members who were not required to move to the monastery were nevertheless permitted to join their relations; in all about 1,500 Jews were concentrated in the monastery. The rest of the Jews were housed together in a few buildings along a single street in the townlet.

On July 27, 1941, all Jewish men in Raseiniai were required to shave their beards. Afterwards, 393 men were taken from the ghetto in accordance with lists prepared in advance. They were taken to a nearby quarry under Lithuanian guard, and shot by the Lithuanians together with about 100 Jews removed from the jail in the townlet. That same day, a group of people composed of the Jewish intelligentsia along with elderly and ill Jews were moved to the ghetto, where they were kept for two days. On July 29, 1941, the entire group was also sent to the quarry and murdered. Before they were killed, a number of the Jews were instructed to write notes to their wives with a request to remit money and valuables with the policemen that brought the notes; many wives complied, turning their valuables over, unwittingly, to their husbands' murderers.

The authorities informed the inhabitants of the ghetto that they could bring all their family members and property to the ghetto in advance of their transfer. In all, about forty men and over 1,000 women and children lived in the ghetto during that period. The overcrowding in the ghetto increased drastically. Lithuanians periodically removed groups of Jews from the ghetto who were never returned. By night, the Lithuanians stole the Jews' meager possessions and raped Jewish women.

In the second half of August 1941, the Jews of the ghetto and surrounding villages were told that they had until August 27 to move to the nearby Biliunu Dvaras estate, located about five kilometers from the monastery. Some 2,000 Jews in all, mostly women and children, were relocated to the estate.

On August 29, 1941, the women and children were taken on trucks to a location near the townlet of Girkalnis, where they were stripped, shot, and buried in pits. Only a few individual Jews survived by hiding with peasants.

RAWA MAZOWIECKA

COUNTY SEAT, WARSAW DISTRICT, POLAND

During the war: General Gouvernement, Radom District

Coordinates:
51°46' | 20°15'

Shortly before World War II, about 2,500 Jews lived in Rawa Mazowiecka, comprising roughly one-third of the townlet's population. Most were merchants and petty artisans. Agudath Israel and various Zionist parties had chapters there. The situation for the townlet's Jews deteriorated in the 1930s. They were the targets of a particularly aggressive economic boycott and a pogrom that was perpetrated in 1934.

The Germans occupied Rawa Mazowiecka on September 8, 1939. They looted Jewish property. Jews were abused, seized for forced labor, and more than twenty were murdered. Several hundred fled to Skierniewice*, but refugees replenished the townlet's population.

The Rawa Mazowiecka ghetto was established in early 1941 in the former Jewish quarter. Since the ghetto was encircled in barbed wire but not sealed, Jews were able to maintain contact with surrounding areas with relative ease. The ghetto was gravely overpopulated, mainly due to a steady influx of refugees that brought its population to some 4,000 in 1942. Those refugees who did not receive permission to live in the ghetto itself settled on the outskirts of the townlet or, in a few cases, lived in the ghetto illegally and without ration cards. Some Jewish artisans did

Rawa Mazowiecka, September 15, 1939
Jewish men were rounded up in the marketplace and ordered to lie face down; twenty-three Jews were murdered that day. (GFH)

odd jobs for the Germans and, illegally, for residents of the area; a few worked on nearby farms. In the fall of 1942, many Jews were sent to a labor camp in Zawady, near Tomaszow Mazowiecki*. About half returned to the ghetto and infected it with typhus, which quickly spread and claimed many casualties.

In early 1942, the situation of the refugees outside the ghetto deteriorated and they, too, were packed into the ghetto by the Germans. The ghetto was sealed and food rations were terminated. On June 23, 1942, the Germans arrested and murdered eighteen Jews.

On October 26, 1942, about 4,000 Jews from Biala Rawska* were brought to the ghetto. The liquidation began the following day, as German and Polish police surrounded the ghetto. During the following days, all inhabitants of the ghetto, including the refugees, were loaded onto trains and deported to Treblinka. Several Jews were murdered during the operation.

RAWA RUSKA

COUNTY SEAT, LWÓW DISTRICT, POLAND
(After World War II in the USSR/Ukraine; Ukrainian: **Rava Rus'ka**; Russian: **Rava Russkaya**)

During the war: General Gouvernement, Galicia District

Coordinates:
50°15' | 23°37'

In the 1930s, about 5,700 Jews lived in Rawa Ruska, representing approximately half of the town's population. Most earned their livelihood from commerce, industry, and artisanship, and were active mainly in the fur industry. The town had a Jewish bank, an artisans' society, and Jewish welfare institutions. Chapters of most of the Jewish parties in Poland were active in the community: the various Zionist parties, the Bund, and Agudath Israel. A number of Jews were active in the outlawed Communist Party. The community had a Hebrew school and an Agudath Israel school, both of which offered supplementary instruction.

On September 10, 1939, Rawa Ruska was occupied by the Germans for about two weeks. During this period, restrictions were imposed on the Jews' freedom of movement, Jewish inhabitants were required to wear a distinctive mark on their clothing, and several were exploited for forced labor. A number of synagogues were broken into and the Torah scrolls defiled. On September 24, 1939, control of Rawa Ruska was handed over to the Soviets, in accordance with the Molotov-Ribbentrop Pact. The political organizations were soon dispersed and community institutions closed, with the exception of several synagogues. Private factories were nationalized and a number of "bourgeois" families were arrested in March

1940, and exiled to the Soviet Union interior. In May–June 1940, the Soviets exiled into the USSR interior many of the Jewish refugees who had fled to the town from western Poland.

On June 28, 1941, Rawa Ruska was occupied by the Germans. In early July 1941, the Ukrainian police arrested and executed in the nearby forest about 100 Jews as per a list of names that included many members of the intelligentsia. Also in July, a Judenrat was established, headed by a Jew of German extraction named Schwitzer, although it was the Zionist leader, Dr. Josef Mandel, the community head until the war, who left the greatest mark on the council. There was considerable tension between the two men owing to Schwitzer's meticulous compliance with all German orders. At a later date, the Germans arrested Josef Mandel, and his fate is unknown. The Germans ordered the Judenrat to conduct a census of the Jewish population, remit large sums of money and valuables to the Germans, and supply people for forced labor. In the winter of 1941/42, many Jews died of hunger and disease. Although the Judenrat ran a public soup kitchen and a hospital, they had scant resources to overcome the difficulties faced by the community.

On March 20, 1942, German police units, under the command of Helmut Tanzmann and aided by Ukrainian policemen, carried out an operation in Rawa Ruska. Jews were arrested in their homes, in the streets, and among the workers headed to their jobs. Some 1,500 Jews were murdered in the operation, many were deported to the nearby Belzec death camp (located only twenty-two kilometers from Rawa Ruska), and still others were murdered in the town or surrounding forests. The following day, the Germans ordered the Jewish cemetery located in the center of town destroyed to allow for the paving of a new road. Jews were forced to uproot tombstones and use the broken pieces for the construction of the road.

In the spring of 1942, the Jews were concentrated in an extremely overcrowded open ghetto in one of the town's quarters. Epidemic typhus soon spread throughout the ghetto. Jews were brought from other localities to the already overcrowded ghetto, raising its population to some 6,700. On July 27, 1942, the Germans carried out an operation and deported about 5,000 Jews to Belzec, some of whom had been brought to Rawa Ruska only a short time earlier because of its proximity to the death camp. Jews discovered in hiding were summarily shot. A few dozen Jews managed to jump off the train on the way to Belzec and return to the ghetto; others were killed during their attempt to escape from the transports.

The Rawa Ruska ghetto became a refuge for many Jews who jumped off trains during their deportation from localities throughout eastern Galicia to Belzec in the summer of 1942, owing to its geographic proximity to Belzec and the railroad tracks leading to the death camp. Many arrived injured and exhausted. The Judenrat and the ghetto inhabitants awarded these refugees asylum and helped them return to their places of origin, risking harsh collective punishment in doing so. In early September 1942, the ghetto was once again full, this time containing numerous Jews from many localities, including Potylicz, Magierow, Uhnow, and Niemirow. The ghetto's population reached about 8,000 at this time.

In early December 1942, the ghetto was sealed off as a preliminary step toward its complete elimination. On December 7, 1942, an operation to liquidate the ghetto was carried out by German police units under the command of Heinz Czimmek and Gerhard Hager. During the operation, the ghetto was set on fire, many Jews (according to one source, some 3,000) were shot to death in the Jewish cemetery and in the forest nearby, while about 2,000 to 2,500 others were deported to the Belzec death camp. This was the final liquidation operation before the ghetto was closed down. Another approximately 750 Jews who were caught attempting to hide were murdered in the forest on December 9, 1942.

About 300 Jews remained in the ghetto. Most were distributed among the labor camps in the area, and about sixty were left in the empty ghetto to tend to the property belonging to the murder victims.

Another approximately 250 Jews managed to survive the operations by hiding with Christian acquaintances, in bunkers in the forest, or in hiding places inside the ghetto itself. The Germans announced that Jews who agreed to emerge from their hiding places would not be punished; due to extreme conditions in the hiding places, dozens were deceived by the offer and came out of hiding. They were transferred to a nearby labor camp in Rawa Ruska, and most were murdered in June 1943, when the camp was liquidated.

RECHITSA

COUNTY SEAT, GOMEL DISTRICT, BELARUS, USSR

During the war: Military Administration Area

Coordinates:
52°22' | 30°23'

At the end of the nineteenth century, about 5,000 Jews lived in Rechitsa, accounting for 60 percent of the total population. In the 1920s, most Jews in the town made their living from crafts and commerce, but many also gained employment as fabric workers and Soviet employees. Yiddish schools operated until the summer of 1938. Many of Rechitsa's Jews, especially youths, left the town as a result of rapid urbanization in the USSR, while migrants arrived from the small townlets in the vicinity. On the eve of the German invasion of the Soviet Union, about 7,000 Jews resided in the town, one-quarter of its population.

When war broke out between the Soviet Union and Germany on June 22, 1941, a number of Jews fled from Rechitsa. The town was occupied by the Germans on August 23, 1941. The terrorization and murders of Jews began immediately. The town's Jewish inhabitants were forbidden to appear in public places. About ten days after the occupation, the ritual slaughterer and an accountant named Yisrael Melinkovitch, who served as a starosta, were instructed to prepare a list of all of the Jews who had remained in Rechitsa. Melinkovitch was murdered before the ghetto was established, apparently because the community had failed to pay a very high ransom. No one was appointed to replace him.

Within two weeks of the occupation, the Jews were required to sew a five-pointed yellow star on their sleeve and to inscribe the word "Jude" in chalk on the back of their garments. In early September 1941, more than 200 Jewish men aged fifteen to fifty were rounded up, ostensibly to repair a bridge, and murdered near Rechitsa; according to one testimony, more than 300 people were murdered, including women. A number of cases are known whereby Jews were murdered by their non-Jewish neighbors seeking to take over their property.

In late November 1941, an injunction was published in Rechitsa ordering the Jewish population to gather at the cultural center. The Jews were then moved into two two-story buildings inside the former prison, which formed a ghetto. According to other sources, the ghetto was established in a match factory. In addition to local Jews, Jewish inhabitants from surrounding localities, as well as prisoners of war and Communists (who were executed on November 25, 1941), were concentrated in it. The ghetto was encircled by a barbed-wire fence two meters high and guarded by policemen. The overcrowded conditions within the ghetto were intolerable, with about forty people per room. Jews were seized from the ghetto daily for forced labor.

About five days after the establishment of the ghetto, some 300 Jews were removed on the pretense that they were to be sent to do farming work. Instead, they were taken out of town and executed. Those who attempted to escape were summarily shot. The murders of the Jews of the ghetto continued until mid-December 1941.

REJOWIEC

TOWNLET IN CHEŁM COUNTY, LUBLIN DISTRICT, POLAND

During the war: General Gouvernement, Lublin District

Coordinates: 51°05' | 23°17'

After World War I, about 350 Jews lived in Rejowiec, accounting for 80 percent of the local population. They were merchants, peddlers, and artisans; some were manufacturers, factory workers, and holders of white-collar positions. Zionist parties, the Bund, and a chapter of Agudath Israel were active there.

The Germans occupied Rejowiec in late September 1939. As they moved in, they confiscated Jewish property, took hostages, imposed ransoms on the community, and abducted Jews for forced labor. SS men from Chelm* often visited Rejowiec and subjected Jews to abuse that ended with murder.

In the spring of 1941, an open ghetto was established in the townlet, to which some 1,300 deportees from Lublin* and Cracow* were brought. Conditions in the ghetto were ghastly; starvation and epidemics claimed many lives. A soup kitchen was established with funds from the JSS in Cracow. By the end of 1941, there were 2,380 Jews in the ghetto.

On April 7, 1942, the Jews in Rejowiec were deported to the Belzec death camp. The ill and the elderly were shot in the ghetto during the roundup. About 10 days later, on April 16–20, about 2,000 Jewish refugees from the Protectorate, Slovakia, and Berlin were brought to the ghetto.

In another roundup on May 2, 1942, Germans transported some 2,700 Jews to Sobibor and about 300 others to a labor camp in Krychow, a satellite of Sobibor. Several weeks later, on May 23–25, 1942, 3,650 additional Jewish refugees from Slovakia were brought to the ghetto. During the arrests and for several months afterwards, many Jews escaped into the forest, but most of them were murdered. In October that year the ghetto was sealed, and on October 10, about 2,400 refugees were deported from the ghetto to Sobibor and Majdanek.

After this deportation, the ghetto functioned as a de facto labor camp, and the group of young Jews who remained there was employed at a sugar factory. Jews who had escaped from the ghetto during the period of arrests began to return, and the Germans initially left them alone. Later, however, they began to murder them systematically.

Nearly all of the rump population of the ghetto was liquidated in two operations perpetrated on April 7 and July 2, 1943, when the last several hundred inhabitants were deported to Majdanek. Sixteen Jews were left behind as service laborers at the local Gestapo headquarters. They were murdered in July 1944, shortly before the area was liberated.

REMBERTÓW

TOWN IN WARSAW COUNTY, WARSAW DISTRICT, POLAND

During the war: General Gouvernement, Warsaw District

Coordinates: 52°15' | 21°10'

On the eve of the World War II, about 2,000 Jews lived in Rembertow, representing approximately 10 percent of the town's population. Most earned their livelihood from commerce and from providing services to vacationers. They were aided by trade unions and a charity and welfare society as well as by a free-loan society. The Jewish schools included traditional Hadarim, a Talmud Torah, a Yeshiva for high school-age students, and a Beit Yaakov school. Zionist parties and youth movements were active in Rembertow and established pioneer training facilities. Agudath Israel and its youth movement and the Bund were active as well. The town had libraries founded by the Zionists and the Bund, and evening classes in Hebrew were held. The Jewish community also enjoyed a drama circle and an orchestra.

The Germans bombed Rembertow on September 1, 1939, and a number of local people were killed. Many Jews fled to Warsaw* and to eastern Poland. Rembertow was occupied by the Germans on September 12, 1939, and they immediately began to plunder Jewish property and seize Jews for forced labor. In December 1939, the Germans ordered the Jews to pay a ransom and supply fifty forced laborers every day. The Germans appointed a Judenrat headed by Meir Tenenbaum.

In 1940, a fenced-in ghetto was established in Rembertow. A food shortage compelled the ghetto residents to pass through the barbed-wire fence in order to trade with the local population. In July 1940, there were 1,380 Jews in Rembertow, including 274 Jewish refugees from Kalisz* and Sieradz*. In early 1941, about 300 Jewish refugees arrived from Lodz*.

In November 1941, the Jewish population of Rembertow reached approximately 1,800. The Judenrat established a public soup kitchen that distributed about 600 hot meals every day. The Jewish butchers risked their lives to obtain beef for slaughter, established a cooperative, and provided the Warsaw ghetto with meat as well. The Jews of Rembertow performed forced labor in two labor camps, Poligon and Pocisk.

In August 1942, the Germans, together with Ukrainian and Polish police, drove out the ghetto Jews to Falenica-Miedzeszyn*, and from there to the Treblinka death camp.

More than 1,000 Jews, the remaining survivors of ghettos that had been liquidated in the vicinity, were brought to the two labor camps in Rembertow, which were still operational. In June 1943, the Gestapo murdered about 1,000 inmates of the Pocisk camp, and in August 1943, they murdered the last remaining Jews in Rembertow.

RIGA

(Yiddish: **Rigeh**)

CAPITAL OF LATVIA, PORT CITY IN VIDZEME (LIFLANDIA)

During the war:
Reichskommissariat Ostland

Coordinates:
56°57' | 24°06'

Before the War: A part of the Russian Empire before World War I, the independent state of Latvia was established after the war, with the city of Riga as its capital. Riga attracted many Jews. Its Jewish residents reached 43,500 by 1935, double the number that inhabited the city on the eve of World War I, representing 11 percent of the population of the capital and half of the Jewish population of Latvia. The Jews fulfilled an important function in the city's economy: in the 1930s, they owned over half of the large factories as well as nearly half of the city's large businesses and five commercial banks. These were established in partnership with wealthy overseas Jews and represented a major financial factor in both the local and the national economy. Jews also occupied the liberal professions, accounting for half of the city's doctors and more than a quarter of its lawyers. Jewish owners of small- and medium-sized businesses as well as artisans and clerks were all organized in trade unions and had Jewish cooperative credit unions at their disposal.

The health institutions of Riga's Jews included two modern hospitals, a *Linat Zedek* association, a *Bikur Holim* hospital (that also treated non-Jewish patients), and a branch of the Jewish health union OZE, which helped the needy. The Riga Jewish community maintained an old-age home and a series of modern and traditional associations and organizations, public soup kitchens, and mutual aid funds.

Religious services were administered in some forty synagogues, Hasidic prayer groups (*minyanim*), and houses of prayer of various sects. The vast majority of the community's children studied in public and private Jewish schools. The Jewish educational network included kindergartens, two evening high schools in Hebrew and Yiddish, a Hebrew seminar for kindergarten teachers, and a popular CYSHO university.

The head of the Mizrachi party was Rabbi Mordekhai Nurok, one of the founders of the movement and a member of the Latvian *Saeima* (House of Representatives); the rabbi eventually immigrated to the Land of Israel. The General Zionists were also active in the community and its institutions. The Zionist youth

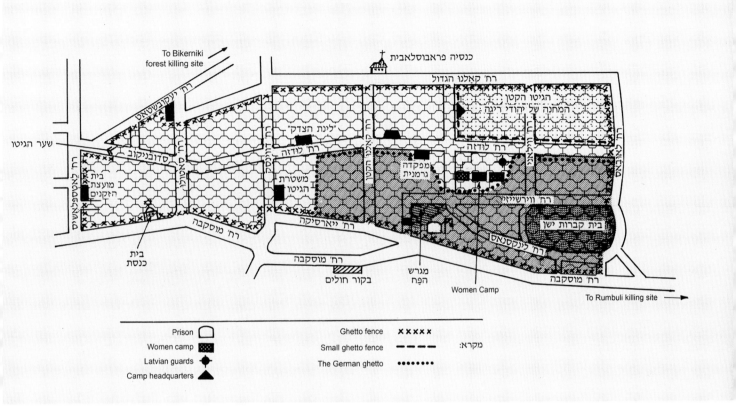

To Bikerniki
forest killing site

כנסיה פראבוסלאבית

רח' קאלנו הגדול

שער הגיטו

הגיטו הקטן
המחנה של יהודי ריגה

רח' לודזה

"לינה הצדק"

רח' לודזה

מפקדה
גרמנית

משטרת
הגיטו

רח' וירשייזי

בית קברות ישן

רח' ייארסיקה

רח' לינקסאס

בית
כנסת

רח' מוסקבה

רח' מוסקבה

בית
מועצת
הזקנים

רח' סדוביניקוב

רח' מוסקבה

בקור חולים   מגרש
הפח

Women Camp

To Rumbuli killing site

Prison ⬭		Ghetto fence ✕✕✕✕✕	מקרא:
Women camp ▨		Small ghetto fence – – – –	
Latvian guards ◆		The German ghetto ••••••••	
Camp headquarters ▲			

**Riga ghetto plan,
reconstructed on the basis of
several sources**
(Dov Levin, ed., *Pinkas Latvia
and Estonia*, Yad Vashem
Publications, Jerusalem 1988)

movements reached their peak of activity in the 1930s. Riga boasted various non-Zionist Jewish parties as well, including the Bund, which ran institutions such as Yiddish schools, a youth movement, a student movement, and a cultural club. Agudath Israel was also very active in the city; its strength and influence were largely due to the works and the stature of Rabbi Mordekhai Dubin, who was elected four times to the Latvian *Saeima* and was considered one of the most prominent Jewish leaders in Latvia.

The Jews of Riga participated in cultural and sporting activities that were organized by the student unions, belonged to various sports unions, including Maccabi, *Hakoah*, and *Hapo'el*, were members of or attended a Jewish theater, a music conservatory, and a choir, and published newspapers and various periodicals in Yiddish and other languages.

In the wake of a coup led by Karlis Ulmanis in May 1934, which put an end to democratic rule in Latvia, Jewish affairs were handed over to the administration of Agudath Israel and its leader, Rabbi Dubin. Once the Jewish schools accepted the curriculum of Agudath Israel and became imbued with the spirit of that organization, many Jewish parents opted to send their children to Latvian public schools instead.

Soviet occupation: In June 1940, the Red Army occupied Riga. In the context of the new economic policy, the banks, industries, and large businesses owned by Jews were nationalized. The new state of affairs nevertheless benefited numerous Jews, who found employment in factories as consultants, experts, officials, and managers. They, moreover, became involved in municipal and national institutions that had previously been closed to them, including the police and security services. The number of Jewish students in academic institutions doubled. Jewish political activity in the community's various organizations and parties was

Riga
Warning sign on the ghetto fence: "Anyone who passes this fence or attempts to make contact with ghetto inhabitants will be shot without warning." (YV)

discontinued, but synagogues remained open. The Jewish educational network underwent a structural and conceptual reorganization in the spirit of the new regime, and in all schools Yiddish was introduced as the language of instruction. Many students joined the Communist youth movement, and young people joined the "Workers' Guard," either of their own free will or under pressure from the authorities. In October 1940, a Yiddish theater opened in Riga.

On June 14, 1941, the authorities began to arrest and deport to Siberia thousands of Riga's Jews, including Zionist activists, and especially Revisionists, Bundists, members of Agudath Israel (including Rabbi Mordekhai Dubin), members of the bourgeoisie, and about 250 Jewish refugees from Germany and Austria.

German (Nazi) occupation: Following the German attack on the Soviet Union in June 1941, the Red Army retreated from Riga as it waged battles with Latvian nationalists. Within Red Army ranks were Jews that fought alongside the Soviets and fell in battle. At least 5,000 Jews left the city together with the Soviets— soldiers, official evacuees, and those who managed to flee on their own. Many Jewish refugees from other localities who attempted to flee from the Germans found themselves trapped in the city.

On the eve of the German occupation of Riga on July 1, 1941, there were approximately 40,000 Jews in the city. From July to October 1941, the German authorities published a series of decrees against the Jews, who were required to register and wear a Star-of-David patch, forbidden to use public transportation or walk on the pavement, and assigned to forced labor. Riga's Jewish inhabitants were thrown out of educational institutions and prohibited from engaging in the liberal professions (with the exception of doctors, who were only permitted to treat Jews); property was confiscated, and harsh supervision was imposed, restricting access to the rest. The purchase of food was limited to three shops in "the Moscow suburb," a poor area in the northern part of the city that was populated by indigent Jews and Russians. Kosher slaughter was outlawed. In that period, the Jews of Riga were unprotected from abductions for forced labor and acts of brutality and rape. Many were cast out of their homes to make way for Germans, and their money, possessions, and valuables were confiscated. They were pushed out of food lines and thrown out of hospitals.

Ghetto setup and internal life: In mid-August 1941, German police, under the command of SS Major Rudolf Lange commander of the SD and SIPO in Riga, began to concentrate the Jews of Riga into a ghetto, which consisted of about 9,000 square meters allocated in the Moscow suburb. The ghetto was sealed on October 23, 1941. According to a German report, 29,602 Jews lived in the ghetto at that time: 8,212 men, 15,738 women, and 5,652 children. The relatively small male population is attributed to the evacuation of many of the men during the Soviet retreat and to the murder of many Jewish men in July.

The ghetto was headed by an Aeltestenrat that had been established even before the ghetto was sealed. The council of elders was headed by the lawyer Mikhael Eliyashev, who had previously led an organization of Jewish fighters for Latvian independence. The Altestenrat included various departments dealing with law, construction, statistics, and other civic matters. The Jewish Order Service was headed by Michael Rosenthal and employed about eighty policemen.

The ghetto was surrounded by a high fence with Latvian policemen posted at its gates. Movement into and out of the ghetto without a special permit was forbidden. Latvian policemen entered the ghetto and committed acts of robbery, violence, and rape. The ghetto was extremely overcrowded, its buildings were dilapidated, and the sanitary conditions and food supply were poor.

The employment office of the Altestenrat regulated the supply of Jewish forced laborers to the Germans. The Jews were employed at unskilled, hard labor and were occasionally sent out in groups to farms and peat mines outside Riga. Artisans worked for army and police units and other German bodies under relatively tolerable conditions, and a small group of skilled technicians was given preferential treatment. Women were employed in cleaning and kitchen work. Jews were removed from the ghetto to various labor camps in and around Riga; a number of them lived in nearby barracks.

The Aeltestenrat made efforts to improve physical conditions in the ghetto. It operated the *Linat Zedek* hospital, headed by Dr. Vladimir Mintz, as well as a clinic, a pharmacy, and an old-age home. The council also ran a laundry and a shoemaker's workshop and provided other similar services to the residents of the ghetto; moreover, it found employment for those of limited work fitness. Schools and soup kitchens were also operating in the ghetto.

Murder operations: Mass murders of Jewish men began in the first month of the occupation. On July 4, Latvian rioters burned down the great synagogue in Riga, with 400 to 500 Jews locked inside. They continued burning synagogues, so that by the end of the month only one Jewish house of prayer remained. Inspired by the German security police, Latvian volunteers, members of ultra-nationalist organizations—who eventually organized as a Latvian auxiliary police unit—began to arrest Jewish men and incarcerate them in jails, in police headquarters, and the cellars of the Latvian fascist organization. Following several days of torture and cruel abuse, the Jewish detainees were taken in groups and killed in pits in the Bikerniki forest. According to a German security police report, 2,400 Jews had been murdered in Riga by July 16, and another 2,000 remained incarcerated in jail. From among those imprisoned, doctors and a few artisans were released, and nearly all others were murdered.

On November 27, the Germans informed the Jews of Riga that they would be resettled in the east. Two days later, the Germans amassed the Jewish workers, about 4,400 men in all, in a separate area in the northeastern corner of the ghetto that later became known as "the small ghetto." That evening, about 300 women who were registered as seamstresses were detained separately, in a prison. On

November 30, 1941, German SS soldiers entered the ghetto under Lange's orders, accompanied by Latvian policemen headed by Herbert Cukurs. Approximately 800 Jews, including babies and old people, were murdered during the operation, and most of the ghetto's residents (about 15,000 Jews, predominantly women) were forced to march in the freezing cold about eight kilometers to the Rumbuli forest, watched by the Latvian population. There, in pits that had been prepared ahead of time, they were murdered by Germans under the command of SS police officer Friedrich Jeckeln; the Germans were helped by Latvians. About 950 German Jews who had arrived in Riga that very day on a transport that had set out from Berlin on November 27, 1941, were also killed then in the Rumbuli forest.

Over 10,000 now people resided in what was called "the large ghetto," including most of the members of the Aeltestenrat, the celebrated eighty-year-old historian Simon Dubnow, and the chief rabbi of Riga, Rabbi Zack. On December 7–9 1941, they were marched to their deaths in Rumbuli forest. The mass killing was carried out under the command of SS officer Franz Stahlecker and the Latvian militia leader, Victor Arajs. Following the murder operation, the 300 seamstresses were released from the prison and returned to the ghetto area; they were allocated a few separate buildings in what later came to be known as the "women's ghetto."

On February 5, 1942, the SS, led by Gerhard Maywald, Lange's deputy, carried out a murder operation in which about 1,500 of the German Jews then living in the large ghetto (see below) were killed. About 1,900 other deportees (2,500 according to another estimate), many of them children and elderly people, were led to their death in another killing operation carried out on March 15, 1942. These operations severely undermined the conviction of the residents of the big ghetto that most would be assured survival if only they worked hard enough.

The German Ghetto (*Reichsjudenghetto*): Immediately after the December 1941 murder operations, as soon as the large ghetto was emptied of Latvian Jews, the Germans began to fill it with Jews deported from Germany, Austria, and Czechoslovakia. The first group arrived as early as December 10, 1941. During the coming weeks, deportation trains pulled in to the ghetto from various cities in the Reich, each transport containing about 1,000 Jews. Upon arrival at the train station, a selection was carried out among the deportees—the ill and elderly were shot to death, and most of the others were taken to the ghetto. All in all, of the approximately 20,000 Jews deported from the Reich area to Riga, about 11,000 are estimated to have reached the ghetto.

Within the ghetto the deportees were organized into ten groups, based on the transport's city of origin: Cologne, Hanover, Stuttgart, Hamburg, Berlin, Bochum, Leipzig, Dresden, Vienna, and Prague. In the big ghetto, which at that time was given the name *Reichsjudenghetto*, the death rate was high among the deportees, who were unaccustomed to living under their harsh new conditions. Both ghettos were under the authority of SS officer Kurt Krause, who introduced a reign of terror. A "Jewish elder" was appointed for each of the two ghettos, as was a chief of the Jewish Order Service. A deportee named Max Leiser, who arrived with the first group, from Cologne, was placed at the head of the Aeltestenrat of the entire large ghetto, while another deportee from the same group, Herbert Schultz, was appointed to be in charge of arranging a framework for Jewish labor. Each day, Jewish laborers marched to their places of work outside the ghetto and returned in the evening. Another central figure in the ghetto was a Jewish man named Günther Fleischel, who managed to develop personal ties with Krause and who became infamous for informing on Jews who attempted to smuggle food into the ghetto.

Riga, August 22, 1941
Jewish woman forced to sweep the city streets (IWM)

Despite the somber mood caused by the mass murder operations carried out on February 1942, the residents of the big ghetto tried to reorganize their lives as best they could. Survivors recall the order and cleanliness of the ghetto's streets, its lovely gardens, the organization of educational frameworks for children and of cultural activities for adults, and a small synagogue that was active in the ghetto.

The relationship between the Jews in the two ghettos was complex. Despite the prejudices and cultural differences that existed between the Jews of eastern Europe and those of central Europe, there were also signs of cooperation and mutual assistance. When the deportees from central Europe arrived, there were attempts by residents of the small ghetto to offer them food supplies. The Latvian Jews whose children had already been murdered sympathized with the distress of the deportees' children. Later, Dr. Hans Aufrecht of Cologne organized a hospital in the big ghetto in which Latvian Jews also received treatment and whose staff featured Jewish Latvian doctors as well.

In the early months of 1942, the institutions of the small ghetto, headed by Arthur (Aron) Kelman, were also reorganized. About 4,000 men and 300 women lived in the small ghetto at that time, in separate areas. Most of the Latvian Jews continued working outside the ghetto for the Germans, and a minority worked inside the ghetto in its internal institutions. The small ghetto, which held Jews without co-dependent family members, was spared starvation and epidemics. While the official food rations were insufficient for survival, they were complemented by additional food received at the workplace, and especially by the constant smuggling of food supplies, medication, and heating fuel, despite the prohibition of such activity and the harsh penalties meted out to those caught. During 1942, close to 700 Jews who had been deported from Kaunas* arrived in the big ghetto, and they organized a school for the few children they had brought with them; they also held cultural activities.

Underground and resistance: In January 1942, an underground was formed in the small ghetto; it acquired arms, trained, and established contact with underground groups outside the ghetto in order to join up with the partisans fighting in the forests. On October 28, 1942, a group of ten underground members left the ghetto to join the partisans, but fell victim to a German ambush. Subsequent to the discovery of the underground, the Germans took punitive measures against the ghetto's residents. In one such instance on October 31, 1942, a group of forty-one Jewish policemen was called up for a routine roll call. Without any warning, they were shot by machine-gun fire in the roll-call yard. Most fell dead, and the few who managed to escape were caught and, after a short struggle, executed. An SS man was also killed during the incident. Meanwhile, the Germans also arrested some 300 Latvian Jews, whom they subjected to a cruel interrogation and murdered.

In the wake of these incidents, the independence of the small ghetto was abolished on November 1, 1942, and it was united with the big ghetto, known, as noted, as "the German ghetto," which was now divided into two sections: the ghetto for the Reich Jews and the ghetto for the Latvian Jews. The latter had one representative on the council of the German ghetto, and its Jewish Order Service was reorganized and made subordinate to that of the German ghetto. These developments stepped up the tensions already manifest between the Reich Jews and the Latvian Jews. For a long time afterwards, searches were performed to uncover underground cells and to arrest their members.

Ghetto liquidation: Workers from the small ghetto had previously begun to stay overnight at their workplaces in the labor camps, including, among others, the Jungfernhof labor camp; once the underground was exposed, this phenomenon increased. The ghetto gradually emptied of its residents, and ties between the different groups of Jews weakened. In the summer of 1943, following Heinrich Himmler's June 21 order to liquidate the remaining ghettos in Ostland, the Germans began to move groups of Jews to the Kaiserwald concentration camp (near Riga) and its satellite camps, where close to 8,000 Jews were held until late August 1943, most of them from the Riga ghetto. Living conditions in these camps were very harsh, and the death rate was high.

The ghetto was liquidated on November 2, 1943. As the Jewish laborers left for their daily routine, German and Latvian policeman led by Lange and Krause invaded the ghetto, gathered up all the children, the elderly and the ill, as well as a few other adults who remained (including teachers and the ghetto hospital staff members) and deported them to Auschwitz, where nearly all were murdered. Between 2,500 and 3,000 Jews (4,000 according to another estimate) were murdered or deported in the operation.

After the ghetto's liquidation, the Jewish laborers were transferred to Kaiserwald and to other camps, and the ghetto ceased to exist. All of the surviving Latvian Jews, including the Jews of Riga (approximately 14,000 according to testimonies), were incarcerated in the Kaiserwald concentration camp and its various satellite camps.

The Red Army liberated Riga in October 1944.

RIMASZÉCS

TOWNLET IN GÖMÖR AND KISHONT COUNTY, HUNGARY

(After World War II in Czechoslovakia/Slovakia; Slovak: **Rimavská Seč**)

Coordinates:
48°18' | 20°15'

The last national census conducted in Hungary prior to the German occupation, taken in January 1941, recorded 126 Jewish inhabitants in Rimaszecs, roughly 7 percent of the total population. Most were merchants and artisans. The townlet's Jewish community was Orthodox and maintained a Talmud Torah.

After World War I, Rimaszecs, which was formerly under Hungarian rule, became part of Czechoslovakia. Later, as per the First Vienna Award (November 2, 1938), the townlet was annexed to Hungary.

The German army occupied Hungary on March 19, 1944, leaving the Hungarian administration intact and operational. Hungarian national and local authorities decreed the ghettoization and deportation of the Jews. The ghetto was established in Rimaszecs in late May 1944. Aside from the local Jews, the Jews from the County-District of Feled were confined in the ghetto, for a total of 466 inhabitants. In June 1944, the ghetto inhabitants were transferred to the entrainment center in the stables of the local mining company in Salgotarjan*, and deported to Auschwitz on June 13, 1944.

RIMASZOMBAT

TOWNLET IN GÖMÖR AND KISHONT COUNTY, HUNGARY

(After World War II in Czechoslovakia/Slovakia; Slovak: **Rimavská Sobota**)

Coordinates: 48°23' | 20°02'

The last national census conducted in Hungary prior to the German occupation, taken in January 1941, recorded 635 Jewish inhabitants in Rimaszombat, approximately 9 percent of the total population. They dominated the local woodworking industry and timber trade, and most were merchants and artisans. Many were also clerks. The townlet had an Orthodox Jewish community, a Talmud Torah, and various Jewish social organizations.

After World War I, Rimaszombat, which was formerly under Hungarian rule, became part of Czechoslovakia. Later, as per the First Vienna Award (November 2, 1938), the townlet was annexed to Hungary. Between the two World Wars, the Jewish Party was the most popular among the Jewish parties in the townlet. The majority of the Jewish youths belonged to various Zionist youth movements.

The German army occupied Hungary on March 19, 1944. A census conducted in the second week of April 1944 showed that 546 Jews belonged to the Orthodox Jewish community of Rimaszombat.

The Hungarian administration remained intact and operational after the occupation. Hungarian national and local authorities decreed the ghettoization and deportation of the Jews. The ghetto in Rimaszombat, located about one kilometer from the townlet, was established at the end of April 1944. A soup kitchen operated in the ghetto.

In June 1944, the inhabitants of the ghetto were transferred to the entrainment center in the stables of the local mining company in Salgotarjan*, and were deported to Auschwitz on June 13, 1944.

ROGACHEV

(**Gomel District, Belarus**)
(Yiddish: **Rohatshov**; Belarussian: **Rahachou**)

COUNTY SEAT, GOMEL DISTRICT, BELARUS, USSR

During the war: Military Administration Area

Coordinates: 53°05' | 30°03'

On the eve of the German invasion of the Soviet Union, there were about 4,600 Jews in Rogachev, roughly one-third of the population. Many practiced artisan trades, some held white- or blue-collar jobs in government factories and institutions, and a few had become farmers. The townlet had a government school that taught in Yiddish.

After the German invasion, many Jewish men in Rogachev were inducted into the Red Army. Quite a few Jewish residents evidently used the railroad that passed through the townlet to evacuate or flee eastward to the Soviet interior. The Germans first occupied Rogachev on July 3–17, 1941, and reoccupied the townlet on August 14, 1941. By the beginning of October, the Jews who had stayed in Rogachev were ghettoized and seized for forced labor.

In October 1941, Jews from the Gorodets* ghetto and, apparently, from additional locations were concentrated in Rogachev.

The ghetto was liquidated on October 31 or in November 1941 (sources vary on the date), when its approximately 1,500 or 2,700 inhabitants (sources vary on the figure) were dispossessed. On the following day, they were murdered near Rogachev by a group of Germans and local police. Children of mixed marriages were murdered later.

ROGACHEV

(Zhitomir District, Ukraine)
(Ukrainian: **Rohachiv**)

TOWNLET IN BARANOVKA COUNTY, ZHITOMIR DISTRICT, UKRAINE, USSR

During the war:
Reichskommissariat Ukraine

Coordinates:
50°30' | 27°30'

In the mid-1920s, there were about 750 Jews in Rogachev, roughly three-quarters of the townlet's population.

The Germans occupied Rogachev in early July 1941. Upon their arrival, they commanded the Jews to relocate to a single street, wear a yellow star, and perform forced labor under the abuse of Ukrainian police. In August 1941, Jewish men aged fifteen to fifty were executed. On Yom Kippur (October 1), all the remaining Jews in Rogachev with the exception of between twenty to twenty-five skilled workers and their families were assembled at the townlet club. The adults were separated from the children and murdered in a nearby forest on the road to Kamennyi Brod. Two days later, Germans assisted by Ukrainian police led the children out of the townlet and murdered them.

About one month later, the skilled workers and their families were transferred to the Novograd-Volynskiy* ghetto.

ROHATYN

COUNTY SEAT, STANISŁAWÓW DISTRICT, POLAND
(After World War II in the USSR/Ukraine; Russian: **Rogatin**)

During the war: General Gouvernement, Galicia District

Coordinates:
49°25' | 24°37'

In the 1930s, about 3,000 Jews lived in Rohatyn, representing approximately half of the townlet's population. They were mostly merchants and artisans, and a number were members of the liberal professions. Various Jewish parties were active in Rohatyn, the Zionist organizations being especially prominent, and the townlet boasted youth movements and sports associations. Some of the townlet's children attended a Talmud Torah or completed their Jewish studies at a supplementary Hebrew school. Jewish aid and welfare organizations operated in Rohatyn.

After the Red Army occupied the townlet on September 18, 1939, all activities of the Jewish community and political parties were discontinued, with the exception of the synagogues, which remained open. As private factories were nationalized and commerce gradually declined, Jews were integrated into the Soviet economic system. About 2,000 Jewish refugees arrived in Rohatyn from western Poland.

In the spring of 1940, Jewish political activists and members of the middle class were exiled to the Soviet interior, and in late June 1940, several hundred refugees were also exiled. When the Soviets retreated eastward in June 1941, a few dozen young Jews joined them.

The Germans occupied Rohatyn on July 2, 1941. A few days later, the Ukrainian police began to humiliate and abuse Jews. In one instance, about 500 Jews were rounded up in the synagogue and forced to pray for Hitler's victory. In late July, a Judenrat was established in the townlet, headed by Shlomo Emernet, and among its members were refugees from western Poland. A Jewish Order Service headed by M. Weisbrum was also established. The Judenrat was ordered to conduct a census of the Jewish population and to supply the Germans with hundreds of Jewish forced laborers and professionals. Through the Judenrat, Germans instructed the Jews to turn over valuables and levied large fines on the Jewish population. In December 1941, they demanded all of the furs in the Jews' possession.

In the fall of 1941, the Jews of Rohatyn were concentrated in a closed ghetto established in a poor, dilapidated neighborhood. Overcrowding and food shortages led to the spread of epidemic typhus, and dozens of Jews died daily. A poorly equipped hospital for contagious diseases was set up in the ghetto, serving mainly quarantine patients. In late 1941, overcrowding in the ghetto was exacerbated by the influx of additional Jews from nearby localities. Members of Ukrainian gangs periodically invaded the ghetto to rob and plunder property. A group of young Jews established a self-defense militia and occasionally succeeded in driving off the rioters.

On March 20, 1942, the first mass murder operation was carried out in Rohatyn. German and Ukrainian policemen under the command of Hans Krueger entered the ghetto, rounded up the Jews, led them to pits prepared near the train station, and shot them to death. Jews who attempted to escape from the round-up area or from the ghetto were summarily shot. About 2,300 Jews were massacred in the operation, including several members of the Judenrat. After the operation, the area of the ghetto was reduced, but once again, Jews from other localities were brought in, causing cases of starvation and epidemics to soar in the summer of 1942. Many of the ghetto inhabitants frantically prepared hiding places in it in anticipation of the impending operation.

On the morning of September 21, 1942, the second operation was launched. The Germans rounded up thousands of Jews brought in from surrounding localities and loaded them on a deportation train that stopped at the Rohatyn station. They carried out a concurrent, large-scale operation in the ghetto. As soon as they learned that the Germans and Ukrainians were approaching the ghetto, many Jews entered the hiding places they had prepared. The Germans and Ukrainians conducted extensive searches and within a few hours had rounded up about 1,000 Jews, whom they loaded onto a deportation train headed to the Belzec death camp. Most of the approximately 300 Jews who attempted to escape from the train cars were killed; few individuals succeeding in returning to the ghetto. In October–November 1942, the Germans continued to concentrate Jews from other communities in the Rohatyn ghetto. On December 8, 1942, the Germans carried out yet another operation. About 250 to 300 elderly and ill Jews were killed on site, while some 1,300 to 1,500 Jews, including the hospital staff, were deported to their deaths in Belzec.

Following the operation, about 2,700 Jews remained in the ghetto. At the beginning of 1943, "small-scale" murders persisted in the ghetto, including the mass murder of all typhus patients in April. The area of the ghetto was continually reduced, and German supervision of life in the ghetto grew more stringent. Jews nevertheless attempted to flee from the ghetto by various means. Dozens found places to hide in and around the city with Ukrainian and Polish families, who risked their lives to save the fugitives; others fled to the forests and organized in bunkers; still others endeavored to obtain forged "Aryan" papers. Many Jews were handed over to the authorities or murdered by hostile locals.

In mid-May 1943, the Judenrat, together with several Jewish policemen, decided to devise plans to obtain weapons and smuggle groups of armed youths out of the ghetto into the forest. A delegation of young Jews was sent to investigate the matter. As soon as the Germans discovered the strategizing, they invaded the ghetto on June 6, 1943, executed the members of the Jewish Order Service, and began to liquidate the ghetto. During the three-day operation, they hurled hand grenades and set fire to buildings to force the Jews out of their hiding places. They then led the Jews to pits that had been dug ahead of time in the new cemetery and shot them to death.

For many weeks after the liquidation of the ghetto, the Germans and their helpers continued to hunt down Jews, apprehending many. They uncovered three bunkers, named Stalingrad, Sevastopol, and Leningrad, which contained arms as well as food sufficient for a protracted underground stay. Sixty armed Jews holed up in one of the bunkers returned fire at the Germans.

ROKIŠKIS

(Yiddish: **Rakishok**)

COUNTY SEAT, LITHUANIA

During the war:
Reichskommissariat Ostland

Coordinates:
55°58' | 25°35'

On the eve of World War II, about 3,500 Jews lived in Rokiskis, representing roughly one-third of the town's population. The Jews of the town, most of whom belonged to the Hasidic movement, earned their livelihood from commerce and artisanship. Several also practiced the liberal professions. The community had active chapters of Zionist parties and Agudath Israel.

After Lithuania was annexed to the Soviet Union in 1940, private businesses were nationalized and the activities of the Jewish parties were discontinued.

Rokiskis was occupied by the Germans on June 28, 1941, and two Jews were murdered that very day. Two days later, the Germans drove out Jews who had traveled to the town from the surrounding area. After several days, the town's Jews were concentrated in one area, with the men separated from the women and children. The men were apparently held in stables, while the women and children were held in a holiday resort located near the town. The Jews were brought daily to work for local farmers. Within a short time, the town instituted a Jewish council headed by Reznikovits and Yaakov Kark.

On August 15–16, 1941, the Jewish men were taken to a nearby village and shot to death in pits. Prior to the murder, Rabbi Zelig Orlovitz spoke words of encouragement and called upon the Jews to die with heads held high in sanctification of God's name. On August 25, 1941, women, children, and the elderly, altogether some 2,000 people, were murdered.

ROKITNO

TOWN IN SARNY COUNTY, VOLHYNIA DISTRICT, POLAND

(After World War II in the USSR/Ukraine; Ukrainian: **Rokytne**; Russian: **Rokitnoye**).

During the war:
Reichskommissariat Ukraine

Coordinates:
51°17' | 27°13'

During the interwar years, there were about 3,000 Jews in Rokitno, approximately one-fifth of the town's population. They made their living from the lumber trade and the manufacture of wood products; they owned a glass factory and plied various crafts. Rokitno's Jews availed themselves of the services of a Jewish savings-and-loan association and a free-loan fund. Their educational institutions included a Talmud Torah, and a Hebrew-language Tarbut school and kindergarten. The community enjoyed the services of both Yiddish and Hebrew libraries. Zionist parties and youth movements were active in the town, as was the Bund.

During the Soviet rule (September 1939–June 1941) all political and religious activities were banned in Rokitno. On July 10, 1941, the Soviets retreated eastward and several hundred Jews left with them. The Ukrainians set up their own municipal regime and police force in the town. Several days later the Germans took over.

On August 5, 1941, the German military administration gave instructions through the Ukrainian regime to establish a five-member Judenrat, headed by Aharon Slutsk. The Jews were forced to wear Star-of-David armbands and remit a ransom.

The Jews of Rokitno and neighboring villages were ghettoized on April 15, 1942. Although the ghetto was unfenced, it was guarded by Ukrainian police and the inmates were not allowed to bring in food.

On August 26, 1942, the Jews were ordered to assemble in the market square. When German and Ukrainian police surrounded the 1,631 Jews who had gathered, inhabitants attempted a mass escape. Between 100 and 400 Jews (sources vary on the figures) were immediately killed, and some 700 managed to flee to the forests. The remaining 800 were transported by train to the Poleska camp in Sarny*. Several of the new arrivals participated in the mass escape from Sarny the following day, but most were murdered along with the Jews of Sarny and the vicinity.

Most of those who fled to the forests were turned over to the Germans by Ukrainians in the ensuing days. The others were assisted by Polish peasants and Ukrainian Baptists.

ROPCZYCE

TOWNLET IN RZESZÓW COUNTY, LWÓW DISTRICT, POLAND

During the war: General Gouvernement, Cracow District

Coordinates:
50°03' | 21°37'

When World War II broke out, about 850 Jews lived in Ropczyce, representing approximately one-quarter of the townlet's population. They earned their livelihood from small-scale commerce and peddling as well as from artisanship, particularly in the garment industry. The needy were supported by the JDC, a free-loan society, and a cooperative bank. The community's children attended a Talmud Torah and a supplementary Hebrew school. Ropczyce had local chapters of the Zionist parties and youth movements, which maintained pioneer training facilities, as well as a branch of Agudath Israel.

The Germans occupied Ropczyce on September 8, 1939, and immediately began to seize Jews for forced labor. They murdered Rabbi Yitzhak Liberman and the synagogue caretaker.

In late 1939, a Judenrat was established in Ropczyce, headed by Arnold Meister. It was ordered to organize the forced labor of Ropczyce's Jews and also assisted refugees and war casualties with housing and money. A clinic was established for babies, children, and nursing mothers, who were also given supplementary food rations.

In April 1940, there were 773 Jews living in Ropczyce of whom sixty were refugees from western Poland. In late 1940, the Judenrat established a public soup kitchen with the help of the townlet's wealthier Jews and the JDC chapter in Cracow*. In 1941, medical assistance was provided to the local Jews. In June 1941, a chapter of the JSS was opened in the townlet.

By the end of 1941, some 1,050 Jews lived in Ropczyce and in the localities subordinate to its Jewish community.

In May 1942, about fifty Jewish men from Ropczyce were transferred to the labor camp in Pustkow. In an operation carried out in June 1942, another 150 men were transferred and 23 Jews were killed in the townlet.

In late June 1942, the last Jews remaining in the surrounding localities were deported to Ropczyce, along with Jews from Wielopole Skrzynskie*, and a ghetto was established in the townlet. On July 23, 1942, the ghetto was liquidated. All the elderly Jews and children were killed on site. Those considered fit for work were brought to Sedziszow*, and from there were sent together with the local Jews to the Belzec death camp.

Ropczyce
Jewish men rounded up in the city square prior to their deportation to the Pustkow labor camp (YV)

ROSLAVL

COUNTY SEAT, SMOLENSK DISTRICT, RUSSIAN FEDERATION, USSR

During the war: Military Administration Area

Coordinates:
53°57' | 32°52'

On the eve of World War II, close to 3,000 Jews lived in Roslavl, representing about 7 percent of the town's total population. The Jews of Roslavl engaged in artisanship, but a number were also employed as blue- or white-collar workers in state-owned enterprises and institutions. In the 1920s, the community ran an orphanage and a Jewish club.

Roslavl was occupied by the Germans on August 3, 1941; most of the town's Jews apparently managed to evacuate to the east immediately beforehand. Once the town was in German hands, all the Jews were registered and required to wear a Star-of-David patch. All contact between the Jews and the local population was outlawed. On August 6, 1941, several Jews were murdered in Roslavl by German soldiers.

In late October 1941, between some 600 and 800 of the Jews remaining in the town were concentrated in a ghetto that consisted of one street encircled by barbed wire. Overcrowding was severe.

The ghetto was liquidated one month later, in late November or early December 1941, when its inhabitants were shot to death and buried in the Jewish cemetery. A Jewish tailor employed by the Germans was spared, although he too was murdered a short time later.

ROSSASNA

(Belarussian: **Rasasna**)

TOWNLET IN DUBROVNO COUNTY, VITEBSK DISTRICT, BELARUS, USSR

During the war: Military Administration Area

Coordinates:
54°38' | 30°52'

In the mid-1920s, there were about thirty Jewish families in Rossasna. The Germans occupied the townlet on July 16–18, 1941.

In early March 1942, a ghetto was established for the Jews in a school building placed under Belarussian police guard. One month later, on April 2, 1942, the Jews were deported to Lyady*, where they were murdered along with the local Jews in the ghetto.

ROSSONY

(Belarussian: **Rason'**)

COUNTY SEAT, VITEBSK DISTRICT, BELARUS, USSR

During the war: Military Administration Area

Coordinates:
55°53' | 28°48'

In the late 1930s, there were about 50 Jews in Rossony and some 400 Jews in the county. The Germans occupied the townlet on July 15, 1941. In late September and early October, Jews from all over the county were concentrated in Rossony, including thirty-three refugees who had fled Poland in 1939.

The Jews were concentrated in a ghetto established in a tailors' workshop building and surrounded with barbed wire. They were required to wear yellow Star-of-David armbands. At first, forced labor was not imposed, and the Jews were permitted to leave the ghetto during the day to engage in trade and obtain food from the local population. Conditions worsened in December 1941, when the ghetto was surrounded by German and Belarussian police guards. The isolation led to hunger and a rise in mortality rates among ghetto residents.

The ghetto was liquidated in early January 1942, when its inhabitants were murdered near the townlet by Germans under the command of Otto Lenz, assisted by Belarussian police.

RÓWNE

**COUNTY SEAT, VOLHYNIA
DISTRICT, POLAND**
(After World War II in the
USSR/Ukraine; Ukrainian:
Rivne; Russian: **Rovno**)

During the war:
Reichskommissariat Ukraine

Coordinates:
50°37' | 26°15'

During the interwar years, about 25,000 Jews lived in Rowne, approximately half of the town's population. Some were merchants and artisans, while others owned large enterprises, including soap and oil factories, the largest brewery in Volhynia, a flour mill, and food factories. The Jews of Rowne constituted a majority of the town's residents who engaged in artisanship, commerce, and liberal professions (law, medicine, and engineering). They belonged to several trade unions. Jewish economic activity was abetted by several Jewish savings-and-loan associations and other financial institutions such as two mutual-aid societies, a loan fund, and an insurance company. The town had an array of traditional Jewish welfare and charitable institutions, including a hospital, an orphanage, an old-age home, and a branch of TOZ. Educational institutions included two Yeshivot, Jewish high schools, and an ORT vocational school. Several Jewish public libraries in the town supplied inhabitants with thousands of volumes. Leisure activities included a drama group and sports clubs. Several regional newspapers were likewise published in Rowne. The town had chapters of Zionist youth movements and parties, as well as the Bund, the Communists (who operated in the underground), and Agudath Israel.

In 1919, dozens of Jews were injured or murdered in a pogrom carried out by forces under Simon Petlyura.

During the Soviet rule (December 1939–June 1941), factories and businesses were nationalized, goods were shipped to the east, and private commerce was abolished. Artisans were required to reorganize and doctors to close down their private practices. All Jewish institutions and organizations were disbanded. The Tarbut Hebrew-language high school was replaced by a high school and three primary schools that taught the Soviet curriculum in Yiddish. Several Jewish manufacturers, wholesalers, and public figures were deported from the town. Many youth movement activists left for the Land of Israel via Vilna* and Romania.

In October 1940, several leaders of the Hashomer Hatzair Zionist youth movement—Tosia Altman, Yishayahu Weiner, Yosef Kaplan, and Adam Rand—gathered in Rowne and moved on to Lwow*. A local leadership remained in Rowne, but a large number of arrests paralyzed the movement's activities by the time of the German invasion.

The Germans occupied Rowne on June 28, 1941. As they approached the city, some 2,000 Jews fled eastward. Ukrainian and German police began kidnapping Jews for forced labor and committing murders. Erich Koch, appointed *Reichskommissar* for the Ukraine, chose Rowne as his base of operations. By the end of July 1941, hundreds of Jews had been murdered, including intellectuals and public figures. One month later, the number of murder victims had risen to several thousand. A great deal of Jewish property was confiscated, and the Jews were required to remit large ransoms.

In early August 1941, Jews were ordered to wear white armbands with blue Stars of David, which were replaced on September 19, 1941, by two yellow badges. A Judenrat was appointed under Dr. Moshe Bergman; his deputy was Leon Sukharchuk. Both subsequently committed suicide, and Bergman was replaced by Chaim Ressner, a Bundist from Warsaw*. An informer for the Germans was placed in command of the Jewish Order Service.

On September 1, 1941, the German army transferred parts of the Ukraine to Reichskommissar Erich Koch, who began to set up his offices in Rowne. It is likely that the decision to exterminate the Jews of Rowne by gunfire in order to make room for clerks in German government institutions was made in a meeting held between Koch and the SS and police commanders in late October 1941.

On November 5, 1941, Koch summoned the heads of the Judenrat and informed them that Jews without labor permits were to report for transport to labor.

On November 6–7, 1941, about 21,000 Jews were taken to pits that Soviet prisoners had excavated outside of town and were shot dead. The murders were committed by between eighty and one hundred members of an external detail of Einsatzkommando 5. German policemen from Police Battalion 320 and a large number of Ukrainian policemen secured and guarded the area.

The Rowne ghetto was established in December 1941 for the 5,000 remaining Jews in the town. Although the ghetto was not fenced, the inmates were forbidden to leave without a permit, other than to perform forced labor. Most Jewish property was looted and some was allotted to Ukrainians.

On July 13, 1942, all the Jews in the ghetto were placed aboard a train to Kostopol*, where they were murdered in pits. On the eve of the liquidation, many Jews barricaded their doors and windows, compelling German and Ukrainian police officers to use hand grenades in order to break into the inhabitants' homes.

There were quite a few individual acts of resistance. Sima Gimberg killed two Germans who had come to arrest him; Nyonya Kopilnik shot and killed three Germans; Yitzhak Schneider acquired a handgun and hand grenades from a Pole and attacked the five Germans who came to arrest him. A woman named Dvorich lured German officers to her home, where she murdered them. As she was being led to prison, she drew a bayonet from the scabbard of one of the policemen, plunged it into his chest, and was shot dead. Liza Gelfand, the wife of a Soviet officer, worked in a restaurant frequented by German officers and helped to smuggle explosives into the restaurant in 1943. Many German officers perished in the explosion.

A number of Jews in the Rowne ghetto were saved by the German engineer Hermann Friedrich Graebe, who employed them as laborers and was subsequently named Righteous Among the Nations.

Many young Jews escaped Rowne shortly before the liquidation operation in July 1942, chiefly to towns in the vicinity such as Tuczyn*. In late 1942, they fled to the forests, where several joined Soviet partisan units.

RÓŻANA

(Yiddish: **Rozhenoy**)

TOWNLET IN IWACEWICZE COUNTY, POLESYE DISTRICT, POLAND

(After World War II in the USSR/Belarus; Belarussian, Russian: **Ruzhany**)

During the war: Bezirk Bialystok

Coordinates:
52°52' | 24°53'

During the interwar period, about 2,400 Jews lived in Rozana, comprising roughly two-thirds of the townlet's population. Most were petty merchants and artisans with access to the services of a free-loan society and a savings-and-loan association. The townlet had a Jewish hospital. Jewish educational establishments in Rozana included a Talmud Torah, a Hebrew-language school, and a Yiddish-language school. Zionist parties, the Bund, and a small group of Communists were active in the townlet, which also featured a pioneering Zionist training commune.

In 1919, Polish soldiers on a looting rampage attacked Jews living in the townlet, murdering six people. During the Soviet occupation, which began in 1939, a Jew from Rozana was delegated to the Belarussian Supreme Soviet in Minsk. Three Jewish factory owners and their families were exiled to the Russian interior. The townlet's Hebrew schools were closed, private trade was abolished, and artisans were organized in cooperatives.

The Germans occupied Rozana in late June 1941. Jews were ordered to wear yellow badges and were conscripted for forced labor. A Judenrat and Jewish Order Service were established. In July 1941, more than fifteen Jewish men, including the Jewish delegate to the Belarussian Soviet, were murdered outside the townlet. The Germans repeatedly demanded high ransoms and confiscated Jewish property.

In August 1941, an unfenced ghetto was established in Rozana. Food was brought in by peasants and Jews from two nearby Jewish farming localities, Pawlowo and Konstantynowo.

In the spring of 1942, several youths in the ghetto began to organize an escape to the forests.

On November 2, 1942, the Jews of the Rozana ghetto were rounded up. Concurrently, eight armed young Jews fled to the forest but returned. The Jews of the ghetto were marched to a bunker camp in Wolkowysk*, where some 20,000 Jews from Wolkowysk and nearby localities were interned. Approximately 500 stragglers and escapees were shot. On November 28, 1942, the Jews of Rozana were taken by train from Wolkowysk to the Treblinka death camp, where all but three were murdered.

ROZSNYÓ

TOWNLET IN GÖMÖR AND KISHONT COUNTY, HUNGARY
(After World War II in Czechoslovakia/Slovakia; Slovak: **Rožňava**)

Coordinates:
48°40' | 20°32'

The last national census conducted in Hungary prior to the German occupation, taken in January 1941, recorded 388 Jewish inhabitants in Rozsnyo, roughly 6 percent of the total population. Most were merchants and artisans; several were factory owners. The Jews in Rozsnyo were organized in a Neolog community and had a Jewish elementary school.

After World War I, Rozsnyo, which was formerly under Hungarian rule, became part of Czechoslovakia. Later, as per the First Vienna Award (November 2, 1938), the townlet was annexed to Hungary. Between the two World Wars, the Jewish Party was the most popular among the Jewish parties in the townlet. The majority of the Jewish youths belonged to various Zionist youth movements.

In 1942, during the deportations from Slovakia, many Jewish refugees arrived in Rozsnyo and were assisted by local Zionist organizations.

The German army occupied Hungary on March 19, 1944. The Hungarian administration remained intact and operational after the occupation. Hungarian national and local authorities decreed the ghettoization and deportation of the Jews. The Rozsnyo ghetto was established along one street, on May 12, 1944. Young people worked outside the ghetto and were required to return every day. After a few days, additional Jews from the County-District of Rozsnyo were forced to move into the overcrowded ghetto, where some 800 people now lived.

At the beginning of June 1944, the ghetto inhabitants were transferred to the entrainment center in a brick factory in Miskolc*. They were deported to Auschwitz in several transports between June 12 and 15, 1944.

ROŻYSZCZE

TOWNLET IN ŁUCK COUNTY, VOLHYNIA DISTRICT, POLAND
(After World War II in the USSR/Ukraine; Ukrainian: **Rozhysche**; Russian: **Rozhishche**)

During the war:
Reichskommissariat Ukraine

Coordinates:
50°55' | 25°16'

During the interwar years, there were about 4,000 Jews in Rozyszcze, accounting for roughly two-thirds of the townlet's population. Most were artisans and merchants who traded in clothing, agricultural produce, and lumber. Others owned looms, workshops, and retail establishments. They received help from the JDC, two Jewish savings-and-loan associations, and mutual-aid societies.

The community had a Talmud Torah, a Tarbut Hebrew-language kindergarten and school, a private school, and, for a while, a Yiddish-language CYSHO school. Libraries, sports clubs and drama groups serviced the population as well. Zionist youth parties and movements established training communes, and the Bund had an active chapter in townlet.

The Soviets assumed control of the area in September 1939. The factories were nationalized, and schools became Soviet institutions teaching in Yiddish.

The Germans occupied Rozyszcze on June 26, 1941, and a large number of Jews were killed in fighting. Dozens of young Jewish conscripts managed to leave the townlet. They were subsequently transferred to labor brigades, which secured their survival. When the Germans arrived, local Ukrainians looted Jewish property. In July 1941, the Germans murdered about 430 of Rozyszcze's Jews in two killing operations. The Jews in the townlet were made to wear white Star-of-David armbands until September 1941, when yellow badges were introduced. A Judenrat and a twenty-member Jewish Order Service were established. Jews were compelled to remit ransoms, surrender their valuables, and perform forced labor. In either October or December 1941 (depending on the source) around 600 of Rozyszcze's Jews were murdered.

In February 1942, the Jews were placed in a sealed ghetto to which Jews from surrounding villages were also brought. The Judenrat established a soup kitchen and a small hospital. Seventy-two young Jews were taken away to build Hitler's headquarters in Vinnitsa; all but one perished.

The Rozyszcze ghetto was liquidated on August 23, 1942. The Jews were taken to pits on the road to the village of Kopaczowka and murdered. About eighty managed to escape and survived with the help of Czech and Polish villagers. Additional fugitives joined Soviet partisan units.

RUBIEŻEWICZE

TOWNLET IN STOŁPCE COUNTY, NOWOGRÓDEK DISTRICT, POLAND
(After World War II in the USSR/Belarus; Belarussian: **Rubyazhevichy**; Russian: **Rubizhevichi**)

During the war:
Reichskommissariat Ostland

Coordinates:
53°41' | 26°52'

About 900 Jews lived in Rubiezewicze when World War II broke out, representing approximately 60 percent of the townlet's population. Most earned their livelihood from small commerce and artisanship. Zionist parties and youth movements were active in the community, as was Agudath Israel.

In the second half of September 1939, the Soviets occupied Rubiezewicze and introduced a Soviet economic, social, and educational system into the townlet.

On June 30, 1941, the Germans occupied Rubiezewicze and, a while later, ordered the establishment of a four-member Judenrat in the townlet. The Jews were required to wear a yellow badge and to submit high ransom payments in cash and valuables to the Germans.

On December 1, 1941, the Jews of Rubiezewicze were herded into an unfenced ghetto, together with Jews from a number of nearby localities. They lived in the ghetto under conditions of severe overcrowding and were permitted to leave only to perform forced labor. On January 25, 1942, about 300 Jews were sent to the Iwieniec* ghetto. Later, the Germans rounded up thirty-six Jewish men and women, forced them to dig a pit, and shot them. They also shot several Belarussian policemen who refused to shoot the Jews. On May 8, 1942, the Germans dispatched another 200 Jews to the Iwieniec ghetto, and on May 18, they sent yet another group.

The ghetto was liquidated on June 8, 1942, when the last remaining survivors of the ghetto were shot to death in the nearby Sienkiewicze forest.

RUDAMINA
(Yiddish: **Rudomin**)

TOWNLET IN SEINIAI – LAZDIJAI COUNTY, LITHUANIA

During the war:
Reichskommissariat Ostland

Coordinates:
54°35' | 25°24'

On the eve of World War II, about twenty Jewish families lived in Rudamina. They earned their livelihood from artisanship and farming.

In June 1940, after Lithuania was annexed to the Soviet Union, a number of Rudamina's businesses and shops were nationalized.

On June 22, 1941, the German army invaded Lithuania, and German soldiers entered Rudamina that same day. Lithuanian rioters took over the townlet. Jewish inhabitants were forced to wear a yellow badge and perform slave labor, and they were abused. The Jews of the townlet were concentrated in a ghetto of sorts in the Beit Midrash and a few partially demolished buildings.

On October 15, 1941, Rudamina's Jews were deported to a ghetto established on the Katkiskes estate, located near Lazdijai*, where they shared the fate of the local Jews.

RUDENSK

(Belarussian: **Rudzensk**)

COUNTY SEAT, MINSK DISTRICT, BELARUS, USSR

During the war:
Reichskommissariat Ostland

Coordinates:
53°36' | 27°52'

Shortly before World War II, there were about 170 Jews in Rudensk, roughly 7 percent of the population. During the era of Soviet rule, many of the townlet's Jewish inhabitants practiced artisan trades (some in cooperatives), and a few farmed at a Jewish kolkhoz.

The Germans occupied Rudensk on June 30, 1941. Some time later, the Jews were concentrated in a ghetto of sorts along a single street. On October 9–11, 1941, the ghetto was liquidated when all its inhabitants were murdered near the townlet in a large-scale operation conducted by Germans and local Lithuanians.

RUDKI

(Yiddish: **Ridik**)

COUNTY SEAT, LWÓW DISTRICT, POLAND
(After World War II in the USSR/Ukraine)

During the war: General Gouvernement, Galicia District

Coordinates:
49°39' | 23°29'

In the early 1930s, about 2,000 Jews lived in Rudki, representing roughly half of the townlet's population. About half of the Jewish breadwinners engaged in commerce, and several among them were prominent businessmen who traded in forest products, wood, and agricultural produce; about one-third were artisans, and a few were doctors, lawyers, and teachers. Rudki had various Zionist parties and youth movements.

In September 1939, the Germans occupied Rudki and controlled the townlet for two weeks, but towards the end of September 1939, it was handed over to Soviet control. Under the Soviets, the Jewish parties and community institutions were dismantled, private commerce was discontinued, large factories were nationalized, the majority of artisans were organized into cooperatives, and a number of Jewish public figures were exiled into the Soviet Union interior.

On June 29, 1941, Rudki was reoccupied by the Germans, who immediately began to seize Jews for forced labor. A number of prayer houses were burned down. In mid-July 1941, Jews aged fifteen to sixty were ordered to report for roll call in the marketplace. Of the assembled Jews, thirty-nine people, largely members of the intelligentsia, were removed and murdered in the nearby Brzezany forest. In November 1941, an operation was carried out in the townlet, and about 800 Jews were deported to the Belzec death camp.

On December 1, 1941, a ghetto was established that also held survivors of Jewish communities in the surrounding localities. In the ensuing months, about 500 of the ghetto's inhabitants died of hunger and epidemic typhus. A number of Jews attempted to escape across the border to Hungary, but most were caught and killed. Many others readied hiding places in preparation for the next operation.

The ghetto was liquidated in an operation carried out on April 9, 1943, by a Gestapo unit from Lwow*, under the command of Erich Engels. About 1,700 Jews were murdered in the operation in the Brzezany forest, and another approximately 300 were sent to the Janowska labor camp on the outskirts of Lwow. A few individuals managed to hide in the surrounding forests, but most were apprehended and murdered by the Germans and their local collaborators.

RUDNYA

COUNTY SEAT, SMOLENSK DISTRICT, RUSSIAN FEDERATION, USSR

During the war: Military Administration Area

Coordinates:
54°48' | 30°41'

In the mid-1920s, about 2,200 Jews lived in Rudnya. Soviet modernization and urbanization led to a decline in the Jewish population of the townlet to some 1,600 people by the eve of World War II, approximately one-quarter of the local population. During the Soviet period, the Jews of Rudnya engaged in various forms of artisanship, while several worked in one of three Jewish kolkhozes that had been established in the townlet.

Rudnya was occupied by the Germans on July 14, 1941. In August 1941, a ghetto was established comprising a single street encircled by barbed wire, where some 1,200 Jews were imprisoned. Living conditions in the ghetto were harsh: a number of families lived in a single room, and everyone's valuables were seized by the authorities. Young Jews were sent to perform forced labor, in exchange for roughly one hundred grams of coarse bread a day. In August 1941, about twenty Jews living in the ghetto were murdered by the Germans, and in September 1941, another approximately 100 Jews were murdered.

On October 21 1941, all of the ghetto's residents were told that their transfer to the city of Smolensk* was imminent, and were asked to bring along their belongings and food. Jews hiding in their homes or those unable to move were summarily killed. All the rest, with the exception of about 300 artisans, were taken outside the city, where they were shot to death.

The ghetto was liquidated in February 1942, when the 300 artisans were murdered together with about 300 Jews from the townlet of Mikulino*.

RYBNITSA
(Moldavian: **Ribniţa**)

COUNTY SEAT IN MOLDAVIAN AUTONOMOUS REPUBLIC, UKRAINE; FROM 1940: THE SOVIET REPUBLIC OF MOLDAVIA; SINCE 1991: MOLDOVA

During the war: Transnistria (under Romanian control)

Coordinates:
47°45' | 29°00'

On the eve of the German invasion of the Soviet Union, on June 22, 1941, about 3,200 Jews lived in Rybnitsa, representing approximately one-third of the town's total population. During the Soviet period, many of the Jews earned their livelihood from artisanship, while several took to farming (there were Jewish kolkhozes in the vicinity) and worked as laborers in the local sugar factory. The town had a Yiddish-language school.

The Germans occupied Rybnitsa on August 5, 1941. A substantial number of the town's Jews managed to evacuate or flee to the east. By late 1941, there remained about 1,500 local Jews in the town.

In the end of August or the beginning of September 1941, the Jews were concentrated in a ghetto. On September 1, 1941, Rybnitsa was annexed to Transnistria, which was under Romanian rule. From October 1941 to January 1942, the town served as a transit point for some 25,000 Jews deported from Bessarabia and Bukovina. About 1,500 of the deportees managed to remain in Rybnitsa, and these Jews, together with Jews from the vicinity, were also placed in the ghetto, raising its population to a total of about 3,000 people.

The inhabitants of the ghetto were employed at forced labor. A number of the deportees worked in offices of the Romanian authorities, and artisans were employed in various state factories and workshops. In the fall of 1942, several of the ghetto's inhabitants were temporarily assigned to farm work near the town.

Overcrowded living conditions in the ghetto, the shortage of food, and outbreaks of epidemic typhus took many lives. In addition, the Romanians periodically murdered groups of ghetto inhabitants. In early 1942, forty-eight of the ghetto's inhabitants who left its boundaries to look for food without permits were executed. In November 1942, there were 1,080 Jews remaining in the ghetto.

On March 17, 1944, as the Red Army drew closer to the town, the Romanian authorities permitted the deportees among the ghetto's inhabitants to return to Romania. The following day, the Romanians withdrew from the town and handed over control to the Germans, who executed more than 200 prisoners concentrated in the local jail, many of whom were Jews.

Rybnitsa was liberated by the Red Army on March 30, 1944.

RYCZYWÓŁ

VILLAGE IN KOZIENICE COUNTY, KIELCE DISTRICT, POLAND

During the war: General Gouvernement, Radom District

Coordinates:
51°41' | 21°26'

About 80 Jews lived in Ryczywol in the interwar period, and by September 1939, their number had grown to 135.

On December 22, 1941, an injunction was issued by the county commander declaring the village a ghetto, into which Jews from nearby localities were transferred.

There are two versions of events regarding the fate of the Jews of Ryczywol during the German occupation. According to the first, they were deported to the Treblinka death camp on September 27, 1942; according to the second account, in August 1942, sixty-nine of Ryczywol's Jews were deported to the Sobibor death camp. The rest were transferred to the Kozienice* ghetto, and on to the Treblinka death camp on September 27, 1942.

RYKI

TOWNLET IN GARWOLIN COUNTY, LUBLIN DISTRICT, POLAND

During the war: General Gouvernement, Lublin District

Coordinates:
51°38' | 21°56'

After World War I, there were around 2,400 Jews in Ryki, more than two-thirds of the townlet's population. Most were merchants and artisans, mainly in clothing, food, and haulage, and a few were innkeepers and bartenders. The community had traditional charitable and welfare institutions, including a free-loan fund and a savings-and-loan association. Zionist parties, Agudath Israel, Hasidic groups, and the Bund were politically active. Children attended private Hadarim as well as Beit Yaakov and Agudath Israel schools.

In September 1939, Ryki received an influx of refugees from western Poland and nearby Deblin-Irena*.

The Germans occupied the townlet on September 17, 1939. Jews were injured, Jewish-owned shops and property looted, and a nighttime curfew was imposed.

In the middle of October 1939, a Judenrat was established under Shmuel Gutveizer, and a ten-member Jewish Order Service was set up. The Judenrat supplied the Germans with hundreds of forced laborers every day. Workers were also sent to labor camps.

Ryki ghetto plan, based on an illustration by Mr. Mandelboim
(Shimon Kanc, ed., *Ryki, A Memorial to the Community of Ryki*, published by Irgun Yotz'e Ryki, Tel-Aviv 1973)

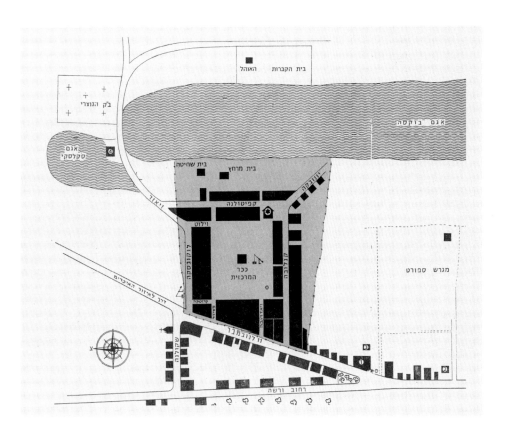

When the Ryki ghetto was established in late 1940, about 1,800 Jews were forced to move there under conditions of severe congestion. In early 1941, the JSS in Cracow* sent relief money to the Judenrat, which used it to open a soup kitchen and a clinic. The ghetto also had a public library that served as a social center.

In June 1941, when the Germans invaded the Soviet Union, they forbade Jews to leave the ghetto for anything but labor. In the winter of 1941/42, about fifty ghetto inhabitants died of epidemic typhus.

On May 6, 1942, Polish police apprehended the members of the Judenrat. That night, SS men came to Ryki and the ghetto was encircled. The SS men and Polish police led the Jews to the market square. The elderly and the ill were summarily murdered there, and the others were marched to Deblin. About 130 Jews who found the march difficult were murdered along the way. About 200 young people were transferred to the labor camp in Deblin; the rest were transported in freight cars to the Sobibor extermination camp.

RYMANÓW

COUNTY SEAT, LWÓW DISTRICT, POLAND

During the war: General Gouvernement, Cracow District

Coordinates:
49°35' | 21°52'

About 1,500 Jews lived in Rymanow when World War II broke out, representing roughly 40 percent of the townlet's population. Most earned their livelihood from commerce and peddling, and a small proportion from artisanship. They were aided by the JDC and by former members of the community who lived in America. Most of the community's children attended traditional Hadarim; Rymanow also had a Beit Yaakov school for girls established by the Agudath Israel party, which was active in the townlet. Zionist parties and youth movements that maintained clubs and libraries also operated in the community. Until 1935, a Yiddish periodical named *Rimanover Vort* was published in the townlet. The Jews of Rymanow were strongly represented on the townlet council.

The Germans occupied Rymanow on September 8, 1939, and on September 17, they drove out all but 160 of the townlet's Jews across the San River, to the area under Soviet control. All of the deportees save 300 people gradually

Rymanow, August 13, 1942
The Jews of the ghetto are rounded up in the town square, then marched on foot to the train station and deported to the Belzec death camp. (YV)

returned to Rymanow, where they were required to perform forced labor and were targeted for abductions to labor camps.

In 1940, Jews from the surrounding and more remote localities, including Cracow*, were brought to Rymanow, and the Jewish population of the townlet rose to about 3,000. In the summer of 1940, Jewish factories and shops were handed over to "Aryan trustees".

A ghetto was established in 1941, and poverty mounted considerably. The JSS helped with the establishment of a public soup kitchen and the provision of medical treatment for the ill. On August 3, 1942, a group of Jewish men was transferred to the Plaszow labor camp.

The Rymanow ghetto was liquidated on August 13, 1942. The Jews were rounded up and following a selection, those considered fit for work were transferred to the Plaszow labor camp, while a few dozen other Jews were killed in Rymanow. A group of Jews was sent to perform forced labor in Barwinek, located south of Rymanow near the Slovakian border. Most of the Jews of Rymanow were deported to the Belzec death camp.

RZEPIENNIK STRZYŻEWSKI

TOWNLET IN GORLICE COUNTY, CRACOW DISTRICT, POLAND

During the war: General Gouvernement, Cracow District

Coordinates:
49°48' | 21°03'

About 300 Jews lived in Rzepiennik Strzyzewski in the interwar period, representing roughly one-eighth of the townlet's population. They earned their livelihood from commerce and artisanship and were aided by a free-loan society, the JDC, and a traditional welfare society. Zionist parties were active in Rzepiennik Strzyzewski. In 1918, a number of Jews were seriously injured in a pogrom.

The Germans occupied Rzepiennik Strzyzewski in early September 1939. In August 1941, dozens of Jews deported from Gorlice* and surrounding localities arrived in the townlet.

In late 1941, a ghetto was established in the townlet. In early 1942, the Germans shot to death 120 of its inhabitants.

The ghetto was liquidated on August 11, 1942. About thirty young men were sent to the Plaszow labor camp, and the rest of the Jews, 364 in all, were taken by German gendarmes from Jaslo* and Gorlice to the Dabry forest near the townlet and shot to death.

RZESZÓW

(Yiddish: **Reyshe**)

COUNTY SEAT, CRACOW DISTRICT, POLAND

During the war: General Gouvernement, Cracow District

Coordinates:
50°03' | 22°00'

Before the War: About 15,000 Jews lived in Rzeszow when World War II broke out, representing more than one-third of the city's population. They earned their livelihood from commerce, small-scale industry, and artisanship, especially in the garment, food, wood, metal, and leather sectors. The Jews were also members of the liberal professions as well as moneychangers and moneylenders. After World War I, Rzeszow's Jews were aided by the JDC, which supported the city's welfare institutions and the Jewish hospital. They also received assistance from free-loan societies, TOZ (which was active in the city), and former Jewish citizens of Rzeszow living in the United States. The welfare institutions included a children's home, an orphanage, and an old-age home. Merchants' and artisans' trade unions also set up welfare institutions for their members.

In 1918 and 1919, about 200 Jews were injured in pogroms carried out by Polish soldiers and civilians and a great deal of Jewish property was stolen. As a result, public soup kitchens were opened and clothing was distributed among the Jews.

Rzeszow had a variety of schools: a modern Heder established by the Mizrachi; Agudath Israel schools—a Beit Yaakov school for girls and *Yesodei ha-Torah* for boys; and an elementary and high school in the community center, which were recognized by the authorities and offered Hebrew instruction. A few young people pursued their studies in the Batei Midrash. The community center featured halls and auditoriums for meetings, plays, and sports events as well as a library and classrooms that hosted varied activities. A Tarbut chapter held evening classes and offered Hebrew and vocational courses. Rzeszow also had a sports club and a drama circle. The local chapter of Agudath Israel published a periodical in Polish called *Promien* that was distributed throughout Galicia. A Yiddish weekly was also published for some time in Rzeszow.

All of the Jewish political organizations in Poland were represented in Rzeszow: Zionist parties, the Bund, and Agudath Israel. A number of Jews were members of the illegal Polish Communist Party. Chapters of Zionist youth movements also operated in the city, in addition to Tze'irei Agudath Israel and pioneer training facilities with hundreds of members, dozens of whom immigrated to the Land of Israel. The Zionist parties maintained libraries and held lectures in their meeting-houses.

German (Nazi) occupation: The Germans occupied Rzeszow on September 10, 1939. In the early days of the occupation, they conducted a separate roll call of the Jews to recruit hundreds of forced laborers, and also seized Jews from the streets and from their homes. The religious Jews were the particular target of German abuse and terror on Rosh Hashanah and Yom Kippur, which fell just a few days after the occupation. The city's synagogues were destroyed and sacred artifacts desecrated as was the Jewish cemetery; Jews were forced to smash its tombstones to pave the streets, turning it into a square. Apartments owned by prosperous Jews and the Jewish hospital were confiscated and used to quarter German officers. The members of the community council opened an alternate hospital.

The Jews' freedom of movement was restricted: they were forbidden to enter certain streets in the city, were subject to a curfew from seven o'clock in the evening, and were permitted to shop in the marketplace only in the afternoon hours. Rzeszow's Jews were periodically forced to make ransom payments and German soldiers and police frequently plundered Jewish property. In the early weeks of the occupation, the Jews were forced to open their shops and mark them with a Star-of-David. The Germans eventually confiscated the Jewish shops, factories, and workshops, handing them over to the management of "Aryan trustees".

In late October 1939, a thirty-member Judenrat was appointed, headed by Dr. Kleinmann, an attorney, and his deputy, Bernard (Benno) Kahana. However, Kleinmann was executed in January 1940 together with several of the members of the Judenrat, after failing to supply the Germans with a sufficient number of forced laborers. Kahana was appointed his successor. The Judenrat was ordered to provide the Germans with forced laborers and to remit periodic ransom payments. A Jewish Order Service with twenty-five policemen was established, headed by Leon Berzaner, a professional photographer.

In the fall of 1939, numerous young Jews fled from the city to the Soviet zone, east of the San River. Prior to the German invasion of the Soviet Union, a number of them returned secretly to their families in Rzeszow. Many of those who remained in the Soviet zone were exiled to the Soviet interior in the summer of 1940.

On November 7, 1939, a very heavy fine was imposed on the Jews of the city. From December 1 onward, all Jews aged twelve and older were ordered to wear a white armband with a blue Star-of-David. Meanwhile, the Germans deported to Rzeszow thousands of Jews from the areas of western Poland annexed to the

Reich, especially from Lodz*, Kalisz*, and Upper Silesia. Thousands of Jewish refugees arrived penniless in the Rzeszow area in early January 1940. On January 22, 1940, the Germans murdered more than thirty Jews in the city.

In late 1939, ten labor camps operated in the area of Rzeszow, with most of the Jews assigned to forced labor working in the nearby military airfield. In mid-1940, close to 12,000 Jews lived in Rzeszow, of whom approximately 4,000 were refugees. By late 1940, numerous Jews had been transferred from their dwellings in the main streets to the quarters populated by Jews; their freedom of movement was further restricted and they were forbidden to move from one residence to another without a permit. The transfer of Jewish property to Germany was completed, and a number of factory machines were relocated there.

Hardship and starvation brought on a dysentery epidemic among the Jews. The forced laborers often received a meager supplementary food ration in payment for their work, and a few managed to establish contact with the Polish population to barter valuables for food.

In April 1941, eighteen Jews were murdered in the Jewish cemetery. On October 3 and 10, 1941, the German police invaded numerous Jewish homes, plundered property, and terrorized the owners.

Ghetto setup, institutions, and internal life: By the summer and fall of 1941, the Jews were moved to a separate quarter of Rzeszow, and Germans and Poles were accommodated in their apartments. In the winter of 1941/42, furs were confiscated from the Jews, and a Jewish furrier was murdered after a piece of fur was found in his possession.

On December 17, 1941, an injunction was published regarding the establishment of the Rzeszow ghetto. That month, the ghetto was encircled by a barbed-wire fence, partitions were built, and the gates were sealed, leaving a total of three exits that were guarded day and night by the German police. On January 10, 1942, the transfer to the ghetto was completed and 12,500 Jews, of whom more than 3,000 were refugees, were concentrated in its now-sealed boundaries.

Those employed at work considered crucial to the German economy received special permits or authorizations from the German employment bureau that granted them temporary immunity from seizure for labor camps. They left the ghetto to work in the plants of the German Air Force, army camps, factories, labor camps in Biesiadka near Rzochow, and on farming estates near the city (including the Milocin estate). Those who worked outside the ghetto struggled to obtain food and smuggle it in. Anyone caught leaving the ghetto without a permit was executed.

Epidemics began to claim victims within the ghetto and a small hospital for contagious diseases was established, although with insufficient beds and medication. The Judenrat and a JSS branch set up public soup kitchens that distributed hundreds of portions of soup daily. The Judenrat managed to persuade the Germans to allow the Jews to cultivate potatoes outside the ghetto and establish a workshop inside, especially for garments and carpentry, as well as a laundry. These plants also provided services for the Germans in exchange for increased food rations for workers. The Judenrat ran a Yiddish elementary school from October 1940 until the deportation in July 1942, and organized vocational courses, among them electricity, carpentry, and nursing, to train young people in professions deemed crucial to the Germans and to prevent their deportation to labor camps.

In June 1942, 10,000 to 12,000 Jews were deported to Rzeszow from the surrounding localities, including Sokolow Malopolski*, Jawornik Polski*, Glogow, Kolbuszowa*, Sedziszow*, Czudec*, Tyczyn*, Blazowa, and Strzyzow*. The population of Rzeszow rose to between 22,000 and 25,000. Responsibility for the Jewish population was turned over to the police and the SD. In July 1942, a ransom of one million zloty was levied on the Jewish population.

After the November 1942 killing operation (see below), about 3,000 Jews remained in the ghetto and its area was once again reduced. The Rzeszow ghetto was one of five ghettos selected for the concentration of the remaining Jews from the entire area. The Germans divided the ghetto into two parts: the eastern ghetto, located east of Baldachowska Street (Ghetto A or 1), became a forced labor camp (*Judisches Zwangsarbeitslager, ZAL*) for those who had work permits, while the western ghetto, Ghetto B or 2, held the family members of the workers: the women, the ill, the elderly, a few children, and additional deportees and survivors. This ghetto was also known as the *Schmelzghetto* or "Melting ghetto." The ghettos were encircled by barbed-wire fences and segregated from one another.

In Ghetto A, the men and women were separated. Frequent searches for people without permits were carried out, and those found were murdered in the Rudna forests or the Jewish cemetery. Inhabitants caught smuggling food into the ghetto were murdered on sight. Every few weeks, Jews were sent from both ghettos to the labor camps in the area: Stalowa Wola, Rzochow, Biesiadka, Romanow, labor camp in Kolbuszowa County, Lisia Gora and to the quarries in Zarnow*, near Strzyzow. The Judenrat endeavored to supply the labor camp inmates with food and clothing. Many perished in these camps.

Hundreds of the inhabitants of Ghetto A worked in the ghetto workshops, especially with garments (repairing the clothing of the murdered Jews that were brought to the ghetto in train cars from the death camps), and in carpentry and glazing. Others worked outside the ghetto, in the train station and factories. The workers in the military factories and camps were marked with a 'W' for Wehrmacht and the workers in armaments were marked with an 'R' for *Rüstung*. These marks were believed to provide laborers with immunity from forced labor or deportation.

Both ghettos had hospitals. Many perished in Ghetto B of epidemic typhus, among them Dr. Hauptman, the director of the hospital.

Deportations and murder operations: On April 28, 1942, the Gestapo murdered about thirty Jews, ostensibly for being Communists.

The first deportations occurred in July 1942, in four waves: on July 7, 10, 14, and 19. On July 7, the patients at the ghetto hospital and old-age home; 150 Jewish inmates of the city jail; the commander of the Jewish Order Service, Berzaner; and Rabbi Halberstam were shot and killed in the Rudna forests on the way to Glogow.

In each deportation wave, the Jews were evacuated from another part of the ghetto to the area that had once held the Jewish cemetery (*Sammelplatz*); the property they brought along was confiscated from them. Following a selection, a number of the people who held work permits were released. About 1,000 ill and elderly Jews were murdered in the cemetery, and almost all the rest were deported from the Staroniwa train station to the Belzec death camp. People who were unable to keep up en route to the station were shot to death.

Some 18,000 to 21,000 Jews are estimated to have been deported and murdered in the operations of July 1942. Afterwards, about 4,000 Jews remained in Rzeszow, people with work permits as well as those who had hidden during the operation. The ghetto area was reduced. The Gestapo periodically inspected and stamped the inhabitants' work permits. In late July, a large group of Jews deported from the Debica* ghetto arrived in Rzeszow.

On August 7, 1942, another deportation of women and children was carried out. The Germans called for the registration of mothers with young children, ostensibly to assign them to less arduous work. About 1,000 women and children reported, only to be sent to the Belzec death camp. A small number of women without children were deported to the Pelkinie camp near Jaroslaw.

In yet another killing operation carried out on November 15, 1942, about 2,000 ill and elderly people, women, and children were executed in the Rudna forests, and others were deported to Belzec.

An additional deportation was carried out on December 15, 1942. Approximately 1,500 people, residents of Ghetto A and deportees from the Krosno* ghetto, were deported to Belzec, while the ill and frail were murdered on site. During the train ride to Belzec, about 200 people jumped off the train and returned to Ghetto A.

In late August or early September 1943, some 2,500 to 3,000 Jews remained in the Rzeszow ghetto. Most were deported to Auschwitz, and the younger Jews were transferred to the Szebnie labor camp. The patients of the hospitals in both ghettos were murdered in their beds. The members of the Judenrat and the Jewish policemen were apparently also executed during this killing operation. Ghetto A ceased to exist. About 150 to 160 people were left to clean up, collect the deportees' belongings, and labor in the workshops. In February 1944, fifteen people remained in the area of the camp. The men were transferred to a labor camp near Rzeszow and to the labor camp in Stalowa Wola, and the women were sent to the Plaszow camp.

Underground and resistance: The members of Hashomer Hatzair sought to establish a fighting underground in Rzeszow. Members included Sala Mol, Hinda Grol, Moshe Traum, and Leib Birman. They attempted to establish contact with the Jewish underground members in Cracow*, Tarnow*, and Jaslo*. Another group, which was organized by a Jewish man named Kobeh, was in contact with the Polish underground in Rzeszow.

Several of the partisan groups in the area had Jewish members from Rzeszow. Several groups of Jews were active in the forests around the city. They had a small number of weapons purchased with the help of Poles.

On February 25, 1944, after being denounced, thirty-five Jews hidden in bunkers in Rzeszow were murdered, together with the Polish man who had hidden them and provided them with food and services.

Of the Jews of Rzeszow, about 100 people survived, either in the ghetto, in hiding places, or in the camps. Another approximately 600 people survived in the area under Soviet control.

RZGÓW

TOWN IN ŁÓDŹ COUNTY, ŁÓDŹ DISTRICT, POLAND

During the war: Wartheland

Coordinates:
51°40' | 19°30'

In 1921, ninety-three Jews lived in Rzgow, representing approximately 5 percent of the local population. The Jewish community had no independent community institutions.

On July 17–18, 1940, a rural ghetto was established in Rzgow, to which the Jews from the villages of Konin, Slupca, Golina, Pyzdry, and Kleczew were deported. On March 9–12, 1941, a number of the ghetto's inhabitants were deported to the Izbica Kujawska* ghetto.

In October 1941, the rest of the Jews were removed from the Rzgow ghetto to the Kazimierz Biskupi forests, where they were placed inside smoldering lime pits and buried alive.

RZHEV

**COUNTY SEAT, KALININ
DISTRICT, RUSSIAN
FEDERATION, USSR**

During the war: Military
Administration Area

Coordinates:
56°15' | 34°20'

On the eve of World War II, about 460 Jews lived in Rzhev, less than 1 percent of the local population. Most were evacuated eastward prior to the German's occupation of the town on October 14, 1941.

As of November 13, 1941, all Jewish inhabitants of Rzhev were required to wear identification bands. It appears that in the spring of 1942, the approximately fifty Jews (belonging to fifteen families) who remained in the town were concentrated in a ghetto housed in the town's former kindergarten. The ghetto had a three-member Judenrat.

The ghetto was liquidated in the summer of 1942, when its thirty-eight inhabitants were shot to death.

S

Saloniki ghetto, Greece

"The ghetto was located in the Baron Hirsch neighborhood for refugees of the fire, near the railroad tracks. The Germans ordered the community to fence in the neighborhood by building walls and a barbed-wire fence. This neighborhood, in which 600 poor families lived isolated from the rest of the city, became a concentration camp of sorts."

Yom Tov Yekuel, "On the way to destruction (a diary)", from Saloniki—A Jewish City *(Tel Aviv: The Research Institute of Saloniki's Jewery, 1967), p. 287 [Hebrew].*

SAJÓSZENTPÉTER

TOWNLET IN BORSOD COUNTY, HUNGARY

Coordinates:
48°13' | 20°43'

The last national census conducted prior to the German occupation, taken in January 1941, recorded 636 Jewish inhabitants in Sajoszentpeter, representing approximately 9 percent of the total population. Most of the Jews were merchants and artisans. The townlet had an Orthodox Jewish community, a Jewish elementary school, and a Talmud Torah.

In the summer of 1941, the Hungarian authorities expelled several Jewish families whose members were not Hungarian citizens to a region in the Ukraine under German occupation; they were murdered on August 27 and 28 at Kamenets-Podolsk*.

The German army occupied Hungary on March 19, 1944. A census conducted in the second week of April 1944 showed that 663 Jews belonged to the Orthodox Jewish community of Sajoszentpeter.

The Hungarian administration remained intact and in force after the occupation. The ghettoization and deportation of the Jews were carried out on the basis of the decrees and orders of the national and local authorities. Dr. Gyula Mikuleczky, the sub-prefect of Borsod County, ordered the establishment of ghettos in the county on May 13, 1944. The Sajoszentpeter ghetto, which had a soup kitchen, was most likely founded in the second half of May 1944.

On June 10, 1944, the inhabitants of the ghetto were brought to an entrainment center in the brick factory on Tatar Street in Miskolc*. A number were then transferred to the Diosgyor* ghetto, and on June 12, 1944, they were deported to Auschwitz. Those who remained in the brick factory were deported to Auschwitz on June 13 and 15, 1944.

ŠAKIAI
(Yiddish: **Shaki**)

COUNTY SEAT, LITHUANIA

During the war:
Reichskommissariat
Ostland

Coordinates:
54°57' | 23°03'

On the eve of World War II, about 600 Jews lived in Sakiai, representing roughly 20 percent of the townlet's population. Most earned their livelihood from artisanship and commerce and had access to Jewish trade associations. Between the World Wars, the townlet had a Jewish Folksbank. The community had active Zionist parties and youth movements.

After Lithuania was annexed to the Soviet Union in 1940, the townlet's private businesses were nationalized and Jewish national activities were discontinued.

Sakiai was occupied by the Germans on June 22, 1941, and administration of the townlet was transferred to the Lithuanians. Orders restricting Jewish movement and contact between Jews and the non-Jewish population of the townlet were immediately enforced. Jewish men above the age of fifteen years were concentrated in a barn on the edge of the townlet. They were sent under Lithuanian guard to dig pits in the nearby forest. On July 5, 1941, the men were brought from the barn to the forest, where they were shot to death in the pits. There were a few individual cases of resistance. Following the killing of the men, forty women from affluent families were also taken to the pits, where they were subjected to abuse and subsequently shot to death.

The Jewish women and children who remained in Sakiai were concentrated in a number of derelict alleys in the townlet that were turned into an open ghetto. The locals were forbidden to bring food to their Jewish acquaintances, while the inhabitants of the ghetto risked their lives in their search for food. Jewish girls were periodically abducted, raped, and murdered by Lithuanians.

The ghetto was liquidated on September 13, 1941, when its women and children were murdered in pits in the forest, together with Jews from nearby townlets.

SALAKAS
(Yiddish: **Saluk**)

**TOWNLET IN ZARASAI
COUNTY, LITHUANIA**

During the war:
Reichskommissariat Ostland

Coordinates:
55°35' | 26°08'

On the eve of the outbreak of the war, about 200 Jewish families lived in Salakas. They earned their livelihood from commerce, fishing, peddling, and small artisanship. The community boasted traditional Jewish religious and educational institutions as well as a Jewish school and active Zionist organizations.

In June 1940, after Lithuania was annexed to the Soviet Union, a number of the townlet's shops were nationalized and Zionist organizations were dismantled.

After the Germans entered Salakas on June 29, 1941, the Jews were required to wear a distinctive sign on their clothing (the letter *J* or a yellow Star-of-David), their freedom of movement was restricted, and they were required to perform forced labor for the Lithuanians. A Judenrat was appointed, with Rabbi Yaakov Ralbe, Feibush Gilinski, and Avraham Bach as its members. (According to a different source, the Judenrat was appointed in August after the Jews of Salakas returned to the townlet and a ghetto was established.)

On August 2, 1941, all of the Jews of Salakas were gathered and taken to the Sungardas forest; 150 of them—the intelligentsia and public figures along with their families—were taken to the village of Paezeriai, where they were shot and buried. The rest of the Jews were returned to Salakas and concentrated in a ghetto.

On August 26, all of the ghetto's inhabitants were gathered under the pretense that they were to be taken to work on farms. Instead, they were brought some ten kilometers away to a forest, where they were concentrated in an area cordoned off with barbed wire, together with Jews from a number of nearby townlets. The following day, all 2,569 of the assembled Jews were murdered by Lithuanians under the supervision of two SS men.

SALANTAI

(Yiddish: **Salant**)

TOWNLET IN KRETINGA COUNTY, LITHUANIA

During the war:
Reichskommissariat Ostland

Coordinates:
56°04' | 21°34'

On the eve of the German occupation, about 500 Jews lived in Salantai, representing approximately one-third of the townlet's residents. Salantai had a Tarbut school, a Talmud Torah, and Beit Yaakov institutions as well as chapters of Agudath Israel and Zionist parties.

After Lithuania was annexed to the Soviet Union in 1940, private businesses in Salantai were nationalized, Jewish national parties and youth movements were disbanded, and Hebrew schools were closed.

Salantai was occupied by the Germans on June 23, 1941. Lithuanians immediately took to plundering Jewish property. In late June 1941, Jewish sacred books were burned in the center of the townlet.

On July 1, 1941, the Jews of Salantai were concentrated in the synagogue, which was surrounded by Lithuanian guards. Each night, ten Jewish men were removed from the premises and murdered, and on July 10, all the remaining men were taken out and shot to death. The older women and children remained in the synagogue, while about 150 young women were assigned to farm work. On July 20, the older women and the children were brought from the synagogue to a place near the village of Sateikiai, where they were murdered and buried in a mass grave. Apparently in early August 1941, the younger women were returned to the synagogue, where they remained until their collective execution in September 1941. One woman was hidden by a Lithuanian and saved.

SALGÓTARJÁN

TOWN IN NÓGRÁD COUNTY, HUNGARY

Coordinates:
48°07' | 19°49'

The last national census conducted prior to the German occupation, taken in 1941, recorded 1,255 Jewish inhabitants in Salgotarjan, accounting for roughly 6 percent of the total population. Most were merchants and artisans. The town's Jewish community was Orthodox.

In 1942, the majority of the young Jewish men were drafted into the Hungarian army for forced labor service. They were deployed to the eastern front, in the Ukraine, where most perished.

The German army occupied Hungary on March 19, 1944. A census conducted in the second week of April, 1944 showed that 1,200 Jews belonged to the Orthodox Jewish community of Salgotarjan. Immediately after the German occupation, several Salgotarjan Jews were arrested and transferred to the internment camps of Garany, Nagykanizsa, and Kistarcsa.

The Hungarian administration remained intact and operational after the German occupation. The ghettoization and deportation of the Jews occurred on the basis of decrees and orders issued by the Hungarian national and local authorities. On the basis of the "ghetto-decree" published by the Hungarian prime minister on April 28, 1944, the Hungarian sub-prefect of Nograd County, Sandor Neogradi Horvath, ordered the "removal of the Jews from all of the localities" of the county and their segregation in "housing estates." Ghettoization in Salgotarjan took place between May 3 and 10, 1944. Aside from the local Jews, 452 Jews from the County-District of Szirak were also concentrated in the Salgotarjan ghetto.

The ghetto was established in three different areas in the town. According to the police regulations, the Jews were permitted to leave the territory of the ghetto between one and four o'clock in the afternoon on workdays. The ghetto had a Jewish Council, headed by the merchant Samu Friedler, the former community president. A hospital was established in it. The approximately thirty to forty Jewish converts to Christianity living in the ghetto petitioned the mayor, Dr. Bela Ratkay, on May 30, 1944, for permission to attend church services.

On May 31, Hungarian gendarmes in search of hidden valuables began to cruelly torture Jews, killing sixteen people in the process. At the beginning of June

1944, able-bodied Jews were drafted into the Hungarian army for forced labor service, thus escaping deportation.

At dawn on June 5, 1944, the inhabitants of the ghetto were transferred to the entrainment center in the stables of the local mining company. The stables, which also held Jews from other ghettos, were full of rats. The Jews, altogether 3,119 people, were deported to Auschwitz on June 13, 1944.

SALONIKA

CITY IN GREECE

Coordinates:
40°38' | 22°58'

Before the War: Dating from the Roman era, the Jewish community of Salonika reached its pinnacle in the early twentieth century when it numbered 80,000 Sephardi Jews. They comprised about half of the population of the city, then under Ottoman rule. Five years after Salonika came under Greek control in 1912, the Jewish quarter was severely damaged in a great fire. That event, together with the economic crisis following World War I and an upturn in manifestations of antisemitism in Salonika, prompted many Jews to leave the city. By the 1930s, the Jewish population had fallen to 56,000, about one-fifth of the city's population.

The Jews of Salonika were prominent in trade, manufacturing, banking, and tourism and played a key role in the economic modernization of the town, especially in the late nineteenth century. Many were unskilled laborers and artisans. Salonika had traditional Jewish schools (Hadarim and Talmudei Torah); schools and vocational training centers affiliated with Alliance Israelite Universelle; a school and kindergarten established by the Jewish-German Hilfsverein; and a school that taught in Hebrew. The city was an important Jewish press center, where Jewish journals and books in Ladino (Judeo-Spanish), French, and other languages were published. The community boasted a variety of Jewish welfare institutions, including a hospital.

Zionist influence in Salonika surged during the interwar years. Most members of the community identified with Zionism and belonged to a variety of Zionist societies and youth movements. Jews were also well represented in the local labor movement and among the Communists.

German (Nazi) occupation: Jews had begun leaving Salonika even before the Germans occupied the city on April 9, 1941. Their preferred destination was the Italian occupation zone, particularly Athens and the countryside. By early 1943, some 3,000 to 7,000 Jews had left Salonika, among them a number of the community's dignitaries and wealthiest people.

Within days of occupying the city, the Germans shut down the Jewish newspapers, confiscated a great deal of Jewish property (including dwellings), closed the Jewish hospital, and arrested leaders and other prominent members of the community. Most of the detainees were released several weeks later. The Germans appointed Sabi (Shabetai) Saltiel as head of the community administration and held him responsible for the administration of nearby peripheral communities and the care of Jewish refugees from Germany, Poland, Hungary, and Romania who reached the city. The Germans stanched the outflow of Jews from Salonika and executed several captured escapees. The Jewish community largely heeded its leadership's plea to be patient and avoid extreme actions.

In the summer of 1941, a German unit under Johann Pohl systematically confiscated thousands of books, manuscripts, and ancient Judaica in Salonika. The racial laws were not officially introduced in Greece in the initial phases of the occupation, but the situation of the Jews in Salonika steadily deteriorated. Hundreds perished in the winter of 1941/42, in the famine that gripped the city and in epidemics in the Jewish quarter.

On Saturday, July 11, 1942 (later known as the "Black Sabbath"), some 6,500 Jews (or, according to another account, 8,500 to 9,000) reported to Lib-

Salonika, July 11, 1942
"Black Sabbath." Jewish
men assemble in the Platia
Eleftheria Square to register
for forced labor. While kept
waiting for many hours in the
square, the Jewish men were
humiliated and beaten. (BA.
Above: BA, 101I-168-0895-07A.
Photographer: Dick)

erty Square at the Germans' behest to be registered for forced labor. Saltiel had managed, with great effort, to ensure the removal of community officials, rabbis, and teachers from the list of inductees. The Jews awaiting enlistment were kept for hours in the sun and were subjected to abuse. By the end of August 1942, at least 2,000 Jews had been sent away for quarrying and road-building; a minimum of another 1,000 joined them later. Labor conditions were harsh; an estimated 700 workers perished, and many who attempted escape were executed. A committee that dealt with worker-related matters was established by the community administration and authorized by the Germans in late August 1942. The committee succeeded in improving conditions in a number of the labor camps and eventually secured the return of workers to Salonika by paying ransoms to the Germans and reluctantly acquiescing to the expropriation of the city's ancient Jewish cemetery.

Saltiel was removed from his post on December 10, 1942, to be replaced the following day by the Galician-born Ashkenazi rabbi Zvi Korets, a graduate of

Left: **Salonika, January 1943**
Destruction of the ancient Jewish cemetery following the expropriation of the site by the authorities (YIVO)

Right: **Salonika, September 1941**
A Jewish family in a slum neighborhood in one of the city's suburbs. *The photograph was taken at the initiative of "Der institut zur Erforsschung der Judenfrage Die Hohe Schule."* (YIVO)

the rabbinical seminary in Vienna. Rabbi Korets, who had been living in Salonika since 1933, conditioned his acceptance of the post on the appointment of a six-member committee to assume collective responsibility.

Preparations for the Final Solution in Salonika began in January 1943, when SS officer Rolf Gunther, Eichmann's deputy, came to the city and was joined several days later by Dieter Wisliceny, Himmler's assistant. Wisliceny's subordinate, Alois Brunner, assisted by Max Merten of the Wehrmacht, planned and implemented the ghettoization and deportation of the Jews of Salonika.

Ghetto setup, institutions, and internal life: On February 6, 1943, Merten issued an order requiring all Jews in Salonika aged five and over to wear a yellow Star-of-David badge and to relocate by February 25 to special quarters, namely, ghettos. Rabbi Korets convened the community committee two days later, after being informed of the Germans' directives. The committee selected two districts as ghettos and appointed committees to conduct censuses of the Jewish population and distribute the numbered yellow badges. Additional German decrees issued in February imposed severe restrictions, including a nighttime curfew; a ban on the use of main streets, public transport, and telephones, and the compulsory marking of Jewish-owned businesses and dwellings in German and Greek. On March 1, 1943, all Jews in Salonika were ordered to submit itemized accounts of their property.

In the hope that compliance would elicit better treatment, the community administration under Rabbi Korets obeyed the German commands, especially the ghettoization order, which was accompanied by severe threats. Eventually, the Jews of Salonika were concentrated in three ghettos in different neighborhoods. While each ghetto was enclosed in barbed wire, the ghetto in the Baron Hirsch quarter near the railroad was also surrounded with a wooden fence and became, in effect, a guarded transit camp for Jews facing deportation. The ghettoization was carried out by a 250-member Jewish Order Service force under Jacques Albala, a German-speaking Jew whom the Germans installed and who collaborated with them closely. The "Baron Hirsch camp" was commanded by the Jewish policeman Vital Hasson. From March 6, 1943, Jews were forbidden to leave or to move between the ghettos, and all Jewish shops outside the ghettos were boarded up. Conditions in the ghettos were dire; epidemics spread and mortality rates escalated amid severe congestion.

Salonika, March 15, 1943
Young Jews. In the background are the ghetto homes (YV)

On March 14, Rabbi Korets and Albala visited the Baron Hirsch camp, where some 16,000 Jews had been concentrated. Rabbi Korets explained to the inhabitants that the unmarried would be transported to labor camps, and their parents would remain in Salonika. In response, a wave of hasty weddings broke out, with a rabbi conducting the ceremonies in groups of ten. By the end of March, up to 100 couples were married daily in an effort to thwart the youths' deportation.

Deportations and the ghetto's liquidation: The first deportation train from Salonika to Auschwitz set out the following day, March 15, 1943, with 2,800 deportees aboard. Four additional trains brought the number of deportees to Auschwitz to 12,800 by the end of March. A fifth train that reached Treblinka on March 28 also apparently departed from Salonika. On March 24, more than 1,000 young Jews were inducted for forced labor in camps across Greece.

After the deportations, Jews from the other ghettos in Salonika were removed to the Baron Hirsch camp in anticipation of future deportations. In late April, they were joined by 316 Jews from Veria and 372 from Florina. The deportations to Auschwitz reached their peak at this time: eleven transport trains left Salonika between early April and May 9.

During May, more than 1,000 Jews from other localities in Greece, including about 900 from Didimoticho, were concentrated in Salonika. On June 1, another deportation train headed for Auschwitz with nearly all members of the community administration aboard. On August 2, deported from Salonika to Bergen-Belsen were 441 Jews; they included 367 who held Spanish citizenship and 74 former community officials, including Rabbi Korets and Jacques Albala, who was appointed the Judenaelteste in Bergen-Belsen. The last two deportation trains from Salonika to Auschwitz departed on August 2 and August 10, the latter carrying 1,810 Jews who had been working in Greek labor camps. In all, more than 48,500 Jews were deported from Salonika to Auschwitz in nineteen transports.

Resistance: A Jewish partisan organization operated in Salonika, its main activity being to gather reports about German military movements in Macedonia and forward them to the Greek resistance. Shortly before the deportation of the Jews of Salonika, representatives of the National Liberation Front (EAM), the Greek resistance organization, contacted Rabbi Korets and asked him to encourage young Jews to join. Although the rabbi did not respond to the request, a group of young Jews managed to slip out of Salonika and join ELAS, the partisan force of the EAM.

Representatives of the EAM implored the Jewish population, by means of leaflets and the underground press, to disobey the Germans and to leave Salonika; they also threatened traitors with severe punishment. The number of Jews from Salonika who enlisted in ELAS during the occupation is estimated at 200 to 450.

About 800 additional Jews left the ghettos and the city with the assistance of the Italian consulate in Salonika, which issued papers that recognized their Italian citizenship. Most of these Jews were placed aboard an Italian military train and transported to Athens, which was under Italian rule until September 1943.

Approximately 2,000 Jews of Salonika survived to the end of the war, most having gone through additional camps.

SAMBOR

COUNTY SEAT, LWÓW DISTRICT, POLAND

(After World War II in the USSR/Ukraine; Ukrainian: **Sambir**)

During the war: General Gouvernement, Galicia District

Coordinates: 49°31' | 23°12'

In the early 1930s, more than 6,000 Jews lived in Sambor, representing approximately one-third of the town's population. They earned their livelihood from commerce, artisanship, and industrial factories as well as wagon driving, farming, and the liberal professions. Sambor boasted Jewish trade unions and welfare organizations as well as various Zionist parties and Agudath Israel. The boys of the ultra-Orthodox families attended a modern Talmud Torah and the girls, a Beit Yaakov school. The community also had a Jewish commercial secondary school and a supplementary Hebrew school. In addition, the town had various Jewish cultural institutions, including a large library and a sports club.

In early September 1939, a few days after the Germans invaded Poland, Sambor was inundated with Jewish refugees attempting to cross the border into Romania. In mid-September 1939, the Germans entered Sambor and immediately began to seize Jews for forced labor and plunder Jewish property. On September 23–24, the town was handed over to Soviet control in accordance with the Molotov-Ribbentrop Pact. Under the Soviets, the Jewish parties were dismantled, private factories were nationalized, and private commerce was almost completely abolished. In late June 1940, the Soviets exiled into the interior of the USSR the Jewish refugees who had come to Sambor from western Poland and refused to accept Soviet citizenship.

On June 30, 1941, the Germans occupied Sambor. The following day, Ukrainians murdered between 50 and 100 Jews. The Germans enacted numerous decrees, severely restricting the hours during which Jewish inhabitants were permitted to shop in the town market, forbidding them to leave the town, and exploiting the Jews for forced labor. Valuables belonging to Jews were confiscated and Jews were evicted from their apartments, which were then turned over to Germans and senior Ukrainian officials. In July 1941, a Judenrat headed by Dr. Schneidsher and a Jewish Order Service under the command of Herman Stal were established.

In February 1942, thirty-two Jewish hostages were murdered in Sambor. In March 1942, Jews were evicted from different parts of the town and concentrated in a number of streets in the ancient Jewish neighborhood in the Blich quarter, which was transformed into an open ghetto.

On August –6, 1942, a large-scale operation was carried out by members of the German and Ukrainian police under the command of Von Willhaus and Richard Rokita (as well as under the district commander Hans-Walter Zinser, who was also present to supervise the operation). At the onset of the operation, numerous Jews from various provincial towns in the district were transferred to the Sambor ghetto. A curfew was imposed and, with the help of the Jewish Order Service, the Germans concentrated thousands of Jews in the sports field near the train station. Either about 150 or 600 Jews (sources vary on the figure) were sent to the Janowska camp on the outskirts of Lwow*; another approximately 150 were murdered in the ghetto. The remaining 4,000 to 6,000 Jews (sources vary on the figure) were deported by train to the Belzec death camp.

On September 4, 1942, the Germans arrested about 300 elderly and ill people according to lists prepared for them by the Judenrat. Those arrested were brought to an area near Drohobycz* and murdered. At least 1,000 Jews were deported from Sambor and its environs to Belzec during two large-scale operations carried out in the ghetto on October 17, 18, and 22, 1942. Units of the German SIPO from Drohobycz, under the command of Hans Block and Jozef Gabriel, conducted the operations. In one of them, Judenrat head Schneidsher was murdered after he refused to submit to the Germans a list of Jews designated for execution. Judenrat member Zausner was appointed to replace him.

On December 1, 1942, the Jewish quarter of Sambor was transformed into a sealed ghetto. Survivors of Jewish communities in the surrounding areas were concentrated in it, raising its population to about 3,000. Harsh conditions, including hunger and epidemic typhus, prevailed in the ghetto. In the winter of 1942/43, groups of young Jews were transferred from the ghetto to the Janowska labor camp.

The Jews attempted escape from the ghetto in various ways. Several hoped to cross the border illegally into Hungary, but most were murdered along the way; others attempted to obtain false "Aryan" papers, flee to the woods, or hide with Christian acquaintances. In early 1943, an underground group organized at the initiative of Dr. Sandauer acquired weapons and planned resistance operations. The group turned to the Judenrat for financial assistance but did not receive it.

On April 10, 1943, another operation was carried out. A few hundred Jews were brought to the Jewish cemetery and murdered—the babies and children first, and a few days later, most of the adults. On May 22–23, 1943, yet another operation was conducted in the ghetto, with about 550 Jews deported to the Majdanek death camp.

The ghetto was liquidated on June 9, 1943. The Germans and their helpers rounded up the Jews, and demolished and set fire to the houses in the ghetto in order to root out anyone still in hiding. They led the approximately 1,500 remaining Jews in the ghetto to the nearby village of Radlowice, some three kilometers outside the town, where they shot them to death.

Hundreds of Jews managed to survive in hiding after the liquidation of the ghetto. In the weeks that followed the liquidation operation, the Germans arrested and executed 170 of the fugitives.

SAMGORODOK
(Ukrainian: **Samhorodok**)

COUNTY SEAT, VINNITSA DISTRICT, UKRAINE, USSR

During the war: Reichskommissariat Ukraine

Coordinates: 49°32' | 28°51'

In the 1920s, there were about 1,300 Jews in Samgorodok, nearly one-third of the townlet's population. In March 1919, Ukrainian soldiers conducted a pogrom in which four Jewish families were murdered. During the Soviet era, a number of Jewish artisans formed cooperatives while others opted for farm work or blue-collar jobs in sugar factories. The townlet's Jewish population declined during the 1930s owing to industrialization and urbanization in the Soviet Union.

The Germans occupied Samgorodok on July 22, 1941. Jewish citizens were obliged to wear Star-of-David armbands, pay ransoms, and perform forced labor. In May 1942, the Jews were ghettoized on one side of the townlet and not permitted to leave to purchase food or draw water, or for any other necessity.

On June 4, 1942, in a pit near the townlet, 500 of Samgorodok's Jews were murdered. About fifty skilled workers and youths who had been separated out during a selection were deported to Kazatin*.

SANDOMIERZ

(Yiddish: **Tsuzmir**)

COUNTY SEAT, KIELCE DISTRICT, POLAND

During the war: General Gouvernement, Radom District

Coordinates: 50°41' | 21°45'

About 2,500 Jews lived in Sandomierz in the interwar period, representing more than one-third of the townlet's inhabitants. Most earned their livelihood from shopkeeping, artisanship, and commerce, especially in wood, grain, and eggs. Sandomierz had a free-loan society, two Jewish banks, traditional Jewish welfare institutions, and a TOZ clinic. Most of the community's boys studied in a traditional Heder, followed by Yeshiva. The girls attended Polish public schools and were tutored separately in Jewish studies and Hebrew. The townlet had chapters of the Zionist parties and pioneering training facilities as well as an active Agudath Israel. Sandomierz also boasted a Yiddish library and a Maccabi sports club.

On September 12, 1939, the Germans occupied Sandomierz and deported its entire Jewish population aged twelve to sixty from the townlet. Several Jews were murdered during the deportation. In the following days, Jews were transferred to a number of townlets in the vicinity, and brutally abused during the process. On September 14, they were returned to Sandomierz.

On November 20, 1939, a Judenrat was established in Sandomierz headed by an attorney, Dr. Goldberg. Large, extortionate "contributions" were exacted, shops were turned over to local Poles, and many Jewish inhabitants were seized for forced labor. As of December 1939, the Jews were ordered to wear white Star-of-David armbands and the letter *J* (for "*Jude*"). They were forbidden to circulate on the sidewalks. Likewise in December, about 1,200 Jews were deported from Kalisz* and Sieradz* to Sandomierz.

In the wake of their severe economic distress, most of the Jews of Sandomierz were compelled to subsist on the support provided by the Judenrat. A special employment bureau affiliated with the Judenrat recruited workers, including women, for very harsh labor.

On November 25, 1941, the Jews were ordered to turn over all furs in their possession, but many preferred to hide or burn the garments.

In June 1942, a ghetto was established in Sandomierz. Although it was not sealed, the Jews were forbidden to leave its grounds. In September 1942, hundreds of Jews were marched on foot from the surrounding localities to the ghetto. Scores of people were unable to keep up the pace were murdered along the way.

The Sandomierz ghetto was among the last to be liquidated in the Radom District (in accordance with the German administrative division). Starting on October 29, 1942, a two-week operation was carried out in the ghetto. More than 3,200 Jews were deported to the Belzec death camp. Some 200 Jews were murdered in their hiding places, while Lithuanian and Ukrainian policemen murdered 78 more people en route to the train station.

Following the deportation, 480 Jews were caught and murdered. Scores of Jews remained in the Sandomierz labor camp, including those with required professions, members of the Jewish Order Service, and dozens of Jews whom the Jewish Order Service had secretly transferred to the camp.

On November 10, 1942, the German reestablished a ghetto in Sandomierz, in which they concentrated about 8,000 Jews from throughout the district. They lured the Jews with assurances that they would be permitted to engage in artisanship and commerce there. Following rumors of an impending operation, approximately 3,000 Jews fled.

On October 10, 1943, about 6,000 Jews were deported from the ghetto to the Treblinka death camp. Some 400 youths were transferred to the Skarzysko-Kamienna labor camp, where most perished within a short time.

It is known that underground activities were organized in Sandomierz that strove from the start to establish a base for partisan activities in the surrounding forests. Contacts made with the local cell of the Armia Krajowa ended tragically:

the Jewish couriers who left the ghetto for a pre-arranged meeting with Armia Krajowa were murdered by members of that group. As a result, the ghetto organization ceased all attempts to send the youth on partisan operations. Jewish youths put up resistance during the liquidation of the ghetto using the few weapons they had managed to obtain. It appears that none survived.

SANNIKI

TOWNLET IN GOSTYNIN COUNTY, WARSAW DISTRICT, POLAND

During the war: Wartheland

Coordinates:
52°20' | 19°52'

About 300 Jews lived in Sanniki in the interwar period, representing approximately one-fifth of the townlet's population. Most earned their livelihood from small-scale commerce and peddling, and a number were artisans.

When World War II broke out, many of Sanniki's Jews fled to the east. The Germans occupied Sanniki in September 1939, and immediately began to terrorize and abuse the townlet's Jews, plundering their property and seizing them for forced labor.

In the summer of 1941, the Jews of Sanniki were forced to move into a separate neighborhood along a number of streets that served as a ghetto of sorts. They were, however, permitted to leave the neighborhood in order to obtain food from the Polish farmers. In the fall of 1941, Jewish men were assigned to forced labor in Konin.

In the summer of 1942, at the same time Gabin* and Gostynin* were liquidated, the Germans deported the Jews of Sanniki to the Chelmno death camp.

SANOK

COUNTY SEAT, LWÓW DISTRICT, POLAND

During the war: General Gouvernement, Cracow District

Coordinates:
49°34' | 22°12'

About 5,000 Jews lived in Sanok when World War II broke out, representing approximately half of the town's population. Most earned their livelihood from commerce, small industry, and artisanship, especially in the garment, metal, and food industries. Others were members of the liberal professions, chiefly in medicine and law. The Jews were aided by the JDC, credit institutions, and free-loan societies. Jewish merchants and artisans formed labor unions. Sanok had an orphanage and welfare and charity societies. Hundreds of pupils attended the local Talmud Torah, and the town also had an Agudath Israel school, a Mizrachi school, and a vocational school that taught weaving. Zionist activities and Hebrew courses were held in a "Jewish House," which also contained a Hebrew library. Sanok had chapters of all the Zionist parties, a branch of the Bund, and chapters of Agudath Israel.

Sanok was occupied by the Germans on September 9, 1939. The Germans imposed a nightly curfew, forbade Jewish inhabitants to purchase provisions in the municipal market, and seized Jews for forced labor. When the Germans torched the town's synagogues, a man named Yosef Rabakh attempted to save a Torah scroll from the fire, but was thrown into the flames and killed.

In the early weeks of the occupation, the Ukrainian town council that presided over Sanok levied a ransom on the town's Jews. In mid-September 1939, the Germans burst into Jewish homes, plundering their property and inflicting beatings. Family heads were ordered to gather, a selection was carried out, and several Jewish inhabitants were ordered to head east with their families across the San River, to the area of eastern Galicia under Soviet control. These Jews were exiled to various areas of the Soviet Union in the summer of 1940.

The Jews who remained in Sanok were required to remit periodic ransom payments, were restricted in their freedom of movement, and were seized for forced labor. In late 1939 or early 1940, a Judenrat was established in the town. It was ordered to supply the Germans with forced laborers, in addition to valuables, furniture, and other assorted items.

Sanok
A view of the ghetto.
Photograph from the Der Stürmer Collection. (YV courtesy Der Stuermer Archive)

In the summer of 1941, a Jewish quarter was established in Sanok that for a time remained unsealed. Jews were brought in from surrounding localities, and the Judenrat and local JSS chapter opened public soup kitchens that distributed hundreds of hot meals every day. In September 1941, the Germans deported a group of Jews they caught praying to the Auschwitz death camp. During this period, Gestapo men randomly murdered Jews in the streets. In early 1942, abductions of Jews for forced labor and as laborers in nearby camps were stepped up.

In the summer of 1942, yet more Jews from surrounding localities were transferred to the Jewish quarter in Sanok. In September 1942, the Jewish quarter was transformed into a closed ghetto. It had a population either of about 8,000 or 13,000 Jews at that time (sources vary on the figure).

An order to deport the Jews from Sanok was issued on September 5, 1942. Those caught in hiding were murdered in the town's cemetery. Most of the Jews were deported to the nearby Zaslaw camp, a place of concentration for Jews from the entire county. They were in turn deported in a number of transports to the Belzec death camp.

Following the deportation, about 1,500 Jews remained in Sanok, with some 300 in the ghetto, while the rest were held in camp conditions in various workplaces. In January 1943, all Jews working in the town were concentrated in the ghetto. In February 1943, the Sanok ghetto was liquidated, and all its inhabitants were deported to the Zaslaw camp, and subsequently to Belzec.

SÁRBOGÁRD

TOWNLET IN FEJÉR COUNTY, HUNGARY

Coordinates:
46°53' | 18°38'

The last national census conducted in Hungary prior to the German occupation, taken in January 1941, recorded 304 Jewish inhabitants in Sarbogard, representing roughly 4 percent of the total population. Most were merchants and artisans. The townlet's Jewish community was Orthodox and maintained a Jewish elementary school, and a Yeshiva.

In 1941, several Jews from Sarbogard were drafted into the Hungarian army for forced labor service.

The German army occupied Hungary on March 19, 1944. A census conducted in the second week of April 1944 showed that 245 Jews belonged to the Orthodox Jewish community of Sarbogard.

The Hungarian administration remained intact and operational after the occupation. Hungarian national and local authorities decreed the ghettoization and deportation of the Jews. On April 3, 1944, gendarmes interned sixty-three Jewish people, thirty-three of whom died in the gas chambers of Auschwitz. On May 8, eight Jews were drafted for forced labor service; since the ration coupons of their families were withheld, they starved until their deportation.

The Sarbogard ghetto was established in May 1944. The Hungarian sub-prefect of Fejer County, Andor Thaisz, boasted that in his county, "not a single Christian had to move out of his home." Most of the Jews in the county were required to move together into Jewish houses marked with yellow stars.

Between June 21 and 23, 1944, Hungarian gendarmes searched the ghetto for concealed valuables and tortured the Jews. From June 26, 1944, Jews from the area were brought to the ghetto of Sarbogard.

On July 1, 1944, the ghetto inhabitants were gathered in the synagogue and then transferred to the entrainment center in Kaposvar*. On July 4, 1944, they were deported to Auschwitz.

SARNAKI

TOWNLET IN SIEDLCE COUNTY, LUBLIN DISTRICT, POLAND

During the war: General Gouvernement, Warsaw District

Coordinates:
52°19' | 22°53'

Before World War II, about 2,000 Jews lived in Sarnaki, representing approximately half of the townlet's population. They earned their livelihood from commerce and artisanship, especially in the garment trade. Many of the townlet's Jews were Hasidim. The townlet also had active chapters of the Zionist Federation and Zionist parties as well as chapters of Agudath Israel and the Bund. The community's children attended a Hebrew school.

The Red Army entered Sarnaki on September 21, 1939. One week later, however, the Soviets retreated to the east in accordance with the Molotov-Ribbentrop Pact, and the Germans entered the townlet. Many of Sarnaki's Jews fled eastward along with the Red Army, and Polish refugees were put up in their abandoned homes.

From the onset of the German occupation, the remaining Jews in Sarnaki were seized for forced labor. In January 1940, a Judenrat was established in the townlet and ordered to provide the Germans with slave laborers. The random abuse and murder of the townlet's Jews began in early 1940. During that period, 1,000 people deported from Kalisz* and Blaszki in Wartheland were brought to Sarnaki.

The townlet was bombed during the German invasion of the Soviet Union in June 1941, and the homes of many Jews were hit.

In September 1941, a ghetto of 1,180 Jews was established in Sarnaki. In May 1942, its residents were evacuated to the ghettos of Losice* and Mordy*, and deported on to the Treblinka death camp on August 22, 1942.

Seventy young and professional Jews remained in the Sarnaki ghetto, which was turned into a labor camp. Most were murdered on July 21, 1942, by German gendarmes and Gestapo, while a few individuals survived in hiding.

SARNY

COUNTY SEAT, VOLHYNIA DISTRICT, POLAND

(After World War II in the USSR/Ukraine)

During the war: Reichskommissariat Ukraine

Coordinates:
51°29' | 26°36'

During the interwar years, there were about 5,000 Jews in Sarny, accounting for almost half of the town's population. The Jews of Sarny manufactured wooden goods and traded in lumber, agricultural produce, leather, and furs with central and western European countries. The town also had Jewish-owned flour mills and edible-oil factories. The Jews of Sarny dominated the town's retail trade and were assisted by trade unions, two Jewish savings-and-loan associations that operated intermittently, and a mutual-aid organization. Traditional charitable and welfare institutions such as a Jewish orphanage and a TOZ clinic were active in the town. Jewish children and youths were educated in a range of institutions: a Hebrew-language Tarbut kindergarten and elementary school, an ORT vocational school assisted by the JDC, a Talmud Torah, and a Yeshiva. The community also boasted three Jewish libraries and a drama group. Political organizations included Bund groups, Communists, and Zionist youth movements and parties whose members were among the founders of the Zionist training facility in Klesow* and who later immigrated to the Land of Israel.

The Soviets occupied the area in September 1939 and then retreated from Sarny on July 4, 1941. The Germans entered the town the following day. For the next three days, local Ukrainians dispossessed Jewish inhabitants of their property. They also attacked Jews.

The Germans forced the Jews of Sarny to wear Star-of-David armbands, which were replaced in the fall of 1941 by yellow badges. A Judenrat was established under the most recent chairman of the organized community, S. Gershonok, but because of his advanced age, the Judenrat was essentially administered by its secretary, Neumann, a German-speaking refugee from Kalisz*. A Jewish Order

Service was set up under the command of Yona Margalit, who later became active in a resistance group.

On April 2–4, 1942, some 6,000 Jews from Sarny and surrounding villages were concentrated in a ghetto that was enclosed by planks and barbed wire and guarded by Ukrainian order police.

In June 1942, when the ghetto received reports about mass murders, three resistance groups formed with assistance from the head of the Judenrat. One of the units was headed by Margalit. The groups equipped themselves with small quantities of firearms and other miscellaneous weapons as well as inflammable materials. They planned to set fire to the ghetto when it was liquidated, break down the fences, attack the guards, and lead a mass escape to the forests.

By August 27, 1942, the Jews had been evacuated from the ghetto to the Poleska camp, already inhabited by Jews from other localities—approximately 13,700 people in all. Neumann, the secretary of the Judenrat, thwarted the resistance groups' planned operation, claiming that the Germans were merely rounding up the Jews for a headcount.

On August 27–28, the Germans began to take the Jews to the pits. Two members of the resistance groups, Tendler and Yosef Gendelman, cut through the barbed wire, gave the order to torch the barracks (the fire was set by a group of Gypsies, according to one testimony), and urged the Jews to escape. Thousands of people attempted to flee, but many were shot while crossing the fences and in the streets of the town. Several hundred managed to reach the forests but only a few dozen survived until the liberation.

SÁRVÁR

TOWN IN VAS COUNTY, HUNGARY

Coordinates:
47°15' | 16°56'

The last national census conducted prior to the German occupation, taken in January 1941, recorded 780 Jewish inhabitants in Sarvar, accounting for roughly 7 percent of the total population. Most were merchants and artisans. The town had both a Neolog and an Orthodox Jewish community. Each Jewish community had various affiliated Jewish social and religious associations as well as an elementary school.

In August 1919, during the White Terror era, members of the detachments and ethnic German (Swabian) youths broke into the homes of Jews, many of whom fled but came back several months later. An elderly Jewish couple was murdered after their return. During the 1930s, Zionism became increasingly popular, especially among young Orthodox Jews. In 1940, Jewish men were drafted into the Hungarian army for forced labor service and were placed in a camp set up in the town.

The German army occupied Hungary on March 19, 1944. A census conducted in the second week of April 1944 showed that 901 Jews belonged to the Orthodox Jewish community and 146 Jews to the Neolog Jewish community of Sarvar.

The Hungarian administration remained intact and in force after the occupation. The ghettoization and deportation of the Jews were carried out on the basis of the decrees and orders of the Hungarian national and local authorities. On May 6, 1944, the Hungarian sub-prefect, Dr. Jozsef Tulok, published a decree designating May 12 as the deadline for moving the Jews into ghettos. According to the decree, as of seven o'clock on the night of May 9, 1944, the Jews of Sarvar were forbidden to leave their homes. From the following day, after submitting a list of their valuables, they were required to move into the ghetto, which was established in the apartments of the workers of the local sugar-beet factory and in one of its storage buildings. Approximately 150 Jews from the Sarvar County-District were also transferred to the ghetto.

Heading the Jewish Council was Erno Fischer, the last serving president of the Orthodox Jewish community. Four physicians practiced in the ghetto. The ghetto inhabitants were prohibited from leaving it and were thus kept from remedying food shortages. Most of the inhabitants were indigent Orthodox Jews in dire need of fat or oil. On June 12, 1944, men under forty-eight years of age who were fit to work were drafted into the Hungarian army for forced labor service; they were thus saved from the later deportation.

In mid-June 1944, there were 950 people living in the ghetto. The ghetto was liquidated on June 29, 1944; its inhabitants were transferred to the Rayon factory of Sarvar, which served as one of the entrainment centers of the county: altogether 5,621 deportees were concentrated in the factory in late June 1944. They were deported on to Auschwitz on July 4 and 6, 1944.

SASHALOM

TOWN IN PEST-PILIS-SOLT-KISKUN COUNTY, HUNGARY

Coordinates:
47°39' | 19°45'

The last national census conducted prior to the German occupation, taken in January 1941, recorded 515 Jewish inhabitants in Sashalom, accounting for roughly 4 percent of the total population. Most were merchants and artisans, and a number were clerks. As Sashalom was a popular summer resort for the residents of Budapest*, many of the town's Jews maintained guesthouses and worked in the catering industry. Sashalom had a Neolog Jewish community and various Jewish social and religious associations.

The German army occupied Hungary on March 19, 1944. On March 21, 1944, German units arrived in the town. As of the following day, Jews were forbidden to leave their homes. A number of people attempted to escape to Budapest by train, but they were ordered by police inspectors to disembark; they were brought to the Kistarcsa internment camp and deported on to Auschwitz.

A census conducted in the second week of April 1944 showed that 326 Jews belonged to the Neolog Jewish community of Sashalom.

The Hungarian administration remained intact and operational after the German occupation. The ghettoization and deportation of the Jews occurred on the basis of decrees and orders issued by the Hungarian national and local authorities. On May 12, Hungarian sub-prefect Dr. Laszlo Endre, a militant antisemite, ordered the establishment of ghettos in his county. The move into the ghettos began at five o'clock in the morning on May 22, 1944. The Sashalom ghetto was not established along a single block; local Jews were required to live in houses marked as Jewish.

At the end of June or beginning of July 1944, the inhabitants of the ghetto were transferred to the brick factory in Monor*, which served as the entrainment center for the ghettos of the county surrounding Budapest from the south and east. They belonged to a group of approximately 8,000 Jews who were deported from the brick factory to Auschwitz in three transports, between July 6 and 8, 1944.

SÁTORALJAÚJHELY

(in Jewish sources: **Újhely**)

COUNTY SEAT IN ZEMPLÉN COUNTY, HUNGARY

Coordinates:
48°24' | 21°40'

The last national census conducted prior to the German occupation, taken in January 1941, recorded 4,160 Jewish inhabitants in Satoraljaujhely, approximately 23 percent of the total population. Most of the Jews were merchants and artisans. Three Jewish communities were active in Satoraljaujhely: Orthodox, Status Quo Ante, and an official "Sephardic" community, which was in fact Hasidic. The town had various Jewish social and religious associations, including a Jewish elementary school and two Talmudei Torah.

The German army occupied Hungary on March 19, 1944. According to a census conducted in the second week of April 1944, about 1,100 Jews belonged to the Sephardic Orthodox, some 900 to the Orthodox, and 877 to the Status Quo Ante Jewish community.

A few days after the German occupation, the German military commander of the town summoned the rabbis of the Jewish communities. He demanded a large sum of money and ordered the dissolution of the Jewish communities and the appointment of a Jewish Council. On April 14, 1944, the German commander of Satoraljaujhely summoned the leaders of the Jewish Council for a brief on the creation of a ghetto in the town.

Despite a highly active German military commander in the town, the Hungarian administration remained intact and in force. The ghettoization and deportation of the Jews were carried out on the basis of the decrees and orders of the Hungarian national and local authorities.

The Hungarian sub-prefect of Zemplen County, Miklos Bornemissza, ordered the mayor of Satoraljaujhely, Dr. Indar Varo, to establish a ghetto in the town. The ghetto was set up in the Gypsy quarter on the banks of the Ronyva and its neighborhood, including the Jewish quarter. Some 15,000 people were required to move into the Satoraljaujhely ghetto, including most the Jews from the Zemplen County (with the exception of Szerencs).

On April 15, 1944, the Hungarian gendarmes began to transfer the Jews from the county to the ghetto in Satoraljaujhely. The entire operation was completed within four days. The authorities were concerned about the extreme overcrowding in the ghetto (with between twenty and twenty-five people to a room) as well as with the primitive water system in the area. Following the official visit of the undersecretary of state for internal affairs, Laszlo Endre, on April 24, 1944, fifteen Jewish physicians practiced in the ghetto and Jewish nurses were recruited. The Jewish hospital in the ghetto accommodated 250 patients, while makeshift hospitals were also set up in the school buildings.

The Jewish Council was headed by lawyer Dr. Lajos Rosenberg, the last serving president of the Status Quo Ante Jewish community. Five young men served as members of the Jewish Order Service. The ghetto also had a Jewish bakery.

The inhabitants of the Satoraljaujhely ghetto were deported to Auschwitz in four transports, on May 16, 22, and 25, and on June 3, 1944. After each transport, the geographic area of the ghetto was reduced.

SAVRAN

COUNTY SEAT, ODESSA DISTRICT, UKRAINE, USSR

During the war: Transnistria (under Romanian control)

Coordinates:
48°08' | 30°05'

In the mid-1920s, about 3,400 Jews lived in Savran, representing nearly half of the townlet's population. In 1920, during the civil war in Russia (1918–1920), a number of Jews were murdered in pogroms carried out in the townlet by Ukrainian farmers along with soldiers of the White Army.

During the Soviet period, Jews were mostly artisans, but several changed over to farming. Savran had a Jewish Ethnic Soviet that conducted its business in Yiddish and a Jewish school that offered instruction in Yiddish. The rise of industrialization and urbanization in the Soviet Union and the accompanying deterioration in economic conditions caused a drop in the townlet's Jewish population, so that by the eve of the German invasion of the Soviet Union, about 1,200 Jews remained in the townlet.

The Germans occupied Savran on July 30, 1941. An unknown number of Jews had managed to evacuate or flee prior to the Soviet withdrawal.

In early September 1941, Savran was annexed to Transnistria, under Romanian rule. In November 1941, the Jews of the townlet were deported to a labor camp established near Obodovka* in the Vinnitsa District. Many perished of cold, disease, and hunger. A number of those who remained managed to reach the Bershad* ghetto, where they were able to survive.

In late 1942, about 150 Jews, mostly children, women, and the elderly, returned to Savran and were concentrated in a ghetto established on the edge of the townlet. They toiled on nearby farms in exchange for food, while the professionals worked in artisans' cooperatives in the townlet and received food products from the local grocery in return.

In May 1943, brought to the townlet were 127 Jewish inmates of the Vapnyarka concentration camp for political prisoners. They were concentrated in a second ghetto consisting of fifteen to twenty buildings that had been confiscated from Ukrainians. The second ghetto was located in the same quarter as the ghetto of the local Jews but had better living conditions. The Ukrainian population related favorably to the Jews, and the local people sold them food at reduced prices. Women were not sent out to work. The deportees organized themselves in the ghetto according to the organizations they had belonged to in the Vapnyarka camp. They had two leaders, one an official leader who maintained contact with the authorities, and another who was unofficially responsible for the organization of the workers' groups. The deportees were in contact with their relatives in Romania through the cooperation of the gendarmes, who brought them money and clothing when they returned from their furloughs. The deportees also received help from the deportees in the Olgopol* ghetto, who were supported by an unofficial organization that extended help to political deportees and prisoners.

Savran had a public soup kitchen that served all of the deportees. The doctors among them organized a tiny medical clinic and a dental clinic. The deportees maintained close relations with the local Jews and strove to improve their situation. Synagogues were established in both ghettos in which services were held on the High Holy Days of fall 1943. A Torah scroll sent from Olgopol was passed from one synagogue to another by Jewish worshippers who wrapped the scroll in their prayer shawls (*tallitot*).

The Jews organized joint self-defense plans against the activities of ultranationalist Ukrainian gangs that entered the ghetto to terrorize and abuse Jews. The head of the deportees' ghetto appealed to the Romanian in charge, requesting protection against the thugs; gendarmes were assigned to protect the ghetto inhabitants.

A number of the ghetto inhabitants made contact with the partisans who were active in the area.

In December 1943, most of the deportees returned home, so that on the day of liberation, March 27, 1944, few deportees and local Jews remained in the townlet.

SEBEZH

COUNTY SEAT, KALININ DISTRICT, RUSSIAN FEDERATION, USSR

During the war: Military Administration Area

Coordinates:
57°06' | 27°04'

In the mid-1920s, there were 1,810 Jews living in Sebezh, more than one-third of the local population. The community had a kindergarten and school that taught in Yiddish. Modernization and industrialization processes in the Soviet Union drove the Jewish population down to 845 people by the eve of World War II.

Many Jewish townspeople apparently managed to escape or were evacuated to the east in the days preceding the German occupation. The Germans occupied Sebezh on July 9, 1941, and within a few days murdered two Jews on charges of arson. In September 1941, the 100 remaining Jews in Sebezh were concentrated in a ghetto, where they were put to assorted humiliating labors. They attempted to ease their plight by bribing the Germans.

The Sebezh ghetto was liquidated in March 1942 and its last inhabitants, some ninety people, were shot to death.

ŠEDUVA

(Yiddish: **Shadeve**; Russian: **Shadov**)

TOWNLET IN PANEVĖŽYS COUNTY, LITHUANIA

During the war: Reichskommissariat Ostland

Coordinates: 55°46' | 23°46'

On the eve of the German occupation, about 800 Jews lived in Seduva, representing more than 20 percent of the local population. Most of the Jews of the townlet earned their livelihood from commerce, artisanship, small industry, and farming. The Jewish community boasted a Heder and a Tarbut school as well as Zionist parties and youth movements.

After Lithuania was annexed to the Soviet Union in 1940, private businesses in Seduva were nationalized, Hebrew schools were closed, and activities of the Zionist parties were discontinued.

Seduva was occupied by the Germans on June 26, 1941, although actual rule was handed over to nationalist Lithuanians. Immediately after the onset of the occupation, Jewish inhabitants were forced to wear a white armband with a yellow Star-of-David. Many of the Jews were employed in forced labor; a number of Jews were arrested, and several were murdered.

In mid-July 1941, all of Seduva's Jews were forced to move into a ghetto of sorts, consisting of two buildings in the nearby village. The ghetto was encircled by a barbed-wire fence, with guards stationed to watch over it. In addition to the Jews of Seduva, twenty-five young Jewish people who worked for farmers in the area were moved into the ghetto. The living conditions there were extremely harsh: the buildings had neither water nor a source of light. The only Jewish doctor, Dr. Paturski, attempted to minister to the inhabitants of the ghetto as best he could. The Jews of the ghetto were at the total mercy of the Lithuanian guards, who stole their possessions.

On August 3, 1941, the Lithuanians removed ten Jews from the ghetto and murdered them on the way to Radviliskis*. In the middle of the month, twenty-seven more Jews were murdered beyond the nearby village. Thirty-five Jews who worked on the nearby Raudondvaris estate were murdered and buried in its grounds. The ghetto was liquidated on August 25, 1941, when its 650 inhabitants were taken to the Liaudiskiai forest and shot to death.

SĘDZISZÓW

TOWNLET IN ROPCZYCE COUNTY, CRACOW DISTRICT, POLAND

During the war: General Gouvernement, Radom District

Coordinates: 50°35' | 20°04'

When World War II broke out, about 1,000 Jews lived in Sedziszow, representing approximately 40 percent of the townlet's population. Most earned their livelihood from artisanship and small-scale industry, especially in the garment and food industries. The JDC and former residents of the townlet living in America helped to establish a free-loan society. Educational establishments included a Tarbut Hebrew school and a Talmud Torah. Zionist parties and youth movements as well as a Zionist sports club were all active in the townlet. A small number of Jews were members of the illegal Communist party.

The Germans occupied Sedziszow in September 1939. In early May 1942, fifty Jewish men were sent from the townlet to a labor camp in Pustkow.

In June or early July 1942, a ghetto was established into which Jews from nearby Ropczyce* and surrounding localities were concentrated along with the local Jewish community. The population of the ghetto grew to about 1,900 people.

The Sedziszow ghetto was liquidated on July 24, 1942, when about 400 elderly and handicapped people and children were murdered near Sedziszow following a selection, and about 1,500 Jews were deported to the Belzec death camp.

SEMELIŠKĖS

(Yiddish: **Semelishok**)

TOWNLET IN TRAKAI-KAISIADORYS COUNTY, LITHUANIA

During the war:
Reichskommissariat Ostland

Coordinates:
54°40' | 24°40'

In 1940, about sixty Jewish families lived in Semeliskes. They earned their livelihood from commerce, artisanship, and light industry. Most of the community's public activities centered on traditional Jewish religious and educational institutions.

In the fall of 1940, after Lithuania was annexed to the Soviet Union, the shops in Semeliskes were nationalized, the Hebrew school closed, and Zionist activity discontinued. During this period, about 200 Yeshiva student refugees from Baranowicze* arrived in Semeliskes.

After Lithuania was occupied by the Germans in late June 1941, nationalist Lithuanians took over Semeliskes. Several weeks later, the Jews of the townlet were concentrated into a ghetto of sorts in a church and four adjacent buildings. Each day, the Jewish men were seized from the ghetto for forced labor; after several weeks, a number of the men were executed by Lithuanians led by the local priest. On September 22, 1941, the remaining Jews from the nearby townlets of Vievis and Zasliai were brought to Semeliskes, and the number of Jews in the severely overcrowded ghetto reached 995, consisting of mostly women and children.

On October 6, 1941, all the inhabitants of the ghetto were taken to a nearby forest and murdered by Lithuanians. According to the Karl Jaeger report, 213 Jewish men, 359 Jewish women, and 390 Jewish children were executed.

Twenty-three Jews managed to escape prior to the ghetto's liquidation and hide with farmers. Several were caught, but others succeeded in joining Soviet partisans.

SEMENOVKA

(Ukrainian: **Semenivka**)

COUNTY SEAT, CHERNIGOV DISTRICT, UKRAINE, USSR

During the war:
Reichskommissariat Ukraine

Coordinates:
52°10' | 32°35'

At the beginning of the twentieth century there were about 1,700 Jews living in Semenovka. The Russian Civil War (1918–20) and subsequent urbanization and industrialization in the USSR led to a significant reduction in the townlet's Jewish population by the eve of World War II, to about 400 people, 5 percent of the local population. Semenovka had a Yiddish-language government school.

The Germans occupied Semenovka on August 25, 1941. A number of Jews managed to flee to the east in advance. Seizures for forced labor and such depredations as property looting were carried out from the onset of the occupation.

In November 1941, the Jews of Semenovka were ghettoized along one street. One day in early December 1941, they were concentrated in a schoolhouse. The following day, all were murdered a short distance from townlet.

SENNO

(Yiddish: **Sene**; Belarussian: **Syanno**)

COUNTY SEAT, VITEBSK DISTRICT, BELARUS, USSR

During the war: Military Administration Area

Coordinates:
54°49' | 29°43'

At the start of the twentieth century, there were about 2,500 Jews in Senno, roughly 60 percent of the population. During the era of Soviet rule, many Jews practiced artisan trades, some in cooperatives, while a few turned to farming.

Senno had both a Jewish Ethnic Council and a school that operated in Yiddish. Urbanization and industrialization in the Soviet Union depleted the Jewish population, so that shortly before the German invasion of the Soviet Union only some 1,000 Jews remained, about one-quarter of the local population.

The Germans occupied Senno on July 5, 1941. In September they established a ghetto in the Jewish neighborhood of Golynka. Over time, Jews from the vicinity were also concentrated in its quarters. At first the ghetto was unfenced, and Jews could go into townlet to buy or barter belongings for food. In October 1941, Belarussian police were deployed to guard the ghetto, and its inhabitants were not allowed to leave without a permit. Jews were required to wear yellow armbands, and forced labor was instituted. Starvation was rampant; the Germans rationed bread at fifty grams per person per day, and often several days passed without the distribution of any provisions. The ghetto was run by a Jewish Council headed by Samuil Svoyskiy, the former principal of the local school.

In October–November 1941, the Germans murdered several Jews on various pretexts. From time to time, Germans and Belarussian police stole Jewish property.

The Senno ghetto was liquidated on December 30, 1941, when SS and Belarussian police murdered some 800 inhabitants near the old Jewish cemetery on the road to Kozlovka. Several Jews survived the operation, a number of whom joined the partisans. Later on, Jews caught in hiding and children of mixed marriages were murdered.

SEPSISZENTGYÖRGY

TOWN IN HÁROMSZÉK COUNTY, HUNGARY
(After World War II in Romania; Romanian: **Sfîntu Gheorghe**)

Coordinates:
46°27' | 24°14'

The last national census conducted in Hungary prior to the German occupation, taken in January 1941, recorded 400 Jewish inhabitants in Sepsiszentgyorgy, roughly 3 percent of the total population. Most were merchants and artisans, while several owned factories. The town had a Status Quo Ante Jewish community and, as of 1937, an Orthodox prayer association.

After World War I, Sepsiszentgyorgy, which was formerly in Hungary, became part of Romania. On August 30, 1940, the town became part of Hungary again. The Hungarian anti-Jewish legislation that applied to the local Jews was enforced more harshly in North Transylvania, where the town was located, than in inner Hungary.

In the summer of 1941, the Hungarian authorities deported to German-occupied Ukraine several Jewish families whose members could not prove their Hungarian citizenship. They were murdered on August 27 or 28 at Kamenets-Podolsk*. In 1942, Jewish men from Sepsiszentgyorgy were drafted into the Hungarian army for forced labor service. Most were deployed to the eastern front in the Ukraine, where many perished.

The German army occupied Hungary on March 19, 1944. A census conducted in the second week of April 1944 reported that 428 Jews belonged to the Status Quo Ante Jewish community of Sepsiszentgyorgy.

The Hungarian administration remained intact and in force after the occupation. The ghettoization and deportation of the Jews were implemented on the basis of the decrees and orders of the Hungarian national and local authorities. Following an April 28, 1944, conference regarding ghettoization in North Transylvania, the ghetto in Sepsiszentgyorgy was established on May 3, 1944, in a partially built building. Some 850 local Jews lived in the ghetto as well as the Jews from the southern parts of Haromszek and Csik counties. The ghetto did not have a Jewish Council. Two Jewish physicians treated the inhabitants in the ghetto.

The residents of the ghetto of Sepsiszentgyorgy were transferred to Szaszregen* on May 31, 1944. They were deported to Auschwitz on June 4, 1944.

SEREGÉLYES

TOWNLET IN FEJÉR COUNTY, HUNGARY

Coordinates:
47°06' | 18°35'

The last national census conducted in Hungary prior to the German occupation recorded, in January 1941, eighty-two Jewish inhabitants in Seregelyes, accounting for approximately 2 percent of the total population. Most were merchants and artisans. The town's Jewish community was Neolog.

The German army occupied Hungary on March 19, 1944. According to a census conducted in the second week of April 1944, eighty-three Jews belonged to the Neolog Jewish community of Seregelyes.

The Hungarian administration remained intact and operational after the occupation. Hungarian national and local authorities decreed the ghettoization and deportation of the Jews. The Seregelyes ghetto was established on May 16, 1944. The Hungarian sub-prefect of Fejer County, Andor Thaisz, boasted that in his county, "not a single Christian had to move out of his home." Most of the Jews in the county, more than 200 Jews from Seregelyes and the vicinity, were required to move together into Jewish houses marked with yellow stars. A curfew was imposed between eight o'clock at night and five in the morning.

On May 31, 1944, local members of the Arrow Cross Party, led by gendarme Sub-Lieutenant Balazsi, tortured the Jews into revealing the whereabouts of their hidden valuables. Later, the ghetto inhabitants were deported to the entrainment center in the Szabo brick factory in Szekesfehervar*, and on to Auschwitz on June 14, 1944.

SERNIKI

TOWNLET IN PINSK COUNTY, VOLHYNIA DISTRICT, POLAND
(After World War II in the USSR/Ukraine; Ukrainian: **Sernyky**)

During the war: Reichskommissariat Ukraine

Coordinates: 51°49' | 26°14'

During the interwar years there were 1,000 Jews in Serniki, about one-fifth of the townlet's population. The Jews of Serniki were petty merchants and artisans, mainly in carpentry and construction. The townlet had a reformed Heder that taught in Hebrew and a chapter of the *Betar* youth movement.

The area came under Soviet rule in September 1939.

When the Germans invaded the Soviet Union in June 1941, the townlet came under the administration of Ukrainian police. The first Germans reached Serniki only on August 8, 1941. SS Cavalry Brigade soldiers murdered 150 Jewish men.

A Judenrat and Jewish Order Service were set up in early September 1941. The Jews were made to wear a Star-of-David armband, which was later replaced by a yellow patch, and were conscripted for forced labor.

In early 1942, the Jews were concentrated in an unfenced ghetto and placed under curfew from seven o'clock at night until morning. Soon afterwards, Jews from villages in the area were transferred to the ghetto.

In early September 1942, rumors spread that pits were being dug in preparation for the murder of Jews. The Judenrat attempted to bribe Ukrainian policemen to turn a blind eye to Jews who tried to escape but to no avail: all were shot.

On September 8, 1942, a large number of Jews gathered at the home of the Judenrat head and decided to escape. About 500 Jews fled the townlet that night and the following morning. The same day, the Germans murdered the remaining 550 Jews of Serniki in the village of Salomir, eight kilometers from the townlet.

About 200 of the fugitives were killed during their escape; 279 men and women, most of them young, hid in groups in the forests.

SHARGOROD

COUNTY SEAT, VINNITSA DISTRICT, UKRAINE, USSR

During the war: Transnistria (under Romanian control)

Coordinates: 48°45' | 28°05'

In the early twentieth century, about 4,000 Jews lived in Shargorod, representing more than half of the town's population. They suffered greatly during the civil war in Russia (1918–20), and in the summer of 1919, about 100 were killed by Ukrainian soldiers.

During the period of Soviet rule, the town had a Jewish Ethnic Soviet and a Jewish school that both operated in Yiddish. In the 1930s, the synagogues in the city were closed; prayers were held in private prayer quorums instead. Two ritual slaughterers, who also performed circumcisions, were active in the town. Many Jews left Shargorod in the interwar period as a result of growing industrialization and urbanization in the Soviet Union. By the eve of the German invasion of the Soviet Union, about 1,600 Jews lived in in the town.

The Germans occupied Shargorod on July 22, 1941, and in early September annexed the town to Transnistria, which was under Romanian control. The Jews of Shargorod were ordered to wear a yellow badge on their clothes and to mark their homes with a yellow metal Star-of-David. They were concentrated in an unfenced ghetto.

In early October 1941, about 3,000 Jews from Bukovina and Bessarabia were transferred to Shargorod. They were put up in the homes of local Jews in the ghetto, the synagogue, and public buildings. Most of the Jews traded in old clothes, cigarettes, and matches, drew water, and worked in other related occupations. Many ghetto inhabitants attempted to obtain food in the nearby villages despite the danger they faced in leaving the site.

During the initial period of the occupation, the local ritual slaughterer, Shlomo Kleiman, was the head of the ghetto. When deportees arrived, a number of their leaders organized themselves on the basis of their towns of origin. In November 1941, a twenty-five member Jewish council was established in the ghetto, which included three or four representatives of each community, as well as three members of the local council. The council elected a six-member committee from among its own members. The committee, headed by Dr. Meir Teich and his deputy Avraham Reicher, both from Bukovina, organized a Jewish Order Service in the ghetto, with seventeen young members, headed by attorney Dr. Koch. The Jewish Order Service defended the ghetto's inhabitants from attacks by local thugs.

With the help of the council, the activities of the public soup kitchen were expanded to 1,500 meals a day, and the bakery stepped up its production. Later, the committee established a farm and organized clothing- and food-storage facilities. It also instituted a registry bureau for the residents of the ghetto, collected various taxes, and set up an employment bureau that prepared work lists according to age, health, and family status.

In the early stages of the ghetto, the local committee received provisions from a local Ukrainian cooperative. The manager of the state flour mill, Julius Andreevich-Mohr, a local German born in Bessarabia, secretly supplied the council with large quantities of flour, and prior to Passover, he koshered the mill and distributed flour for matzo to the Jews. In February 1942, help began to reach the ghetto from Bucharest, and in June of that year, assistance was arranged on a regular basis. Groups of deportees also received aid from Bucharest as well as from Jews from various towns and from Zionist organizations.

To fight the spread of epidemic typhus, disinfection ovens were set up in the ghetto as early as December 1941, the public bathhouse was reopened, and a hospital with 100 beds was established in February 1942. Later, a power station that generated power to pump water in the ghetto, a soap factory, and a pharmacy were established. These initiatives succeeded to some extent in mitigating the impact of the epidemic in the ghetto, but the death rate was nevertheless high: about 1,400 people, including roughly half of the doctors active in the ghetto, fell victim to epidemic typhus, mainly in the winter of 1941/42.

Few of the ghetto's children studied formally, but in time, an orphanage for 600 children was organized with help from Romania; the children were instructed in both Jewish and general studies. The orphanage also became the cultural center in the ghetto, holding play productions and concerts. In the fall of 1942, before the High Holy Days, the great synagogue was reopened and remained active throughout the remainder of the ghetto's existence. Weddings, circumcisions, and other religious services were held in the synagogue. Activities of Hano'ar Hatziyyoni were held secretly in the ghetto and a newspaper was published.

In time, Jews from the area slipped into the ghetto, including several who had fled from the German occupation zone. Despite the prohibition against accepting any additional Jews into the ghetto and the evacuation of a number of Jews to nearby villages on June 30, 1942, more than 400 Jews who were not recorded in the official registry or who were registered under false names secretly entered it. According to the figures of the Bucharest aid committee, some 1,800 local Jews and about 3,500 deportees lived in the ghetto in March 1943. In late December, approximately 650 of the deportees returned to Dorohoi, and from there to their homes.

The ghetto committee maintained close contact with the partisans who were active in the area and helped them; in special circumstances, partisans hid in the ghetto. During the Romanian withdrawal, partisans entered the ghetto in order to protect the Jews, if the need arose, from extermination units.

Shargorod was liberated by the Red Army on March 20, 1944.

SHAROVKA

(Ukrainian: **Sharivka**)

TOWNLET IN YARMOLINTSY COUNTY, KAMENETS-PODOLSK DISTRICT, UKRAINE, USSR

During the war: Reichskommissariat Ukraine

Coordinates: 49°25' | 26°55'

In the 1920s, there were 650 Jews in Sharovka, approximately one-quarter of the townlet's population. Most worked in a nearby kolkhoz.

The Germans occupied Sharovka on July 8, 1941. Although a few Jewish families managed to escape in advance of the occupation, after the Germans' arrival the townlet received an influx of Jews deported from nearby towns as well as refugees from Poland and Bessarabia.

A ghetto was established in one part of the townlet. It was not fenced; Jews were permitted to leave its confines and Ukrainians entered to barter food for possessions. The yellow Star-of-David requirement was instituted and the community was forced to pay ransoms. A head of the Jews and a two-member Jewish Order Service were appointed to assign labor duties and collect ransoms. The Jews of Sharovka performed forced labor in nearby Yarmolintsy. Many ghetto inhabitants died owing to conditions of overcrowding, starvation, and poor sanitation. In late summer 1941, Jews from the Frampol* ghetto were transferred to Sharovka.

In October 1942, the Jewish Order Service, acting on the orders of Germans who had come from Yarmolintsy, rounded up all the young men in the ghetto, ostensibly for labor. They were taken to a quarry and murdered. The rest of the inhabitants were killed in late October or early November 1942, along with the other Jews in the district.

SHCHEDRIN

(Belarussian: **Shchadryn**)

VILLAGE, FORMER JEWISH FARMING COLONY IN PARICHI COUNTY, POLESYE DISTRICT, BELARUS, USSR

During the war: Military Administration Area

Coordinates: 52°53' | 29°33'

Shchedrin was established in 1842 at the initiative of the third *Lubavitcher* Hasidic leader, Menachem Mendel Schneersohn (the "*Tzemach Tzedek*"). In the early twentieth century, there were some 4,000 Jews in Shchedrin. During the Soviet era, half of the residents worked in a Jewish kolkhoz that was established in the village; the others practiced artisan trades. The village had a school that taught in Yiddish. In the early 1930s, there were about 370 Jewish families in Shchedrin.

After the German invasion of the Soviet Union, only a few Jews from the village managed to escape to the Soviet interior. The Germans occupied Shchedrin on July 1, 1941. By November 9, all the Jews had been concentrated in a ghetto of sorts along a single street. Some were assigned to labor in a workshop. Several young Jewish women were housed in a building that was used as a brothel.

The ghetto was liquidated on March 8, 1942, when Germans who had come from Parichi murdered its population near the Jewish cemetery. A few Jews managed to escape and join the partisans.

SHEPETOVKA

(Ukrainian: **Shepetivka**)

COUNTY SEAT, KAMENETS-PODOLSK DISTRICT, UKRAINE, USSR

During the war:
Reichskommissariat Ukraine

Coordinates:
50°11' | 27°04'

In the early twentieth century, there were about 3,800 Jews in Shepetovka, roughly one-third of the local population. Under Soviet rule, a number of Jews in Shepetovka continued to work in their professions as artisans, several formed trades cooperatives, and still others took on white- or blue-collar jobs in state-owned enterprises such as a local sugar factory. The town had a Yiddish-language government school. During the Soviet era, Jews from nearby localities were attracted to Shepetovka, raising the town's Jewish population to about 4,800, one-fifth of the total, shortly before the German invasion of the Soviet Union.

The Germans occupied Shepetovka on July 5, 1941. Shortly before their arrival and in the ensuing days, Jewish refugees from western Ukraine and other areas in the vicinity thronged to the town. On July 28, 1941, the Germans ordered the Jewish population to report to the town square, where members of German Order Police Battalion 45 and Ukrainian police conducted a selection and took away 800–1,000 childless young men and women, ostensibly for transfer to a labor camp. They were trucked to a nearby forest and murdered.

The Shepetovka ghetto was established in December 1941, along three streets that were surrounded with barbed wire and guarded by Ukrainian police. Many Jews from the area were also concentrated in the ghetto, including 2,000 people from Sudilkov, bringing its population to some 6,000, including numerous children. Later on, the offspring of mixed marriages were likewise placed in it. Adults performed forced labor, leaving only the elderly and children there during the daytime. Occasionally Ukrainian police murdered one or two Jews in the ghetto, usually near the synagogue. A harsh regimen was imposed, under the command of Filip Svoyachenko; within the ghetto itself, movement was limited to certain times of day. Non-Jews were forbidden to enter the ghetto to trade with the residents.

Excessive congestion in the ghetto (twelve to eighteen people per house) led to high mortality from starvation and disease. Dr. Stetsiuk, a Ukrainian physician who was appointed to monitor sanitation in the ghetto but was forbidden to treat patients, defied her orders, filling out prescriptions under Ukrainian names and delivering the medication to the ghetto.

On June 25, 1942, Germans and predominantly Ukrainian police murdered most of the ghetto's approximately 3,000 residents. Skilled workers in high-demand occupations and their families were spared, until their elimination in early September 1942, during the final liquidation of the ghetto.

SHKLOV

COUNTY SEAT, MOGILEV DISTRICT, BELARUS, USSR

During the war: Military Administration Area

Coordinates:
54°13' | 30°18'

At the beginning of the twentieth century there were about 5,400 Jews in Shklov, roughly 80 percent of the population. During the era of Soviet rule, many Jews practiced artisan trades. When private commerce was abolished in the early 1930s, a number of Jews took up farming, while others accepted jobs at a paper factory in the town. Shklov had a government school that taught in Yiddish. Industrialization and urbanization in the Soviet Union caused the Jewish population to plummet; by the eve of the German invasion of the USSR, only about 2,100 Jews remained, approximately one-quarter of the population.

After the German invasion, many Jews in Shklov were inducted into the Red Army. Others tried to escape to the Soviet interior, but many failed and were compelled to return. The Germans occupied the townlet on July 12, 1941. About one week later, some of the Jews were taken to the nearby village of Ryzhkovichi and subjected to a selection, after which eighty-four men aged between fifteen and sixty-five years were shot dead. Some of the survivors were lodged in the homes of local Jews; others were concentrated in an open-air ghetto in the village square, under Belarussian police guard. Food supplies were so scanty that the Jews were required to seek handouts from Belarussian farmers.

Most Jews who remained in Shklov were concentrated in a second ghetto that the Germans established on a street lined with demolished houses. About 100 additional Jews were concentrated in a building at the Iskra kolkhoz near the townlet. All Jews were ordered to wear a yellow Star-of-David armband. On October 2, 1941, Germans, Finns, and Belarussian police transferred the Jews in Ryzhkovichi across the Dnieper River to a location near the village of Zarechye, where they were all murdered. At roughly the same time, Germans trucked 1,459 Jews from the ghetto in Shklov (including Jews from the Iskra kolkhoz) to Zarechye, and exterminated them all.

SHPIKOV

TOWNLET IN TULCHIN COUNTY, VINNITSA DISTRICT, UKRAINE, USSR

During the war: Transnistria (under Romanian control)

Coordinates:
48°47' | 28°34'

About 900 Jews were living in Shpikov on the eve of the German invasion of the Soviet Union, representing approximately 20 percent of the townlet's population. After the Soviet regime abolished private commerce beginning in the early 1930s, most of the townlet's Jews worked as laborers, artisans, and clerks, several became farmers, and others formed a Jewish kolkhoz. Shpikov had a Jewish Ethnic Soviet and a Jewish school, both of which operated in Yiddish.

The Germans occupied Shpikov on July 22, 1941; in early September 1941, the townlet was annexed to Transnistria, which was under Romanian rule. The Romanian authorities established a ghetto in one of the townlet's streets, in which local Jews were concentrated together with Jews from the surrounding localities. Asher Kartsovnik was appointed to head the ghetto, and David Zarotskii was appointed his deputy. The Jews were required to perform forced labor cleaning government offices and harvesting sugar beets and potatoes.

On December 6, 1941, about 850 Jews were deported to a camp located in the nearby village of Rogozna, leaving twenty-seven Jews in Shpikov. The deportees were severely abused by the Ukrainian police, and many perished from hunger and disease. In July 1942, the surviving deportees were transferred to the Pechera camp, where many died or were seized by the Germans for forced labor, from which they did not return.

Shpikov was liberated on March 18, 1944.

SHPOLA

COUNTY SEAT, KIEV DISTRICT, UKRAINE, USSR

During the war: Reichskommissariat Ukraine

Coordinates:
49°02' | 31°25'

At the dawn of the twentieth century, there were about 5,400 Jews in Shpola, approximately half of the town's population. During the Russian Civil War (1918–1920), many Jewish homes were torched and about forty Jews were murdered in pogroms conducted by Ukrainian gangs.

During the era of Soviet rule, many Jews took white- or blue-collar jobs in state-owned institutions and factories, while several people turned to farm work. The town had a Jewish Ethnic Soviet and two Jewish government schools. The number of Jewish inhabitants in the town dwindled considerably during the Soviet regime; shortly before the German invasion, some 2,400 Jews remained, accounting for 16 percent of the total population.

Shpola's proximity to a railroad line enabled a significant portion of the Jewish population to flee to the east before the Germans occupied the town on July 30, 1941. On August 22, a group of Jews (apparently men) was executed. On September 3 and 9, 1941, Einsatzkommando 5 murdered 160 members of the Jewish intelligentsia.

The remaining Jews in Shpola were concentrated in a ghetto mockingly named "Palestine" by the Germans. The inhabitants of the barbed-wire–enclosed ghetto were compelled to wear armbands, were not allowed to visit the market, and did not receive regular food supplies. Many starved to death.

In March 1942, about 800 Jews were led to a concentration camp near the town. On May 15, 1942, all were murdered by Ukrainian auxiliary police on German orders. Thirteen of the last remaining skilled workers in the Shpola ghetto were murdered in 1943.

SHUMILINO

(Belarussian: **Shumilina**)

SIROTINO COUNTY SEAT, VITEBSK DISTRICT, BELARUS, USSR

During the war: Military Administration Area

Coordinates:
55°18' | 29°37'

In the late 1930s, there were about 370 Jews in Shumilino, roughly 15 percent of the population. The townlet had a government school that taught in Yiddish.

In 1939, Jewish refugee families from Poland reached Shumilino and reported on the German persecution of Polish Jews. Only a few families, including several refugees, managed to escape to the east during the two weeks following the German invasion of the Soviet Union.

The Germans occupied Shumilino on July 8, 1941. Some time later, twelve young Jews were murdered near the village of Starinovichi. In August 1941, the Jews of Shumilino and several refugees were concentrated in a ghetto that was set up in ten houses along a street at the edge of the townlet. The severely overcrowded ghetto was fenced in with barbed wire and guarded by Belarussian police. Men were assigned to forced labor. The inhabitants managed to obtain food from Belarussians by bartering goods and valuables. Several ghetto residents committed suicide.

The ghetto was liquidated on November 19, 1941, when its inhabitants were murdered near the townlet.

SHUMYACHI

COUNTY SEAT, SMOLENSK DISTRICT, RUSSIAN FEDERATION, USSR

During the war: Military Administration Area

Coordinates:
53°47' | 32°24'

At the beginning of the twentieth century, about 2,500 Jews lived in Shumyachi, representing a majority of the local population. The movement toward modernization and urbanization, coupled with Soviet policies, led to a decline in the number of Jews in the townlet to about 700 people by the eve of World War II.

Under the Soviet regime, the Jews of the townlet were largely employed by one of two Jewish agricultural cooperatives and practiced various forms of artisanship. The Jews of Shumyachi were aided in their economic activity by an artisans' organization as well as a loan fund. The town had a Yiddish elementary school with about forty-five pupils in the 1930s.

Shumyachi was occupied by the Germans on August 1, 1941. In September 1941, the Germans ordered the Jews to wear a badge on their back and chest and to hang signs bearing a Star-of-David on their homes. A Jewish resident of Shumyachi was appointed Aeltester, and the Jews of the townlet were required to perform forced labor. Prior to the establishment of the ghetto, the Germans announced that all Jews with impaired vision or hearing were required to report themselves in order to be transferred to a sanitarium. A number of elderly Jews who trusted the Germans' intentions were sent away from the townlet, never to be seen again.

In October 1941, between 400 and 500 Jews were concentrated in a ghetto established in a part of Shumyachi emptied of its non-Jewish residents. The ghetto was liquidated on November 17–18, 1941, when all its inhabitants were shot and killed. A number of Jews who had hidden in nearby villages were murdered in the summer of 1943.

ŠIAULIAI

(Yiddish: **Shavl, Shavli**)

COUNTY SEAT, LITHUANIA

During the war:
Reichskommissariat Ostland

Coordinates:
55°56' | 23°19'

On the eve of the German occupation, about 6,600 Jews lived in Siauliai, representing approximately 20 percent of the city's population. While most earned their livelihood from commerce, industry, and artisanship, there were also hundreds of Jewish workers and clerks as well as members of the liberal professions in Siauliai. Leather factories owned by the Frenkelis family employed hundreds of Jews. A Jewish Folksbank fulfilled an important role in the economic life of the city, as did the Mutual Credit Union. A community council was active in the city for a number of years. Siauliai boasted chapters of Zionist parties and youth movements, Agudath Israel and the Bund, as well as kibbutzei hachshara. A number of Jews were pro-Communist. The community's educational institutions included a religious Hebrew school, a Heder, Tarbut schools, a Hebrew high school, and a Yiddish-language school. The city had numerous charitable and welfare societies, such as *Linat Zedek, Gmilut Hessed, Bikur Holim*, and the Jewish health union OZE, which cared for the health of the Jewish schoolchildren.

After Poland was divided between Germany and the Soviet Union in the winter of 1939, throngs of refugees flooded Siauliai. Following the annexation of Lithuania to the Soviet Union in 1940, political activity among the Jews was discontinued, and private businesses were nationalized.

Siauliai was occupied by the Germans on June 26, 1941. Hundreds of Jews managed to escape into the Soviet Union during the first few days of the war, while refugees continued to pour into the city.

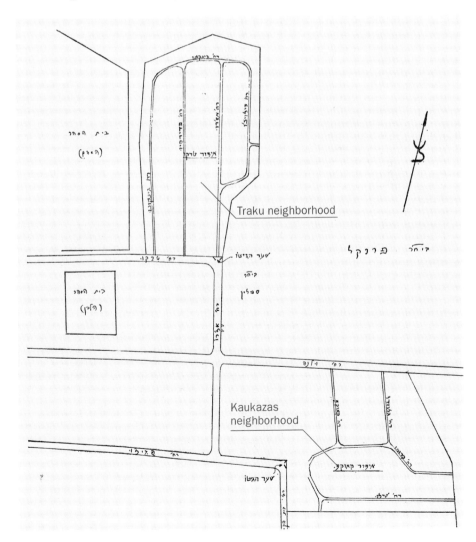

Siauliai ghetto plan. Prepared by Eng. Y. Lavi (Leibowitz), based on his memory
(*Yahadut Lita*, vol. 4, *The Holocaust in Lithuania 1941–1945, A Book of Remembrance*, published by Igud Yotzey Lita B'Israel, Tel-Aviv 1984)

Traku neighborhood

Kaukazas neighborhood

Murders of local Jews began immediately after the occupation. Nationalist Lithuanians seized Jews (including the city's rabbi and high school principal) from their homes and imprisoned them. On the night of June 28, 1941, all of the incarcerated Jews were murdered and buried in the Kuziai forest, some fifteen kilometers from Siauliai.

As of July 1941, Siauliai's Jewish inhabitants were ordered to wear a yellow badge and were forbidden to walk or ride on the paved street. During that period, a plan was devised at the initiative of the Lithuanians to drive out all of the Jews of Siauliai to Zagare*, located dozens of kilometers from the town. However, the Jewish Delegation (later the official representative body of the Jews of the Siauliai ghetto) managed to influence, through daily contact, high-ranking German officials as well as local Lithuanians, to permit the Jews to remain in Siauliai. The decree was rescinded, but not before all of the town's elderly Jews were deported to Zagare and murdered. The decision not to move the Jews from Siauliai was initially based on economic considerations, as 400 Jewish expert artisans worked in the Frenkelis leather factories; the Jews' lobbying also played a role. The experts were housed in the Kaukazas slum neighborhood along with their families. Once the plan to deport the Jews was shelved, the remainder of the Jews of Siauliai were also moved into the slum quarter, and the neighborhood was turned into a ghetto. Following the publication of the order to move Jewish inhabitants into the ghetto by August 1941, the authorities realized that the Kaukazas neighborhood, with its 200 run-down buildings, was too small to accommodate the anticipated number of residents. Therefore another neighborhood, Traku, with its 110 buildings a half-kilometer distant from the Kaukazas ghetto, was allocated to it. Despite the supplementary space, the ghetto suffered from severe overcrowding. About 1,000 of the Jews who were still residing outside the ghetto were massed in the Landkremer prayer house and in an old-age home. A short time later, several were murdered and buried in pits in Bubiai, while others perished in Zagare.

On September 1, 1941, both sections of the Siauliai ghetto were officially sealed and fenced in; Lithuanian guards were placed at their gates. Only those with special permits were allowed to enter or leave the ghetto. Its internal life was organized by the Jewish Delegation, whose members were not elected, but rather applied for positions they felt were suitable. Its composition was authorized by the person accountable for the ghetto to the municipality. The chairman of the Delegation was Mendel Leibovich; the secretary was Aaron Katz, and later, Eliezer Yerushalmi. It included numerous departments, such as provisions, housing, social aid, and the hospital. The ghetto also had a court and a Jewish Order Service.

Overcrowding was one of the ghetto's most pressing problems. Not only did some 5,500 local Jews and refugees live in an area of about 8,000 square meters, but its size was reduced a number of times, exacerbating the situation.

On the Friday following the closure of the ghetto, forty-seven children of the orphanage were removed together with their teacher Avraham Katz and administrator Zhenia Karpel, and murdered. Four days later, on September 10, 1941, altogether 130 elderly and infirm people were killed. On September 12, thirty members of the intelligentsia were removed from the ghetto and murdered, as well.

Two weeks after the ghetto was sealed, its members were examined to determine their "fitness for work." Ninety people were found unfit for work and were sent to their deaths in Zagare. The Delegation managed to obtain 500 blank work permits, and distributed the forms among the Jews. Hundreds of Jews were employed in a Frenkelis factory outside the ghetto, as well as in the airport near Siauliai. Others were employed in the workshops established by the Delegation.

Siauliai, June 26, 1941
Jewish men, including rabbis and community leaders, led to the local jail. On June 29, they were brought to the Kuziai forests, about fifteen kilometers from the town, and executed. (YV)

Another 750 Jews worked in nearby villages with the permission of the authorities. In fall-winter 1941, numerous refugees arrived in the ghetto from nearby townlets.

Cultural activities were held in the ghetto, and various classes were organized. The Hehalutz, Betar, Communist, and other youth movements organized underground activities. They also marked the various holidays and memorial days and published underground newspapers in Hebrew. In August 1942, the Massada organization was established in the ghetto as an apolitical framework; its 120 members were youths from the Zionist circles. In the context of Massada's activities, arms were collected and military training was carried out. In February 1943, the members of the organization, together with the Delegation, proposed a plan to escape and join the partisans or to conduct an uprising in the ghetto prior to the Germans' retreat. These plans, however, were never executed.

Owing to the efforts of the Delegation members, a hospital with forty beds was set up in the Kaukazas ghetto in February 1942, under the management of Dr. Wolf Peisakhovich; clinics were also established in both sections of the ghetto. In February 1942, a decree forbidding women from giving birth in the ghetto was published and went into effect on August 15. As a result, the doctors were forced to perform hundreds of abortions in the ghetto and were compelled to put to death newborn babies with injections.

Jews were transported to labor camps throughout the Siauliai ghetto's existence. In May 1942, the first transport containing hundreds of Jews departed from the ghetto for the Radviliskis, Baciunai, and Rekyva camps. In 1943, a group of Jews was transferred to the Linkaiciai camp.

In the summer of 1943, the situation of the Jews in the Siauliai ghetto degenerated. Security at the gates was intensified, Jews caught smuggling food were imprisoned, and at least one Jew was publicly hanged. In September 1943, the Siauliai ghetto was placed under SS control. The Lithuanian policemen were joined by SS guards, and the ghetto was officially designated the "Siauliai Concentration Camp." Most of the Jewish Delegation's powers were revoked. During the months of September–October 1943, most of the Jews of the Siauliai ghetto were sent to six labor camps that were opened; by the end of the transfer, the Kaukazas ghetto was emptied of its inhabitants and, in fact, ceased to exist.

On November 5, 1943, the "children's Aktion" began: the ghetto was encircled by SS men and Ukrainians who proceeded to seize 574 children, 190 elderly people, 26 handicapped people, and 4 women and send them to their deaths. During the operation, the Jews were promised that their children would be sent to children's homes in Germany. As many Jews did not believe this promise, two members of the Delegation accompanied the children in order to ascertain their fate. A similar operation was carried out in the labor camps: dozens of children, women, and elderly people were sent to their deaths.

As the front drew closer in spring 1944, preparations for the liquidation of the Siauliai ghetto began. In early July 1944, all the Jews were returned to the ghetto from the labor camps, and all work outside the ghetto ceased.

On July 15, 1944, the liquidation of the Siauliai ghetto was set in motion when the first train carrying Jews left for Germany. The trains, which departed on July 17 and 19, brought the inhabitants of the ghetto to the Stutthof transit camp. One group was transferred to a concentration camp in Riga. Only a few dozen of the ghetto's inhabitants managed to survive the Riga camp and the labor camps.

Of the 3,000 Jews who were transferred from the Siauliai ghetto to the camps, 500 lived to see the day of liberation. The empty ghetto was destroyed in the bombings that preceded the liberation of Siauliai.

SIEDLCE

COUNTY SEAT IN LUBLIN DISTRICT, POLAND

During the war: General Gouvernement, Warsaw District

Coordinates: 52°10' | 22°18'

About 15,000 Jews lived in Siedlce when World War II broke out, representing nearly half of the city's population. They earned their livelihood mainly from commerce and artisanship, while a segment of the community practiced the liberal professions. Many owned shops and stalls. Siedlce boasted four Jewish banking institutions and Jewish trade unions as well as charity and welfare facilities such as an orphanage, an old-age home, and a Jewish hospital. The Jewish community also maintained a number of reformed Hadarim and Yiddish and Hebrew kindergartens, a Tarbut Hebrew school, a Yiddish elementary school, and several Jewish libraries.

A variety of Zionist parties and youth movements held activities in Siedlce and pioneer training facilities were established. Chapters of the Bund and Agudath Israel also operated in the city. A number of Jewish periodicals were published that were largely politically oriented.

In 1920, some twenty-five Jews suspected of collaborating with the Soviets (who had occupied the city for several weeks) were murdered in Siedlce by Polish soldiers.

Siedlce, August 22, 1942
The Jews of the "Large Ghetto" and of surrounding localities are loaded on a train for deportation to the Treblinka death camp. *Photograph taken by German soldier Hubert Pfoch while on his way to the eastern front* (YV)

The Germans occupied Siedlce on September 11, 1939, and immediately set about plundering Jewish shops, abducting Jews for forced labor, and murdering Jews. After a few days, the Germans withdrew from Siedlce and the Red Army entered the city, only to withdraw two weeks later in accordance with the Ribbentrop-Molotov Pact. Hundreds of the city's residents, mostly Jews, fled Siedlce together with the retreating Red Army.

When the Germans returned to Siedlce on October 10, 1939, they renewed the looting and abductions for forced labor in the Wegrow camp. Jews were severely discriminated against in the supply of food, which was administered by the Poles.

In late November 1939, the Jews were ordered to establish a twenty-five member Judenrat, which was initially headed by Nachun Weintraub, a local Zionist activist. The leadership duties were actually performed by Dr. Henryk Lebel, the director of the Jewish Hospital, who was in charge of health issues on the Judenrat. A fifty-member Jewish Order Service was also set up, with Yeshayah Goldberg as the organization's head.

In December 1939, a fine of 20,000 zlotys was levied on the Jewish community. On the night of December 24, 1939, Christmas Eve, the Germans, aided by Polish policemen, burned down the great Synagogue, the study hall, and the offices of the Jewish community, which were located nearby. All of the refugees who were sheltered in the synagogue at the time perished. On January 1, 1940, the Jews were ordered to wear a yellow armband with a Star-of-David.

In March 1940, about 1,200 refugees arrived in Siedlce from Kalisz* and other localities in western Poland.

On June 12, 1940, numerous Jews were seized for work involving the draining of the Liwiec River, during which one man was murdered and a number of others were injured. During this period, the Jews of Siedlce were transferred to labor camps in the area of Lublin.

In October 1940, the Germans authorized the Judenrat's initiative to establish workshops in Siedlce and even allowed some of the forced laborers to return to the city. In November 1940, a census was conducted in the streets containing many Jews residents. A further ransom was levied upon the Jews. Some of the Jewish shops were confiscated, and the others were ordered marked with a

Star-of-David. In March 1941, six Jews were murdered in a pogrom in the city's Jewish neighborhood.

On August 1, 1941, the Germans ordered the establishment of two ghettos in Siedlce. The "large ghetto" was situated in the area of the old market and a number of nearby streets and had two gates. About 10,000 Jews were moved into its confines. The "small ghetto," also known as the "triangle" ("*Draiek*"), was established in a poor neighborhood and was home to approximately 2,000 Jews.

Both ghettos were sealed and encircled by a barbed-wire fence in October 1941, with Poles and Germans barred from entering them. Harsh living conditions and severe overcrowding led to an outbreak of epidemic typhus that caused the deaths of about twenty-five people each day. The Jewish Hospital was moved inside the large ghetto and was instrumental in the effort to control the epidemics that struck the ghettos. The Judenrat also supported a daycare center for orphans inside the ghetto, where the children received meals and educational activities were held. In December 1941, the Jews were ordered to hand over all furs in their possession to the Germans, and in 1942, an additional ransom was levied.

In March 1942, ten Jews who had been taken for forced labor to the Stok Lacki camp were murdered. During this period, the Judenrat managed to obtain exemptions from work for three groups of Jews in the ghetto: functionaries (especially Judenrat members, Judenrat clerks, and Jewish policemen); employees of Polish institutions; and the ill, who were released from work by the doctors of the Jewish Hospital. The doctors strove to exempt as many people as possible, but in the spring and summer of 1942, the forced-labor quotas demanded by the Germans were stepped up.

In June 1942, forced laborers were sent from the ghetto to the Majdanek camp. In July, thirteen Jewish laborers who were late for work were executed.

On August 21, 1942, the large ghetto was encircled by Ukrainians as well as by members of the Polish blue police and the SS. The following day, August 22, 1942, an operation was launched lasting through to August 24, 1942, in which the Jews of Siedlce together with about 9,300 people from Mordy* and Losice* were rounded up in a square near the Jewish cemetery and in the area of the destroyed synagogue. Following a selection, about 2,300 Jews were murdered in the square and in the Jewish cemetery and about 600 Jewish men aged sixteen to forty were transferred to the small ghetto. The rest, about 10,000 in all, including the members of the Jewish Order Service, were deported to the Treblinka death camp. About 2,000 Jews who could not be packed into the excessively overcrowded train cars were murdered on site. The head of the Judenrat, Lebel, declined an offer to be transferred to the small ghetto and was murdered on the first day of the operation in the ghetto hospital, together with the entire medical staff and about 100 patients. In all, about 13,000 Jews were murdered during the operation. Another approximately 200 Jews who were discovered later in searches in the large ghetto were also murdered. The few deportees who managed to escape from the train returned to Siedlce and slipped back into the small ghetto. On August 26, 1942, about thirty Jewish women were removed from the small ghetto to sort through the deportees' belongings; when they completed their task they were executed in the Jewish cemetery.

About 2,000 Jews were concentrated in the small ghetto, among them laborers, about 550 workers employed by the Germans, and others who were still allowed to remain in the city. A new Judenrat was established, charged foremost with organizing the employment of the ghetto residents as well as with collecting ransom payments. It was headed by Hersz Eizenberg, the deputy head of the first Judenrat.

The ghetto suffered from a severe shortage of food and extreme overcrowding. In September 1942, most of the ghetto residents were dispersed among small labor camps in the vicinity. Many people perished owing to the harsh labor conditions. On September 26, 1942, a further deportation to Treblinka was carried out.

The small ghetto was liquidated on November 25, 1942, when its inhabitants were marched to a labor camp near Gasie-Barki, where they remained for a few days in an open ghetto together with about 1,000 Jews from nearby localities. On November 30, 1942, the Jews of Siedlce were marched back to the city. Along the way, several hundred of them were murdered by Ukrainian guards. The rest were deported from Siedlce to Treblinka. A Jewish blacksmith named Simkha Vilik managed to smash through the door of one of the train cars and dozens of Jews escaped, although most were shot by the Ukrainian guards.

About 500 Jews remained in Siedlce, working in five different workplaces. January 1943 saw the murder of 150 of them. A few dozen managed to flee during the winter and the rest were killed by the Germans in mid-March 1943.

SIEMIATYCZE

TOWNLET IN BIELSK PODLASKI COUNTY, BIAŁYSTOK DISTRICT, POLAND

During the war: Bezirk Białystok

Coordinates:
52°27' | 22°53'

About 3,700 Jews were living in Siemiatycze when World War II broke out, representing roughly two-thirds of the townlet's population. Most earned their livelihood from commerce and artisanship. The community had a synagogue, six Batei Midrash and charity societies as well as a Yeshiva, a Tarbut Hebrew school and a Jewish library. Jewish political organizations and youth movements were active in Siemiatycze, including Zionist parties, Agudath Israel, and the Communists.

In early September 1939, the Germans occupied Siemiatycze, but in the second half of September 1939, the townlet was handed over to Soviet control in accordance with the Molotov-Ribbentrop Pact. During the period of Soviet rule, a Soviet economic, social, and educational system was instituted in the townlet. Privately owned shops were nationalized or closed and cooperatives were formed. Numerous Jewish refugees thronged to the townlet from the areas of Poland occupied by the Germans.

On June 25, 1941, the Germans reoccupied Siemiatycze, and on the very same day, seven Jews were executed outside of the townlet. In the early days of the occupation, the Jews of Siemiatycze were ordered to wear a yellow badge, their freedom of movement was restricted, and they were seized for forced labor. A thirteen-member Judenrat was established, charged with collecting ransom payments and recruiting Jews for forced labor that often ended in murder. Yisrael Rosenzweig was appointed chairman of the Judenrat.

On August 1, 1942, the Jews of Siemiatycze were transferred to a fenced-in ghetto together with Jews from Mielnik and various other localities. In all, close to 7,000 Jews were packed into it under conditions of very severe overcrowding. Former members of Zionist youth movements formed an underground. Beginning in October 1941, the Jews of the ghetto were required to display residents' names on the outside of each building.

On September 2, 1942, the Germans encircled the ghetto and kept it surrounded for a week. During this period, a number of young Jews attempted to escape from the ghetto; several were successful. The members of the underground who remained in the ghetto considered an attack on the Germans as the preferred course of action but were deterred by opposition on the part of many of the ghetto's inhabitants.

On the morning of November 9, 1942, most of the Jews, about 4,500 people, were deported to the Treblinka death camp. Altogether 290 tried to escape from the train. Some 140 people succeeded, but close to half were eventually shot or opted to return to the ghetto, lacking an alternative.

The ghetto was liquidated on November 12, 1942, when its last inhabitants were deported to Treblinka. The manhunt for the townlet's Jews continued until the end of 1943.

SIENIAWA

TOWNLET IN JAROSŁAW COUNTY, LWÓW DISTRICT, POLAND

During the war: General Gouvernement, Cracow District

Coordinates:
50°12' | 22°38'

When World War II broke out, about 1,300 Jews lived in Sieniawa, representing more than half of the townlet's population. Most earned their livelihood from commerce and artisanship. The JDC distributed food and clothing, especially to children; it also supported the townlet's *Bikur Holim* and free-loan society and provided loans to merchants and artisans. Zionist parties and youth movements were active in the community, whose members were also offered Hebrew courses.

In September 1939, Sieniawa was occupied by the Germans, then handed over to the Soviets that same month in accordance with the Molotov-Ribbentrop Pact. The Soviets closed most of the Jewish shops or levied heavy taxes on Jewish shopkeepers. Most of the artisans formed cooperatives, while other Jews were employed in government and public offices.

The Germans reoccupied Sieniawa after their invasion of the Soviet Union on June 22, 1941. In the early days of the occupation, the Jews were ordered to wear an armband and mark their property with a Star-of-David; a number of Jews were murdered for disobeying the order. A Judenrat was established soon after the occupation and was headed by Shmariahu Schmidt, the former leader of the Jewish community. Schmidt was replaced a short time later by Eliahu Gross. The Judenrat was required periodically to pay ransoms and to supply the Germans with forced laborers.

About two weeks after occupying the townlet, the Germans murdered fifteen Jews accused of collaborating with the Soviet regime.

Jewish inhabitants were required to perform forced labor, and a group of Jewish youths was recruited to work under the supervision of the Ukrainian police. The Jews bartered their possessions for food with local Ukrainians. Towards the end of 1941, the Jews were forbidden to leave the townlet.

In early 1942, a ghetto was established in Sieniawa (according to another testimony, the ghetto was established in August 1942, following the killing operations). The ghetto was fenced in and guarded by Polish police. In June 1942, Jews from Jaroslaw, Lancut, and other localities were transferred to Sieniawa, and the townlet's Jewish population grew to about 1,800. Gross was appointed head of the central regional Judenrat, which encompassed fifteen Judenräte.

In July and August 1942, a number of operations were carried out in Sieniawa. During the operations, several Jews committed suicide, and others were murdered in the townlet. The Jews were brought to the Pelkinie camp, where a selection was carried out. The elderly, the infirm, and children were murdered in a nearby forest, and most of the women and some of the men were deported to the Belzec death camp. A few dozen young Jews were sent to a labor camp.

In October 1942, Gross, his deputy Yudel Rotenburg, and six other members of the Judenrat were murdered. Eventually, a new Judenrat was appointed, headed by Lazer Fass, who was from Lancut. Murders and deportations reduced the ghetto population to about 600 by the end of 1942.

In November 1942, the ghetto was encircled. Its inhabitants were loaded onto train cars and transported to Belzec. Hundreds of Jews jumped off the train and sought out hiding places, but food and water shortages drove most to eventually emerge from hiding; the escapees were caught and murdered.

SIENNO

TOWNLET IN WIERZBNIK COUNTY, KIELCE DISTRICT, POLAND

During the war: General Gouvernement, Radom District

Coordinates: 51°05' | 21°28'

Sienno
Jewish residence in the ghetto (YV)

After World War I, about 750 Jews lived in Sienno, representing approximately half of the townlet's population. Most earned their livelihood from peddling and small-scale commerce.

The Germans occupied Sienno in September 1939. A Judenrat was established, charged with recruiting forced laborers for the Germans. About 1,000 refugees from western Poland and nearby localities arrived in the townlet, and by the winter of 1941 the number of Jews there had escalated to about 2,000. The JSS provided assistance to the Judenrat.

In December 1941, an open ghetto was established in Sienno. In the second half of October 1942, the inhabitants of the ghetto were deported to the Treblinka death camp.

SIERADZ

COUNTY SEAT, ŁÓDŹ DISTRICT, POLAND

During the war: Wartheland

Coordinates: 51°36' | 18°45'

During the interwar period almost 3,000 Jews lived in Sieradz, about one-third of the town's population. Most were artisans and merchants. Zionist parties were active there, and Agudath Israel was particularly influential. The community had a ramified education system, a branch of TOZ, sports associations, and a library. The Jews of Sieradz inhabited a harsh antisemitic climate in the 1930s, especially with regard to their economic affairs. Many were forced to close their shops and workshops.

The Germans occupied Sieradz on September 4, 1939. On September 15, German troops killed seventeen civilians in the town, including eleven Jews. Several Jews were taken to concentration camps in Germany. In December, hundreds of Jews were deported to Sandomierz*.

An unfenced ghetto was established in Sieradz in March 1940. Some Jews were employed at a weaving workshop that had been set up in the town prison. In 1940–41, many Jews were deported to Zdunska Wola* and labor camps in the Poznan area. By early 1942, only 1,100 to 1,400 remained in the ghetto. Living conditions severely deteriorated during the final six months of its existence. Jews were ordered to report twice a day for roll call, leaving their dwellings open to looters.

In the spring and summer of 1942, several thousand Jews from ghettos in the vicinity were concentrated in the Sieradz ghetto, bringing the population to 4,500 by the eve of the liquidation. On August 22, 1942, German policemen stormed

Sieradz
A group of Jews are led to the local train station and then deported to other towns and cities in the General Gouvernement. (GFH)

the ghetto and forced all inhabitants into a nearby convent, shooting anyone who attempted to hide or who was incapable of moving. The Jews were held in the convent for three days. From there, most were deported to the Chelmno death camp, while 184 others were sent to the Lodz* ghetto for forced labor.

SIERPC

(Yiddish: **Sheps**)

COUNTY SEAT, WARSAW DISTRICT, POLAND

During the war: Bezirk Zichenau

Coordinates: 52°53' | 19°40'

About 3,100 Jews lived in Sierpc in the interwar period, representing approximately 30 percent of the townlet's population. Most earned their livelihood from commerce, artisanship, and clerical work, while others were factory owners or members of the liberal professions. The Jews of Sierpc were aided in their economic activity by five trade and craft associations, three Jewish popular banks, the JDC, and by an organization of former members of the Sierpc community who lived in the United States. The community's children attended a Szabasow- ka school, Hadarim, a Talmud Torah, two Yeshivot, Agudath Israel elementary schools, and a Tarbut kindergarten and elementary school. Sierpc had Zionist parties and youth movements that established pioneer training facilities and held evening Hebrew classes. Agudath Israel and the Bund each had their own youth movements. Some of the parties maintained libraries, which served as cultural and social centers. Sierpc had three sports clubs, two affiliated with the Zionists and one with the Bund.

When World War II broke out, a number of Sierpc's Jews fled to the east. The Germans occupied the townlet on September 8, 1939, and immediately began to plunder Jewish property with the help of local ethnic Germans (Volksdeutsche) and Poles. They also seized Jews for forced labor. In the second half of September 1939, the Jews were required to wear a yellow badge and were forbidden to use the sidewalks. On September 28, 1939, about forty young Jews were deported east from Sierpc, to the area under Soviet control. The following day, the Germans burned down the synagogue. The Jews were required to pay a collective fine.

After Sierpc was annexed to the Third Reich as part of Bezirk Zichenau (which was annexed to eastern Prussia), a decision was reached to deport the Jews from the townlet. On November 8, 1939, the SS and the Volksdeutsche auxiliary police deported 3,000 of Sierpc's Jews to Nowy Dwor* and Warsaw*. About 400 Jews remained in Sierpc. Most were artisans who worked in German factories; they were soon joined by deportees who returned to the townlet following the mass deportation.

Between March and April 1940, about 500 Jews were concentrated in an unfenced ghetto guarded by German police. The German mayor appointed a Judenrat, which was required to send forced laborers, including children, to perform various types of work outside the ghetto in return for a meager wage. Religious rites and the kosher slaughter of meat were forbidden; they were carried out in secret. A Jewish Order Service was not established in the ghetto. During the first year of the ghetto's existence, Jews were permitted to travel to Warsaw to visit relatives and bring them food and belongings. When their freedom of movement was restricted at the orders of the governor, contact was terminated.

On January 6, 1942, the Gestapo deported the remaining Jews to Strzegowo*. A number of Jews who resisted during the deportation were shot dead.

SIROTINO
(Yiddish: **Sirotshin, Sirotin**; Belarussian: **Sirotsina**)

COUNTY SEAT, VITEBSK DISTRICT, BELARUS, USSR

During the war: Military Administration Area

Coordinates: 55°23' | 29°37'

In the early twentieth century, there were about 1,700 Jews in Sirotino, roughly 90 percent of the local population. Urbanization and industrialization in the Soviet Union induced Jews to leave the townlet, drastically lowering its Jewish population to about 300 on the eve of World War II. The townlet had a government school that taught in Yiddish.

When Germany invaded the Soviet Union, many Jews in Sirotino did not leave the townlet, despite learning from Jewish refugees from Poland who had settled in the neighboring townlet of Shumilino* about German actions against the Jews. A number of Jews who had gone into hiding in surrounding villages even returned to the townlet, since German soldiers did not harm its residents at the occupation's inception, on July 6–10, 1941. Within a few days, however, the Germans began to dispossess Jews and induct Jewish men for forced labor. In late July, early August, or September 1941 (depending on the source), about forty young Jewish townspeople were taken away, ostensibly for work in Vitebsk*, and murdered at an unknown location. At that time, most of the Jews were sent to forced labor, including the elderly, women, and children.

In autumn 1941, all Jews in Sirotino were concentrated in a ghetto composed of several old houses on the outskirts of the townlet. They were allowed to bring possessions and, uncustomarily, to leave the ghetto during the day. Germans and Belarussian police periodically entered the ghetto to seize Jewish property.

On November 18, 1941, the ghetto was liquidated when Germans and Belarussian police murdered all its inhabitants at the nearby Gniloi Most ravine.

ŠIRVINTOS
(Yiddish: **Shirvint**)

TOWNLET IN UKMERGĖ COUNTY, LITHUANIA

During the war: Reichskommissariat Ostland

Coordinates: 55°03' | 24°57'

On the eve of the German occupation, about 700 Jews lived in Sirvintos, representing approximately one-third of the townlet's population. Most of the Jews earned their livelihood from commerce, artisanship, and farming. The community's children were educated at a Tarbut school, a Yiddish school, and a number of Hadarim. Chapters of Zionist parties and youth movements were opened in the townlet as well.

After Lithuania was annexed to the Soviet Union in 1940, private businesses in Sirvintos were nationalized and the activities of the Jewish parties were discontinued.

When the Germans occupied Sirvintos in late June 1941, the synagogues in the townlet were torched and the holy books desecrated. After the German soldiers left Sirvintos and advanced to the east, nationalist Lithuanians took power in the townlet, and Jews suspected of maintaining connections with the Soviet regime were arrested and murdered. From mid-July 1941 onward, young Jews were assigned to various forms of forced labor. During the months of July and August, dozens of the townlet's Jews were murdered by Lithuanians.

In late August 1941, the Jews of the townlet were ordered to gather in a ghetto comprising some twenty buildings in the old part of Sirvintos. The attempts of Rabbi Avraham Leib Grossberer and his son-in-law Zundel Krok to organize Jewish life in the ghetto were unsuccessful owing to the perpetual plunder of Jewish property.

The ghetto was liquidated on September 18, 1941, when the Jews were taken to the Fivonija forest and shot to death. Following the operation, a sign was posted in Sirvintos stating that the townlet was "*Judenrein.*"

SKAŁAT

COUNTY SEAT, TARNOPOL DISTRICT, POLAND
(After World War II in the USSR/Ukraine; Ukrainian, Russian: **Skalat**)

During the war: General Gouvernement, Galicia District

Coordinates:
49°26' | 25°59'

In the early 1920s, about 3,000 Jews lived in Skalat, representing roughly half of the townlet's population. Most earned their livelihood from commerce and artisanship. Chapters of various Jewish parties and youth movements were active there. In 1933, control of the community council passed from the Hasidim to the Zionists. The townlet had a number of Jewish schools, including a supplementary Hebrew school and a kindergarten.

In the second half of September 1939, Skalat was occupied by the Red Army. Under Soviet rule (1939–41), private commerce was gradually abolished and the pressure mounted on artisans to organize into cooperatives. Jewish political and national-cultural activities were halted, with the exception of the synagogues, which remained open. Jews held important positions in the new administration. About 200 Jews managed to evacuate with the Soviets to the USSR as they withdrew to the east in late June 1941.

On July 7, 1941, the Germans entered Skalat and murdered twenty Jews. The following day, the Ukrainian militia began to terrorize the Jews. Together with the local citizens and with the active support of the Germans, the Ukrainian militia murdered about 560 Jews. In mid-July 1941, the Germans ordered the establishment of a Judenrat headed by Meir Nikhler and a Jewish Order Service under the command of Dr. Yosef Brits. The Judenrat ran a public soup kitchen and an old-age home.

On July 19, 1941, the Judenrat was compelled to remit to the Germans, within five days, a ransom totaling 600,000 rubles. In the summer and fall of 1941, the Judenrat was forced to supply about 300 Jews for forced labor daily. In the fall of 1941 and winter of 1942, hundreds of youths were sent to labor camps, and in July 1942, a group of young women was sent to the Jagielnica labor camp. To alleviate the difficult conditions endured by camp inmates, the Judenrat established a women's council that shipped food packages. In the months of February and March 1942, the Jews were evicted from their apartments in the center of the townlet, which were then transferred along with their contents to members of the German and Ukrainian administration. The evicted Jews moved into the Jewish quarter located near the market, which now began to serve as an open ghetto of sorts. In late August 1942, the Germans demanded that the Judenrat turn in 600 Jews unfit for work, threatening the welfare of all the Jews for non-compliance. The 600 elderly and ill Jews who were handed over to the Germans were sent on August 31,

1942, to the Belzec death camp. This act caused considerable dispute within the Jewish community as well as within the Judenrat itself.

Fearing another operation, many Jews prepared hiding places and bunkers. In the first half of October 1942, Jews from surrounding communities were concentrated in Skalat. On October 21–22, 1942, a large-scale operation was carried out. German and Ukrainian police burst into Jewish homes, conducted searches, and rounded up close to 2,700 Jews in the synagogue. The Jews were deported to Belzec. During the operation, 153 Jews were shot to death in the streets and hiding places. Additional Jews were killed when they jumped off the death train to Belzec. However, fifty Jews managed to escape from the train cars and return to Skalat. During the operation, about 200 Jews were also sent to the Janowska camp on the outskirts of Lwow*. On November 9, 1942, the Germans carried out another operation in which some 1,100 Jews were sent via Tarnopol* to their deaths in Belzec.

In December 1942, after a series of operations and the murder of thousands of Jews from Skalat and its environs, the Jews who remained in Skalat were concentrated in a sealed ghetto established in the townlet's Jewish quarter. Harsh conditions led to starvation and epidemic typhus. The Germans concurrently established a labor camp outside the ghetto in which about 300 Jews, including thirty women, were concentrated. The separation of the working Jews from the rest of the Jews caused serious concern, and many attempted to obtain jobs in the labor camp. On April 7, 1943, altogether 750 Jews were removed from the ghetto, among them patients of the hospital and its medical staff, and shot to death in pits that had been prepared ahead of time.

After the massacre, an underground group consisting of youths led by Mechel Glanz began to purchase weapons and seek contact with the ghetto survivors wandering in the forests. However, when the liquidation operation of the ghetto occurred on June 9, 1943, they were unable to implement their plan, and the last 500 Jews of the Skalat ghetto were shot to death in pits.

The approximately 400 Jews who remained in the labor camp were executed on June 30 and July 28, 1943.

About 300 Jews managed to escape from the ghetto and labor camp and organized into armed groups. Some 30 or 100 Jews (sources vary regarding the figure) joined Kovpak's partisan brigade, and most fell in battle. Seven of the partisans survived until the end of the war.

SKALBMIERZ

TOWNLET IN PIŃCZÓW COUNTY, KIELCE DISTRICT, POLAND

During the war: General Gouvernement, Cracow District

Coordinates:
50°20' | 20°25'

When World War II broke out, about 400 Jews lived in Skalbmierz, representing approximately one-quarter of its population. Most earned their livelihood from petty commerce and artisanship, but there were also a few large-scale grain merchants among them. The Skalbmierz Jewish community had traditional charity and mutual aid societies as well as a chapter of the Zionist Organization.

The Germans occupied Skalbmierz in the early days of the war. They began immediately to seize Jewish property and demanded large ransoms. Jewish inhabitants were constrained to wear a yellow badge, later replaced by an armband marked with a Star-of-David. The occupiers also recruited Jews for forced labor.

In September 1940, an open ghetto was established and a Judenrat appointed. More than 1,000 deportees were brought to the ghetto from Cracow*.

On August 29, 1942, German gendarmes, SS men, and Polish policemen deported the Jews of Skalbmierz to the Slomniki transit camp, where they were held without shelter together with thousands of Jews from throughout Miechow County. The Germans carried out a selection in early September 1942. About

1,500 young people were sent to a labor camp, including youths from Skalbmierz. The ill and elderly were murdered on site, while the rest were deported to the Belzec death camp.

A few Jewish families remained in the Skalbmierz ghetto, including the members of the Jewish Order Service, who were employed at collecting and sorting the deportees' belongings. When they completed their assigned task, they were sent to the nearby labor camp.

SKARYSZEW

TOWNLET IN RADOM COUNTY, KIELCE DISTRICT, POLAND

During the war: General Gouvernement, Radom District

Coordinates:
51°19' | 21°15'

After World War I, about 850 Jews lived in Skaryszew, representing roughly half of the local population. They earned their livelihood mainly from small-scale commerce and artisanship; several owned vegetable gardens and fruit groves. A Zionist association was active in the townlet.

Skaryszew was occupied by the Germans in early September 1939. A Judenrat was established and charged with recruiting Jews for forced labor. Life in the townlet continued relatively peacefully, and in early 1941, a number of Jewish families from Warsaw* moved into it. In April 1941, they were joined by several dozen Jews deported from nearby Przytyk. In the summer of 1941, the Judenrat opened a public soup kitchen for the refugees, aided by the JSS.

In April 1942, an initially unsealed ghetto was established in Skaryszew. By the summer of 1942, it had a population of about 1,800 Jews.

On August 18, 1942, the Jews were moved to the Szydlowiec* ghetto together with Jews from the nearby Radom* and Kielce* localities. They were later deported to the Treblinka death camp.

SKARŻYSKO-KAMIENNA

TOWN IN THE KOŃSKIE COUNTY, KIELCE DISTRICT, POLAND

During the war: General Gouvernement, Radom District

Coordinates:
51°07' | 20°54'

On the eve of World War II, about 2,000 Jews lived in Skarzysko-Kamienna, representing just over 10 percent of the local population. Most earned their livelihood from small-scale commerce, peddling, and artisanship. Several were employed in the local metal industry. The town had a small Jewish bank. As a Hasidic center, Skarzysko-Kamienna was home to fifteen shtiblech belonging to the various Hasidic courts. The town had chapters of the Zionist parties, Agudath Israel, and the Bund. The Zionists operated a small public library, a short-lived Hebrew kindergarten, Hebrew courses, and drama classes. The town also had Zionist and Bund youth movements. In 1918, pogroms perpetrated in the town took the life of one Jew and injured many others, with several Jews seriously wounded.

The Germans occupied Skarzysko-Kamienna on September 6, 1939, and immediately seized Jews for forced labor; five Jews were murdered within the first few days of the occupation. Several weeks later, a Judenrat and a Jewish Order Service were established in the town. The Judenrat was headed by Dov Hirsh Feldman. The Germans ordered the Judenrat to collect large ransom payments and confiscated a great deal of Jewish property.

In early 1940, the Jews were ordered to wear an armband marked with a Star-of-David. The Judenrat, following the Germans' demands, began to recruit slave laborers. In January 1940, refugees were brought to the city from Przytyk.

In the summer of 1940, a large labor camp of the Hasag industrial company was established in Skarzysko-Kamienna, composed of a series of weapons and ammunition factories that were established in the town during World War I. The camp was under the command of SS officer Egon Dalski. Of the 23,000 Jewish laborers in the Skarzysko-Kamienna camp, some 17,000 perished.

In late 1940, the JSS assisted the Judenrat in organizing a public soup kitchen. The Judenrat also ran a makeshift hospital.

In March 1941, the local Jews and the refugees were transferred to a closed ghetto. Although it was guarded by Polish police and members of the Jewish Order Service, individuals managed to periodically slip out and obtain food. During the winter of 1941/42, the ghetto's death rate rose owing to an outbreak of epidemic typhus, severe overcrowding, and poor sanitary conditions.

In early 1942, Jewish refugees were brought to the ghetto from Plock* and Lodz*. The population of the ghetto swelled to about 5,000. During that same period, Jewish workers were recruited as forced laborers for the camp in the town. Many of the camp's laborers who died owing to the extremely harsh working conditions were buried in the Skarzysko-Kamienna ghetto.

A few days before the liquidation of the ghetto, refugees from Szydlowiec* arrived there.

On September 28, 1942, contingents of SS soldiers and Lithuanian and Ukrainian units encircled the ghetto and rounded up about 4,000 of its inhabitants. Those that sought to hide were summarily shot, along with the elderly, the infirm, and pregnant women. About 500 Jews were taken from the round-up area to the labor camp; according to another version of events, they were taken to the Kielce* prison on the eve of the deportation and were deported from there to Auschwitz. The rest of the Jews were deported to Treblinka. Among the deportees were most of the members of the Judenrat.

SKAWINA

TOWNLET IN CRACOW COUNTY, CRACOW DISTRICT, POLAND

During the war: General Gouvernement, Cracow District

Coordinates:
49°59' | 19°50'

After World War I, about 280 Jews lived in Skawina, representing approximately one-ninth of the local population. Most earned their livelihood from commerce, while a number engaged in small-scale industry. The only Jewish school in the townlet was a traditional Heder. The Tarbut organization held Hebrew courses, and the Zionist Akiva movement was active in the townlet.

The Germans occupied Skawina in September 1939. On April 7, 1941, the governor of Cracow* permitted Jews to live in a few of the county's localities, including Skawina. Nevertheless, about 150 Jews were deported from the townlet that same month to Miedzyrzec Podlaski*. A Judenrat was established in Skawina, headed by M. Filman from May 1941 onward.

In 1942, Skawina had a chapter of the JSS, which in February of that year assisted about 100 Jews. It also had a public soup kitchen and a clinic. The approximately forty Jews who worked on farms in the area thereby received immunity from deportation to a labor camp. In the summer of 1942, Jewish workshops also operated in the townlet.

A ghetto was apparently established in Skawina, in which a number of "shops" operated.

On July 8, 1942, the Germans transferred 200 Jews from Liszki, Czerniechow, Teczynek, and Nowa Gora to Skawina. Towards the end of August 1942, the Jews of Kalwaria Zebrzydowska, Myslenice, and according to some testimonies, Gdow and Dobczyce as well, were deported to Skawina. On August 28, 1942, Jews from Wieliczka* who were classified as professionals, 128 in number, arrived in Skawina. That same month, the townlet's Jews were ordered on three occasions to pay a ransom to the Germans.

On August 29, 1942, a unit of the German police carried out a selection among the approximately 2,000 Jews who were in Skawina at the time. Those considered fit for work were sent to the Plaszow labor camp. About 180 children as well as elderly and handicapped people were murdered in the Podbory forest near the townlet, while the remaining men, women, and children were deported the following day to the Belzec death camp.

SKIDEL

TOWNLET IN GRODNO COUNTY, BIAŁYSTOK DISTRICT, POLAND

(After World War II in the USSR/Belarus; Belarussian: **Skidzel'**)

During the war: Bezirk Białystok

Coordinates:
53°35' | 24°15'

According to German estimates, about 2,300 Jews lived in Skidel when World War II broke out, representing approximately two-thirds of the townlet's population. Most of the Jews earned their livelihood from small commerce, peddling, and artisanship. Zionist parties, the Bund, and a branch of the Communist party were active in Skidel. The Jewish community held educational and cultural activities.

From the beginning of the fighting between Germany and Poland, the Polish government in the area ceased to function, and gangs of thugs carried out pogroms against the Jews of Skidel, who were accused of collaborating with the Soviets. With the Soviet occupation of the townlet in the second half of September 1939, its economic activity was nationalized and the private property of the Jews, including their apartments, was confiscated by the authorities.

On June 23, 1941, Skidel was occupied by the Eighth German Division. The occupation was accompanied by heavy shelling, which set houses in the townlet ablaze. The Jewish quarter in the center of the townlet burned to the ground, and many of the Jews fled to the forest and to nearby townlets. Those who remained were forced to crowd into the few houses still standing and into buildings across the Skidel River. Immediately after the occupation, on June 27, 1941, Jews were seized for forced labor, and a few days later were ordered to wear a yellow badge.

The ghetto was established in Skidel in two stages. At first, a group of workers was put up in a number of buildings at an airfield across the nearby river. The second group, which included cobblers, tailors, and carpenters, remained in the townlet. In August 1942, the remaining Jews of Skidel were transferred to the fenced-in ghetto across the river, leaving most of their property behind. The Germans appointed a Judenrat, headed by a man named Volkovyski. In the ghetto, the Jews suffered from harsh conditions, extreme overcrowding, and cruel abuse at the hands of the Germans.

On the morning of November 2, 1942, the elderly and ill were shot in their residences while the balance of the Jews were rounded up. Once the Germans robbed Skidel's Jewish inhabitants of their few remaining possessions, all 2,330 Jews were led to the Kielbasin camp. In November 1942, they were deported on to the Treblinka death camp and to Auschwitz-Birkenau.

SKIERNIEWICE

COUNTY SEAT, WARSAW DISTRICT, POLAND

During the war: General Gouvernement, Warsaw District

Coordinates:
51°58' | 20°09'

Skierniewice, 1940
Jews accused of trading with Poles outside the ghetto to observe the *kapparot* ceremony on the eve of Yom Kippur. Four of the accused were released after paying a large fine, while the rest were sent to a jail in Warsaw. (YV)

During the interwar years, about 4,300 Jews lived in Skierniewice, comprising one-fifth of the town's population. Skierniewice was known as an important Hasidic center, and Jewish social and cultural life in the town revolved around the court of the local Hasidic rabbi. Agudath Israel had considerable influence on community life, and Zionist parties were also active. Children attended a Hebrew-

The order to establish a ghetto in Skierniewice
(YVA 0.6/21)

speaking kindergarten and primary school, and an Agudath Israel primary school. In the 1930s, Jewish merchants endured an economic boycott and other forms of antisemitic abuse.

The Germans occupied Skierniewice in early September 1939. On September 17, German authorities announced the dispossession of the town's Jews and filmed as they looted Jewish property. In late 1939, the Great Synagogue was torched and the Beit Midrash and mikve were demolished.

Meanwhile, hundreds of refugees flowed in from nearby localities. The community leadership continued to function and, during the first weeks of the occupation, they elected a special panel of officials to care for the refugees, and recruit forced laborers to thwart ad hoc abductions of Jews by the Germans. This body was initially known as the *va'ad* (board) or *ve'ida* (committee). At the Germans' command, it became a twelve-member Judenrat under Herman Guzik and his deputy, Avraham Rosenblum. The Judenrat had several departments: finance, maintenance, supplies, sanitation, court of law, labor, and postal service. A Jewish Order Service was established under Grajek.

The Skierniewice ghetto was established in October 1940 in the most squalid neighborhood in the town. Some 7,000 Jews were packed into rickety buildings under abysmal sanitary conditions. Piotrkowska Street was excluded from the ghetto area and a pedestrian bridge was built over it. The ghetto was unsealed most of the time, enabling inhabitants to leave for large cities and to obtain food from people in the vicinity with relative ease. The refugee population climbed from about 600 to 2,400 in early 1941. Mindful of the refugees' worsening plight, the Judenrat requested a grant from the JDC office in Warsaw*, which it received. The Judenrat also took action to obtain official residency permits for refugees from nearby Rawa Mazowiecka* by paying large bribes to the Germans.

The ghetto was sealed in January 1941, ahead of the deportation of its inhabitants to Warsaw. When the Jews realized that their deportation was imminent, the Judenrat asked the Germans to let them leave on their own, without German intervention. Indeed, on January 24, 1941, it was announced that Jews would be given until March 3, 1941, to leave for Warsaw without special permits. Affluent Jews departed by their own devices. The Judenrat attempted to hire wagons for the poor, but were only able to procure transport for the elderly and the frail. Some Jews decided to head for Rawa Mazowiecka, Piotrkow Trybunalski*, and Lublin District. The final inhabitants to leave were the mentally and terminally ill, escorted by Azriel Kuchinski, the last member of the Judenrat remaining in the ghetto.

SKRZYNNO

TOWNLET IN OPOCZNO COUNTY, KIELCE DISTRICT, POLAND

During the war: General Gouvernement, Radom District

Coordinates:
51°22' | 20°43'

On the eve of World War II, about 100 Jews lived in Skrzynno. An influx of refugees during the early stages of the war boosted the Jewish population to between 300 and 400 by 1941–42. They were all put to work in a quarry.

In January 1942, the Polish population of Skrzynno was evacuated, and the townlet was declared a ghetto. Any Jew found outside its limits was condemned to death. The ghetto was liquidated in October 1942, as 200 Jews were deported to Opoczno* and from there, along with the Jews of Opoczno, to the Treblinka death camp. In November 1942, an additional twenty-two Jews were shot in Skrzynno. They were apparently members of a labor group left behind after the deportation.

SLAVNOYE

(Belarussian: **Slaunaye**)

TOWNLET IN TOLOCHIN COUNTY, VITEBSK DISTRICT, BELARUS, USSR

During the war: Military Administration Area

Coordinates:
54°18' | 29°27'

On the eve of the German invasion of the Soviet Union, several dozen Jewish families lived in Slavnoye. During the Soviet era, most Jewish wage earners practiced artisan trades, while several turned to farming. The townlet had a government school that taught in Yiddish.

The Germans occupied Slavnoye on July 6, 1941. Many Jews tried to leave the townlet before the occupation, but most subsequently returned. On July 9, 1941, altogether 143 Jews were concentrated on one street of the townlet in a ghetto established under local police guard. The ghetto was surrounded with barbed wire only on the side facing the townlet. The Germans instituted forced labor and required Jews to wear a yellow star on their backs. A well located inside the ghetto that was used by the Jewish inhabitants for bathing did not sufficiently mitigate the effects of congestion and lack of food, which fanned epidemic typhus. During July 1941, the Germans murdered several Jews in the ghetto.

The ghetto was liquidated on March 16, 1942, when an SS unit murdered its inhabitants near the village of Glinniki. A few Jews managed to escape before or during the slaughter, and several men joined the partisans.

SLAVUTA

COUNTY SEAT, KAMENETS-PODOLSK DISTRICT, UKRAINE, USSR

During the war: Reichskommissariat Ukraine

Coordinates:
50°18' | 26°52'

In the late 1930s, there were about 5,100 Jews in Slavuta, one-third of the town's population. During the Russian Civil War (1918–20), several Jewish inhabitants were murdered in pogroms conducted by Ukrainians. Under Soviet rule, many Jews were artisans, while a number organized in cooperatives and yet others went to work in state-owned factories. Slavuta had a Jewish Ethnic Soviet and Yiddish-language government schools. For nearly the entire duration of the interwar period, the town had a functioning synagogue and mikve.

The Wehrmacht occupied Slavuta on July 4 or July 7, 1941 (sources vary on the date). Members of German Military Police Battalion 45 shot 322 Jewish townspeople on August 18, 1941, and another 1,000 on August 30.

The Slavuta ghetto was established in January 1942 and held Jews from nearby localities as well. The inmates wore armbands, surrendered all valuables to German headquarters, and were put to forced labor. The ghetto was congested; starvation and disease claimed many lives.

Most of the ghetto inhabitants were murdered in a large operation conducted on July 26, 1942, with some 5,000 Jews shot to death near the town. Skilled workers and their families remained in the ghetto until September 10, 1942, when they, too, were exterminated.

SŁAWATYCZE

TOWNLET IN WŁODAWA COUNTY, LUBLIN DISTRICT, POLAND

During the war: General Gouvernement, Lublin District

Coordinates: 51°45' | 23°33'

During the interwar period, about 950 Jews lived in Slawatycze, representing approximately half of the townlet's population. They earned their livelihood through artisanship and from small-scale commerce, especially in grain and wool. The townlet had chapters of the Zionist parties and a chapter of Agudath Israel, most of whose members were Hasidim.

The Germans entered Slawatycze in early October 1939. By then, many of the townlet's Jews, especially the youths, had fled to the area controlled by the Soviets, east of the river Bug. Upon their entry, the Germans ordered Jewish inhabitants to wear a yellow badge, later replaced by a white armband marked with a blue Star-of-David. They were forbidden to use the townlet's sidewalks or to buy food from the local farmers. Their businesses and factories were appropriated. Jews were seized for forced labor.

In December 1939, Jewish refugees from Radzyn* were brought to Slawatycze; they were, however, returned home a short time later. In early 1940, a Judenrat was established in Slawatycze. In February 1940, SS officers murdered thirty-two of the townlet's Jews.

In 1941, a ghetto was established in Slawatycze. In January 1942, altogether 149 Jews from villages in the Biala Podlaska county were transferred to the ghetto.

On June 13, 1941, most of the ghetto residents were evacuated to the Lomazy* ghetto, and in August 1942, nearly all were murdered together with the Jews of Lomazy. In September 1942, the remaining Jews living in Slawatycze were evacuated to the Miedzyrzec Podlaski* ghetto.

SŁAWKÓW

TOWNLET IN OLKUSZ COUNTY, KIELCE DISTRICT, POLAND

During the war: Wartheland

Coordinates: 50°18' | 19°24'

About 650 Jews lived in Slawkow when World War II broke out, representing approximately one-sixth of the townlet's population. Many of the younger people had emigrated earlier, especially to South America. The Jews of Slawkow earned their livelihoods as workers in the local iron foundry and from petty commerce and small-scale industry, especially in garment manufacturing. They received aid from the JDC and a free-loan society. Slawkow boasted chapters of Zionist parties as well as a Hachshara training farm. The townlet also had a chapter of Agudath Israel. Most of the community's children studied in private Hadarim.

The Germans occupied Slawkow in early September 1939. A few days later, they murdered ninety-eight men who attempted to escape to the area under Soviet occupation in eastern Poland. Large, extortionate "contributions" were exacted from the Jews.

In November 1939, a Judenrat headed by Laks and a three-member Jewish Order Service were established in the townlet. The Jews were ordered to wear Star-of-David armbands, which were later replaced by a yellow Star-of-David on the chest. The Judenrat was subordinate to the central Judenrat in the Upper Central

Silesian region, which was located in Sosnowiec*. After its establishment, the Judenrat opened a public soup kitchen, a clinic, and a metalworking course. The Jews were recruited or seized for forced labor.

In late 1941 or early 1942, a ghetto was established in Slawkow in which some 850 Jews were concentrated. Although the ghetto was not fenced in, Jews were forbidden to leave its confines, and a nightly curfew was imposed.

On June 10, 1942, the Jews of Slawkow were rounded up outside the townlet. Following a selection, those qualified as fit were taken to work in the "shops" in Sosnowiec and Bedzin*, while the rest were deported to Auschwitz two days later.

About twenty Jews remained in Slawkow: the members of the Judenrat and skilled workers, along with their families. A few months later, they were deported to towns in the Silesian region still inhabited by Jews, whose fate they shared.

SŁONIM

COUNTY SEAT, NOWOGRÓDEK DISTRICT, POLAND

(After World War II in the USSR/Belarus; Belarussian, Russian: **Slonim**)

During the war:
Reichskommissariat Ostland

Coordinates:
53°06' | 25°19'

About 16,000 Jews lived in Slonim on the eve of World War II, representing approximately half of the town's population. Most earned their livelihood from artisanship and industry. Zionist parties and youth movements were active in Slonim, as were the Bund and Agudath Israel. Educational institutions included a Tarbut Hebrew school, a Beit Yaakov school for girls, a *Tachkemoni* school, a Yiddish school, a Yeshiva, and a Jewish high school. The community partook of Jewish cultural and recreational institutions, including clubs and libraries, and a number of Jewish newspapers were published in the town.

The Soviets occupied Slonim on September 18, 1939. During the period of Soviet rule, privately owned shops were nationalized or closed and cooperatives were opened. Jewish community institutions were dismantled. Following the occupation, Jewish public figures and members of youth movements fled from Slonim, while thousands of refugees inundated the town from the areas of Poland occupied by the Germans. These new arrivals raised the town's Jewish population during the period of Soviet occupation to some 22,000 people.

The Germans occupied Slonim on June 26, 1941, and that same day began to loot Jewish property and murder Jews. Within a few days, Jews and non-Jews were forbidden to reside in the same buildings, and many of Slonim's Jews were forced to relocate. In early July 1941, the Jews reinstated the Jewish community council and appointed Wolf Berman as its head. The council worked to renew the food supply to the town's Jewish inhabitants and to introduce order into the recruitment of Jews for forced labor. As of July 10, 1941, the Jews of Slonim were ordered to wear a yellow badge.

On July 24, 1941, an murder operation was carried out in Slonim by Einsatzkommando 8, during which close to 1,400 Jewish men and boys were removed from their homes and taken to a forest near the village of Pietralewicze, where about 1,250 of them were executed. Among the killed were the community's rabbi, Rabbi Yehuda-Leib Fein, as well as members of the intelligentsia and the community council. The survivors, fewer than 200 people, were returned to Slonim. After the operation, the Jews of Slonim established a fifteen-member Judenrat at German orders, headed by Wolf Berman. They also set up a Jewish Order Service headed by Moshe Lots, as well as an employment bureau.

Towards the end of the summer of 1941, the military administration in Belarus was replaced by a civil administration. The man placed in charge of Jewish affairs in the new administration, staff officer Hiek, was known as the "Angel of Death" among Jews. He periodically summoned members of the Judenrat from Slonim, levied fines on the Jewish community, and imposed new restrictions on the Jews. In one instance, the Jews were helped by a Polish priest named Adam Sztark, who collected gold crosses from the members of his parish to help the Jews pay their fines (Sztark was recognized as a Righteous Among the Nations). Later, Hiek ordered the execution of ten members of the Judenrat and their families after he was informed that they were withholding funds. The Jews then established a new Judenrat at German orders, headed by Gershon Kvint. The Jewish Order Service personnel were increased to thirty policemen.

In late August 1941, a ghetto was established in Slonim. The Zabinka quarter was included in the ghetto and became known as the "island" owing to the river that flowed through its grounds, separating it from the rest of the ghetto. Those with required professions and their families were placed on the "island" and were permitted to visit the other section of the ghetto, whereas entry into the "island" was restricted to its inhabitants. Several weeks later, the ghetto was divided into quarters according to the inhabitants' professions. The administration issued yellow documents to the inhabitants of the "island" and to those living in one of the other quarters in the ghetto. Several Jewish inhabitants were allowed to continue residing in their own apartments outside of the ghetto, including a number of families who billeted army officers in their homes, twelve doctors who treated non-Jews, and a number of artisans. These Jews assisted the inhabitants of the ghetto by bartering for food with farmers. The Judenrat established a small hospital and a public soup kitchen in the ghetto.

In September 1941, about sixty inhabitants of the ghetto were seized to perform forced labor—the digging of pits; they were never seen again. On November 7, 1941, about 200 Jews were murdered, including most of the Judenrat members and their families. Gershon Kvint attempted to save all of the members of the Judenrat by paying the Germans a ransom, but his efforts secured the lives of only three people. On the morning of November 14, 1941, a large-scale murder operation was carried out. Between 9,000 and 10,000 of the ghetto's Jews, specifically the people who did not hold permits, were sent in the direction of Czepielow, where most were shot to death in the pits that had been dug some two months earlier. Hundreds of Jews managed to escape from the pits and return to the ghetto. The wounded, treated in the ghetto hospital, were caught and taken once again to the murder site, where they were killed.

Following the November 1941 operation, a hundred young people organized in the ghetto and formed an underground. Judenrat head Gershon Kvint and a number of additional community leaders helped them by warning about searches in the ghetto and by bribing the Germans to free underground members who had been arrested. The members of the underground managed to hoard arms and smuggled weapons to the partisans.

In December 1941, the Slonim ghetto was sealed off, reduced in size, and encircled by a barbed-wire fence with two gates. The "island" remained within its boundaries. The Germans ordered the establishment of a Judenrat with a single member, and a man named Yelishevich volunteered to serve. Many of the reduced ghetto's Jews prepared underground bunkers and various other places to hide, and fled to the forests or to other ghettos, mainly to that of Bialystok*. From January through March 1942, hundreds of Jews were deported from other localities and concentrated in the Slonim ghetto, raising its population to about 15,000. In April 1942, the doctors and artisans who had lived outside the ghetto until then, about 200 people in all, were also moved into the ghetto with their families.

In late May 1942, Kvint, who continued to manage the affairs of the employment bureau, was ordered to recruit 500 workers to be sent to Mogilev* in east Belarus. When he refused, about 400 Jews were seized and sent to Mogilev.

In June 1942, the Jews who worked for the civil administration, the municipality, and the medical staff were given green permits. Hiek, who had been dismissed from his job a month earlier and who sought to sabotage the work of his successor, Rietmeyer, smuggled the Jewish administration employees to a place distant from Slonim, where many hid in the forests.

The Slonim ghetto held several thousands of the Jews from the area, and its liquidation was carried out between June 29 and July 15, 1942. On June 29, at dawn, local police units and a Lithuanian unit encircled the ghetto. When Kvint passed through the front gate to determine what was taking place, Rietmeyer shot him on the spot. The Germans began shooting into the ghetto homes, and set them on fire if their residents did not emerge. Many Jews were killed either in the fires or shot in the streets as they fled from the fire. In all, between 8,000 and 10,000 of the ghetto's Jews were killed in the operation, which lasted over two weeks. Most were shot at the killing site in Pietralewicze. The operation was carried out with the active participation of the district governor, Gerhard Erren.

During the liquidation operation, Jews committed of acts of resistance and escape. Two armed groups from among the ghetto's Jews that were under the command of Zerach Kerman and Aharon Band had fled in July 1942 and laid the foundations for a Jewish partisan unit. At the height of its activity, the unit was 150- to 160-member strong and became famous for its daring exploits, including an attack on the garrison in Kosow Poleski*.

By the end of the operation, fewer than 1,000 Jews, mostly craftsmen, remained in Slonim; about 400 of them were shot on August 20, 1942, while several hundred fled to the forests in the following months. Some 300 of the remaining Jews were concentrated in a number of places throughout Slonim and performed various jobs, until the final liquidation of the Slonim ghetto in December 1942.

SLOVENI/SLAVENI

TOWNLET IN TOLOCHIN COUNTY, VITEBSK DISTRICT, BELARUS, USSR

During the war: Military Administration Area

Coordinates:
54°20' | 29°32'

In the late 1930s, there were several dozen Jewish families in Sloveni. Since the townlet was near the Minsk–Moscow railroad, a few Jewish families presumably managed to flee to the east after the German invasion of the Soviet Union on June 22, 1941. The Germans occupied Sloveni in early July 1941. Near the beginning of the following year, the approximately 110 Jews remaining in townlet were concentrated in a ghetto that the Germans set up on a single street. After a period of starvation and abuse inflicted by the Germans, the ghetto was liquidated on March 16, 1942, and its population was murdered in a pit near the townlet.

SLUTSK

COUNTY SEAT, MINSK DISTRICT, BELARUS, USSR

During the war:
Reichskommissariat Ostland

Coordinates:
53°01' | 27°33'

At the beginning of the twentieth century, there were about 10,200 Jews in Slutsk, nearly 80 percent of the local population. During the era of Soviet rule, many Jews in the town held white-collar jobs or practiced artisan trades, and several hundred turned to farming near the town. No modern industry developed. As Slutsk declined in its commercial viability, many Jews left. By the late 1930s, some 7,400 Jewish inhabitants remained, about one-third of the population. The town had two government schools that taught in Yiddish.

The Germans occupied Slutsk on June 27, 1941. Only a few Jews, chiefly those with connections in the Soviet administration, were able to flee eastward in time. As soon as the Germans settled in, they required Jews to wear a yellow Star-of-David on their chests. Some seventy Jews who had been active Communists under the Soviets were murdered during the first two days of the occupation. In late September or October 1941, many Jews were taken from Slutsk to the nearby village of Selishche, where they were murdered by Order Police Battalion 11, which had come from Kaunas* and had Germans and Lithuanians in its ranks.

In October 1941, a ghetto was established in a neighborhood of Slutsk that had several synagogues. It was fenced in with barbed wire and guarded by Belarussian and Lithuanian police. Jews were not allowed out and non-Jews were denied entry. Jewish artisans who had skills in demand remained in their previous workplaces; others were sent to forced labor. Jews from surrounding towns and villages, including Starobin and Krasnaya Sloboda (formerly Vizna), were also concentrated in the Slutsk ghetto.

The Germans appointed a Judenrat with several members; there was also a Jewish Order Service. Later, the ghetto was divided into an "urban ghetto," located at the original site and designated for skilled workers and their families, and a "rural ghetto," established a short distance from town, where most of the Jews were taken. The inhabitants, particularly those in the rural ghetto, suffered from intense overcrowding and hunger. At one stage, the Germans used the records of a doctor who worked in the ghetto to execute the chronically ill. After that, ghetto inhabitants refrained from visiting the doctor in a bid to conceal their illnesses. Now and again, the Germans ordered the Judenrat to round up groups of Jews, ostensibly for labor but in fact to be murdered near the town.

In March or April 1942, the rural ghetto was liquidated and its 3,000 to 4,000 inhabitants were murdered near the nearby village of Sloboda.

In winter 1943 (apparently in January), the Germans decided to establish a brothel for soldiers and employed Jews from the ghetto to build it, using tombstones from the Jewish cemetery in Slutsk for the foundations. According to several testimonies, when the construction workers completed their labors, they were shot by the Germans and buried in the foundation.

The urban ghetto was liquidated on February 8–9, 1943. Its inhabitants, apart from some twenty to fifty-three skilled craftsmen (sources vary in their estimates), were murdered at Sloboda. Those spared spent two days in prison and were then sent to the Minsk* ghetto.

SŁUŻEWO

TOWNLET IN NIESZAWA COUNTY, WARSAW DISTRICT, POLAND

During the war: Wartheland

Coordinates:
52°51' | 18°39'

About 250 Jews lived in Sluzewo in the interwar period, representing approximately one-sixth of the townlet's population. They earned their livelihood from commerce and artisanship and were aided by a free-loan society and the traditional welfare societies. Some of the community's children attended Hadarim, while others studied with private teachers or in Polish public schools. The townlet had a Jewish library.

The Germans occupied Sluzewo in the early days of September 1939, and immediately began to seize Jews for forced labor; they also periodically murdered Jews.

The Nieszawa area was annexed to the Third Reich as part of the Wartheland. In the fall of 1940, a ghetto was established in the townlet. In mid-May 1942, the ghetto was liquidated and the Jews of Sluzewo were apparently deported to the Chelmno death camp.

SMOLENSK

DISTRICT SEAT, RUSSIAN FEDERATION, USSR

During the war: Military Administration Area

Coordinates:
54°46' | 32°02'

On the eve of World War II, 15,000 Jews lived in Smolensk, accounting for just under 10 percent of the city's population. In the 1920s, the community had two Yiddish schools, a Yiddish drama group, and a branch of the Hehalutz movement. These institutions ceased to exist in the 1930s. In 1929, a Yiddish-language teachers' college was relocated from Gomel* to Smolensk.

The Germans occupied Smolensk on July 16, 1941. A majority of the Jewish residents (about 12,000) had fled or been evacuated in advance.

Several dozen Jewish townspeople, mostly members of the intelligentsia, were murdered during the first weeks of the occupation. In August 1941, Jewish inhabitants aged ten years and over were ordered to wear yellow armbands and to sew Jewish patches onto their clothing. The ghettoization of between 1,200 and 2,000 Jews from Smolensk and refugees from Belarus began on August 5, 1941 (or at the end of July, according to German sources). The selected area, located across the Dnieper River and near the Jewish cemetery, was enclosed in barbed wire and purged of its original inhabitants. The Jews were compelled to carry their belongings to the ghetto area within a one-week period. The ghetto was severely congested, with six to eight families occupying each of a number of small houses. Jews who could not find a place to sleep were forced to sleep sitting up.

As the ghetto was being established, a Judenrat was set up under a dentist named Peinson. Its duties were to mobilize Jews for forced labor and maintain order in the ghetto. Despite the barbed-wire fence, the ghetto Jews remained in contact with the surrounding population, mainly to obtain food. Jews also procured food in the form of a daily ration of 200 grams of coarse bread, in exchange for forced labor. They cleaned the streets of Smolensk and, later on, worked at the railroad station. Those who became too exhausted to continue working were shot and buried locally. In the early months of the ghetto, several artisans were assigned to shoemaking and sewing work for the Germans. They evidently continued to hold these jobs notwithstanding an order that was issued to assign Jews to only the harshest forms of labor, and to confiscate their tools.

One of the gravest problems facing residents in the Smolensk ghetto was its lack of a water source. The Jews were compelled to draw water from the Dnieper River, and Russian or German police would often empty the Jews' pails before they reached home. The shortage of clean water coupled with acute congestion led to rampant disease. In the winter of 1941/42, more than 200 Jews, mostly children and the elderly, died in the ghetto. The Jews were not allowed to bury their dead in the cemetery despite its proximity to the ghetto; burials were restricted to the ghetto confines.

Despoliation took place intermittently; in September 1941, for example, the Germans confiscated all Jewish-owned furs. Russian and German police entered the ghetto at night and perpetrated robberies that were sometimes accompanied by beatings, gunfire, and rape. Elderly people stood watch at night to warn women of impending danger. In June 1942, the ghetto population was assessed a fine that members of the Judenrat were obliged to collect.

The Smolensk ghetto was liquidated on July 15, 1942. On the night of July 14–15, Russian police ringed the ghetto. All inhabitants were marched to a nearby grove roughly one kilometer from the village of Magalenshchina. The Jews were either shot or gassed to death in vans.

SMOLEVICHI

(Belarussian: **Smalyavichy**)

COUNTY SEAT, MINSK DISTRICT, BELARUS, USSR

During the war:
Reichskommissariat Ostland

Coordinates:
54°02' | 28°05'

On the eve of the German invasion of the Soviet Union, there were about 1,400 Jews in Smolevichi, roughly one-fifth of the local population. During the era of Soviet rule, many Jews practiced artisan trades, some held blue- or white-collar jobs, while others turned to farming. The townlet had a Jewish Ethnic Council and a school that functioned in Yiddish.

The Germans occupied Smolevichi on June 26–27, 1941, and promptly established an open-air, barbed-wire fenced ghetto in a part of townlet that had been destroyed. On July 28, 1941, some 120 young Jewish men were taken from the ghetto to the Kurovshchina area, where they were murdered by the Germans for having ostensibly been in contact with partisans.

The ghetto was liquidated on August 28, 1941, when all its inhabitants were murdered in the nearby Gorodishche forest by a regiment of the Division SS "Galizien" under the command of Franz Lechthaler, and by Lithuanians.

SMOLYANY

(Yiddish: **Smilian**; Belarussian: **Smalyany**)

TOWNLET IN ORSHA COUNTY, VITEBSK DISTRICT, BELARUS, USSR

During the war: Military Administration Area

Coordinates:
54°36' | 30°04'

In the mid-1920s, there were about 900 Jews in Smolyany. During the era of Soviet rule, many Jews practiced artisan trades, while a few became farmers or white-collar workers in government institutions.

The Germans occupied Smolyany in early July 1941; they required Jews to wear a yellow mark and imposed forced labor. On March 8, 1942, between 700 and 800 local Jews and refugees from Borisov,* Minsk,* Orsha* and Dubrovno* were concentrated in a ghetto composed of a single street. It was surrounded by a barbed-wire fence but was not guarded closely. Inhabitants occasionally left the ghetto to barter belongings for food. Starvation, congestion, and cold led to high mortality. Inhabitants unfit for labor were summarily murdered.

The ghetto was liquidated on April 5, 1942, when Germans and Belarussian police murdered all 560 inhabitants in a forest near the Gubinskaya dacha.

SMORGONIE

(Yiddish: **Smargon**)

TOWNLET IN OSZMIANA COUNTY, VILNA DISTRICT, POLAND
(After World War II in the USSR/Belarus; Belarussian: **Smarhon'**; Russian: **Smorgon**)

During the war:
Reichskommissariat Ostland

Coordinates:
54°29' | 26°24'

About 2,300 Jews lived in Smorgonie on the eve of World War II, representing less than half of the townlet's population. Most earned their livelihood from artisanship, shopkeeping and small commerce. Jewish parties and youth movements were active in Smorgonie, including Zionist parties and the Bund. The townlet's community also boasted a Tarbut Hebrew school, a Jewish library, and a sports club.

After the Soviets occupied Smorgonie in the second half of September 1939, economic activity in the townlet was restricted and Jewish political activity was banned.

On June 26, 1941, Smorgonie was occupied by the Germans, who immediately burned down the Tarbut school building and executed twelve young Jews. In early July 1941, the Jews of Smorgonie were ordered to wear a yellow badge, their freedom of movement was restricted, and they were required to submit ransom payments. At German orders, a Judenrat was established, headed by Rabbi Yitzhak Markus and Y. Badnes. The Judenrat was mainly responsible for recruiting Jews aged twelve years and older for forced labor.

In September 1941, the Jews of Smorgonie were concentrated in two closed ghettos, one of which was situated on a farming settlement near the townlet that was already inhabited by Jews. Many Jews from the "farming ghetto" were sent outside to perform forced labor, and the ghetto's population dwindled. In the summer of 1942, the "farming" ghetto was liquidated, and its inhabitants were transferred to the other ghetto, which was closed and guarded.

In October 1942, about 1,600 of the Smorgonie ghetto's inhabitants were evacuated to the Oszmiana* ghetto and shared the fate of local inhabitants. A number of the Jews who remained in Smorgonie were concurrently sent to labor camps in Lithuania. In April 1943, the last remaining Jews in Smorgonie were taken to Ponary and murdered.

ŚNIATYN

COUNTY SEAT, STANISŁAWÓW DISTRICT, POLAND
(After World War II in the USSR/Ukraine; Ukrainian: **Snyatyn**; Russian: **Snyatin**)

During the war: General Gouvernement, Galicia District

Coordinates:
48°27' | 25°34'

About 3,250 Jews lived in Sniatyn during the interwar period, representing approximately one-third of the town's population. They earned their livelihood mainly from commerce and artisanship. The community ran traditional charity and welfare organizations, including an orphanage and a public soup kitchen for needy children. Sniatyn had a Hebrew school, a Jewish cultural center, and a sports club. The Bund and Agudath Israel were active in the community, as were Zionist parties and youth movements, which maintained a Jewish library.

In September 1939, hundreds of Jewish refugees from western Poland passed through Sniatyn on their way to Romania. Following the Soviet occupation in the second half of September 1939 and the closure of the passage to Romania, numerous Jewish refugees remained in the town. In June 1940, many of the refugees were exiled to remote locations in the Soviet Union for refusing to accept Soviet citizenship.

In late June 1941, after Germany invaded the Soviet Union, a small group of young Jews managed to flee to the east. In early June 1941, Sniatyn was occupied by units of the Romanian army (allies of the Germans). The Romanian soldiers plundered Jewish property and seized Jews for forced labor. One week later, Romanians and local Ukrainians murdered more than twenty Jews, including refugees from Bukovina and Bessarabia. After two weeks of Romanian rule, Sniatyn was handed over to the Hungarians. Jews continued to be seized for forced labor, but the Hungarian governor restrained the Ukrainians somewhat.

In September 1941, Sniatyn was handed over to German control. The seizure of Jews for forced labor continued. Cows, horses, and wagons were confiscated, and a Judenrat was established, headed by a dentist named Cohen. The Judenrat was required to supply the Germans with forced laborers and to take care of the refugees.

In September and October 1941, hundreds of Jews from surrounding localities were concentrated in Sniatyn. In late September 1941, thirty Jews who had been taken hostage were shot to death in the nearby Potoczek forest, despite the high ransom that had been paid for them. In October to December 1941, another approximately 500 Jews were murdered in this forest, and in the second half of March 1942, another approximately seventy Jews were killed.

In early 1942, the Germans began to concentrate the Jews in a ghetto. Many died of hunger and disease. In early April 1942, a large-scale operation was carried out by units of the German police, under the command of Paul Behr and the supervision of Peter Leideritz, with the assistance of Ukrainian policemen. The town's several thousand Jews were concentrated in the municipal sports center building; within the following days, Jews were brought to the location from other localities, as well. Many Jews were beaten or shot to death in the building, and many died because of the harsh conditions of their detainment, including dehydration. On April 6, 1942, about 2,000 of those kept in the sports facility were deported to the Belzec death camp. A group of skilled artisans whose occupations were in demand were handed over to the local Wehrmacht commanders.

The survivors of the community were once again concentrated in the ghetto, and several started to dig out bunkers in preparation for coming operations.

On September 8, 1942, German SIPO police launched the ghetto's liquidation operation, in accordance with Leideritz's instructions and under the direct command of Albert Westermann. The operation continued through to September 10, 1942. The Germans set fire to buildings in the ghetto in order to uncover hiding places, and they concentrated the Jews they found in the sports center. Several people were murdered in the facility or on the way to the train station. Approximately 1,500 Jews were deported to Belzec in this operation. A number of people jumped off the moving train, many were shot to death by German guards, and others were handed over to the police by the local population.

SNITKOV
(Ukrainian: **Snitkiv**)

TOWNLET IN MUROVANNYE KURILOVTSY COUNTY, VINNITSA DISTRICT, UKRAINE, USSR

During the war:
Reichskommissariat Ukraine

Coordinates:
48°48' | 27°38'

In the mid-1920s there were about 1,200 Jews in Snitkov. Under Soviet rule, Jewish private commerce was gradually phased out, artisans formed cooperatives, and a number of Jews became farm workers at a Jewish kolkhoz. A government school that taught in Yiddish functioned until the mid-1930s.

Once Germany invaded the Soviet Union on June 22, 1941, Jewish men in Snitkov were drafted into the Red Army. The Germans occupied the townlet on July 23, 1941. A few days later, they participated with local collaborators in a pogrom. By decree of the occupation authorities, Jews were ordered to post a black Star-of-David on the door of their residence and to wear a white armband.

Several weeks later, a fenced ghetto comprising a single street and an area near the market was established in Snitkov. The Jews were constrained to move into the ghetto within two hours, while Ukrainian police and the local population looted their abandoned property. Jews from the Jewish kolkhoz were also concentrated in the ghetto. The ghetto inhabitants were escorted to their forced labor service every morning and were given one hour per week to visit the market and barter possessions for food. Many died of starvation or as a consequence of poor hygiene in the ghetto. The Germans appointed Moshe Krym and, subsequently, Perelman as ghetto leaders, charging them with collecting valuables and money and delivering forced laborers. A Hungarian army unit stationed for a period in the townlet also paid periodic visits to the ghetto leader to demand warm clothing, boots, and money.

In early 1942, Jewish refugees from Bessarabia reached Snitkov and were provided with food and housing by the ghetto population. In March 1942, a group of about sixty young people was sent from the ghetto to a labor camp at Letichev.

The ghetto was liquidated on August 20, 1942, when most of the inhabitants were transferred to Murovannye Kurilovtsy*, where they were murdered along with Jews from the vicinity. Several dozen youths who were separated out during the operation were deported to the labor camp at Letichev.

SOBIENIE JEZIORY
(Yiddish: **Sabin**)

TOWNLET IN GARWOLIN COUNTY, LUBLIN DISTRICT, POLAND

During the war: General Gouvernement, Warsaw District

Coordinates:
51°56' | 21°19'

When World War II broke out, about 1,400 Jews lived in Sobienie Jeziory, representing approximately three-quarters of the local population. They eked out a living from commerce and artisanship. The townlet had a free-loan society, a bank, and a library as well as chapters of Zionist parties and Agudath Israel.

In the first week of September 1939, a large number of refugees from the area and western Poland, including from Garwolin, arrived in Sobienie Jeziory. In 1940, another wave of refugees arrived from Pilawa, Warsaw*, Piaseczno*, and Gora Kalwaria*. In 1941, the Jewish population of Sobienie Jeziory reached about 2,250, and by the end of that year, it had swelled to about 3,680.

In September 1941, the Germans established a ghetto in Sobienie. The Judenrat was responsible for recruiting hundreds of Jews for forced labor. The workers were sent to the Wilga labor camp and replaced every few weeks.

During the winter of 1941/42, epidemic typhus broke out in the ghetto, and many of its inhabitants perished. A number of people were shot to death while leaving the ghetto to purchase food. The Judenrat opened a public soup kitchen.

In September 1942, the Jews of the area were concentrated in Sobienie Jeziory, and on October 2, 1942, approximately 8,000 Jews were deported to the Treblinka death camp by SS men and German gendarmes.

SOBKÓW

TOWNLET IN JĘDRZEJÓW COUNTY, KIELCE DISTRICT, POLAND

During the war: General Gouvernement, Radom District

Coordinates: 50°42' | 20°28'

On the eve of World War II, 565 Jews lived in Sobkow, representing more than half of the townlet's population. They earned their livelihood from commerce and artisanship, especially tailoring and shoemaking, in addition to a small-scale farming. The townlet had a Jewish school.

Immediately upon entering Sobkow in September 1939, the Germans, along with the Poles, plundered Jewish property.

By September 1940, a ghetto was established in Sobkow. Its inhabitants were struck by epidemic typhus. The residents of the ghetto were assigned to forced labor, while professionals were sent to labor camps. In September 1940, Jews from the Jedrzejow* ghetto were brought to the ghetto, followed by refugees from other localities.

On August 28, 1942, the Germans deported the 800 residents of the ghetto to the Jedrzejow ghetto, and from there, most were sent to the Treblinka death camp between September 16 and 25.

SOBOLEVKA

(Ukrainian: **Sobolivka**)

TOWNLET IN TEPLIK COUNTY, VINNITSA DISTRICT, UKRAINE, USSR

During the war: Reichskommissariat Ukraine

Coordinates: 47°42' | 29°33'

Shortly before the German invasion of the Soviet Union, there were about 400 Jews in Sobolevka. Under Soviet rule, many changed their occupations from commerce to artisanship or took up jobs as blue-collar workers or bureaucrats in the state sector. The townlet had a Jewish Ethnic Soviet that operated in Yiddish. A Yiddish-language government school closed in 1938.

The Germans occupied Sobolevka on July 28, 1941. They established a ghetto in September under a man surnamed Zhurakovski, who was in charge of recruiting Jews for forced labor. In April 1942, a group of about 100 young Jews was sent to a labor camp in Raigorod.

The ghetto was liquidated on May 27, 1942, when its remaining 382 inhabitants were murdered at a nearby location.

SOBOLEW

TOWNLET IN GARWOLIN COUNTY, LUBLIN DISTRICT, POLAND

During the war: General Gouvernement, Warsaw District

Coordinates: 51°44' | 21°40'

About 800 Jews lived in Sobolew when World War II broke out, representing more than half of the townlet's population. They earned their livelihood from peddling and artisanship as well as by providing services to vacationers. A Zionist chapter, Zionist youth movements, and Agudath Israel were active in Sobolew. The townlet had a Beit Yaakov school for girls and a traditional Talmud Torah.

The Germans occupied Sobolew on September 17, 1939. A twelve-member Judenrat was established in late 1939, headed by Yisrael Farber, and its main function was to recruit forced laborers for the Germans. In early 1940, there arrived in Sobolew 680 Jewish refugees; while most were from Garwolin, several had also fled from Warsaw* and western Poland.

In early fall 1940, an open ghetto was established in the townlet. On October 23, 1940, about 400 Jews deported from Maciejowice* arrived in Sobolew, and the ghetto's population swelled to over 2,000. In June 1941, the ghetto was sealed off and encircled by a barbed-wire fence. The Judenrat opened a public soup kitchen and a clinic.

The ghetto was liquidated in October 1942, when SS soldiers and policemen deported its inhabitants to the Treblinka death camp.

On December 1, 1942, the Germans reestablished a ghetto in Sobolew for some 1,400 Jews who had fled or hidden during the deportations in the area. On January 10, 1943, they were deported to Treblinka by German police and SS men.

SOCHACZEW

COUNTY SEAT, WARSAW DISTRICT, POLAND

During the war: General Gouvernement, Warsaw District

Coordinates: 52°14' | 20°15'

About 3,000 Jews lived in Sochaczew in the interwar period, representing approximately 30 percent of the townlet's population. They earned their livelihood from commerce and artisanship, formed trade and craft associations, and were aided by a Jewish bank supported by the JDC. Sochaczew had the traditional welfare societies as well as a free-loan society. The community's children attended traditional Hadarim, a modern Heder, a Hebrew Yavne school, a Beit Yaakov school for girls and a *Yesodei Torah* school for boys, both founded by Agudath Israel, as well as a Szabasowka school. Sochaczew had a Jewish library with a reading room, a drama circle, and a sports organization that held summer camps for poor children. Political organizations included Zionist parties and youth movements that established pioneer training facilities, the Bund and Agudath Israel and their youth movements, and a group of Jewish Communists.

When World War II broke out, many Jews fled from Sochaczew to the east. About 100 people found asylum in the parts of Poland that later were occupied by the Soviet Union.

On September 9, 1939, the Germans took control of Sochaczew. They murdered a number of the elderly and ill and burned down the homes of Jews who were away from the townlet. When a number of the people who had fled returned to the townlet, they were forced to live with other Jews under conditions of terrible overcrowding. In the coming months, the remaining approximately 2,000 Jews in the townlet were joined by 400 to 500 Jewish refugees from surrounding localities and from Lodz*.

In mid-October 1939, the Germans began to seize hundreds of Jews every day for forced labor, building fortifications and a bridge over the Bzura River. Tombstones from the Jewish cemetery were used to build the fortifications, and several Jews drowned while building the bridge.

In January 1940, the Jews of Sochaczew were ordered to establish an eighteen-member Judenrat, headed by a merchant named Yaakov Biderman, and a Jewish Order Service, headed by Menachem Knat. The Judenrat supplied the Germans with forced laborers, putting an end to the random seizure of Jews from the street. On January 18, 1941, about 900 of Sochaczew's Jews were deported to Zyrardow*.

On January 19, 1941, the Germans ordered the establishment of a ghetto in Sochaczew. It was encircled by a high barbed-wire fence and was guarded from the outside by German gendarmes and from within by members of the Jewish Order Service. The Judenrat, with the help of the JDC, established a public soup kitchen that supplied half of the ghetto's population with hot meals.

On February 13 or 14, 1941, the Germans murdered Knat, the head of the Jewish Order Service. On February 15, 1941, the Germans ordered the deportation of Sochaczew's Jews to the Warsaw* ghetto. Prior to their deportation, the Jews were ordered to undergo disinfection, during which all valuables they had on their person were stolen. Initially, only half of Sochaczew's Jews were ordered to leave the local ghetto and move over to Zyrardow. The Judenrat began to draw up lists of those designated for deportation and panic ensued. There were Jewish inhabitants of the ghetto who could afford to pay to evade deportation, and consequently, the poor were the first to be removed. Meanwhile, the members of the Judenrat managed to rent a car for themselves, load it with their personal property, and leave for Warsaw as quickly as possible. At a later stage, however, the wealthier Jews were also unable to escape deportation.

A few weeks after the deportation, the Germans returned 150 of Sochaczew's Jews from the Warsaw ghetto to the townlet for forced labor. When the work was completed, they were brought back to Warsaw, with the exception of a few Jews who hid out in Sochaczew and were murdered, as well as twenty-one Jews who were left in the townlet and were executed a short time later in the nearby forests. The Jews of Sochaczew in Warsaw shared the fate of Warsaw's Jews. Most died in the ghetto or were deported to the death camps in the summer of 1942.

During the deportations from Sochaczew, a few dozen Jews, especially children, scattered in the area. Most were handed over to the Germans and murdered, while a few were saved by Poles living in the area. These Poles would later be designated "Righteous Among the Nations."

SOKAL
(Yiddish: **Sikol**)

COUNTY SEAT, LWÓW DISTRICT, POLAND
(After World War II in the USSR/Ukraine; Ukrainian: **Sokal'**)

During the war: General Gouvernement, Galicia District

Coordinates:
50°29' | 24°17'

In the 1930s, about 5,200 Jews lived in Sokal, representing approximately half of the town's population. In addition to merchants and artisans, Sokal's Jews counted members of the liberal professions and owners of factories that engaged in light industry. Sokal had a merchant bank of the Jewish merchants' union and a number of welfare societies. Hasidism was very strong in the town, and Agudath Israel was active there, in addition to several Zionist movements and the Bund. The various parties ran youth movements and cultural clubs. Sokal had traditional Hadarim, a Beit Yaakov school for girls, and a Tarbut Hebrew school.

In September 1939, Sokal was inundated with hundreds of Jewish refugees who thronged to the town from western Poland, and the local Jews established a council to assist them. The Soviets entered Sokal in the second half of September 1939. Under Soviet rule, the factories were nationalized, commerce was significantly cut back, and Jewish parties were abolished. In the summer of 1940, a few middle-class families along with some of the refugees that refused to accept Soviet citizenship were exiled into the Soviet Union interior.

On June 23, 1941, the Germans occupied Sokal and murdered eight Jews. On June 28, 1941, at the initiative of SS officer Paul Blobel, the Germans and the Ukrainian ultra-nationalists began to hunt down Jews who had been active in the former Soviet governmental institutions. They killed either 183 or 400 Jews (sources vary on the figure) accused of Communism.

In July 1941, the Germans appointed a seven-member Judenrat headed by G. Yanoshcinski that was ordered to supply hundreds of Jews every day for forced labor. In November 1941, all the Jewish men aged fourteen to sixty were registered in the German employment bureau. Those who were employed in jobs vital to the Germans received special work permits. On December 27, 1941, the Jews were ordered to turn over all furs in their possession to the Germans. That same winter, the community suffered from a severe shortage of food and many people died of starvation. The Judenrat established a public soup kitchen that distributed hundreds of portions of soup each day. In February 1942, the Germans demanded that the Judenrat hand over 500 people from Sokal and its environs for forced labor. A bribe reduced the quota to 200 Jews. In March 1942, about 450 Jews were deported to labor camps. The Judenrat and their family members shipped the laborers packages of food and clothing. In most cases the packages did not reach their destination, and by summertime, all contact was lost with the camp detainees, the vast of majority of whom perished or were murdered. On

August 3, 1942, thirty-two Jewish men were sent to perform forced labor near the Bug River and were apparently murdered.

On September 17, 1942, a mass operation was carried out in Sokal. German and Ukrainian police blocked all entrances to the town, combed through the Jews' homes, took all the Jews they found to the marketplace, where they killed some 160 of them. About 2,000 others were transported to the Belzec death camp.

On October 15, 1942, one month after the operation, the Jews were concentrated into a ghetto. On October 22–24, 1942, the Germans transferred about 3,000 additional Jews to Sokal from surrounding localities, including Radziechow* and Mosty Wielkie*. In all, more than 5,000 people were packed into the ghetto in a state of extreme overcrowding; they had four wells from which to draw water. An epidemic of typhus (*rickettsia*) soon broke out, killing more than twenty people a day. The Judenrat established a hospital and clinic, which barely addressed the inhabitants' health needs.

Two weeks after the establishment of the ghetto, on November 28, 1942, a second operation was carried out during which about 2,500 Jews were deported to Belzec. Most of the Jews who jumped off the train cars were killed by the jump or shot by the guards. Judenrat head G. Yanoshcinski attempted to escape from the ghetto and was murdered. After the second operation, the Germans appointed David Kindler as head of the Judenrat. When he refused, they appointed the engineer Schwartz; his refusal to take on the post cost him his life.

After the two operations, attempts to escape from the ghetto to the forests and to Christian acquaintances increased. But these attempts were hindered by a combination of an indifferent local population, searches by Germans, and gangs of Ukrainian ultra-nationalists led by Stefan Bandera that wandered the forests and killed Jews. In the ghetto itself, poor sanitary conditions continued to take a heavy toll in Jewish lives. Some 1,500 people are estimated to have perished from hunger and disease in the ghetto in the winter of 1942/43.

In the spring of 1943, groups of Jews that were living in the forests began to emerge from their hiding places and return to the Sokal ghetto in wake of the German rumors that they would be employed in factories.

On May 27, 1943, an operation to finally liquidate the ghetto was carried out. During the operation, there were attempts to organize a mass escape, but most of those fleeing were shot on sight and buried in the local cemetery. The inhabitants of the ghetto were led to pits located about three kilometers from Sokal and shot to death.

SOKÓŁKA

COUNTY SEAT, BIAŁYSTOK DISTRICT, POLAND

During the war: Bezirk Białystok

Coordinates:
53°25' | 23°30'

About 2,800 Jews were living in Sokolka when World War II broke out, representing less than half of the townlet's population. Most earned their livelihood from commerce and artisanship. Zionist parties, the Bund, and Agudath Israel were active in Sokolka, and a number of the townlet's youths participated in the outlawed Communist party. The community also boasted a Tarbut Hebrew school, a Yeshiva, and community welfare institutions.

The Germans occupied Sokolka in September 1939, but in the second half of that month the townlet was handed over to the Soviets. Jewish refugees began to throng to the townlet from the areas of Poland occupied by the Germans. During the period of Soviet rule in Sokolka, a Soviet economic, social, and educational system was instituted in the townlet. Privately owned shops were nationalized or closed and cooperatives were formed.

The Germans reoccupied Sokolka on June 24, 1941, and immediately afterwards, Jewish property was plundered. On June 28, 1941, two Jews were executed. As of June 29, 1941, the Jews of Sokolka were required to wear a yellow badge, their freedom of movement was restricted, and they were seized for arduous forced labor, some of which ended in murder. Some time later, at German orders, the Jews of Sokolka established a five-member Judenrat headed by an attorney named Friedberg.

In the fall of 1941, the Germans established on three streets a fenced-in ghetto, into which the Jews of Sokolka were concentrated under very harsh conditions of overcrowding. A Jewish Order Service was set up, headed by Paltiel Stein.

The Judenrat was ordered to maintain very precise records of all the inhabitants of the ghetto and to recruit Jews for forced labor. It opened a hospital in the ghetto as well as a bakery and a shoe factory that employed 200 people. The Germans periodically entered the ghetto and terrorized the Jews, on one occasion executing twenty-five Jewish youths. In March 1942, the community's rabbi, Rabbi Yitzhak Halevi Shuster, was arrested and taken to the jail in Bialystok*, where he was executed.

On November 5, 1942, the Jews were rounded up, and a selection was carried out in which about 200 people with required professions were separated from the rest. Their number was supplemented by an additional 200 Jewish workers from nearby localities. The rest of the ghetto's inhabitants were sent to the Kielbasin camp, and were again deported in late December 1942, to the Treblinka death camp.

The workers who remained in the Sokolka ghetto continued to work in the shoe factory. In January 1943, the last remaining Jews of Krynki* were also brought to the ghetto. Most of the ghetto's inhabitants were deported to the Auschwitz-Birkenau extermination camp on February 23, 1943. The last approximately twenty workers were deported to the death camp in March 1943.

SOKOŁÓW MAŁOPOLSKI

TOWNLET IN KOLBUSZOWA COUNTY, LWÓW DISTRICT, POLAND

During the war: General Gouvernement, Cracow District

Coordinates: 50°14' | 22°07'

After World War I, about 1,350 Jews lived in Sokolow Malopolski, representing roughly one-third of the townlet's population. To alleviate the poverty of the townlet's Jews after World War I, the JDC established a public soup kitchen and organized the distribution of food and clothing. Sokolow Malopolski also had a free-loan society, established with the help of former residents of Sokolow Malopolski living in New York. Zionist parties, associations, and youth movements were active in Sokolow Malopolski, and ran Hebrew classes, a library, and a drama circle. A pioneer training facility was operated by Tze'irei Hamizrachi. A Jewish sports club was also active in the townlet for some time.

In 1941, a ghetto was established in Sokolow Malopolski. Jews from surrounding localities and nearby townlets such as Wola Ranizowska and Ranizow Zielonk were moved into the ghetto. In the fall of 1941, Jewish families from Kolbuszowa* were also deported into it, raising its population to about 3,000.

Sokolow Malopolski had a Judenrat as well as a Jewish Order Service, under the command of Marcuse. Aided by the JDC and the JSS, the Judenrat established a public soup kitchen that distributed food and provided monetary support to the poor. The Judenrat and JSS supplied jobs and set up vocational courses for young Jews. One of their aims was to enable the youths to obtain work permits that would protect against deportations. In the spring of 1942, efforts were made to secure work for Jewish youths on farms in nearby villages.

In early May 1942, members of the Gestapo from Rzeszow* arrived in Sokolow Malopolski and murdered a number of Jews who were apparently accused of being Communists.

The ghetto was liquidated in June 1942, when a German police unit arrived in the townlet and carried out a selection followed by an operation, in which thirty-five Jews were killed, mostly the elderly and handicapped. The rest of the Jews were deported to Rzeszow, although some were returned to Sokolow Malopolski to collect and sort through the deportees' belongings. In July 1942, the Jews of Sokolow Malopolski were deported together with the Jews of Rzeszow to the Belzec death camp.

SOKOŁÓW PODLASKI

COUNTY SEAT, LUBLIN DISTRICT, POLAND

During the war: General Gouvernement, Warsaw District

Coordinates:
52°24' | 22°15'

When World War II broke out, about 5,000 Jews lived in Sokolow Podlaski, representing about half of the town's population. Most earned their livelihood from commerce and artisanship in the garment, food, wood, metal, and construction industries. They were aided by a free-loan society, a bank, trade unions, and traditional charity societies. The town had chapters of the Zionist parties, the Bund, and Agudath Israel. The Zionists established a workers' club and library, while the Bund chapter ran its youth movement, Tsukunft, and children's movement, *Skif*. Despite legal prohibitions, many Jews secretly supported the Polish Communist Party and its youth movement. The town also boasted a youth club and a Jewish TOZ clinic. A number of Hasidic courts were established in Sokolow Podlaski. The children of the community studied in the traditional Heder and Talmud Torah, a Yavne school of the Mizrachi movement, a public elementary school, and a Beit Yaakov school for girls.

In 1920, six Jews from Sokolow Podlaski accused of aiding the Bolsheviks were murdered by Polish soldiers. In 1937, pogroms against the Jews were perpetrated once again in Sokolow Podlaski. A number of Jews were injured and a great deal of Jewish property was damaged and looted. Many of Sokolow Podlaski's Jews left the town during the interwar period, heading primarily to Western Europe and overseas.

In the latter part of September 1939, a unit of the Red Army entered the town, but one week later, the Soviets retreated in accordance with the Molotov-Ribbentrop Pact, and many young people followed them eastward. The town was handed over to the control of the Germans, who immediately began to seize Jews for forced labor.

In late 1939, a Judenrat with six members was established in the town, headed by Chaim Yaakov Spadel, who was succeeded by Chaim Levin. The Judenrat was ordered to collect ransom payments from the Jews and recruit forced laborers. The Germans sent about 1,000 Jews to labor camps; one camp was established within the town and another in Korczew, located fifteen kilometers away.

Later, apparently sometime during 1940, the Jews were moved into three streets in the vicinity of the large synagogue, which served as an open ghetto of sorts. On September 28, 1941, as per the orders of the German county governor, Ernst Grams, the ghetto was sealed and encircled by a brick wall topped by barbed wire. Residents were forbidden to leave it. A Jewish Order Service that was established by the Judenrat maintained order.

Following the arrival of about 2,000 Jews deported from the areas of Lodz* and Kalisz*, epidemic typhus broke out, claiming many lives daily. In the summer of 1942, about 5,800 Jews were imprisoned in the ghetto.

The Sokolow Podlaski ghetto was liquidated on September 22, 1942, the day after Yom Kippur, when SS soldiers, aided by Ukrainian auxiliary forces and Polish policemen, deported the inhabitants of the ghetto to the Treblinka death camp. Many who resisted were summarily shot.

About fifty Jews were left behind in Sokolow Podlaski to collect the deportees' belongings. When they completed this task, they, too, were deported to Treblinka.

SOLEC ON THE VISTULA

TOWNLET IN WIERZBNIK-STARACHOWICE COUNTY, KIELCE DISTRICT, POLAND

During the war: General Gouvernement, Radom District

Coordinates:
51°08' | 21°46'

After World War I, some 850 Jews lived in Solec on the Vistula, about a quarter of the population. Most were merchants and artisans. A chapter of the Zionist movement organized Hebrew classes and lectures. The Jewish community employed a teacher, but religious services were provided by the community of Radom*.

On September 9, 1939, the Germans occupied Solec and executed several Jews. In December 1941, an open ghetto was established. In June 1942, the Germans set up a labor camp near Solec and employed some 150 prisoners there. The labor camp was liquidated in October 1942.

By October 29, 1942, the 800 inhabitants of the ghetto had been moved to the Tarlow* ghetto, whence they were deported along with the local Jews to the Treblinka death camp.

SOLIPSE

FORT IN WŁOCHY COUNTY, WARSAW DISTRICT, POLAND

During the war: General Gouvernement, Warsaw District

Coordinates:
52°12' | 20°55'

The ghetto was established in December 1940, in an uninhabited area in the Solipse fort near Wlochy, located on the left bank of the Vistula. The area was in a state of disrepair and lacked the most fundamental sanitary requirements. From the outset, the ghetto was intended to contain no more than 700 Jews who had lived in a number of communities in the area, including Falenty, Ozarow*, Mlociny, and Wlochy. Prior to their deportation from these localities to Solipse, Jewish inhabitants represented by Dr. Velikovski (one of the leaders of the JSS in Warsaw*) appealed to the occupation authorities to be allowed to settle in Pruszkow*. When the request was refused, many decided to flee to Warsaw, while others were concentrated in Solipce. Some 300 Jews of means fled from Mlociny to Warsaw, while the poor were left behind and transferred to Solipse. On January 1, 1941, the ghetto held 247 people, mostly women and children with no means of supporting themselves. In late January 1941, the Solipse ghetto was liquidated and its inhabitants were deported to Warsaw.

SOLOBKOVTSY

(Yiddish: **Solobkovets**; Ukrainian: **Solobkivtsi**)

COUNTY SEAT, KAMENETS-PODOLSK DISTRICT, UKRAINE, USSR

During the war: Reichskommissariat Ukraine

Coordinates:
49°05' | 26°55'

Shortly before World War II, there were about 900 Jews in Solobkovtsy, accounting for approximately one-fifth of the local population. Under Soviet rule, many were skilled craftspeople, some of whom organized in cooperatives. Others became farm workers in a Jewish kolkhoz that was established nearby. The townlet had a Jewish Ethnic Soviet and a government Jewish school that taught in Yiddish.

The Germans occupied Solobkovtsy on July 9, 1941, and established a ghetto, which was liquidated in the fall of 1942, when German gendarmes and Ukrainian auxiliary police led its 700–800 inhabitants into a nearby forest and murdered them.

SOLTVADKERT

(in Jewish sources: **Vadkert**)

TOWN IN PEST-PILIS-SOLT-KISKUN COUNTY, HUNGARY

Coordinates:
46°35' | 19°23'

The last national census conducted prior to the German occupation, taken in January 1941, recorded 412 Jewish inhabitants in Soltvadkert, accounting for approximately 2 percent of the total population. Most traded in agricultural produce. The town's Jewish community was Orthodox and maintained several educational institutions: a Heder, a Talmud Torah, a Yeshiva, a Beit Midrash, and a Jewish elementary school.

The German army occupied Hungary on March 19, 1944. The Hungarian administration remained intact and operational. The ghettoization and deportation of the Jews occurred on the basis of decrees and orders issued by the Hungar-

Soltvadkert
The Jews of the village are transferred to the Kecskement ghetto and deported on to Auschwitz in late June 1944. (YV)

ian national and local authorities. On May 12, Hungarian sub-prefect Dr. Laszlo Endre, a militant antisemite, ordered the establishment of ghettos in his county. While the decree did not designate Soltvadkert as a locality wherein a ghetto should be established, the chief administrative officer of the Kiskoros County-District, Dr. Janos Benedek, nevertheless ordered the establishment of a ghetto in the town on May 24, 1944. The 295 local Jews were ordered to move on May 30 and 31 into the ghetto, which consisted of four houses and the school building. The local rabbi, Rabbi Mozes Pollak, organized the prayers in the ghetto and continued to teach the children.

On June 17 or 18, 1944, the ghetto inhabitants were marched twenty-six kilometers from Soltvadkert to the copper factory in Kecskemet*, which served as an entrainment center. They were deported along with many other Jews to Auschwitz on June 25 and 27, 1944.

SOŁY

TOWNLET IN OSZMIANA COUNTY, VILNA DISTRICT, POLAND
(After World War II in the USSR/Belarus; Belarussian, Russian: **Soly**)

During the war:
Reichskommissariat Ostland

Coordinates:
54°31' | 26°11'

About 130 Jewish families lived in Soly during the interwar period, representing roughly half of the townlet's population. Most earned their livelihood from commerce, leasing, and artisanship, and were supported by Jewish welfare organizations. The community had educational facilities, among them, a Tarbut Hebrew school.

The Soviets occupied Soly in the second half of September 1939, and instituted a Soviet economic system in the townlet, abolishing all Jewish political and cultural organizations.

The Germans occupied Soly in late June 1941. The Jews were required to wear a yellow badge, their freedom of movement was restricted, and several people were seized for forced labor. A Jewish Order Service was established, as was a Judenrat headed by Michael Magid. The main function of the Judenrat was to recruit Jews for forced labor.

A few days after the onset of the occupation, about sixty-five Jewish families living in Soly were concentrated in a fenced-in ghetto on a side street in the townlet. The ghetto was guarded only by members of the Jewish Order Service, and the Jews were forbidden to leave its gounds. In the summer of 1942, about sixty Jews, mostly youths, were sent from Soly to the Olkieniki labor camp in the Troki County.

In August 1942, the Germans decided to liquidate the smaller ghettos in Lithuania and to concentrate all of their inhabitants in four ghettos, one of which was the Soly ghetto. By early 1943, there were between 900 and 1,000 Jews living in it. Epidemic typhus spread, but the Judenrat strove to conceal the disease from the Germans.

In March 1943, the Germans decided to liquidate the remaining four ghettos. The Soly ghetto was liquidated on April 4, 1943, when all its inhabitants were deported to Ponary and murdered.

SOMPOLNO

TOWNLET IN KOŁO COUNTY, ŁÓDŹ DISTRICT, POLAND

During the war: Wartheland

Coordinates:
52°23' | 18°31'

During the interwar period, there were about 1,200 Jews in Sompolno, almost one-third of the townlet's population. Most were artisans and merchants. Zionist parties, Agudath Israel, and the Bund were all active in Sompolno's Jewish community.

After the Germans occupied the townlet in September 1939, they confiscated Jewish property, imposed restrictions on movement, obliged Jews to wear a yellow badge, and seized those fit for forced labor.

In 1940, the Jews of Sompolno were concentrated in a ghetto comprising several streets. Until the summer of 1941, Jews were allowed to leave the ghetto. Jewish men in Sompolno, like those in other nearby ghettos, were sent to labor camps in the vicinity of Poznan.

The Sompolno ghetto was one of the first ghettos in the area to be liquidated. On February 2, 1942, the Germans deported its inhabitants to the Chelmno death center, where no selection was conducted: all the Jews of Sompolno were murdered.

SOPOĆKINIE

(Yiddish: **Sopotkin**)

TOWNLET IN AUGUSTÓW COUNTY, BIAŁYSTOK DISTRICT, POLAND

(After World War II in the USSR/Belarus; Belorussian: **Sapotskin**; Russian: **Sopotskin**)

During the war: Bezirk Białystok

Coordinates:
53°50' | 23°39'

About 900 Jews lived in Sopockinie in the interwar period, representing approximately half of the townlet's population. They earned their livelihood from small commerce, peddling, and artisanship, and were aided by a trade and craft association, a Jewish bank, and a free-loan society. Sopockinie had Zionist parties and youth movements that established pioneer training facilities as well as Agudath Israel and its youth movement, and the Bund. Most of the parties and youth movements maintained libraries, clubs, and sports circles.

In September 1939, Sopockinie was annexed to the area under Soviet control, in accordance with the Molotov-Ribbentrop Pact. Many large homes belonging to Jews were seized, and their residents were deported at least 100 kilometers into the Soviet interior. Many Jews were deported to Siberia. Jewish businesses were confiscated and transformed into cooperatives. The Beit Midrash was seized and turned into a cinema and entertainment site.

On June 22, 1941, Sopockinie was occupied by the Germans. Fires and aerial bombings caused the townlet damage. Many Jews were killed during the occupation, while others escaped. After the occupation, Poles denounced Jews who had worked with the Soviet authorities. The Germans murdered Rabbi Mordechai Eliyahu Rabinovits, as well as other major figures in the Jewish community accused of collaborating with the Soviets. They also seized many Jews for forced labor. The Jews were deported to a camp established in a nearby settlement. The men, with the exception of artisans, were sent to work in Starocielce, and the rest were returned to Sopockinie. In December 1941, a ghetto was established in a single building at the edge of the townlet that had previously served as a theater hall. Poverty and overcrowding were extreme.

On November 1, 1942, the ghetto was liquidated. Its inhabitants were told that they were to be transferred to work in the Ukraine, but they were actually transported to the Kielbaszin transit camp, near Grodno*, which was liquidated on December 19, 1942.

SOPRON

(in Jewish sources:
Ödenburg)

COUNTY SEAT, HUNGARY,

Coordinates:
47°41' | 16°36'

The last national census conducted prior to the German occupation, taken in January 1941, recorded 1,861 Jewish inhabitants in Sopron, roughly 4 percent of the total population, which was mostly German. Most of the Jews were merchants and artisans. The town had both a Neolog and an Orthodox Jewish community as well as a Jewish elementary school and various Jewish social and religious associations. The Orthodox community operated a Talmud Torah and a Yeshiva. In 1941, Jewish men were drafted into the Hungarian Army for forced labor service.

The German army occupied Hungary on March 19, 1944. On April 7, 1944, an SS lieutenant arrived in Sopron from Szekesfehervar* and summoned the leaders of the Neolog and Orthodox Jewish communities. He ordered them to dissolve both Jewish communities and establish a five-member "Elders' Council." As no one was willing to volunteer to be president of the Jewish Council, the lieutenant appointed clothier Zsigmond Rosenheim to the position. Dr. Bela Hasler, who was a Jewish convert to Christianity, became a member of the Jewish Council by order of Antal Rupprecht, the prefect of Sopron County, to represent the interests of Jewish converts.

According to a census conducted in the second week of April 1944, about 900 Jews belonged to the Neolog Jewish community and some 600 Jews to the Orthodox community of Sopron.

After the German occupation, the Hungarian administration remained intact and operational. The ghettoization and deportation of the Jews occurred on the basis of decrees and orders issued by the Hungarian national and local authorities. The Hungarian officials designated a ghetto area in the town center in mid-May 1944, in which altogether 1,801 local Jews lived. The Jewish Council was in charge of moving the Jewish inhabitants into the ghetto.

In mid-June 1944, men from the ghetto were drafted for forced labor service and were thereby saved from immediate deportation.

Sopron
The gate of one of the ghetto entrances (YV)

On the morning of the June 29, Hungarian gendarmes, led by Captain Takacs, began searching for hidden valuables. They subjected ghetto inhabitants to cruel and humiliating interrogation and torture for three days. Following the search, from June 29 onward, the Jews were moved into the refectory building of the Technical College in Sopron, which was still in the stages of construction, and into the adjacent Jakobi factory building. Jewish inhabitants of the other three county ghettos—Csepreg*, Csorna*, and Kapuvar*—as well as fored laborers on leave, were also transferred to the Sopron entrainment center by Rupprecht's decree of June 15, 1944. The 3,385 Jews lived on starvation rations, as they were supplied dry bread and water in the morning and evening, and salty cooked beans at noon.

About 3,000 of the Jews who were concentrated in the Sopron entrainment center were deported to Auschwitz on July 5, 1944. The remaining 385 Jews were deported to Auschwitz on the following day via Sarvar* (Vas County).

SOROKSÁR

TOWN IN PEST-PILIS-SOLT-KISKUN COUNTY, HUNGARY

Coordinates:
47°24' | 19°07'

The last national census conducted prior to the German occupation, taken in January 1941, recorded 243 Jewish inhabitants in Soroksar, approximately 1 percent of the total population. Most of the local Jews worked in Budapest*. The town's Jewish community was Orthodox and maintained a Jewish school.

From the end of the 1930s on, the ethnic German majority population (the Swabians) became increasingly hostile toward the Jews. In 1943, a local Jewish physician who went to visit a patient at night was beaten to death.

The German army occupied Hungary on March 19, 1944. According to a census conducted in the second week of April 1944, sixty-six Jews belonged to the Orthodox Jewish community of Soroksar (most of the other Jewish inhabitants had likely left for Budapest).

The Hungarian administration remained intact and operational after the German occupation. The ghettoization and deportation of the Jews occurred on the basis of decrees and orders issued by the Hungarian national and local authorities. In April 1944, the Jews of Soroksar were ordered to move into a few designated houses within the town. Their ghettoization took place prior to the publication of the decree ordering the establishment of ghettos in the county on May 12, 1944.

In late June 1944, the inhabitants of the ghetto of Soroksar were forbidden to leave its confines. On June 30, 1944, they were taken to Budapest and transferred by boat on to Bekasmegyer*, to one of the entrainment centers for the ghettos of the Pest-Pilis-Solt-Kiskun County surrounding Budapest from the north. They were deported to Auschwitz between July 6 and 8, 1944.

SOSNOWIEC

COUNTY SEAT, KIELCE DISTRICT, POLAND

During the war: Upper Silesia

Coordinates:
50°18' | 19°10'

Before the War: In 1931, about 31,000 Jews lived in Sosnowiec, roughly 30 percent of its total population. The Jews of Sosnowiec made their living at trade and crafts, primarily in tailoring, food, and metal products. A minority were wealthy merchants. The Jews availed themselves of Jewish trade unions, a savings-and-loan association, and a free-loan fund subsidized by the JDC. The community had traditional charitable and welfare institutions, including a hospital, an old-age home, a convalescent home, orphanages, and summer camps for the children of the poor. TOZ was active in the city. Among the educational institutions were an Orthodox Heder, a Talmud Torah, and Jewish schools including Beit Yaakov, a high school associated with the Mizrachi movement, the Radomsk Yeshiva, and an ORT high school that offered trade courses and evening classes in crafts. Zionist parties and youth movements, the Bund, and Agudath Israel were rep-

Sosnowiec, December 15, 1940
A group of Judenrat members with Aharon Menczer, the director of Aliyat Hanoar in Vienna, who arrived in Sosnowiec to help organize youth activities. Sitting in the center, Moshe Merin and Fany Charna (YV)

resented in the city, along with professional and merchant parties. A number of the Communists in Sosnowiec were Jewish, including several leading figures. The community also boasted a Jewish public library, and hundreds of local Jews belonged to the Maccabi and *Shimshon* Jewish sports associations. Several Yiddish periodicals were published in Sosnowiec, including two important weeklies, *Unzer Telefon* and *Zaglembier Lebn*.

In antisemitic incidents in the city in the 1930s, several Jews were injured and a Jewish boy was killed.

In May 1939, some 120 German-Jewish refugees in Sosnowiec received assistance from the local Jewish community. During the first days of the war, thousands of Jews fled from the city to the east. A number were compelled to return to their homes to evade the Wehrmacht.

German occupation: The Germans occupied Sosnowiec on September 4, 1939. During the next two days, about thirty Jews were murdered in a series of abusive attacks perpetrated by the Germans. In the first days of the occupation, the Germans ordered one of the members of the community council to identify himself so that they could establish a Judenrat. As the leading members of the council were afraid to comply, young Zionist activist Moshe (Moniek) Merin, lacking any community leadership experience, identified himself as the council chair and was ordered to establish a twenty-four-member Judenrat. The Judenrat had several departments, including welfare, health, and labor. The Health Department was charged with maintenance of the only hospital in the Zaglebie area that served Jews. In late 1939, a two-hundred-member Jewish Order Service was established in Sosnowiec and placed under the command of Romek Goldmintz. Its members wore yellow-and-white armbands.

In late October 1939, forced labor was introduced for all Jews under the age of fifty-five. The Germans accepted Merin's offer to provide them with forced laborers and stopped abducting people in the streets. In early November 1939, Sosnowiec's Jewish residents were ordered to pay a ransom, and their property and businesses were confiscated. Many carried on as employees of their erstwhile businesses for paltry wages. That month, the wearing of a white armband with a blue Star-of-David was imposed. Several Jewish families were forced to evacuate their dwellings in affluent city neighborhoods to make room for Volksdeutsche.

In January 1940, the Germans established the Zentrale der Jüdischen Aeltestenrate in Ostoberschlesien (the Central Office of the Jewish Councils of

Elders in Eastern Upper Silesia) and installed the versatile Moshe Merin at its head. The Zentrale controlled twenty-seven Jewish communities with a total population of over 100,000 people. It had various departments, including welfare and health, which supervised the work of the corresponding departments of local Judenraete and provided them with funding. The Zentrale eventually employed some 1,500 workers.

In the spring of 1940, the Welfare Department opened public kitchens and clothing warehouses to assist the hundreds of Jewish refugees from Silesia who poured into Sosnowiec. From that time on, "shops" were established in Sosnowiec—enormous workshops that exempted employees from deportation to labor camps. The shops formed part of the Zentrale's policy under Merin, rendering the Jews in the area as economically efficient as possible. These enterprises manufactured clothing and leather, braided straw, and wood products, among other goods. Positions were highly sought after despite offering grim working conditions, as employees earned wages. In the spring of 1942, the number of Jewish workers in the shops reached about 3,000.

In early 1941, Merin established a Youth Department at the Zentrale. After a dispute among its members, Hanoar Hatziyyoni movement agreed to operate within the framework of the Judenrat. Its leader in Sosnowiec, Josek Kozuch, was placed at the head of the department and was appointed to the Judenrat. The Youth Department disbursed a budget from the Judenrat exchequer for youth movements and protected the movements' members from deportation to labor camps until 1942.

In March 1941, Jews were evacuated from the town of Oswiecim. Jewish policemen in Sosnowiec and Bedzin* took part in sorting the deportees' belongings. When the evacuees reached Sosnowiec, several hundred were sent on to labor camps, about 3,000 were transferred to nearby Bedzin, and hundreds were moved to other localities in the area. The remainder stayed in Sosnowiec, where the Judenrat quickly arranged jobs and housing for most of them.

Forced labor: In October 1940, the Germans established a new entity to coordinate forced labor in Upper Silesia. This body, titled "Organisation Schmelt" after Albrecht Schmelt, the SS officer who was appointed to head it, established labor camps and also assumed responsibility for the shops. The shop workers were required to contribute a portion of their wages to the organization, while factory owners turned over some of their earnings. That same month, Schmelt ordered Merin to draw up a list of able-bodied Jews. Merin addressed the young members of the Jewish population, couching his demand in terms of participation in a volunteer project for the advancement of the Jews' productivity, and promising the youths decent wages and conditions. He thereby managed to persuade a number of the activists in Sosnowiec, nearby Bedzin, and other localities, to enlist. By the end of October, the first groups, comprising some 500 young people, set out from Sosnowiec and Bedzin, and by the late fall, the number of workers in the camps reached approximately 2,800. When the Jews in Sosnowiec discovered that the conditions in the camps were harsh and brutal, they accused Merin of being a traitor and a collaborator.

The Jews in Sosnowiec were confronted by yet another wave of labor inductions in March 1941. With the local population now aware of the dreadful working conditions in the camps, the Jewish Order Service performed the induction by force. To evade the transports, Jews attempted to find jobs in the shops. A few secured exemptions from transport to the camps by ransoming themselves, while others married. Merin applied pressure by canceling the ration cards of families whose children did not report for induction.

Murder operations in 1942: In late April 1942, the Judenrat issued call-up orders to several thousand deportation candidates, comprising chiefly families with two or more children, refugees, the elderly, and persons who lacked labor permits. The Judenrat received the guidelines from the SS officers Heinrich Lindner and Friedrich Kuczynski of Organisation Schmelt, who were charged with carrying out the deportation. The Jews of Sosnowiec were told that the deportees' destination would be Theresienstadt*.

In early May 1942, Merin convened the senior officials of the Zentrale and the local ghettos for a discussion of the deportation program. He claimed at the conference that the Germans had demanded the deportation of 10,000 Jews and that he had managed to lower this number to 5,000. While contentious, Merin's proposal to cooperate with the deportation plan was ultimately accepted. A minority group, composed largely of members associated with the Youth Department and led by Josek Kozukh, dissented with the officials' decision and seceded from the Judenrat.

The deportation of Jews from Sosnowiec to the Auschwitz death camp began on May 10, 1942. Few of the deportation candidates (those on public support, families with children, the elderly, and the "unproductive") reported willingly, leaving the transport 300 persons shy of its quota. To rectify the shortage, the Gestapo encircled several large buildings on Targowa and Kollataja Streets and arbitrarily removed their Jewish occupants. The Germans received assistance from the Jewish Order Service and the active support of Judenrat member Fany Charna, an especially close associate of Merin's. The first deportation train set out on May 12, 1942, with 1,500 Jews aboard. In June 1942, approximately 2,000 additional Jews were transported from Sosnowiec to Auschwitz.

In early August 1942, the Germans decided to perform mass selections in Sosnowiec, Bedzin, and Dabrowa-Gornicza*. Accordingly, they ordered all Jews in the area to report on August 12 to a place of assembly, ostensibly to be registered but in fact for a mass selection ahead of deportation. On August 8, 1942, Chaim Merin, chair of the local Judenrat and the brother of Moshe Merin, ordered the Jews of Sosnowiec to report with their labor documents for censuses. Most of the Jews in Sosnowiec did not conceive that they were being led to their deaths, notwithstanding the general climate of suspicion in the city and agitation in the Jewish street, especially among youth movement members, the refugees, and the poor classes (from whom most victims of the first deportation had originated). The Judenrat's propaganda prevailed: at seven o'clock on the morning of August 12 (a day known in retrospect to the Jews of Sosnowiec as the "Big Punkt," after the *punkt*, the athletic grounds where they were concentrated) a large majority of the Jews of Sosnowiec, about 22,000 in number, reported for the roll call either at the field or at the seven large shops where they were collected and brought to the field. Hours later, SS forces surrounded the field and a riot broke out in which many people were trampled to death, mainly children. On August 13, 1942, after the Jews spent the night standing in the field under pouring rain, the Germans began to perform a selection, which lasted several days. The Jews chosen for deportation were packed into four houses that had been emptied of their inhabitants. Those who were selected for life—the Judenrat officials and their families, men with labor permits, and people aged sixteen to eighteen—were gradually allowed to return to city.

Between August 15 and 18, 1942, about 4,000 Jews were deported from Sosnowiec to Auschwitz. (Some estimate their number at approximately 8,000.)

Deportations of Jews from Sosnowiec to Auschwitz, involving mainly refugees, the jobless, and those in need of public support, persisted in the following months, although on a smaller scale. Following the August deportation, Sosnowiec's Jews were aware that the trains headed to Auschwitz.

Ghetto setup, institutions, and internal life: The SS was eager to proceed with the ghettoization of the Jews of Zaglebie, including the Jewish inhabitants of Sosnowiec. However, while Jewish residents on certain streets were required to vacate their homes and the isolation of the Jews at large steadily intensified, no sealed ghetto as such operated in Sosnowiec until 1943, and Jews continued to circulate within and sometimes outside the city, subject to various restrictions.

Many of the remaining Jews strove, after the spring and summer 1942 murder operations, to obtain jobs at the shops in the hope of evading further deportations. Among the new workers were children, women, the elderly, and undocumented refugees from the General Gouvernement and Zaglebie. In early 1943, the Held textile shop employed approximately 4,000 Jews from Sosnowiec. Concurrently, operations at the Organisation Schmelt labor camps increased perceptibly, as did the number of Jews employed in the camps.

Although the Germans had decided in the fall of 1942 to ghettoize the Jews of Sosnowiec in the remote and neglected Srodula quarter, the implementation of the decision was long postponed. By March 15, 1943, however, the transfer of Poles from the designated ghetto area was completed. Altogether 14,000 Jews were packed into the Srodula ghetto and another 6,000 into a ghetto in the Old City (Stary Sosnowiec), a preferred neighborhood among the Jews, many of whom paid to be included among its residents. The Srodula ghetto was not bordered by a fence; instead, signs posted on its periphery proclaimed that Jews were forbidden to leave its confines. Jewish residents thus brought food into the ghetto and thousands of workers commuted daily to work in the shops located outside the ghetto, all with greater facility. Inside the ghetto, a care center for children up to age six was established, and the Jewish hospital and public kitchens continued to function.

Murder operations in 1943 and the ghetto's liquidation: In early June 1943, Himmler decided to obliterate what remained of Polish Jewry, including the Jews of Eastern Upper Silesia. On the morning of June 19, a group of thirty-four Jews who had received South American passports and were supposed to go abroad were deported from the Sosnowiec ghetto to Auschwitz. In the middle of that day, Moshe Merin, his brother Chaim, Fany Charna, and several of Merin's senior aides were summoned to the German police and deported to Auschwitz. Some sources say that they were deported owing to their involvement in the passport incident, after they had demanded to replace several of those slated for rescue with their own acquaintances and friends.

On June 23–24, 1943, about 1,200 Jews were deported from the Sosnowiec ghetto to Auschwitz, in an operation commanded by Chief Gestapo Dreier. Many people avoided the deportation by going into hiding. Twenty-two Jews were shot to death during the operation. Several members of the underground went into hiding in a bunker that they had prepared. However, they did not manage to organize an uprising, and several of their comrades were captured and added to the transport.

After the murder operation, the remaining Jews in the ghetto began to prepare for subsequent operations. Many organized bunkers and hideouts, and resistance members attempted to obtain weapons. The strength of the ghetto Judenrat, now run by Vebek Shmetana, plummeted at this time; a climate of "every man for himself" prevailed.

On August 1, 1943, the Germans returned to the ghetto with reinforcements and carried out a large-scale murder operation through to August 7. Most of the Jews went into hiding in bunkers. About 400 who resisted or attempted to escape were shot to death. The number of deportees to Auschwitz in this operation, which coincided with a similar operation in the Bedzin ghetto, reached approximately 30,000 in both ghettos combined.

For several months after the liquidation of the ghetto, the Germans continued to maintain a labor camp in Sosnowiec that employed several hundred Jewish prisoners, mainly at cleaning homes and sorting the deportees' belongings. Occasionally, additional Jews who had been hiding in bunkers were placed in the camp. Some 800 people were deported to Auschwitz on December 7, 1943. The last remaining Jews in the camp in Sosnowiec, about 400 in number, were likewise transported to Auschwitz, on January 15, 1944.

Resistance: In 1941, the Jewish youth movements in the area strengthened their relations with their counterparts elsewhere in Poland. The upturn in autonomous movement activities became a permanent source of tension with the Zentrale. In early June 1942, Mordechai Anielewicz visited Sosnowiec for the first time and told the members of Hashomer Hatzair about the murder of the Jews of Vilna* and the vicinity at Ponary as well as about the waves of extermination operations in eastern Poland. A Jew who had escaped from Auschwitz and gone into hiding with members of Hano'ar Hatziyyoni in Sosnowiec recounted the existence of "gas showers" in Auschwitz. In response to these disclosures, the members of Hashomer Hatzair decided to establish a local Jewish resistance organization. They distributed leaflets about the exterminations, published an underground newspaper, and urged Jews to refuse to report for deportation and to sabotage operations in the "shops." Other youth movements took similar actions. Hashomer Hatzair's underground comprised ten members and was headed by twenty-one-year-old Tzvi Dunski.

On August 11, 1942, shortly before the Jews were scheduled to assemble for registration ahead of deportation, the youth movement leaders in Sosnowiec held a meeting in the presence of Mordechai Anielewicz. Anielewicz urged the Jews to disobey the census order, but the members in attendance did not emerge from the meeting with a united call for defiance. On August 13, 1942, during the Big Punkt, Hano'ar Hatziyyoni members carried out acts of relief and rescue, smuggling out a number of the people who were packed into houses, selected for and awaiting deportation.

From late 1942 onward, the Jews of Sosnowiec's youth movement underground became increasingly active and attempted to obtain weapons. Underground couriers traveled to the vicinity of Warsaw and returned with plans for the construction of bunkers and instructions for the preparation of homemade bombs. Also in late 1942, the Jewish Order Service placed the members of the Hashomer Hatzair underground and their leader, Tzvi Dunski, under surveillance. Merin wanted to arrest the underground members, convinced the existence of the underground constituted a menace to the Jews. When the members went into hiding, Merin pressured their families. The conflict peaked when members of the Jewish Order Service arrested all members of Hashomer Hatzair, turning over Dunski and Lipek Mintz to the Germans; the two were deported in the spring of 1943 to Auschwitz and hanged.

Another clash between the underground activists and Moshe Merin took place in the spring of 1943, instigated by an attempt to rescue hundreds of Jews from Zaglebie by means of South American passports. Merin opposed the method for posing a threat to the entire Jewish population. The Jewish underground tried Merin in absentia and sentenced him to death.

After the Warsaw ghetto uprising in April 1943, the members of Hashomer Hatzair and Dror argued in favor of fight to the end. Many local members of Hano'ar Hatziyyoni, however, argued that nothing could be achieved through an uprising that necessarily ended in death, and preferred instead to attempt to smuggle members over the border.

During the August 1943 liquidation operations, the underground had access to two bunkers in the Srodula ghetto, but the Germans captured many of the members before they could organize.

In late August 1943, after the liquidation of the ghetto, dozens of youth movement members in Sosnowiec managed to escape to Slovakia and Hungary. Among them were thirty-two members of Hano'ar Hatziyyoni along with several of their parents, who had been at the labor camp in Sosnowiec. A number of these survivors reached the Land of Israel in 1944.

STALINO

(Formerly **Yuzovka**, from 1961: **Donetsk**; Ukrainian: **Yuzivka, Donets'k**)

DISTRICT SEAT, UKRAINE, USSR

During the war: Military Administration Area

Coordinates:
48°00' | 37°48'

In the early twentieth century, there were about 3,100 Jews in the city, which was renamed Stalino under the Soviets. It developed into an important industrial center, attracting many Jews. Shortly before the German invasion, 25,000 Jews lived in Stalino, accounting for approximately 5 percent of the population. Most Jewish wage earners held blue- or white-collar jobs in factories, quarries, and state institutions. A number of Jews, however, were skilled craftsmen, primarily tailors and shoemakers. A Jewish government school in the city taught in Russian and Yiddish.

After the Germans crossed into the USSR and prior to their occupation of the town on October 20, 1941, most of Stalino's Jewish inhabitants were evacuated or managed to flee to the east. The Jews who remained there were abducted for forced labor, and often abused and murdered. In November 1941, the Germans ordered the establishment of a Jewish Council responsible for collecting ransoms from the community under the supervision of local police and mobilizing Jews for labor. Jews were forced to wear white armbands.

Some 450 Jews were murdered in November 1941, and Einsatzkommando 6 killed hundreds more in December. The same German unit murdered another 150 Jews between January 10 and February 6, 1942.

In March 1942, the Jews were concentrated in a ghetto in the suburb of Belyi Karier. According to German statistics, there were approximately 3,000 ghetto inhabitants. The ghetto was fenced in with barbed wire and guarded by police. Its residents were deprived of food and medical assistance. Many were denied shelter altogether. Dire conditions caused hundreds of deaths daily.

The ghetto was liquidated in an operation that began on April 3, 1942. A number of inhabitants were shot dead; others were murdered in gas vans, and their bodies thrown into a mine near the city. According to several testimonies, a certain number of Jews, predominantly small children, were thrown into the mine alive. During the liquidation operation, one of the ghetto inhabitants grabbed two Germans and leaped into the mine with them.

STANISLAVCHIK

(Ukrainian: **Stanislavchyk**)

COUNTY SEAT, VINNITSA DISTRICT, UKRAINE, USSR

During the war: Transnistria (under Romanian control)

Coordinates:
50°10' | 24°54'

On the eve of the German invasion of the Soviet Union, about 300 Jews lived in Stanislavchik. In the interwar period, the Jewish population of Stanislavchik had continually decreased owing to the growing trends of industrialization and urbanization in the Soviet Union. Jewish artisans formed cooperatives, while other Jews were employed as clerks or laborers in state factories. From the mid-1920s onward, the town had a Yiddish-language school and a Jewish Ethnic Soviet that conducted its meetings in Yiddish. As the German army drew closer to Stanislavchik, a number of its Jewish inhabitants fled to nearby Zhmerinka*.

The Germans occupied Stanislavchik on July 16, 1941. On September 1, 1941, the town was annexed to Transnistria, which was under Romanian rule. In the fall of 1941, some 250 Romanian Jews from Bessarabia and Bukovina were deported to the town. They were put up in the homes of local Jews. Later, the Jews were concentrated on a single street, which was an open ghetto of sorts. A Jewish doctor headed the ghetto. The Romanian gendarmes permitted the Jews to draw water from the town well once a day. Jews were assigned to forced labor, and a small number managed to obtain permission to work with farmers in the area. In the winter of 1941/42, many of the ghetto's inhabitants perished from epidemic typhus, the lack of food and medicine, and poor sanitary conditions.

In the summer of 1942, all of Stanislavchik's Jews, with the exception of some of the artisans, were transferred to an area near the village of Zatishye. Several of the artisans among the transferees were returned a few months later to the ghetto, along with others who bribed officials. According to the figures of a Bucharest aid committee delegation, there were about 120 local Jews and 80 deported Jews in Stanislavchik in January 1943.

In late 1943 and early 1944, the Jews of Stanislavchik feared that they might be killed by a German unit that had recently arrived, but the Germans abandoned the town in February 1944. In March 1944, the Romanians also withdrew from the town, and on March 14, partisans entered Stanislavchik.

Stanislavchik was liberated by the Red Army on March 18, 1944.

STANISŁAWÓW

TOWNLET IN MINSK MAZOWIECKI COUNTY, WARSAW DISTRICT, POLAND

During the war: General Gouvernement, Warsaw District

Coordinates: 52°18' | 21°33'

About 500 Jews lived in Stanislawow in the interwar period, representing approximately one-quarter of the townlet's population. They earned their livelihood from artisanship and commerce.

Stanislawow was occupied by the German army in the early days of September 1939. Jewish refugees from Dobre were brought to the townlet.

A ghetto was established in Stanislawow, into which about 400 Jews were concentrated. A number of the ghetto residents were assigned to forced labor, manufacturing railroad tracks. The ghetto was liquidated on September 25, 1942, and its inhabitants were transported to the Treblinka death camp. A number of Jews were saved by Poles.

STANISŁAWÓW

DISTRICT SEAT, POLAND
(After World War II in the USSR/Ukraine; Ukrainian: **Ivano-Frankivs'k**; Russian: **Ivano-Frankovsk**)

During the war: General Gouvernement, Galicia District

Coordinates: 48°56' | 24°43'

Before the War: In the early 1930s, about 25,000 Jews lived in Stanislawow, representing approximately one-third of the population. During the Polish-Russian war (1919–20) that followed World War I, Ukrainian gangs carried out pogroms in the city, killing two Jews.

The Jews of Stanislawow were the leading figures in local commerce, and also earned their livelihoods in trades, especially the garment industry and construction, as well as in the liberal professions. During the 1930s, the poor economic climate drove many of the city's Jews to accept social-welfare support. The community had a ramified system of Jewish social-welfare aid services, including a Jewish hospital and a large chapter of TOZ. A number of Jewish banks also operated in the city.

Stanislawow's Jewish community was characterized by the vigorous political activity of Zionist parties, Agudath Israel, the Bund, and Jewish youth movements. The city had a Jewish high school, vocational schools, and various Zionist educational institutions as well as a Talmud Torah, a Beit Yaakov school for girls, and a Yeshiva. During the interwar period, about twenty Jewish periodicals were published, although most were short-lived. The city also boasted a number of Jewish public libraries and sports unions plus a Jewish arts and culture union.

Soviet occupation: When World War II broke out, thousands of refugees from elsewhere in Poland thronged to Stanislawow. The city was occupied by the So-

Stanislawow
Sign on one of the entrances to the ghetto: "Jewish living area. Entry and exit prohibited." A Ukrainian guard stands at the guard post near the gate; a member of the Jewish Order Service is posted inside the ghetto. (YV)

viets on September 18, 1939. In the wake of the Soviet occupation, Jewish community institutions active in the city were dismantled, and several of the leaders of the Jewish parties were imprisoned while others were exiled to remote areas of the Soviet Union. Factories and warehouses filled with merchandise were confiscated, and hundreds of Jews were organized into cooperatives. In the summer of 1940, the Soviets also exiled many of the Jewish refugees living in the city to remote areas of the Soviet Union.

German (Nazi) occupation: When the Germans invaded the Soviet Union on June 22, 1941, a few hundred Jewish youths managed to escape from Stanislawow to the east of the Soviet Union, and a number of them were conscripted into the Red Army. When the Soviets retreated from the city, the local Ukrainian population carried out pogroms against the Jews. The pogroms ceased once the Hungarians (allies of the Germans) occupied the city on July 2, 1941. During the month of July, Stanislawow was flooded with thousands of Jewish refugees who had been deported from Carpatho-Ruthenia by the Hungarian occupation authorities. They were joined by numerous refugees from nearby townlets and villages who fled in fear of Ukrainian pogroms. This influx of refugees raised the number of Jews in Stanislawow to more than 40,000 by the end of July 1941. Most of the refugees were incarcerated under very harsh conditions in an unfinished three-story flour mill known as the Rudolf Mill. Despite receiving food, clothing, and medical services from the city's solicitous Jews, most of the refugees perished from hunger and cold within a few months.

On July 20, 1941, Stanislawow was handed over to German control. An Einsatzkommando unit for special functions under the command of Oskar Brandt arrived in the city, joined by SS-Captain Hans Krueger. A branch of the regional command of the SIPO and SD was established in Stanislawow. The German police, along with Ukrainians and Poles, immediately began to abuse and attack the Jews. As early as July 1941, Krueger established an auxiliary police force composed of ethnic Germans (Volksdeutsche), Romanians, and Hungarians. From August onward, the force was under the command of a Schupo unit that had arrived from Vienna.

A few days after they entered the city, the Germans ordered Moshe Yisrael Zeibeld, a member of the Jewish community administration prior to the war, to establish a Judenrat in the city. It was made up of members of the former community administration: the attorney Mikhael Lam was appointed deputy while the attorney Dr. Tanenbaum was appointed the organization's liaison with the Gestapo. On August 2, some 800 Poles and Jews of liberal professions were ordered to register in the Gestapo offices. About 200 of them were sent home; the rest were taken the following day to the nearby Pawelce forest, where they were murdered.

In early August 1941, the Jews of Stanislawow were ordered to wear a Star-of-David armband, their movements were severely restricted, and many were abducted for forced labor. The Judenrat established an employment bureau, requiring all unemployed Jews to report in order to regulate their recruitment for work and prevent abductions. The Germans made various demands of the Judenrat regarding the supply of equipment and the performance of various jobs and issued orders calling for the Jews of the city to hand over all their valuables.

Ghetto setup, institutions, and internal life: In September 1941, Friedrich Katzmann and Helmut Tanzmann of the SIPO command in Lwow* resolved to start the liquidation of the Jews of Galicia. To this end, they decided to establish a ghetto in Stanislawow, which from the outset was intended to be small in size.

On October 12, 1941, the German police, helped by Ukrainians, massacred between 10,000 and 12,000 Jews in the old cemetery of Stanislawow, including close relatives of Judenrat officials (see below). Judenrat chairman Lam and his family were released. After the mass murder operation, Zeibeld (who apparently managed to escape) was replaced by Lam as head of the Judenrat. Lam held the position until the summer of 1942, nominating Mordekhai (Markus) Goldshtein as his deputy. By September 1941 the German authorities had already begun discussions with the Judenrat regarding the concentration of the city's Jews in the ghetto. They initially planned to build a block of shacks to house the Jews. In light of the reduction in the city's Jewish population following the murder operation of October 1941, however, they opted instead to place the city's Jews within the boundaries of the traditional Jewish quarter, the most neglected neighborhood in Stanislawow, covering about one-eighth of the city's territory. The Germans officially announced the establishment of the ghetto in October or November 1941, but its boundaries were not clearly demarcated for some time, and the Judenrat attempted to expand the number of allotted streets. The "Aryans" living in the area were ordered to move out of the ghetto by the end of November, allowing them time to harvest crops from their plots and gardens. Stanislawow's Jews were ordered to move into the ghetto between December 1 and 15, 1941.

The more affluent members of the Jewish community moved to the ghetto immediately; they were able to bring along their possessions and procure the best apartments. For thousands of poor Jews, the move to the ghetto proved a great hardship, and many found themselves living in warehouses, garages, prayer houses, and any other free space that could be found. The ghetto was separated from the "Aryan side": the doorways and windows of the peripheral buildings were bricked up or nailed down with wooden planks, and a two-and-a-half to three-meter- high wooden fence was built, topped by barbed wire. The outer side of the fence was painted with a white stripe and yellow Stars of David. At first, contact with the outside world was maintained by means of the ghettos' three gates, which were guarded by the SCHUPO and Ukrainians as well as by Jewish policemen. The ghetto bordered the Bystrzyca River on one of its sides, also with a police presence.

The ghetto was officially sealed on December 20 or 22, 1941. At that time, between 28,000 and 30,000 Jews were living in it. It is possible that the ghetto's population was even higher, in light of an influx of Jewish survivors from surrounding localities who arrived in Stanislawow in the fall of 1941. Very difficult conditions soon developed in the closed ghetto. The inhabitants' food rations were substantially diminished. Jews were permitted to possess cows and goats for only a very short time. Some of the milk was confiscated by the authorities, and the rest supplied the ghetto's needs, particularly at the hospital.

Social disparities among the ghetto population were blatant. The plight of people without children, orphans, the elderly, and the Hungarian refugees was especially harsh. Many destitute ghetto inhabitants lay in the streets and died of starvation and exposure from the very first winter (1941/42). The more affluent inhabitants managed to survive by selling their possessions and buying food smuggled in on the black market, which flourished in the ghetto. Jews employed outside the ghetto received sustenance at their workplace in addition to some form of payment, and were also in a position to smuggle merchandise out of the ghetto and food supplies in. People caught smuggling by the guards, however, were usually sent to labor camps or executed. Beyond the workers, permission to leave for the "Aryan" side on a regular basis was also granted to the members of the Judenrat and the Jewish policemen as well as to people with connections who were able to buy exit permits.

Many Jews were "permanently" employed by various German enterprises as artisans, engineers, officials, and laborers performing menial work. Jews also toiled on farms and in various private factories. In addition to the employment bureau and supply departments, which were established to fulfill the German authorities' requirements, the Judenrat also established a number of departments responsible for areas such as welfare, health, and food distribution for the more vulnerable inhabitants of the ghetto. Beside the Jewish Order Service, the Judenrat set up a fire department, whose members supervised the refugee camp operating in the Rudolf Mill.

The Germans conducted sporadic raids on the ghetto and assigned youths to work in forced-labor camps, from which few returned. Visits by German police to the ghetto were accompanied by acts of brutality and murder. In December 1941, the residents of the ghetto were ordered, under penalty of death, to hand over all of the furs in their possession.

On Passover eve March 31, 1942, about 5,000 Jews, mostly the elderly, the ill, and beggars, were killed in a murder operation.

From ghetto to camp: After the March 1942 murder operation (see below), the ghetto was officially designated as a camp for fit Jews employed in the service of the Germans. The inhabitants were ordered to report to the Jewish employment bureau on certain days. They appeared before Gestapo officials and underwent a selection in order to receive work permits, a document that in effect determined their chances of survival.

In April–May 1942, a number of new workplaces employing hundreds of Jews were established inside and outside the ghetto. However, this "productivity plan" did not improve living conditions within it, nor did it halt the murder of its inhabitants—many of whom were deported to Belzec.

The Rudolf Mill was concurrently turned into a "camp" to hold Jews designated for extermination, both residents of Stanislawow and thousands of Jews who had been transferred there from the surrounding townlets and villages immediately after the March 1942 operation, including the residents of Tysmienica*, Wojnilow, Tlumacz*, and other localities. Occasionally, up to 3,000 Jews were held in the mill and the nearby factory building under conditions of severe overcrowding, sometimes for a few days at a time. They were deported on to the Belzec extermination camp or murdered by German and Ukrainian guards in the cemetery or the building. These acts of murder were carried out under the command of Krueger and Brandt. The mill was guarded by Ukrainian guards as well as by members of the Jewish Order service under the command of Zigo Veis. The Jewish fire brigade members helped to strip the victims before they were murdered, sort through their clothing afterwards, bury their bodies, and clean up the murder site.

In late June or in July 1942, treatment of the ghetto's inhabitants worsened, as the supervision of the Jews' work was transferred to the Gestapo and the Jewish employment bureau was dismantled. The Germans executed five members of the Judenrat, including the chairman, Lam. The deputy chairman, Goldshtein, was forced to take on the role of chairman of the Judenrat, which now had twenty-four members. During this period, the number of Jews employed in German factories was reduced drastically, and inhabitants were permitted to leave the ghetto only in groups guarded by Ukrainians or Germans. The ghetto's contact with the "Aryan side" was further restricted when only a single gate into and out of the ghetto remained. During the same period, the Germans liquidated the Rudolf Mill camp.

In August 1942, following yet another operation, the area of the ghetto was once again reduced. A barbed-wire barrier, not a fence, marked its new boundaries. The Germans appointed a new Judenrat, the ghetto's fourth, now headed by Sheinfeld, the director of the Jewish *Baudienst* or building service, who had not previously been a resident of Stanislawow. Sheinfeld also served as the head of the Jewish Order Service. At this stage, about 11,000 Jews remained in the ghetto.

In September and October 1942, work permits were confiscated from numerous Jews and a substantial number of the workplaces were liquidated or scaled down. Many of the Jews who were dismissed were sent to various labor camps, including the Janowska camp in Lwow. The ghetto was reduced further in size, and the Germans carried out frequent acts of murder.

In November and December 1942, a number of enterprises that wanted to retain their Jewish workers began to house them in camps set up next to the factories. Owing to the superior conditions in the camps as compared with the ghetto, many attempted to gain entry into the camps, sometimes by means of bribery or connections. Meanwhile, Jewish residents also tried to arrange hiding places in the ghetto or on the "Aryan side," and a few people who still had the means obtained "Aryan" documents. A number of Jews attempted to flee to the forests, but many were forced to return to the ghetto after being turned in by local Ukrainians. Only a few individuals managed to escape to Hungary or Romania.

Murder operations and the ghetto's liquidation: On August 3, 1941, hundreds of Jewish liberal professionals were taken to the nearby Pawelce forest and murdered.

On October 12, 1941, the German police, under the command of Hans Krueger and Oskar Brandt and helped by Ukrainians, massed about 20,000 of the city's Jews in the old cemetery of Stanislawow; between 10,000 and 12,000 were massacred. Tanenbaum chose to die with his brothers, despite an offer of release by the Germans. The massacre became known as "Bloody Sunday."

On Passover eve, March 31, 1942, a large-scale murder operation was carried out in the ghetto by the German police, under the command of Hans Krueger and assisted by the Ukrainians. About 5,000 Jews were killed in the operation, mostly the elderly, the ill, and beggars, and their residences were set ablaze. According to one version of events, they were placed on trains headed for Belzec on April 1, 1942.

In the second half of July or early August 1942, another operation was launched in the ghetto, on the pretext that Jews had struck a Ukrainian guard. The Judenrat was ordered to supply 1,000 men within three days, but apparently failed to fulfill this command. The Germans carried out a retaliatory massacre, killing about 1,000 people in the ghetto, in front of the members of the Judenrat. Afterwards, several of the Judenrat members were executed, beginning with the chairman, Goldshtein.

On September 12, 1942 (Rosh Hashanah 5703), between 3,000 and 4,000 Jews were deported to the Belzec extermination camp. The patients of the two hospitals in the ghetto were also murdered in this operation, but a few of the doctors were spared, owing to the Germans' fear of epidemic typhus. Operations were also carried out in the smaller towns and townlets in the surrounding areas, as Jewish residents were taken to the Stanislawow cemetery and murdered. The most outstanding was the deportation of the Jews of the Kalusz* ghetto to Stanislawow and their murder in the city's cemetery on September 15–17, 1942.

In January 1943, the Germans launched an approximately two-month-long liquidation of the Stanislawow ghetto. With the help of Ukrainians, the German police cordoned off blocks of streets designated for liquidation, rounded up their Jewish residents, freeing some and shooting most of the rest. To instill a false sense of security, the Germans all the while reassured Jews living in the nearby streets that they had a chance of survival. The most exhaustive hunt for Jews during the period occurred on January 24–25, 1943, when some 1,000 Jews without work permits were shot and another approximately 1,500 to 2,000 were deported to the Janowska camp. At the end of this process, all of the Jews were amassed under extreme conditions of overcrowding in the few buildings that remained in the ghetto.

The liquidation of the ghetto was completed on February 22 or 23, 1943, in an operation that was carried out under Brandt's command. The inhabitants of the last buildings (including Sheinfeld) were shot to death, with the exception of a few hundred railroad workers and economic service employees. Searches for Jews and executions of those found in hiding persisted until April 1943.

Jews concentrated in camps adjacent to the factories were gradually exterminated through to June 25, 1943, by which time only a few dozen experts, engineers, technicians, and seamstresses had been kept alive by the Germans in the municipal jail. The women were shot on September 29, 1943, and the rest of the prisoners apparently managed to survive until the spring of 1944.

When Stanislawow was liberated by the Red Army on July 27, 1944, remaining in the area were 100 Jews who had managed to hide with the help of a number of Poles and Ukrainians.

STARAYA RUSSA

COUNTY SEAT, LENINGRAD DISTRICT, RUSSIAN FEDERATION, USSR

During the war: Military Administration Area

Coordinates:
58°00' | 31°23'

On the eve of World War II, there were about 830 Jews living in Staraya Russa, about 2 percent of the town's total population.

Staraya Russa was occupied by the Germans on August 9, 1941. In September 1941, all of the local Jews were registered and required to wear white identification bands.

In September–October 1941, the Jewish inhabitants of Staraya Russa were imprisoned in a ghetto of sorts located in the local jail and a nearby monastery. Some weeks later, the ghetto was liquidated, and all of its inhabitants were shot and buried in mass graves.

STARAYA SINYAVA

(Yiddish: **Altsinave**;
Ukrainian: **Stara Synyava**)

COUNTY SEAT, KAMENETS-PODOLSK DISTRICT, UKRAINE, USSR

During the war:
Reichskommissariat Ukraine

Coordinates:
49°36' | 27°37'

On the eve of World War II, there were some 1,200 Jews in Staraya Sinyava, constituting approximately one-third of the population. Under Soviet rule, the townlet had a Jewish Ethnic Soviet and a government school that taught in Yiddish.

On July 14, 1941, the Germans occupied Staraya Sinyava and immediately subjected the Jews to abuse and confinement in a barbed-wire enclosed ghetto. Three hundred ghetto inhabitants were murdered and buried near a sugar factory on August 19, 1941.

The ghetto was liquidated in mid-1942, when the remaining Jews were deported to Starokonstantinov* and subsequently murdered there. During the summer of 1943, eighty Jews found in and around the townlet were killed by the Germans.

STARODUB

COUNTY SEAT, OREL DISTRICT, RUSSIAN FEDERATION, USSR

During the war: Military Administration Area

Coordinates:
52°35' | 32°42'

In the 1920s, about 4,100 Jews lived in Starodub. The trends toward modernization and urbanization in the Soviet Union at the time contributed to a decline in the town's Jewish population to about 1,620 people by the eve of World War II, at which time Jews constituted 13 percent of the local population. During the Soviet regime, most of the Jews of Starodub engaged in various forms of artisanship; the town also had a Jewish kolkhoz. The community's educational institutions consisted of a Jewish elementary and high school in which the language of instruction was Yiddish.

Starodub was occupied by the Germans on August 18, 1941. In late September 1941, about 1,400 Jews were concentrated in a ghetto that was established on the outskirts of the town. The Jews were forced to perform slave labor in exchange for 100 grams of bread per day. On October 1, 1941, between 272 and 400 Jews (sources vary on the exact figure) were shot to death. In the course of the ghetto's five-month existence, over 150 Jews died, victims of extremely harsh living conditions.

The ghetto was liquidated on March 1, 1942, in an operation that killed its approximately 800 remaining Jews. The Russian police actively participated in gathering and transporting the Jews prior to their murder.

STAROKONSTANTINOV

(Yiddish: **Altkonstantin**;
Ukrainian:
Starokostiantyniv)

COUNTY SEAT, KAMENETS-PODOLSK DISTRICT, UKRAINE, USSR

During the war:
Reichskommissariat Ukraine

Coordinates:
49°45' | 27°13'

At the beginning of the twentieth century, there were about 9,200 Jews living in Starokonstantinov. By the eve of World War II, urbanization and modernization in the Soviet Union during the interwar period had reduced the town's Jewish population to 6,700, one-third of its total. During the Soviet era, many Jews continued to work as artisans and organized in cooperatives. Others accepted blue- or white-collar jobs in state-owned institutions and factories, and several became farm workers. During this time, the town's Jewish inhabitants had access to government schools that taught in Yiddish and, briefly, an unofficial Yeshiva.

The Germans occupied Starokonstantinov on July 8, 1941, and immediately began to prey on the Jews. On August 3, the Germans loaded hundreds of local Jews aboard trucks and drove them to a large former Soviet army camp. There, they subjected the Jews to cruel abuse and separated out and shot dead the elderly and the ill, murdering a total of 439 people. The survivors were driven back to the town.

At the end of the month, a Jewish Council was appointed. Two of its three members were lawyers named Langer and Shprit. The council was responsible for paying ransoms, helping the Germans confiscate property such as bicycles and sewing machines, and supplying people for forced labor. During another operation, conducted in August 1941, Germans and Ukrainian police murdered some 800 Jews in the neighboring Novogorodskiy forest. Additional Jews—members of the local intelligentsia—were murdered later.

In late August 1941, the survivors were concentrated in a ghetto in the northern part of the city. The ghetto was fenced in and its gate guarded by members of the Jewish Order Service. Jews were forced to wear a yellow star; skilled workers were required to wear a black band, as well. The skilled workers labored from sunrise to sundown and received 100 grams of bread per day; the others received no provisions and were compelled to barter possessions for food. Congestion, starvation, and epidemic typhus led to high mortality; suicides were widespread. In mid-1942, a large number of Jews from nearby localities, notably Gritsev*, Ostropol, and Staraya Sinyava*, were transferred to Starokonstantinov. In the beginning of summer 1942, about 4,000 Jews, apparently deportees who had recently arrived, were murdered near the city.

The Starokonstantinov ghetto was liquidated on November 29, 1942, when SD members and military police rounded up the entire Jewish population, brought them to a place near the Novogorodskiy kolkhoz, and shot them dead. The operation, orchestrated by the local SD commander, Graf, was carried out with the assistance of the commander of the Military Police station.

STARY SĄCZ

TOWNLET IN NOWY SĄCZ COUNTY, CRACOW DISTRICT, POLAND

During the war: General Gouvernement, Cracow District

Coordinates:
49°34' | 20°39'

About 550 Jews lived in Stary Sacz when World War II broke out, representing approximately one-eighth of the townlet's population. Most earned their livelihood from small-scale commerce and peddling; several ran inns and a few were artisans. Most of the community's children studied in traditional Hadarim and Batei Midrash. Zionist parties and youth movements were active in the townlet, which also featured a sports club and a drama circle.

Prior to the Germans' occupation of Stary Sacz in early September 1939, a number of the townlet's Jews, primarily the youths, had fled to the area under Soviet control to the east. After the occupation, German soldiers and police seized

Jews for forced labor. The Jews were required to pay a ransom and wear a yellow badge on their clothing, and their freedom of movement was restricted.

In late 1939, a Judenrat was appointed in Stary Sacz and was ordered to regularly supply the Germans with forced laborers.

In 1940, the Germans began to carry out mass punishments of Jews accused of forgoing the yellow badge requirement or of violating restrictions on their freedom of movement. The Judenrat and JSS established mutual-aid activities. Groups of pupils were formed that studied various subjects, including Hebrew, clandestinely. By the end of 1940, altogether 148 Jewish refugees had arrived in Stary Sacz.

The Germans began to send young Jews from Stary Sacz to labor camps. Inhabitants sought out permanent jobs in factories considered indispensable to the German economy, hoping to obtain immunity from labor camp work. In April 1941, a chapter of JSS was established in the townlet to address the care of the needy. In late 1941 and early 1942, attempts were made to secure work for Jews at nearby farms. On September 13, 1941, twenty Jewish women were shot in the townlet.

In the spring of 1942, a ghetto was established in Stary Sacz. Jews from surrounding localities were also concentrated there, and its population reached about 1,000.

In July 1942, dozens of Jews died of epidemic typhus and rubella. In the same month, the Jews were ordered to remit a high ransom.

The ghetto was liquidated on August 17, 1942, and its inhabitants were deported by foot to the Nowy Sacz* ghetto, at a distance of ten kilometers. Ninety-five or nearly 150 elderly and ill Jews (sources vary on the figure) were murdered in the townlet. A short time later, the Jews of Stary Sacz were deported from Nowy Sacz to the Belzec death camp.

STASZÓW

TOWNLET IN SANDOMIERZ COUNTY, KIELCE DISTRICT, POLAND

During the war: General Gouvernement, Radom District

Coordinates: 50°33' | 21°10'

On the eve of World War II, about 4,800 Jews lived in Staszow, representing over half of the townlet's population. Most earned their livelihood from artisanship, especially in the fields of leatherwork and shoemaking, and from the trade of products generated by the grain, wood, and alcoholic beverage industries, among others. The townlet boasted the traditional Jewish charity and welfare associations as well as two Jewish-owned banks. Staszow had a chapter of the Zionist Federation, alongside which various Zionist parties and youth movements were active, as well as Hachshara training farms. The Zionist parties established a large library in the townlet. Staszow also had a sizable branch of Agudath Israel and a Bund chapter. The boys of the Jewish community studied in modern Heder-type schools. The girls largely attended Polish schools, but nevertheless received Hebrew and Jewish history lessons, along with courses in Judaic studies sponsored by Agudath Israel. The townlet also had a Talmud Torah and a Yeshiva. The townlet's Jewish sports association organized self-defense classes whose lessons were applied on several occasions, leading to a reduction in the volume of violent antisemitic incidents in Staszow.

The Germans occupied Staszow on September 7–8, 1939, and immediately demanded payment of an exorbitant ransom. In October 1939, the Germans confiscated the shops, workshops, and other property owned by Jews. In November 1939, a Judenrat was established in Staszow, headed by A. Singer. The Judenrat was charged with collecting the large ransom on pain of deportation of the Jews from the townlet.

In December 1939, the Jews were ordered to wear a white armband marked with a blue Star-of-David. That same month, Jews who had been driven out of Kalisz* and Lodz* were brought to Staszow. The Judenrat established a public

Staszow

A member of the Jewish Order Service (Chaim Feferman) standing at the entrance to the ghetto. Inscription on the sign: "Caution, boundary of Staszow Jewish living area. Entrance of local Jewish residents without permission punishable by death." (YV)

soup kitchen in the Hasidic shtibl. On January 29, 1940, the Germans completed their confiscation of all Jewish-owned shops, businesses, and merchandise. In May 1940, the recruitment of slave laborers from among Staszow's Jews began, and by September 1940, hundreds of the townlet's Jewish men had been seized. In January 1942, an order was issued prohibiting the Jews of Staszow from leaving the townlet. On January 6, the Jews were ordered to turn over all the furs in their possession.

On June 15, 1942, the Germans established a ghetto in Staszow. It was encircled by a barbed-wire fence and guarded by Polish policemen. That same month, the Judenrat was ordered to compile a list for the SS command of 100 young Jews to be assigned to a labor camp. These youths were murdered.

In August 1942, two sewing workshops that produced Wehrmacht uniforms were established in the ghetto. Rumors began to circulate at this time of deportations to the death camps, and many of the Jews sought out places to hide and built bunkers. Members of the youth movements devised plans for an uprising; the Judenrat and adults opposed the notion, however, the Judenrat contending that at least those Jews performing work essential to the Germans would be saved.

In October 1942, members of the Gestapo seized a group of Jews for work in Skarzysko-Kamienna. Several were murdered.

On October 8, 1942, Gestapo and SS soldiers aided by Ukrainian and Polish policemen rounded up all of the ghetto's residents. Singer, the head of the Judenrat, was murdered in front of the members of the community. About 6,000 of the ghetto's residents were deported to the Treblinka death camp; 189 of those found in hiding were summarily killed.

About 330 Jewish employees of the sewing workshops remained in the ghetto. They were joined by the Jews who emerged from hiding, fifty of whom were arrested by the Gestapo and sent to a ghetto reestablished in Sandomierz* on November 17, 1942. On January 10, 1943 they were added to a transport leaving for Treblinka, together with hundreds of other Jews from Staszow who had moved to the re-established ghetto from their hiding places in the forests or with local farmers. On October 19, 1943, a total of twenty-three Jews found hiding in Staszow were shot to death by German policemen.

In the course of the ghetto's existence, about 1,000 Jews managed to escape its confines and reach the forests. The vast majority perished within a short time.

STAWISKI

TOWNLET IN ŁOMŻA COUNTY, BIAŁYSTOK DISTRICT, POLAND

During the war: Bezirk Białystok

Coordinates:
53°22' | 22°09'

About 1,900 Jews lived in Stawiski in the interwar period, representing approximately two-thirds of the townlet's population. Most earned their livelihood from commerce and artisanship; they were aided by traditional welfare institutions, including a free-loan society. The community's children attended a public elementary school, a modern Heder, and traditional Hadarim. Stawiski had Zionist parties and youth movements, which in addition to running a club and a library, offered Hebrew courses and established a pioneer training facility. The Bund and the underground Polish Communist Party were active in the townlet.

In September 1939, the Germans occupied Stawiski and deported all of the townlet's men to a detention camp in east Prussia, some fifty kilometers from Grajewo*. Germans and Poles plundered Jewish shops. In October 1939, the townlet was handed over to the Soviets in accordance with the Molotov-Ribbentrop Pact, and the Jewish men returned to Stawiski. Many were killed or had died of disease during the brief period of German occupation.

Following the German invasion of the Soviet Union on June 22, 1941, numerous youths fled to the east together with the retreating Red Army. Many were killed in German bombings. Local Poles murdered a number of Jews before the Germans reentered the townlet.

The Germans reoccupied Stawiski on June 27, 1941, and aided by local Poles, immediately began to seize Jewish inhabitants for forced labor and to murder Jews. A number of Jews were murdered by Poles on a day of pogroms and looting, which, according to several testimonies, took place in the first week of July 1941. On the night of the reoccupation, about 300 Jews were killed by Polish peasants armed with non-firearms and were buried by their murderers in pits outside the townlet. The Germans assisted the Poles and photographed the pogrom. Murders continued for about one month.

On August 15, 1941, the townlet was encircled by the Gestapo. The younger Jews were led to the nearby townlet of Matwica, murdered, and buried. About 500 elderly Jews and children were led to the Kisielnica Forest, where they were all executed and buried.

After most of Stawiski's Jews had been murdered, a few professionals remained in the townlet, and the Germans and local farmers exploited their labor. On August 17, 1941, about sixty professionals and their families, among them a doctor, cobblers, tailors, carpenters, and blacksmiths, were rounded up in the ghetto. Its area was confined to a number of dilapidated houses known as the "Crooked Wheel" (*Krzywe Kolo*). A Jewish council was in charge of the open and unguarded ghetto. The Germans periodically demanded ransom payments. A few Jews worked on nearby Polish farms. Peasants murdered a group of Jews that worked in fields near Swirydy. A small number of Jews who managed to hide in the forests around Stawiski occasionally visited the ghetto. Each visit posed great danger to their lives, as the Germans paid bounties for Jews.

The ghetto was liquidated on November 2, 1942, when the Gestapo transferred the Jews to the Bogusza camp. The site had previously served as a concentration camp for Soviet POWs, in which tens of thousands had been murdered. Jews were also brought to the camp from villages in the area. Many of Stawiski's Jews perished in Bogusza from starvation and the filthy conditions. The handicapped and ill were shot, and the others were transported to Treblinka and Auschwitz. Many were gunned down along the way, before even boarding the train.

Individual Jews managed to flee from the Stawiski ghetto. Several people found shelter with farmers in the area, but many were handed over to the Germans and murdered. By the end of 1943, nearly all of the Jews who had escaped had been killed. According to hearsay evidence, all of Stawiski's murdered Jews were buried near Maly Plock.

STEPAŃ

TOWNLET IN KOSTOPOL COUNTY, VOLHYNIA DISTRICT, POLAND
(After World War II in the USSR/Ukraine; Ukrainian: **Stepan'**; Russian: **Stepan**)

During the war: Reichskommissariat Ukraine

Coordinates: 51°08' | 26°18'

During the interwar period, there were about 1,300 Jews living in Stepan, roughly one-third of the townlet's population. Most were petty merchants and artisans. Several Jews were mill owners or large-scale grain and cattle merchants, while others rented out rooms to vacationers. The Jews of Stepan received financial assistance from a self-help organization and a savings-and-loan association supported by the JDC. The community boasted chapters of Zionist youth movements and parties, a library, a drama group, and a Tarbut school.

When the Soviet occupation began in September 1939, the Tarbut school adopted the Soviet curriculum and Yiddish replaced Hebrew as the language of instruction.

The Germans occupied Stepan on July 17, 1941. During the early days of the occupation, local villagers and German soldiers dispossessed Jews of their property. Jewish inhabitants were conscripted for forced labor in the townlet and in Kostopol*. A Judenrat and a Jewish Order Service were set up.

The ghetto in Stepan was established on October 5, 1941. Jews from eleven neighboring villages were brought in, increasing its population to some 3,000. The ghetto was divided into three sections: one for skilled workers in high-demand occupations, one for standard workers, and one for "useless persons"— the elderly, women, and children.

On August 24, 1942, some 500 Jews fled from the ghetto. Ukrainian peasants captured about 300 of the escapees who were then sent back to the ghetto.

The Stepan ghetto was liquidated on August 25, 1942, and its residents were taken to pits near Kostopol, where they were murdered. Dozens more escapees were later caught and murdered. Most of the Jewish refugees from Stepan, however, were helped by Polish villagers. A number of Jews joined and fought with Polish and Soviet partisan units.

STERDYŃ

TOWNLET IN SOKOŁÓW COUNTY, LUBLIN DISTRICT, POLAND

During the war: General Gouvernement, Warsaw District

Coordinates:
52°35' | 22°18'

Sterdyn was a townlet located six kilometers southwest of the Bug River. Out of a total population of 800 during the interwar period, about 700 were Jews. Most worked as petty merchants and artisans, mainly as tailors, shoemakers, and furriers.

The townlet was occupied by the Germans on September 22, 1939. In late 1939, a Judenrat was established, charged with recruiting Jews for forced labor. In early 1941, a number of Jews deported from other localities were brought to Sterdyn, mostly refugees from Kalisz*. They were housed in the local synagogue. The new arrivals brought the Jewish population of the townlet to about 900 by February 1941.

A ghetto was established in Sterdyn in late March 1941. Conditions of overcrowding and poor hygiene were abysmal. The ghetto was open, but Jews were forbidden to leave the townlet or maintain ties with the local inhabitants. A hospital was established in the Beit Midrash and the Judenrat hired the services of a Polish doctor who secretly treated ill Jews. During their time in the ghetto, Jews (mainly refugees from other localities) were seized for forced labor in the labor camp near Siedlce*.

As the invasion by the Soviet Union drew closer, seizures of Jewish men and women for forced labor were increased owing to the townlet's proximity to the Bug River. When Poles related stories of the liquidation of Jews from nearby villages, panic broke out in the ghetto, and numerous youths fled in all directions to escape deportation.

The ghetto was liquidated in September 1942, when the townlet's Jews were deported to the Treblinka death camp.

STOCZEK

TOWNLET IN WĘGRÓW COUNTY, LUBLIN DISTRICT, POLAND

During the war: General Gouvernement, Warsaw District

Coordinates:
52°33' | 21°54'

When World War II broke out, about 3,000 Jews lived in Stoczek, representing approximately three-quarters of the townlet's population. They earned their livelihood from small-scale commerce and artisanship, and were helped by an artisans' trade union for mutual aid, two bank branches, and traditional welfare and charity societies. Most of Stoczek's Jews were Hasidim, and the townlet had a number of Hasidic courts. Nonetheless, Zionist parties, the Bund, and Agudath Israel also operated in the community, and a number of Jews were active in the outlawed Polish Communist Party. Stoczek had five Hadarim and a Beit Yaakov school for girls.

In 1937, forty-two Jews were injured in antisemitic riots that erupted in the townlet's marketplace.

Stoczek, 1942
The deportation of the ghetto's Jews (USHMM, courtesy of Morris Rosen)

Stoczek was occupied by the Germans in mid-September 1939. They torched Jewish homes, plundered Jewish property, and seized Jews for forced labor. About 200 young Jews were sent to the Chyzyny labor camp.

In late 1939, the Germans appointed a Judenrat, ordered Stoczek's Jewish inhabitants to wear Star-of-David armbands, and forced them into a ghetto. Owing to severe overcrowding, epidemic typhus soon erupted there, and many inhabitants perished. In November 1941, a few hundred Jews from the surrounding areas were deported into the Stoczek ghetto.

The ghetto was liquidated on September 22, 1942, when all of its inhabitants were deported to the Treblinka death camp.

STOCZEK ŁUKOWSKI

TOWNLET IN ŁUKÓW COUNTY, LUBLIN DISTRICT, POLAND

During the war: General Gouvernement, Lublin District

Coordinates:
51°53' | 21°31'

About 2,000 Jews lived in Stoczek Lukowski during the interwar period, representing roughly two-thirds of the townlet's population. Most earned their livelihood from artisanship and peddling, although several were also small-scale farmers. The townlet had a Jewish bank that aided Jewish merchants and artisans, and also boasted chapters of the Zionist parties and youth movements, Agudath Israel, and the Bund.

During the summer of 1937, more than thirty Jews were injured in antisemitic riots in the marketplace.

The Germans occupied Stoczek Lukowski in mid-September 1939. A great deal of Jewish property was confiscated from the Jews in October–December 1939, and harsh restrictions were imposed on the Jews' movements. In late 1939 or early 1940, a Judenrat headed by Aharon Haler was established and charged with recruiting Jews for forced labor outside the townlet. A small Jewish Order Service was also set up.

At an unknown date, an open ghetto was established in Stoczek Lukowski. In the winter of 1940/41, epidemic typhus broke out in the ghetto, and many of its inhabitants perished. In the summer of 1941, the Jews were ordered to hand over all furs in their possession to the Germans.

In late August 1942, German and Polish policemen deported the majority of the ghetto's inhabitants to the Parysow* ghetto, leaving only a small number of people they qualified as fit for work in Stoczek Lukowski. About 100 of the deportees were murdered en route to Parysow. On September 27, 1942, when the Jews of Parysow were deported to the Treblinka death camp, most of Stoczek Lukowski's Jews were included in the transport.

STOLIN

COUNTY SEAT, POLESYE DISTRICT, POLAND

(After World War II in the USSR/Belarus)

During the war:
Reichskommissariat Ukraine

Coordinates:
51°53' | 26°51'

During the interwar period, about 3,000 Jews lived in Stolin, approximately two-thirds of the townlet's population. Several earned their living as merchants and artisans, while others worked in the lumber industry and exported grain and agricultural produce via the Horyn River. They availed themselves of a Jewish free-loan society and savings-and-loan association. Jewish educational institutions included a Yeshiva, a modern religious school, and a Hebrew-language Tarbut school and kindergarten. Zionist youth movements and parties were active in the townlet, as was the Bund.

When the Soviets occupied Stolin in 1939, they arrested twenty Zionist and Bund activists and exiled them along with their families to the Russian interior. The Hebrew-language school was transformed into a Soviet school that taught in Yiddish. The townlet's economy was Sovietized.

After the Soviets fled in late June 1941, Stolin was left without a government for about two months. During that time, local residents attempted to stage pogroms against the Jews. The Jews organized in self-defense, albeit without firearms. On July 14, 1941, the Jews of Stolin heard that a group of released Soviet prisoners was planning a pogrom; a bribe foiled the scheme. On August 22, 1941, the German Gebietskommissar (territorial commander) and his staff arrived. The commander appointed a Judenrat with Natan Bergner, a refugee from Lodz*, as its head. The Jews of the townlet were periodically compelled to pay high ransoms and wear armbands, and those aged sixteen years and over were conscripted for forced labor. Imposed sanctions included bans against public prayer, contact with the Christian population, and meat consumption. In late August 1941, some 1,500 women and children who were deported from Dawidgrodek* were brought to Stolin.

Also in late August 1941, the mayor of Stolin and several Germans were killed in a partisan ambush near the village of Chemin. The entire Jewish population of Chemin was murdered in an act of retaliation. The Germans also planned to kill the Jews of Stolin, but the Judenrat staved off a massacre.

The Stolin ghetto was established on May 22–23, 1942. Many Jews from the neighboring villages had by that time been brought to Stolin, raising the population to some 7,000 people. The ghetto Jews were employed in workshops and various forms of forced labor.

On September 10, 1942, all of the Judenrat members were murdered at the local SIPO-SD office. The Stolin ghetto was liquidated the following day. The ghetto was quarantined, and all of its inhabitants were removed from the townlet in groups of 500 and murdered in the forest in specially dug pits. Jews who were ill, weak, or caught in hiding were murdered inside the ghetto. About thirty Jews managed to escape to the forests.

A resistance movement formed in the ghetto. It dispatched two messengers to establish contact with the partisans in the forests; they were, however, caught and hanged. The movement stockpiled kerosene and made other preparations to set the ghetto ablaze and flee, but the plan failed for unknown reasons.

STOŁOWICZE

TOWNLET IN BARANOWICZE COUNTY, NOWOGRÓDEK DISTRICT, POLAND
(After World War II in the USSR/Belarus; Belarussian: **Stalavichy**; Russian: **Stolovichi**).

During the war:
Reichskommissariat Ostland

Coordinates:
53°13' | 26°02'

About 250 Jews lived in Stolowicze on the eve of World War II, representing approximately one-third of the townlet's population. They earned their livelihood mainly from farming, small commerce, and artisanship.

On September 19, 1939, Stolowicze was occupied by the Soviets. During the period of their rule, a Soviet economic, social, and educational system was instituted in the townlet. Stolowicze's Jewish population rose to about 350, apparently due to an influx of refugees.

On June 27, 1941, the Germans reoccupied Stolowicze and a few days later executed fourteen Jews. On September 1, 1941, a Judenrat was established, and the Jews were required to wear a yellow badge and were seized for forced labor.

In January 1942, the Jewish inhabitants of Stolowicze were concentrated in a ghetto; it was enclosed by a fence in March 1942. On May 6, 1942, sixteen Jews with required professions were transferred with their families to the Baranowicze* ghetto. The rest of the ghetto's inhabitants were shot to death outside of the townlet on May 12, 1942. A number of Jews hid during the operation; several were found and shot to death by the Germans, and about forty were persuaded to return to the ghetto a few days later. On June 20, 1942, they, too, were executed.

STOŁPCE

(Yiddish: **Stoybets, Shtuptsi**)

COUNTY SEAT, NOWOGRÓDEK DISTRICT, POLAND
(After World War II in the USSR/Belarus; Belarussian: **Stoubtsy**; Russian: **Stolbtsy**)

During the war:
Reichskommissariat Ostland

Coordinates:
53°29' | 26°44'

When World War II broke out, about 2,000 Jews were living in Stolpce, representing roughly one-third of the townlet's population. Most earned their livelihood from small commerce and artisanship. Jewish parties and youth movements, such as the Zionists, were active in Stolpce. The townlet boasted a Tarbut Hebrew school, a Yiddish school, and a Jewish library.

After the Soviets occupied Stolpce in the second half of September 1939, privately owned business and economic activity in the townlet were nationalized. In the weeks following the occupation, about 2,000 Jewish refugees thronged to the townlet from the areas of Poland occupied by the Germans. Several were exiled into the Soviet Union's interior after refusing to accept Soviet citizenship.

When the Germans occupied Stolpce on June 27, 1941, there were about 3,000 Jews living in the townlet. The day after the occupation, about 200 Jews were murdered. In early July 1941, a Judenrat was established at German orders, headed by Witenberg, a refugee from Lodz* who devoted himself to taking care of the Jews' needs. Immediately after the Judenrat was established, the Jews of Stolpce were ordered to wear a distinctive badge and their freedom of movement was restricted. Ransom payments were periodically levied on the Jews, and each day, about 400 Jews left to perform forced labor. On July 25, 1941, eighty-seven Jewish public figures and members of the liberal professions were executed, and on August 19, 1941, nineteen young Jewish forced laborers were murdered.

In the summer of 1941, the Jews of Stolpce were concentrated in a poor neighborhood. Having learned of the killing operations in Kleck* and Nieswiez*, they began to prepare hiding places and bunkers in the ghetto. On August 3, 1941, about 400 young Jews were sent to work in Baranowicze*, and on August 30, 1941, another 230 young Jews were sent to work in Minsk*. On November 5, 1941, the ghetto area was fenced in and closed to passage. Inhabitants experienced a severe shortage of food and a rise in the mortality rate. Latvian policemen who guarded the ghetto together with members of the Jewish Order Service severely terrorized and abused the Jews.

In late February 1942, an underground formed, made up of local Jewish youths and refugees from Warsaw* and Lodz; it was headed by Hershel Posesorski and Fogel. The members dug out a bunker, obtained weapons, and established contact with partisans.

Stolpce
Jewish women aged 18–40 were required by the German authorities to perform forced labor. (YV)

On the morning of September 23, 1942, about 450 Jewish workers living in the ghetto were taken to their usual places of work. The same day, some 750 Jews, mostly women, were taken from the ghetto under guard and shot to death outside of Stolpce by a unit of the SD from Minsk. Among the murdered were the members of the Judenrat and the Jewish Order Service. On the eve of and during the operation, hundreds of Jews (about 850 according to a German source) hid, while others fled from the ghetto. During the operation, individuals resisted in various ways, such as setting fire to buildings and attacking policemen. In the manhunt carried out by the Germans between September 24 and October 1, close to 500 people attempting to hide or flee were discovered (488 according to a German source) and executed.

The Jews who were sent to work on the first day of the operation were held in detention for an extended period and returned to the ghetto on October 2, 1942. Within a few days, Jews who had been in hiding or who had fled returned to the ghetto, and the ghetto population reached 560. On October 11, 1942, a German police unit under the command of Schulz, with the help of Lithuanian policemen, carried out another operation in the ghetto in which about 350 Jews were murdered. After this operation, small groups of armed Jews from among those remaining in the ghetto—estimated by the Germans at a little more than 200—persisted in their attempts to flee to the forests and join the partisans.

The Stolpce ghetto was liquidated on January 31, 1943, after a mass escape of about 200 Jews from the Swierzen Nowy* ghetto.

STOPNICA

TOWNLET IN BUSKO COUNTY, KIELCE DISTRICT, POLAND

During the war: General Gouvernement, Radom District

Coordinates:
50°26' | 20°57'

Following World War I, about 3,300 Jews lived in Stopnica, representing approximately three-quarters of the townlet's population. They earned their livelihood from commerce and artisanship. Two Jewish banks were established in the townlet with the assistance of the JDC, and an Agudath Israel bank was also instituted. The townlet had numerous Hasidim. The Zionist parties were also active; they established a library, opened a clubhouse, and held courses in Hebrew. Community members belonged to Agudath Israel and Bund chapters as well. About 150 girls studied in the townlet's Beit Yaakov school, while a number of the boys studied in a traditional Heder-type school.

In 1919, the Jews of Stopnica were attacked by Polish antisemites. A great deal of property was plundered, and a number of Jews were injured.

When World War II broke out, the local Poles looted shops and apartments belonging to the townlet's Jews. On September 8, 1939, the Germans occupied

Stopnica, torched the Jewish residential quarter, and murdered four Jews. In early 1940, the German governor of the townlet, Niedermann, ordered the Jews to wear a white armband with a Star-of-David. A Judenrat was established in the same period, charged with collecting ransom money for the Germans.

In April 1940, on Passover eve, the Germans murdered thirteen Jews as they sat at the Seder table. During the summer of 1940, the Judenrat recruited forced laborers for the Germans.

In early 1941, a ghetto was established in Stopnica. The ghetto was not sealed, but the Jews were forbidden to leave its confines other than for work. The Judenrat established workshops in the ghetto, mostly in the textile industry, which employed about 200 professionals.

In 1941, hundreds of Jewish refugees from Lodz*, Cracow*, Radom*, and Plock* were brought to Stopnica. In May 1941, the number of Jews in the ghetto reached 4,600, leading to an outbreak of epidemic typhus. The Judenrat opened a public soup kitchen and clinic with the help of the JSS in Cracow.

In April 1942, the population of the ghetto stood at approximately 5,300. By June 1942, some 400 refugees had perished of starvation and disease.

On September 5, 1942, SS men, Polish police, and Ukrainian auxiliary units surrounded the ghetto. On September 6, 1942, about 400 mostly elderly and disabled Jews who had not reported as required were murdered near the ghetto. Some 1,500 youths were sent to the labor camp in Skarzysko-Kamienna*, and the remaining 3,000 ghetto residents were deported to the Treblinka death camp.

About seventy Jews were left behind in the ghetto to bury the murder victims and collect the deportees' belongings. About seven weeks later, these workers were sent to a ghetto reestablished in Sandomierz*.

STOROJINEȚI

COUNTY SEAT, BUKOVINA, ROMANIA

Coordinates:
48°10' | 25°43'

About 2,500 Jews lived in Storojineti in the interwar period, representing approximately one-quarter of the town's population. They earned their livelihood from commerce and artisanship, and as owners of three leather-tanning factories. A small number of Jews were clerks or members of the liberal professions. The Jewish community had traditional charitable and welfare institutions. Its children studied in traditional private Hadarim, a Talmud Torah in which Hebrew was taught for two hours daily, a Yeshiva, and a Hebrew high school that was active until 1934. Storojineti boasted a Jewish sports association, Zionist youth movements and a pioneer training facility as well as a chapter of the Jewish Romanian party. A number of the town's Jews were members of the Bund and Communist parties.

In 1940, Storojineti was annexed together with northern Bukovina to the Soviet Union, and Soviet law was imposed. The Jewish community's institutions were shut down, and Jewish businesses were closed and their merchandise confiscated. In the spring of 1941, dozens of Jewish families were exiled from the town, including merchants, industrialists, Zionists, and members of the Bund.

On July 3, 1941, the Red Army retreated from Storojineti, which was damaged in German aerial bombings. Romanian army units occupied the town and carried out acts of looting and murder. For two days, Romanian soldiers indiscriminately fired their weapons in the streets and into homes and courtyards. About 200 Jews were murdered, including the former heads of the Jewish community, Solomon Drimmer and Simon Schaeffer. Meanwhile, nearly all of the Jews in the villages surrounding Storojineti, thousands of Jews in all, were murdered. Local Ukrainians looted Jewish homes. Dozens of Jews managed to escape, either to the forests or across the Dniester River. About 300 Jews fled in wagons to Czernowitz*.

Two weeks after the Romanian occupation of the town, the Jews were transferred into a ghetto that was established in the southern part of the town on about five streets. The local population looted the Jews' homes, and Christians seized the homes that were not demolished. The Jews were assigned to forced labor and required to wear a yellow badge. Every day, groups of Jews were deported from the ghetto to the Edineti camp in Bessarabia, and eventually to Transnistria. The heads of the ghetto council were humiliated and forced to sweep the streets. Jewish hostages were seized and the Jews' freedom of movement was restricted, as were the hours they were permitted to shop in the market.

All of the ghetto inhabitants were deported on foot in groups of a few hundred each to the Edineti camp, with the exception of eleven Jewish families needed to guarantee the provision of vital services (members of these families included three doctors, a pharmacist, and experts in wood processing and alcohol production). On October 13, 1941, the final transport left by train for the Marculesti camp, and on to Transnistria.

On August 5, 1941, a group of about 300 deportees from Storojineti arrived in Volcineti on the Dniester River, near Atachi. Many were shot or drowned in the river by the Romanian police guards who escorted them and wished to get rid of them, while the Germans would not yet allow them to cross the Dniester into German-occupied territory. Others were concentrated in camps on the Romanian side of the river until October–November 1941.

The deportees who arrived in Transnistria were dispersed among the camps and ghettos. Roughly 10 percent survived.

STRESHIN
(Belarussian: **Streshyn**)

COUNTY SEAT, GOMEL DISTRICT, BELARUS, USSR

During the war: Military Administration Area

Coordinates:
52°43' | 30°07'

At the start of the twentieth century, there were about 1,200 Jews in Streshin, roughly 60 percent of the population. During the era of Soviet rule, many Jews practiced artisan trades—some in cooperatives—and a few farmed at a Jewish kolkhoz. The townlet had a Jewish Ethnic Council and a school that operated in Yiddish. Urbanization and industrialization drew Jews away from the townlet. By the eve of the German invasion of the Soviet Union, only about 530 remained, around one-third of the population.

The Germans occupied Streshin in mid-August 1941, by which time many Jews had already evacuated. In September of that year, the Germans ghettoized and dispossessed those who remained. The ghetto was guarded by police, and no one was allowed to leave without a permit. In April 1942, Germans and Belarussian police led 280 Jews from the Streshin ghetto in the direction of Zhlobin*. On April 14, 1942, they were murdered on the road between Zhlobin and the village of Lebedevka.

STRYJ
(Yiddish: **Satriye**)

COUNTY SEAT, STANISŁAWÓW DISTRICT, POLAND
(After World War II in the USSR/Ukraine; Ukrainian, Russian: **Stryy**)

During the war: General Gouvernement, Galicia District

Coordinates:
49°15' | 23°51'

In the early 1930s, about 11,000 Jews lived in Stryj, representing approximately one-third of the city's population. They earned their livelihood mainly from commerce and artisanship and endured a grave economic decline. The community operated a hospital and an orphanage as well as various welfare societies. Zionist parties, the Bund, and Agudath Israel were active in the community. The various parties ran cultural institutions as well as libraries. The longtime chapter of Hashomer Hatzair active in Stryj was the largest in Galicia. Most of the community's children attended general schools and a complementary Tarbut Hebrew school, and the children of the ultra-Orthodox studied in a Talmud Torah that included general studies as well. Stryj also had a vocational school for boys established by the JDC in 1919.

In 1939, Stryj was occupied by the Germans and handed over to the Soviets a few days later. During this period, hundreds of refugees from the German occupation zone in western and central Poland arrived in the city. Under Soviet rule, the activities of the parties and community institutions were discontinued and only the synagogues remained open. Free commerce gradually ceased and the artisans organized into cooperatives. In mid-1940, the Soviets exiled to the USSR interior a group of Zionist activists, Bundists, and middle-class Jews as well as hundreds of Jewish refugees from western Poland who refused to accept Soviet citizenship.

When the Red Army withdrew from the city in the wake of the German invasion of the Soviet Union on June 22, 1941, they were joined by about 300 Jewish recruits. On the eve of the withdrawal, the Soviets arrested a number of Zionist activists and murdered them in the local jail together with other political activists.

On July 2, 1941, the Germans entered Stryj. Some 300 Jews were murdered in riots carried out by local Ukrainian and Polish citizens. In late July, another twelve Jews allegedly "sympathetic to the Soviet regime" were executed. On German orders, a Judenrat was established, headed by Oscar Hutterer, along with a Jewish Order Service, whose first commander was an attorney named Kahane. He was later replaced by Dolik Laufer. The Jewish Order Service was initially made up of members of the city's elite families and members of the youth movements, but in time it began to attract Jews who lived on the margins of society.

A number of harsh decrees were imposed on the Jews of Stryj: they were required to wear a white Star-of-David armband, severe restrictions were imposed on their freedom of movement, and they were seized for forced labor. Hundreds of Jews worked in city institutions, labor camps, and private German factories, which were the preferred places of employment because they provided a certain amount of protection from forced labor seizures.

On September 16, 1941, an operation was carried out in Stryj. German and Ukrainian police removed between 800 and 1,000 Jews from their homes and, after three days of cruel abuse, led them to a forest outside the city and murdered them.

In late 1941, the Germans began to concentrate the Jews from throughout the city into the Jewish quarter, which became an open ghetto. The ghetto was severely overcrowded, and its sanitary conditions were very poor. In December 1941, the Germans ordered the Jews to turn over all furs in their possession. In the first half of 1942, groups of Jews were periodically seized from the ghetto and shipped to labor camps, where many perished.

In July 1942, altogether 9,377 Jews lived in the Stryj ghetto. Nearly one-quarter received support from the JSS. The ghetto ran a hospital and five public soup kitchens, one of which was located in an orphanage and helped feed its fifty-five children.

For three days starting on September 3, 1942, German SIPO units, a unit of the SS Police Battalion 133, and the Ukrainian police carried out a large-scale operation. Some 3,000 Jews were rounded up and held in a synagogue under very harsh conditions, and another 500 to 600 were shot during their arrest. The detainees were sent under especially cruel conditions to the Belzec death camp together with another approximately 2,000 Jews from the nearby townlet of Skole.

In the second half of September 1942, about 1,700 Jews from surrounding localities, including Zydaczow, Zurawno*, Rozdol, and others were deported to Stryj. On October 22, 1942, the Germans carried out another operation, which was especially violent and brutal. Although the Jews had prepared elaborate hiding places, the Germans and their helpers combed through the streets of the ghetto and the surrounding areas, using dogs, destroying floors and walls, flooding cellars with water, and setting houses on fire to find those in hiding. Some 2,300 people are estimated to have been killed as a result of this operation;

most were deported to Belzec, and several hundred were killed in the city. A few Jews jumped off the trains, but most were killed by the fall, shot by guards, or handed over to the Germans. Few managed to return to the ghetto.

After the October 1942 operation, another 700 Jews designated "unfit for work" were concentrated in the ghetto. The area of the ghetto was reduced, its boundaries closed in with wooden planks, free entry and exit were abolished, and food smuggling into the ghetto now incurred the death penalty. The ghetto held some 4,000 Jews, and hunger and epidemic typhus were rampant. The ghetto inhabitants were divided into two groups: several hundred workers in factories producing essential products, who wore a square patch on their bodies bearing the letter *W*, and all the rest—Jews considered "not vital" to the Germans. Initially the laboring Jews lived in the ghetto and left its grounds each day for work, but after some time, they were concentrated in a separate "workers' ghetto" set up near the factories in which they toiled.

On November 15, 1942, the Germans carried out yet another operation in the ghetto in which they deported about 1,500 Jews to the Janowska labor camp in the suburbs of Lwow* and to Belzec.

In the fall and winter of 1942/43, the efforts of Jews to escape from the ghetto redoubled. Dozens attempted to flee to Hungary, while others escaped to the forest where they built bunkers for hiding. Most, however, were caught and murdered. Jews who managed to obtain false "Aryan" papers attempted to move to other cities.

On February 28, 1943, an operation was launched that lasted through to March 3, 1943. This time about 1,000 Jews were killed, including those with work permits, which were no longer honored. Jews who attempted to break through the well-guarded walls of the ghetto were shot, and their bodies were scattered on both sides of the fence. After the operation, the survivors in the ghetto strove to obtain jobs in the labor camps in the city, which as yet remained undisturbed.

The Stryj ghetto was liquidated in an operation carried out on May 22, 1943. The ghetto was encircled by a tight ring of German and Ukrainian policemen. More than 1,000 Jews were rounded up and packed into the large synagogue, where they were held for several days without food or water. A few days later they were brought to the local cemetery and shot.

On June 3, the Germans and their helpers set about removing the last remaining Jews from their hiding places: they torched houses, flooded cellars, and threw bombs into bunkers. The Judenrat building was burned, and the last members of the Judenrat and Jewish Order Service were murdered.

In July and August 1943, the labor camps in Stryj were also liquidated and their Jewish workers murdered.

STRYKÓW

TOWNLET IN ŁÓDŹ COUNTY, ŁÓDŹ DISTRICT, POLAND

During the war: Wartheland

Coordinates:
51°54' | 19°36'

On the eve of World War II, there were about 2,000 Jews living in Strykow, nearly half of the townlet's total population. Most were petty merchants and artisans who were assisted by a free-loan society and traditional charities. Children attended a Zionist school that taught Hebrew, a reformed Heder, and other schools. A Jewish library held evening classes and gave Hebrew instruction. The community also enjoyed the services of a Jewish sports association. While Strykow was renowned as a Hasidic center, Zionist parties and groups, Agudath Israel, and the Folkspartey were also active in the townlet.

The Germans occupied Strykow on September 7, 1939, and annexed it to the Reich. In December 29, most of the approximately 1,600 Jews remaining in the townlet were deported to Glowno*, a part of the General Gouvernement; however when the mayor of Glowno refused to receive them, they were returned to Strykow. When the mayor of Strykow refused to re-admit the group of Jews from his town, they were shuttled back to the periphery of Glowno, where they were imprisoned in a camp until the spring of 1940, when they were sent to Warsaw*. Left behind in Strykow were 378 Jewish artisans, factory workers, and their families; several refugees later joined them.

In the spring of 1940, the Strykow ghetto was established and enclosed in barbed wire. In April or May 1942, the ghetto's population was deported to Brzeziny*. When the Brzeziny ghetto was liquidated in the middle of May 1942, some 300 skilled workers from Strykow were transported from Brzeziny to the Lodz* ghetto, along with Jews from Brzeziny who had survived the selection. Eventually, they shared the fate of the Jews of Lodz. Very few survived.

STRZEGOWO
(Yiddish: **Strezegove, Stshegov**)

TOWNLET IN MŁAWA COUNTY, WARSAW DISTRICT, POLAND

During the war: Bezirk Zichenau

Coordinates:
52°54' | 20°17'

About 600 Jews lived in Strzegowo in the interwar period, representing approximately one-third of the townlet's population. They earned their livelihood mainly from commerce and artisanship, and a few were laborers. They were aided by a joint Jewish-Polish loan fund and traditional charity and welfare societies. A number of the Jewish children attended traditional Hadarim. Strzegowo had a Tarbut Hebrew school and a Beit Yaakov school for girls. The Jews of Strzegowo enjoyed a library and drama circle. The Bund, the Communist Party, and Zionist parties and youth movements were active in Strzegowo, as was Agudath Israel and its youth movement.

Jewish refugees arrived in Strzegowo from Mlawa*, which was on the German border, on September 2, 1939. On September 3, the townlet was bombed, and a number of Jews were killed. Many fled in the direction of Plonsk*.

The Germans occupied Strzegowo on September 4, 1939. Local ethnic Germans (Volksdeutsche) took power in the townlet and proceeded to plunder Jewish property, confiscate homes belonging to wealthy Jews, and seize Jews for forced labor.

The first Jews were murdered in Strzegowo in late 1939 or early 1940, during the ransacking of Jewish businesses.

In October 1939, Strzegowo was included in the Bezirk Zichenau and annexed to the Third Reich. A unit of the German gendarmerie was stationed in Strzegowo. At the demand of the unit commander, a Jewish help council was established in the townlet. In late 1939 or early 1940, a number of Jewish families moved to Warsaw*. In the summer of 1940, the local government was handed over to a German civilian official, and at his orders a Judenrat was established in Strzegowo, headed by Ben-Zion Bogan, as well as a four-member Jewish Order Service, headed by Feldman. The Judenrat was required to recruit Jews for forced labor, but as employers were required to pay Jews wages, the demand for Jewish labor fell in the second half of 1940.

In the second half of 1941, the Germans began to concentrate the Jews of the Bezirk Zichenau in ghettos. A ghetto was established in Strzegowo and was apparently sealed off on either October 14 or November 1, 1941 (sources vary regarding the date). With the establishment of the ghetto, the number of Jewish Order Service members was increased.

In 1941/42, most of the Jews of Strzegowo were performing forced labor, mainly outside the ghetto, which enabled them to occasionally smuggle in food for their families. The Jews were forbidden to gather in groups in the ghetto. Gendarmes often shot randomly into it, injuring and killing Jews. Local Volksdeutsche periodically invaded the ghetto to ransack Jewish homes and murder Jews.

On January 6, 1942, about 1,000 refugees from Sierpc* and Biezun were transferred to the ghetto, and in the following months another approximately 200 Jews who had fled from operations in ghettos in the area also arrived, raising the ghetto's population to nearly 2,000. The Judenrat and local aid council extended assistance to the fugitives, and a public soup kitchen that distributed 400 hot meals daily was established. Epidemic typhus broke out in the ghetto, and a tiny hospital with a Polish doctor, Dr. Grokhovski, was established. Contributions by the affluent Strzegowo Jews served as the main source of funding for welfare activities. Despite the organized help, about 200 people—10 percent of the ghetto's population—perished due to the harsh conditions.

On April 20, 1942, the gendarmes demanded that the members of the Judenrat be handed over, threatening the murder of all of the ghetto's Jews if the demand was not obeyed. The following day, Ben-Zion Bogan gave himself up to the Germans. On August 6, 1942, twenty men from the ghetto were arrested, and on September 2, they were publicly hanged in the presence of all of Strzegowo's Jews.

Apparently sometime in 1942, a man named Neufinkel arrived in Strzegowo, after escaping from Treblinka. Neufinkel, who had lived in Warsaw* and was the son-in-law of a resident of Strzegowo, told the townlet's Jews about the death camp. He was eventually arrested by the Gestapo of Ciechanow* and murdered.

On November 2, 1942, all of the elderly Jews in the Strzegowo ghetto were sent to Mlawa, and deported on November 10, 1942, on to Treblinka, together with a number of the Jews of the Mlawa ghetto.

The Strzegowo ghetto was liquidated on November 24, 1942. All of its inhabitants were sent to Mlawa, and from there to Auschwitz, where nearly all were murdered.

Throughout the ghetto's existence, youths attempted to form resistance, without success. During the liquidation of the Strzegowo ghetto, a number of Jews escaped, and in 1943, they joined the Polish partisans that were active in the area.

STRZEMIESZYCE WIELKIE

TOWN IN BĘDZIN COUNTY, KIELCE DISTRICT, POLAND

During the war: Upper Silesia

Coordinates:
50°19' | 19°17'

Note: Up until World War II, Strzemieszyce Wielkie, located near the larger city of Dabrowa Gornicza, was considered a separate town; since the war, it has been designated as a neighborhood of the city, and appears on maps accordingly.*

After World War I, about 1,300 Jews lived in Strzemieszyce Wielkie, representing more than one-tenth of the town's population. Most of Strzemieszyce Wielkie's Jews earned their livelihood from small-scale commerce and artisanship, and a small proportion engaged in the liberal professions. The town had a number of Hasidic courts but did not have a modern Jewish school. Strzemieszyce Wielkie boasted the traditional Jewish charity societies and a Jewish bank, a chapter of Agudath Israel established by the Orthodox Jews, chapters of the Zionist parties and youth movements, a public library established by the Zionists, and a drama class.

Strzemieszyce Wielkie was occupied by the Germans on September 3, 1939. In November 1939, a Judenrat was established, subordinate to the regional Judenrat in Sosnowiec*. The Judenrat in Strzemieszyce Wielkie was headed by Flashenberg, the head of the Jewish community prior to the war, and Horwitz. The Judenrat established two "shops" in the town, a tailor shop and an ironsmith shop.

In April 1940, Jewish refugees were brought to Strzemieszyce Wielkie, raising the town's Jewish population to about 1,800. In May 1940, the Germans confiscated Strzemieszyce Wielkie's Jewish-owned businesses and apartments.

In 1940, an open ghetto was established in the town. The Judenrat set up a public soup kitchen and an improvised Yiddish school in the ghetto. From mid-

1940 on, Jews from Strzemieszyce Wielkie were assigned to forced labor in near-by camps.

In December 1940, the Jews were ordered to wear a white armband marked with a Star-of-David, replaced by a yellow badge in October 1941.

In early 1942, about 500 workers and their families were transferred to Bedzin*. In May 1942, Jews from nearby villages were moved into the Strzemieszyce Wielkie ghetto. In June 1942, about 400 of the town's Jews were deported to Auschwitz.

Following the deportation, the head of the central Judenrat in Sosnowiec, Moshe Merin, arrived in the town along with his assistants. They conducted a census and provided the Jews of the ghetto, approximately 1,000 in number, with new work documents.

On June 15, 1943, the SS and German police deported the residents of the ghetto to Auschwitz. Forty-three elderly and infirm people and young children who were unable to report for the deportation were murdered on site. Dozens of Jews considered fit for work were sent to Bedzin.

STRZYŻÓW
(Yiddish: **Strizhov**)

TOWNLET IN RZESZÓW COUNTY, LWÓW DISTRICT, POLAND

During the war: General Gouvernement, Cracow District

Coordinates:
49°52' | 21°48'

When World War II broke out, about 1,100 Jews lived in Strzyzow, representing roughly half of the townlet's population. Most earned their livelihood from commerce, peddling, artisanship, and farming in the surrounding villages. They were aided by a free-loan society and for some time by the JDC. The townlet boasted Zionist parties and youth movements that ran a pioneer training facility, a club, a library, Hebrew courses, and a Hebrew kindergarten. Strzyzow also had chapters of Agudath Israel and a Talmud Torah supported by the JDC. For a time in the 1930s, a Yeshiva and a Beit Yaakov school for girls operated by Agudath Israel were also active.

After the German invasion of Poland in September 1939, Jewish refugees arrived in the townlet from various places near the Slovakian border. About 200 members of affluent families, the community rabbi, the chairman of the community, and a number of young Jewish men fled to the east. A number of the fugitives were killed by German soldiers, while others reached the area under Soviet control, particularly Lwow. The Soviet authorities exiled a number of those who reached Lwow to the USSR interior in the summer of 1940.

On September 10, 1939, the Germans occupied Strzyzow and immediately began to plunder Jewish shops and terrorize Jews. Apartments belonging to wealthy Jews were confiscated for use as army offices and to house German officers. Many of Strzyzow's Jews were seized for forced labor. Anti-Jewish decrees included the order to wear a Star-of-David as well as a prohibition against leaving the townlet, boarding a train without a permit, and conducting commercial dealings with or receiving food from local farmers.

A Judenrat with eight to ten members and a Jewish Order Service were appointed. The Judenrat was ordered to pay the Germans a periodic ransom, to supply them with items and products at their demand, and to provide male and female forced laborers every day. Jews were sent from Strzyzow to the Pustkow and Biesiadka labor camps.

In late 1939, refugees arrived in Strzyzow from Kalisz*. In May 1941, there were about 300 refugees in Strzyzow.

In April or May 1941, about 1,000 Jewish men arrived from Warsaw* to perform forced labor in the area. The Judenrat helped the laborers as best it could. After some time, most were transferred to labor camps outside the townlet. Some 300 remained in a camp near the townlet, and were transferred in June

1941 to the labor camp in Pustkow. The Jews of Strzyzow were forbidden to have any contact with the laborers. In the winter of 1941/42, Jewish inhabitants were ordered to turn over all furs in their possession on pain of death.

On December 17, 1941, an open ghetto was established in Strzyzow; the Jews were required to obtain permission from the Germans to leave its confines. An increasingly stringent guard was kept on the ghetto, and many Jews were executed for leaving its grounds without a permit or for trading with the local population. Only a small number of Jews managed to obtain work permits from the German employment bureau that protected them against seizure for the labor camps.

On May 4, 1942, SS men arrived in the townlet and murdered an attorney named Rosenthal, who was suspected of belonging to leftist organizations.

On May 15, 1942, another eight Jews were shot to death.

On June 26–28, 1942, the Jews of Strzyzow were deported to Rzeszow* in farmers' wagons. The ill and weak unable to leave their homes were shot on site. Most of the others perished in July 1942, in a mass deportation operation from Rzeszow to the Belzec death camp.

SUBAČIUS
(Yiddish: **Subotsh**)

TOWNLET IN PANEVĖŽYS COUNTY, LITHUANIA

During the war:
Reichskommissariat Ostland

Coordinates:
55°44' | 24°47'

On the eve of the war, about twenty Jewish families lived in Subacius.

In the fall of 1940, after Lithuania was annexed to the Soviet Union, a number of Jewish-owned shops were nationalized and Zionist activity was outlawed.

Subsequent to the occupation of Lithuania by the Germans in June 1941, nationalist Lithuanians took over Subacius, looted Jewish property, and concentrated the Jews in a ghetto of sorts. In late July 1941, eighty Jews were murdered in the Ilciunai forests located some three kilometers west of the townlet.

SUCHA BESKIDZKA

TOWNLET IN ŻYWIEC COUNTY, CRACOW DISTRICT, POLAND

During the war: Upper Silesia

Coordinates:
49°44' | 19°36'

When World War II broke out, about 330 Jews lived in Sucha Beskidzka, representing roughly 6 percent of the townlet's population. Most earned their livelihood from small-scale commerce and peddling, while a few were clerks, artisans, or employed by the resort industry. They were aided by a free-loan society and contributions received from former residents of the townlet living in America. Sucha Beskidzka had a Jewish public building with rooms to accommodate guests and a study room for children. Chapters of Zionist organizations were active in the townlet, but Agudath Israel's influence was especially strong.

After Sucha Beskidzka was occupied by the Germans on September 4, 1939, the townlet was annexed to the Third Reich, to the district of eastern Upper Silesia. As it was located on the border of the General Gouvernement, the townlet became a transit point for Jews fleeing from the region, especially to Austria. In late 1939, a Judenrat was established in Sucha Beskidzka, subordinated to the Zentrale, which was headed by Moshe Merin. A man named Buchenbaum was appointed to head the Judenrat in Sucha Beskidzka; he was later replaced by Erwin Klapholtz from Rajcza. The Judenrat maintained a bakery and a food shop and employed three Jewish Order Service members.

Most of the young Jews, about 200 in number, were regularly employed as forced laborers. In 1940, a commune was established in Sucha Beskidzka by a group of teenagers from Rajcza and Zywiec. The commune was dismantled when the young people's families arrived in the townlet.

It was decided that Sucha Beskidzka would be a concentration site for the Jews of Zywiec County. In 1940/41, all of the Jews who remained after the deportation of the county's Jews to the General Gouvernement in the fall of 1939, were deported to Sucha Beskidzka. In March 1941, there were 480 Jews living in Sucha Beskidzka, and it is possible that the number later rose to 600. In 1941, the Germans began to send Jews to labor camps. At first, some fifty young Jews were sent to the labor camp near Breslau; seventy young Jews were sent daily to a labor camp in Wadowice.

Initially, Dr. Rauk Belsko cared for the ill. In late 1941, a clinic was established in the townlet, and its physician, Dr. Kornhauser, offered treatment free of charge. Every month, he visited each Jewish home to verify its sanitary conditions.

In March 1942, members of the Jewish Order Service of the Zentrale in Sosnowiec* sent thirty youths from Sucha Beskidzka to a transit camp in Sosnowiec.

In late June 1942, an operation was conducted in Sucha Beskidzka by SS and Gestapo men in the presence of Moshe Merin; following a selection, about 220 of Sucha Beskidzka's Jews were deported to the Auschwitz death camp. Merin succeeded in preventing the deportation of another fifty Jews, as well as the transport of fifty Jews to the Sosnowiec transit camp.

Jews considered fit for work remained in the townlet; in early 1942, they were concentrated in the area of a former beer brewery that had been transformed into a ghetto. The ghetto was encircled by a wall one and a half meters high. Only inmates setting out for work in groups or inhabitants with special permits were allowed to leave. About 200 of those imprisoned in the ghetto were employed regulating the Skawa River. A kitchen and dining room were established in the ghetto, and the Jews participated in cultural activities, including *Kabbalat Shabbat* parties and the production of a play.

On May 8, 1943, the ghetto was encircled by German and local policemen together with Gestapo men under the command of Linder; they were aided by the Jewish Order Service from Sosnowiec. A selection was carried out, and 120 mothers with children, along with the elderly and the ill were loaded onto trucks and deported to the Auschwitz death camp, where they were killed. The remaining approximately 120 people, who were considered fit for work, were sent by train to the Sosnowiec transit camp, and from there were distributed among various labor camps. In all, approximately 300 of Sucha Beskidzka's Jews perished in the Holocaust.

SUCHEDNIÓW

TOWNLET IN KIELCE COUNTY, KIELCE DISTRICT, POLAND

During the war: General Gouvernement, Radom District

Coordinates:
51°04' | 20°50'

After World War I, about 900 Jews lived in Suchedniow, representing roughly one-quarter of the population. They earned their livelihood from small-scale commerce and artisanship. Many were supported by the Jewish local free-loan society as well as by the traditional charity societies. Suchedniow had chapters of Zionist parties, which operated a public library and drama class. The townlet also had a Beit Yaakov school for girls.

The Germans occupied Suchedniow on September 7, 1939, and seized Jewish inhabitants for forced labor. In November 1939, a Judenrat was established in the townlet, headed by Zelig Warszawski, one of the leaders of the community.

As of January 1940, the Jews of the townlet were ordered to wear an armband with a Star-of-David. In April 1940, a group of young Jews from Suchedniow was assigned to slave labor in Skarzysko-Kamienna*. In February 1941, about 2,000 Jews deported from Plock* were brought to Suchedniow.

In June 1941, a closed ghetto was established along three streets in the center of the townlet. A Jewish Order Service with about forty members was established. A short time later, the Germans moved another approximately 500

Jews from the nearby localities of Blizyn, Samsonow, and Bodzentyn into the Suchedniow ghetto, raising the ghetto population to more than 3,000. With the assistance of the JSS in Cracow*, the Judenrat opened a public soup kitchen, a clinic, and a children's house.

In June 1942, the Jews were assigned to forced labor in the area of Kielce and in a camp established near Suchedniow under the supervision of the SS officer Engelbert Kirschner. The Judenrat was charged with providing workers for these camps.

In August 1942, hundreds of Jews were brought to the ghetto from Blizyn, Zagnansk, and Samsonow, inflating the number of Jews in the ghetto to about 5,000.

At dawn on September 22, 1942, German and Polish policemen ordered the members of the Jewish Order Service to round up all of the ghetto's Jews. About 200 Jews qualified as fit for work and were sent to the camp in Skarzysko-Kamienna, while approximately 4,500 others were deported to the Treblinka death camp. Some thirty Jews remained in Suchedniow in hiding.

SUCHOWOLA

TOWNLET IN SOKÓŁKA COUNTY, BIAŁYSTOK DISTRICT, POLAND

During the war: Bezirk Białystok

Coordinates: 53°35' | 23°06'

About 1,500 Jews were living in Suchowola when World War II broke out, representing approximately half of the townlet's population. Most earned their livelihood from small commerce and artisanship. Jewish parties and youth movements were active in Suchowola, and the townlet boasted a library as well as a Tarbut Hebrew school and Hadarim.

After Suchowola was occupied by the Soviets in the second half of September 1939, a Soviet economic, social, and educational regime was introduced into the townlet. Privately owned shops were nationalized or closed and cooperatives were formed. Numerous refugees thronged to Suchowola from the areas of Poland occupied by the Germans.

In late June 1941, the Germans occupied Suchowola. From the first day of the occupation, the Jews were ordered to wear a yellow badge, their freedom of movement was restricted, and several people were seized for forced labor. On July 26, 1941 (known to the Jews of Suchowola as "Black Shabbat"), Jewish residents were severly abused and tortured by the Germans and their helpers, and a number of young men and women accused of being Communists were murdered. A short time later, a Judenrat was appointed and charged with recruiting Jews for forced labor.

In either the fall of 1941 or February 1942 (sources vary on the date), the Jews of Suchowola were concentrated in a fenced-in ghetto located on two-and-a-half streets. Jews from other localities were also brought to it, raising its population to some 5,000. All inhabitants lived under very harsh conditions of overcrowding. In the spring of 1942, Mordechai Tenenbaum, Hershel Rosental, and Mishkinski, leaders of the Hehalutz underground in Bialystok,* slipped into the ghetto and reported on the mass murders carried out in other ghettos. Equipped with this information, youths in the Suchowola ghetto attempted to organize for resistance and escape, but their plans failed, in part owing to the heavy guard placed around the ghetto.

On November 2, 1942, the Jews of the Suchowola ghetto were ordered to prepare for evacuation and leave the ill and elderly behind. Many Jews tried to escape, but most were caught and shot. The rest were transferred to the Kielbasin transit camp near Grodno* and deported on to the Treblinka death camp.

Suchowola map indicating ghetto boundaries
(H. Steinberg, ed., *Sefer Suhovolah*, Jerusalem, 1957. Map prepared by Mr. Y. Tzaban, based on his memory)

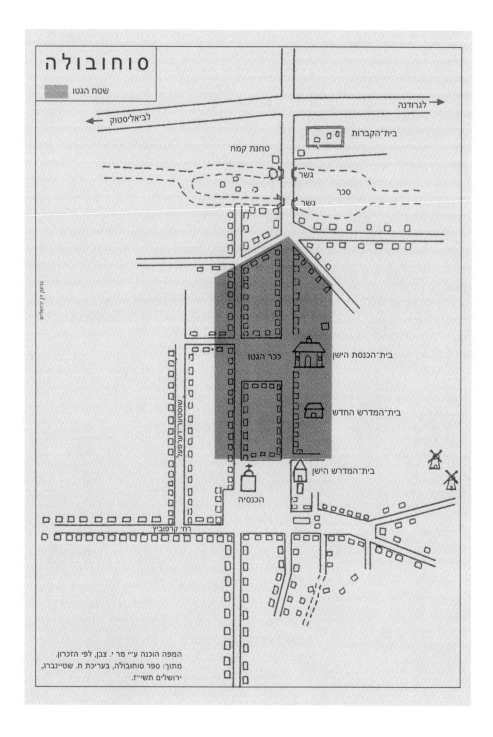

SÜMEG

TOWNLET IN ZALA COUNTY, HUNGARY

Coordinates:
46°59' | 17°17'

The last national census conducted prior to the German occupation, taken in January 1941, recorded 226 Jewish inhabitants in Sumeg, approximately 4 percent of the total population. Most were merchants and artisans. Jews dominated the townlet's wine trade. Sumeg's Jewish community was Neolog. In 1942, local Jewish men were drafted into the Hungarian army for forced labor service.

The German army occupied Hungary on March 19, 1944. A census conducted in the second week of April 1944 reported that 192 Jews belonged to the Neolog Jewish community of Sumeg.

After the German occupation the Hungarian administration remained intact and operational. The ghettoization and deportation of the Jews were carried out on the basis of the decrees and orders of the Hungarian national and local authorities. On May 4, 1944, the Hungarian sub-prefect of Zala County, Laszlo Hunyadi, ordered the establishment of a ghetto in Sumeg for the 316 Jews living in the settlement and its vicinity. The decree assured the Jews freedom of worship and allowed each person to bring along fifty kilograms of luggage.

The Jewish population of the townlet and the county-district of Sumeg were moved into the ghetto on May 31, 1944. On June 19, 1944, Hunyadi ordered the mandatory vaccination of the inhabitants of the ghettos in his county against typhoid fever.

On June 20, 1944, the Jews in the Sumeg ghetto were transferred to Zalaegerszeg*, to one of the entrainment centers of Zala County. They were deported on to Auschwitz on July 5, 1944.

ŚWIĘCIANY
(Yiddish: **Sventsyan**)

TOWNLET IN ŚWIĘCIANY COUNTY, VILNA DISTRICT, POLAND
(After World War II in the USSR/Lithuania; Lithuanian: **Švenčionys**)

During the war: Reichskommissariat Ostland

Coordinates: 55°09' | 26°10'

About 2,750 Jews lived in Swieciany when World War II broke out, representing more than half of the townlet's population. Most earned their livelihood from commerce, peddling, and artisanship. The community boasted chapters of Zionist parties and youth movements, Agudath Israel, the Bund, and the Communist party.

When the war broke out, numerous Jewish refugees thronged to the townlet from the areas of Poland occupied by the Germans. After Swieciany was occupied by the Soviets on September 18, 1939, privately owned businesses in the townlet were nationalized and cooperatives were formed. On the eve of the German occupation, about 8,000 Jews lived in Swieciany.

When the Germans invaded the Soviet Union on June 22, 1941, more than 1,000 Jews fled eastward from Swieciany together with the retreating Red Army. About 6,500 Jews remained in the townlet, both locals and refugees. The Germans occupied Swieciany on July 1, 1941. On July 15, 1941, about 100 Jewish residents were executed for alleged Communist activity. At German orders, a Judenrat was established, headed by a man named Shechman. Many of the townlet's Jews were seized for forced labor.

On September 22, 1941, Rosh Hashanah, a rumor spread regarding an impending operation. A local Jew interrupted prayers in the synagogue beseeching the Jews to flee. Several Jewish youths managed to escape.

On September 27, 1941, the Jews were rounded up, and following a selection, about 170 required workers with their families were separated from the rest, who were then taken to the regional transit camp known as Poligon. Most of the inmates, including the majority of Swieciany's Jews, were murdered about two weeks later, on October 7–8, 1941. Only a few individual survivors returned and slipped back into Swieciany.

The Jewish workers and their families, as well as a few Jews who returned from Poligon with their families, were moved into a fenced-in street that was turned into a ghetto. They toiled in workshops located both inside and outside of the ghetto. A new Judenrat was selected, headed by Moshe Gordin, and a ten-member Jewish Order Service was appointed. In addition to arranging forced laborers, the Judenrat also provided assistance to the needy and ill. The population of the ghetto grew when young Jews from Swieciany who had been in hiding slipped back in.

In the summer of 1942, after the area was annexed to the administrative area of Lithuania, Jews from Widze* and later from Lyntupy* were also brought to the ghetto, boosting its population to some 2,850; only about 550 people were originally from Swieciany. Overcrowding in the ghetto was severe, and many were forced to live in public buildings. The extreme conditions led to an outbreak of epidemic typhus, which two doctors and a number of nurses who were ghetto inhabitants strove to contain.

In February 1942, a twenty-five-member underground that managed to obtain and smuggle in weapons formed in the ghetto. On March 5, 1943, about fifty members of the underground escaped to the Narocz forests, where they joined the partisan unit in the area.

Despite the Judenrat's efforts to impede the ghetto's liquidation, it went ahead on April 4, 1943, in the context of a German order to remove all the Jews from a fifty-kilometer strip along the Belarussian-Lithuanian border. About 500 of the ghetto's inhabitants who had required professions were transferred to the Vilna* ghetto. The rest of the Jews, whom the Germans promised to transfer to the Kaunas* ghetto, were sent together with Jews from the vicinity to the Ponary murder site. When the deception was discovered, the deportees attacked the Germans; 600 of the Jews were killed and a few dozen managed to escape. All of the others were shot to death in Ponary.

ŚWIERŻE

TOWNLET IN CHEŁM COUNTY, LUBLIN DISTRICT, POLAND

During the war: General Gouvernement, Lublin District

Coordinates:
51°13' | 23°44'

About 300 Jews lived in Swierze in the interwar period, representing approximately 80 percent of the townlet's population. They engaged in commerce and artisanship. The townlet had a small Yeshiva.

After the occupation's onset in September 1939, the Germans began to confiscate Jewish property and seize Jews for forced labor. Jews from other localities were sporadically brought to the townlet, including eighty Jews from Cracow*, bringing its Jewish population to about 800 in late 1939. This figure apparently includes the refugees who came to Swierze immediately after the outbreak of the war.

An open ghetto was established in the townlet. A Judenrat complete with public health and welfare departments was appointed, headed by Moshe Perlstein, and charged with recruiting forced laborers. In 1940, the JSS helped the Judenrat to set up a public soup kitchen.

In October or November 1942, the Jews of Swierze were deported via Wlodawa* to the Sobibor death camp. Only a few individuals managed to flee to the forests and survive.

ŚWIERŻEŃ NOWY

(Yiddish: **Sverzhen, Sverzhna**)

TOWNLET IN STOŁPCE COUNTY, NOWOGRÓDEK DISTRICT, POLAND
(After World War II in the USSR/Belarus; Belarussian: **Novy Sverzhan'**; Russian: **Novyi Sverzhen**)

During the war: Reichskommissariat Ostland

Coordinates:
53°27' | 26°44'

About 430 Jews lived in Swierzen Nowy on the eve of World War II, representing roughly one-third of the townlet's population. Most earned their livelihood from small commerce, peddling, and artisanship.

After Swierzen Nowy was occupied by the Soviets in the second half of September 1939, privately owned businesses in the townlet were nationalized and cooperatives were formed.

On June 27, 1941, the Germans occupied Swierzen Nowy, and immediately murdered a Jewish couple. The Jews were forced to adhere to a number of decrees; for instance, they were compelled to wear a special badge and their freedom was restricted. The Germans appointed a five-member Judenrat headed by Yisrael Tselkovich. In August 1941, the Germans lined up the Jews and confiscated their valuables and money, and then shot two Jews to death. Later, two members of the first Judenrat resigned, and the Germans appointed a new Judenrat, this time with twelve members. On October 4, 1941, the secretary of the Judenrat, a man named Shvatag, at German orders rounded up about thirty young Jewish men and women, as well as the community's rabbi, Rabbi Alpert, his daughter, and a member of the Judenrat. With the exception of one young woman who managed to escape to the forest, all were shot in the cemetery as the youths' parents and Judenrat members looked on.

On October 25, 1941, the Jews of Swierzen Nowy were moved into a severely overcrowded, closed ghetto established in a number of ramshackle buildings along a side street. On November 5, 1941, after the workers had left for work, the remaining Jews were rounded up and most were loaded onto trucks. A number of Jews resisted but to no avail: all were shot dead outside the townlet. About 220 Jews remained in the ghetto, including those who had been sent off to work that day as well as those who worked in the ghetto. That same evening, about 150 Jews from Turzec were brought to the ghetto and were housed in one section of it encircled by a fence.

An underground made up of about fifty youths formed in the ghetto, and was headed by Binyamin Vielitovski and Monek Yoselevski. The members of the Judenrat were opposed to the activities of the underground and endeavored to impede its plans. Jews from the labor camp in Stolpce*, including a refugee from Warsaw* named Zvi Hershel Posesorski, occasionally appeared at the saw mill where the Jews worked and attempted to convince the members of the underground to flee. On January 28, 1943, Posesorski entered the Swierzen Nowy ghetto, and the following day he fled to the forest along with some 220 youths.

The last remaining Jews in the ghetto were executed the following day by a German police unit under the command of Schulz. A few individuals managed to escape.

ŚWIR

TOWNLET IN ŚWIĘCIANY COUNTY, VILNA DISTRICT, POLAND
(After World War II in the USSR/Belarus; Belarussian, Russian: **Svir**)

During the war: Reichskommissariat Ostland

Coordinates: 54°51' | 26°24'

About 800 Jews lived in Swir in the interwar period, representing approximately half of the townlet's population. Most earned their livelihood from small commerce, shopkeeping, and artisanship. Zionist parties and the Bund were active in Swir's community, which also had a Tarbut Hebrew school and a Jewish library.

The Germans occupied Swir on June 26, 1941, and established a police force composed of Polish and Belarusian collaborators who were granted extensive powers of authority. Even from the initial days of the occupation, the Jews were terrorized and abused by the local police, their property was looted, and they were seized for forced labor. As of July 29, 1941, the Jews were ordered to wear a yellow badge. At German orders a Judenrat was established, headed by Chaim Reznik. The Judenrat handed over a monthly bribe payment to the Germans.

On November 5, 1941, the Jews of Swir were transferred to a ghetto located in a side alley. About 1,500 Jews lived in its confines, including refugees from the areas of Poland occupied by the Germans. On December 1, 1941, the Judenrat arrested and executed twelve young Jews at German orders. On February 15, 1942, about 200 Jews were taken to a labor camp in Lithuania and later murdered.

In April 1942, Swir was annexed to the Reichskommissariat Ostland as part of the Vilna-land County. The governor of the county, Horst Wulff, ordered the Jews of the ghettos removed from a fifty-kilometer strip (which included the Jews of Swir) and concentrated in four central ghettos: Oszmiana*, Swieciany*, Soly*, and Michaliszki*.

The Swir ghetto was liquidated in August 1942, when almost all of its inhabitants were transferred to the nearby Michaliszki ghetto. A small group of Jews with required professions was left behind for a short time to work on estates located near Swir; they were later murdered.

ŚWISŁOCZ

(Yiddish: **Sislevitsh**)

TOWNLET IN WOŁKOWYSK COUNTY, BIAŁYSTOK DISTRICT

(After World War II in the USSR/Belarus; Belarussian: **Svislach**; Russian: **Svisloch**)

During the war: Bezirk Białystok

Coordinates:
53°02' | 24°06'

About 2,000 Jews lived in Swislocz when World War II broke out, representing approximately two-thirds of the townlet's population. Most earned their livelihood from small commerce and artisanship. Various Jewish political organizations and youth movements were active in Swislocz, including Zionist parties and the Bund. The community also boasted a Tarbut Hebrew school, a Yiddish school, and a modern Heder.

Swislocz was occupied by the Germans for a few days in early September 1939, but in the second half of the month, control of the townlet was handed over to the Soviets. During the period of Soviet rule, a Soviet economic, social, and educational regime was introduced into the townlet. Privately owned shops were nationalized or closed and cooperatives were formed. Numerous Jewish refugees thronged to Swislocz from the areas of Poland occupied by the Germans.

On June 26, 1941, the Germans reoccupied Swislocz and immediately instigated a regime of terrorization, abuse, and even murder of Jews, aided by locals. The Jews were required to wear a yellow badge on their clothes from the first day of the occupation.

In July 1941, a Judenrat was established at German orders, headed by Shlekhter, the former principal of the Hebrew school. The Jews of Swislocz were moved into a ghetto in an area near the synagogue. Acts of plunder and looting persisted, and Jews were seized for forced labor.

The Swislocz ghetto was liquidated on November 2, 1942. Following a selection, 300 Jews, including the elderly, ill, women and children, were murdered outside of the townlet. The remaining 3,000 Jews were taken to a transit camp near Wolkowysk*, where they were kept for several weeks. Many of them perished owing to the harsh conditions in the camp. The rest were deported in groups to Treblinka and Auschwitz-Birkenau by the end of January 1943.

SZABADKA

CITY IN BÁCS-BODROG COUNTY, HUNGARY

(After World War II in Yugoslavia/Serbia; Serbian: **Subotica**)

Coordinates:
46°06' | 19°40'

The last national census conducted prior to the German occupation, taken in January 1941, recorded 3,549 Jewish inhabitants in Szabadka, approximately 3 percent of the total population. Most were merchants and artisans, and several owned factories. After World War I, the city belonged to Yugoslavia (which was called the Serbo-Croatian-Slovenian Kingdom until 1929). In April 1941, Szabadka was annexed by Hungary. The city had a Neolog Jewish community and an Orthodox minority as well as various Jewish associations and welfare organizations. Co-educational Jewish schools and a kindergarten operated in Szabadka. In 1923, the Jewish hospital opened its doors. The Zionist movement became increasingly popular throughout the 1930s.

In 1942, many of the city's men were drafted into the Hungarian army for forced labor service; most of them died in the Ukraine, on the eastern front.

The German army occupied Hungary on March 19, 1944. According to a census conducted in the second week of April 1944, nearly 3,400 Jews belonged to both Jewish communities of Szabadka.

The Hungarian administration remained intact and in force after the occupation. The ghettoization and deportation of the Jews were carried out on the basis of the decrees and orders of the Hungarian national and local authorities. At the beginning of April 1944, Hungarian authorities declared several towns in Bacs-Bodrog County zones of hostility. Consequently, the Jews of the town of Ujvidek, some 1,900 people, were packed into the local synagogue on April 26 and 27, 1944. They were transferred to Szabadka the following day and housed in a mill that served as an internment camp. The local Jews were responsible for providing them with food. The Jewish Council, which had already been established in Szabadka and was headed by Dr. Zoltan Lorant, provided the Ujvidek Jews with food from a soup kitchen. Szabadka's Jews were also allowed to invite their relatives and acquaintances to live with them. Men were taken to work in the forest, and young women were assigned to work in the fields. The internment camp was closed down on May 17, and its inhabitants were taken to Baja* and deported on May 27 or 28, 1944.

The ghetto for the Jews of Szabadka was established about one week after the Jews of Ujvidek were brought into the city's internment camp. According to the Central Council of the Hungarian Jews in Budapest, the Jews of Szabadka were required to move into the ghetto of the local Jews, situated near the train station, by May 10, 1944. Jews who lived in mixed marriages were instructed to settle in the outskirts of the ghetto. Both a hospital and a labor ward operated in the ghetto.

The inhabitants of the ghetto were transferred to Bacsalmas* on June 16. They were deported to Auschwitz on June 26, 1944.

SZACK

VILLAGE IN LUBOML COUNTY, VOLHYNIA DISTRICT, POLAND
(After World War II in the USSR/Ukraine; Ukrainian: **Shats'k**; Russian: **Shatsk**)

During the war:
Reichskommissariat Ukraine

Coordinates:
51°30' | 23°57'

During the interwar period, about 200 Jewish families lived in Szack, accounting for approximately half of the village's population. The Jews of Szack were petty merchants and artisans; many had auxiliary farms.

The area came under Soviet rule in September 1939. The Germans occupied Szack on June 25, 1941. Some time later, Jewish inhabitants from the vicinity were brought to Szack; a ghetto was established, surrounded by a barbed-wire fence and confining some 700 Jews. Every day, several Jews were murdered while performing labor.

In mid-August 1942, eighty young Jews were removed from the ghetto to dig pits. After they completed their task they were shot. The adults were then removed from the ghetto, while the children were tied together. When shots were heard, a mass escape was attempted. Most of the escapees were shot as they fled, but about fifty people managed to reach the forest. The youngsters organized a fighting group that collaborated with a Soviet partisan unit. The rest of the escapees gathered in a family camp but were murdered by the Germans in early 1943.

SZADEK

TOWNLET IN SIERADZ COUNTY, ŁÓDŹ DISTRICT, POLAND

During the war: Wartheland

Coordinates:
51°41' | 18°59'

Before World War II began, about 500 Jews lived in Szadek, mainly petty merchants and artisans. Zionist parties were particularly influential in the community.

During the first months of the German occupation, about 100 Jews were removed to nearby Zdunska Wola*; the remainder were moved to a local ghetto that was established in May–June 1940.

The Szadek ghetto was liquidated on August 14, 1942, and its inhabitants deported to the Chelmno death camp.

Szadek
Jews in the ghetto near a sign prohibiting passage through the ghetto (YV)

SZAMOSÚJVÁR

TOWN IN SZOLNOK-DOBOKA COUNTY, HUNGARY
(After World War II in Romania; Romanian: **Gherla**)

Coordinates:
47°02' | 23°55'

The last national census conducted in Hungary prior to the German occupation, taken in January 1941, recorded 847 Jewish inhabitants in Szamosujvar, representing roughly 13 percent of the total population. Most were merchants and artisans, but several were also factory and landowners. The town had an Orthodox Jewish community, a Jewish elementary school, and a Talmud Torah.

After World War I, Szamosujvar, which was formerly in Hungary, became part of Romania. In August 30, 1940, the town once again became part of Hungary.

In the summer of 1941, the Hungarian authorities deported to German-occupied Ukraine a Jewish family of six who could not prove their Hungarian citizenship. They were murdered on August 27 or 28 at Kamenets-Podolsk*.

In 1942, Jewish men from Szamosujvar were drafted into the Hungarian army for forced labor service. Most were deployed to the eastern front in the Ukraine, where many perished. In 1943/44, additional local Jews were drafted for forced labor service, this time in Hungary; most survived.

The German army occupied Hungary on March 19, 1944. According to a census conducted in the second week of April 1944, about 800 Jews belonged to the Jewish Orthodox community of Szamosujvar.

The Hungarian administration remained intact and in force after the occupation. The ghettoization and deportation of the Jews were implemented on the basis of the decrees and orders of the Hungarian national and local authorities. The ghetto in Szamosujvar was established on May 3, 1944, according to the order of the mayor, Dr. Lajos Gyorffy, in the local brick factory. Aside from the Jews of Szamosujvar, the Jews of the villages in the Szamosujvar County-District were required to move into the ghetto, which held some 1,600 Jews. Its sheds could not contain all of the ghetto inhabitants, and the rainy weather muddied the ground. The Jews of the ghetto did not initially receive any cooked food, and later, food remained scarce.

Border police soldiers guarded the ghetto and tortured the inhabitants into revealing the whereabouts of their hidden valuables. A Jewish Council operated in the ghetto.

On May 18, 1944, the ghetto was liquidated and its inhabitants were transferred to the brick factory in Kolozsvar*. They were deported to Auschwitz between May 25 and June 9, 1944.

SZARKOWSZCZYZNA
(Yiddish: **Sharkeyshtshine**)

TOWNLET IN GŁĘBOKIE COUNTY, VILNA DISTRICT, POLAND
(After World War II in the USSR/Belarus; Belarussian: **Sharkaushchyna**; Russian: **Sharkovshchina**)

During the war:
Reichskommissariat Ostland

Coordinates:
55°22' | 27°28'

About 800 Jews lived in Szarkowszczyzna in the interwar period, and they earned their livelihood mainly from small commerce and farming. Zionist parties and youth movements were active in Szarkowszczyzna, as was the Bund. The townlet's community boasted a number of educational institutions, including a Yiddish school, a Tarbut Hebrew school, Batei Midrash, a library, and study circles.

Following the Soviet occupation of Szarkowszczyzna on September 18, 1939, economic activity in the townlet was restricted and Jewish political parties were outlawed.

After the Germans occupied Szarkowszczyzna on June 30, 1941, Jewish property was plundered, Jewish inhabitants were required to wear a yellow badge, their freedom of movement was restricted, and Jews were compelled to perform humiliating forced labor. At German orders, a Judenrat headed by Hirsh Brekhan was established. In the summer of 1941, the Germans murdered eleven Jewish youths who had held jobs in the Soviet administration of the townlet.

In October 1941, the Jews of Szarkowszczyzna were concentrated in a ghetto located in two different parts of the townlet. Both sections were encircled by a barbed-wire fence with gates. Jews from other localities were also concentrated there, raising its population to about 1,900. Hunger and disease soon led to a

Szarkowszczyzna, 1942
German administrative officials during a visit to a shoe factory in the ghetto (USHMM, courtesy of Mark Fintel)

high mortality rate in the ghetto, especially in the spring of 1942, when the Germans ordered the Judenrat to restrict bread distribution to the workers only.

On July 17, 1942, a German SS officer ordered the Judenrat head to collect a ransom payment and valuables from the inhabitants of the ghettos. Suspecting that the demand of the ransom was a precursor to the ghettos' liquidation, Brekhan warned the inhabitants and urged them to prepare to flee; to this end he stationed guards at various lookout points in the ghettos. The following day, when the Germans and their helpers approached the gates, young Jews set fire to the two ghettos, but rainfall prevented the fire from spreading. As chaos broke out, about 700 Jews broke through the fences, and several hundred people managed to escape. The rest of the approximately 1,200 Jews were murdered outside the townlet by the Germans and their helpers. Some of those who escaped hid in the forests, while others, unable to find hiding places, moved to a new ghetto for workers that the Germans established in Glebokie*, where they were murdered when the ghetto was liquidated in August 1943.

SZARVAS

TOWN IN BÉKÉS COUNTY, HUNGARY

Coordinates:
46°52' | 20°33'

The last national census conducted prior to the German occupation, taken in January 1941, recorded 686 Jewish inhabitants in Szarvas, approximately 3 percent of the total population; most were merchants and artisans. Both Neolog and Orthodox Jewish communities were active in the town, and each ran an elementary school.

The German army occupied Hungary on March 19, 1944. A census conducted in the second week of April 1944 showed that 412 Jews belonged to the Orthodox Jewish community of Szarvas.

The Hungarian administration remained intact and in force after the occupation. The ghettoization and deportation of the Jews were carried out on the basis of the decrees and orders of the Hungarian national and local authorities. The Szarvas ghetto, which was established in the buildings of both Jewish communities and in the main and auxiliary buildings of the Bolzor mansion, was established on May 15, 1944, and the local Jews moved in through May 22. Jews from the county-district of Szarvas were also confined ithere. Doctors and pharmacists treated the sick. In the last week of May 1944, a kosher soup kitchen was established.

In mid-June 1944, the ghetto inhabitants were transferred to the entrainment center of Bekescsaba*. On June 25, 1944, most of the Jews were deported on to

Strasshof, Austria, via the entrainment center of Szolnok*. Those who remained in Bekescsaba were deported to Auschwitz on June 26, 1944.

SZÁSZRÉGEN

TOWN IN MAROS-TORDA COUNTY, HUNGARY
(After World War II in Romania; Romanian: **Reghin**)

Coordinates:
46°46' | 24°42'

The last national census conducted in Hungary prior to the German occupation, taken in January 1941, recorded 1,635 Jewish inhabitants in Szaszregen, comprising approximately 16 percent of the total population. Most were merchants and artisans and were mainly involved in wine production and the wine trade, as well as in the wood trade. The town's Jewish community was Orthodox with Hasidic groups, a Jewish school, a few private Hadarim, and a Talmud Torah.

After World War I, Szaszregen, which was formerly in Hungary, became part of Romania. During the interwar period, Zionist movements and Agudath Israel were active in the town.

On August 30, 1940, the town became part of Hungary again. The Hungarian anti-Jewish legislation that applied to the local Jews was enforced more harshly in North Transylvania, where Szaszregen was located, than in inner Hungary.

In the summer of 1941, the Hungarian authorities deported to German-occupied Ukraine ten Jewish families whose members could not prove their Hungarian citizenship. The Hasidic rabbi of Sulita, Rabbi Yaakov Israel Yeshurun Rubin, who settled in Szaszregen with his followers after World War I, endeavored to help those whom the Hungarian authorities intended to deport, through such measures as hiding (two) families in his home. The deportees were murdered on August 27 or 28 at Kamenets-Podolsk*.

In 1942, many Jewish men from Szaszregen were drafted into the Hungarian army for forced labor service. Most were deployed to the Ukraine, where many perished. Operating in the town was a drafting center for forced labor service to which Jews drafted for it were required to report. The rabbi hid several runaway forced laborers or arranged to hide them with others.

The German army occupied Hungary on March 19, 1944. A census conducted in the second week of April 1944 reported that 1,682 Jews belonged to the Orthodox Jewish community of Szaszregen.

The Hungarian administration remained intact and in force after the occupation. The ghettoization and deportation of the Jews were implemented on the basis of the decrees and orders of the Hungarian national and local authorities. Following an April 28, 1944, conference regarding ghettoization in North Transylvania, Imre Schmidt, the mayor of Szaszregen, ordered the establishment of the ghetto in the town. It was set up in the local brick factory on May 3, 1944.

Aside from the local Jews, the Jews from the localities in the southern part of Maros-Torda County and the northern part of Csik County were concentrated there, too. Altogether, some 4,000 Jews lived in the brick factory. A few families were allowed to move into adjacent houses. The commander of the ghetto was local deputy commissioner of police Janos Dudas. Major Laszlo Komaromi, the local commander of the Hungarian army, and Gyorgy Feleki Kugler, the leader of the Arrow Cross Party in Szaszregen, conducted several raids on the ghetto. Police and gendarme officers interrogated and tortured the inhabitants of the ghetto into revealing the whereabouts of their hidden valuables.

Many Jewish men were assigned to work on the construction of a nearby military airfield, while bakers labored in the military bakeries. About twenty women were sent to clean and cook for the German forces stationed in the town.

The inhabitants of the ghetto of Sepsiszentgyorgy* were transferred to the Szaszregen ghetto on May 31, 1944. They were deported along with the local Jews to Auschwitz on June 4 (according to other sources, also on June 10), 1944.

SZATMÁRNÉMETI

(in Jewish sources: **Szatmár**)

TOWN IN SZATMÁR COUNTY, HUNGARY

(After World War II in Romania; Romanian: **Satu Mare**)

Coordinates:
47°48' | 22°53'

The last national census conducted in Hungary prior to the German occupation, taken in January 1941, showed 12,960 Jewish inhabitants in Szatmarnemeti, representing approximately one-quarter of the total population. Most were merchants and artisans, but a number were owners of factories and model farms employing mainly Jewish workers. The town had both an Orthodox and a Status Quo Ante Jewish community, two Jewish schools, a Yeshiva, and a Talmud Torah. From the late nineteenth century onward, the Orthodox Jewish community became one of the centers of Hasidism in Hungary. From 1928, Rabbi Joel Teitelbaum, the founder of the Satmarer Hasidic dynasty, held his court in the town. Various Jewish social and religious associations also operated in Szatmarnemeti.

After World War I, Szatmarnemeti, which was formerly in Hungary, became part of Romania. Zionism, especially the religious Zionist movements, became popular during the 1930s.

On August 30, 1940, Szatmarnemeti became an integral part of the Hungarian civil administration. The Hungarian anti-Jewish legislation that applied to all the Jews there was enforced more harshly in North Transylvania, where the town was located, than in inner Hungary.

In the summer of 1941, the Hungarian authorities deported from Szatmarnemeti to German-occupied Ukraine several Jewish families whose members could not prove their Hungarian citizenship. They were murdered on August 27 or 28 at Kamenets-Podolsk*.

In 1942, the overwhelming majority of Jewish men from Szatmarnemeti' aged between twenty-one and forty-five were drafted into the Hungarian army for forced labor service. Most were deployed to the eastern front in the Ukraine, where many perished.

The German army occupied Hungary on March 19, 1944. According to a census conducted in the second week of April 1944, about 12,000 Jews belonged to the Orthodox Jewish community and some 750 Jews belonged to the Status Quo Ante Jewish community of Szatmarnemeti.

The Hungarian administration remained intact and in force after the occupation. The ghettoization and deportation of the Jews were implemented on the basis of the decrees and orders of the Hungarian national and local authorities. An April 26, 1944, conference regarding ghettoization with Laszlo Endre, the undersecretary of state for internal affairs, was held in Szatmarnemeti for the administrative leaders of North Transylvania. The Szatmarnemeti ghetto was established on May 3, 1944, in the neighborhood that was most densely populated by Jews, according to the decrees of the Hungarian sub-prefect, Dr. Endre Boer, and the mayor, Dr. Laszlo Csoka. Aside from the local Jews, the Jews from the county-districts of Erdod, Nagykaroly, and Szatmarnemeti (Szatmar County) were required to move into the ghetto, altogether nearly 17,000 people. The Jews moved into the ghetto from May 3 through 6, 1944. Upon arrival, all Jews were subjected to a thorough body search for hidden valuables. On May 13, 1944, an additional 2,000 Jews from the ghetto of Nagykaroly* were concentrated in it.

The ghetto was extremely overcrowded: each person had 160 by 40 centimeters of living space in the apartments. The use of beds was forbidden; people lay on regular or straw mattresses.

The president of the Jewish Council that operated in the ghetto was Zoltan Schwartz. Jewish physicians organized medical care there, a hospital was established in one of the factory buildings inside the ghetto, and a hospital for infectious diseases operated as well. A soup kitchen was set up despite a severe shortage of food. The Hevra Kadisha premises were turned into the ghetto synagogue.

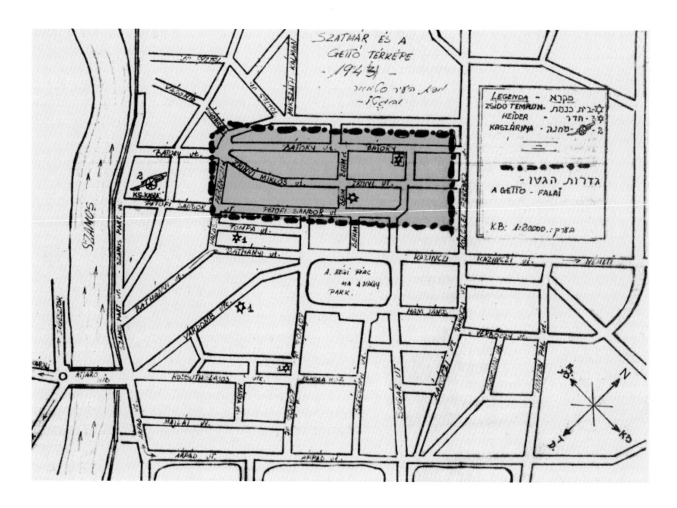

Szatmarnemeti streetmap indicating ghetto boundaries, illustrated by Simon Rozenberg
(*Emlekezz Szatmarra, a Zatmari Zsidosag Emlekkonyve*, szerkesztette Harav Naftali Stern, Bnei Brak 1964)

The commander of the ghetto was the Hungarian police officer Dr. Bela Sarkozi, referred to by the locals as "the second Hitler." Sarkozi personally oversaw the torture of the ghetto inhabitants, inflicted to determine the whereabouts of hidden valuables. Several people died as a result of the torture, and others committed suicide in order to escape it.

The 18,863 inhabitants of the ghetto were deported in six transports to Auschwitz between May 19 and June 1, 1944. Rabbi Schwartz, holding a Torah scroll and praying in a commanding voice, led one of the processions of Jews towards the trains.

A few courageous gentiles attempted to help Jews. Kalman Galffy, the commander of the 110/67 forced labor battalion in Szatmarnemeti, saved the lives of about 250 Jewish forced laborers.

SZCZEBRZESZYN

TOWNLET IN ZAMOŚĆ COUNTY, LUBLIN DISTRICT, POLAND

During the war: General Gouvernement, Lublin District

Coordinates:
50°42' | 22°58'

After World War I, there were around 2,600 Jews in Szczebrzeszyn, about one-third of the townlet's population. They were petty merchants and artisans. The community had traditional charitable and relief institutions and Jewish trade unions. Zionist parties, Agudath Israel, the Bund, and various youth movements were active there. In addition to the traditional Heder, the townlet had a Yeshiva, a Yavne religious school, and a Yiddishist CYSHO school.

The Germans occupied Szczebrzeszyn on September 13, 1939, and began to plunder Jewish property. On September 27, 1939, they retreated, and the Red Army stayed there until October 5, 1939. Then, the Soviets retreated under the Molotov-Ribbentrop Pact, accompanied by many Jews from the townlet.

The Germans reoccupied Szczebrzeszyn on October 9, 1939. Mistreatment of Jews resumed, the community was charged occasional ransom payments, and Jews were abducted for forced labor each day.

On December 19, 1939, from Wloclawek* 180 deportees were brought to Szczebrzeszyn. On December 20, the Jews were ordered to wear a yellow badge on their clothing and a white armband with a yellow Star-of-David. In early 1940, the Germans appointed a six-member Judenrat.

July 1940 saw 130 Jewish workers sent from Szczebrzeszyn to the labor camp in Bialobrzegi. During 1941, the Jews of Szczebrzeszyn were placed under severe movement restrictions, including an injunction against being in various parts of the townlet. This had the effect of concentrating them in certain quarters that amounted to an open ghetto. In December 1941, the Jews were ordered to surrender their furs to the Germans; two Jews who concealed furs were murdered.

In January 1942, epidemic typhus among the Jews of Szczebrzeszyn claimed many lives. In April, an eight-member Jewish Order Service was established in the townlet, where the Jewish population had grown to more than 3,000.

On May 8, 1942, the Gestapo rounded up about 2,000 Jews in the townlet square and opened fire. About 100 Jews were killed, and many were wounded. Some 280 Jews were deported to the Belzec death camp.

On June 23, 1942, the Germans murdered twenty Jews outside of the townlet and led scores of others toward Bilgoraj*. Their fate is unknown.

On August 8, 1942, some 400 Jews were deported to Belzec, and 200 elderly Jews were shot to death out of townlet. Several days later, the Germans sent 700 Jews from Szczebrzeszyn to a labor camp near Chelm*, where they were murdered.

The Jewish community of Szczebrzeszyn was liquidated on October 21–24, 1942, when some 2,000 Jews were sent to Belzec, and about 500 others were shot to death during the arrests and deportations or in escape attempts. Some who managed to survive were denounced by Poles; others were murdered by peasants with whom they sought refuge. Nonetheless, hundreds of Jews from Szczebrzeszyn managed to escape to the forests, where they operated as partisans. Although many were killed, a few did survive until liberation.

Szczebrzeszyn
Humiliation of Jews by German police in the city hall courtyard (USHMM, courtesy of IPN)

SZCZEKOCINY

TOWNLET IN WŁOSZCZOWA COUNTY, KIELCE DISTRICT, POLAND

During the war: General Gouvernement, Radom District

Coordinates: 50°38' | 19°50'

About 2,500 Jews lived in Szczekociny in the interwar period, representing nearly half of the townlet's population. Most earned their livelihood from small-scale commerce and artisanship, especially in the garment and construction industries, while a number either worked in or owned a factory. The townlet had a Jewish bank, a free-loan society, and trade unions. Szczekociny had chapters of the Zionist parties, Agudath Israel, and the Bund, which held cultural and youth activities. The children of the community studied in Hadarim and a Beit Yaakov school.

On the eve of World War II, about 2,800 Jews lived in the townlet. In early September 1939, more than 1,000 of Szczekociny's Jews fled to the east, to the area under Soviet control.

On the morning of September 4, 1939, the Germans occupied Szczekociny and immediately instituted a regime of forced labor and persecution. All Jewish-owned businesses were confiscated, and Jews were ordered to wear a white armband marked with a blue Star-of-David.

The Jewish refugees who returned from the Soviet-controlled zone found their homes destroyed; most moved on to other towns. In September 1939, the German military governor deported more than 200 Jews to Jedrzejow* and Zarnowiec, claiming danger of an epidemic owing to poor living conditions.

The governor also ordered the establishment of a Judenrat, whose thirteen members had all belonged to the previous Jewish community council. The Judenrat was headed by the community leader, Yaakov Moshe Feibish. A Jewish Order Service was set up alongside the Judenrat. Later, the governor ordered the number of Judenrat members reduced, because of their internal disputes. The Judenrat opened a school and a public soup kitchen with the help of the JSS; it was also charged with recruiting slave laborers on a daily basis. By 1942, the number of laborers had risen to 350.

Beginning in 1940, Jews were sent from Szczekociny to distant labor camps, including Sedziszow and Skarzysko-Kamienna. That same year, an open ghetto was apparently established in Szczekociny. The Germans periodically entered the ghetto and killed inhabitants.

In June 1940, there were 1,254 Jews living in Szczekociny. By June 1941, 140 refugees had arrived. With starvation becoming increasingly rife, the JSS opened a branch in the ghetto and funded the maintenance of the soup kitchen.

On June 22, 1941, the day of the German invasion of the Soviet Union, the ghetto was enclosed by a fence. Jews caught outside the ghetto were executed or deported to Auschwitz. In August 1941, Feibish, the head of the Judenrat, died, and was replaced by Yechiel Mordechai Richt.

In mid-September 1942, the Germans transferred the Jews of the surrounding small localities to the Szczekociny ghetto. They were marched on foot, and those who had difficulty walking were shot. Many of the ghetto's inhabitants realized that their end was near and searched for hiding places in the nearby villages and forests. The majority were murdered by the Germans or by Polish ultranationalists. Others reached Koniecpol or the ghetto reestablished in Radomsko* in November 1942, and from there, most were deported, with a minority transferred to the Skarzysko-Kamienna labor camp. Some of the Jews of Szczekociny were saved by Poles.

The Szczekociny ghetto was liquidated on Yom Kippur Eve on September 20, 1942, when the Germans, with the help of the mayor, Frote, deported 1,500 Jews to the Treblinka death camp via the Sedziszow train station. A number of Jews were murdered by German gendarmes in the station. The elderly and infirm were murdered in their places of residence.

Following the deportation, twenty-seven Jews remained in Szczekociny and were employed as slave laborers. Two Jews—the former head of the Judenrat, Yechiel Richt, and the secretary of the Zionist youth in Szczekociny, Yehuda Rafalovits—were accused of illegally monitoring radio broadcasts and executed.

SZCZUCZYN
(Białystok District)

COUNTY SEAT, BIAŁYSTOK DISTRICT, POLAND

During the war: Bezirk Białystok

Coordinates:
53°34' | 22°18'

About 2,500 Jews lived in Szczuczyn, representing nearly half of the townlet's population. They earned their livelihood from small industry, commerce, and artisanship, especially in the garment industry. They were aided by trade unions, traditional welfare institutions, a free-loan society, and a Jewish bank that was supported by the JDC; they also received help from Jewish émigrés from Szczuczyn living in the United States. The townlet had a Tarbut Hebrew school, a Beit Yaakov school for girls, a Yeshiva, and a Szabasowka school. A Yiddish elementary school operated there for some time. The townlet also boasted two Jewish libraries, a Bund cultural organization (*Kultur Lige*), a drama circle, and a Maccabi sports union. Chapters of Agudath Israel, its youth movement, and the Bund were active in Szczuczyn, as were Zionist parties and youth movements that established pioneer training facilities.

The Germans controlled Szczuczyn from September 8–23, 1939. They transferred 350 of the townlet's men, mostly Jews, to Germany for forced labor. Five months later, the thirty surviving members of the group returned. The Germans torched the townlet's synagogue and two Batei Midrash.

Following the Molotov-Ribbentrop Pact, Szczuczyn was annexed to the Soviet-occupied zone. A unit of the Soviet army entered Szczuczyn on September 27, 1939, and proceeded to arrest numerous wealthy people, many of whom were Jews. Some twenty Jewish families were deported to Siberia on June 21, 1941.

After the Germans invaded the Soviet Union on June 22, 1941, a small number of Szczuczyn's Jews fled to the east, while about 2,000 Jews remained. On the night of June 25, 1941, mass murders were carried out at three different locations in the townlet. For two weeks after the Soviets' withdrawal, no official body ruled Szczuczyn. On June 28, 1941, Poles murdered about 300 Jews there, without using firearms; the Poles threw the bodies into anti-tank ditches near the townlet. The victims included entire families, especially well-to-do and educated Jews. The arrival of German soldiers in the townlet put a stop to these murders.

On August 8, 1941, the Gestapo arrived in the townlet and ordered the Polish police to establish a ghetto encircled by a barbed-wire fence (according to another testimony, the ghetto was established on July 20, 1941). A fifteen-member Judenrat headed by Yona Levinovich was set up the same day, as was a Jewish Order Service with four members; at the same time, all Jewish patients in the municipal hospital were murdered in the cemetery. Shortly thereafter, Germans and Poles apparently murdered about 600 Jews in the Jewish cemetery, including Rabbi Eliyahu Zvi Efron, the community's rabbi.

Women with children and a few dozen young men were moved into the ghetto, as were artisans and the members of the Judenrat and Jewish Order Service. They lived in conditions of extreme overcrowding, with fifteen to twenty-five people to a room. Many people fell ill and died owing to the shortage of food and heating fuel.

The Szczuczyn ghetto was liquidated on November 2, 1942. The Jews were transported to the Bogusza transit camp. In December 1942 and early January 1943, they were transported on to the Treblinka and Auschwitz death camps.

SZCZUCZYN

(Nowogródek District)

**COUNTY SEAT,
NOWOGRÓDEK DISTRICT,
POLAND**

(After World War II in the
USSR/Belarus; Belarussian:
Shchuchyn; Russian:
Shchuchin)

During the war: Bezirk
Białystok

Coordinates:
53°36' | 24°45'

About 2,000 Jews were living in Szczuczyn when World War II broke out, representing more than half of the townlet's population. Most earned their livelihood from small commerce, peddling, and artisanship. Szczuczyn had chapters of Jewish parties and youth movements, a Yeshiva, and Jewish libraries.

After Szczuczyn was occupied by the Soviets on September 18, 1939, commercial activity was nationalized, private commerce was abolished, and cooperatives were formed. Jewish refugees thronged to the townlet from the areas of Poland occupied by the Germans, raising its Jewish population to about 3,000 people.

The Germans occupied Szczuczyn on June 25, 1941, and immediately hanged a Jew accused of Communism in the marketplace. From the first days of the occupation, the Jews were required to wear a yellow badge, their freedom of movement was restricted, a great deal of their property was confiscated, and many were seized for forced labor. In early July 1941, the Germans appointed a seven-member Judenrat and gave it the task of collecting ransom payments and recruiting forced laborers. A small Jewish Order Service was also established. The Jews of Szczuczyn were periodically summoned for roll calls during which they were terrorized and abused.

In late August 1941, the Jews were concentrated in an open ghetto that they were permitted to leave daily, with certain restrictions. In mid-September 1941, near the village of Topiliszki, the Germans murdered dozens of Jewish intellectuals and community leaders, including the community rabbi, Rabbi Yechiel Mechel Rabinovich. A Jewish ritual slaughterer survived the killing and returned to Szczuczyn. In late September 1941, dozens of Jewish forced laborers were marched to Ejszyszki and executed. Approximately twenty Jews living in the Szczuczyn ghetto were murdered in January 1942.

In early May 1942, the Germans fenced in the ghetto in preparation for a large-scale murder operation. The Jews were forbidden to leave the ghetto, and they were joined by another 600 Jewish laborers from the surrounding area. In a extensive operation that was carried out on May 9, 1942, some 2,000 of the ghetto's inhabitants were shot to death. Between 500 and 600 Jews were spared by the Germans in this operation, and they were concentrated in the ghetto, now reduced in size. A new Judenrat was established; it reopened the public soup kitchen and also arranged schooling for about thirty orphans.

During the following year, the Germans deported various groups of the ghetto's inhabitants to different labor camps, until the ghetto's final liquidation in the summer of 1943, when the last remaining laborers were dispatched to the Lida* ghetto. From there, they were sent on September 17, 1943, to the Majdanek concentration camp together with the Jews of Lida.

SZÉCSÉNY

**TOWNLET IN NÓGRÁD
COUNTY, HUNGARY**

Coordinates:
48°05' | 19°31'

The last national census conducted prior to the German occupation, taken in January 1941, reported 280 Jewish inhabitants in Szecseny, approximately 7 percent of the total population. Most were merchants and artisans. The townlet's Jewish community was Orthodox and maintained a Jewish elementary school.

From 1940, Jewish merchants and artisans who were competitors of the local gentiles were interned. They, and other young Jewish men, were drafted into the Hungarian army in 1941, for forced labor service.

The German army occupied Hungary on March 19, 1944. The Hungarian administration remained intact and operational after the German occupation. The ghettoization and deportation of the Jews occurred on the basis of decrees and orders issued by the Hungarian national and local authorities. On the basis of the "ghetto-decree" published by the Hungarian prime minister on April 28, 1944, the

Hungarian sub-prefect of Nograd County Sandor, Neogradi Horvath, ordered the "removal of the Jews from all the localities" of the county and their segregation in "housing estates." A "temporary settlement", that is, a ghetto, was already established in Szecseny on May 5, 1944. In addition to the local Jews, 445 Jews from the county-district of Szecseny were ordered to move into it.

The Szecseny ghetto was severely overcrowded, with sixteen to twenty people to a room. Its inhabitants were permitted to visit the townlet between one and two o'clock in the afternoon, but they were not allowed to make any purchases. With the exception of children under the age of fourteen and the elderly, all ghetto inhabitants were required to work in army depots. Nevertheless, the inhabitants were not starving and the sick received medical treatment. Jews were interrogated and tortured by the gendarmes in search of hidden valuables.

On June 1, 1944, the inhabitants of the ghetto were transferred to the ghetto in Losonc*. They were then sent on to the entrainment center of Nyirjestanya, and were deported to Auschwitz in two transports, on June 11 and 14, 1944.

SZEGED

CITY IN CSONGRÁD COUNTY, HUNGARY

Coordinates:
46°15' | 20°10'

The last national census conducted prior to the German occupation, taken in January 1941, recorded 4,161 Jewish inhabitants in Szeged, approximately 3 percent of the total population. Most were merchants; a number were clerks. The town's Jewish community was Neolog and maintained a Jewish elementary school, and various Jewish social and religious associations.

From 1930 onward, antisemitic riots and Jew-beatings organized by right-wing Christian students were common at the local university. In 1942, many Jewish men from Szeged were drafted into the Hungarian army for forced labor service. Most were sent to the eastern front in the Ukraine.

The German army occupied Hungary on March 19, 1944. A census conducted in the second week of April 1944 reported that 2,852 Jews belonged to the Neolog Jewish community of Szeged. Many of the Jews were baptized.

In April 1944, several Hungarian towns in Bacs-Bodrog County were declared zones of hostility. Jews from Zombor, Zenta, and Magyarkanizsa—altogether more than 2,200 people, among them sixty-three baptized Jews—were therefore brought to Szeged from April 27, 1944, onward. Dr. Robert Pap, a lawyer, the last serving president of the Jewish community, and head of the Central Jewish Council of the Jews of Szeged, was charged with finding buildings to accommodate the arriving Jews. Pap designated for the purpose various buildings of the Jewish community such as the old synagogue, the school, and the community headquarters. As these structures were not sufficiently large to lodge all of the Jews, a number of the inhabitants were also placed in the abandoned pigsties of the Pick Salami Factory. On May 17, 1944, nearly all of the internees were transferred to Baja*. They were deported to Gaenserndorf (near Vienna) on May 27 or 28, 1944, and then to Auschwitz.

The Hungarian administration remained intact and in force after the German occupation. The ghettoization and deportation of the Jews were carried out on the basis of the decrees and orders of the Hungarian national and local authorities. On April 29, 1944, Dr. Sandor Tukats, the prefect of Szeged, ordered Bela Toth, the deputy mayor of Szeged, to begin preparations for the establishment of a ghetto in the city. On May 17, 1944, Toth ordered the establishment of a ghetto in one contiguous block around the synagogue. Jews who had converted to Christianity were placed in a separate block of houses within the ghetto. That day, Dr. Pap addressed a petition to the mayor in which he requested a space of seven to eight square meters per person, permission to establish a hospital, and

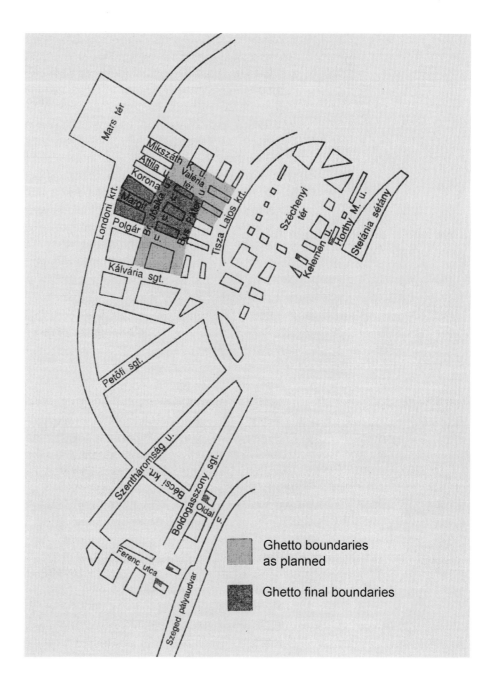

Szeged ghetto plan, reconstructed
(Molnar Judit, *Zsidósors 1944-ben*, Cserépfalui Kiadó 1995)

the settling of the issue of the furniture left behind in the Jews' homes. Dr. Pap also suggested that Jews with a Christian spouse be permitted to remain in their own apartments, with their entire families.

The process of moving into the ghetto lasted for eight days beginning on May 22, 1944. The ghetto was overcrowded, with three to eight people to a room. Each person had scarcely more than two square meters of living space. Jews with a Christian spouse were required to move into the ghetto only on the last day of the moving-in process. About 500 converted Jews were also compelled to move into the ghetto, but they were put up in special houses within its grounds. The deputy mayor permitted the establishment of a hospital.

The severely overcrowded ghetto nevertheless had insufficient space to contain every Jew. Thus, the deputy mayor designated a second ghetto, and at the end of May 1944, the first ghetto was also enlarged. Altogether 3,827 people were confined in the Szeged ghettos. A forty-member Jewish Order Service, led by Sandor Gerle, was established. On June 10, the authorities discontinued supplying gas and water to the ghetto.

The ghettos of Szeged were evacuated between June 16 and 20, 1944, following body searches by midwives and physicians in search of hidden valuables. Altogether 3,095 of their inhabitants (Jews who were married to non-Jews and several others were exempted) were moved to the Szeged entrainment center, which was located in a brick factory and initially also in the nearby sports complex; thirty-four Jews died on the night before the transfer, eighteen of whom committed suicide. The living conditions in the brick factory, in which eventually more than 8,000 people from various ghettos were packed together, were very poor, exacerbated by an acute shortage of water. The commander of the brick factory was the gendarme captain Imre Finta. Franz Abromeit commanded the SS.

The Jews were deported from the brick factory in several transports between June 25 and 28, 1944, to either Auschwitz or Strasshof, Austria. One car from the final transport was detached from the train in Budapest*. The sixty-six Jews who were on the car were selected to leave Hungary on the Kasztner train. One of the passengers was the ninety-one-year-old Rabbi Dr. Immanuel Low, the world-famous rabbi of Szeged. Low died in the Jewish Hospital in Budapest several weeks later.

SZEGHALOM

TOWNLET IN BÉKÉS COUNTY, HUNGARY

Coordinates:
47°02' | 21°10'

The last national census conducted prior to the German occupation, taken in January 1941, recorded 159 Jewish inhabitants in Szeghalom, approximately 2 percent of the total population, and most were merchants and artisans. The townlet had a Neolog Jewish community and several Jewish associations.

The German army occupied Hungary on March 19, 1944. As of the following day, local Jews were forbidden to leave Szeghalom. A census conducted in the second week of April 1944 showed that 140 Jews belonged to the Neolog Jewish community of Szeghalom.

The Hungarian administration remained intact and in force after the occupation. The ghettoization and deportation of the Jews were carried out on the basis of the decrees and orders of the Hungarian national and local authorities. The Szeghalom ghetto was established in the buildings surrounding the synagogue, according to a decree published on May 26, 1944, by the chief administrative officer of the county-district of Szeghalom, Dr. Bela Toth. Aside from the local Jews, the Jews from the Szeghalom County-District were confined in the ghetto. The men slept without shelter owing to the overcrowded conditions.

In mid-June 1944, the ghetto inhabitants were transferred to the entrainment center of Bekescsaba*. On June 25, 1944, most of the Jews were deported on to Strasshof, Austria, via the entrainment center of Szolnok*. Those who remained in Bekescsaba were deported to Auschwitz on June 26, 1944.

SZÉKESFEHÉRVÁR

COUNTY SEAT IN FEJÉR COUNTY, HUNGARY

Coordinates:
47°12' | 18°25'

The last national census conducted in Hungary prior to the German occupation, taken in January 1941, recorded 2,075 Jewish inhabitants in Szekesfehervar, representing roughly 4 percent of the total population. Most were merchants and artisans. The town had both Neolog and Orthodox Jewish communities, various Jewish aid organizations, a Jewish school, and a Talmud Torah.

From 1940, Szekesfehervar functioned as an enlistment center where approximately 12,000 Jews, including local men, were enlisted for forced labor service into the Hungarian army. They worked in agriculture in the vicinity of the town. After about two months, elderly people were released. In 1942, also drafted for forced labor were 250 Jewish youths from Szekesfehervar; they were sent to Komarom*. After a few months, many of them were deployed to the eastern front, in the Ukraine, where the majority of them perished. At the beginning of 1943, living in the town and its vicinity were 7,018 forced laborers.

The German army occupied Hungary on March 19, 1944. According to a census conducted in the second week of April 1944, about 1,500 Jews belonged to the Neolog Jewish community, and 230 Jews to the Orthodox Jewish community of Szekesfehervar.

Soon after the occupation, the Gestapo made its appearance in the town, arrested more than fifty Jews, and demanded 120,000 pengo (Hungarian currency) from the Jewish communities.

The Hungarian administration remained intact and operational after the occupation. Hungarian national and local authorities decreed the ghettoization and deportation of the Jews. The Hungarian sub-prefect of Fejer County, Andor Thaisz, boasted that in his county, "not a single Christian had to move out of his home." Most of the Jews in the county were required to move together into Jewish houses that were selected by the mayor of Szekesfehervar, Lajos Kerekes, and marked with yellow stars. Between May 23 and 31, 1944, altogether 2,148 Jews—654 Jewish families, 110 of which had converted to Christianity—moved into the ghetto, whose houses were scattered all around the town. The move was organized by the Jewish Council, headed by Dr. Imre Neuhauser, a lawyer and the last serving president of the Neolog Jewish community. A curfew was imposed between eight o'clock at night and five in the morning. A wedding between a thirty-seven-year-old forced laborer and a local Jewish woman was held in the ghetto.

Between June 1 and 5, 1944, the inhabitants of the ghetto were systematically brought to the local headquarters of the Gestapo, where gendarmes tortured them into revealing the whereabouts of their hidden valuables. The Roman Catholic bishop Lajos Shovy attempted to persuade Hungarian officials to put a stop to the torture and intervened on behalf of converted Jews, but to no avail. On June 5, 1944, the mayor ordered the Jewish Council to demolish the towers of the synagogue.

On the morning of June 6, the inhabitants of the ghetto were ordered to begin evacuation. They were transferred by the Hungarian gendarmes in a cruel manner to the entrainment center in the Szabo brick factory, beside the railway, where they were kept with neither water nor shelter. A few days later, they were deported to Auschwitz.

On June 23, 1944, Jews living in mixed marriages and their children were confined in the stud farm in Szekesfehervar. They were transferred to the entrainment center of Kecskemet* through to June 5, 1944, and deported on to Auschwitz.

SZEKLENCE

TOWNLET IN MÁRAMAROS COUNTY, HUNGARY
(After World War II in the USSR/Ukraine; Ukrainian: **Sokyrnytsya**; Russian: **Sokirnitsa**)

Coordinates:
48°07' | 23°23'

The last national census conducted in Hungary prior to the German occupation, taken in January 1941, recorded 685 Jewish inhabitants in Szeklence, making up approximately 19 percent of the total population. Most were merchants and artisans. According to the 1941 census, the vast majority of the Jews in Szeklence declared their mother tongue to be Yiddish. The townlet's Jewish community was Orthodox.

After World War I, Szeklence, which was formerly in Hungary, became part of Romania. After August 30, 1940, the townlet again became an integral part of the Hungarian civil administration, whose anti-Jewish legislation was enforced more harshly in North Transylvania, where Szeklence was located, than in inner Hungary.

The German army occupied Hungary on March 19, 1944. The Hungarian administration remained intact and in force after the occupation. The ghettoization and deportation of the Jews were implemented on the basis of the decrees and orders of the Hungarian national and local authorities. The ghetto in Szeklence was established in the second half of April 1944 and held the Jews of the nearby villages as well. The Germans devised various ways to humiliate the Jews in it. Hungarian gendarmes guarded the ghetto, and a Jewish Order Service was set up to maintain internal order. A Jewish Council ran a soup kitchen. Both men and women were assigned to work outside of the ghetto.

On May 15, 1944, the inhabitants of the ghetto were gathered in the courtyards of one of the local schools. They were subjected to a thorough body search and then marched on foot to the train station of nearby Szaldobos, and deported to Auschwitz.

SZENDRŐ

TOWNLET IN BORSOD COUNTY, HUNGARY

Coordinates:
48°24' | 20°44'

The last national census conducted prior to the German occupation, taken in January 1941, recorded 233 Jewish inhabitants in Szendro, accounting for roughly 7 percent of the total population. Most of the Jews were merchants and artisans. The townlet's Jewish community was Orthodox and maintained a Jewish elementary school, a Talmud Torah, and a Yeshiva.

In 1938, a few local Jews were arrested and taken to the internment camp in Nagykanizsa*. In 1942, fifteen prominent members of the Jewish community were arrested and held in the internment camp of Kistarcsa, according to the order of the antisemitic mayor of the townlet. They were released after several months of captivity, but were immediately drafted into Hungarian forced labor service together with many Jewish men from Szendro. Most of them died on the eastern front, in the Ukraine.

The German army occupied Hungary on March 19, 1944. A census conducted in the second week of April 1944 reported that 228 Jews belonged to the Orthodox Jewish community of Szendro.

The Hungarian administration remained intact and in force after the occupation. The ghettoization and deportation of the Jews were carried out on the basis of the decrees and orders of the Hungarian national and local authorities. The Hungarian sub-prefect of Borsod County, Dr. Gyula Mikuleczky, ordered the establishment of the ghettos in the county on May 13, 1944. On May 18, 1944, the Hungarian chief administrative officer of the county-district of Edeleny, Emil Bizony, ordered the local Jews to move into the Edeleny* and Szendro ghettos. The former mine and distillation plant buildings and their vicinity were marked out for the Szendro ghetto. Local Jews and Jews from the surrounding area, altogether about 400 people, were held in its grounds. A bakery whose owner and building were both within the ghetto, supplied the inhabitants with bread.

A Jewish Council was established, headed by Jeno Groszmann, the last serving president of the Jewish community, as well as a Jewish Order Service consisting of fifteen to twenty policemen armed with batons. A fifteen-bed hospital operated within the ghetto. The Jews were permitted to write strictly Hungarian-language letters on unsealed postcards. They could receive similar letters addressed to the "Jewish ghetto."

At the beginning of June 1944, the inhabitants of the ghetto were taken to an entrainment center in the brick factory on Tatar Street in Miskolc*. A number of the Jews were then transferred to the Diosgyor* ghetto and a few days later, on June 12, 1944, were deported to Auschwitz. Those who remained in the brick factory were deported to Auschwitz on June 13 and 15, 1944.

SZENTENDRE

TOWN IN PEST-PILIS-SOLT-KISKUN COUNTY, HUNGARY

Coordinates:
47°40' | 19°05'

The last national census conducted prior to the German occupation, taken in January 1941, recorded 206 Jewish inhabitants in Szentendre, accounting for approximately 2 percent of the total population, comprising mainly ethnic Germans (Swabians). Most of the Jews traded in vines and vegetables or were vine-growers. The town's Jewish community was Neolog and maintained a Jewish school. During the White Terror following World War I, the majority population repeatedly assaulted the local Jews.

In 1940, Szentendre became a drafting center for forced labor service in the Hungarian army. Jewish men were called up and were deployed to the eastern front, in the Ukraine, where many perished.

The German army occupied Hungary on March 19, 1944. German units arrived in Szentendre on April 10, 1944, and shot five local Jews. A census conducted in the second week of April 1944 reported that 170 Jews belonged to the Neolog Jewish community of Szentendre.

The Hungarian administration remained intact and operational after the German occupation. The ghettoization and deportation of the Jews occurred on the basis of decrees and orders issued by the Hungarian national and local authorities. At the end of April 1944, the Jews of Szentendre were required to move together into a few designated houses. Their ghettoization took place prior to the publication of the decree ordering the establishment of ghettos in the county on May 12, 1944. Since Jews were not permitted to leave the Szentendre ghetto under any circumstances, they soon began to starve.

On June 30, 1944, the residents of the ghetto were transferred to Bekasmegyer*, to one of the entrainment centers for the ghettos of Pest-Pilis-Solt-Kiskun County surrounding Budapest* from the north. They were deported to Auschwitz between July 6 and 8, 1944.

SZENTES

COUNTY SEAT IN CSONGRÁD COUNTY, HUNGARY

Coordinates:
46°39' | 20°16'

The last national census conducted prior to the German occupation recorded, in January 1941, 510 Jewish inhabitants in Szentes, approximately 2 percent of the total population. Most were merchants and artisans; a number were clerks. The town's Jewish community was Neolog, and maintained a Jewish elementary school and a Talmud Torah.

The German army occupied Hungary on March 19, 1944. A census conducted in the second week of April 1944 showed that 464 Jews belonged to the Neolog Jewish community of Szentes. In April 1944, the Germans arrested several prominent members of the Jewish community and confined them in the Topolya internment camp; they were deported on to Auschwitz.

The Hungarian administration remained intact and in force after the occupation. The ghettoization and deportation of the Jews were carried out on the basis of the decrees and orders of the Hungarian national and local authorities. Andor Dobay, the Hungarian sub-prefect of Csongrad County, commanded on May 6, 1944, the establishment of ghettos in his county. The mayor of Szentes, Dr. Sandor Kanasz-Nagy, ordered the Jews to move into a ghetto on the outskirts of the town between May 9 and 12, 1944. The groups of Jews moving into the ghetto were unloaded from carts by forced laborers. Rabbi Dr. Jozsef Berend, the rabbi of the Jewish community, was appointed president of the Jewish Council.

On June 16, the Jews from the Szentes ghetto, altogether 398 people, were transferred to the entrainment center in Szeged* following a cruel body search. From Szeged they were deported, along with many other Jews, to Auschwitz and to Strasshof, Austria, on June 25, 27, and 28, 1944.

SZENTGOTTHÁRD

TOWNLET IN VAS COUNTY, HUNGARY

Coordinates:
46°57' | 16°17'

The last national census conducted prior to the German occupation, taken in January 1941, recorded 134 Jewish inhabitants in Szentgotthard, roughly 4 percent of the total population. Most of the Jews were merchants and artisans. The townlet's Jewish community was Neolog.

After the German occupation of Hungary on March 19, 1944, the Hungarian administration remained intact and in force. The ghettoization and deportation of the Jews were carried out on the basis of the decrees and orders of the Hungarian national and local authorities. On May 6, 1944, the Hungarian sub-prefect, Dr. Jozsef Tulok, published a decree designating May 12 as the deadline for moving the Jews into ghettos. Based on the decree, the ghetto in Szentgotthard was established in the barracks of the local scythe factory; 119 local Jews and 30 from the vicinity were required to move into the ghetto on May 10–11, 1944, with two to three families to a room. A Christian physician who was granted a permit from the authorities to enter the ghetto offered medical treatment to the Jews.

In mid-June 1944, the inhabitants of the ghetto were transferred to the premises of the Mayer Engine and Machine Factory Share Company in Szombathely*, which served as an entrainment center. They were deported to Auschwitz on July 4 and 6, 1944.

SZILÁGYSOMLYÓ

(in Jewish sources: **Somlyó**)

TOWNLET IN SZILÁGY COUNTY, HUNGARY
(After World War II in Romania; Romanian: **Şimleul Silvaniei**)

Coordinates:
47°14' | 22°48'

The last national census conducted in Hungary prior to the German occupation, taken in January 1941, recorded 1,496 Jewish inhabitants in Szilagysomlyo, comprising approximately 17 percent of the total population. Most were merchants and artisans; several Jews owned factories and model farms. The townlet had an Orthodox Jewish community, within which a Sephardic community operated its own prayer house. Educational institutions included two Jewish schools (for boys and for girls), a Talmud Torah, and a Yeshiva.

After World War I, Szilagysomlyo, which was formerly in Hungary, became part of Romania. In August 30, 1940, Szilagysomlyo once again became an integral part of the Hungarian civil administration. The Hungarian anti-Jewish legislation that applied to the local Jews was enforced more harshly in North Transylvania, where Szilagysomlyo was located, than in inner Hungary.

In the summer of 1941, the Hungarian authorities deported several Jewish families that could not prove their Hungarian citizenship to German-occupied Ukraine. They were murdered on August 27 or 28 at Kamenets-Podolsk*. In 1942, many Jewish men from Szilagysomlyo were drafted into the Hungarian army for forced labor service. Most were deployed to Ukraine, where many perished.

The German army occupied Hungary on March 19, 1944. According to a census conducted in the second week of April 1944, about 1,300 Jews belonged to the Orthodox Jewish community of Szilagysomlyo.

The Hungarian administration remained intact and in force after the occupation. The ghettoization and deportation of the Jews were implemented on the basis of the decrees and orders of the Hungarian national and local authorities. Following an April 26, 1944, conference regarding ghettoization in North Transylvania, the ghetto of Szilagysomlyo was established on May 3, 1944, in the Klein Brick Factory situated near the road leading from Szilagysomlyo to Somlyocsehi. Ultimately, the entire Jewish population of Szilagy County, some 8,500 people, were concentrated in the ghetto. Inhabitants suffered from a shortage of both water and food. The brick sheds had no walls and the territory of the brick factory was muddy. Only the women, the elderly, and the ill had roofed accommodation.

The notorious commander of the ghetto, Dr. Laszlo Krasznay, forbade prayers in the ghetto, and when the elderly rabbi of Szilagysomlyo, Rabbi Samuel (Shlomo Zalman) Ehrenreich was caught engaged in prayer in a prayer shawl, Krasznay ordered the rabbi's hands to be bound behind his back and hanged him in a tree by his tied hands. Krasznay also hosted orgies for his friends in the ghetto, in which Jewish girls were sexually humiliated and abused. The inhabitants of the ghetto were habitually interrogated and tortured into revealing the whereabouts of their hidden valuables.

Two groups escaped from the ghetto. One group comprised five young boys and girls who were hidden by Romanian peasants and who survived. Another group of Jews fled to the nearby forest; as they were denounced by locals, only one person survived.

The inhabitants of the ghetto were deported to Auschwitz between May 31 and June 6, 1944.

SZOLNOK

COUNTY SEAT IN JÁSZ-NAGYKUN-SZOLNOK COUNTY, HUNGARY

Coordinates:
47°11' | 20°12'

The last national census conducted in Hungary prior to the German occupation, taken in January 1941, recorded 2,590 Jewish inhabitants in Szolnok, roughly 6 percent of the total population. Most were merchants and artisans, many were also clerks. The town had a Neolog Jewish community, an Orthodox Prayer Association, a Jewish school, a Talmud Torah, and several Jewish religious and social associations. During the days of the Hungarian Soviet Republic following World War I, several local Jews were arrested and seven were executed. The ensuing White Terror claimed three more Jewish victims.

In 1940, the community's cultural center was expropriated by the army and was transformed into an enlistment center for forced laborers. In 1941, Jewish men aged eighteen to fifty-five were drafted into the Hungarian army for forced labor service. Many were deployed in 1942 to the eastern front, to the Ukraine, where they died. Between 1939 and 1942, forced laborers from other parts of the country were working under poor conditions in Szolnok and its vicinity.

The German army occupied Hungary on March 19, 1944. A census conducted in the second week of April 1944 reported that 1,359 Jews belonged to the Neolog Jewish community of Szolnok.

In March and April 1944, the Germans and the Hungarians arrested and interned several prominent Szolnok Jews as well as Jewish members of the underground Social Democrats' Party; most were transferred to the internment camp at Hajduszentgyorgypuszta near Debrecen*.

The Szolnok Jewish Council, consisting of leading community officials and headed by Dr. Sandor Mandel, was active within a few days of the German occupation.

The Hungarian administration remained intact and operational after the occupation. The ghettoization and deportation of the Jews were carried out on the basis of the decrees and orders of the Hungarian national and local authorities. On May 1, 1944, the Hungarian sub-prefect, Imre Alexander, published a decree ordering the ghettoization of the Jews in the county. The mayor, Ferenc Szabó, designated for the ghetto the buildings of the Jewish community, including the synagogue and its vicinity. He also charged the Jewish Council with moving Jews into the ghetto. The process took place between May 15 and 22; 1,070 people, including converts to Christianity, were concentrated into the ghetto. Each person was allowed to bring along fifty kilograms of luggage. Dr. Mandel and his wife were permitted to remain in their home outside the ghetto. The internal order of the ghetto was maintained by the Jewish Order Service, headed by Jeno Schenker. The bread supply to the ghetto was provided by Lipot Schwarcz's bakery, which was situated within the ghetto boundaries. Men from the ghetto were called up for forced labor service, and were thus saved from immediate deportation.

On May 20 and 21, 1944, Szolnok Jews, 144 in number, and 78 people from the area were moved into a second ghetto, which was located in a distillery in Szandapuszta, near the town. They were lodged in the hayloft of the cattle-shed rather than the previously designated distillery building. The Hungarian gendarme officer Antal Szekely was the commander of the second ghetto. A three-member committee was appointed by the Szolnok Jewish Council to serve as the local Jewish Council; among its members was the ghetto's physician, Gyorgy Gyarfas. The committee appealed to the mayor in a petition on May 24, 1944, protesting the appalling conditions; the authorities granted them two cauldrons for cooking. After June 5, 1944, the able-bodied were allowed to work on the nearby Simay estate, in exchange for a small amount of food.

At the end of May, Dr. Mandel also appealed to the mayor in a petition concerning the part of the ghetto located in the inner town. By this time, as 400 poor Jews had moved into the ghetto without provisions, its food supply had dwindled.

On June 16, 1944, the inhabitants of both parts of the Szolnok ghetto were transferred to the entrainment center at the town sugar factory, which held many Jews from other ghettos. They were all interrogated and tortured into revealing the whereabouts of their hidden valuables; twenty-nine people perished, many succumbing to the torment.

On June 25, 1944, the first transport, containing 2,628 people, left the sugar factory for Strasshof, Austria. They worked on farms and in factories in various localities in eastern Austria and in Vienna. The families lived together in camps.

On June 28, 1944, the second transport left the Szolnok sugar factory, carrying 2,083 deportees to Auschwitz.

SZOMBATHELY

(In Jewish sources: **Steinamanger**)

COUNTY SEAT IN VAS COUNTY, HUNGARY

Coordinates:
47°14' | 16°37'

The last national census conducted prior to the German occupation, taken in January 1941, recorded 3,088 Jewish inhabitants in Szombathely, accounting for roughly 7 percent of the total population. Most were merchants and artisans, and many were clerks. The town had both a Neolog and an Orthodox Jewish community, each with various affiliated Jewish social and religious associations, as well as a Jewish elementary school. Zionism became increasingly popular during World War I and in its aftermath, when Jewish refugees arrived from Galicia. During the interwar period, Zionist ideas spread in Szombathely, mainly due to the activities of the Neolog rabbi, Rabbi Dr. Jozsef Horovitz.

During the period of the White Terror following World War I, anti-Jewish riots in the town claimed the lives of several Jews.

In 1942, the majority of young Jewish men were drafted into the Hungarian army for forced labor service; many perished.

The German army occupied Hungary on March 19, 1944. According to a census conducted in the second week of April 1944, about 1,800 Jews belonged to the Neolog Jewish community and 1,068 to the Orthodox Jewish community of Szombathely.

On March 19, 1944, an SS armored regiment led by Standartenfuehrer Baecker entered Szombathely. In the following days a Jewish Council was nominated, headed by Mano Valyi. The SS officer, Heinz von Arndt, the local commander of the Eichmann Sonderkommando, refused to communicate with Valyi. A new ten-member Jewish Council was established, headed by Dr. Imre Wesel.

The Germans arrested Wesel on April 24, 1944, and sent him to the internment camp of Nagykanizsa for refusing to satisfy the incessant German requests for

Szombathely, June 30, 1944
The Jews of the ghetto are transferred to an engine factory near the train station and then deported to Auschwitz on July 4, 1944. (YV)

various goods and supplies. Arndt again changed the membership of the Jewish Council on April 25, and appointed Ferenc Zalan president. From that time forward, aside from a daily list of requests, the Germans also demanded laborers.

The Hungarian administration remained intact and in force after the occupation. The ghettoization and deportation of the Jews were carried out on the basis of the decrees and orders of the Hungarian national and local authorities. On May 6, 1944, the Hungarian sub-prefect, Dr. Jozsef Tulok, published a decree designating May 12 as the deadline for moving the Jews into ghettos. The mayor of Szombathely, Dr. Hugo Meszaros, designated the territory of the ghetto on May 8, 1944, in the inner city around the synagogues. The Jews of the city, 2,615 people (926 families), and the Jews from the vicinity, 103 people (sixteen families), were required to move into the ghetto between May 9 and 12, 1944.

Jewish converts to Christianity wished to live in a separate block in the ghetto, a request denied by the Jewish Council. The council did however set up a chapel for the converts, and a Franciscan monk was granted an entrance permit for the observance of Sunday mass.

Life in the ghetto was controlled by the ghetto regulations issued by the head of the police department of Szombathely, Dr. Geza Russay. A Jewish Order Service was formed. The mayor ordered the establishment of a maternity home, an old-age home, a hospital, and a hospital for infectious diseases.

The local police raided the ghetto for the first time on May 22, in search of hidden valuables. The raid was led by police officer Dr. Kalman Fordos. Several raids followed the first, in the second half of June and beginning of July. The policemen of Szombathely also interrogated and tortured the inhabitants of the ghetto in one of the Jewish school buildings; cash, jewels, and other valuables worth millions were confiscated.

The food supplies of the ghetto were exhausted by the second half of June. The Jewish Council appealed to the municipality for assistance numerous times, but their pleas were ignored. The Roman Catholic bishop of Szombathely, Sandor Kovacs, firmly protested against the anti-Jewish measures, and he saved a number of Jews.

As of June 28, 1944, the Jews were transferred from the Szombathely ghetto to the premises of the Mayer Engine and Machine Factory Share Company, which was used as an entrainment center. Until June 20, the Jews from the various ghettos of Vas County (Kormend*, Koszeg*, Szentgotthard*, and Vasvar*), and from a nearby settlement called Beled in Sopron County, were also brought to the center.

Neither water nor cooking facilities were available on the premises. The local authorities twice delivered cooked food, enough to feed several hundred people.

The approximately 3,000 Jews who were concentrated in the entrainment center were deported to Auschwitz on July 4 and 6, 1944.

SZUMSK

TOWNLET IN KRZEMIENIEC COUNTY, VOLHYNIA DISTRICT, POLAND
(After World War II in the USSR/Ukraine; Ukrainian: **Shums'ke**; Russian: **Shumskoye**)

During the war: Reichskommissariat Ukraine

Coordinates: 50°07' | 26°07'

During the interwar period, about 1,700 Jews lived in Szumsk, approximately three-quarters of the townlet's population. Some were grain and lumber merchants and artisans. Others owned food processing plants, including flour mills and factories that manufactured construction materials. They received financial assistance from a savings-and-loan association and a mutual aid society. Szumsk's children attended a Tarbut kindergarten and school that taught in Hebrew. Inhabitants enjoyed a large public library and a drama group. Zionist parties and youth movements held activities in the townlet.

The Soviets took control of the area in September 1939. The Germans occupied Szumsk on July 5, 1941. Five days later, Ukrainians and German soldiers murdered several Jews and looted Jewish property. On July 17, a German military administration was established in the townlet, and the pillaging and murders ceased.

All Jewish valuables, including furs and warm clothing, were confiscated in the early days of the occupation. The Jews were forced to wear Star-of-David armbands and were conscripted for forced labor. A Judenrat was established under Rabbi Yosef Rabin, who was soon replaced by a German-speaking refugee from Katowice. A forty-member Jewish Order Service was set up.

Jewish inhabitants were themselves required to provide the funding for the March 3, 1942, establishment of the fenced-in ghetto in Szumsk. The Judenrat opened a soup kitchen and a hospital in the ghetto. Jews from villages in the vicinity were brought in. During the ensuing months, the ghetto Jews were charged frequent ransoms in valuables and crops. When the Jews were unable to meet one such demand in early June 1942, thirty were murdered.

The Szumsk ghetto was besieged on August 9, 1942. It was liquidated on August 18, and its 1,792 Jewish inhabitants (a population figure cited in a German report) were taken to pits outside the townlet on the road to the village of Krylich and murdered. Several young Jews resisted, with one killing a Ukrainian policeman. The following day, about 1,000 Ukrainians broke into and looted the ghetto homes, and Jews found in hiding were largely turned in to the Germans. The Germans left about 100 Jews in the ghetto to gather the belongings of those murdered; another roughly fifty inhabitants remained in hiding.

On September 9, 1942, the Germans began to murder the ghetto's rump Jewish population. Several of those who attempted escape were shot dead as they fled. Of the fifteen inmates who had attempted to escape a day before the murder operation, nearly all succeeded.

Ukrainian Baptists and Polish villagers sheltered approximately sixty Jews. Several of the survivors joined the Soviet partisan units.

SZYDŁÓW

TOWNLET IN BUSKO COUNTY, KIELCE DISTRICT, POLAND

During the war: General Gouvernement, Radom District

Coordinates:
50°36' | 21°00'

About 660 Jews lived in Szydlow after World War I, representing roughly one-quarter of the townlet's population. Most earned their livelihood from commerce and artisanship. The townlet had a chapter of the Zionist movement.

In September 1939, Szydlow was occupied by the Germans, who confiscated Jewish property and seized Jews for forced labor. The synagogue was demolished.

In May 1940, a Judenrat was established in Szydlow. Later, the Germans moved Jewish refugees from Plock* into the townlet. The German invasion of the Soviet Union in the summer of 1941 led to a rise in the Jewish population of Szydlow to about 1,500. The Judenrat operated a public soup kitchen with the assistance of the JSS in Cracow*.

On January 1, 1942, a ghetto was established in Szydlow, which the Jews were only permitted to leave for work. In the winter of 1941/42, rampant starvation in the ghetto contributed to a high mortality rate.

The ghetto was liquidated in early October 1942. After SS men and Ukrainian auxiliary forces surrounded the ghetto, the Jews were rounded up in the townlet square. A number of people attempted to hide in attics or basements, but most were caught and murdered on the spot. About 1,000 of the ghetto's Jews were transferred to the Chmielnik* ghetto, and a few days later were deported to the Treblinka death camp.

SZYDŁOWIEC

TOWN IN THE KONSKIE COUNTY, KIELCE DISTRICT, POLAND

During the war: General Gouvernement

Coordinates:
51°14' | 20°51'

On the eve of World War II, about 7,200 Jews lived in Szydlowiec, representing approximately three-quarters of the town's population. They earned their livelihood mainly from the garment, food, and construction industries. Among the Jews were owners of flour mills and quarries as well as large-scale merchants. The town had two Jewish banks and Jewish trade unions, most of whose members belonged to the Bund.

Zionist parties were active in Szydlowiec, as was Agudath Israel. Most of the community's children received Jewish and religious instruction in the afternoon hours. The town had twenty private Hadarim, a Talmud Torah, a Po'alei Zion Hebrew school, a Beit Yaakov school for girls, and a small Yavne school.

The Germans occupied Szydlowiec on September 9, 1939, and immediately instituted a regime of forced labor and persecution. The local synagogue was burned

Szydlowiec
Jewish policemen lined up next to the Judenrat building (YV)

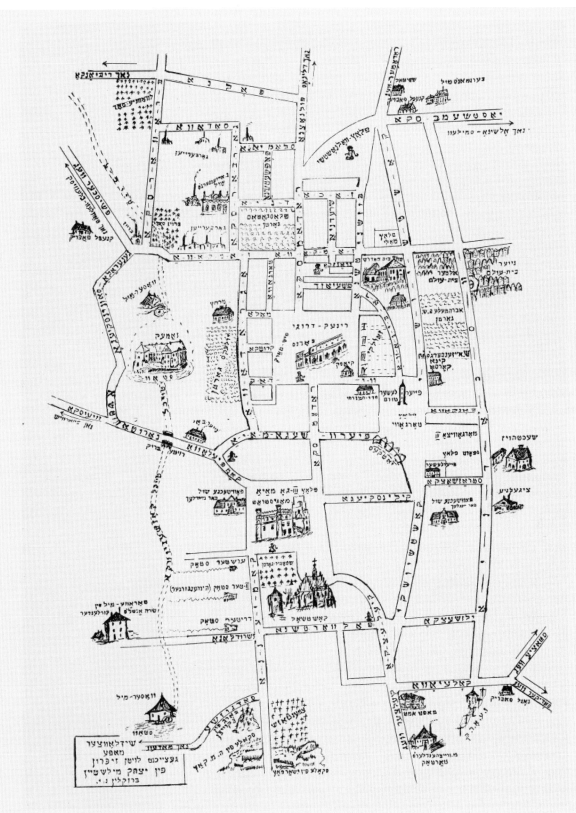

Szydlowiec illustrated plan, illustrated by Yitzhak Milshtein, based on his memory
(*Shidlovtser Yizkor Book*, published by Irgun Yotzey Szydłowiec in New York, 1974)

Left: **Szydlowiec,
September 23, 1942**
Jews marched from the ghetto
to the train station and then
deported to Treblinka (YV)

down. Within a few days, a Judenrat was appointed with a Betar activist, Avraham Redlich, as chairman. A labor bureau headed by Yechiel Zuker and Kalman Rosenboim was also set up as well as a Jewish Order Service under the command of a refugee from Cracow* named Ostroveitz. The Germans straight away imposed a series of restrictions on the Jews, including a nighttime curfew, the requirement to wear a special armband, and a prohibition against practicing any public religious rituals. Jews, mainly young men, were periodically seized for forced labor.

In August 1940, SS officers from Lublin sent groups of Jews from Szydlowiec to the Wolanow, Janiszow, and Jozefow labor camps.

The leaders of the Judenrat determined early on that in forging personal ties with the various occupation officials in Radom*, and in offering them steady bribes, they might improve the lot of the local Jews. Two members of the Judenrat traveled by train every day to Radom, where they presented money and "gifts" to various leading administrative officials and their associates. The secretary of the Szydlowiec Judenrat, Avraham Finkler, related in his testimony that he regularly transferred money and valuables to the district governor's young mistress, who in return extended considerable assistance to the Jews of Szydlowiec. The decision to establish the ghetto was published in December 1941, and confirmed on April 27, 1942. The original plan was to move the town's Jews, who represented 80 to 90 percent of Szydlowiec's population, into an overcrowded area; however, following the intervention of the district governor's lover, the entire town with the exception of two streets was turned into an open ghetto, allowing the Jews of Szydlowiec a decent standard of living. These relatively favorable conditions earned the town renown beyond its borders, attracting throngs of Jewish refugees from the surrounding localities, who thus raised the Jewish population of the town to more than 10,000. About 4,000 of these inhabitants were refugees, for whom the Judenrat opened a public soup kitchen. By the beginning of 1942, the Jews numbered about 12,000.

The personal ties that the heads of the Judenrat forged with the German occupation officials in Radom led to the release of hundreds of young Jews working as forced laborers in the nearby Janiszow camp.

On September 3, 1942, fifty Jews from Szydlowiec were sent to the Skarzysko-Kamienna labor camp.

On September 23, 1942, the ghetto was encircled by Lithuanians and Ukrainians, Polish police, and local firefighters, under the command of the SS Obersturmführer Matilka and Franz Schippers. The inhabitants of the ghetto were rounded up. The patients of the Jewish hospital, which was located in the synagogue, were among the first to be executed. Some 10,000 ghetto Jews were marched several kilometers to the train station and deported to the Treblinka death camp. Close to 5,000 people were herded onto an abandoned, ruined estate on the outskirts of the town; two days later, they were also deported to Treblinka. About 100 Jews who futilely paid a ransom in exchange for their release were among them. Another approximately 600 Jews who were caught in various hiding places were executed.

About 600 Jews remained in Szydlowiec, including the Jewish policemen, Jews who had come out of hiding, and workers employed in the factory or assigned the task of collecting the belongings of the deportees and burying the hundreds of bodies.

During November 1942, the last Jews of Szydlowiec were transferred to the Skarzysko-Kamienna labor camp.

In December 1942, the Germans reestablished a ghetto in the leather-tanning factory in Szydlowiec and instructed the surviving Jews to move into the premises, threatening anyone caught outside the ghetto boundaries with death. Within a short time, about 5,000 Jews from nearby localities had been rounded up into the new ghetto, whose two separate quarters were encircled by a barbed-wire fence, while another 1,000 deportees were brought in from Radom. The Germans appointed a new Judenrat, which was headed by Shmuel Weissbrot. Lack of water, very meager food rations, and overcrowding led to an epidemic typhus outbreak. Many perished.

A few days before the ghetto's liquidation, hundreds of exhausted prisoners from the Hasag camp in the Skarzysko-Kamienna labor camp were brought to the ghetto and were replaced by some 1,000 Jewish youths. On January 8, 1943, the ghetto was encircled, and on January 13, SS men entered the ghetto. About eighty people were murdered on the spot. The rest of the Jews were deported to the Treblinka death camp.

T

Terezin ghetto, Czechoslovakia

"Dear God, what a life! Multifaceted, terrible, filled with contrasts and flowing fast, very fast. A cabaret show, on the one hand, and next to it, elderly people dying. New transports arrive daily in the city, which is capable of absorbing about 3,000 people under normal conditions. A chess game: Today, there are more than 30,000 people here. There are days in which up to 2,000 people arrive all at once. There are problems of disinfection, lice de-infestation, living space, kitchen, mattresses, manufacture of beds—a colorful mosaic of life and death." (July 18, 1942)

Seemingly Alive, Diary of Egon Redlich of the Terezin Ghetto (1942–1944), (Beit Lochamei Hagetaot, 1983) p. 105 [Hebrew].

TAB

TOWNLET IN SOMOGY COUNTY, HUNGARY

Coordinates:
46°44' | 18°02'

The last national census conducted prior to the German occupation, taken in January 1941, recorded 459 Jewish inhabitants in Tab, approximately 11 percent of the total population. Most were merchants and artisans. The town's Jewish community was Orthodox and maintained a Jewish elementary school, and a Talmud Torah.

During the period of the White Terror following World War I, the members of the detachments murdered three Jews from Tab.

The German army occupied Hungary on March 19, 1944. A census conducted in the second week of April 1944 reported that 500 Jews belonged to the Orthodox Jewish community of Tab.

The Hungarian administration remained intact and in force after the occupation. The ghettoization and deportation of the Jews were carried out on the basis of the decrees and orders of the Hungarian national and local authorities. At the beginning of May 1944, the Hungarian sub-prefect of Somogy County, Dr. Pal Stephaich, ordered the establishment of ghettos in his county. In addition to the local Jews, more than 1,100 Jews of the county-districts of Tab, Lengyeltoti, and Marcali were ordered to move into the Tab ghetto in late May 1944. The gendarmes confiscated most of the incoming Jews' valuables, including watches, watch chains and rings. The Jewish Council in Tab filed a protest, to no avail. Several people committed suicide prior to or just following the move into the ghetto. Jewish refugees from Poland, whom the local chief administrative officers were especially determined to arrest, were also confined in the Tab ghetto.

The ghetto consisted of a single street; its approximately 1,500 inhabitants lived in severely overcrowded conditions. A soup kitchen operated in it.

Men were removed from the ghetto for different kinds of agricultural labor and fieldwork. If the gendarmes supervising work determined that progress was too slow, the Jewish Council was forced to imprison every tenth laborer upon his return to the ghetto in the detention room set up within the ghetto. Later, fit men were drafted into the Hungarian army for forced labor service, and were thus saved from immediate deportation.

On July 3, 1944, the inhabitants of the ghetto were transferred to the artillery barracks in Kaposvar*, which served as one of the entrainment centers of the county. They were deported on to Auschwitz on July 4, 1944.

TAMÁSI

TOWNLET IN TOLNA COUNTY, HUNGARY

Coordinates:
46°38' | 18°17'

The last national census conducted prior to the German occupation, taken in January 1941, recorded 187 Jewish inhabitants in Tamasi, less than 3 percent of the total population. Most were merchants and artisans and several were farmers. The town's Jewish community was Neolog and maintained a small Jewish school.

The German army occupied Hungary on March 19, 1944. The Hungarian administration remained intact and operational after the German occupation. The ghettoization and deportation of the Jews were carried out on the basis of the decrees and orders of the Hungarian national and local authorities. In April 1944, the Hungarian local authorities arrested a few Jewish residents who failed to prove their Hungarian citizenship. On May 1, 1944, Edvin Szongott, the Hungarian sub-prefect of Tolna County, ordered the establishment of ghettos in his county. According to his decree, 165 local Jews and were concentrated in the Tamasi ghetto along with about 70 additional Jews from the vicinity. The houses belonging to the ghetto were marked with mandatory "canary-yellow" stars.

At the end of June or beginning of July 1944, the inhabitants of the Tamasi ghetto were transferred to the artillery barracks in Kaposvar*, which served as an entrainment center. On July 4 and 5, 1944, the 5,159 Jews concentrated in the barracks were deported to Auschwitz.

TAPOLCA

TOWNLET IN ZALA COUNTY, HUNGARY

Coordinates:
46°53' | 17°26'

The last national census conducted prior to the German occupation, taken in January 1941, recorded 508 Jewish inhabitants in Tapolca, accounting for approximately 7 percent of the total population. Most were in the wine trade dealing in the local distribution and export of the famous Badacsony wines. The local bank and all the shops in Tapolca were owned by Jews. The townlet's Jewish community was Neolog and maintained a Jewish elementary school and various other Jewish social and religious associations.

On September 2 and 9, 1919, during the period of the White Terror, the synagogue was damaged and eleven Jews were murdered during pogroms.

From 1938, the Hungarian government introduced a series of anti-Jewish laws as part of its anti-Jewish policy; among other enforced measures, licenses to trade in wine were revoked. In 1940, Jewish forced laborers drafted into the Hungarian army for forced labor service were posted in Tapolca to work in the local military airfield.

The German army occupied Hungary on March 19, 1944. A census conducted in the second week of April 1944 reported that 503 Jews belonged to the Neolog Jewish community of Tapolca.

The Hungarian administration remained intact and operational after the German occupation. The ghettoization and deportation of the Jews were carried out on the basis of the decrees and orders of the Hungarian national and local authorities. On May 4, 1944, the Hungarian sub-prefect of Zala County, Laszlo Hunyadi, ordered the establishment of a ghetto in Tapolca for the Jews living in the townlet and in the county-districts of Tapolca and Balatonfured. The decree assured for the Jews freedom of worship; each person was also allowed to bring along fifty kilograms of luggage. Hunyadi also ordered the immediate establishment of a maternity home, an old-age home, a general hospital, and a hospital for infectious diseases.

The move into the Tapolca ghetto, which was established near the synagogue, was carried out from May 17 to 22, 1944. The inhabitants of the ghetto were interrogated and tortured by the authorities into revealing the location of their hidden valuables.

In June 1944, the Jews were transferred to Zalaegerszeg*, to one of the entrainment centers of Zala County. They were deported on to Auschwitz on July 5, 1944. The forced laborers working in Tapolca remained in the townlet after the liquidation of the ghetto.

TARCZYN

TOWNLET IN GRÓJEC COUNTY, WARSAW DISTRICT, POLAND

During the war: General Gouvernement, Warsaw District

Coordinates:
51°58' | 20°50'

About 1,400 Jews lived in Tarczyn in the interwar period, representing approximately 60 percent of the local population. They earned their livelihood from small commerce, artisanship, and peddling. The community was aided by a charity fund and a chapter of TOZ, which provided medical care. The Agudath Israel Party, the Zionist parties and Zionist youth organizations, and a chapter of the Bund were active in Tarczyn.

With the approach of the German army, many of the townlet's Jews fled. Tarczyn was occupied in mid-September 1939. The Germans set fire to it, burning down one-third of the townlet's houses. The Germans appointed a Judenrat, and in either the fall of 1940 or January 1941 (testimonies vary on the date), a ghetto was established that was guarded by Poles. The Jews were employed in forced labor. The ghetto was open, and Jews bartered with Poles for food.

The ghetto was liquidated in February 1941. The Jews of Tarczyn were deported to the Warsaw* ghetto and shared the fate of its Jews: they, too, were deported to the Treblinka death camp.

TARLÓW

TOWNLET IN WIERZBNIK COUNTY, KIELCE DISTRICT, POLAND

During the war: General Gouvernement, Radom District

Coordinates:
51°00' | 21°43'

After World War I, about 1,000 Jews lived in Tarlow, roughly half of the townlet's population. They practiced petty trade and crafts; a few cultivated small parcels of land near their homes. A greater part of the community members were Orthodox, while a minority was Zionist.

The Germans occupied Tarlow in September 1939. They dispossessed the Jews, established a Judenrat responsible for turning over large sums of money in ransoms, and mobilized Jewish residents for forced labor.

The Tarlow ghetto was established in December 1941. In June 1942, seventy young Jews were sent from the ghetto to the Skarzysko-Kamienna labor camp. That fall, the Germans transferred Jews from nearby towns to the Tarlow ghetto, raising the ghetto population to approximately 7,000 people.

On October 29, 1942, the ghetto inhabitants were deported to Treblinka. More than 100 Jews were murdered in Tarlow during the deportation, and dozens who were captured in hiding were murdered at the Jewish cemetery.

TARNOBRZEG-DZIKÓW

TOWNLET IN TARNOBRZEG-DZIKÓW COUNTY, LWÓW DISTRICT, POLAND

During the war: General Gouvernement, Cracow District

Coordinates: 50°35' | 21°41'

About 2,100 Jews lived in Tarnobrzeg-Dzikow during the interwar period, representing approximately two-thirds of the townlet's population. Most earned their livelihood from commerce and artisanship in the garment, food, wood, and construction industries. A few dozen were members of the liberal professions. Tarnobrzeg-Dzikow had a Jewish Folksbank and a free-loan society. After World War I, the JDC established a public soup kitchen, distributed food and clothing, and supported a clinic and three Jewish schools. In the 1920s, most of the community's children attended Jewish schools: a Talmud Torah under the supervision of Agudath Israel, a Tarbut Hebrew school, a Hebrew Heder run by Mizrachi, and a Hebrew kindergarten. The community had three libraries at different periods as well as a Jewish sports union. Chapters of Zionist parties and youth movements were active in the townlet, and pioneer training facilities operated with scores of members.

Immediately after the war's onset, a few dozen young Jews fled to eastern Galicia.

In September 1939, the Germans occupied Tarnobrzeg-Dzikow and immediately murdered five Jews. The Germans plundered Jewish property and seized Jews for forced labor. A curfew was imposed on the townlet's Jewish inhabitants and their freedom of movement was restricted. During the first two weeks of the occupation, Jews who had been deported from nearby localities were brought to the townlet. A few days later, the Jews were rounded up and forced to sign a declaration stating that they were leaving the townlet of their own free will. Their property was seized, and a number of Jews who attempted to hide cash or valuables were murdered. After the search was completed, Jews unable to walk were murdered, while the rest were deported across the San River to the area of eastern Galicia under Soviet control. In the summer of 1940, many were exiled to the Soviet Union interior for refusing to accept Soviet citizenship.

In the summer of 1941, a labor camp was established in Tarnobrzeg-Dzikow, in which about 500 Jews from the area were imprisoned. Dozens perished from spotted fever, while others died as a result of starvation and hard labor.

In June 1941, about fifteen families that had been hiding in various localities were permitted to return to the townlet. The Jewish population of Tarnobrzeg-Dzikow gradually grew; it was mostly made up of people who had been displaced from Nisko, Jaroslaw, Rozwadow, and nearby villages. The Jews were concentrated in a quarter, which in late 1941 was turned into a ghetto.

On July 19, 1942, the Tarnobrzeg-Dzikow ghetto was liquidated and its inhabitants were transferred to Baranow*. From there they were sent to the Debica* ghetto, where they shared the fate of the ghetto's Jews—all were deported either to the Belzec or Auschwitz death camp or to labor camps in the area of Cracow.

TARNOGRÓD

TOWNLET IN BIŁGORAJ COUNTY, LUBLIN DISTRICT, POLAND

During the war: General Gouvernement, Lublin District

Coordinates: 50°22' | 22°45'

During the interwar period, some 2,500 Jews lived in Tarnogrod, about half the townlet's population. Most were petty merchants, principally in agricultural products, and artisans, chiefly in the clothing industry. The Jewish community ran traditional charitable and welfare institutions, and there was a Jewish savings-and-loan association. Tarnogrod had chapters of Zionist youth movements and parties and of Agudath Israel. Most schools were of the traditional Orthodox type.

The Germans occupied Tarnogrod on September 15, 1939. Many Jews were beaten and one was killed. Jews were forbidden to leave their homes after 6:00 p.m. and had to pay a steep ransom.

The Germans withdrew a week later and the Soviets entered, but after a four-day stay the Soviets pulled back to the demarcation line in eastern Poland set forth in the Molotov-Ribbentrop Pact. Many young Jews joined the retreating Soviet troops as the Germans returned to Tarnogrod.

Some 370 refugees from Lodz*, Wloclawek*, and Kalisz* reached Tarnogrod in December 1939. In early 1940, a Judenrat was established in the townlet, chaired by Jewish community leader Hersh Blutman. Most of its members had been active in the community before the war. The Judenrat was tasked with the mobilization of forced laborers. In early 1940, groups of young Jews were sent from Tarnogrod to the labor camp in Belzec, where they took part in building the extermination camp.

About 200 refugees from Bilgoraj* arrived in March 1941. The Judenrat established a soup kitchen for them and, until June 1941, received financial support from the JSS. By June, there were 2,730 Jews in the ghetto, including 600 laborers.

The Tarnogrod ghetto was established in May 1942, and Jews from Lukowa, Biszcza, and other villages were brought there. By the summer, its population exceeded 3,000 amid mass mortality caused by the harsh conditions.

The Germans reconstituted the Judenrat shortly after the ghetto was established. The chairman of the second Judenrat was Sinai Grauer. On August 9, 1942, deported from the ghetto to the Belzec death camp were 800 Jews, including Grauer. The Tarnogrod ghetto was liquidated on November 2, 1942. Its 2,500 Jews were marched to Bilgoraj, whence they were deported to Belzec the next day. About fifty ill and elderly Jews were murdered at the Jewish cemetery in Tarnogrod.

A few young people escaped from the ghetto into the forests and joined the partisans or found refuge with peasants.

TARNOPOL

COUNTY SEAT, POLAND
(After World War II in the USSR/Ukraine; Ukrainian: **Ternopil'**; Russian: **Ternopol**)

During the war: General Gouvernement, Galicia District

Coordinates:
49°33' | 25°35'

Before the War: During the interwar years, Tarnopol's 14,000 Jews accounted for 40 percent of the town's population. Tarnopol was famed in the nineteenth century as a center of the Haskala (Jewish Enlightenment movement) in Galicia and was an important Hasidic center as well. The Jews of Tarnopol earned a living mainly at trade and crafts and were assisted by related professional associations. Hundreds of Jews held white-collar jobs or practiced liberal professions. Various Jewish mutual-assistance societies operated within the community, a number subsidized by the JDC; several Jewish savings-and-loan associations; a Jewish hospital; and a TOZ medical center. A long-standing Jewish primary school adopted Polish as its language of instruction during the interwar period; the town also had a Talmud Torah and Beit Yaakov and Tarbut schools. Jewish residents partook of Jewish public libraries, drama groups, and sports clubs. Zionist political parties and youth movements were dominant in Jewish public life. Branches of the Bund and Agudath Israel were active in Tarnopol, as was an underground group of Polish Communists.

Soviet occupation: After the Soviets occupied Tarnopol on September 17, 1939, Jewish political activities ceased, private businesses were nationalized, and workers were organized in cooperatives. Thousands of refugees from western Poland raised the Jewish population of the town to more than 20,000 in early 1940. Many refugees, along with Jewish townspeople deemed "unproductive" or "hostile", were exiled to nearby localities or, in some cases, to the Soviet interior. Thus, the Jewish population receded to some 17,000 by the time of the German invasion.

German (Nazi) occupation: As the Germans moved into Tarnopol on July 2, 1941, several hundred Jews in Tarnopol followed the Soviet authorities in their re-

Tarnopol, July 4–11, 1941
Bodies of Jewish men murdered
in the courtyard of the prison
on Mickiewicz Street (DOEW)

treat to the east. A pogrom broke out in the town two days later. By the time the violence subsided on July 11, a group of Germans, Ukrainian police, and the local rabble had murdered thousands of Jews. The victims, nearly all of them men, included 1,000 Jewish members of the local intelligentsia who were arrested by order of the SS officer Guenther Hermann, as well as 600 additional Jews who were murdered by the Ukrainian militia following Hermann's command.

In the weeks following the pogrom, the Germans imposed a series of sanctions on the Jews including confiscation of property, limitation of freedom of movement, and forced labor. In early August 1941, Jews were ordered to wear a Star-of-David armband and to mark their homes. In August 1941, a twelve- to eighteen-member Judenrat was established under the attorney Gustav Fischer (chairman) and Yaakov Lipa (deputy). The Judenrat's first task was to collect a large fine from the Jews; afterwards it served as an instrument of the Germans' theft of Jewish property. A sixty-member Jewish Order Service was established with the assistance of a Jewish Order Service officer whom the Germans brought in from Warsaw*.

Ghetto setup, institutions, and internal life: In September 1941, the Germans announced the establishment of a Jewish ghetto in a rundown slum district that occupied 5 percent of the town area. By the end of September, some 12,000 Jews were packed into the quarter that had previously been home to 5,000 Jews. Construction of a barbed-wire fence around the ghetto began several weeks later and was completed on December 1, 1941. The fence had two gates through which hundreds of Jews passed each day for forced labor as well as clandestine trade.

The ghetto population was polarized, with an impoverished majority and a wealthy minority that had connections with the Judenrat and the "Aryan" side of town. The Judenrat labor bureau provided the Germans with daily quotas of Jews for forced labor in military camps and other locations near the ghetto. The Judenrat and Jewish Order Service were also in charge of conscripting Jews for service in nearby labor camps, where they worked in quarries and built roads, and in a women's farm labor camp. The Germans exerted a great deal of pressure, compelling the Order Service to abduct young men and women in the streets for dispatch to the labor camps. The Judenrat was required to provide the Jewish workers in the labor camps with tools, food, and clothing, and to replace workers who had died owing to the harsh conditions. To ease the lives of the ghetto inhabitants, the Judenrat, aided by affluent Jews, established a soup kitchen, an orphanage, an old-age home, and a hospital. These institutions, however, did little to alleviate the severe distress of the population. In the winter of 1941/42, mortality in the ghetto escalated to such a degree that the Judenrat was constrained to bury the dead in a common grave.

In early 1942, the Germans replaced Gustav Fischer as chair of the Judenrat with his deputy, Yaakov Lipa.

After the murder operation in March 1942 (see below) and in anticipation of further operations, the remaining ghetto inhabitants set up hideouts and strove to obtain jobs in German institutions. Affluent Jews paid bribes to sign up for labor. In April–May 1942, the Judenrat opened several workshops in which men and women were employed in carpentry, shoemaking, and tailoring. Abductions of Jews for service in labor camps continued intermittently, and Jews were executed for smuggling, pilfering, or illegally crossing to the "Aryan" side.

In July–August 1942, Jewish survivors of mass murder actions perpetrated by Ukrainians in nearby villages were concentrated in the Tarnopol ghetto.

Murder operations and ghetto's liquidation: On March 23, 1942, the German SIPO commander in Tarnopol, Hermann Mueller, ordered the Judenrat to prepare a list of about 500 elderly, ill, and indigent Jews, ostensibly for deportation. Lipa complied, rationalizing that he sacrificed some of the ghetto in order to save the rest. Among the victims arrested with the help of the Jewish Order Service were children from the ghetto's orphanage and residents of its old-age home as well as the inhabitants of the ghetto's poorest quarter. The arrested Jews were concentrated in the synagogue and then taken to a nearby forest and shot to death by German and Ukrainian police, under the command of the SIPO officer Lex, Mueller's deputy.

On August 31, the ghetto was surrounded. German and Ukrainian police, with the assistance of the Order Service, rounded up thousands of Jews and inspected their labor permits. The operation, which was initiated by Mueller, was especially brutal. The Jews were held for long hours without food or water. The children were murdered in front of their mothers, at least one by Mueller personally. Those employed by the police and the German army were released, young men were transferred to the labor camps, and the others, about 5,000 (most of whom were elderly or ill), were loaded into railroad cars and transported two days later to the Belzec death camp.

After this murder operation, the Germans reduced the size of the ghetto. The Jewish residents continued to prepare hideouts and a number attempted to acquire forged "Aryan" papers. By order of the Germans, the Judenrat began to compile a list of all ghetto inhabitants over the age of sixty. Small numbers of surviving Jews from nearby localities continued to arrive in the ghetto. Karol Fohorlis chaired the Judenrat at this time.

On September 30, 1942, the Germans ordered the Judenrat to hand over Jews whose names appeared on their lists. The Jewish Order Service rounded up several hundred people, and the Germans set out afterwards to arrest more. By the time the operation ended on October 5, some 1,200 mostly poor and elderly Jews had been arrested and deported to Belzec.

In early November 1942, some 2,500 Jews from Tarnopol and the vicinity were murdered in two additional murder operations, initiated by Mueller. A brief moratorium followed. The Germans appointed Pinchas Grynfeld, a refugee from western Poland who had headed the Judenrat in the peripheral town of Zbaraz*, to chair the Judenrat of Tarnopol and to head the Jewish Order Service.

After the November murder operation, a *Julag* ("Jew camp") was established and separated from the rest of the ghetto by a barbed-wire fence. A satellite of the Janowska camp in Lwow*, it was placed under the command of Wilhelm Rokita of the SS, previously the deputy commander of the Lwow camp. The Judenrat was ordered to equip the camp with a kitchen, a bakery, storerooms, and a clinic. "Useful" Jewish men and women from Tarnopol and other locations were concentrated in the new facility, which became a concentration and labor camp. A number of inmates worked on the "Aryan" side of Tarnopol each day; others toiled in workshops in the camp. Camp residents lived in better conditions than the rest of the ghetto inhabitants, and received larger food rations. A few prisoners were able to see their families across the barbed-wire fence that separated the camp from the ghetto.

A new spate of murders in the ghetto began in mid-March 1943. Groups of elderly and indigent Jews were murdered every few days, as were others, including 150 employees of the Judenrat and of the Order Service in late March. In a new murder operation on April 8–9, 1943, headed by Mueller and Lex, thousands of Jews were removed from the ghetto, transferred to a camp, and put through a selection. People who were young and strong, along with those who ransomed themselves, remained in the camp. The others, about 1,000 in all, were shot to death near Petrykow. After the operation, Germans and Ukrainians spent weeks combing the ghetto for Jews in hiding; those found were either taken to the camp or murdered.

As of late March 1943, about 700 Jews remained in the ghetto by official count, but several hundred others were likely in hiding. By this time, many of the ghetto inhabitants were attempting to leave the ghetto in any possible way: by slipping into the camp, arranging a hideout on the "Aryan" side, or finding refuge in the German plants where they worked.

The ghetto was liquidated on June 20, 1943, in a murder operation that claimed the lives of its rump Jewish population of about 500.

The number of Jews in the *Julag* peaked at 5,000 in the spring of 1943 and declined in June 1943 to between 2,000 and 2,500, including a number of people from the Tarnopol ghetto and nearby localities. By that time, many inmates had been killed in numerous murder operations. In mid-July 1943, the prisoners discovered that the camp was to be liquidated, and several hundred escaped. On July 22, 1943, German police ringed the camp, evicted its inhabitants, and shot most of them to death near Petrykow. The operation saw several attempts by Jews to defend themselves, some with weapons. The Germans kept several hundred Jews alive to clean up the camp; they were murdered two weeks later.

About 100 expert artisans were spared and sent to the *Julag* in Lwow. A few hundred Jews from Tarnopol and its vicinity attempted to survive by hiding within the town limits. Many were denounced to the Germans, including some 200 people shortly before the Soviets liberated the area. Peasants and Ukrainian partisans murdered others. A number of Jews survived by hiding with Poles.

TARNÓW

COUNTY SEAT IN CRACOW DISTRICT, POLAND

During the war: General Gouvernement, Cracow District

Coordinates: 50°01' | 20°59'

About 15,600 Jews lived in Tarnow after World War I, representing approximately 40 percent of the city's population. Most earned their livelihood from commerce and artisanship, especially in the garment, glasswork, and jewelry-making industries. They were aided by a number of merchants' and artisans' trade unions, credit unions, a free-loan society, and various loan funds and Jewish banks. Jews of Tarnow belonged to the liberal professions, primarily as attorneys and physicians, and counted a number of industrialists and wholesalers. After World War I, the Tarnow Jewish community received assistance from the Joint Distribution Committee, while welfare organizations cared for orphans and refugees. TOZ and CENTOS health and children's-aid organizations were also active in the city. Many members of the community were supported by a public pension fund established by former members of the community who had emigrated from Poland. A Jewish hospital and an old-age home also operated in the city.

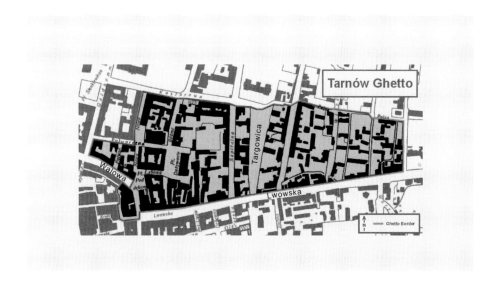

Reconstructed Tarnow ghetto plan based on an original German document
(Michael Peters, Germany)

The Jewish community maintained a wide variety of schools, including a Talmud Torah for the children of the poor, a number of schools that offered Hebrew-language instruction, a popular university established by the Tarbut organization (which also held Hebrew courses), a Beth Jacob school for girls, and a vocational school for the clothing, carpentry, and metalwork trades, in which Jewish studies were also taught. Tarnow's Jewish library held about 15,000 volumes, and Yiddish and Polish weeklies were published in the city. A *Shimshon* sports union was active there.

The city's Zionist parties and youth movements held various activities in Hebrew and established pioneer training facilities that boasted dozens of members. Also active in Tarnow were the Agudath Israel party and its youth movement as well as the Bund; a number of Jews were members of the illegal Communist party and its youth movement.

Before World War II, about 25,000 Jews lived in Tarnow, representing approximately half of the local population. At the war's outbreak, thousands of refugees from Silesia and Cracow* thronged to the city. In the early days of the war, numerous Jews, mainly men, also fled from it.

The Germans occupied Tarnow on September 8, 1939, and immediately began to confiscate Jewish property, levy ransom payments, and seize Jews for forced labor. On September 12, 1939, the Germans ordered that all Jewish shops in the city be marked. On September 18, 1939, all Jewish bank accounts in the city were frozen, and the amount of cash Jews were permitted to possess was restricted. On October 20, 1939, the Jews were ordered to wear a white armband with a blue Star-of-David. On November 4, 1939, Jewish employees were dismissed from their jobs in the municipality and public service. Jewish doctors were forbidden to treat non-Jewish patients, although many Poles ignored this decree.

On November 9, 1939, most of the city's synagogues and study halls were set aflame, as was the Jewish community building. The "Aryanization" of all Jewish property, businesses, and factories was underway. Meanwhile, in the fall of 1939, Jewish public activity was discontinued: community institutions and schools were closed, and the political parties ceased their activities. Several welfare activities were allowed, and the orphanage, hospital, and old-age home continued to function.

In late October or early November 1939, a Judenrat was established with members who were well-known public activists. It was headed for a short period by attorney Dr. Yosef Offner, followed by David Lenkowicz, who was in turn succeeded by Wolf Schenkel and then Dr. Shlomo Goldberg, both Zionist activists deported a few weeks later to Auschwitz, where they perished. Arthur Folkman was then appointed to head the Judenrat. The organization was required to supply the Germans with forced laborers, to collect and pay ransoms, and to turn over valuables to the Germans. The Judenrat also distributed clothing and meager food rations among the Jews, and established a public soup kitchen. Its employment bureau screened prospective forced laborers and allocated workers for various jobs. Employees of factories considered essential enjoyed immunity from random seizures for forced labor by the Germans, which persisted even after the Judenrat had fully filled the quotas of workers.

In the spring of 1940, public figures in Tarnow were arrested and in mid-1940 deported to Auschwitz, where they perished. At the same time, Tarnow Judenrat member Dr. Schpeiser was murdered. In the summer of 1940, numerous Jewish families were evicted from their homes, which were then placed at the disposal of officers and members of the civil administration. Concurrently, thousands of Jews from surrounding localities were deported to Tarnow, and the Jewish population of the city rose substantially.

On August 25, 1940, a German employment bureau opened in the city, which stepped up the supervision of the Jewish labor force. All Jews aged twelve and older were required to obtain work permits with photo identification. Jews who came to register in the bureau were often promptly seized and sent to the Pustkow or Stalowa Wola labor camps.

In September 1940, a Jewish Order Service with thirty to forty members was established in Tarnow. It was headed first by a man named Miller, who was followed by Wasserman and finally by a Viennese Jew named Diestler. In mid-1942, the number of Jewish policemen rose to 120.

In late 1940, a number of Jews accused of black marketeering were deported to Auschwitz, where they perished. The Gestapo seized Jews for interrogation while others were sent to dig pits outside the town. All were murdered in the pits. In early 1941, essential workers permits were distributed, which Jews paid large bribes to obtain. In the course of February 1941, a number of Jews were murdered in the city's streets.

In mid-October 1941, the city's Jews were forbidden to leave their neighborhoods without a permit and were ordered to shave off their beards "for reasons of sanitation." In December 1941, the Jews were ordered to hand over all furs in their possession.

On December 9, 1941, when the United States entered the war, more than 100 Jews were arrested, of whom 17 were shot and the rest released a few days later.

On February 19, 1942, a ghetto was established in Tarnow, in the Grabowka neighborhood. Jews from Germany, Austria, and Czechoslovakia were deported to the ghetto, and its population rose to about 40,000. it was severely overcrowded, and its buildings were disconnected from the city's power grid. In April 1942, more than sixty Jews were murdered, including Dr. Hirshfeld, one of the leaders of the Mizrachi movement in western Galicia, as well as other well-known figures. A number of the victims were refugees who had come from the Soviet occupation zone, while others were executed for practicing kosher slaughter. In May 1942, a heavy ransom was levied on the Jews in the form of property and furniture designated for the apartments that the Germans had confiscated.

In June 1942, the Germans decreed that work permits needed to be reauthorized, and Tarnow's Jews scrambled to obtain them from essential work places in order to receive immunity from deportation. Several attempted to establish new factories and workshops for this purpose. Hundreds of Jews worked in a factory that manufactured juices and jams for the German army, and a portion of the factory's income supported the Jewish orphanage and hospital.

On June 11, 1942, a murder operation notable for its extreme brutality was carried out. The operation was "unique," according to the Germans, as it was a "local deportation," a euphemism for the mass murder of local Jews, especially the elderly, the ill, and those unable to withstand the conditions of the transport. The Polish auxiliary police and construction services assisted the German police units in carrying out the operation. The people designated for immediate deportation were selected by a branch of the German security police (K.d.S) in Tarnow. On June 11, the first day of the deportation, some 8,000 Jews were separated from the others and led to the nearby Zbilitowska Gora and Skrzyszow forests and murdered by soldiers of the Waffen SS. On June 15 and 18, 1942, about 2,000 more Jews were murdered in this manner in the Jewish cemetery and various other places. In addition, about 10,000 Jews were deported to the Belzec death camp. The Jewish policemen were recruited to help round up the Jews; those who declined to participate were also sent to Belzec. Paul Reis, a German refugee who was in charge of the Judenrat's social-welfare department, refused to supply the Germans with lists of Jews and was executed together with a number of Judenrat employees.

When the operation was over on June 19, 1942, about 20,000 people remained in the ghetto, which was then reduced in size and encircled by a barbed-wire fence with four gates. The ghetto was guarded from the outside by the Polish police and from the inside by the Jewish Order Service.

The Jews were given forty-eight hours to move into the smaller ghetto, leaving nearly all of their belongings behind. Many became destitute. The Judenrat ran four public soup kitchens that supplied thousands of hot meals daily. The Jewish hospital, which had been relocated into the ghetto, helped to contain the typhus epidemic that broke out due to hunger and deficient sanitary conditions.

In the early days following the establishment of the ghetto, the German police and Gestapo randomly murdered dozens of Jews in their ghetto apartments. Many Jews attempted to obtain false documents or prepare hiding places, both inside and outside the ghetto. These shelters were often designed to hold scores of people for a protracted stay: they were equipped with food and water and were connected to the electrical grid. Most people's efforts to save themselves were directed at obtaining work permits in places both inside and outside the ghetto that supplied the German army, such as sewing and metal shops. People also took to forging work permits, as the bearers of work permits were thought to be immune from deportation and as employment outside the ghetto enabled one to obtain food.

After the June 1942 operation, a fighting underground began to organize in the ghetto among the members of the Hashomer Hatzair movement, who were joined by the members of other political movements. The organization was headed by Yosef Broder, Rivka Shusler, Shmuel Shpringer of Hashomer Hatzai'ir (also a member of the Jewish Order Service), and Melech Binstok, a Communist. The members of the organization contacted the Polish underground in the city and acquired four guns. Shpringer helped the members of the underground to enter and leave the ghetto as needed. He was murdered while smuggling arms.

In early September 1942, Jewish identity papers were once again collected for inspection. When the elderly, women, and children saw that their papers were not stamped, they began to hide in the bunkers, fearing deportation. On September 9, 1942, notices were put up announcing that the deportation of the Jews of Tarnow would begin the next day, that all the exit permits from the ghetto were canceled, and that anyone leaving it would be shot. The following day, the ghetto was encircled by the German police. A few dozen Jews were shot dead in the early stages of the roundup. A selection was carried out during which many bearers of work permits were moved into the group of imminent deportees, because the quota of

Jews designated for extermination had not been filled. The ghetto was searched, and hundreds of Jews were discovered in hiding and executed in the streets by the Germans and their helpers, while many others were added to the deportation transports. Some 6,500 Jews were deported to Belzec in this operation.

Following the September operation, a group of underground fighters fled to the Tuchow forests; all but three of its members were killed in a battle with an SS unit, and of those three, two were injured. They returned to the ghetto, where they continued their underground activities. There were also attempts by members of the underground and groups of youths who joined them to set out in the direction of the Hungarian border to find asylum in Hungary, but few succeeded.

By October 1942, there were some 15,000 Jews in the Tarnow ghetto, including deportees from surrounding localities. Many perished in typhus epidemics. In late October 1942, the number of German and Polish policemen stationed along the fence and at the gates was increased. All personal exit permits were canceled, and laborers set out to work outside the ghetto only in groups, heavily guarded by Polish police. Most of the attempts to smuggle food into the ghetto were thwarted.

In early November 1942, in advance of a further operation, the Germans lured the Jews who were hiding outside the ghetto into the ghetto boundaries by announcing that they would be permitted to return and suffer no punishment. On the morning of November 15, 1942, after the workers had left the ghetto, the ghetto was encircled by the Polish auxiliary police. Gestapo members rounded up more than 2,500 Jews, some from workplaces outside the ghetto, and deported them to Belzec. A number of the ghetto inhabitants managed to hide.

Following the third operation, the ghetto was divided into two quarters. Ghetto A was designated for employees of factories inside the ghetto and was organized as a labor camp, with separate living quarters for men and women; Ghetto B was inhabited by all the unemployed, who were starving. Passage between the two ghettos was prohibited.

In the first half of 1943, the German police and the Gestapo periodically raided the ghetto to examine work permits and randomly murder Jews. In August 1943, a unit of the German police, together with groups of Ukrainian and Latvian collaborators, was deployed in the ghetto. Amon Goeth, the commandant of the Plaszow camp, also arrived. The Jews responded by preparing more hiding places in the ghetto.

On September 2, 1943, the Germans and their helpers, armed with heavy machine guns, stationed themselves along the ghetto fences. The fences separating Ghetto A from Ghetto B were removed. The members of the Judenrat and Jewish Order Service were ordered to inform the Jews that the inhabitants of the ghetto were to be taken to the Plaszow camp. Only a few managed to find a place to hide. Some 11,000 people, almost the entire population of the ghetto, were rounded up in Magdeburg Square. About 2,000 workers were indeed transferred to Plaszow, while some 7,000 were deported to Auschwitz. A few were sent to the Szebnie camp. The patients of the Jewish hospital were murdered in a ghetto alleyway. Some of the factories and workshops in the ghetto were dismantled and transferred to Plaszow. During the operation, the members of the underground waged a battle with the Germans, but none of them survived. There were also individual cases of physical resistance to the Germans and their helpers.

About 300 men and women remained in the ghetto to collect and sort through the deportees' belongings. They were put up in two buildings and lived as in a labor camp. They were joined by 300 to 400 people who came out of hiding, but in late September 1943, the Jews whose names did not appear on the list of workers were sent to the Szebnie camp. Most were murdered in forests en route to the camp.

Tata, June 1944
Transfer to the Komarom district of the Jews of the town, who were later deported to Auschwitz (YV)

TATA

TOWN IN KOMÁROM COUNTY, HUNGARY

Coordinates:
47°39' | 18°19'

The last national census conducted prior to the German occupation, taken in January 1941, recorded 527 Jewish inhabitants in Tata, approximately 4 percent of the total population. Most were merchants and artisans; several were factory owners. The town's Jewish community was Neolog and maintained a Jewish elementary school.

The German army occupied Hungary on March 19, 1944. A census conducted in the second week of April 1944 reported that 559 Jews belonged to the Neolog Jewish community of Tata.

The Hungarian administration remained intact and operational after the German occupation. The ghettoization and deportation of the Jews occurred on the basis of the decrees and orders of the Hungarian national and local authorities. The ghetto of Tata was established in May 1944, in the Gypsy quarter of the town and in a barn on the Deutsch estate. Later, its inhabitants were moved to the school building. The ghetto residents were mainly children, women, and elderly people, as younger men had been drafted into the Hungarian army for forced labor service, prior to the ghettoization.

In early June 1944 the ghetto inhabitants were transferred to the entrainment center in Komarom*. They were deported to Auschwitz in two transports, on June 12 and 15, 1944.

TATARSK

TOWNLET IN MONASTYRSHCHINA COUNTY, SMOLENSK DISTRICT, RUSSIAN FEDERATION, USSR

During the war: Military Administration Area

Coordinates:
54°15' | 31°34'

Beginning in the mid-nineteenth century, Tatarsk had a Jewish agricultural colony, which under the Soviet regime was converted into a Jewish kolkhoz. In the 1920s, about 850 Jews lived in Tatarsk, representing approximately half of the townlet's population. The townlet had two Jewish schools in which the language of instruction was Yiddish.

Tatarsk was occupied by the Germans on July 18, 1941. In mid-September 1941, a Judenrat was established in Tatarsk, which had at least three members, but they were murdered by the Germans a short time later. According to German sources, in September 1941, about twenty Jewish men were shot to death.

In late September or early October 1941, a ghetto was established in Tatarsk, and about 600 Jews were moved into its confines under very harsh conditions of overcrowding. The ghetto existed for a few weeks. A short time after its establishment, about thirty Jewish men and three women living in the ghetto were murdered as punishment for leaving the area of the ghetto and attempting to drive out the Russians who had taken over their apartments. The women who remained in the ghetto were abused and raped. The residents of the ghetto were murdered in a series of operations that took place in October 1941.

TAURAGĖ

(Yiddish: **Tauvrig**)

COUNTY SEAT, LITHUANIA

During the war:
Reichskommissariat Ostland

Coordinates:
55°15' | 22°17'

On the eve of the German invasion, about 2,000 Jews lived in Taurage, representing roughly 19 percent of the population. They earned their livelihood from banking, commerce, customs, artisanship, and smuggling. The Taurage Jewish community boasted varied religious, welfare, and educational institutions, including youth movements and a Hebrew high school. A fifteen-member community council was elected in accordance with the Jewish autonomy law passed by the independent Lithuanian government and was active in Taurage for a number of years.

After Lithuania was annexed to the Soviet Union in 1940, the factories and most of the shops in Taurage were nationalized and their owners exiled to the Soviet Union. Jewish institutions were shut down and Jewish political activity was outlawed.

On June 22, 1941, the Germans invaded Lithuania, occupying Taurage that same day. A few days later, at Gestapo orders, the Lithuanian police arrested about 300 Jewish men. Most were shot to death on July 2, 1941, near the village of Vizbutai. Another 122 Jewish men were murdered on the way to Siauliai* on July 3–10, 1941.

In early September 1941, all of Taurage's Jews were concentrated in a number of shacks that had previously served as truck sheds, in an area termed a "ghetto." The ghetto was encircled by a barbed-wire fence and guarded by Lithuanian guards. The Jews were sent out to perform forced labor and were not permitted to bring food back into the ghetto, which was rife with hunger, filth, and disease.

On September 16, 1941, the Jews were transported by truck to the Taurage and Vizbutai forests, where they were brutally murdered by the Lithuanians.

According to Soviet sources, about 3,000 and 900 people are buried in the Taurage and Vizbutai forests, respectively.

TÉCSŐ

TOWN IN MÁRAMAROS COUNTY, HUNGARY
(After World War II in the USSR/Ukraine; Ukrainian: **Tyachiv**; Russian: **Tyachev**)

Coordinates:
48°00' | 23°34'

The last national census conducted in Hungary prior to the German occupation, taken in January 1941, recorded 2,150 Jewish inhabitants in Tecso, representing approximately 20 percent of the total population. Most were merchants and artisans who were also engaged in seasonal agricultural work, though a few were wholesalers. The town's Jewish community was Orthodox and maintained Hadarim and several Yeshivot.

After World War I, Tecso, which was formerly in Hungary, became part of Czechoslovakia. In mid-March 1939, Tecso was re-annexed to Hungary. The Hungarian anti-Jewish legislation was implemented more harshly in Carpatho-Ruthenia, where the town was located, than in inner Hungary. In 1939, local youths broke into the synagogue and ransacked it. From then on, young Jewish men kept constant guard over the synagogue. Beating Jews on the streets and disturbing prayers in the synagogue became commonplace.

As of 1940, many Jewish men were drafted into the Hungarian army for forced labor service. From 1942, most were sent to the Ukraine, where a large percentage perished.

In the summer of 1941, the Hungarian authorities declared dozens of Jewish families whose members could not prove their Hungarian citizenship to be stateless and deported them to German-occupied Ukraine. They were murdered on August 27 or 28 at Kamenets-Podolsk*.

The German army occupied Hungary on March 19, 1944. The Hungarian administration remained intact and in force after the occupation. The ghettoization and deportation of the Jews were implemented on the basis of the decrees and orders of the Hungarian national and local authorities. On April 15, 1944, Israel Weisz, the president of the Jewish community, was informed that a ghetto would be established in Tecso the following day and that he was appointed to head the Jewish Council. Weisz, however, did not accept the position, and Jeno (Yaakov) Roth was nominated in his stead.

In addition to the local Jews, Jews from the county-districts of Tecso and Taracvolgy were concentrated in the Tecso ghetto established in the vicinity of the synagogue. Altogether, about 10,000 Jews lived in the ghetto. The gentiles moved out of the territory of the ghetto, but their houses were boarded up and off-limits to the Jews. The town ghetto was thus severely overcrowded, with ten to fifteen people to a room. A number of the Jews from the vicinity were locked in a camp built outside of the town.

Several physicians lived in the ghettos. A soup kitchen was set up, but as food supplies were insufficient, the inhabitants were starving. Men under the age of fifty-five were assigned to work outside of the ghetto, mainly as a means of humiliation. The Hungarian gendarmes interrogated and tortured the inhabitants of the ghetto into revealing the whereabouts of their hidden valuables. Several people were beaten to death. A few people attempted to escape from the ghetto, but they were unsuccessful, mainly owing to the enmity of the locals, who hunted down the Jews hiding in the forests and handed them over to the gendarmes.

The inhabitants of the ghettos of Tecso were deported to Auschwitz between May 22 and 26, 1944.

TELŠIAI
(Yiddish: **Telz, Telzh**)

COUNTY SEAT, LITHUANIA

During the war:
Reichskommissariat Ostland

Coordinates:
55°59' | 22°15'

On the eve of the German invasion, about 2,800 Jews lived in Telsiai, representing roughly half of the townlet's population. From the late nineteenth century, Telsiai's large Yeshiva produced rabbis and leaders who later became active and important contributors in various countries and communities abroad. The Jews of Telsiai earned their livelihood mainly from commerce, artisanship, and light industry as well as from providing accommodations to the hundreds of Yeshiva students who settled in the townlet. Jewish educational institutions included a high school and a seminary for girls. While Agudath Israel was the primary political force among the townlet's Jews, Zionist parties and youth movements were active as well.

After Lithuania was annexed to the Soviet Union in 1940, the townlet's factories were nationalized, parties and youth movements were disbanded, and Hebrew institutions were closed. In June 1941, a number of Jewish businesspeople and Zionist activists were exiled to Siberia.

The German army entered Telsiai on June 26, 1941. The following day, the townlet's Jewish inhabitants were driven out of their homes and their property was plundered. They were then imprisoned under very harsh conditions in cowsheds and barns on the Rainiai estate.

The commander of the Lithuanians appointed a council to represent the Jews, which strove to improve living conditions. On July 14, 1941, a number of Germans and Lithuanians appeared at the estate and began to abuse the Jews as a crowd of Telsiai residents looked on. That day and the next, all the Jewish men at the estate were murdered, as were Jews from Alsedziai* and from a number of nearby townlets and villages.

On July 22, 1941, the women and children were taken from the Rainiai estate to the Geruliai camp, where they endured severely overcrowded conditions. They were held together with the women and children of nearby townlets, totaling close to 2,000 people. On Saturday, August 30, 1941, the women and children were driven out of their huts. Five hundred women and young girls were then marched to Telsiai, while the others were murdered by Lithuanians.

In Telsiai, the 500 women and children were imprisoned in a ghetto near the lake under very harsh conditions. The ghetto was encircled by a high wooden fence topped by barbed wire; its ghetto gate was guarded by Lithuanians. A number of the women toiled for Lithuanian farmers, who fully exploited their workers, while others worked in Lithuanian homes as servants.

Female doctors who were inhabitants of the ghetto, Dr. Blat, Dr. Shapira, and Dr. Srolovits, established an makeshift clinic to treat women who were ill or in labor. Despite their efforts, all of the babies born in the ghetto died shortly after their birth. Epidemic typhus also raged in it.

On Rosh Hashanah and Yom Kippur (September 1941), the women of the ghetto gathered to pray—as several led the prayers—in the Beit Midrash inside the ghetto. Other women, having undergone brutal hardships and suffering, turned to the local priest seeking to convert to Christianity.

From December 22, 1941, the women who worked in the villages were returned to the ghetto. The development was construed as a sign of the ghetto's impending liquidation, prompting many women to flee from there via the lake or under the fence. Dozens of the women who escaped reached the Siauliai* ghetto.

On December 24–25, 1941, all of the women who remained in the ghetto were taken to the vicinity of the Rainiai estate, where they were murdered.

Of those that escaped, sixty-four survived and lived to see the day of liberation.

TEOFIPOL

(Ukrainian: **Teofipol'**)

COUNTY SEAT, KAMENETS-PODOLSK DISTRICT, UKRAINE, USSR

During the war:
Reichskommissariat Ukraine

Coordinates:
49°50' | 26°25'

At the dawn of the twentieth century, there were 2,900 Jews living in Teofipol, more than half of the local population. Under Soviet rule, the townlet had a Jewish Ethnic Soviet and a Jewish government school that offered instruction in Yiddish. Many Jewish townspeople organized in a Jewish kolkhoz. Urbanization and industrialization in the Soviet Union reduced the Jewish population of the townlet to about 1,200 shortly before the German invasion in June 1941.

The Germans occupied Teofipol on July 6, 1941. According to survivors' testimonies, a ghetto was established that also held Jews from neighboring villages. In January 1942, about 970 Jews from Teofipol were shot dead.

TEPLIK

(Ukrainian: **Teplyk**)

COUNTY SEAT, VINNITSA DISTRICT, UKRAINE, USSR

During the war:
Reichskommissariat Ukraine

Coordinates:
48°40' | 29°44'

On the eve of the German invasion of the USSR, there were 1,200 Jews in Teplik, one-fourth of the townlet's population. In February 1919, during the Russian Civil War, 200 Jewish inhabitants were murdered in a pogrom perpetrated by a Ukrainian gang. Under Soviet rule, many of the Jews became farmers. A Jewish Ethnic Soviet and a Jewish government school were established, both operating in Yiddish. In the 1920s and 1930s, more than half of Teplik's Jews left the townlet as a result of urbanization and industrialization.

The Germans occupied Teplik on July 26, 1941. They immediately established a Judenrat, restricted Jews' movements, required Jewish inhabitants to wear a white Star-of-David armband, and barred them from the townlet's market. Shortly after the occupation's onset, the Germans established a ghetto on two streets near the river. Jews were assigned to forced labor outside of the ghetto, enduring harassment from the Germans as they traveled to the labor site. The ghetto received no food rations; inhabitants were obliged to barter possessions to obtain provisions. Ransoms were periodically imposed on the community.

On March 2, 1942, able-bodied inhabitants of the ghetto aged between fourteen and forty-five were rounded up and trucked to labor camps. Most were murdered or perished owing to the appalling conditions in the camps.

On the morning of May 27, 1942, altogether 769 Jews from the Teplik ghetto were murdered in pits near the townlet. The same day, 520 Jewish deportees from Bukovina were murdered in the same pits. The deportees had been imprisoned in a camp established in Teplik in the fall of 1941. Following a selection near the pits, ten to fifteen skilled workers in high-demand occupations were housed under guard in a single house in Teplik. An influx of Jews who had been in hiding eventually brought the population of the building up to forty. These people were killed in 1942 and replaced by Jews from Bukovina.

TERNOVKA

(Yiddish: **Ternevka**;
Ukrainian: **Ternivka**)

**TOWN IN DZHULINKA
COUNTY, VINNITSA
DISTRICT, UKRAINE, USSR**

During the war:
Reichskommissariat Ukraine

Coordinates:
48°32' | 29°58'

In the mid-1920s, Ternovka had a Jewish population of about 3,000. A number of Jews continued to run private businesses in the early years of Soviet rule, but many eventually took up white- and blue-collar jobs in the state sector, while others turned to farming on kolkhozes. The town had a Jewish Ethnic Soviet and a Jewish government school, both of which operated in Yiddish. In the mid-1930s, the town's synagogues were closed.

After the German invasion of the Soviet Union on June 22, 1941, a number of Jewish townspeople fled to the Soviet interior. The Germans occupied Ternovka in late July 1941, and shortly thereafter established an unfenced open ghetto. Jews were forced to wear white Star-of-David armbands and paint Stars of David on their homes. The Germans appointed two Jews, one surnamed Nokhe, to head the community.

Survivors of massacres in Uman*, Teplik*, Gaysin*, and other locations arrived at the Ternovka ghetto. During the fall and winter of 1941, Germans and Ukrainian police murdered several ghetto inhabitants. Men were seized for forced labor. A number of men were sent to the Krasnopolka labor camp in the Gaysin area and did not return.

After a selection was conducted on May 27, 1942, SS forces and Ukrainian police murdered 2,400 ghetto inhabitants at a location near the town. The following day, the German commander of the town murdered forty-five Jews who had been hiding. Several skilled workers, the two leaders of the ghetto and their families, and a few people who had managed to hide during the killings, survived. They were later concentrated in two houses, and, over time, were joined by Jews from other localities. The Ternovka ghetto was liquidated on April 2, 1943.

THERESIENSTADT/ TEREZIN

**A FORTRESS CITY
IN NORTHWEST
CZECHOSLOVAKIA**

During the war: Protectorate of Bohemia and Moravia

Coordinates:
50°31' | 14°09'

The Theresienstadt ghetto, as the Germans called it, or Terezin, as it was known to the Czechs, was distinctive in many respects. It was the only ghetto that was located in central Europe, that was erected in a town without a pre-existing Jewish community (with but a few Jewish families), and that spanned an entire locality (albeit a small fortress town), which in ordinary times had some 7,000 inhabitants, equal parts soldiers and civilians. The livelihood of the town's residents was largely derived from providing services to the army. During the peak of Theresienstadt's overcrowding, some 59,000 Jews were packed into a 750-square-meter area.

Theresienstadt was deemed a ghetto, but resembled a concentration camp in certain respects: it featured separate living quarters for men and women, received regular food supplies (for the most part, starvation rations) for the entire

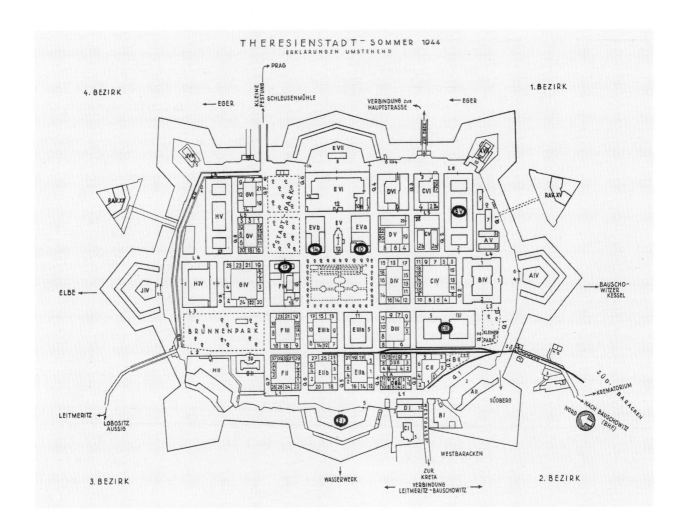

Terezin ghetto map, summer 1944 (Ruth Bondi, *Edelstein Against Time*, Zmora-Bitan Publishing, Tel Aviv 1990)

population, and was governed by a centralized administration under the control of the SS command.

Most of the Jews incarcerated in Theresienstadt were eventually sent to death camps, but the ghetto was not destroyed, liquidated, or set afire until the end of the war. Consequently, a relatively large proportion of documentation concerning the ghetto remains, enabling a unique glimpse into the lives of its Jewish inhabitants, trapped in the Holocaust, and their struggle for survival. Theresienstadt was the only ghetto with a number of surviving Jewish prisoners, including elderly people and children, at the end of World War II, in May 1945.

The last census carried out in the Czechoslovakian Republic before World War II was conducted in 1930, with altogether 117,551 people in Bohemia and Moravia declaring themselves members of the Jewish religion. After the German occupation on March 15, 1939, and the establishment of the Protectorate of Bohemia and Moravia, which was directly annexed to the German Reich, 118,310 Jews were tallied. From the time the Sudetenland was annexed to the Reich in the fall of 1938 through 1940, about 30,000 Jews managed to leave the area of the Protectorate, either legally or illegally. The rest, approximately 88,000 people, remained trapped inside.

Ghetto setup: In September 1941, Hitler declared his objective to empty the Reich and the Protectorate of Jews as soon as possible. From October 17 to November 3, 1941, to that end, 5,000 Jews of the Protectorate were deported to Lodz*, located in the General Gouvernement. The Lodz ghetto was filled to capacity even before the deportees' arrival, and due to the danger of an out-break of epidemics that threatened the surrounding non-Jewish area, an interim solution was needed to render the area of the Protectorate *Judenrein*. Indeed, the ghetto in Theresienstadt was initially intended to serve exclusively as a transition camp, to concentrate the Jews of Bohemia and Moravia designated for later deportation.

On September 27, 1941, Reinhard Heydrich, head of the ministry of Reich Security, was appointed Reichsprotektor of Bohemia and Moravia. Of the two towns that were contenders for the temporary (several weeks long) concentration of the Protectorate's Jews, Heydrich favored Theresienstadt. In a discussion on October 17, 1941, he said, "For that purpose, Theresienstadt has been evacuated of all army units.... It can easily be populated with 50,000 to 60,000 Jews. From there, the Jews will be taken eastward. Minsk* and Riga* have already agreed to take in 50,000 Jews each. After the complete evacuation of the Jews, Germans will be settled in Theresienstadt in accordance with the model planning, and it will become a center of German life."

The Jewish representatives of the Prague community, which was now responsible for all the Jews in the Protectorate, were not informed of the temporary nature of the ghetto that was to be established in Bohemian territory, as testified by the records of the conversations held between the leaders of the community and Hans Guenther. Guenther, the head of the center for Jewish emigration in Prague, was subordinate to Adolf Eichmann. The community's representatives were instructed to seek out suitable cities for the concentration of Jews and devise a ghettoization plan. They were reassured by the idea of setting up a ghetto on Czech soil, which was preferable to deportation to Poland. The Prague community began to work feverishly to plan a Jewish city that would be self-sufficient—publish its own newspaper, establish a fire station, open restaurants, and operate a post office. In the course of their otherwise thorough planning, there was one critical element they did not foresee: that they had been lured into a hoax by the Germans.

Ultimately, only one ghetto was established in the Protectorate, in Theresienstadt, and from the point of view of the Nazi regime, it was a sound choice. Theresienstadt was a fortress city with a tiny Czech population that could be easily evacuated; surrounded by walls, ramparts, and trenches, it had only a few gates that could be easily guarded; inside were eleven barracks suitable for mass accommodations.

On November 24 and December 4, 1941, two construction units of engineers, technicians, artisans, and workers were sent from Prague to Theresienstadt to prepare the city for its new purpose. Despite all of the plans drawn up on paper, the model city was not built, for as early as November 30, even before the arrival of the second construction unit, mass transports containing 1,000 people each began to arrive. Moreover, instead of living in planned family-style housing, the men were separated from the women and children.

In June 1942, the last Czech residents of Theresienstadt were evacuated and the entire city within the walls was turned into a ghetto, with the exception of the area reserved for the SS headquarters and the headquarters of the Czech policemen, who were in charge of guarding the gates and the work units that left the city to work. Housed in separate barracks, for seven months family men were restricted to meeting with their wives and children after work hours and prior to the evening curfew, which usually began at eight o'clock in the evening.

Theresienstadt, January 20, 1944
Arrival in the ghetto of a transport of 870 Dutch Jews. *Photograph taken by Ivan Vojtech Fric, a crew member of a Czech film company shooting a propaganda film in the ghetto* (YV)

Internal life: One of the main purposes of Theresienstadt was to serve as a ghetto for the elderly and the disabled veterans of World War I from the Reich and Austria, who could not be placed on transports headed east, allegedly for fortification work at the front. The idea was conceived by Josef Goebbels and further developed by Heydrich at the infamous Wannsee conference held near Berlin on January 20, 1942. The Jewish leadership in Theresienstadt learned of the new purpose of the ghetto only in late May 1942, just a few days before a steady stream of transports began to arrive, filled with the elderly and handicapped from Germany and Austria. Many of the elderly had been promised accommodations in an old-age home in a resort town, with all the necessary conveniences, and a number of people had signed contracts, agreeing to pay with everything they owned. Their arrival changed the face of the Theresienstadt ghetto dramatically. For lack of room, the elderly people were housed in the attics of the barracks, which were airless and hot in the summer and freezing in the winter, or within the walls of the city, in dark, dank cellars. Occasionally they were forced to sleep on the floor, or if they were fortunate, on straw mattresses. By the thousands, these elderly people began to die of exhaustion, diarrhea, and lack of desire to live.

During the forty-two months of the Theresienstadt ghetto's existence, it was presided over by three Jewish elders (*Judenaelteste*). The first, Yaakov Edelstein, born in Horodenka*, Galicia, was a Zionist and a Socialist; he understood that the Germans intended to destroy the Jewish people but hoped to at least save the younger generation and those fit for work, a nucleus for the future of the nation. Edelstein covered up escapes from the ghetto and was subsequently arrested in November 1943 and shot to death in Auschwitz.

Dr. Paul Eppstein, born in Manheim, Germany, was a brilliant sociologist and a major figure in the National Union of Jews in Germany and the Berlin community. He was appointed as Jewish council leader by orders from Berlin in January 1943. He followed SS orders more closely. However, he too was eventually executed, on September 27, 1944, in the Gestapo prison in the small fortress of Theresienstadt.

Dr. Benjamin Murmelstein, born in Vienna, a rabbi and researcher of the history of Judaism, was appointed Jewish elder after Eppstein's death and remained in Theresienstadt until the liberation of the ghetto.

A twelve-member Aeltestenrat worked alongside the Jewish elder. Even before the establishment of the ghetto, it was agreed that the council would be made up of an equal number of Czech Jews and Zionists. The first Aeltestenrat was made up entirely of young men. In October 1942, following orders from Berlin, six of the representatives of the Protectorate Jews were replaced by six older representatives of German and Austrian Jews. In October 1944, sixteen of the former and current members of the Aeltestenrat were sent to their deaths in Auschwitz. In December 1944, a new Aeltestenrat was appointed with representatives from five countries. It was headed by Rabbi Leo Baeck, who held the position until the ghetto's liberation.

All ghetto prisoners aged fifteen to sixty-five (and as of October 1944, younger inmates as well) were required to work, and most did so faithfully, without SS supervision, in the knowledge that their employment contributed to the welfare of the general prisoner population of the ghetto, as well as to their own well-being. In the early days, there was still some hope that, despite circumstances, the ghetto could support and become an integral part of the war economy. In the spring of 1942, however, men's work units were shipped to Kladno and other mines, 1,000 women were sent to labor in the forests of Krivoklat, while the elderly inhabitants were required to carry out nearly all of the work within the ghetto. A number of factories were opened, in which soldiers' socks were patched, uniforms were sprayed with camouflage colors, and parachute parts were sewn, but these facilities were not vital for the German war effort. Only two factories essential for the war industry were active throughout the entire existence of the ghetto. In June 1942, a mica-splitting (*Glimmerspalten*) factory was opened, for the manufacture of the thin leaves used as insulation material in the aircraft industry. It employed on average close to 850 women (who were largely protected from transports) and continued to exist until February 1945. On July 1, 1943, a huge tent was set up in the city square to pack winter equipment for motorized military vehicles used on the eastern front. The K (for *Kisten*, boxes) production, which employed about 1,000 people, was halted in mid-November that same year.

Living conditions in the ghetto gradually improved. Inhabitants benefited from three-story bunks made of raw wooden planks; pots were added in the public kitchens; hospitals and nursing homes were established, and most importantly, the expansion of the water and sewage plumbing system (which had been planned 150 years earlier for a much smaller population), largely owing to the professional skills of Jewish engineers and technicians. This last improvement was made possible after the SS command agreed to the plan (tons of pipes were brought to the ghetto) over fears of an outbreak of epidemics that might pass through the Eger River and on to the general population, and especially the nearby Reich territories.

While all of the synagogues in the Protectorate were shut down even before the ghetto was established, improvised prayer rooms were set up in most of the barracks, a small synagogue operated in one of the houses, and prayer corners were organized in venues that hosted both plays and lectures. Yaakov Edelstein, the first Jewish elder, appointed a chief rabbi and two deputies. There was no dearth of rabbis and cantors to lead the services. The rabbis prepared boys for their bar mitzvah, conducted wedding ceremonies, were present at the purification of the dead, and recited the *Kaddish* prayer for the dead. Early on, the dead of the Theresienstadt ghetto were buried in cemeteries outside the wall. However, in order to contend with the mounting death rate, a crematorium with a burning capacity of 160 to 180 bodies per day was built and started to operate in the summer of 1942. The ashes were preserved according to lists in numbered cardboard boxes; however, in November 1944, as the front approached and with it the fear of the Reich's impending defeat, the ashes of over 30,000 people were dumped into the River Ohre(Eger in German) in order to destroy the evidence.

Members of other religions, who were considered Jewish only according to the Nazi racial laws, were also brought to the ghetto, and they gathered on Sundays and Christian holidays for prayers led by the Catholic priests and Protestant ministers among the prisoners.

Children's rooms were set up in the men's and women's barracks, even during the period when men and women were housed separately. Some of the children remained in the rooms while their mothers and fathers were at work; others lived with counselors, most of whom were members of Zionist youth groups. After the evacuation of the town, the Jewish leadership allocated the best buildings—the school and town hall—as houses for children aged ten to fifteen, with girls and boys housed separately. Parents were not required to transfer their children to the children's houses (which, in any case, did not have room for all the children who were brought to the ghetto), but many did so for the children's benefit. Living conditions in the children's houses were better than in the large sleeping rooms in the barracks, even as thirty to forty boys or girls slept, ate, played, and studied in each room, known as *Heim* in the ghetto. The children received slightly more food, and, most importantly, were under the supervision of teachers and counselors. The children held competitions, published single-copy newspapers, painted, and drew. They participated in plays for children that were performed dozens of times in the ghetto, the most popular of which was the children's opera *Brundibar*. Jewish studies were forbidden to children as of 1940, but they were nevertheless given regular secret lessons in Judaism, to the extent that it was possible without paper, writing implements, or textbooks.

Cultural events were also held at the prisoners' initiative to satisfy their urgent need for distraction and leisure. Immediately after the arrival of the first transports in the ghetto, entertainment evenings were held separately in the men's and women's barracks, featuring poetry readings, improvised humorous sketches, and scenes from theatrical plays that former actors among the prisoners remembered by heart. Musical accompaniment to these productions was provided by harmonicas and tin bowls that served as drums, since the possession of musical instruments was forbidden. Over time, various instruments were smuggled into the ghetto, and a broken piano was found in an attic. Secret concerts were held. The ghetto contained an extensive Jewish library of 60,000 books. After the evacuation of the city, cultural activities were institutionalized by what was known as the Department for the Administration for Free Time Activities (*Freizeitgestaltung*), and the Jewish elder or his deputy passed on a list to the SS command for approval, including lectures, theater plays, cabarets, and operas performed without staging (including Smetana's *The Bartered Bride* and Mozart's *The Marriage of Figaro*).

It has often been stated that the Germans brought the finest Jewish artists of central Europe to Theresienstadt, but the claim is misleading. The Germans simply brought to the ghetto the Jews of central Europe, many of whom happened to be musicians, actors, directors, and artists who sought outlets to express their existential distress. A group of artists worked in the technical bureau of the

Theresienstadt, January 1942
Burial of Jews murdered in the ghetto. Photographs taken by Karel Salaba, a Czech gendarme stationed as a guard in the ghetto (YV)

Jewish administration building, creating graphic work for the ghetto's needs and for the SS command. However, the group also took advantage of its access to paper and drawing materials to secretly sketch pictures of the harsh reality in the ghetto. While a number of the pictures were concealed in various hiding places, others were smuggled out by a collector with connections outside the ghetto, where they fell into the Germans' hands. Five of the finest artists in the ghetto were arrested in July 1944, interrogated, and transferred with their families to the small fortress—the infamous Gestapo prison near the ghetto, intended mainly for political prisoners. From there they were sent to extermination camps. Only two of the artists survived, in addition to Tomas, artist Bedrich Fritta's infant son.

Deportations to the east: Two events in early 1942 put an end to the Jews' illusions of Theresienstadt constituting a "city of refuge" until the end of the war: two executions by hanging were carried out for disobeying SS orders concerning contact with the Czech population still living in Theresienstadt and for corresponding by mail with relatives outside the ghetto; and two transports—the first of their kind to depart from Theresienstadt—were sent to the east, to Riga. In the coming stages, the transports were dispatched to undisclosed destinations. Theresienstadt's inmates only learned through postcards following the September 1943 transport that the deportees' destination was indeed "the Birkenau labor camp," none other than Auschwitz.

The SS headquarters in Theresienstadt gave orders regarding the departure date of each transport, the number (ranging from 1,000 to 2,500) of ghetto inhabitants to be transferred, the identity of the passengers—prisoners from the Reich or from the Protectorate, or both—and the ages of the deportees. The Germans compiled the names of those tried for disobeying SS orders and designated for transfer as punishment, but the complete list of names was drawn up by a transport committee of the ghetto leadership. The leadership was entitled to release vital workers from transports, and consequently found itself under enormous pressure. Occasionally people were sent to the "east" after spending just a few days in the ghetto; in some cases, connections and favoritism determined who would go and who would remain.

Theresienstadt
Members of the Judenrat headed by Dr. Paul Eppstein (standing in the center). Benjamin Murmelstein is standing on his left and Otto Zuker on his right. *From a propaganda film made about the ghetto* (USHMM)

The first half of 1942 saw 20,000 men, women, and children (who up to the age of sixteen were sent together with their parents) transported from the Theresienstadt ghetto to unknown destinations generally referred to as the "east", which, it was learned only after the war, were in fact the camps of Izbica, Zamosc, and others in the Lublin district. The death rate at that time in the Theresienstadt ghetto itself was still relatively low—thirty to forty people each month. However, the wave of transports of elderly people brought the death rate to a record high in September 1942, when close to 4,000 people, predominantly seniors, died in one month. But the Germans were not satisfied with that mortality rate. The proportion of elderly people in the ghetto reached 57 percent, and there were not enough working hands to take care of them. In order to "expedite the situation", between September 19 to September 29, 1942, six transports containing some 11,000 people, most over the age of sixty-five, were sent, supposedly, to "another ghetto". In fact, the Jews were transported to the Maly Trostenets extermination camp near Minsk. One of these Jews survived. From October 5 to October 22, 1942, five additional transports carrying 8,000 people left for the Treblinka extermination camp. Of them, two people survived.

The ghetto as a "model Jewish city": Another function of the Theresienstadt ghetto was as a "model Jewish city," as conceived in early 1943, contrary to the claims of numerous publications. In December 1942, after the world media published for the first time authoritative news reports about the mass extermination of Jews in occupied Europe, the Nazis sought ways to refute the "enemy's outrageous propaganda." Moreover, high-level personages had been brought to the ghetto, such as former government ministers, world-renowned scientists, and people under the protection of prominent individuals in the top Nazi ranks. Of them, 225 were given the status of *Prominenten*, most of whom, together with their close families, were by and large protected from deportation to the east. In addition, in October 1943, brought to the camp were 466 Danish Jews who had not been able to escape in time to Sweden, and the Danish Red Cross, by means of the International Red Cross in Geneva, requested a visit.

A visit of that nature required meticulous planning on the part of the Germans. A beautification campaign was thus launched in the fall of 1943. The streets of the ghetto, which until then had been marked only with letters and numbers, received poetic names. A bank was established and special ghetto money was printed—bills that bore on one side a likeness of Moses with side-locks, and on the other, the signature of Yaakov Edelstein, the first Jewish elder. Dummy shops were created, with barely any stock. A "café" with a resident jazz band was opened. Theresienstadt was no longer known as a ghetto, but rather a "Jewish settlement area."

In their original request, the representatives of the International Red Cross had asked to visit the Theresienstadt ghetto as well as one of the camps in the east. Thus in September 1943, the B/2/b camp, also known as the Birkenau Family Camp, was established in the Auschwitz complex. Five thousand prisoners from Theresienstadt were sent to the camp, where they were granted special conditions. Unlike the rest of the prisoners in the Auschwitz-Birkenau complex, their hair was not sheared, they were not required to wear striped uniforms, and men and women lived in the same camp (albeit in separate barracks). Most importantly, the arrivals did not undergo a selection, thus sparing, provisionally, both the children and the elderly. The prisoners were permitted to receive packages, and to write postcards to the Theresienstadt ghetto as well as to Jews outside the ghetto. The ruse was mounted to prove that contrary to the rumors of extermination, the Jews sent to the east were in fact alive and well.

In December 1943, another 5,000 prisoners from Theresienstadt were transferred to the family camp, and in May 1944, a short time before the planned visit of the International Red Cross delegation, another 7,500 were sent, to alleviate the overcrowding in the ghetto.

In preparation for the visit itself, which was held on June 24, 1944, the ghetto pavement on the designated route of the delegation was scrubbed clean, and a kindergarten was established for one day. A large proportion of the prisoners who were usually packed into overcrowded rooms on the ground floor of the buildings along the planned route were evacuated, and the three members of the delegation—including two representatives of the Danish Red Cross—visited the "family rooms". They were exclusively permitted to speak with privileged prisoners, Danish Jews, and representatives of the Jewish leadership, and only in the presence of SS guards. They watched a football match and children's opera and listened to Verdi's *Requiem* (the performance of which had been decided on by the conductor Rafael Schechter long before anyone knew about the city-beautifying campaign).

The hoax succeeded beyond expectation: Dr. Moritz Resel, the representative of the International Red Cross from Geneva, wrote a report that very evening characterizing Theresienstadt as a "city like all other cities," whose residents even benefited from larger food rations than the general population, and lacked nothing, with the exception of alcoholic drinks and cigarettes. The delegation viewed Theresienstadt as a "final destination" and did not inquire after the whereabouts of the tens of thousands of Jews who had passed through the ghetto on their way east.

In the family camp in Auschwitz-Birkenau, the prisoners of the September 1943 transport, 3,792 men, women, and children who had survived until then under conditions of starvation, cold, and filth, were all exterminated (without a prior selection) in the gas chambers on March 8, 1944, six months after their arrival. The December 1943 transport was designated for extermination six months later, towards the end of June 1944. When it was clear that the Red Cross delegation viewed the Theresienstadt ghetto as a final destination and therefore had no interest in visiting another camp, the family camp was completely liquidated in July 1944. Some 3,000 young men and women were sent to work in Germany, mostly

Theresienstadt
Chorus from children's opera
*Brundibar. From a propaganda
film made about the ghetto.* (YV)

in subsidiary camps of the large concentration camps, and all the remaining approximately 11,000 people were murdered in the gas chambers.

Before the scenery for the large-scale deception in the Theresienstadt ghetto itself was dismantled, a propaganda film was recorded, entitled *Theresienstadt, The Jewish Settlement Area*, cynically named "The Führer Gives the Jews a City" by the prisoners. The film was never screened before the general public because the Reich fell before it could be completed. Most of the cast and staff were sent to Auschwitz. And then, after the fate of the war had already been decided, 18,500 prisoners from Theresienstadt were sent to Auschwitz within a single month, from September 28 to October 28, 1944. The men of working age were supposedly sent to a new labor camp, followed by the women and children, and finally the entire Jewish leadership, all of whom were brought directly to the gas chambers. The same fate awaited the children in the children's houses, the elderly, and mothers of young children. These were the last transports from Theresienstadt that were liquidated in the Auschwitz facilities before they ceased operations, as the eastern front grew closer.

The final period: Approximately 11,000 prisoners remained in the ghetto: a few men fit for work, women who worked in the mica-splitting factory and farming, the privileged prisoners, the Danish Jews, and a few elderly people and children. To them were added transports of women and children who had been brought from the Sered detention camp in Slovakia after it was no longer possible to transport them to Auschwitz, along with the Jewish spouses of "Aryans" in valid marriages, who until then had been protected from deportation.

In February 1945, sealed rooms that could be used to asphyxiate prisoners with gas began to be built within the ghetto walls, and a huge pit was dug. These preparations indicate that the SS command intended to liquidate the remaining ghetto inhabitants. Yet the tumultuous events unfolding in advance of the anticipated defeat of the Nazi regime precluded these plans. On February 3, 1945, a change of fortune: an announcement to the effect that a transport would soon leave for Switzerland—and for the first time, it was not a trap, but the truth. Altogether 1,200 people actually left the ghetto and reached their destination as part of a deal struck by Heinrich Himmler with Swiss authorities.

On April 6, 1945, Paul Dunant of the International Red Cross arrived for a visit to Theresienstadt. Once again, the Red Cross representative was shown a sham "model ghetto", but on a far smaller scale than in June 1944. Another auspicious event involved the transfer of all the Danish prisoners to Sweden by Swedish Red Cross buses on April 15, 1945.

The surviving residents of Theresienstadt learned about the extermination on April 20, 1945, when survivors of the death marches began to arrive, emaciated from starvation. Only then did the Theresienstadt residents fully discover the fate that their loved ones had met in the "east". The survivors of the death march were infected with epidemic typhus, which took the lives of hundreds of victims, including a number of the doctors and nurses that cared for them.

Underground and resistance: Three undergrounds were active in the Theresienstadt ghetto: one made up of Czech Jews, one of Communists, and one of Zionists. Their members built improvised radio receivers and monitored BBC broadcasts, and, occasionally with the help of the Czech guards, smuggled into the ghetto food, money, medications, and other forbidden but vital provisions. The underground organizations maintained secret contact with the outside world, prepared sketches of the barracks and walls of the ghetto, and discussed the possibility that the Germans might want to liquidate the ghetto. They had brass knuckles but no firearms. No armed uprising was planned, mainly in the hope that thousands would survive in the ghetto until the end of the war, but also because the underground members were unable verify the news and rumors of the total extermination of the Jews in "the east".

Liberation: The first units of the Red Army entered Theresienstadt on May 8, 1945, after the members of the SS command had fled. Owing to the fear of a spreading typhus epidemic, the city was declared closed territory. Following the gradual return of the liberated prisoners to their native countries, the ghetto officially ceased to exist on August 15, 1945.

During the three and a half years of its existence, 155,650 prisoners from the Protectorate of Bohemia and Moravia, the German Reich, including Austria, Holland, Denmark, Slovakia, and small numbers from other countries, passed through the gates of the Theresienstadt ghetto. Of them, about 34,000 perished in the ghetto itself; close to 87,000 were sent to extermination camps from Theresienstadt in sixty-three transports; of these, about 3,000 survived. As noted above, after the extermination transports in the fall of 1944, about 11,000 prisoners remained in the ghetto, of whom only about 400 were men of working age. At the time of the liberation of the ghetto by the Red Army on May 1945, there were 29,469 prisoners living in the ghetto. This figure can be attributed to the arrival in the final months of the war of Jewish spouses married to "members of the Aryan race," who until then had been protected from deportation, as well as to the arrival of survivors of the death marches who made their way to the camp during its final days.

The three SS commanders of the Theresienstadt ghetto were, like Hitler himself, natives of Austria. The first, Dr. Siegfried Seidl, stood as the head of the ghetto until July 1943. Anton Burger, a teacher by profession and a particularly brutal man, served as the commandant of the ghetto from July 1943 until February 1944. Burger was replaced by Karl Rahm, who was a mechanic by profession with a personality that was apparently better suited to carry off the hoax of the model Jewish city.

Ruth Bondi

TIRASPOL

SEAT OF THE MOLDAVIAN AUTONOMOUS REPUBLIC, UKRAINE; FROM 1940, COUNTY SEAT IN THE SOVIET REPUBLIC OF MOLDAVIA/MOLDOVA

During the war: Transnistria (under Romanian control)

Coordinates:
46°03' | 28°49'

On the eve of the German invasion of the Soviet Union, there were about 12,000 Jews living in Tiraspol, representing approximately one-quarter of the city's population.

During the period of Soviet rule, many of the Jews were artisans and several had formed cooperatives. The city had two Jewish schools that offered instruction in Yiddish, one of which was a vocational school. In the interwar period, Jews moved to Tiraspol from surrounding localities, boosting the city's Jewish community.

The Germans and Romanians occupied Tiraspol on August 8, 1941. An unknown number of Jews had managed to evacuate or flee to the east prior to the occupation. The German forces murdered most of the Jews who remained in the city in the early days of the occupation. Only a few managed to survive in hiding with the help of Christians.

On September 1, 1941, Tiraspol was handed over to Romanian rule after it was annexed to Transnistria. A few dozen young Jewish women who survived the massacre were raped and then murdered by Romanian civil administration officials and soldiers. From September 1941, Tiraspol became a central transit point for thousands of Jewish deportees from Romania; few managed to remain in the city.

In the summer of 1942, about 100 Jews lived in Tiraspol, of whom 30 to 40 were artisans. These Jews were concentrated in the city hospital, which was turned into a ghetto. In 1943, additional Jews reached the city, and the ghetto's population gradually grew to about 800. The building and surrounding park were encircled by a barbed-wire fence.

The Romanian authorities set up two sewing shops, a cobbler's workshop, a small soap factory, and a barbershop in the ghetto. The Tiraspol ghetto became a model of mutual self-aid and internal organization, in part owing to the favorable treatment exhibited by Iacobescu, the commander of the local Romanian gendarmerie. The Jews employed in the workshops and the various institutions allocated half of their wages to a common fund that went toward establishing a public soup kitchen that served all of the ghetto's inhabitants and for assistance to hundreds of Jews who temporarily lodged in Tiraspol on their way to other locations in Transnistria. The ghetto had a dental clinic as well as a medical clinic with six to eight beds. The deportees farmed the area around the building and cultivated agricultural produce. A small number of epidemic typhus cases were discovered in the early days of the Jews' stay in the ghetto, but the favorable sanitary conditions that were maintained in the ghetto staved off further spread of the disease.

The Tiraspol ghetto became a place of asylum for Transnistrian deportees owing to its relatively adequate living conditions. The ghetto inhabitants established a house of prayer and managed to acquire a Torah scroll and a *shofar* from one of the nearby towns. On the Jewish holidays, they were permitted to take time off from work. The Jews also organized parties and artistic performances. In December 1943, the ghetto population received assistance from the aid committee in Bucharest, which endeavored to organize the return of the deportees from the Dorohoi District to Romania.

As the front drew closer, the deportees received permits from the Romanian gendarmes to return to their homes, and on March 17–19, 1944, they crossed the Dniester together with other deportees from south Transnistria. After the Romanians left, the Germans took over the city and executed many of the inmates of the local prison, some of whom were Jewish.

Tiraspol was liberated by the Soviets on April 12, 1944.

TISZAFÖLDVÁR

TOWNLET IN JÁSZ-
NAGYKUN-SZOLNOK
COUNTY, HUNGARY

Coordinates:
46°59' | 20°15'

The last national census conducted in Hungary prior to the German occupation recorded, in January 1941, ninety-five Jewish inhabitants in Tiszafoldvar, approximately 1 percent of the total population. Most were merchants and artisans. Tiszafoldvar had a Status Quo Ante Jewish community, which became increasingly poverty stricken in the interwar period as several of its members moved after World War I to other nearby localities.

The German army occupied Hungary on March 19, 1944. According to a census conducted in the second week of April 1944, seventy-one Jews belonged to the Status Quo Ante Jewish community of Tiszafoldvar.

The Hungarian administration remained intact and operational after the occupation. The ghettoization and deportation of the Jews were carried out on the basis of the decrees and orders of the Hungarian national and local authorities. On May 1, 1944, the Hungarian sub-prefect, Imre Alexander, published a decree ordering the ghettoization of the Jews in the county. A ghetto was subsequently established in Tiszafoldvar.

In mid-June 1944, its inhabitants were transferred to a copper sulfate factory in Kecskemet*, which served as an entrainment center, and deported on to Auschwitz between June 25 and 27, 1944.

TISZAFÜRED

TOWN IN HEVES COUNTY,
HUNGARY

Coordinates:
47°37' | 20°46'

The last national census conducted in Hungary prior to the German occupation, taken in January 1941, recorded 442 Jewish inhabitants in Tiszafured, representing roughly 4 percent of the total population. Most were merchants and artisans; several were landowners. The town's Jewish community was Orthodox and had a Yeshiva and a Jewish elementary school.

In 1942, fifteen local Jews were arrested by the Hungarian authorities and sent to the Kistarcsa internment camp. From July 1942, a decree by the Hungarian local chief administrator forbade Jews to buy provisions in the county before nine o'clock in the morning, by which time the markets were usually emptied.

The German army occupied Hungary on March 19, 1944. A census conducted in the second week of April 1944 showed that 416 Jews belonged to the Orthodox Jewish community of Tiszafured.

The Hungarian administration remained intact and operational after the occupation. Hungarian national and local authorities decreed the ghettoization and deportation of the Jews. On May 6, 1944, Hungarian sub-prefect Gyula Szabo published a decree concerning the establishment of Jewish Councils and the ghettoization of the Jews from Heves County. The Jews of Tiszafured and the area were ordered to move into the town ghetto as of May 8. The ghetto was established in the brick factory, as the two previously suggested options (next to the synagogue and near the railway station) would have involved the eviction of too many Christians. Altogether about 800 people from Tiszafured and the area moved into the ghetto through to May 14, 1944.

Ferenc Kiss, the last serving president of the Jewish community, headed the Jewish Council (which in Tiszafured was referred to as the Quintet Council). The Jewish Council organized community prayers and created rooms for the sick as well as a delivery room. The soup kitchen soon ran out of provisions, leaving the ghetto inhabitants starving.

At the end of May 1944, police detectives arrived in the ghetto, forcing the Jews to reveal the whereabouts of their hidden valuables. At the beginning of June 1944, between sixty and seventy Jewish men aged sixteen to sixty were drafted into the Hungarian army for forced labor service, saving them from immediate deportation.

On June 8, 1944, the ghetto inhabitants were transferred from the ghetto to an entrainment center at the Kerecsend brick factory, near Eger*, and deported on to Auschwitz.

TŁUMACZ
(Yiddish: **Tolmitsh**)

COUNTY SEAT, STANISŁAWÓW DISTRICT, POLAND
(After World War II in the USSR/Ukraine; Ukrainian, Russian: **Tlumach**)

During the war: General Gouvernement, Galicia District

Coordinates: 48°52' | 25°00'

In the early 1930s, about 2,100 Jews lived in Tlumacz, representing approximately one-third of the townlet's population. Most earned their livelihood from petty commerce and artisanship, while several were factory owners and large-scale businesspeople. Tlumacz boasted Zionist parties and youth movements, the ultra-Orthodox *Machzikei Hadas*, and a chapter of the Bund. The parties operated cultural clubs, libraries, and sports organizations, and the children of the community received complementary education in Hebrew in a *Safa Brurah* school. A number of young Jews joined the illegal Polish Communist Party. In 1937, Ukrainian farmers looted Jewish shops in the townlet.

In the second half of September 1939, Tlumacz was occupied by the Red Army and handed over to Soviet control. Jewish public life was discontinued, factories and large commercial enterprises were nationalized, and retail commerce was phased out. Artisans were organized in cooperatives. In the spring of 1940, a number of "bourgeois" families and Jews accused of profiteering were exiled into the Soviet interior; in June 1940, Jewish refugees from western Poland who refused to accept Soviet citizenship were also exiled. After the Soviets withdrew from the townlet, Jews who had held positions in Soviet governmental institutions and who were members of the Polish Communist Party also headed east, but not all were able to reach the Soviet interior.

On July 7, 1941, Tlumacz was occupied by the Hungarians (allies of the Germans). A few weeks later, in August or September 1941, the townlet was handed over to German control. Eliyahu Redner was appointed the first head of the Judenrat; according to one source, he and his deputy were murdered in September 1941, for refusing to comply with Gestapo demands to hand over eight Jews. The second Judenrat head was Dr. Steinberg, and Chaim Reitser was placed in charge of the Jewish Order Service. In October 1941, the Jews of Tlumacz were ordered to remit their gold and silver to the Germans, and in December, they were commanded to turn over their furs and to furnish thirty-two apartments for the Germans at their own expense.

Tlumacz, 1942
The Jews of the ghetto are deported to Stanislawow, where they were executed. (YV)

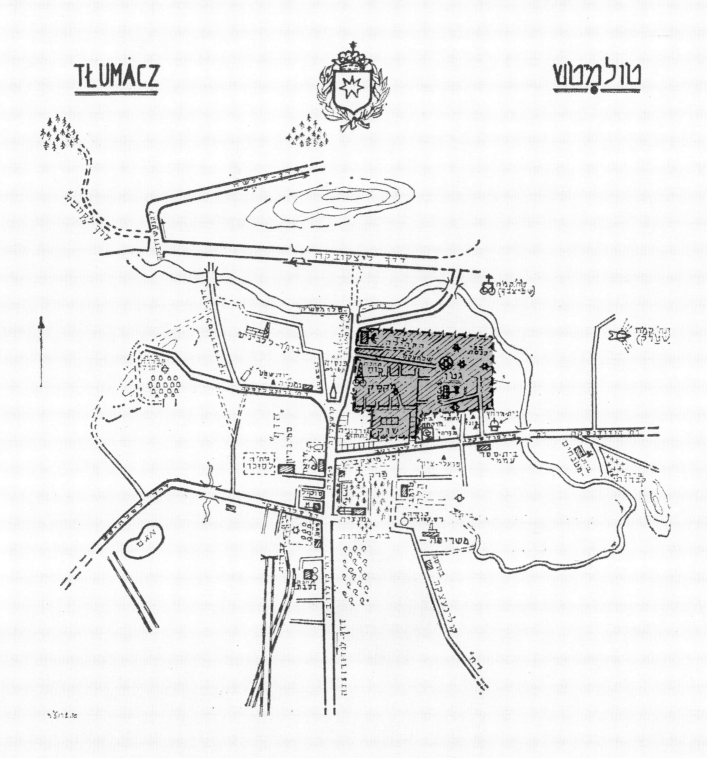

Tlumacz plan indicating ghetto boundaries, illustrated by A. Shrayer, based on his memory
(*Memorial Book of Tlumacz, The Life and Destruction of Jewish Community*, published by the Tlumacz
Societies in Israel and the USA, Israel 1976)

On April 5–6, 1942, the Germans carried out the first mass deportation from the townlet. The police ordered the Jews to gather in the Polish school building "for transfer to another location." To complete the deception, the Jews were permitted to bring along luggage weighing twenty kilograms each. The approximately 1,000 Jews who assembled at the round-up site were transferred to the Stanislawow* ghetto and murdered.

In early May 1942, a ghetto was established in Tlumacz in which the Jews from surrounding localities were also concentrated. The ghetto was very overcrowded and the living conditions were harsh. Some 280 Jews died of hunger and disease. A hospital, a public soup kitchen, and an orphanage were set up but were scarcely equipped to alleviate the general suffering. On May 18, 1942, about 180 Jews were murdered by members of the German SIPO, and in June 1942, another 70 elderly and ill people were murdered. During the same period, hundreds of young Jews were sent to the Janowska labor camp on the outskirts of Lwow* as well as to other camps. In the summer of 1942, the Judenrat was ordered to supply 200 Jewish men each day for forced labor. The population of the ghetto at this stage is estimated at about 1,200.

The Germans began to liquidate the ghetto in early August 1942. For one month, groups of Jews were executed either in the Jewish cemetery or in Stanislawow. Eighty Jews remained in the ghetto to sort through the Jewish property; when they completed their task they, too, were executed. On September 10, 1942, Tlumacz was declared *"Judenrein."*

TŁUSZCZ

TOWNLET IN RADZYMIN COUNTY, WARSAW DISTRICT, POLAND

During the war: General Gouvernement, Warsaw District

Coordinates:
52°25' | 21°27'

About 440 Jews lived in Tluszcz, representing approximately 35 percent of the population. They earned their livelihood from commerce, artisanship, and transportation. Traditional charitable institutions assisted the needy. The community had a Jewish school, a Beit Midrash, and a library. The Zionist parties and pioneering youth movements were amply represented.

Tluszcz was bombed early in the war. Most of the townlet's buildings were destroyed, and many of its Jewish inhabitants fled. The Germans occupied Tluszcz on September 14, 1939, and they immediately began to seize Jews for forced labor. In October 1939, the Germans appointed a Judenrat headed by Gutman Popovski. In late 1939, the townlet's Jews were ordered to wear a yellow patch and a yellow Star-of-David armband.

In the winter of 1939/40, many of the Jews left for the east to the Soviet zone, while hundreds of displaced Jews sought asylum in the townlet. The situation worsened with the arrival of SS officer Lipsche. In the wake of the large-scale destruction caused by the occupation, the German authorities ordered the local inhabitants to rebuild; however, the Jews of Tluszcz were unable to bear the reconstruction expenses, owing to their devastated circumstances.

In the winter of 1941, an order was issued regarding the establishment of a ghetto and a Jewish Order Service. The ghetto was closed and encircled by a barbed-wire fence, and held about 750 Jews from Tluszcz and the surrounding localities. In the winter of 1941/42, many Jews suffering from disease and hunger fled, including Tluszcz's rabbi, Rabbi Yaakov Yosef Brikman, who escaped to Jadow*.

The Tluszcz ghetto was liquidated on May 27, 1942. On the night of May 25, 1942, the Jews were ordered to gather in the marketplace. Their belongings and money were robbed, and the women and children were sent in wagons to Radzymin*, and from there to Warsaw*. The men, meanwhile, were taken on foot; during the march, more than 100 were shot and killed. Some 600 Jews from Tluszcz arrived in Warsaw. A small number of artisans were transferred to the Wilanow forced-labor camp. The Jews of Tluszcz in Warsaw shared the fate of the entire Jewish population of the Warsaw ghetto.

TOLNA

TOWNLET IN TOLNA COUNTY, HUNGARY

Coordinates:
46°26' | 18°47'

The last national census conducted prior to the German occupation, taken in January 1941, recorded 205 Jewish inhabitants in Tolna, less than 3 percent of the total population. Most were merchants and artisans and several were farmers. The Jews in Tolna were organized in a Status Quo Ante community and maintained a Jewish school.

In 1937, the local branch of the *Volksbund*, composed largely of ethnic Germans (Swabians), was established in Tolna, causing much suffering to the Jewish residents of the townlet. In 1939, Jewish men were drafted into the Hungarian army for forced labor service. In 1942, Jewish men from Tolna were again drafted for forced labor service in the Ukraine; many perished.

The German army occupied Hungary on March 19, 1944. A census conducted during the second week of April 1944 reported that 180 Jews belonged to the Status Quo Ante Jewish community of Tolna.

The Hungarian administration remained intact and operational after the German occupation. The ghettoization and deportation of the Jews were carried out on the basis of the decrees and orders of the Hungarian national and local authorities. On May 1, 1944, Edvin Szongott, the Hungarian sub-prefect of Tolna County, ordered the establishment of ghettos in his county. In addition to the local Jews, 230 Jews from the Kozponti county-district were required to move into the Tolna ghetto, which was established along three blocks of houses marked with mandatory "canary-yellow" stars.

At the end of June or beginning of July 1944, the Jews were transferred to Paks*, to the entrainment center of Tolna County. They were deported to Auschwitz in a single transport, on July 5, 1944.

TOLOCHIN

(Belarussian: **Talachyn**)

COUNTY SEAT, VITEBSK DISTRICT, BELARUS, USSR

During the war: Military Administration Area

Coordinates:
54°25' | 29°42'

At the beginning of the twentieth century, there were about 2,000 Jews in Tolochin, two-thirds of the local population. During the era of Soviet rule, Jews worked as artisans, some in cooperatives. Urbanization and industrialization in the interwar period prompted many Jews to leave Tolochin, so that by the late 1930s only some 1,300 remained, about 20 percent of the population. The townlet had a school that taught in Yiddish.

On July 4, 1941, a number of Jews left Tolochin when the townlet came under German bombardment. German occupation began four days later.

In September 1941, the Germans ordered all Jews to move into a ghetto consisting of one street and a few alleys in a slum quarter from which all non-Jewish inhabitants had been evicted. Jews from the nearby townlets of Krugloye*, Drutsk, and Sloveni* were concentrated there as well. The ghetto was guarded initially by Belarussian police and later by more brutal Ukrainian police. The Jews were ordered to wear a "badge of shame" with a yellow Star-of-David. Although the ghetto was not fenced, the Jews were not allowed to leave. Given no food rations, they obtained food in what remained of vegetable plots in the ghetto and by bartering with the local population. The Jews brought water into the ghetto from the local river, under police supervision. In October 1941, seven Jewish men who refused to help carry water were hanged. In the winter of 1941/42, about 150 inhabitants of the ghetto died from the cold and starvation.

The ghetto was liquidated on March 13, 1942, when approximately 1,300 Jews were apparently murdered near the townlet.

TOMASHPOL

(Ukrainian: **Tomashpil'**)

COUNTY SEAT, VINNITSA DISTRICT, UKRAINE, USSR

During the war: Transnistria (under Romanian control)

Coordinates:
48°32' | 28°31'

In the late nineteenth century, about 4,500 Jews lived in Tomashpol, representing more than half of the town's population. In March 1920, during the civil war in Russia (1918–20), soldiers from a White Army unit murdered 25 of Tomashpol's Jews and injured another 210.

During the Soviet period, Tomashpol had a Jewish Ethnic Soviet that conducted its affairs in Yiddish as well as a Yiddish-language school and kindergarten. Most of the town's Jews engaged in private commerce until its abolishment in the early 1930s and in artisanship. Some of the Jews took up farming and formed a Jewish kolkhoz. On the eve of the German invasion of the Soviet Union, about 1,800 Jews lived in Tomashpol.

In the wake of the German invasion of the Soviet Union on June 22, 1941, many Jewish men from Tomashpol were recruited into the Red Army. The Germans occupied the town on July 20, 1941. A few days later, the Jews were ordered to wear a white armband with a black Star-of-David. On July 25, 1941, six Jews were shot to death. The Germans rounded up either 160 or 240 Jews (sources vary on the figure), apparently on August 11, 1942, murdering all in the Jewish cemetery.

In late August 1941, Tomashpol was annexed to Transnistria, which was under Romanian rule. In December 1941, a ghetto encircled by a barbed-wire fence was established, into which the Jewish population of the town was concentrated under conditions of severe overcrowding. Zalman Bronffman was appointed head of the twelve-member ghetto council. Jews from nearby localities and from Bessarabia were also concentrated in the ghetto. The Jews were permitted to leave it in small groups in order to collect water. They were required to perform forced labor. Many fell ill with epidemic typhus owing to overcrowding and hunger. Groups of Jewish women disobeyed the council's orders and collected donations for the needy and ill. Individual Ukrainians helped by passing food through the barbed-wire fence. Religious services were held daily in the ghetto. In 1943, its population numbered 1,100 Jews.

Tomashpol was liberated on March 16, 1944.

TOMASZÓW LUBELSKI

COUNTY SEAT, LUBLIN DISTRICT, POLAND

During the war: General Gouvernement, Lublin District

Coordinates:
50°27' | 23°25'

During the interwar years, some 5,600 Jews lived in Tomaszow Lubelski, more than half the town's population. Most were merchants and artisans who worked mainly in the clothing industry and at a foundry. The Jewish community had mutual-assistance trade associations, charitable and welfare societies supported by organizations and Jewish communities out of town, a free-loan fund, and a savings-and-loan association.

Tomaszow Lubelski was an important Hasidic center and the seat of rebbes of various courts. Zionist parties and pioneering movements were active there, as were Agudath Israel and the Bund. A Jewish weekly was published in Tomaszow Lubelski, and there were several Jewish cultural associations.

The Germans occupied the town on September 13, 1939, and immediately began abducting Jews for forced labor. Six Jews were murdered. On September 20, the Germans withdrew and the Soviets entered the town. A week later, the Soviets pulled back to the demarcation line established in the Molotov-Ribbentrop Pact. They were joined by some 2,000 local Jews, including the Hasidic rebbe Aryeh Leibush Rubin. Some 3,500 Jews remained in Tomaszow Lubelski.

When the Germans returned, the persecutions resumed. Several Jews were murdered in December 1939. At the end of 1939, the Jews were required to affix a yellow badge to their clothing and wear a Star-of-David armband. Shortly after the occupation began, the Germans appointed a Judenrat and installed Yehoshua

Fishelson at its head. The Judenrat was ordered to mobilize Jews aged twelve to fifty for forced labor and to pay large ransoms. It opened a soup kitchen.

Eventually, two streets in the town became an open ghetto. In the spring of 1942, the Gestapo executed Fishelson and his family for refusing to provide the Germans with a list of Jews to be deported.

In March 1942, the Germans deported all Jews aged thirty-two and over to the Belzec death camp. Another transport set out on May 22, 1942, and, on October 27, 1942, Poles and members of the Gestapo deported the remaining Jews in the ghetto to Belzec.

Some Jews managed to escape to the forests, but most were caught by Polish collaborators and handed over to the Germans. Several young people managed to mount an organized resistance.

TOMASZÓW MAZOWIECKI

TOWN IN BRZEZINY COUNTY, ŁÓDŹ DISTRICT, POLAND

During the war: Wartheland

Coordinates:
51°32' | 20°01'

In the interwar period, Tomaszow Mazowiecki had a Jewish population of about 10,000, one-third of the town's population. Most Jews in Tomaszow Mazowiecki were merchants or artisans, although a substantial number also held blue- or white-collar jobs at an artificial silk factory. A number belonged to Jewish trade unions. The community had many charitable institutions, including an orphanage and an old-age home that were supported by donations from Polish expatriates. A range of educational institutions included three Szabasowka schools, a Talmud Torah run by Agudath Israel, a bilingual Polish-Hebrew Jewish high school, a Jewish popular college that was also attended by non-Jews, and Polish high schools. Zionist political parties and youth movements ran a pioneering training center. The Bund, its youth movement, and Agudath Israel were active as well. Many Jews belonged to a local chapter of the Communist Party. Most parties sponsored cultural associations, drama groups, and libraries. By the eve of World War II, the Jewish population had climbed to about 13,000.

The Germans occupied Tomaszow Mazowiecki on September 5, 1939. By September 13, they had arrested about 1,000 townspeople, including some 300 Jews, and sent 90 Jewish men to the Buchenwald concentration camp. Only thirteen were alive at the end of the war. The Germans also abducted Jews for forced labor. Jews were only allowed to circulate in the town streets between eight

Tomaszow Mazowiecki
A group of Jews, including a member of the Jewish Order Service, near the ritual bath in the ghetto (YV)

o'clock in the morning and noon. The Germans torched the Great Synagogue on October 16 and burned two other houses of worship on November 7 and 14.

During the first few months of the occupation, a number of Tomaszow Mazowiecki's Jews, including many youths, fled to Soviet-controlled territory. Nevertheless, the town's Jewish population increased due to a large influx of refugees from Lodz* and Warsaw*.

In late 1939, a Judenrat was established under Baruch Shoeps and his deputy, Leibush Warsager. A Jewish Order Service was set up under Josef Goldberg. In late 1940, after the Gestapo arrested Shoeps and beat him to death, Warsager took over as chairman of the Judenrat. In early December, the Judenrat was ordered to furnish the Germans with 1,000 Jewish laborers every day. In 1940–42, hundreds of Jewish men in Tomaszow Mazowiecki were sent to villages and the Zawada labor camp for forced labor.

In June 1940, the Jewish population of Tomaszow Mazowiecki stood at 16,500.

The Jews of Tomaszow Mazowiecki were ghettoized on December 20, 1940. The ghetto, commanded by the county governor, Karl Glehn, was established in three different parts of town. While Jews were not allowed to leave the ghetto without permits, they violated this injunction liberally.

In March 1941, about 1,000 Jewish refugees from Plock* reached the ghetto, prompting the Judenrat to organize a soup kitchen. The kitchen's output gradually increased, and it soon served 1,500 meals per day. In May 1941, there were 15,306 Jews living in Tomaszow Mazowiecki, including 3,536 refugees.

In October 1941, about 1,500 Jews were deported from Tomaszow Mazowiecki to the nearby towns of Zarnow*, Drzewica*, Biala Rawska*, and Nowe Miasto*. On December 25, 1941, two of the three sectors of the ghetto were evacuated. Their inhabitants were either placed in the third sector or deported to Opoczno*. Congestion in the ghetto became unendurable, at more than ten people per room.

Primary and secondary studies were conducted clandestinely until the end of 1941. One of the teachers was Dr. Bornstein, a former principal of the town's Jewish high school. The soup kitchen was shut down in November or December 1941 because of lack of food. The sixty-bed ghetto hospital, run by Dr. Efraim Mordkovich of Lodz, struggled to cope with epidemic typhus, which broke out in 1941 owing to poor sanitary conditions in the ghetto.

Hundreds of Jews, including many children, were shot to death by German police while attempting to smuggle food into the ghetto. In late April and early May 1942, the Germans murdered between 100 and 200 Jews, including intellectuals and almost all members of the Judenrat.

Rumors about the liquidation of the ghettos of Warsaw and Piotrkow Trybunalski* reached Tomaszow Mazowiecki in the summer and fall of 1942. On the night of October 28, 1942, German and Polish police, along with Ukrainians and Latvians, surrounded the ghetto and trained their machine guns on it. Many Jews who attempted to flee were killed or wounded. The following day, the Germans informed the Judenrat that the entire ghetto population would be deported "to the east". Hundreds of Jews from Biala Rawska, Rawa Mazowiecka*, Ujazd*, and villages in the vicinity reached the town that night and were concentrated in a yard surrounded by barbed wire. Many were killed during this operation.

On October 31, 1942, German police rounded up all Jews in the Tomaszow Mazowiecki ghetto, townspeople and refugees alike. In the ensuing deportation operation, which lasted until November 2, hundreds of Jews were murdered and some 15,000 were sent to Treblinka. The operation to liquidate the Tomaszow Mazowiecki ghetto excluded between 900 to 1,300 Jews, mostly young people and refugees, who were left behind along with several hundred Jewish townspeople. This group comprised artisans, a few practitioners of liberal professions, and remaining members of the hospital staff, the Judenrat, and the Jewish Order Service. Yosef Goldberg was placed in charge of the Jewish Order Service; his deputy was Mulek Milstein. The rump community was housed in a confined area known as the "small ghetto", enclosed in barbed wire, and guarded by Germans, Poles, and Ukrainians. Most of its inhabitants set out for work every day under guard. A few gathered and sorted belongings that were left behind in the ghetto; others toiled in workshops in the ghetto and factories on the "Aryan" side of town.

On January 5, 1943, German and Ukrainian police surrounded the ghetto as trucks and wagons were brought in. Over the course of the following two days, 250 Jews were deported to Ujazd and on to Treblinka. One day in February 1943, two German policemen murdered twenty-one Jews, among them Jewish policemen and several physicians, including Dr. Mordkovich. The casualties were buried in the Jewish cemetery. In March, four Jews were murdered in the ghetto and the others were dispossessed. Two groups of artisans were sent from the ghetto to labor camps in Blizyn and Pionki.

By May 1943, only 600 to 900 Jews inhabited the ghetto. A selection was performed on May 31, and all of Tomaszow Mazowiecki's remaining residents were taken to the labor camp in Blizyn. Thirty-six to thirty-eight Jews were left behind to clean up the ghetto area and, on September 5, 1943, were taken to the labor camp in Starachowice.

TOPOLYA

TOWN IN BÁCS-BODROG COUNTY, HUNGARY
(After World War II in Yugoslavia/Serbia; Serbian: **Bačka Topola**)

Coordinates:
45°49' | 19°39'

The last national census conducted prior to the German occupation, taken in January 1941, recorded 319 Jewish inhabitants in Topolya, approximately 2 percent of the total population. Most were merchants and artisans. The town's Jewish community was Neolog.

After World War I, the town belonged to Yugoslavia (until 1929, it was called the Serbo-Croatian-Slovenian Kingdom). In April 1941, Topolya once again came under Hungarian rule.

In 1941, following the invasion by the Hungarian army, the Hungarian authorities established an internment camp in Topolya that held many Jews.

According to a census conducted in the second week of April 1944, a few weeks after the German occupation of Hungary, 217 Jews belonged to the Neolog Jewish community of Topolya.

After the occupation on March 19, 1944, the Germans took control of the internment camp at Topolya, concentrating within its grounds the local Jews as well as other Jews from the vicinity and throughout the country.

The Hungarian administration remained intact and in force after the occupation. The ghettoization and deportation of the Jews were carried out on the basis of the decrees and orders of the Hungarian national and local authorities. At the beginning of April 1944, Hungarian authorities declared several towns in Bacs-Bodrog County zones of hostility. As a consequence, some eighty Jews from the town of Zombor were sent to Topolya on April 28, 1944. On the same day, seventeen Jewish refugees from Poland also arrived in Topolya's internment camp. On May 7, 1944, there arrived in Baja* from the internment camp in Topolya, which was closed down, 200 Jews. They were deported to Gaenserndorf (near Vienna) from Baja on May 27 or 28, 1944. Following a selection, able-bodied people were assigned to work in the fields while the balance was sent to Auschwitz.

TORCZYN

TOWNLET IN ŁUCK COUNTY, VOLHYNIA DISTRICT, POLAND

(After World War II in the USSR/Ukraine; Ukrainian: **Torchyn**; Russian: **Torchin**)

During the war: Reichskommissariat Ukraine

Coordinates: 50°46' | 25°00'

During the interwar years, there were about 1,500 Jews in Torczyn, accounting for roughly half of the townlet's population. They engaged in crafts relating to clothing, construction, and food as well as in petty trade. The services of Jewish savings-and-loan associations and self-help organizations were available to the community. Torczyn's children attended a Hebrew-language Tarbut primary school, Hadarim, and a Talmud Torah. The Bund was active in the townlet. Torczyn also enjoyed a popular drama circle.

After the Soviets took control of Torczyn in September 1939, the Tarbut school was transformed into a Yiddish-language Soviet school.

The Germans occupied Torczyn on July 25, 1941. Jews were made to wear a Star-of-David armband and were abducted for forced labor. During the first few months of the occupation, about 300 Jews were murdered.

In January 1942, the Jews were ordered to remit a ransom of gold, clothing, and assorted possessions. That month some 1,500 Jews were brought to Torczyn from other locations in the vicinity.

About a month later, a ghetto was established that concentrated about 3,000 Jews into its quarters. Seventy artisans and their families were allowed to live outside of it. In May 1942, of the 150 Jewish youths removed from the ghetto and sent to Kiev, ostensibly for labor, all but one were murdered.

The Torczyn ghetto was liquidated on August 23, 1942, and its inmates murdered at the Jewish cemetery outside its confines. Several Jews committed acts of resistance during the operation. The blacksmith Moshe Zoberman grabbed a rifle from a Ukrainian policeman and struck him with the weapon, but was shot and killed. Several dozen Jews fled. A number of the escapees returned to Torczyn and joined the thirty-three skilled workers who had remained in the townlet. When it came time for their liquidation three days later, seven inhabitants fled and obtained weapons. Later, they fought against Ukrainian collaborators, committed acts of sabotage, and ultimately joined a Soviet partisan unit.

TORNALJA

TOWNLET IN GÖMÖR AND KISHONT COUNTY, HUNGARY

(After World War II in Czechoslovakia; Slovak: **Tornala**)

Coordinates: 48°25' | 20°20'

The last national census conducted in Hungary prior to the German occupation, taken in January 1941, recorded 629 Jewish inhabitants in Tornalja, accounting for approximately 17 percent of the total population. Most were merchants and artisans. The townlet's Jewish community was Orthodox and had a Jewish elementary school.

After World War I, Tornalja, which was formerly under Hungarian rule, became part of Czechoslovakia. Later, as per the First Vienna Award (November 2, 1938), the townlet was annexed to Hungary. Between the two World Wars, the Jewish Party was the most popular among the Jewish parties in the townlet. The majority of the Jewish youth belonged to various Zionist youth movements.

In the summer of 1941, the Hungarian authorities deported from Tornalja to a region in the Ukraine under German occupation eight Jewish families whose members could not prove their Hungarian citizenship,. They were murdered on August 27 and 28 at Kamenets-Podolsk*. In July 1941, gendarmes rounded up about 100 Jewish men in Tornalja and transferred them to nearby Putnok*. The Hungarian authorities intended to deport the men to Kamenets-Podolsk, but the Jewish leadership in Budapest intervened and they were released.

The German army occupied Hungary on March 19, 1944. The Hungarian administration remained intact and operational after the occupation. Hungarian national and local authorities decreed the ghettoization and deportation of the Jews. On April 21, 1944, Hungarian gendarmes transferred the local Jews into a ghetto, which was sealed off on May 8, 1944. A total of 620 Jews lived in eighteen houses. Another 200 Jews from the County-District of Tornalja were brought to Tornalja. They were placed in a second ghetto established in a local hotel.

Samuel Krakovits, a merchant and the last serving president of the Jewish community, was appointed president of the Jewish Council. In May 1944, able-bodied men were called up for forced labor and were transferred to the nearby Jolsva (today: Jelsava, Slovakia). They were in turn deployed to the eastern front. Many of the men perished.

On June 4, 1944, gendarmes liquidated both ghettos, whose inhabitants were brought to tobacco warehouses on the outskirts of the townlet near the train station. On June 6, 1944, they were transferred to the entrainment center in a brick factory in Miskolc*. They were deported to Auschwitz in several transports between June 12 and 15, 1944.

TÖRÖKSZENTMIKLÓS

TOWN IN JÁSZ-NAGYKUN-SZOLNOK COUNTY, HUNGARY

Coordinates:
47°11' | 20°25'

The last national census conducted in Hungary prior to the German occupation, taken in January 1941, recorded 520 Jewish inhabitants in Torokszentmiklos, accounting for approximately 2 percent of the total population. Most were merchants and artisans. The town's Jewish community was Neolog and had a Jewish school. Following World War I, a number of Jews were arrested and three Jews were killed, during the days of the White Terror. In 1942, several Jews from Torokszentmiklos were drafted into the Hungarian army for forced labor service. Twenty-two of the men perished on the eastern front, in the Ukraine.

The German army occupied Hungary on March 19, 1944. A census conducted in the second week of April 1944 reported that 420 Jews belonged to the Neolog Jewish community of Torokszentmiklos. In April 1944, six local Jews were arrested and sent to an internment camp, and deported on to Auschwitz.

The Hungarian administration remained intact and operational after the occupation. The ghettoization and deportation of the Jews were carried out on the basis of the decrees and orders of the Hungarian national and local authorities. On May 1, 1944, the Hungarian sub-prefect, Imre Alexander, published a decree ordering the ghettoization of the Jews in the county, and a ghetto was subsequently established in Torokszentmiklos; 683 Jews from the town and the six small localities nearby were concentrated in its grounds.

At the beginning of June 1944, the inhabitants of the ghetto were transferred to the entrainment center at the Szolnok* sugar factory. On June 25, 1944, the first transport of deportees left for Strasshof in Austria, with 2,628 people aboard. The second transport left on June 28, 1944, carrying 2,083 people to Auschwitz.

TOROPETS

COUNTY SEAT, KALININ DISTRICT, RUSSIAN FEDERATION, USSR

During the war: Military Administration Area

Coordinates:
56°30' | 31°39'

In the early 1920s, about 1,400 Jews lived in Toropets, more than one-tenth of the municipal population. During the interwar years, the town's Jewish population declined considerably, falling to 500 people by 1939. The town had a Yiddish government school and a Jewish club.

The Germans occupied Toropets on August 29, 1941. Many Jews managed to flee the town prior to its occupation. A three-member Judenrat chaired by a physician was established. The Jews were forced to wear a white Star-of-David armband and to perform forced labor; they endured German abuse, humiliation, and mistreatment. A number of Jewish residents of the town were murdered.

On September 20, 1941, some sixty Jews who remained in Toropets were interned in a ghetto of sorts established in a linen factory on the outskirts of town.

During their confinement, they were sent out to perform forced labor. The local population looted Jewish-owned property.

The ghetto was liquidated in October or November 1941 when the Jews were removed from the factory and shot to death.

TÓTKOMLÓS

TOWN IN BÉKÉS COUNTY, HUNGARY

Coordinates:
46°25' | 20°44'

The last national census conducted prior to the German occupation, taken in January 1941, recorded 153 Jewish inhabitants in Totkomlos, approximately 1 percent of the total population; most were merchants and artisans. The town had an Orthodox Jewish community.

From 1940, the majority of the Jewish men from Totkomlos were drafted into the Hungarian army for forced labor service.

The German army occupied Hungary on March 19, 1944. A census conducted in the second week of April 1944 reported that 146 Jews belonged to the Orthodox Jewish community of Totkomlos.

The Hungarian administration remained intact and in force after the occupation. The ghettoization and deportation of the Jews were carried out on the basis of the decrees and orders of the Hungarian national and local authorities. The Totkomlos ghetto was established in May 1944, in the house of a local Jew. Non-Jews of Totkomlos were permitted to enter the ghetto freely, and they brought in food and, occasionally, mail.

At the end of June 1944, the inhabitants of the ghetto, about 120 Jews, were brought to the Bekescsaba* entrainment center. They were then transferred to the entrainment center in Debrecen*, and finally deported on to Strasshof, Austria, on June 24 and 25, 1944.

TREMBOWLA

COUNTY SEAT, TARNOPOL DISTRICT, POLAND
(After World War II in the USSR/Ukraine; Ukrainian, Russian: **Terebovlya**)

During the war: General Gouvernement, Galicia District

Coordinates:
49°18' | 25°43'

In the early 1920s, about 1,500 Jews lived in Trembowla, representing roughly 20 percent of the townlet's population. The Jewish community boasted chapters of various Jewish parties and youth movements, among them those of the Zionists, as well as welfare institutions.

In the second half of September 1939, Trembowla was occupied by the Soviets. Under their rule, the townlet's economic life was nationalized, the Jews' commercial activity was impaired, and the Jewish parties were abolished. In late June 1941, the Soviets withdrew from the townlet, and they were joined as they headed eastward by groups of young Jews.

On July 7, 1941, the Germans occupied Trembowla, and on that same day, German army units murdered a number of Jews in the streets. On July 11, 1941, Ukrainians murdered thirty-eight Jews, claiming that they had collaborated with the Soviets. Additional Jews were assigned to forced labor, and several were murdered. In late July, a Judenrat was established and headed by attorney Seret or Moshe Milman (sources vary regarding the identity), and a twelve-member Jewish Order Service was set up. The Judenrat was ordered to conduct a census of all Jewish males and females aged fourteen to sixty, who were then required to perform forced labor, such as quarry work, road paving, and farm work. In the fall of 1941, the Judenrat was ordered to supply lists of Jews to be shipped to labor camps. After the Jews learned of the very harsh conditions in the camps, the Judenrat encountered difficulty filling the quotas, so the German and Ukrainian policemen seized those designated for the camps themselves. To alleviate the suffering of the camp inmates, the Judenrat shipped clothing, food, and medication, until all contact with the laborers was lost. In the winter of 1941/42, the Judenrat organized a public soup kitchen that distributed hundreds of portions of soup daily to alleviate hunger. In the spring of 1942, groups of young Jews were sent to farm in camps established on estates in the area. Conditions were tolerable initially, but in time, they deteriorated, and the female inmates in the camps especially suffered from abuse at the hands of the Ukrainian guards.

In late September and during October 1942, Jews from the surrounding localities were concentrated in Trembowla, and all the Jews were ordered to move into a ghetto. About 4,000 Jews were living in the ghetto when it was sealed on October 28, 1942. Only groups of forced laborers accompanied by Ukrainian policemen were permitted to leave the ghetto.

On November 5, 1942, one week after the ghetto was sealed off, an operation was carried out, and about 1,400 Jews were deported for extermination in the Belzec death camp. More than 100 Jews were murdered during the operation when their hiding places were discovered or when they attempted to escape from the ghetto.

After the operation, the size of the ghetto was reduced, leading to the spread of hunger and epidemic typhus. The Judenrat hid the severity of the epidemic from the Germans and organized two quarantine rooms with forty beds, but was unable to contain the epidemic.

On April 7, 1943, a second operation was conducted in the ghetto. Many people hid in various types of hiding places, some of which were stocked with food and water in preparation for a long stay. The Germans and their helpers used bloodhounds, burned down houses, and destroyed walls and floors in their efforts to uncover the hiding places. At the end of the day, they led some 1,100 inhabitants to a forest located near the village of Plebanowka, about three kilometers away from the townlet, and shot the Jews to death. A few Jews attacked the murderers, and several took advantage of the chaos that ensued to escape. After the operation, a group of young people convened in the ghetto and planned to head to the forest and join the partisans. It is not known whether they succeeded in their escape.

On June 2–3, 1943, the Trembowla ghetto was liquidated by a unit of the German police under the command of Friedrich Hildebrand. About 1,000 Jews were rounded up in the market place and led to Plebanowka. Dozens of Jews attempted to escape to the nearby Kopyczynce* ghetto, but most were caught and murdered.

TROJANÓWKA

TOWNLET IN KOWEL COUNTY, VOLHYNIA DISTRICT, POLAND
(After World War II in the USSR/Ukraine; Ukrainian: **Troyanivka**; Russian: **Troyanovka**)

During the war: Reichskommissariat Ukraine

Coordinates: 49°50' | 26°30'

On the eve of World War I, there were about 350 Jews in Trojanowka, approximately half of the townlet's population. They engaged in agriculture, petty trade, and crafts.

After the Soviets took control of Trojanowka in September 1939, the local community was joined by 150 refugees from central and western Poland.

On June 28, 1941, the Germans occupied Trojanowka. They handed over the municipal governance of the townlet to the Ukrainians, who murdered several Jews and conscripted inhabitants for forced labor.

On August 11, 1941, some 200 Ukrainian bandits invaded the townlet. Fifteen Jewish men, including three armed former soldiers, united to repel the attack. They fired at the assailants, killing their leader and driving the others away.

In the summer of 1941, a Judenrat was established in Trojanowka under a refugee lawyer named Gold. The Jews were ordered to pay a ransom. An open and unfenced ghetto was established.

On September 3, 1942, the Jews of Trojanowka were led in the direction of Maniewicze. The elderly and the ill were shot near the village of Czerewacha. About 150 Jews fled to the forests; the rest reached Maniewicze where they were murdered along with the local Jewish population. About seventy escapees, including Rabbi Yitzhak Melamed, returned to Trojanowka after the Germans promised their safety. All were murdered. While most of the others died of starvation and disease in the forests, a number of young escapees survived and joined Soviet partisan units in early 1943.

TROKI
(Yiddish: **Trok**)

TOWNLET IN VILNA COUNTY, VILNA DISTRICT, POLAND
(After World War II in the USSR/Lithuania; Lithuanian: **Trakai**)

During the war: Reichskommissariat Ostland

Coordinates: 54°38' | 24°56'

About 420 Jews lived in Troki on the eve of World War II, representing roughly one-eighth of the townlet's population. The Jews earned their livelihood from peddling, small commerce, and artisanship. Troki had Jewish parties and youth movements, a Hebrew school, and a library. The townlet was occupied by the Red Army in the second part of September 1939 but was annexed to Lithuania several days later. Once Lithuania was annexed to the Soviet Union in June 1940, the townlet's economy and public life were Sovietized.

When news spread of the German invasion of the Soviet Union on June 22, 1941, a few dozen Jews fled from Troki to the east. The Germans occupied the townlet in late June 1941.

A few days later, the Jews were rounded up in a ghetto inside the townlet. There were also Karaites in Troki who were initially treated no differently from the other Jews by the Germans. Later, however, when they decided that the Karaites were members of the Mongol-Tartar race, their lives were spared.

The Troki ghetto was liquidated in September 1941, when its inhabitants were taken to an island in the Troki Lake, where they were held together with some 2,200 Jews from a number of nearby localities. On September 30, 1941, the Jews were shot to death on the island by a Lithuanian murder unit.

TROŠKŪNAI
(Yiddish: **Trashkun**)

TOWNLET IN PANEVĖŽYS COUNTY, LITHUANIA

During the war: Reichskommissariat Ostland

Coordinates: 55°36' | 24°51'

On the eve of the German occupation, about ninety Jewish families lived in Troskunai. Most earned their livelihood from commerce and artisanship. The townlet boasted a Jewish Folksbank and a credit company for Jewish farmers, as well as a Tarbut school and Zionist parties.

In autumn 1940, when Lithuania was annexed to the Soviet Union, several of the local businesses were nationalized and Jewish national activity was outlawed.

Following the German occupation of the townlet, Lithuanians murdered a group of Jewish youths. There were a number of cases of Jewish resistance.

In July 1941, all of the Jews of Troskunai were concentrated in a ghetto of sorts consisting of a number of buildings in the poor quarter of the townlet. On August 21 or 22, they were all taken to Pajuoste, near Panevezys*, where they were murdered on August 23, 1941.

TRUDY

VILLAGE IN POLOTSK COUNTY, VITEBSK DISTRICT, BELARUS, USSR

During the war: Military Administration Area

Coordinates: 55°38' | 29°22'

In the mid-1920s, about 120 Jews lived in Trudy. The Germans occupied the village in mid-July 1941. Some time later, they concentrated the Jews of Trudy in a ghetto composed of three or four houses, along with several Jewish families from Sirotino* and Polotsk*. On February 4, 1942, all the Jews were packed into a single house and ordered to surrender their remaining valuables. Then they were given a two-day supply of food and promised that they would be released.

The ghetto was liquidated on February 7, 1942, when a police unit (apparently Belarussian) from Polotsk murdered the remaining seventy-six Jews in a forest near the village.

TRYŠKIAI
(Yiddish: **Trishek**)

TOWNLET IN ŠIAULIAI COUNTY, LITHUANIA

During the war:
Reichskommissariat Ostland

Coordinates:
56°04' | 22°35'

On the eve of the German occupation, about 200 Jews lived in Tryskiai, representing more than 10 percent of the local population. Most earned their livelihood from artisanship, small-scale commerce, and farming. The townlet had a Tarbut school and a Jewish Folksbank.

After Lithuania was annexed to the Soviet Union in 1940, most of the factories and shops in Tryskiai were nationalized and the Tarbut school was closed.

After the townlet was occupied by the Germans on June 25, 1941, Lithuanians plundered the homes of the Jewish inhabitants.

In mid-July 1941, all of Tryskiai's Jews were transferred to a ghetto of sorts located in a granary on an estate on the outskirts of the townlet. The ghetto was encircled by barbed wire and guarded by Lithuanians. After several days, its seventy male Jewish inhabitants were removed from the granary on the pretext that they were being taken for forced labor. Instead, they were shot to death by Lithuanians. The women and children continued to live in the granary. In early August, told that they were reuniting with the men, the women and children were led to Gruzdziai, where they remained for one week in an open field, subject to the abuse of the Lithuanian guards. In mid-August 1941, they were all moved to the ghetto in Zagare*, where they were murdered on October 2, 1941, together with the local Jews.

TRZEBINIA
(Yiddish: **Tshebin**)

TOWNLET IN CHRZANÓW COUNTY, CRACOW DISTRICT, POLAND

During the war: General Gouvernement

Coordinates:
50°10' | 19°29'

About 1,346 Jews (329 families) lived in Trzebinia in the interwar period, representing approximately 70 percent of the townlet's population. They earned their livelihood from small-scale commerce as well as in the electrical and oil refining plants, the coal mines, the iron foundry, and the cement factory. The JDC and former residents of Trzebinia living in the United States assisted in the renovation of Trzebinia's bathhouse and clinic and contributed to the local free-loan society. The townlet had a Talmud Torah, a modern Heder, and two Yeshivot. From 1932 to 1937, the Hasidic court of the Bobowa Rebbe was active in Trzebinia. Zionist parties and youth movements held ongoing activities, Hebrew lessons, and a drama circle, and maintained a 1,500-volume library.

In early September 1939, the Germans occupied Trzebinia, which was situated at the junction of the Cracow–Vienna train lines. The train station was bombed and close to 100 Jews fled on foot from the townlet during the shelling by the German army. German soldiers and police murdered many of the Jews as they returned home to Trzebinia via Chrzanow*. They were buried in a mass grave near the bridge that joined Trzebinia and Chrzanow.

In the early days of the occupation, Jewish shops and homes were plundered by the Germans, Volksdeutsche, and Poles. Many Jews were recruited for forced labor through an arrangement between the Germans and the community, while others were seized in the streets of the townlet. Most of the laborers were employed loading military equipment onto trains or in cleaning work in the army barracks. A ransom was periodically levied on the community, paid in money or valuables and home furnishings. The Jews' freedom of movement within Trzebinia was restricted, and Jewish residents were forbidden to leave the townlet. The atmosphere of terror prompted many young Jews to flee Trzebinia. A number of the youths who managed to reach the Soviet occupation zone were exiled deep into the Soviet interior.

In October 1939, the Jews of Trzebinia were ordered to wear an armband, which in early 1940 was replaced by a yellow badge inscribed with the word

Trzebinia, 1941

Portrait photograph of Ruzia Reich-Lehrer. The Jews of the town were photographed for identity cards. On June 13, 1942, Ruzia and the daughter born to her in the ghetto were sent to Auschwitz, where they perished. (YV)

Jude. A night curfew was imposed and in early 1940, a branch of the central Judenrat in Sosnowiec* was established in Trzebinia, headed by Yissachar Mandelbaum. The Judenrat had fifteen members and was subordinate to Moniek (Moshe) Merin, the head of the central Judenrat in Sosnowiec. All of the Jewish-owned factories were confiscated and transferred to "'Aryan' trustees."

In late 1940 and the first half of 1941, the Germans began to seize groups of Jewish men and transfer them to labor camps, where the death rate was high. In an attempt to prevent their deportation to the camps, the Jews of Trzebinia strove to find work in the local industrial plants.

In the summer of 1940, about 1,100 Jews lived in Trzebinia. They were ordered to move into another part of the townlet, which had four streets. This area became a ghetto. It was initially open, and inhabitants were permitted to leave for up to one hour, but this allowance was gradually reduced. Later, a curfew was imposed on the Jews of the ghetto, from the evening hours until the following morning. While gatherings of more than six Jews were forbidden, Jews endangered themselves to pray in a *minyan* (prayer quorum of ten) in private homes. A public soup kitchen was established in the ghetto, and secret educational activities were organized.

Over time, about 1,000 Jewish refugees arrived in Trzebinia from Rybnik, Oswiecim, and Pszczyna. Most of the ghetto's Jews worked in German factories, in exchange for seventy marks a month. The Jews of the ghetto supplemented their income by selling their personal belongings to the local population. Inside the ghetto, a number of Jews were permitted to own shops for the sale of food, which was paid for with ration slips.

In June 1942, the ghetto was surrounded by units of the SS and German police and the inhabitants were rounded up. Following a selection, a number of the Jews were sent to the labor camp in Sosnowiec or to the Chrzanow ghetto, while others were deported to Auschwitz.

At the war's end, 235 of Trzebinia's Jews were alive.

TSIBULEVKA

(Ukrainian: **Tsybulivka**)

VILLAGE IN OBODOVKA COUNTY, VINNITSA DISTRICT, UKRAINE, USSR

During the war: Transnistria (under Romanian control)

Coordinates:
48°23' | 29°08'

Staraya Tsibulevka and Novaya Tsibulevka, two adjacent villages, were occupied in July 1941 by German and Romanian units. A number of the villages' Jewish residents joined the retreating Red Army, and the remaining Jews were murdered by the Germans in the early days following the occupation and buried locally in a mass grave.

November 1941 saw 1,270 Jews brought from Bukovina to Staraya Tsibulevka, and 1,200 Jews from Bukovina and Bessarabia brought to Novaya Tsibulevka. The deportees were housed in two cowsheds encircled by a barbed-wire fence that were declared a ghetto and guarded by Romanian gendarmes and Ukrainian police. Only artisans were permitted to leave the cowsheds. A typhus epidemic soon broke out among the deportees, killing some 2,000 people within the first three months of their confinement. The deportees had no access to medication, and the only doctor among them also fell ill and died. The dead were buried in three mass graves that were covered by a thin layer of dirt, and the bodies soon fell prey to dogs. By January 1942, only about 200 of the deportees remained alive.

The high death rate among the deportees caused the commander of the Obodovka* gendarmerie to allow the Jews who had belongings and money to enter the village. In the evening, however, they were required to return to the cowsheds and be present for a roll call that was held for all the deportees. They were removed daily to perform forced labor for twelve hours at a time and were treated cruelly and barely fed by their employers. After help began to arrive in Tsibulevka from the aid committee in Bucharest, the Jewish Council that had been established organized a public soup kitchen in the ghetto. Jews arrived in Tsibulevka from other localities as well, where the situation was even more dire. Despite the sympathy the locals felt for the deportees, they kept their distance from the Jews for fear of reprimand from the Germans, who were stationed in a German command post in the village.

Based on the lists of the help committee in Bucharest, there were 40 deportees in Tsibulevka in March 1942. According to the figures of the gendarmerie command in Transnistria, there were 390 deportees in Tsibulevka in September 1943, of whom 373 were from Bukovina and 17 from Bessarabia.

In March 1944, the Red Army liberated the two villages, and the surviving deportees returned to their homes.

TUCHÓW

TOWNLET IN TARNÓW COUNTY, CRACOW DISTRICT, POLAND

During the war: General Gouvernement, Cracow District

Coordinates:
49°54' | 21°04'

About 300 Jews lived in Tuchow during the interwar period, representing approximately one-eighth of the local population. They earned their livelihood from small commerce and artisanship. The community boasted Zionist parties and youth movements that ran a library serving also as a Jewish cultural center.

When the war broke out, a small number of Tuchow's Jews managed to flee to the east.

Tuchow was occupied by the Germans in early September 1939. Immediately after the occupation, the Germans plundered Jewish property, burned down a synagogue, seized Jewish inhabitants for forced labor, and murdered a number of Jews. In December 1939, fifteen Jews were killed close to the nearby village of Tarnowiec. Their bodies were discovered three months later.

In late 1939, a Judenrat headed by Wachs was established in the townlet. It was required to provide the Germans with forced laborers.

In 1940, the Germans murdered a prayer quorum caught holding a service in the apartment of the Weiss family. At German orders, the victims were buried in the yard of the house in which they were killed.

In 1941, displaced Jews deported from Ryglic, Gromnik, Ciezkowice, and other localities in the area were brought to Tuchow. The refugees were aided by the Judenrat and the local chapter of the JSS. On the eve of the establishment of the ghetto, the head of the Judenrat was murdered after a Pole who coveted his apartment accused him of being a Communist.

In June 1942, a ghetto with seventeen buildings was established in the southern part of the townlet. After its establishment, displaced Jews from other localities were also moved in, raising the population to about 3,000. In early 1942, a workshop involved mainly in tailoring was set up in the ghetto at the initiative of the Judenrat, aimed at preventing further seizures of Jews for labor camps. In late summer 1942, the Germans ordered the registration of all of the ghetto's Jews.

In September 1942, German and Polish police encircled the ghetto, and, following a selection, deported most of its inhabitants to the Belzec death camp. The surviving members of the community were employed sorting through the belongings abandoned by the deportees, while others worked on farms in the area.

The Tuchow ghetto was liquidated on August 18, 1943, when most of its inhabitants were murdered on site and others were transferred to Tarnow*.

TUCZYN

TOWNLET IN RÓWNE COUNTY, VOLHYNIA DISTRICT, POLAND
(After World War II in the USSR/Ukraine; Ukrainian: **Tuchyn**; Russian: **Tuchin**)

During the war:
Reichskommissariat Ukraine

Coordinates:
50°42' | 26°34'

During the interwar years, there were about 2,200 Jews living in Tuczyn, accounting for three-fourths of the townlet's population. They engaged in trade and crafts, mainly in clothing. They availed themselves of the services of a Jewish savings-and-loan association and self-help organizations. Zionist youth movements, a Bund group, and Communists were all active in the townlet. Most children in Tuczyn attended a special Polish government school for Jews that had a large number of teachers as well as a principal who were Jewish. The townlet also had a Tarbut kindergarten and primary school that taught in Hebrew, a Polish high school that taught in Hebrew, a Talmud Torah, a Yeshiva, and a Jewish public library.

After the Soviets took control of Tuczyn in September 1939, private businesses were nationalized and the Hebrew-language primary school became a Yiddish-language Soviet school. When the Germans invaded the Soviet Union on June 22, 1941, many of the townlet's Jews left for the USSR.

The Germans occupied Tuczyn on July 6, 1941. Not long after their arrival, local Ukrainians murdered some seventy Jews and a squad of Einsatzkommando 4a murdered another thirty.

By the end of July 1941, the Jews of Tuczyn were required to wear a Star-of-David armband and a Judenrat had been appointed under Getsel Schwartzman. The community was repeatedly dunned for ransoms in valuables and gold, and Jews were conscripted for forced labor in and near the townlet.

Construction of a fence for a ghetto in Tuczyn began in July 1942 and was completed in early September. The ghetto held 3,000 Jews from Tuczyn and nearby villages.

Upon hearing reports about the liquidation of the Rowne* ghetto in July 1942, the head of the Judenrat, Schwartzman, his deputy, Meir Himelfarb, and Jewish youths in Tuczyn began to plan an uprising. They gathered weapons, prepared flammable material to set ghetto buildings on fire, and organized groups of fighters equipped with rifles, handguns, hand grenades, and a small quantity of ammunition.

On September 24, 1942, German and Ukrainian policemen surrounded and fired into the ghetto. As the fighters returned fire, the Jews in the ghetto torched all the ghetto buildings, including synagogues that the Germans had been using as warehouses, and broke through the fence in several places. About 2,000 Jews fled to the nearby Pustomyty forests. Seven hundred and fifty-seven Jews remained in the ghetto and were murdered. In the course of fighting, two Ukrainian policemen and several Germans were killed, and an unknown number of Germans and Ukrainians were wounded.

Within three days about 1,000 escapees were captured and murdered. Some 300 women and children returned to the ghetto owing to the harsh conditions in the forest. On September 26, 1942, the two leaders of the Judenrat, Schwartzman and Himelfarb, turned themselves in to the Germans, identifying themselves as the organizers of the uprising. The men asked to be allowed to die at the Jewish graveyard, and their request was granted: they were shot and buried in the cemetery.

Almost all of the 600 to 700 Jews who remained in the forest perished, were denounced, or were murdered by members of the local population. A few young escapees joined Soviet partisan units.

Tuczyn
Gecel Szwarcman, head of the Judenrat in the ghetto (YV)

TULCHIN

(Ukrainian: **Tul'chyn**)

COUNTY SEAT, VINNITSA DISTRICT, UKRAINE, USSR

During the war: Transnistria (under Romanian control)

Coordinates:
48°41' | 28°52'

In the early twentieth century, about 16,000 Jews lived in Tulchin. During the civil war in Russia (1918–20), Ukrainian gangs carried out pogroms in the town, murdering more than 200 Jews.

During the Soviet period, a Jewish court was established in Tulchin as well as a Jewish Ethnic Soviet that conducted its affairs in Yiddish and a school that offered instruction in Yiddish. While many Jews earned their livelihood from commerce until the abolition of private commerce in the early 1930s, as well as from artisanship, many others worked in sugar and other factories, and a few were farmers. The civil war and the pogrom, coupled with the growing trend of industrialization and urbanization in the Soviet Union, prompted the majority of Tulchin's Jews to leave the town in the 1920s and 1930s. On the eve of the German invasion of the Soviet Union, about 5,500 Jews lived in Tulchin.

The Germans occupied Tulchin on July 23, 1941. Many Jews attempted to flee into the Soviet hinterland, but the vast majority discovered that escape was no longer an option, and were forced to return to Tulchin. In early September 1941, Tulchin was handed over to Romanian rule and annexed to Transnistria.

On Yom Kippur of 1941 (October 1), the Jews were concentrated in a ghetto in a poor quarter of the town. A council headed by Zabakritski, Vitner, and Veshler was established, as was a Jewish Order Service. The Romanian authorities ordered the Jews to wear a round black badge with a yellow Star-of-David on their clothing.

On December 13, 1941, about 3,000 of Tulchin's Jews were transferred to a concentration camp in Pechera, where many perished; 118 people with vital professions remained in the town. In late December 1942, about 230 Jews deported from Bukovina were also brought to Tulchin, including deportees from Romania, who had lived until then in villages in the area, and Ukrainian Jews from Yampol*. In March 1943, the population of the ghetto reached 500.

In early 1943, the Bucharest aid committee sent clothing, food, and medicine to Tulchin. This assistance enabled the local Jewish council to organize a public soup kitchen for the needy and to run a number of workshops. With permission from the authorities, the ghetto council also set up a school for about ninety children. In April 1943, deportations from the ghetto to forced labor and German camps were renewed. All the deportees were murdered by December 1943.

In late January 1944, the Tulchin ghetto was encircled by a unit of the German police intent on its liquidation; however as Fetecau, the commander of the Romanian gendarmerie, opposed the operation, the Jews were saved.

Tulchin was liberated on March 15, 1944.

TULISZKÓW

TOWNLET IN KONIN COUNTY, ŁÓDŹ DISTRICT, POLAND

During the war: Wartheland

Coordinates:
52°05' | 18°18'

There were about 260 Jews living in Tuliszkow in the 1920s; most were farmers, merchants, or petty artisans. A weakening economy drove approximately 30 percent of the Jews out of the townlet in the 1930s.

After the German occupation, the Jews faced restriction of movement, heavy taxes, and forced labor. In late November 1939, they were ordered to wear yellow Star-of-David armbands. In December, a Judenrat was established and ordered to prepare a register of the townlet's Jewish population.

In January 1940, the Jews of Tuliszkow were concentrated in a ghetto, one of the first in the area. The Germans cut off electricity to the ghetto houses. They also forbade inhabitants to bring in furniture, furs, or new clothing, instead confiscating these items for distribution among the local population.

In October 1941, the entire ghetto population was moved to the rural ghetto in Kowale Panskie*.

TUREK

COUNTY SEAT, ŁÓDŹ DISTRICT, POLAND

During the war: Wartheland

Coordinates:
52°02' | 18°30'

On the eve of World War II, there were about 2,700 Jews living in Turek, accounting for approximately one-quarter of the town's population. Most were merchants and artisans. Zionist parties, Agudath Israel, and an influential chapter of the Bund were established in the community. Children were educated in a Heder, a kindergarten affiliated with the Mizrachi movement, and a primary school called the Torah School. The town's Jews also participated in sports and amateur drama groups.

When the Germans occupied Turek, fifteen Jews were murdered and others were robbed or seized for forced labor. On September 24, 1939, the Germans torched a synagogue along with worshippers trapped inside the building. In November 1939, altogether 700 Jews were sent to perform forced labor in Bochnia*, near Cracow*. For some time, the community kept in contact with the deportees and shipped them parcels of food.

In February 1940, after all Jewish shops and factories had been expropriated, a number of Jews were relocated to a special quarter in the area of Wide Street. The remainder of the town's Jews followed in July 1940, and the quarter was declared a ghetto. The Turek ghetto was initially open, and while food was thus easier to obtain, many Jews starved. The Judenrat, chaired by Hershl Zimnovoda, established a soup kitchen for the needy. Mordechai Strykovski was appointed head of the Jewish Order Service.

During the summer of 1940, some ninety Jews were taken from the Turek ghetto to the Poznan area for labor. Others left the town of their own volition, attempting to find asylum by moving to Warsaw* or crossing into Soviet territory. The liquidation of the Turek ghetto began on October 1, 1941 (*Yom Kippur*), under the command of SS Major Georg Glaustein. In the course of the liquidation, the inhabitants were moved to the rural ghetto in Kowale Panskie*.

TÚRKEVE

TOWN IN JÁSZ-NAGYKUN-SZOLNOK COUNTY, HUNGARY

Coordinates:
47°06' | 20°45'

The last national census conducted in Hungary prior to the German occupation, taken in January 1941, recorded 179 Jewish inhabitants in Turkeve, approximately 1 percent of the total population. Most were merchants and artisans. The town's Jewish community was Neolog and had a Jewish school.

In 1942, twenty-one Jewish men were drafted into the Hungarian army for forced labor service. Most perished on the eastern front, in the Ukraine.

The German army occupied Hungary on March 19, 1944. The Germans arrested four members of the Jewish community, who were sent to the Kistarcsa internment camp and deported on to Auschwitz. A census conducted in the second week of April 1944 showed that 172 Jews belonged to the Neolog Jewish community of Turkeve.

The Hungarian administration remained intact and operational after the occupation. The ghettoization and deportation of the Jews were carried out on the basis of the decrees and orders of the Hungarian national and local authorities. On May 1, 1944, the Hungarian sub-prefect, Imre Alexander, published a decree ordering the ghettoization of the Jews in the county. A ghetto was subsequently established in Turkeve.

In early June 1944, the inhabitants of the ghetto were transferred to the entrainment center at the Szolnok* sugar factory. On June 25, 1944, the first transport of deportees left for Strasshof in Austria, with 2,628 people aboard. The second transport left on June 28, 1944, carrying 2,083 people to Auschwitz.

TURZYSK

TOWNLET IN KOWEL COUNTY, VOLHYNIA DISTRICT, POLAND
(After World War II in the USSR/Ukraine; Ukrainian: **Turiys'k**; Russian: **Turiysk**)

During the war:
Reichskommissariat Ukraine

Coordinates:
51°06' | 24°32'

During the interwar years, there were about 1,200 Jews living in Turzysk, more than half of the townlet's population. Most engaged in petty trade and crafts; a few were involved in the trade and export of lumber and grain. Zionist and Bund circles were active in Turzysk, and there were also supporters of the underground Communist Party. The Tarbut and CYSHO associations ran schools and libraries in the townlet.

After the Soviets took control of the townlet in September 1939, all Jewish institutions and organizations were disbanded.

German forces occupied Turzysk on June 28, 1941, and along with local Ukrainians looted Jewish property. Ten Jews were murdered on the basis of a list prepared by the Ukrainian municipal administration. Jews were ordered to wear a Star-of-David armband, were dispossessed of valuables, jewelry, furs, and livestock, and were conscripted for forced labor.

A Judenrat was established, and the Jews of Turzysk were concentrated into several streets that were not fenced in. On August 19, 1942, the community was ordered to pay a steep ransom in valuables and clothing. That very day, several ghetto inhabitants, including a member of the Judenrat, were murdered.

The ghetto was liquidated on August 23, 1942. The Jews of Turzysk were murdered in trenches that had been excavated outside the townlet. Several people were killed committing acts of resistance: Berish Segal grabbed a German's submachine gun and wounded several policemen before he was fatally shot; and two women attacked the German commander of the operation, wounding him, before they were shot. A number of Jews managed to set half of the ghetto houses on fire.

TYCZYN

TOWNLET IN RZESZÓW COUNTY, LWÓW DISTRICT, POLAND

During the war: General Gouvernement, Cracow District

Coordinates:
49°58' | 22°02'

About 950 Jews lived in Tyczyn in the interwar period, representing approximately one-third of the townlet's population. They earned their livelihood from artisanship and petty commerce, especially in the trade of onions, for which the area was famous. Tyczyn was a Hasidic center, and until the Hasidic court moved away in 1927, a number of the townlet's Jews earned their livelihood from transportation and restaurants. After World War I, the JDC aided the Jews of Tyczyn with food and clothing, and the *Bikur Holim* Society helped with rehabilitation. The Jews of the townlet were also assisted by a free-loan society. The Zionist *Beit Yehuda* Society ran a library and drama circle in the townlet, which also boasted Zionist parties, a chapter of *Akiva,* and a chapter of the Tarbut organization. The community also had a branch of the *Bar Kochba* sports club.

The Germans occupied Tyczyn in September 1939. In the initial months following the occupation, numerous refugees arrived in the townlet, especially from Lodz*.

In 1941/42, the Germans transformed the Jewish quarter into a ghetto that was neither fenced in nor guarded. A JSS chapter was established in the ghetto. A Judenrat was also most likely set up, although no details are available regarding its activities.

In June 1942, Jews from nearby localities were concentrated in the ghetto. Its entire population was first transferred to the Rzeszow* ghetto and in July 1942, on to the Belzec death camp.

TYŚMIENICA

TOWNLET IN TŁUMACZ COUNTY, STANISŁAWÓW DISTRICT, POLAND

(After World War II in the USSR/Ukraine; Ukrainian: **Tysmenytsya**; Russian: **Tysmenitsa**)

During the war: General Gouvernement, Galicia District

Coordinates: 48°54' | 24°51'

In the early 1930s, about 1,200 Jews lived in Tysmienica, representing 16 percent of the townlet's population. The Jewish community had a number of Jewish political organizations, including Zionist parties, as well as Jewish welfare organizations.

In the second half of September 1939, Tysmienica was occupied by the Red Army. Under the Soviets, the Jewish parties were abolished, but the Jews were accepted into public jobs that had previously been closed to them, and their religious life remained unimpeded. In 1940, a number of wealthy families were exiled into the Soviet interior. When the Soviets withdrew in June 1941, they were joined by a number of Jewish leftist activists.

On July 2, 1941, Tysmienica was occupied by the Hungarians (allies of the Germans). The Hungarians did not harm the Jews and impeded their terrorization by Ukrainian ultra-nationalists. Jewish refugees from Hungary received help from the Jewish community.

In late August 1941, Tysmienica was handed over to German control. At German orders, a Judenrat was established, headed by Yaakov Tsigler. A Jewish Order Service was also set up, under the command of Eliyahu-Ber Buchhalter. In September 1941, groups of Jews were seized, transferred to Stanislawow*, and murdered.

Just prior to Passover in the spring of 1942, the Jews were concentrated in a ghetto established on a number of neglected, narrow streets; Jews from nearby localities were also crowded into the confined area. A Jewish doctor received permission to live outside the ghetto. Hunger and spotted fever spread throughout the ghetto, and its hospital experienced difficulty containing the epidemic.

The ghetto was liquidated in August 1942. A number of its inhabitants were murdered in the local cemetery, while others were deported to the Belzec death camp. The Germans left about thirty Jewish artisans in Tysmienica. They were moved some time later to the prison in Stanislawow, where they worked manufacturing gloves for the German army until their murder in the spring of 1943.

TYSZOWCE

TOWNLET IN TOMASZÓW LUBELSKI COUNTY, LUBLIN DISTRICT, POLAND

During the war: General Gouvernement, Lublin District

Coordinates: 50°37' | 23°42'

After World War I, some 2,500 Jews lived in Tyszowce, more than half the townlet's population. Most wage earners were petty merchants and artisans, chiefly shoemakers. The community had an association of craftsmen, a savings-and-loan association, and a free-loan fund.

While the Tyszowce community was predominantly Orthodox, Zionist parties and the Bund maintained local chapters there. There were traditional Hadarim, a Hebrew-language Tarbut primary school, a Jewish library, and drama and literary clubs.

The Germans occupied Tyszowce on September 17, 1939. A week later, they withdrew and were replaced by the Soviets. Several days afterwards, the Soviets retreated to the east, in accordance with the Molotov-Ribbentrop Pact, and were joined by about 1,000 Jews from Tyszowce, part of whom spent the war years in the Soviet Union.

From the spring of 1940, the Jews of Tyszowce had to wear a yellow badge on their clothing and a Star-of-David armband. The Germans ordered them to establish a ten-member Judenrat, headed by Zelig Tsuker, and a Jewish Order Service under Meir Shak. The Judenrat had to mobilize forced laborers and collect ransoms from the populace. In the spring and summer of 1940, SS men sent hundreds of Jews to labor camps including Zamosc, Bialobrzegi, and Belzec. A labor camp was set up at Tyszowce as well, where hundreds of local Jews toiled alongside hundreds of others from Lublin*, Otwock*, and elsewhere.

On May 25, 1942, SS and Gestapo forces came to Tyszowce and deported some 800 Jews to the Belzec death camp. About 200 Jews resisted and were shot on the spot, as were the chairman of the Judenrat, Zuker, and his deputy. Hundreds of Jews fled to the forests during the roundup. The remaining some 600 Jews were moved into one neighborhood, which became a ghetto. A German Jew by the name of Fishleber replaced Zuker as chairman of the Judenrat.

The Germans executed forty-nine Jews in September 1942. In early October of that year, more Jews fled to the forests upon hearing rumors about the extermination of the Jews of Zamosc*. Some of the escapees established a fighting company in the forests. They used their meager supply of arms, which they had purchased from Poles, to attack Germans and appropriate their weapons.

The Tyszowce ghetto was liquidated in November 1942. Most of the rump population was deported to Belzec; several dozen were shot dead on the spot. The head of the Judenrat committed suicide, as did his mother and his sister.

TYVROV

COUNTY SEAT, VINNITSA DISTRICT, UKRAINE, USSR

During the war: Transnistria (under Romanian control)

Coordinates:
49°01' | 28°30'

On the eve of the German invasion of the Soviet Union, about 400 Jews lived in Tyvrov, representing approximately 10 percent of the townlet's population. In the interwar period, most engaged in commerce until its abolishment in the early 1930s and in various forms of artisanship. A number of Jews began working in government institutions.

A few Jewish families managed to evacuate to the east of the USSR before the Germans entered the townlet on July 18, 1941. The Jewish population was immediately subjected to persecution. That same day, twenty-eight Jewish men were executed in a nearby forest. Men were seized for forced labor and severely beaten by their Ukrainian supervisors.

In September 1941, Tyvrov was handed over to Romanian control as part of Transnistria. Germans and their Ukrainian abettors surrounded the townlet and ordered the entire Jewish population to gather in the synagogue building. Anyone who disobeyed the order or who was delayed was shot on sight. At the end of that day, about 400 Jews were transported by trucks to the area of the beer factory and murdered in pits. Sixteen young Jews managed to escape and flee to the forests.

In December 1941, deportees from Dorohoi, 450 in number, were brought to Tyvrov, and in February 1942, another 850 deportees arrived, mostly from Bukovina. In September 1942, several hundred more deportees from Bukovina and Bessarabia arrived from the Skazintsy camp, which had been liquidated. In addition, Jewish refugees fleeing from the German occupation zone in Ukraine also arrived in Tyvrov.

A ghetto was established in the center of the townlet on the site of the former Jewish quarter. The ghetto was not encircled by a barbed-wire fence, but its inhabitants were forbidden to leave its boundaries or have any contact with the Ukrainian population. Although the Jews were required to wear a yellow patch and were sent by the local Romanian gendarmerie commander to perform forced labor, they were generally treated fairly. In the spring of 1943, a group of Jewish workers was sent to work in Nestervarka. In the fall of that year, another group was transferred to the German labor camp in the area of Ochakov. Few returned after the liberation.

Internal affairs in the ghetto were controlled by a Jewish council, headed by a deportee from Dorohoi. A Jewish Order Service was organized, with a staff of three deportees who were paid wages, headed by the brother of the council head. Many of the deportees worked for Ukrainian farmers or as artisans, while those who lacked professional skills worked in the fields in exchange for food. Still others were reduced to begging in the streets, for lack of any alternative. The Romanian government prohibited Jews from working for the Ukrainians, a directive that was exploited by the head of the council, who accepted bribes from Jewish workers in exchange for his silence.

The Jewish community of Tyvrov was assisted by the Bucharest aid committee via the regional council in Mogilev-Podolskiy*. However, the council members distributed the clothing contributions among the deportees once or twice, and kept the rest. They also neglected to establish welfare institutions to help the needy in the ghetto.

As of September 1, 1943, there were 418 Jews from Bukovina and 40 from Bessarabia in the Tyvrov ghetto. The townlet was liberated on March 16, 1944.

Isaac Celnikier (b. 1923)
"Et vous dites que Dieu est absent!"
1946, oil on canvas

Collection of the Yad Vashem
Art Museum, Jerusalem

Tzvi Hirsch Szylis (1909–1987)
"The Bridge", Lodz Ghetto, 1942, gouache and oil
crayon on paper

Collection of the Yad Vashem Art Museum, Jerusalem

Gift of Eli Shilat, Haifa

A brooch engraved with a depiction of the Lodz
ghetto including the bridge that connected the
two parts of the ghetto, the church spire seen from
inside the ghetto, and a guard. Beneath the image is
the word "Getto" and the year "1943".

Yad Vashem Artifacts Collection

Gift of Dr. Ilana Kozin, Ra'anana, Israel.

Jacob Lifshitz
(1903–Dachau, 1945), "Beaten",
Kovno Ghetto, 1941–1944,
watercolor on paper

Collection of the Yad Vashem
Art Museum, Jerusalem

Leo Haas (1901–1983), "Execution"
Terezin Ghetto, 1943, India ink and wash on paper

Collection of the Yad Vashem Art Museum, Jerusalem

Gift of the Mr. Edward Singer, New Jersey

Haim Bargal (1922–1985), "My Town"
1956, India ink on paper

Collection of the Yad Vashem
Art Museum, Jerusalem

Gift of Kibbutz Sha'ar Hagolan and the Bargal family, Israel

A powder compact that Avraham Tory
gave as a gift to Pnina Sheinson in the
Kovno ghetto. The compact was a gift that
he had commissioned from a silversmith in
the ghetto for the price of a slice of bread.

Yad Vashem Artifacts Collection

Avraham and Pnina Tory Collection

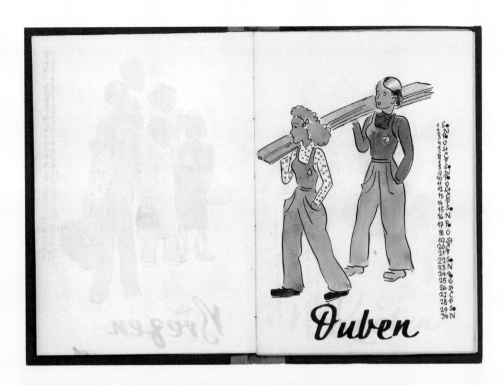

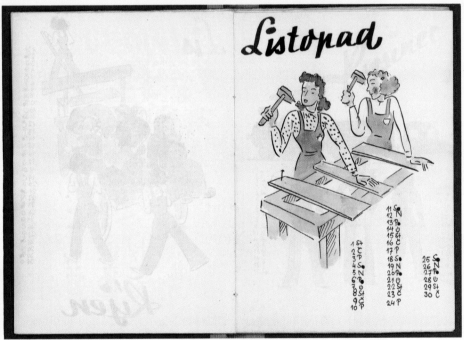

Top: **A calendar** illustrated by Ruth Freund depicting daily scenes of women at work in Terezin ghetto.

Yad Vashem Artifacts Collection

Gift of Uri Naor, Israel

Left: **Halina Olomucki** (1920–2008), "After Removing the Beard" Warsaw Ghetto, 1943, pencil on paper

Collection of the Yad Vashem Art Museum, Jerusalem

Gift of the artist

Top: **Jacob Lifshitz** (1903–Dachau, 1945), "Kriśćiukaićio Street", Kovno Ghetto, 1944, watercolor on paper

Collection of the Yad Vashem Art Museum, Jerusalem

Bottom: **Samuel Bak** (b. 1933), "Refugees", 1947, gouache on paper

Collection of the Yad Vashem Art Museum, Jerusalem

Gift of the artist

Top: **A page from a miniature Bible** written in micrographic script by Solomon Knobel in the Lodz ghetto and dedicated to the head of the Judenrat, Chaim Rumkowski.

Bottom: **A page from the miniature Bible** with a portrait of the head of the Judenrat, Chaim Rumkowski.

Yad Vashem Artifacts Collection

Gift of Bela Bialik, Tel Aviv, Israel

Moshe Rynecki (1881–Majdanek, 1943), "Refugees"
 Warsaw Ghetto, 1939, watercolor on paper

Collection of the Yad Vashem Art Museum, Jerusalem

Gift of Alex Rynecki, California

Top: **Box and two "Ex Libris"** bookplates made by Petr Ginz for his sister Eva in Terezin ghetto.

Bottom: **One of the Ex Libris bookplates** engraved with the name "Eva Ginzova".

Yad Vashem Artifacts Collection

Gift of Eva (Ginz) Pressburger, Jerusalem, Israel

Doll made by Paulina Klauber in Terezin Ghetto. She was deported with her daughter Gertrude to Terezin in 1943. Paulina used her talents to make various handicrafts, which she exchanged for food, and survived. Her daughter Gertrude was deported to Auschwitz where she was murdered.

Yad Vashem Artifacts Collection

Gift of Gusti (Klauber) Felton,
White Plains, NY, U.S.A

The teddy bear "Mishu" that Ina Rennert received as a gift from her grandfather upon her birth in Cracow in 1935 in Poland. She kept "Mishu" with her when she and her parents moved to Warsaw, moving from one hiding place to another, both in the Ghetto and on the "Aryan" side. After the Polish uprising, Ina and her mother were deported to Auschwitz with other Polish (non-Jewish) residents of Warsaw. "Mishu" was tied to Ina's backpack on their journey to Auschwitz, and so she was nicknamed "the girl with the teddy bear."

Yad Vashem Artifacts Collection

Loaned by Ina Rennert-Rechavy,
Jerusalem, Israel

Arnold Daghani (1909–1985), "Waiting for Doles"
Bershad Ghetto, 1943, watercolor on paper

Collection of the Yad Vashem Art Museum, Jerusalem

These are the Laws According to the Customs of Ashkenaz [Nazi Germany], a clandestine book by Avraham Tory, general secretary of the Kovno Aeltestenrat. The book documents the edicts and hardships imposed by the Germans on the ghetto's inhabitants. It was designed by Fritz Gadiel.

Yad Vashem Artifacts Collection

Avraham and Pnina Tory Collection

The Monopoly game was made in the graphics workshop in Terezin as part of the ghetto's underground activity. It was drawn by Oswald Poeck, an artist who was expelled from Prague to Terezin in November 1941 and was later deported to his death in Auschwitz in September 1944. In addition to entertaining the children, it was intended to provide them with information about ghetto life. The board displays a drawing of the ghetto. Major ghetto sites are stations in the game: the prison, the barracks, the fort, the warehouse, the kitchen, the expellees induction site, and others. Those who were deported would often leave belongings with friends who remained in the ghetto; in this way, the Monopoly game was passed on to Pavel and Tomaš Glass in Terezin.

Yad Vashem Artifacts Collection

Gift of Micah Glass, Jerusalem, Israel, & Dan Glass, Ramat Gan, Israel

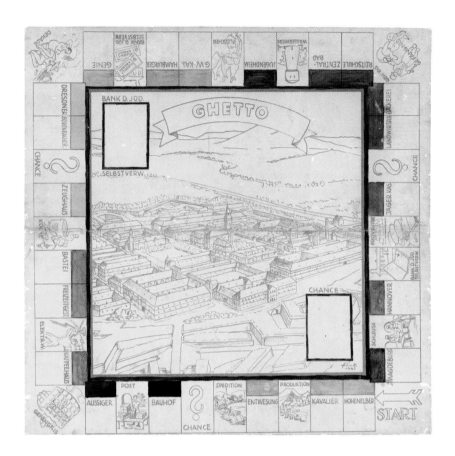

Armbands worn by officials appointed by the Aeltestenrat in the Kovno ghetto.

Yad Vashem Artifacts Collection

Józef Kowner (1895–1967), "Self-portrait"
Lodz Ghetto, 1941, watercolor on paper

Collection of the Yad Vashem
 Art Museum, Jerusalem

Gift of Leon and Carmela Kowner, Haifa

Martin Spett (b. 1928), "My Sister and I"
1993, oil on canvas

Collection of the Yad Vashem
Art Museum, Jerusalem

Gift of the artist

Ungvár ghetto, Hungary

"My One and Only Dear Son!

We are standing here, ready for the way, after packing our most necessary belongings, in order for them to take us shortly with all the Jews of the city to an unknown place for an unknown purpose, under orders of the Hungarian government. They gathered all the Jews of the area and placed them in the brick factory. They number approximately 10,000 people, and among them are Grandmother and Aunt Malevene.

The Jews of the city gave them food for a few days, but now, when we're ready for the way, there is no one to care for us …"

A letter sent to Yehoshua Szeremi on April 20, 1944, from Zvi Bachrach, These are My Final Words: Last Letters from the Holocaust *(Jerusalem: Yad Vashem Publications, 2003), p. 198 [Hebrew].*

UJAZD

TOWNLET IN BRZEZINY COUNTY, ŁÓDŹ DISTRICT, POLAND

During the war: General Gouvernement, Radom District

Coordinates:
50°23' | 18°21'

During the interwar period, there were about 130 Jewish families in Ujazd; most breadwinners were petty merchants and artisans. An antisemitic climate led to a string of violent attacks against the townlet's Jewish population. In July 1937, a female Jewish shopkeeper was murdered.

When World War II broke out, there were about 800 Jews in Ujazd. Heavy bombardment destroyed most of the townlet's buildings during the first days of the war. Hundreds of Jews fled their homes; a diminished number returned after the bombing, gathering in three houses that had remained intact. In June 1941, Jewish deportees and refugees from other areas began to arrive in Ujazd, and by the fall of 1942, the townlet's Jewish population had risen to about 1,000. Residents were crowded into three buildings, and were put to various forms of labor by the Germans.

The ghetto in Ujazd was most likely established in the summer of 1942, when many young Jews were deported to labor camps, and about twenty were shot.

In October 1942, most of the ghetto inhabitants were sent to the Treblinka extermination camp. On November 10, SS and Police Chief Friedrich Wilhelm Krueger selected Ujazd as the location of one of four "re-established ghettos" in the Radom District. These ghettos were meant to house surviving Jews in the Tomaszow Mazowiecki area and to induce Jews who had fled during German deportation and liquidation operations to come out of hiding. Some 2,000 local Jews were concentrated in Ujazd, along with others who had fled to the forests while the ghettos in the county were liquidated. Surrounded by barbed wire and protected by German guards, the ghetto became a de facto transit camp. A Jewish Order Service performed guard duties in the ghetto itself. The Ujazd ghetto was liquidated on January 6, 1943, and its inhabitants were deported to Treblinka. German police murdered about seventy Jews during the evacuation.

ÚJPEST

TOWN IN PEST-PILIS-SOLT-KISKUN COUNTY, HUNGARY

Coordinates:
47°34' | 19°05'

The last national census conducted prior to the German occupation, taken in January 1941, recorded 10,882 Jewish inhabitants in Ujpest, approximately 14 percent of the total population. The town was founded by Jewish settlers in the 1830s, under the name Ujmegyer. Ujpest was one of the leading industrial towns of Hungary and held this prominent position throughout the interwar period, during which most inhabitants worked in the local factories owned by Jews. The town had a Neolog as well as a small Orthodox Jewish community and various religious and social associations, including a school and a Talmud Torah. In the 1930s, the Zionist movement gained popularity in Ujpest. A local branch of the Hungarian Zionist Association was established in 1935.

In 1942, many of the Jewish men were drafted into the Hungarian army for forced labor service; most were sent to work in the infamous copper mines of Bor.

The German army occupied Hungary on March 19, 1944, and soon thereafter German units arrived in Ujpest. On March 20, 1944, German soldiers broke into and robbed Jewish shops and homes.

According to a census conducted in the second week of April 1944, about 12,000 Jews belonged to the Neolog Jewish community and 460 Jews to the Orthodox Jewish community of Ujpest.

The Hungarian administration remained intact and operational after the German occupation. The ghettoization and deportation of the Jews occurred on the basis of decrees and orders issued by the Hungarian national and local authorities. On May 12, Hungarian sub-prefect Dr. Laszlo Endre, a militant antisemite, ordered the establishment of ghettos in his county. On that same day, the area of the main local ghetto was marked out in the industrial sector of the town. In addition, individual apartment blocks along several streets near the Cotton Factory and the Chinoin-Plant were designated as part of the ghetto area. A four-member Jewish Council was established, charged with organizing the move into the ghetto.

The move into the ghetto took place en masse between May 22 and 29, 1944, by order of the mayor, Pal Hess. During that period, more than half of Ujpest's Jews, about 7,500 people, moved into the ghetto. Between June 21 and 23, 1944, the rest were lodged in houses marked Jewish by yellow Stars of David in different parts of the town. About 300 Jews from the Ujpest ghetto were rescued by various Zionist organizations that were active in Budapest*; most of the people who escaped to the capital survived.

The Jews from the marked houses were transferred on June 24, 1944, to the brick factories of Budakalasz and Bekasmegyer*, which were the entrainment centers for the ghettos of the Pest-Pilis-Solt-Kiskun County surrounding Budapest from the north. The Ujpest Jews who lived in the main ghetto were transferred to Budakalasz between July 1 and 3, 1944, by infamously cruel gendarmes brought from Nagyvarad*. Prior to the transfer, the Jews were mercilessly tortured into revealing the whereabouts of their hidden valuables.

The Jews from the brick factories of Bekasmegyer and nearby Budakalasz were deported to Auschwitz between July 6 and 8, 1944. In the fall of 1944, Arrow Cross men discovered about 150 Jewish children hiding in a local convent. They brought the children to the bank of the Danube and shot them.

UKMERGĖ
(Yiddish: **Vilkomir**)

COUNTY SEAT, LITHUANIA

During the war:
Reichskommissariat Ostland

Coordinates:
55°15' | 24°45'

About 8,000 Jews lived in Ukmerge during the interwar period, representing more than one-third of the town's population. They earned their livelihood from commerce, farming, and artisanship and owned most of the shops and factories in the city. The community boasted Jewish welfare, religious, and educational institutions, including Hadarim and a Talmud Torah, two Hebrew schools, a high school, a Yeshiva, a hospital, and assorted other institutions. Zionist political parties and youth movements were active in Ukmerge, as was Agudath Israel. By that time, an elected twenty-five-member community council had operated in Ukmerge for a number of years, in conformity with a law calling for autonomy for Jews that had been passed by the independent Lithuanian government.

After Lithuania was annexed to the Soviet Union in 1940, most of Ukmerge's shops and factories were nationalized, Jewish national activity was discontinued, and Hebrew schools were transformed into Soviet schools. Several schools adopted Yiddish as their language of instruction.

When the German army entered Ukmerge on June 26, 1941, the plunder of Jewish property and abuse of Jewish inhabitants began immediately. During the same period, Jewish refugees from all over Lithuania thronged to the town on their way to the east. The Germans arrested and executed a number of Jewish public figures. Some 200 Jews were arrested for collaborating with the Communists; on July 4, 1941, they were taken to the Pivonija forest and executed by Germans and Lithuanians.

In early August 1941, the Jews were ordered to move into a ghetto that was established in two alleyways in the city's poorest quarter. The ghetto was not fenced in but was surrounded by a heavy guard of armed Lithuanians. The Jews of the ghetto were removed for forced labor, during which several were killed.

On September 5–18, 1941, armed Lithuanians carried out a large-scale murder operation of the Jews of Ukmerge and the surrounding towns, in the Pivonija forest. The ill, elderly people, women, and children who remained in the ghetto were murdered on September 26, 1941.

After the war, 6,354 bodies were discovered in the forest.

ULANOV
(Ukrainian: **Ulaniv**)

COUNTY SEAT, VINNITSA DISTRICT, UKRAINE, USSR

During the war:
Reichskommissariat Ukraine

Coordinates:
49°42' | 28°08'

In the late 1930s, about 1,200 Jews lived in Ulanov, representing approximately two-thirds of the total population. The townlet had both a Jewish Ethnic Soviet and a school that offered instruction in Yiddish.

Ulanov was occupied by the Germans on July 15, 1941, and the local Jewish population was immediately subjected to abuse. This included the plundering of Jewish property, forced labor seizures, and sporadic murders. The Jews were concentrated in a ghetto that was confined to one street and surrounded with a barbed-wire fence.

In December 1941, about 300 Jews from the nearby localities were moved into Ulanov; in the spring of 1942, another approximately 150 Jewish inhabitants were brought from the nearby village of Salnitsa. In April 1942, a few hundred Jews were sent to build the Kalinovka airfield.

The Ulanov ghetto was liquidated between June 10 and 14 or on July 10 (sources vary regarding the date) when approximately 900 Jews, including Jews from the area, were murdered in a huge pit in the Polish cemetery located near the townlet.

ULANÓW

TOWNLET IN NISKO COUNTY, LWÓW DISTRICT, POLAND

During the war: General Gouvernement, Cracow District

Coordinates:
50°29' | 22°16'

After World War I, about 900 Jews lived in Ulanow, representing nearly half of the townlet's population. They earned their livelihood from small-scale commerce and artisanship, especially in the garment, food, and wood industries. Institutions that provided financial aid included the JDC, CENTOS, a free-loan society, and an association of former residents of Ulanow living in the USA. The townlet had a union of Jewish merchants and held vocational courses for Jewish youth. Zionist parties and the *Akiva* youth movement were active there.

During the first week of World War II, Jewish refugees fleeing from the German army arrived in Ulanow from western Poland. The Germans occupied the townlet on September 10, 1939, and immediately began to seize men for forced labor. In late September 1939, the Germans evacuated Ulanow and turned it over to the Soviets, who in turn withdrew to the east two weeks later. Dozens of Jews from Ulanow who followed the Soviets were exiled deep into the Soviet Union in the summer of 1940.

The Germans returned to Ulanow and terrorized its Jewish inhabitants, especially targeting the more traditional Jews. In the second half of October 1939, the Germans seized the apartments of the Jews who had fled to the Soviet Union and confiscated all their contents.

In late 1939, Jews from Niski, Tarnobrzeg-Dzikow*, Rozwadow, and Rudnik were deported to Ulanow. In early 1940, a Jewish Order Service was established, as was a Judenrat, headed by Moshe Reikh. The Judenrat carried out a census and provided the Germans with forced laborers, but random abductions of forced laborers and sporadic murders of Jews persisted nevertheless.

In January 1942, a ghetto was established in Ulanow, with 1,400 people concentrated in its grounds. JSS representatives supplied food, clothing, and medication.

In October 1942, most of the Ulanow's Jews were deported to Zaklikow. Dozens of Jews who hid in the forests and surrounding localities were apprehended and murdered by Germans and by local collaborators.

ULLA

(Yiddish: **Ule**; Belarussian: **Ula**)

TOWNLET IN BESHENKOVICHI COUNTY, VITEBSK DISTRICT, BELARUS, USSR

During the war: Military Administration Area

Coordinates:
55°14' | 29°15'

In the early twentieth century, there were some 1,500 Jews in Ulla, about 60 percent of the population. During the era of Soviet rule, many practiced crafts, others became white-collar workers, and a small number turned to farming. In the late 1930s, only 520 Jews remained in the townlet. A Jewish Ethnic Council was created and children attended a government school that taught in Yiddish.

The Germans occupied Ulla on July 5–7 1941. A number of Jewish residents managed to evacuate to the east before the occupation. Those who remained were ordered to wear yellow badges.

In December 1941, a ghetto was established in the center of the townlet, and Belarussian police were posted as guards. The inhabitants were permitted to leave its quarters to obtain food but were required to return every evening.

The ghetto was liquidated on January 17, 1942, when between 200 and 350 inhabitants (sources vary on the figure) were murdered at the site of a nearby former Soviet army camp.

UMAN

(Ukrainian: **Uman'**)

COUNTY SEAT, KIEV DISTRICT, UKRAINE, USSR

During the war:
Reichskommissariat Ukraine, USSR

Coordinates:
48°45' | 30°13'

Uman, August 1941
Jews rounded up in the marketplace area, near city hall, awaiting deportation (BPK)

In the early twentieth century, there were about 18,000 Jews in Uman, nearly two-thirds of the city's population. The Jews suffered acute losses during the Russian Civil War (1918–20). In May 1919, approximately 500 members of the community were murdered in two pogroms conducted by Ukrainians. Red Army soldiers perpetrated another pogrom in the city at a later date. During the 1920s and 1930s, many Jews left Uman as a result of industrialization and urbanization in the Soviet Union. By the time the Germans invaded the USSR, about 13,000 Jews remained, accounting for approximately one-third of the city's population. During the Soviet era, many Jewish inhabitants continued to work as artisans, and quite a few formed cooperatives. Others accepted white- and blue-collar jobs in state-owned factories and institutions. The police in Uman had a Yiddish-language department, and several government schools taught in Yiddish. Many Jews continued to visit the grave of the Hasidic leader Nachman of Braslaw.

When the Germans occupied Uman on August 1, 1941, there were some 15,000 Jews in the city, including refugees. In the ensuing days, the Germans executed six Jewish doctors. On August 13, 1941, eighty Jewish members of the city's intelligentsia were summoned, ostensibly to establish a body of Jewish leaders. The group was murdered by Sonderkommando 4b. Later, the military headquarters in the city appointed two Jews to head the community and a Jewish Order Service composed of a small group of members. The wearing of Star-of-David armbands was made compulsory. On September 22–23, 1941, a detail of Einsatzkommando 5 murdered 1,412 men outside the city. Concurrently, some 3,000 women and children were gathered in the cellars of the local Communist youth organization building, where most were asphyxiated when the air vents were sealed. Only 300 survived.

Two days after the operation, the Germans ordered the Jews to settle, by October 1, into a ghetto near the municipal market. Although the ghetto was unfenced, inmates were forbidden to leave on pain of death. As the Jews moved into the ghetto, many were robbed of their possessions by Ukrainians. German and Ukrainian policemen frequented the ghetto at night to dispossess and abuse its inhabitants. A forced-labor requirement was imposed.

The Germans appointed a man surnamed Samburski as head of the Jews, while Tabachnik was appointed as his deputy. A Jewish Order Service was established; one of its members, a woman named Ida who was nicknamed *Glekele* ("little bell"), was notorious for her brutal treatment of Jews.

On October 8, 1941, Order Police Battalion 304 conducted a massive operation in the ghetto, murdering most of its inhabitants. On German instructions, Ukrainian volunteers and police selected some 900 Jewish skilled workers in high-demand occupations together with their families and escorted the remaining 6,000 or 9,000 Jews (sources vary on the figure) to a location out of the city and murdered them.

Those who passed the selection returned to the ghetto and over subsequent weeks were gradually joined by hundreds who had survived in hiding, bringing the ghetto population to about 1,800. They were assigned to harsh labor. Occasionally, the head of the Jews forced relatively affluent Jews to raise the sum demanded for periodic ransoms. On January 8, 1942, the inhabitants of the ghetto were ordered to replace their armbands with two yellow stars affixed to the front and back of their clothing.

The ghetto was liquidated on April 22, 1942. In the spring of 1942, a labor camp was established in Uman that held Jews from Bessarabia and Bukovina who were assigned to road construction. By liberation day (March 10, 1944), most inhabitants of the camp were dead.

UNECHA

COUNTY SEAT, OREL DISTRICT, RUSSIAN FEDERATION, USSR

During the war: Military Administration Area

Coordinates:
52°52' | 32°42'

On the eve of World War II, about 1,700 Jews lived in Unecha, approximately one-tenth of the local population. Unecha boasted a Yiddish library and a Jewish school, with Yiddish as its language of instruction.

Unecha was occupied by the Germans on August 17, 1941. Many of the town's Jews had managed to flee or were evacuated eastward in the weeks preceding the occupation.

In October 1941, the Germans murdered about 600 of the town's residents, some of whom were apparently Jews. In late December 1941–early January 1942 (according to one testimony), the approximately 300 Jews remaining in Unecha were concentrated in a ghetto that was established in a chicken factory. They were not permitted to leave the ghetto building. Living conditions were extremely harsh, and as the Jews were forbidden to bury their dead, they were confined in the ghetto building along with corpses.

On March 15, 1942, the Unecha ghetto was liquidated. About 300 Jews were shot together with a number of Gypsies (Romany) and buried in a mass grave.

UNGVAR

COUNTY SEAT OF UNG COUNTY, HUNGARY
(After World War II in the USSR/Ukraine; Ukrainian, Russian: **Uzhgorod**)

Coordinates:
48°37' | 22°18'

The last national census conducted in Hungary prior to the German occupation, taken in January 1941, recorded 9,576 Jewish inhabitants in Ungvar, comprising roughly 27 percent of the total population. Most were merchants and artisans, but many were also clerks or practiced the free professions. The town had both an Orthodox and a small Neolog Jewish community. The Orthodox Jewish community ran a Yeshiva, a Talmud Torah, and an elementary school. The Neolog Jewish community maintained an elementary school and a high school.

After World War I, Ungvar, which was formerly in Hungary, became part of Czechoslovakia. As of August 30, 1940, Ungvar again became an integral part of the Hungarian civil administration. The Hungarian anti-Jewish legislation was implemented more harshly in Carpato-Ruthenia, where Ungvar was located, than in inner Hungary.

From 1940, many Jewish men were drafted into the Hungarian army for forced labor service. In 1940, they were assigned to work in Hungary, but as of 1942, the majority of the forced laborers were sent to the eastern front, in the Ukraine, where many perished.

In the summer of 1941, the Hungarian authorities declared several Jewish families whose members could not prove their Hungarian citizenship to be stateless and deported them to German-occupied Ukraine. They were murdered on August 27 or 28 at Kamenets-Podolsk*.

The German army occupied Hungary on March 19, 1944. The Hungarian administration remained intact and in force after the occupation. The ghettoization and deportation of the Jews were implemented on the basis of the decrees and orders of the Hungarian national and local authorities. Following an April 12, 1944, conference concerning ghettoization with Laszlo Endre, the undersecretary of state for internal affairs, held for the administrative leaders of Carpatho-Ruthenia, sub-prefect Janos Kossey and mayor Dr. Laszlo Megay directed the ghettoization in Ungvar. SS-Hauptsturmfuerer Theodor Dannecker, a member of the Eichmann Sonderkommando, acted as advisor. Two ghettos were established in the town for the local Jews and the Jews of the vicinity. The Jews from the countryside were required to begin moving into the ghetto on April 16, 1944, and the local Jews from April 21 to 23, 1944. More than 14,300 Jews from the town and the vicinity were concentrated in the Moskovits brick factory. An additional 2,600 Jews from the countryside were concentrated in the Glueck lumberyard ghetto. Altogether, about 17,000 Jews lived in the ghettos, a majority without shelter.

A five-member Jewish Council operated in the ghettos, headed by Dr. Laszlo. The Jewish Council established a soup kitchen, but food was very scarce. The Jewish Order Service was responsible for maintaining order in the ghettos. Sixty physicians practiced in them, several in a hospital in the brick factory ghetto. However, hygienic conditions in the ghettos were exceedingly poor. Once warned of the dire situation, the mayor, Megay, petitioned minister of interior Andor Jaross to remove the Jews, as they posed a health hazard to the other inhabitants of his town.

A secret courier service operated between the ghettos and the various Jewish organizations in Budapest*. The Germans arrested one of its messengers, Dr. Ackermann, a lawyer from Ungvar.

The inhabitants of the Ungvar ghetto were deported to Auschwitz in five transports from May 17 to 31, 1944.

UNIEJÓW

TOWNLET IN TUREK COUNTY, ŁÓDŹ DISTRICT, POLAND

During the war:
Wartheland

Coordinates:
51°58' | 18°48'

On the eve of World War II there were about 130 Jewish families in Uniejow, out of a total population of 3,660. A majority of the townlet's Jews worked as merchants and artisans. Several Zionist parties were active in the community, and a library hosted a range of cultural activities. In the 1930s, an economic boycott of the Jews of Uniejow, a product of a national economic crisis, was accompanied by a surge in antisemitism.

The Germans occupied Uniejow one week into the war. They plundered Jewish property, evicted many families from their homes, and abducted Jews for forced labor. In December 1939, a Judenrat was established in the townlet and Jews were ordered to wear a yellow badge.

In 1940, the Jews of Uniejow were moved into a special quarter that was transformed into a ghetto in October. It comprised four buildings that accommodated 491 people.

The Uniejow ghetto remained unsealed until June 1941, although its inhabitants were forbidden to enter the "Aryan" side of the townlet. It was subsequently downsized and sealed, exacerbating the overcrowded conditions, starvation, and disease. In 1941, young Jews were sent to labor camps in the Poznan area.

The ghetto was liquidated on October 20, 1941. All its inhabitants were deported to the Kowale Panskie area and lodged in the village of Dzierzbotki, one part of a rural ghetto into which the Jews of the Turek County were concentrated.

Uniejow, 1940
Jews rounded up in the town square to be taken to perform forced labor (YV)

UŚCIŁUG

TOWNLET IN WŁODZIMIERZ WOŁYŃSKI COUNTY, VOLHYNIA DISTRICT, POLAND

(After World War II in the USSR/Ukraine; Ukrainian: **Ustyluh**; Russian: **Ustilug**)

During the war: Reichskommissariat Ukraine

Coordinates: 50°52' | 24°09'

After World War I, there were about 2,700 Jews in Uscilug, three-fourths of the townlet's population. They engaged in trade and crafts and were organized in Jewish trade unions that owned two savings-and-loan associations. Schools affiliated with the Hebrew-language Tarbut and Yavne organizations were active in Uscilug. The community also enjoyed the services of both Hebrew and Yiddish libraries. Most Zionist political parties were represented in the townlet.

The Soviets took control of Uscilug in September 1939. Owing to the townlet's proximity to the German occupation zone, the Soviets restricted its inhabitants' movements. One-third of the Jews in the townlet left, primarily for Wlodzimierz Wolynski*.

The Germans occupied Uscilug on June 22, 1941, and soon began abducting Jews for forced labor. Several days later thirty Jews were murdered. In late July 1941, the Germans appointed a Judenrat in the townlet and established a Jewish Order Service.

In late October 1941, 890 Jewish men, including dignitaries and intellectuals, were rounded up and murdered. Afterwards, groups of young Jews were intermittently arrested and murdered near the Jewish cemetery.

The Uscilug ghetto was established in March 1942, with some 2,000 persons interned within its confines. The ghetto was liquidated in the first half of September 1942; its inhabitants were transported to Wlodzimierz Wolynski and murdered in a nearby village, Piatyden, along with Jews from the local ghetto. Some 300 of Uscilug's Jews fled during the murder operation; although most were tracked and murdered, a few found refuge with Poles or joined the partisans.

A small group of workers from Uscilug was left behind after the liquidation to work in a military camp near Wlodzimierz Wolynski. These Jews, too, were murdered in early 1943.

USHACHI

(Yiddish: **Ushats, Ushatsh**; Belarussian: **Ushachy**)

COUNTY SEAT, VITEBSK DISTRICT, BELARUS, USSR

During the war: Military Administration Area

Coordinates: 55°11' | 28°37'

In the early twentieth century, there were about 1,100 Jews in Ushachi, approximately 70 percent of the population. During the Soviet era, many Jews practiced artisan trades, some in collectives. Others became white-collar workers in Soviet institutions or turned to farming. A Jewish Ethnic Council and a government school both functioned in Yiddish.

In the late 1930s, about 500 Jews remained in the townlet. After World War II began, Jewish refugees from Poland arrived in Ushachi with reports of German brutality toward Polish Jews.

The Germans occupied Ushachi on July 3, 1941. Only ten families, most of them headed by white-collar workers in party or state-owned institutions, are known to have evacuated to the east in advance. The Germans, upon their arrival, subjected Jews to abuse and instituted a requirement that the Jews wear a yellow Star-of-David on their chests and backs. Jews were forbidden to shop, even in the market, and were put to grueling forced labor.

In October 1941, the 460 Jews in Ushachi were concentrated into a ghetto established on the street where the synagogue was located. About a month later, the ghetto was surrounded with barbed wire and placed under Belarussian police guard. Living conditions in the ghetto were appalling; the buildings were little more than hovels and some residents starved or froze to death. The Germans appointed a man named Azriel Nemtsov as head of the Jews.

When several Belarussians warned the inhabitants that pits were being readied in the days preceding the liquidation of the ghetto, a few Jews managed to escape. The remaining Jews were murdered on January 12, 1942, near the townlet. Several days after the operation, about 200 Jews from Kublichi* were brought to the Ushachi ghetto. They set fire to a house in the ghetto and tried to escape. Some perished in the fire, while all the rest but two were captured and murdered.

USVYATY

(Yiddish: **Usviat**)

COUNTY SEAT, SMOLENSK DISTRICT, RUSSIAN FEDERATION, USSR

During the war: Military Administration Area

Coordinates:
55°44' | 30°45'

On the eve of the German occupation, there were 136 Jews living in Usvyaty. A Jewish kolkhoz had been established in the townlet at the onset of Soviet rule and operated through to 1922, when the antisemitic harassment and murder of Jews by local inhabitants forced its closure.

The Germans occupied Usvyaty on July 14, 1941, and along with local inhabitants immediately began to dispossess the Jews, who were required to wear a white Star-of-David armband. Three Jewish townspeople were murdered on July 25, 1941.

In late September 1941, a ghetto was established for between 100 and 170 Jews in the townlet and its vicinity as well as refugees from various localities, including Riga*.

The Usvyaty ghetto was set up in several buildings on the shore of a lake and enclosed in barbed wire. Its inhabitants were put to various forms of forced labor, such as cleaning, and were paid in the form of meager food rations. Occasionally, local inhabitants tossed food over the fence in the direction of Jewish acquaintances.

A Jew named Baskin, identified by testimonies as a Communist Party activist before the war, was accused of contact with partisans and executed on November 7, 1941. Twenty-five more Jews were murdered on November 10.

The Germans began to liquidate the Usvyaty ghetto on January 28, 1942, but the arrival of Soviet forces thwarted the planned mass murder of Jewish inhabitants.

UZDA

(Yiddish: **Uzde**)

COUNTY SEAT, MINSK DISTRICT, BELARUS, USSR

During the war:
Reichskommissariat Ostland

Coordinates:
53°27' | 27°13'

In the early twentieth century, there were about 2,000 Jews in Uzda, approximately two-thirds of the local population. During the era of Soviet rule, many Jews practiced crafts, in some instances in cooperatives that they organized. Others became white-collar workers in Soviet institutions, and a few turned to farming. Urbanization and industrialization induced many Jews to leave Uzda, so that by the late 1930s only about 1,100 Jews remained, approximately one-third of the population. The townlet had a Yiddish-language Jewish Ethnic Council and government school.

The Germans occupied Uzda on June 28, 1941. About a month later, they concentrated the Jews in a ghetto established along two streets. All Jews over the age of ten years were ordered to wear yellow identifying marks on the front and back of their clothing. The ghetto was enclosed in barbed wire, and Jews were forbidden to leave its premises.

The Uzda ghetto was liquidated on October 17, 1941, when the Germans, assisted by local collaborators, led all inhabitants to a nearby location and shot them dead. In all, 1,740 people were murdered in the operation, including hundreds of Jews from the vicinity.

UŽPALIAI
(Yiddish: **Ushpol**)

TOWNLET IN UTENA COUNTY, LITHUANIA

During the war:
Reichskommissariat Ostland

Coordinates:
55°39' | 25°35'

More than 500 Jews lived in Uzpaliai during the interwar period, representing approximately one-third of the townlet's population. They earned their livelihood from small-scale commerce, artisanship, and farming. The Jewish children of the townlet attended a Heder or the local school, which was the cultural and social center of the entire area. Many of the Jews of Uzpaliai were active Zionists.

A large fire in 1932 destroyed most of the townlet's homes. After Lithuania was annexed to the Soviet Union in 1940, a number of Jewish shops were nationalized, Hebrew schools were closed, and Jewish parties and youth groups were dissolved.

On June 26, 1941, the Germans entered Uzpaliai and ordered the Jews to move into a ghetto set up along a few narrow streets around the Beit Midrash and bathhouse. Shortly thereafter began acts of plunder and rape, as well as murders of Jewish men and occasionally of entire families, some of whom were led out of the townlet to be killed.

On August 29, 1941, all of Uzpaliai's Jews were brought from the ghetto to the nearby county seat of Utena. They were murdered together with the Jews of nearby localities by Lithuanians near the Rase grove, some fifteen kilometers from the townlet. Most of the Jews who tried to hide in the area were caught and murdered.

Vilnius ghetto, Poland

"We were slaves to Pharoah in Egypt... Matzo for the Ghetto
Despite everything, there is no anarchy in the world. Jews, even this year, will not remain without matzo in the Vilna ghetto. The committee of Orthodox [Jews] has already taken care of that. The residents of the ghetto will receive in their March [1942] ration cards, a 'matzo ration' of a quarter kilogram for 10 rubles. Some of the residents may be able to secure another half kilo. In short, as stated, there is still some order in the world. There will be matzos and Jews will be able to say: 'We were slaves to Pharaoh in Egypt...'"

Herman Kruk, The Diary of Vilna Ghetto, *ed. Mordecai W. Bernstein (New York, 1961) [Yiddish].*

VABALNINKAS
(Yiddish: **Vabolnik**)

TOWNLET IN BIRŽAI COUNTY, LITHUANIA

During the war:
Reichskommissariat Ostland

Coordinates:
55°58' | 24°45'

On the eve of the German occupation, about 600 Jews lived in Vabalninkas, representing approximately one-third of the townlet's population. They earned their livelihood from small-scale commerce, artisanship, light industry, and farming. Most of the shops and a considerable proportion of the factories in the townlet were owned by Jews. Many of Vabalninkas's Jews were active Zionists.

After Lithuania was annexed to the Soviet Union in 1940, all the shops and factories in the townlet were nationalized, the Zionist movements dispersed, and the Hebrew schools closed.

On June 27, 1941, the Germans occupied Vabalninkas. Nationalist Lithuanians took over the townlet, arresting numerous Jews and murdering eighty-six of them in the marketplace.

In mid-July 1941, the Jews of Vabalninkas were ordered to move into a ghetto established along an alleyway located in the poorest quarter of the townlet. The ghetto was not fenced in but was guarded by a number of armed Lithuanians. According to a census, some 600 Jews lived in the Vabalninkas ghetto, including refugees from nearby townlets. The Jews in the ghetto were employed at forced labor.

On August 18, 1941, the ghetto's inhabitants were ordered to gather in the Shulhoyf Beit Midrash and bring along food for three days. The Jews turned over their money and were transferred to the nearby townlet of Pasvalys*. On August 26, 1941, they were murdered in the Zadeikiai forest, located about four and a half kilometers from Pasvalys, together with 1,349 of the local Jews.

While the Jews were living in the Vabalninkas ghetto, a local priest proposed that they convert to Christianity in order to be saved. Either forty or seventy of the ghetto's Jews (testimonies vary on the figure) agreed and were kept separate from the other inhabitants. However, their conversion did not ultimately spare their lives.

VÁC

(in Jewish sources: **Vaytzen**)

TOWN IN PEST-PILIS-SOLT-KISKUN COUNTY, HUNGARY

Coordinates:
47°47' | 19°08'

The last national census conducted prior to the German occupation, taken in January 1941, recorded 1,854 Jewish inhabitants in Vac, representing roughly 8 percent of the total population. Most were merchants; a number were industrialists and landowners. The town had a Status Quo Ante Jewish community, which became Orthodox in 1930, as well as an independent Orthodox Jewish community. Various Jewish social and religious associations, two Jewish schools (elementary and middle school), and a Talmud Torah operated in the town. Both Jewish communities had their Yeshivot. Vac, one of the centers for Hebrew publishing in Hungary, had two Hebrew printing houses.

The German army occupied Hungary on March 19, 1944. The Hungarian administration remained intact and operational after the German occupation. The ghettoization and deportation of the Jews occurred on the basis of decrees and orders issued by the Hungarian national and local authorities. On May 12, the Hungarian sub-prefect, Dr. Laszlo Endre, a militant antisemite, ordered the establishment of ghettos in his county. The mayor of Vac, Dr. Kalman Karay, commanded the ghettoization in his town. From May 22 on, 518 local Jewish families (altogether 1,515 people) moved into the Vac ghetto, consisting of sixty-seven houses, two schools, and two prayer houses. In addition to the local Jews, about 500 Jews from the county-district of Vac were moved into the ghetto between May 22 and 30, 1944. The former presidents and rabbis of both Jewish communities became the members of the newly founded Jewish Council.

At the end of June or beginning of July 1944, the inhabitants of the ghetto were transferred to the brick factory in Monor*, which served as the entrainment center for the ghettos of Pest-Pilis-Solt-Kiskun County surrounding Budapest* from the south and east. According to the report of gendarme Lieutenant-Colonel Laszlo Ferenczy, some 8,000 Jews were deported from the brick factory of Monor to Auschwitz in three transports between July 6 and 8, 1944.

VÁGSELLYE

TOWNLET IN POZSONY-NYITRA COUNTY, HUNGARY

(After World War II in Czechoslovakia/Slovakia; Slovak: **Šala on the Váhom**)

Coordinates:
45°52' | 17°51'

In 1941, about 441 Jewish inhabitants lived in Vagsellye, accounting for roughly 10 percent of the total population. Most were merchants and artisans. The townlet's Jewish community was Orthodox and maintained a Jewish elementary school. After World War I, Vagsellye (which was formerly in Hungary) became part of Czechoslovakia. In the interwar period, Agudath Israel was the most popular Jewish organization in the townlet. The Jewish Party and several Zionist organizations were also active ithere.

As a result of the First Vienna Award in November 1938, Vagsellye became part of Hungary again. The Hungarian authorities expelled and pushed through the new Slovakian-Hungarian border several Jewish families whose members did not have Hungarian citizenship.

In 1940/41, many of the townlet's Jewish men were drafted into the Hungarian army for forced labor service. They were deployed to the eastern front, in the Ukraine. In 1942, when the Jews were deported from Slovakia, a few dozen Jewish refugees arrived from there. The Jewish community assisted the refugees and helped many of them to reach Budapest*.

The German army occupied Hungary on March 19, 1944. A census conducted in the second week of April 1944 reported that 451 Jews belonged to the Jewish community of Vagsellye.

The Hungarian administration remained intact and operational after the German occupation. The Vagsellye ghetto, established at the beginning of May 1944 according to national and local decrees of the Hungarian administration, was located in the local Jewish quarter. About 850 Jews from the townlet and the vicinity were ordered to move into its grounds by May 10, 1944. The ghetto was not fenced in. Signs on its apartments read "Jewish housing." The Jews were allowed to bring along essential furnishings and food.

On June 5, 1944, the inhabitants of the ghetto were transferred to the Kurzweil brick factory in Ersekujvar*, which served as an entrainment center. They were deported to Auschwitz on June 11 and 14, 1944.

VANDŽIOGALA
(Yiddish: **Vendzigole**, **Vendzegole**)

TOWNLET IN KAUNAS COUNTY, LITHUANIA

During the war:
Reichskommissariat Ostland

Coordinates:
55°07' | 23°58'

On the eve of the German occupation of Lithuania, there were about 350 Jews living in Vandziogala, representing 58 percent of the population. They earned their livelihood from commerce, artisanship, and farming and were aided by a Jewish Folksbank. The community boasted three synagogues, a Heder, and a Hebrew school.

In the fall of 1940, after Lithuania was annexed to the Soviet Union, a number of the townlet's businesses and factories were nationalized, Jewish national activity was outlawed, and the Hebrew schools were closed.

On June 25, 1941, the Germans entered Vandziogala and immediately imposed severe restrictions on the Jewish inhabitants' freedom of movement. Jews were required to wear a yellow badge, their homes were marked, and they were recruited for forced labor.

On July 8, 1941, the Lithuanians arrested sixty-eight Jews, robbed them of their clothing, and murdered them in the Borekas grove near the cemetery. The rest of Vandziogala's Jewish inhabitants were concentrated in a ghetto of sorts. During Sabbath prayers on August 9, 1941, the synagogue was surrounded by armed Lithuanians. They removed about 100 Jewish men and several women from the synagogue and brought them to the townlet of Babtai, where they were held for two weeks in a synagogue and then murdered. On August 28, 1941, the remaining Jews were removed from the ghetto and concentrated in the townlet's marketplace. They were then brought to Babtai and murdered. A few Jews from Vandziogala managed to reach the Kaunas* ghetto, while several joined the partisans.

VARAKLĀNI
(Yiddish: **Varklian**)

TOWNLET IN RĒZEKNE COUNTY, LATGALE DISTRICT, LATVIA

During the war:
Reichskommissariat Ostland

Coordinates:
56°37' | 26°44'

In the 1930s, about 950 Jews lived in Varaklani, representing nearly 60 percent of the townlet's population. Many of the townlet's leaders and members of the municipal council were Jews; until the anti-democratic coup of 1934, most of the council's meetings were held in Yiddish. The Jews engaged in commerce, artisanship, and transportation, supplementing their modest earnings with money sent by former members of the community who lived in the United States. The community boasted a Jewish savings-and-loan bank, various welfare organizations, and three synagogues. Among the Jewish political activities conducted in Varaklani, the Bund operated a Yiddish kindergarten and elementary school, Agudath Israel supported a Talmud Torah, and the Zionist movement ran a chapter of *Tzeirei Zion* and various youth movements. During the period of Soviet rule (1940/41), Jewish public institutions were abolished and private property was gradually nationalized. Leftist Jews were appointed to various key positions, and a Jewish Communist named Lazer Zelekovich became the chairman of the townlet council.

When World War II broke out, Jewish refugees thronged to Varaklani from Latvia and Lithuania. On June 28, 1941, the Soviets evacuated the townlet, joined by several hundred Jews. Dozens of Jews enlisted in the Red Army, and many were killed in battle. A short time afterwards, the Germans occupied the townlet and imposed forced and demeaning labor on the Jews. The homes and shops of Jewish inhabitants were seized, and they were forced into a ghetto in a suburb near the Jewish cemetery. Although the ghetto was not fenced in, Jews were forbidden to enter the center of the townlet. They were allowed to purchase food at only one specific shop, and they were required to perform forced labor.

On August 4, 1941, the ghetto and all its inhabitants were liquidated. The Jews were ordered to report for work, and the approximately 540 Jews who appeared at the appointed place were taken to the cemetery and shot next to a pit that they dug with their own hands. Two Jews who managed to hide with a farmer were discovered a few months later, and drowned in the swamps as they fled from their pursuers. A number of young Jewish women who converted to Christianity were murdered in the course of a campaign that was carried out several months after the liquidation of the Jewish community, to trace Jews who had converted. Before they retreated, the Germans ordered local farmers to open the pits and burn the bodies of the murder victims.

VASVÁR

TOWNLET IN VAS COUNTY, HUNGARY

Coordinates:
47°03' | 16°48'

The last national census conducted prior to the German occupation, taken in January 1941, recorded 184 Jewish inhabitants in Vasvar, roughly 4 percent of the total population. Most were merchants and artisans; several were factory owners and landowners. The townlet's Jewish community was Neolog and maintained a Jewish elementary school.

The German army occupied Hungary on March 19, 1944. The Hungarian administration remained intact and in force after the occupation. The ghettoization and deportation of the Jews were carried out on the basis of the decrees and orders of the Hungarian national and local authorities. On May 6, 1944, the Hungarian sub-prefect, Dr. Jozsef Tulok, published a decree designating May 12 as the deadline for moving the Jews into ghettos. According to the decree, the 180 local Jews and 180 Jews from the vicinity were required to move into the ghetto of Vasvar, which was established in the "Hungarian King" restaurant, a café, and the townlet cinema. The Jews moved into the ghetto on May 10–11, 1944; just prior to the move, four Jews committed suicide.

Life in the ghetto was controlled by the ghetto regulations, which were issued by Dr. Karoly Lipp, the chief administrative officer of the Vasvar County-District. A Jewish Council operated in the ghetto; two of its members were permitted to leave it daily for two hours to maintain contact with the authorities. On May 30, 1944, there were 322 Jewish inhabitants living in the Vasvar ghetto.

On June 20, 1944, the inhabitants of the ghetto were transferred to the premises of the Mayer Engine and Machine Factory Share Company Szombathely, which served as an entrainment center. They were deported to Auschwitz on July 4 and 6, 1944.

VATRA-DORNEI

TOWN IN CÂMPULUNG COUNTY, BUKOVINA, ROMANIA

Coordinates:
47°21' | 25°22'

About 1,700 Jews lived in Vatra-Dornei in the interwar period, representing approximately one-quarter of the town's population. They earned their livelihood from artisanship and commerce, which included trade in wood and wood products, as well as from banking, the liberal professions, and the provision of vacation services. The Romanian authorities did not consent to the formation of a separate Jewish school network, requiring instead that the Jewish children attend state schools. A number of Zionist parties and youth movements were active in the community.

When northern Bukovina was annexed to the Soviet Union in June 1940, many Jews from the region fled to Vatra-Dornei, which was in southern Bukovina and remained under Romanian control. In the summer of 1941, Jews were deported there from the small villages and localities in the area, including Iacobeni and Dorna-Candreni.

In August 1941, all 2,029 of Vatra-Dornei's Jews were rounded up in a ghetto and ordered to wear a yellow badge; dozens were seized as hostages. Jewish men were assigned to forced labor. The Jews' freedom of movement was restricted.

On October 9, 1941, deportation orders were issued, and on October 10, 1941, the Jews of Vatra-Dornei were deported by train to Atachi on the banks of the Dniester River, with the exception of twenty-one people belonging to two Jewish families who owned a wood factory needed by the German army. A few days later, on October 17–18, 1941, the deportees were transferred in rafts to the opposite side of the river and deported to various destinations.

VCHERAYSHE
(Ukrainian: **Vchoraishe**)

COUNTY SEAT, ZHITOMIR DISTRICT, UKRAINE, USSR

During the war:
Reichskommissariat Ukraine

Coordinates:
49°52' | 29°09'

In the early twentieth century, about 1,000 Jews lived in the townlet. During the Russian Civil War (1918–20), Red Army soldiers carried out a pogrom in it. During the period of Soviet rule, modernization and urbanization prompted many Jews to leave the townlet; by the late 1930s, about 500 Jews remained. The townlet had both a Jewish Ethnic Soviet and a Yiddish-language school. A considerable proportion of the Jews were employed in artisanship, and many were organized in cooperatives.

The Germans occupied Vcherayshe on July 16, 1941. In August 1941, a number of Soviet and Jewish activists were murdered. The Germans ordered the Jews to wear a yellow Star of David on their chest and right arm.

All of the townlet's Jews were concentrated in a ghetto set up along a single street on the edge of the townlet. The ghetto was not fenced in but was encircled by a steep ravine that rendered access and clear passage difficult on three sides. The Jews were forbidden to leave the ghetto without a permit. The Germans appointed a German-speaking Jew named Davidov as a head of the Jews. All orphans in the ghetto were divided among the families of the artisans (such as shoemakers and carpenters) and others.

The living conditions in the ghetto were relatively reasonable. Food was obtained by people who performed forced labor outside of the ghetto or in exchange for valuables; Ukrainians were permitted to bring food into the ghetto. A female doctor and a nurse lived among the Jews in the ghetto. As winter approached, Jews from the vicinity, including Verkhovnya and later Pavoloch and other localities, were concentrated in the ghetto.

The inhabitants of the ghetto became aware that Jews from the area were being executed. A number attempted to flee upon learning on April 30, 1942, that the Ukrainians had been dispatched to dig a murder pit. The head of the Jews appealed to the Ukrainian authorities, who denied the rumors. The Jews nevertheless organized themselves to guard the ghetto. The following day, on May 1, 1942, some 300 of the ghetto's Jews, one-third of them children, were murdered in a forest near the townlet. About six weeks later, a second murder operation was carried out, after which only about thirty artisans remained in the ghetto. In late August 1943, six Jews fled from the ghetto, and all the others were murdered, with the exception of seven Jews who were incarcerated in the prison and three artisans.

VELIZH
(Yiddish: **Viliz**)

COUNTY SEAT, SMOLENSK DISTRICT, RUSSIAN FEDERATION, USSR

During the war: Military Administration Area

Coordinates:
55°36' | 31°12'

In the early twentieth century, about 3,300 Jews lived in Velizh, more than one-third of the town's population. Modernization and urbanization under the Soviets reduced the Jewish population to some 1,800 by 1939. The Jews of Velizh were compelled to abandon private commerce and turn to crafts and employment in state institutions. The Jewish community ran a club with a drama circle and a Yiddish government school.

The Germans occupied Velizh on July 15, 1941. They immediately established a Judenrat and appointed a former teacher as its chair. Members of the Judenrat were required to wear a Star of David armband, while the remaining Jews wore yellow patches on the front and back of their clothing. A Jewish Order Service was also established in the town.

About 150 Jewish men in Velizh were shot to death in September 1941. Additional groups of Jews met the same fate at other times.

The Velizh ghetto, established on November 7, 1942, housed between 1,400 and 1,500 Jewish townspeople and inhabitants from the vicinity, along with refugees who had made their way to the area. The ghetto was comprised of twenty-seven houses and two pigsties on the outskirts of town. A number of Jews, primarily tailors who were employed by the Wehrmacht, continued to live outside the ghetto.

Officially, the ghetto received no food supplies. The inhabitants initially subsisted on food already in their possession; later on, they relied on smuggling. Although leaving the ghetto was forbidden and violators were flogged, a few inmates slipped in and out to obtain food.

The refugees who had reached the ghetto faced an especially challenging plight; several starved to death. The ghetto inhabitants suffered from the severe cold and used their bunks as firewood. Occasionally, young Jews were permanently removed from the ghetto. When Jews in the ghetto fell ill, a Russian doctor named Zhukov, who had moved into the ghetto with his Jewish wife and their children, tended to the patients without charging a fee.

The ghetto was liquidated on January 30, 1942, when Red Army forces closed in on the town. The Germans placed the Jews under curfew and set their homes ablaze. More than 1,500 ghetto inhabitants were murdered that day. Several attempted to escape by climbing out of windows and were shot by local police. Only twenty managed to escape.

VENTSPILS
(Yiddish: **Venden/Vindoy**)

COUNTY SEAT, KURZEME DISTRICT, LATVIA

During the war: Reichskommissariat Ostland

Coordinates:
57°24' | 21°31'

In the 1930s, about 1,000 Jews lived in Ventspils, a major port city on the Baltic Sea, representing about 8 percent of the city's population. Most earned their livelihood from commerce and artisanship. A majority of the doctors and dentists in Ventspils were Jews. The Jewish community had a merchants' club, two credit unions, and three schools: an elementary school, a high school, and a Talmud Torah. Ventspils had chapters of the Zionist organizations as well as a chapter of the Maccabi sports club with its own sports field.

In August 1940, Ventspils was handed over to Soviet control. The Jewish high school was closed, Jewish public life was paralyzed, and Jewish businesses were gradually nationalized. Many Jews found work in the Red Army naval base that had been set up in the port. On June 27, 1941, the Soviets retreated from Ventspils, and a small number of Jews left with them, either as part of the official evacuation or at their own initiative.

The Germans entered Ventspils on July 1, 1941. In the second week of the occupation, they began to drive Jews out of their homes and confiscate their property. A number of Jews destroyed valuables rather than hand them over to the Germans, and several committed suicide. The Jews were crowded into a ghetto established in a synagogue and in a number of dilapidated houses near the river. A senior Latvian police officer was appointed commander of the ghetto. The Jews were ordered to wear a yellow badge on their clothing, their freedom of movement was restricted, and they were conscripted for forced labor. Both women and men worked for German army units, cleaned the market, and weeded. They were the target of severe abuse and humiliation, such as the public shaving of beards and sexual harassment of the women.

In the third week of July 1941, a three-day-long operation was carried out during which hundreds of Jewish men were murdered. A unit made up of twenty members of the German security police with the assistance of fifty Latvian policemen rounded up the Jewish men in a cabin in the Kasin forest, about two kilometers south of the town. The Jews were grouped according to a list of names, and made to run to a pit between two rows of guards that prodded them on by beating and shooting at them. The firing squad was made up of Germans, who were later replaced by Latvian policemen.

The second operation was carried out in the last ten days of September 1941, during which another 200 Jews were murdered in the Kasin forest. On October 3–17, 1941, the last 533 Jews (according to a German report) of Ventspils were murdered, mostly women and children. In early 1942, the district commissar declared that there were no remaining Jews in Ventspils and its environs.

VEREBÉLY

TOWNLET IN BARS-HONT COUNTY, HUNGARY

(After World War II in Czechoslovakia/Slovakia; Slovak: **Vráble**)

Coordinates:
48°15' | 18°19'

The last national census conducted prior to the German occupation, taken in January 1941, recorded 223 Jewish inhabitants in Verebely, accounting for roughly 7 percent of the total population. Most of the Jews were merchants and artisans; several were factory and landowners. The townlet had an Orthodox Jewish community that maintained an elementary school. After World War I, Verebely became part of Czechoslovakia. During the interwar period, the majority of the local Jewish youths belonged to the various Zionist youth movements.

As per the First Vienna Award (November 2, 1938), Verebely reverted to Hungary. In the winter of 1938, the Hungarian authorities deported ten Jewish families without Hungarian citizenship through the newly established Hungarian-Slovakian border. In 1941, many of the Jewish men were drafted into the Hungarian army for forced labor service.

The German army occupied Hungary on March 19, 1944. A census conducted in the second week of April 1944 reported that 249 Jews belonged to the Orthodox Jewish community in Verebely.

The Hungarian administration remained intact and in force after the occupation. The ghettoization and deportation of the Jews were carried out on the basis of the decrees and orders of the Hungarian national and local authorities. On the basis of the decree of the Hungarian sub-prefect concerning the designation of the ghettos in the county, published on May 4, 1944, a ghetto was established in Verebely on May 9, 1944, in the grounds of the steam mill. Aside from the local Jews, the Jews from the Verebely County-District, about 500 individuals (eighty-five families), were concentrated in the ghetto. Adults under the age of forty were assigned daily to work outside of the ghetto.

On June 10, 1944, the inhabitants of the ghetto were transferred to the tobacco factory on the outskirts of Leva*, which served as the entrainment center of the county. They were deported to Auschwitz on June 13, 1944.

VERKHOVKA

(Ukrainian: **Verkhivka**)

**TOWN IN OBODOVKA
COUNTY, VINNITSA
DISTRICT, UKRAINE, USSR**

During the war: Transnistria
(under Romanian control)

Coordinates:
48°26' | 29°10'

In May 1919, during the civil war in Russia (1918–20), dozens of Verkhovka's Jewish residents were injured and about forty were murdered in a pogrom. Numerous Jews left in the wake of the war and the pogrom; by the mid-1920s, 400 Jews remained in Verkhovka. The town had a Yiddish-language school.

The Germans occupied Verkhovka in late July 1941. In September 1, 1941, the town was annexed to Transnistria, which was under Romanian control, and a ghetto was established.

In the fall of 1941, about 1,200 Jews from Bukovina and Bessarabia were deported to Verkhovka. All were put up under conditions of harsh overcrowding in the homes of local Jews and in a Jewish public building in the town. The ghetto inhabitants were forbidden to leave its grounds and were ordered to wear a yellow badge. Several were assigned to forced labor in distant camps. In the winter of 1941/42, about half of the ghetto's residents perished from epidemic typhus, cold, and hunger. Two doctors who worked in the ghetto strove to prevent further spread of the epidemic. A council that ran a public soup kitchen for the ill and for orphans was established. In December 1942, the list of inhabitants receiving assistance contained 800 names. The Jews in the Verkhovka ghetto observed the Jewish holidays and held public services in a cowshed.

In 1943, the Romanian authorities permitted Jewish women from the ghetto to work in nearby villages in exchange for food. In the summer of 1943, money collected among Romanian Jews was transferred to the ghetto and was used to open a small hospital.

Verkhovka was liberated on March 15, 1944.

VESZPRÉM

**TOWN IN VESZPRÉM
COUNTY, HUNGARY**

Coordinates:
47°06' | 17°55'

The last national census conducted prior to the German occupation, taken in January 1941, recorded 887 Jewish inhabitants in Veszprem, roughly 4 percent of the total population. Most were merchants and artisans. The local Neolog Jewish community operated a Jewish school and various Jewish social and religious associations. In 1942, many of the town's Jewish men were drafted into the Hungarian army for forced labor service.

The German army occupied Hungary on March 19, 1944. Immediately after the onset of the occupation, forty Jews were arrested in Veszprem. They were tortured and freed after several days.

The Hungarian administration remained intact and operational after the German occupation. The ghettoization and deportation of the Jews were carried out on the basis of the decrees and orders of the Hungarian national and local authorities. The Hungarian sub-prefect, Dr. Istvan Buda, published the ghettoization decree of Veszprem County on May 17, 1944. The ghetto for the Jews of Veszprem was established along one block: in the synagogue, the Jewish school, various other buildings of the Jewish community, and three private houses. On June 1, 1944, about 750 local Jews moved into the crowded ghetto. Each of the school's classrooms lodged about thirty to thirty-five people. The main synagogue was emptied out to accommodate 250 people; services were held in the smaller synagogue. On weekdays, the smaller synagogue was used as the office of the Jewish Council, which had ten members, five of whom were allowed to leave the ghetto for two hours daily in order to communicate with the authorities.

Jewish converts to Christianity were placed together with other Jews. Ten soup kitchens cooked kosher meals for about 180 people. A kindergarten and a summer school were established, and the inhabitants organized outdoor activities for the children. A room for the sick, a consulting room, and a room for people with infectious diseases were all organized.

In addition to the town ghetto, a ghetto was established in the old buildings of the Komakut army barracks in Veszprem for about 500 Jews from the county-districts of Enying and Veszprem. They had a separate Jewish Council. The Jews in the Komakut barracks built a toilet and a bathroom at their own expense and established a small hospital. The ghetto had four physicians and a soup kitchen that ran out of provisions by the second half of June 1944. Eventually, fifty-three Jews were moved to the town ghetto in order to ease the overcrowded conditions of the army barracks ghetto. In late June 1944, the Jews from the town ghetto were transferred to the Komakut army barracks; all ghetto inhabitants were deported to Auschwitz on June 29, 1944.

VETRINO

(Belarussian: **Vetryna**)

COUNTY SEAT, VITEBSK DISTRICT, BELARUS, USSR

During the war: Military Administration Area

Coordinates:
55°24' | 28°27'

In the late 1930s, there were about sixty Jews in Vetrino, accounting for less than 10 percent of the population. The wage earners were artisans and farmers.

The Germans occupied Vetrino on July 11, 1941. They promptly registered and dispossessed the Jews and instituted forced labor. In late July or early August 1941, they transferred the Jews to Polotsk* but reversed the decision three days later and sent them back to Vetrino.

In September or October 1941, the remaining Jews in the townlet, about forty in number, were concentrated in three houses. The ghetto was surrounded with barbed wire and guarded by Germans. The inhabitants were subjected to abuse and starvation. Non-Jewish townspeople were forbidden to approach the ghetto on pain of death.

The ghetto was liquidated on January 11, 1942, when Germans murdered its inhabitants near the village of Kosari.

VIDUKLÉ

TOWNLET IN RASEINIAI COUNTY, LITHUANIA

During the war:
Reichskommissariat Ostland

Coordinates:
55°24' | 22°54'

On the eve of World War II, about 160 Jews lived in Vidukle; most earned their livelihood from commerce, artisanship, and farming. The townlet had a Heder and a Tarbut school.

After Lithuania was annexed to the Soviet Union in 1940, Jewish political life in the townlet came to an end and private businesses were nationalized.

Vidukle was occupied by the Germans on June 23, 1941, and decrees were enacted against the Jews almost immediately. The townlet's Jewish inhabitants were required to wear a yellow badge and were robbed and seized for humiliating slave labor. A number of Jewish men accused of maintaining contact with Communists were arrested and disappeared without a trace.

After some time, all men over the age of fourteen years were ordered to report to the local council building. With the exception of the elderly, who were imprisoned in the Beit Midrash, all of the men were concentrated together with Jewish men from Nemaksciai and employed in hard labor service. On July 24, 1941, they were murdered together with the elderly men of the community.

The Jewish women and children who remained in Vidukle were moved into the synagogue and four nearby houses, forming a ghetto of sorts, and employed in cleaning work. On August 22, 1941, they were all taken by Lithuanians to the Jewish cemetery, where they were murdered and buried in a mass grave.

VIEKŠNIAI

TOWNLET IN MAŽEIKIAI COUNTY, LITHUANIA

During the war:
Reichskommissariat Ostland

Coordinates:
56°14' | 22°31'

On the eve of the German occupation, about 600 Jews lived in Vieksniai. Most earned their livelihood from artisanship, commerce, and farming. Vieksniai had Yavne and Tarbut schools, and the influence of Zionist parties was strong.

Following the annexation of Lithuania to the Soviet Union in 1940, a number of businesses and shops were nationalized and the activities of the Jewish parties and youth movements were outlawed.

After the German army invaded the Soviet Union on June 22, 1941, Lithuanian nationalists took over the townlet. In early July, the Jewish men were gathered in the Beit Midrash and on July 7, following abusive and humiliating treatment, were transferred to granaries. They were held for four weeks under conditions of torture and starvation and assigned to forced labor. A few days later, political prisoners, among them Jews, were also brought to the granaries, three of whom were murdered on July 20.

The women and children were meanwhile concentrated in the Beit Midrash, where they remained for several weeks under harsh conditions that caused many to fall ill. They received treatment in a makeshift hospital set up near the Beit Midrash.

In late July or early August 1941, the Lithuanians registered the Jewish men in the granaries and the women in the Beit Midrash, all the while inflicting harsh abuse.

On August 4, 1941, the Jews of Vieksniai were transferred to Mazeikiai, gathered in the local cemetery, and murdered along with the local Jews and those of the environs.

VIĻAKA
(Yiddish: **Vilyaki**)

TOWNLET IN ABRENE COUNTY, LATGALE DISTRICT, LATVIA

During the war:
Reichskommissariat Ostland

Coordinates:
57°11' | 27°41'

In the mid-1930s, about 450 Jews lived in Vilaka, representing approximately 30 percent of the townlet's population. The Jews controlled most of the local commerce. In the 1920s, leftist circles established a Yiddish elementary school and a cultural club of *Kultur Fareyn*, which ran a library and a drama circle. Chapters of Beitar and Hashomer Hatzair–*Netzah* were active in Vilaka. During 1940/41, Vilaka was under Soviet control.

After war broke out between Germany and the Soviet Union in June 1941, about 200 Jewish refugees arrived in the townlet from Lithuania. The Jewish community took them in, and several found asylum in the synagogue. On July 2, 1941, the Germans occupied Vilaka and immediately imposed anti-Jewish decrees: Jews were forbidden to use the sidewalk, were ordered to wear a yellow Star of David patch on their back and chest, and were only permitted to leave their homes between four and six o'clock in the evening. Many Jews were beaten or murdered by the Germans. The local rabbi, Rabbi Chernens, had his beard shaved.

After a short time, the Jews were driven out of their homes and concentrated in a ghetto located in the poorest quarter of the townlet. Lack of space forced most to live in the streets. The ghetto was guarded by local policemen. The Jews were required to perform forced labor and fell victim to acts of murder. Jewish women were raped and severely abused. Only Jews who worked received rations; the rest were left to die of starvation. Local residents who attempted to smuggle food into the ghetto were beaten and imprisoned.

On the night of August 11, 1941, the Jewish men of Vilaka were taken to the local fire station, while the women were brought to the synagogue. All of their valuables were confiscated. As dawn approached, the first group of men was taken to a location about two kilometers from the townlet, where they were forced to dig pits. All were shot in groups of eight to ten people by units of the Arajs Kommando in cooperation with local police. The German commanders who were present photographed the massacre. After the men were killed, the units massacred the remaining Jews; in all about 650 Jews were murdered, of whom 145 were children. Among the murder victims were refugees from Lithuania.

On the eve of their retreat, the Germans burned the bodies of their victims.

VILKAVIŠKIS
(Yiddish: **Vilkovishk**)

COUNTY SEAT, LITHUANIA

During the war:
Reichskommissariat Ostland

Coordinates:
54°39' | 23°02'

On the eve of the war, about 3,000 Jews lived in Vilkaviskis, representing roughly 40 percent of the local population of the townlet. They earned their livelihood mainly from commerce and industry, and the majority of the townlet's shops and factories were owned by Jews. Vilkaviskis boasted various welfare, religious, and educational Jewish institutions, including a Beit Midrash, a Heder and Talmud Torah, as well as Hebrew primary schools and a Hebrew high school. Zionist parties and youth movements hosted extensive activities.

After Lithuania was annexed to the Soviet Union in 1940, the townlet's factories were nationalized, the Hebrew schools were closed, and the Zionist parties and youth movements were disbanded.

When the German army invaded the Soviet Union on the morning of June 22, 1941, Vilkaviskis was bombed from the air, and most of the townlet's Jewish homes and its old synagogue were destroyed. That same day, nationalist Lithuanians began to attack Jews. Owing to the townlet's proximity to the German border, Vilkaviskis came under the supervision of the Tilsit Gestapo unit, commanded by Hans-Joachim Boehme.

On June 24, Jewish men were ordered to gather in the marketplace. They were assigned to forced labor in the townlet and in units of the German army. All Jewish inhabitants were ordered to wear a yellow patch on their clothing. One week later, most of the Jews of Vilkaviskis, including nearly all of the men, were transferred to barracks outside the townlet that were encircled by a barbed-wire fence. The area was declared a ghetto, and a committee of four Jews—a "Jewish council"—was placed at its head.

On July 27, 1941, Lithuanian guards surrounded the barracks and seized 250 Jewish men to dig pits in the area. The following day, about 800 Jewish men were abducted from the ghetto and murdered in the pits, together with sixty-five non-Jewish Communists. These murders were administered by the Tilsit Gestapo unit in cooperation with the German border police and Lithuanian nationalists. On August 1, 1941, the Jewish women and children who remained in the townlet were transferred to the ghetto; several managed to escape. About two months later, on September 24, 1941, the women and children were murdered in the nearby pits, as well. A number of the Vilkaviskis ghetto inhabitants fled, but most were caught and later murdered.

According to official Soviet records, the Germans and Lithuanians collectively killed 3,056 Jews between June and September 1941.

VILKIJA
(Yiddish: **Vilki**)

TOWNLET IN KAUNAS COUNTY, LITHUANIA

During the war:
Reichskommissariat Ostland

Coordinates:
55°03' | 23°35'

On the eve of World War II, about 500 Jews lived in Vilkija, representing approximately one-quarter of the townlet's population. Jews owned the majority of the townlet's businesses and factories as well as the local bank branch. Jews likewise earned their livelihood by transporting trees along the local river. During the 1930s, the number of Jews in Vilkija decreased as a result of the deteriorating economic conditions in Lithuania coupled with the rising antisemitism incited by the Verslas movement.

After Vilkija was annexed to the Soviet Union in 1940, shops and factories were nationalized, Jewish national activity was discontinued, and Hebrew schools closed.

When the Soviet forces retreated from the advancing German army, Lithuanian nationalists took over Vilkija. They attacked Jews whom they accused of collaborating with the Soviets; two were summarily murdered, and another twenty-one were executed on July 15. The German army occupied Vilkija on June 26, 1941.

The German authorities levied an exorbitant tax on the Jews of the townlet and also confiscated Jewish property. The Jews were ordered to move into a ghetto; some of the men were imprisoned in the Beit Midrash while the women and children were crowded into the home and barns of Shimon Friedland. Lithuanian auxiliary police guarded the Jews. Young Jewish men and women were occasionally seized from the ghetto for forced labor.

On August 28, 1941, all of the Jews of Vilkija and its environs were taken to the Pakarkle forest located near the village of Jaucakiai, where they were shot to death and buried in pits. In all, 402 people were murdered.

VILNA, VILNIUS
(Yiddish: **Vilne**)

DISTRICT SEAT, POLAND
(After World War II in the USSR/capital of Lithuania)

During the war:
Reichskommissariat Ostland

Coordinates:
54°41' | 25°19'

Before the War: Vilna, one of the most important Jewish historical sites in Eastern Europe, was renowned from the mid-eighteenth century onward as a major center of Torah scholarship. Under the leadership of the Vilna Gaon, Rabbi Eliyahu of Vilna, the community spearheaded the opposition to Hasidism. Toward the mid-nineteenth century, Vilna was celebrated as a leading center of Jewish Enlightenment in Eastern Europe as well as of Torah scholarship publications, and hence was known to Jews throughout the world as the "Jerusalem of Lithuania." In the early twentieth century, when the Jewish population of Vilna exceeded 100,000, the city also became a hub of Yiddish and Hebrew literature and journalism, as well as of Jewish political activity, which included Zionist parties and the Bund. During the Soviet-Polish war of 1919–20 (after World War I), dozens of Vilna's Jews were murdered, mainly by Polish rioters. The war prompted many of the city's Jewish residents to leave, and once it was over, control of the city passed over to Poland.

In the late 1930s, close to 60,000 Jews lived in Vilna, representing more than one-quarter of the city's population. In the interwar period, the underdeveloped local market coupled with a surge in Polish antisemitism plunged the Jewish community into an economic depression. About half of Vilna's Jews earned their livelihood from various forms of industry and artisanship or from commerce; the remainder worked in education and the liberal professions. All of the community's standard political parties participated in the Jewish political activity that flourished in the city, including Zionist parties, the Bund, and Agudath Israel. The Zionist parties and institutions held gatherings nearly every year.

Vilna had a vibrant and highly developed Jewish intellectual life, with Jewish schools of every kind and level. Jews and their children attended kindergartens, elementary schools, high schools (including the Yiddish Real-Gymnasium and the Hebrew Tarbut Gymnasium), seminars for school and kindergarten teachers (teaching in Hebrew and Yiddish), Talmud Torahs, technical-vocational schools, and assorted courses. In the 1920s and 1930s, Vilna boasted large Jewish public libraries. A number of daily Jewish newspapers were published in Yiddish and Polish, in addition to party periodicals and other Hebrew- and Yiddish-language publications. Vilna was also a center of Jewish cultural activity, with a Yiddish theater named *Vilner Trupe* (Vilna Troupe) and a Jewish symphony orchestra. The year 1924 saw the establishment of YIVO, the Jewish Institute for the Study of Yiddish Language and Culture, which developed into the world's foremost research center for all matters related to Yiddish writing.

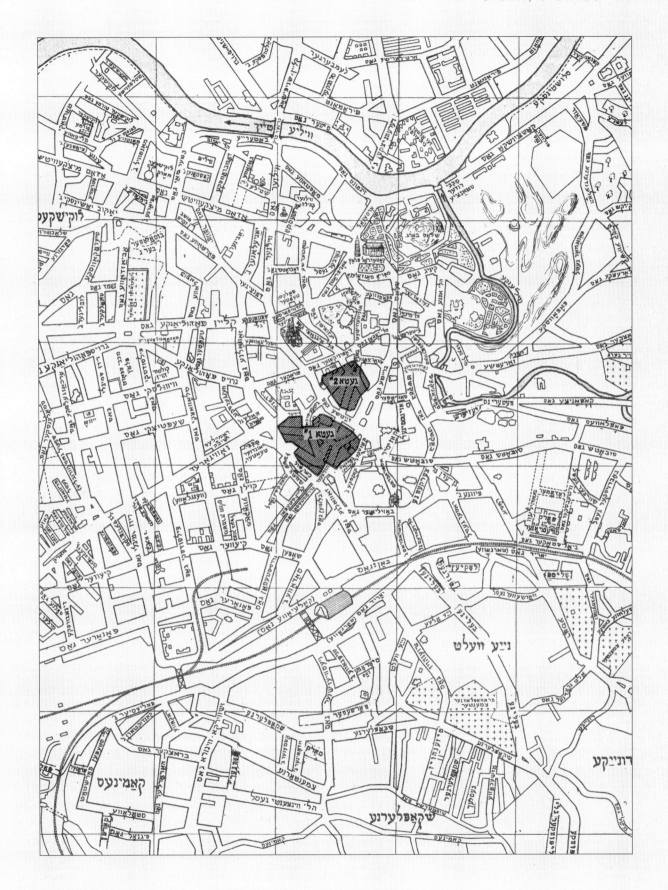

Vilna map indicating ghetto boundaries (Leyzer Ran, ed., *Jerusalem of Lithuania*, New York 1974)

Soviet occupation: Following the Molotov-Ribbentrop Pact, the Red Army invaded Poland on September 17, 1939, occupying Vilna after two days. Several weeks later, on October 28, 1939, Vilna was handed over to the control of independent Lithuania, after which pogroms were carried out against the Jews. Jewish groups organized for self-defense. By the spring of 1940, some 14,000 Jewish refugees from the areas of the German and Soviet occupation zones as well as individuals from various movements, together with their leaders, found refuge in Vilna. Among them were Menachem Begin, Betar leader and eventual prime minister of Israel; Moshe Sneh (Kleinboim), the leader of the General Zionists (*Tzionim Klaliim*) party and head of the Zionist Organization and later a member of the Israeli Knesset and leader of the Israeli Communist party; Zerach Warhaftig, leader of Mizrachi–Hapoel Hamizrachi and in time an Israeli Knesset member and minister. During this period, new branches of Jewish youth movements and party organizations were formed in Vilna.

In June 1940, Lithuania was annexed to the Soviet Union and Vilna came under Soviet control. Vilna's Jewish community institutions and parties were disbanded, the Jewish schools were Sovietized, and the nationalization process of private commerce began. About 6,000 of the Jewish refugees who flocked to Vilna ultimately left the city (especially during this period) for the Land of Israel, for the Soviet interior, and for other destinations. On June 13–14, 1941, the Soviets exiled about 3,500 Jews from Vilna to the Soviet interior.

German (Nazi) occupation: Heavy bombing of Vilna succeeded the German invasion of the Soviet Union on June 22, 1941. Many Jews attempted to flee to the east, but most were prevented by the rapid advance of German troops. In the period prior to the German occupation of Vilna on June 24, 1941, fewer than 3,000 Jews managed to flee eastward, while 57,000 to 60,000 Jews remained in the city.

Immediately after the occupation, the Germans seized sixty Jews hostage and held them for about one month in jail, where most were murdered. June 26, 1941, saw the first in a wave of abductions of Jews for forced labor; a number of the Jews were never seen again. Within a few days, anti-Jewish decrees were issued in Vilna: the Jews' freedom of movement was severely restricted, Jewish residents were required to wear a Star of David armband (and later on the front and back of the garment), Jewish schools and bank accounts were closed, and Jews were dismissed from public jobs.

About one month following the onset of the occupation, Einsatzkommando 3 of Einsatzgruppe A replaced Einsatzkommando 9 of Einsatzgruppe B.

On July 4, 1941, the Germans instructed the synagogue beadle of Vilna, Chaim Meir Gordon, to form a Judenrat within one day. The Judenrat had ten members, but by the end of the month, the organization was expanded at German orders to include twenty-four members. The first Judenrat head was Shaul Trotski, and Anatol Fried was his deputy. The members of the Judenrat represented nearly the entire cross section of Vilna's Jewish population, earning them the trust of the community as representatives willing to fight for the people's rights. The Judenrat's first task was to regulate the recruitment of forced laborers, to avert the arbitrary abduction of Jews. Jews who worked in the German administration unit received certificates (*Scheinen*) that offered them temporary protection from forced labor seizures.

On August 1, 1941, control of Lithuania was transferred from the German military administration to the German civil administration. Hans Christian Hingst was appointed governor, and responsibility for the Jews was handed over to Franz Murer; upon his appointment, he ordered the Judenrat to remit a large ransom.

First murder operations: On July 2, 1941, the Einsatzkommando 9 unit of Einsatzgruppe B entered Vilna together with auxiliary forces of the German Orpo. The Germans integrated Lithuanian policemen and volunteers into their own forces to assist with the liquidation of the Jews of Vilna. The 150-man *Ypatingi Buriai*—a "special" unit of Lithuanian volunteers—accomplished its work with tremendous efficiency. In early July 1941 and for about three weeks' duration, abductions were carried out, ostensibly for forced labor. Some 5,000 Jewish men from Vilna were seized in the streets and from their homes, brought to the Ponary (Paneriai) forest about ten kilometers south-west of Vilna and to various other murder sites, and shot to death. After Eiensatzkommando 3 took command, the murders of Jews persisted, although on a more limited scale. According to German reports, more than 400 Jews were murdered in August 1941.

From August 31 to September 3, 1941, the Germans carried out a large-scale murder operation in Vilna as part of the Germans' policy to decrease the size of the Jewish population, especially in the area allocated to the future ghetto. Some 5,000 to 8,000 Jewish men, women, and children, including those with work permits, were transferred to the notorious Lukiszki prison and on to Ponary, where they were murdered. The massacre later became known in the ghetto as the "Great Provocation Operation," because the people who were murdered had been evicted by the German administration from the streets designated for the ghetto, as punishment for the alleged killing of two German soldiers by Jews. On September 2, 1941, the Judenrat was dissolved and ten of its members were murdered in Ponary, including the Judenrat head, Trotski. About 6,000 Jews were transferred to Ponary on September 6, 1941, and murdered.

Ghetto setup and formation of the ghetto institutions: The ghettoization of Vilna's Jews began almost immediately after the murder operation, in the beginning of September 1941. On September 6, all Jews, including workers, were ordered to move into the ghetto by the end of the day and were permitted to take with them only as much as they could carry. They were concentrated in two fenced-in ghettos with gates. In all, about 29,000 to 30,000 Jews were densely crowded into Ghetto 1, and 9,000 to 11,000 into Ghetto 2. The following day,

Vilna
Members of the Jewish Order Service and Lithuanian police near the entrance gate to the ghetto (USHMM, courtesy of William Begell)

Vilna
Members of the Jewish Order
Service in the ghetto watching
an event organized at the
initiative of the Judenrat. Jewish
Order Service chief Jacob
Gens can be seen sitting in the
audience (sixth from the left).
(JNUL)

the Germans appointed two Judenraete; Anatol Fried was appointed to head the Judenrat of Ghetto 1, and Yitzhok Leibovits headed the Judenrat of Ghetto 2. Both Judenraete established special departments to deal with various issues. Concurrently, a Jewish Order Service unit was established in each of the ghettos, with many Betar members serving in their ranks. The commander of the Jewish Order Service in Ghetto 1 was Jacob Gens, a former officer in the Lithuanian army, and an attorney named Fawiarski was appointed commander of the Jewish Order Service in the second ghetto.

The mass murders continued during the first months of the ghettos' existence (see below) and had a major impact on their development. The murder operation that was carried out on October 1, 1941, was considered a significant milestone in the activities of Vilna's Judenrat and Jewish Order Service. They now began to cooperate with the German arrests in the belief (shared by many of the inhabitants of Ghetto 1) that those with work permits would be saved from deportation. As time passed, this conviction motivated the Vilna ghetto's Judenrat to exert every effort to ensure the ghetto's productivity.

In the early weeks of October 1941, the Germans were involved in regulating Jewish labor in the ghetto. The German work department issued new yellow work permits, which from that time forward were considered the sole key to survival in the ghetto, to 3,000 workers and 9,000 of their family members. The distribution of the yellow permits, *Gelbscheinen*, to about 12,000 inhabitants of the ghetto's 28,000 inhabitants created considerable strife, primarily directed toward the Judenrat, whose 400 employees were among those who received permits. For its part, the Judenrat did whatever it could to increase the number of people granted permits. Ghetto 2 was totally liquidated in October 1941, leaving from that time on a single ghetto in Vilna.

Murder operations—September–November 1941: On September 15, 1941, the Germans rounded up about 3,500 of the Jews of Ghetto 1 who lacked work permits, predominantly elderly, ill, and orphaned inhabitants, supposedly for transfer into Ghetto 2. About 2,950 of the people seized were taken to Ponary and murdered, while the rest actually were sent to Ghetto 2. Meanwhile, people from Ghetto 2 with work permits were transferred along with their families to Ghetto 1. The killing operation prompted additional Jews from Ghetto 2 to slip into Ghetto 1.

On October 1, 1941, Yom Kippur, the Germans carried out another murder operation in the Vilna ghetto with the help of the Lithuanians. Some 1,700 Jews were arrested in Ghetto 2, while 2,200 Jews were seized in Ghetto 1, with the help of the Judenrat and Jewish Order Service. The following day, the Germans released several hundred of those arrested, mostly people with work permits, while all the others were led to Ponary and murdered.

The Germans liquidated Ghetto 2 in three additional operations carried out on October 3–4, 15–16 and 21, 1941, in the course of which some 8,000 Jews were murdered. During these killing operations, the first cases of passive resistance in the Vilna ghetto took place. A group of Jews who realized that they were being led in the direction of Ponary refused to keep moving and lay on the ground. The Germans opened fire, killing several dozen of the Jews. A few others escaped, but after failing to find refuge, they were forced to slip back into the ghetto. The surviving Jews from Ghetto 2 managed to sneak into Ghetto 1, and a number of people considered fit for work were even transferred in by the Germans.

On October 24, 1941, all yellow permit holders were ordered to gather at their work places or in the Judenrat building. Germans and Lithuanians invaded the ghetto to arrest all the others, many of whom attempted to hide but were shot on sight by the Germans. In the murder operation, altogether about 3,500 Jews without permits were arrested, led to Ponary, and killed. Afterwards, some 1,500 people who did not have permits were lured by German promises to transfer from Ghetto 1 into Ghetto 2. However, they too were murdered in Ponary on October 29, 1941.

In early November 1941, the Germans and Lithuanians carried out another murder operation (known as "The Second Yellow *Scheinen* 'Aktion'"), during which all permits were scrutinized to identify those who lacked permits and were in hiding. There is some disagreement concerning the role played by Jacob Gens and the members of the Judenrat during the process. A number of people maintained that they doomed to death numerous Jews, especially children, while others credited them with saving the lives of Jewish children by matching parentless children with childless workers. During the murder operation, about 1,200 "illegals" were apprehended and murdered in Ponary, in addition to several dozen Jews caught hiding in bunkers in the ghetto.

Ghetto institutions and internal life: In November 1941, following the mass killings, the ghetto was reorganized; the workers were put up in blocks of houses in accordance with their jobs, further increasing the anxiety among inhabitants who did not hold permits.

On December 3–4, 1941, about 160 Jews with criminal records were arrested in the ghetto based on lists that had been prepared by the Judenrat. The arrests, which were carried out by Lithuanian police and members of the Jewish Order Service, represented a precedent in the planned handing over of Jews by the Judenrat and the Jewish Order Service. On the night of December 15, 1941, the Germans ordered about 500 Jewish workers and their family members to leave the ghetto. Until that time, these particular workers, known as "Gestapo employees," were employed as service providers for the German security police and enjoyed certain privileges, and as such did not suspect the Germans' intentions. They were taken to jail, where it was decided to send 300 of them to Ponary and to return the remaining 200 to the ghetto.

On December 20, 1941, the Judenrat completed the distribution of new work permits, this time colored pink, to the ghetto workers. An additional killing operation was carried out in the ghetto on December 20–22, 1941, termed the "Pink *Scheinen Aktion*," during which about 400 Jews were seized and sent to Ponary. Many others were murdered where they were found hiding. In one case, Jews found hiding in a bunker attacked the Lithuanians, killing several during the fighting that ensued. The "Pink *Scheinen* 'Aktion'" ended the first phase of the liquidation of Vilna's Jews. Altogether 34,000 Jews had been murdered.

By late 1941, close to 20,000 Jews remained in the ghetto, a number of them illegally. About 3,000 of Vilna's Jews managed to escape during this period to the areas of Belarus where Jews still resided in relative peace, and the rest hid outside the ghetto in various hiding places, some in the possession of false "Aryan" papers.

From early 1942 to the spring of 1943, the ghetto experienced a relatively quiet period, although the murder of individuals and the elderly and infirm at Ponary persisted. During this period, most of the "illegal" inhabitants managed to attain resident status. A new lifestyle took shape in the ghetto. The activities of the ghetto leadership reflected its desire for the ghetto to appear as productive as possible to the Germans. The official number of ghetto inhabitants registered as workers rose from about 4,000 in early 1942 to more than 9,000 toward the end of the year, and to more than 14,000 by June 1943. While the bulk of the increase was attributable

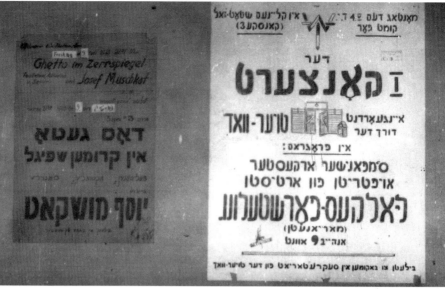

Left: **Vilna**
Teacher Muschkat and his students in a ghetto classroom (JNUL)

Right: **Vilna**
Announcement of a concert held in the ghetto in the small hall on Kanska Street. On the program: a symphony orchestra, artists' performance, and marionette show (YV)

to the supply of workers for German services and industries outside the ghetto, factories and workshops were opened inside the ghetto as well.

The official food rations the Jews received were meager. The Germans strove to prevent the smuggling of food into the ghetto, inflicting death as punishment for the activity. Food smuggling continued despite the penalty, occasionally sponsored by the Judenrat. The Judenrat ran five public soup kitchens as well as health services, a clinic, and a hospital. Despite explicit German prohibitions, Jewish women continued to give birth in the ghetto, with doctors hiding the babies from the Germans. Almost immediately after the establishment of the ghetto, the educational system was reinstated, and included two kindergartens and three elementary schools, a high school, and classes offered on assorted subjects that were held in Yiddish and later in Hebrew as well.

Extensive cultural activities were held in the ghetto. The Judenrat's culture department ran a very popular public library and put on theatrical and musical productions. In early 1942, a theater was established that initially was the target of very harsh public criticism (posters in the streets protested "No theater in a graveyard"), but later became very popular and quite successful. A symphony orchestra performed and choirs sang in Yiddish and Hebrew.

In 1942, the ghetto hospital operated, at great risk, a secret department for epidemic typhus patients for a number of months until the disease was eradicated. A special project was commissioned by the Gestapo, namely a three-dimensional plastic map of Vilna and its environs. The project employed most of the ghetto's artists, sculptors, and architects, as well as students of art and architecture—a total of thirty to thirty-five people. The project was located in the Judenrat building, and the artists were granted a special permit to freely roam the city. Many were underground members who exploited the privilege. The unit also surreptitiously mapped out the Jewish holy places in the city. In all, about forty map sections were prepared. They disappeared after the war, with the exception of five or six that can be found in the cellars of the Jewish museum in Vilna.

In February 1942, the special Rosenberg unit (Einsatzstab Reichsleiter Rosenberg) became active in Vilna, given the task of collecting and transferring to Germany cultural treasures from the occupied Soviet Union, including Jewish cultural treasures. The members of Rosenberg's staff were German academics cognizant of Jewish Vilna's cultural riches, and took a special interest in the collections in the YIVO institute and the Strashun library. Overseen by Herman Kruk, the staff members recruited the employees of the ghetto library for this purpose and managed to hide a large part of Vilna's Jewish cultural treasures, thus saving them from destruction.

Beginning in early 1942, the Jewish Order Service, which had been established to serve as the executive arm of the Judenrat, became an independent power center, largely owing to the Germans' preference for its commander Gens to Judenrat head Fried. The Jewish Order Service, which had close to 200 members, was gradually granted authority over jobs and food distribution. By mid-July 1942, the Germans had decided to dissolve the Judenrat, appointing Gens as the representative (head) of the ghetto and Salek Desler as head of the Jewish Order Service. The Judenrat members were then appointed to various jobs within the new ghetto administration.

In October 1942, the Germans ordered Gens to help them carry out a roundup in the Oszmiana* ghetto. On October 19, about twenty Jewish policemen, led by Salek Desler, were sent to Oszmiana, where they rounded up about 400 people, most the elderly and infirm, and handed them over to the Germans. These people were murdered by Lithuanians. Gens was condemned in Vilna for collaborating with the Germans. He took full responsibility for his actions, arguing that the sacrifice of a few Jews might save numerous others. Gens dismissed one of his harshest critics on this matter, Josef Glazman, from his job, and sent him to prison. Glazman was released within a few days, following the intervention of several underground members, and was transferred for a short period to a labor camp in the Vilna vicinity.

Final murder operations and the ghetto's liquidation: In March 1943, the Germans informed Gens and the Judenrat head in Kaunas* (Kovno) of their intention to liquidate the ghettos of Oszmiana, Swieciany*, Soly*, and Michaliszki*, and to transfer their inhabitants to the Vilna and Kaunas ghettos. Horst Wulff, the governor of the area, gave orders to select Jews from among these ghettos' inhabitants for an initial transfer to Vilna, with the promise that the rest would be

Vilna, April 1943
Collection and sorting of books in the YIVO institute for the study of Yiddish, instigated by ERR—the Rosenberg unit (YV)

sent later to Kaunas. On March 26–April 2, 1943, about 1,300 of the residents of these four ghettos were transferred to the Vilna ghetto, with the help of Gens's men, and close to 1,500 other Jews were transferred to various labor camps.

The last remaining Jews of these ghettos, close to 4,000 people, were rounded up on April 3–5, 1943. They were assured that they would be taken to the Kaunas ghetto. Accompanied by a group of members of the Jewish Order Service, they arrived to Vilna in two transports. The first transport left the city on the night of April 4 and the second left early in the morning on the following day, accompanied by Gens and a number of policemen, carrying Jews who believed that they were being transferred to the Kaunas ghetto. In fact all of the trains traveled to Ponary (Gens and his people were sent back and were kept some hours in the Gestapo headquarters). When the people realized where they were brought, a mass resistance broke out and many attempted to escape. About 600 Jews were killed during the struggle, a few dozen managed to get away and reach Vilna, and all the rest were eventually murdered.

The murder operation severely undermined Vilna's Jews' already limited sense of security. It caused a great shock among the Jewish population and triggered extremely harsh public criticism of Gens. Alarm increased following the liquidation of the labor camps in the area in June and July of 1943, and murder of most of the camps' inmates. On July 25, 1943, the Germans invaded the ghetto demanding the arrest of the families of those who had fled from the ghetto as well as their work managers. Gens's attempt to hand over elderly Jews in place of the work managers failed, and on July 27, the thirty-two family members and work managers were murdered at Ponary. The following day, the Germans murdered the last remaining inmates of the nearby Nowa Wilejka labor camp in retaliation for the escape from the ghetto. They then announced that all family members of the escapees would be executed.

On June 21, 1943, Himmler ordered the liquidation of the remaining ghettos in the Reichskommissariat Ostland and the transfer to labor camps of all their inhabitants fit for work. The implementation of the order in the area of Vilna was carried out in three separate killing operations that became known as the "deportations to Estonia." The first was carried out on August 6, 1943, when about 1,000 Jewish workers were arrested at their workplaces outside the ghetto by the Germans, with the help of Estonian police. Fearing that they were being sent to Ponary, the workers resisted, and dozens were shot during the evacuation. The second operation was carried out on August 24, 1943, and the third on September 1–4, 1943, during which women were also deported. In all, about 7,000 Jews were transferred to camps in Estonia in the deportation operations. Gens continued to cooperate with the Germans during the operations, encouraged by the return on August 11 of one of the deportees, who testified that the workers had indeed been taken to labor camps and not murdered.

After the deportations to Estonia, about 12,000 Jews remained in the Vilna ghetto. They were no longer permitted to leave its boundaries for work. On September 14, 1943, Gens, ignoring warnings that his life was in danger, responded to a summons and together with his deputy Desler, reported to the headquarters of the German security police. He was executed a short time later and Desler was appointed to replace him. Desler fled from the ghetto a few days later, however, and soon a new ghetto administration was appointed, headed by Boria Biniakonski, as well as a Jewish Order Service under the command of Oberhart.

On September 23, 1943, the liquidation of the Vilna ghetto was launched, carried out by SS officer Bruno Kittel. Germans and Ukrainians encircled the ghetto and the inhabitants were ordered to assemble in an area near the Rosa monastery. On arrival, an abrupt selection took place and the men were separated from the women, children, and elderly. Families clung together with their last ounces of strength, refusing to separate. The Ukrainians beat their victims violently and confiscated any valuables they found on them. The following day, 1,600 to 2,000 people were transported to camps in Estonia. Those who remained underwent a further selection, after which 1,400 to 1,700 young women were transferred to the Kaiserwald camp near Riga*, Latvia. Hundreds of sick and elderly people were sent to Ponary while all the rest, about 4,000 people, were transported to the Sobibor extermination camp, where they were gassed. The liquidation of the Vilna ghetto was complete.

More than 2,000 people managed to escape death by hiding in or outside the ghetto or infiltrating into the Kailis and HKP (Heeres-Kraftfahrpark) labor camps.

Resistance: The remnants of the various Jewish parties that had flourished in Vilna prior to the war—Zionist parties, the Bund, and the Polish Communists—continued to be active and meet regularly in the ghetto. The main pioneering youth movements were Hehalutz Hatza'ir–Dror, Hashomer Hatzair, Hanoar Hatziyyoni, Akiva, and Betar. During the period of murder operations, these movements made every effort to save their members and families, organized hiding places, and smuggled a few activists over to the "Aryan" side of the city with the help of false papers. Even at this early stage, the activities of the youth movements in the ghetto created the infrastructure for underground activity, and in late October 1941, the movements, together with the Zionist parties, established a seven-member joint council. The most significant activities of the youth movements at this time included collecting information about other locations and spreading news about mass murders perpetrated in the Vilna ghetto to other ghettos in Belarus and Poland (including the Warsaw* ghetto), where mass killing operations had not yet been carried out.

On January 1, 1942, Hashomer Hatzair leader Aba Kovner read a manifesto that he had written to 150 members of the youth movements in Vilna. The manifesto publicly stated, for the first time in the history of the public discourse during the Holocaust, that the Germans were planning to exterminate the entire Jewish people in Europe and that their only hope for survival was resistance. Subsequent to the reading of the manifesto, on January 21, 1942, the decision was made to establish the United Partisans Organization (*Fareynikte Partizaner Organizatsye*), or FPO. The organization was led by a three-member team: Communist movement commander Yitzhak Wittenberg and two deputies, Aba Kovner of Hashomer Hatzair and Yosef Glazman of Betar. Within a short time, the Bund also joined the FPO, and the leadership team was expanded to include two more members: Abrasha Khvoinik of the Bund and Nissan Reznik of *Haoved Hatziyyoni*. Yosef Glazman served as Gens's deputy in the Jewish Order Service, but was nevertheless trusted by the members of the underground. The FPO managed to obtain arms through its connections with the partisans and other anti-Nazi forces outside the ghetto and by stealing German weapons. They established regular fighting units, collected information on German activities and movements, and formulated an action plan. The FPO intended to fight inside the ghetto and launch an uprising when the danger of the ghetto's liquidation became imminent. The number of fighters in the FPO increased gradually to about 300 by the fall of 1943. The FPO members also sabotaged the German infrastructure and disseminated an underground newspaper that reported to the ghetto inhabitants on important events, such as the defeats of the German army at the front.

Aside from the FPO, another, smaller underground known as "Yechiel's Group" was active in the ghetto, composed of members of Hehalutz Hatza'ir–Dror and headed by Yechiel Sheinboim. In late 1942, the group's members joined forces with the "Combat Group," which was headed by Borke Friedman and had Betar activists among its members, including Natan Ring (who was also a member of the Jewish Order Service). The numbers in the united group, which later became known as "Yechiel's Combat Group," reached about 200 in the summer of 1943, and their primary objective was to fight the Germans in the forests as part of the partisan groups. Gens was aware of the existence of the underground in the ghetto, but until 1943, there was no great tension between the head of the ghetto and the underground groups; according to certain sources, Gens occasionally extended assistance to the underground. In the summer of 1943, all of the underground groups united to form a single underground resistance group.

The renewal of the mass murders in the Vilna area, along with the arrival of the news of the Soviet victory at Stalingrad and the Warsaw ghetto uprising, once again stirred up clashes among Vilna's underground resistance groups. In the spring and summer of 1943, they argued over whether it was preferable to implement resistance and uprising inside the ghetto (the position supported by the FPO) or escape from the ghetto to join the partisans (the favored position of the Yechiel Combat Group). In May 1943, the FPO and Yechiel's Combat Group agreed to step up their mutual coordination and decided a number of the members of the underground should leave the ghetto that month to join the partisans.

A confrontation between the ghetto administration and the underground organizations broke out in the spring of 1943, fueled by the growing threat to the future of the ghetto, the collaboration of Gens and his people in the killing operations in the nearby ghettos, and the pressure exerted by the Germans to prevent escapes from the ghetto. On June 12, 1943, a member of the Jewish Order Service shot an underground activist to prevent him from escaping from the ghetto. In the wake of the incident, the FPO resolved to resist any attempts by Gens to use force against the underground. As escapes from the ghetto increased, Gens decided on June 25, 1943, to arrest Yosef Glazman, but the members of the FPO freed him by force. An agreement with the FPO, however, sent Glazman for some time to the labor camp Rzesza in the neighborhood. The Germans' discovery of a Lithuanian Communist underground led to the exposure of the identity of Yitzhak Wittenberg, who had worked in cooperation with it. The Germans demanded that Gens hand Wittenberg over. Public pressure in the ghetto and fear of major retribution against the entire ghetto caused Wittenberg to give himself up on July 16, 1943, and the following day he committed suicide in the German prison. On July 24, a group of twenty-one underground members led by Glazman left the ghetto to the forest, where they were joined by fourteen others. The group was ambushed by the Germans: nine underground members were killed and the others escaped.

The members of the FPO, however, decided to launch armed resistance to the deportations to Estonia that were carried out on June 21, 1943. On September 1, a struggle took place within the ghetto in which Sheinboim was killed. The majority of the inhabitants of the ghetto did not respond to their appeal to join them. Consequently, the underground decided to transfer its activities outside the ghetto, joining the partisans in the forest. From late August to mid-September, more than 200 members of the FPO left the ghetto (several with Gens's knowledge), finding their place within the Lithuanian and Belarussian partisan brigades.

During the liquidation of the Vilna ghetto, about 100 FPO members who had remained inside the ghetto managed to escape through sewer tunnels to the "Aryan" side of the city and joined the partisans in the forest.

Ponary, July 1941
Jewish men with their eyes covered are brought to pits to be shot. *Photographed by a German soldier who arrived in the area with his unit* (YV)

After the liquidation of the ghetto, about 350 Jews from Vilna fought in the surrounding forests in four separate Soviet partisan groups. A number of them were killed in action, while others were murdered by antisemitic partisans.

Camps: Before the operation which led to the final liquidation of the ghetto, about 2,500 Jews were concentrated into two large labor camps, Kailis and HKP, and in another two small camps of about seventy-five people each in the Gestapo headquarters and the city's military hospital.

On March 27, 1944, a murder operation was carried out in the labor camps in Vilna, in which about 200 children under the age of fifteen were found and murdered by Germans. Several dozen elderly Jews were caught and executed at Ponary. The labor camps in the area of Vilna were liquidated on July 2–3, 1944, when Jewish inmates were murdered in Ponary.

A group of about 150 HKP prisoners managed to escape on July 3, 1944. Hundreds had been in hiding, and about 350 were found by the Germans and killed inside the camp.

On July 13, 1944, the Red Army liberated Vilna. Jewish fighters who emerged from the forests entered Vilna together with the Soviet forces. Several thousand Vilna Jews survived.

VIRBALIS

(Yiddish: **Virbalen** and **Verzhbelov**)

TOWNLET IN VILKAVIŠKIS COUNTY, LITHUANIA

During the war:
Reichskommissariat Ostland

Coordinates:
54°38' | 22°49'

On the eve of the war, about 600 Jews lived in Virbalis, representing approximately 13 percent of the population. The Jews of Virbalis earned their livelihood from commerce, artisanship, industry, and farming, and were assisted by a Jewish-owned Folksbank and a credit union for Jewish farmers. The community boasted the traditional Jewish educational institutions, a Hebrew school, two synagogues, and Jewish welfare institutions, as well as Zionist activity.

In June 1940, after Lithuania was annexed to the Soviet Union, all of the townlet's factories were nationalized; in early June 1941, the authorities began to exile the families of factory owners.

On June 22, 1941, the Germans entered Virbalis, located near the German border. The occupiers immediately released from jail Lithuanian prisoners, who formed groups and took revenge on Communists and Jews. A local government was organized within several days and imposed restrictions on the townlet's Jewish inhabitants; the edicts, among others, required Jews to wear a yellow badge, forbade them to work or to own a radio set, and imposed a nightly curfew.

Between July 7 and 10, 1941, the Lithuanians arrested all the Jewish males aged sixteen years and older. The Jews were led to a farm located north of Virbalis to deepen existing anti-tank trenches. On July 10, 1941, the Jewish men were shot to death at the trenches by Lithuanians.

Following the murder of the Jewish men and youths, all the women and children of Virbalis, along with the Jewish women and children of Kybartai, were concentrated in a ghetto. The ghetto was headed by Dr. Sheina Poziski, a dentist. Young women and boys were assigned to slave labor. In late July or early August, 1941, all the elderly women, the sick, and the unemployed were removed from the ghetto, murdered in ditches, and buried. On the night of September 11, 1941, the remaining women and children were murdered in the same location.

VITEBSK

(Belarussian: **Vitsebsk**)

DISTRICT SEAT, BELARUS, USSR

During the war: Military Administration Area

Coordinates:
55°12' | 30°11'

Many Jews in Vitebsk became white- or blue-collar workers in state-owned factories and institutions during the Soviet era, though a significant proportion continued to practice artisan trades. In 1918, Marc Chagall was appointed director of the newly founded Academy of Art in Vitebsk, where many Jews studied or taught. The city boasted government schools that conducted classes in Yiddish, a Yiddish-language teachers' college, and (in the 1930s) a Yiddish department at the municipal pedagogical institute. In the early 1920s, the first Yiddish-speaking law court in the Soviet Union opened in Vitebsk. All the Yiddish-speaking institutions in the city were shut down by the late 1930s, at which time there were about 37,000 Jews living in the city. In the months following the outbreak of war in September 1939, some 4,000 Jewish refugees from Poland arrived in the Vitebsk District, many of whom settled in the city.

The Germans heavily bombarded Vitebsk during the invasion of the Soviet Union, but the authorities did not announce the city's evacuation until July 3, 1941. Some Jews—mostly employees of the state —were evacuated, and many men were inducted into the Red Army. The Germans' rapid advance and a shortage of railroad cars prompted many to flee eastward on foot, but most were unsuccessful and were compelled to return to the city.

The Germans occupied Vitebsk on July 9–11, 1941, after the retreating Soviets had set many buildings ablaze. During the first week of the occupation, German soldiers murdered several dozen Jewish townspeople. Twenty-seven Jews were shot on the street for refusing to do forced labor. On July 18, 1941, about forty Jews were murdered on the banks of the Zapadnaya Dvina River. A local Jewish Council composed of both men and women was formed in the first weeks of the occupation; one of its tasks was the selection of Jews for forced labor. A Jewish Order Service was established later. On German orders, the Jewish Council registered all Jews, including children and grandchildren of mixed families. The Germans selected about 300 Jewish males between the ages of fourteen and fifty-five for forced labor. On July 24, 1941, they accused all the men of arson and murdered them in the nearby locality of Mazurino. Jews were required to wear a yellow mark on the front and back of their clothing. During these first weeks, a resistance group operating in the area helped twenty-five families to cross the front and reach the Soviet interior.

During the first two weeks of the occupation, Jews in Vitebsk were concentrated in several locations. On July 25, 1941, the Germans gave all Jews two days to move into a ghetto on the west bank of the Zapadnaya Dvina River, in and around a metalworkers' club. The Germans drowned 200–300 of the Jews as they crossed the river. The ghetto was initially unfenced, but later a wooden fence was erected; on September 8, 1941, barbed wire and a gate were added. The ghetto was guarded by Belarussian police.

On August 26, 1941, nearly 500 members of the Jewish intelligentsia (doctors, teachers, and students) were murdered by Einsatzkommando 9, and in early September, 397 Jews imprisoned in a POW camp set up by the Germans in Vitebsk were murdered, as well.

A daily ration of 300 grams of bread was given to forced laborers; the other ghetto inhabitants, apart from a few exceptions, were not provided with food at all. In the first few weeks of the ghetto's existence, Belarussians entered in order to trade with the Jews and barter food for possessions. The ghetto received water from a pipe installed by the Germans. Numerous young Jews, having heard of the murder of many forced-labor conscripts, evaded conscription by going into hiding.

On September 16, 1941, the Germans barred non-Jews from the ghetto, and conditions inside worsened. Although residents were forbidden to leave the ghetto without official permission, many Jews (particularly the youths) did slip out to obtain food. In September 1941, the Germans captured and murdered Jews who had tried to escape via the sewers.

The ghetto inhabitants lived in severe congestion, some in demolished buildings or without shelter altogether. The overcrowding worsened when they were joined by Jews from villages in the vicinity and others found hiding in the city. Mortality was high.

A few Jewish artisans who worked for the Germans, eight Jewish doctors, several pharmacists, and—according to some sources—the families of members of the Jewish Council remained outside the ghetto. By the end of September 1941, very few Jewish men remained in the ghetto.

The Vitebsk ghetto was liquidated on October 8–10, 1941, ostensibly to impede a typhus epidemic. The Germans trucked its 4,090 inhabitants to the nearby Ilovskiy (Tulovskiy) ravine and murdered them. According to another testimony, the last massacre of Jews in Vitebsk took place on November 5, 1941.

After the liquidation of the ghetto, a number of Jewish pharmacists and doctors were still living outside of the ghetto. Some were murdered in 1942; others escaped and joined the partisans.

VOLOCHISK
(Ukrainian: **Volochys'k**)

COUNTY SEAT, KAMENETS-PODOLSK DISTRICT, UKRAINE, USSR

During the war:
Reichskommissariat Ukraine

Coordinates:
49°32' | 26°10'

In the early twentieth century, about 3,200 Jews lived in Volochisk, representing approximately half of the townlet's population. During the Soviet regime, many were artisans, while a number worked in cooperatives or as factory workers in an iron forge. Others worked in a Jewish kolkhoz that had been established near the townlet. The townlet had both a Jewish Ethnic Soviet and a school that offered instruction in Yiddish. As a result of industrialization and urbanization in the Soviet Union, most of the Jews moved to larger cities; by the late 1930s, only some 500 Jewish residents remained in Volochisk, constituting roughly 20 percent of the total population.

The Germans occupied Volochisk on July 5, 1941. All of the Jews of the townlet and the county were rounded up and concentrated in a single location, in a ghetto of sorts, which was encircled by a barbed-wire fence and guarded by German policemen. The Jews were forbidden to leave the area of the ghetto, and a number of those who disobeyed the order paid with their lives. The Jews were ordered to wear a yellow badge in the shape of a Star of David on their chest and back. The Germans demanded exorbitant ransom payments from the Jews every month.

The ghetto was liquidated in August 1942 (according to one source on September 21, 1942), and its approximately 4,000 inhabitants, mostly women and children, were executed next to a brick factory.

VOLYNTSY
(Yiddish: **Volynets**;
Belarussian: **Valyntsy**)

**VILLAGE IN DRISSA
COUNTY, VITEBSK DISTRICT,
BELARUS, USSR**

During the war: Military
Administration Area

Coordinates:
53°12' | 31°00'

In the mid-1920s, there were about 450 Jews in Volyntsy, roughly 60 percent of the population. During the era of Soviet rule, some practiced artisan trades, and many turned to farming.

The Germans occupied the village on July 10, 1941. In January 1942, they concentrated the Jews in a ghetto surrounded by barbed wire.

In late February 1942, Germans from Drissa* murdered about eighty Jews in a forest near the village.

VORONICHI

**VILLAGE IN POLOTSK
COUNTY, VITEBSK DISTRICT,
BELARUS, USSR**

During the war: Military
Administration Area

Coordinates:
55°19' | 28°38'

In the 1920s, twenty-six Jewish families lived in Voronichi, seven of which engaged in farming.

Voronichi was occupied by the Germans on July 4, 1941. The small Jewish community was headed by a starosta named Konstantin Gorbuk.

In December 1941, some sixty Jews from the area, including twenty-eight children, were concentrated in a ghetto established in two buildings, in which they lived for about one month under extremely harsh conditions. On January 16, 1942, all of the inhabitants of the ghetto were shot to death. Anyone who attempted to flee was summarily shot.

VYŽUONOS
(Yiddish: **Vizhun**)

**TOWNLET IN UTENA
COUNTY, LITHUANIA**

During the war:
Reichskommissariat Ostland

Coordinates:
55°36' | 25°30'

On the eve of the German occupation of Lithuania, about fifty Jewish families lived in Vyzuonos. During the interwar period, the Jews of the townlet earned their livelihood from small-scale commerce and artisanship. It had Jewish educational and religious institutions including a Hebrew school, synagogue, mikve, Beit Midrash, and library. Many of Vyzuonos's Jews were active Zionists.

After Lithuania was annexed to the Soviet Union in 1940, the townlet's shops and businesses were nationalized, the Zionist organizations were disbanded, and the Hebrew school was closed.

The German army entered Vyzuonos a few days after the German invasion of the Soviet Union on June 22, 1941. On June 26, 1941, the Jews of the townlet were ordered to move into two small alleyways, which served as a ghetto. The following day, the members of a few Jewish families were murdered in a nearby forest. On June 29, additional Jews were seized by the Lithuanians, abused and tortured for several days, and murdered. The remaining Jews of Vyzuonos were brought to Utena, where they were murdered in the Rase forest on August 7, 1941.

Warsaw, Poland

"The tens of thousands of deportees, hungry and thirsty, barefoot and naked, their hands empty, without a penny in their pockets, and among them many ill, handicapped, diseased—are crammed into the ghetto, which in economic terms is no more than a huge body without legs, like a prisoner unable to move or support itself."

> *H.A. Kaplan,* Scroll of Anguish, Warsaw Ghetto Diary, November 27, 1941 *(Tel Aviv: Am Oved 1966) [Hebrew].*

WADOWICE

TOWNLET IN WADOWICE COUNTY, CRACOW DISTRICT, POLAND

During the war: Ost-Oberschlesien

Coordinates:
49°53' | 19°29'

On the eve of World War II, about 1,400 Jews lived in Wadowice, representing one-fifth of the townlet's population. They earned their livelihood from small-scale industry, artisanship (mainly tailoring), and commerce, some as wholesalers. The Jews also counted among their ranks a few members of the liberal professions, in particular attorneys and physicians. Associations of Jewish businesspeople and artisans assisted their members with loans, as did the Jewish Folksbank (which was supported by the JDC), and a free-loan society. The community had access to traditional charity and welfare associations. CENTOS helped feed the needy Jewish children of the townlet. Zionist parties and youth movements were active in Wadowice, which was a stronghold of both the secular enlightenment movement and Hasidism, particularly the Bobow Hasidic sect. Wadowice had traditional Hadarim and two Yeshivot, a Hebrew kindergarten, and a Beit Yaakov school for girls established by Agudath Israel, which also operated a kindergarten for some time. Wadowice also boasted a Jewish library, a cultural hall, sports clubs, and, for a time, a Zionist Hebrew school.

After World War II broke out, a small number of Jews managed to head east across the San River, to the area controlled by the Soviets. Several reached other towns in eastern Galicia, such as Cracow*, Tarnow*, and Rzeszow* as well as a number of small townlets.

On September 4, 1939, the region of Zaglembia, which included Wadowice, was occupied by the German Tenth Army. Some of the area's Jews had fled beforehand, but many returned within a short time, and in the second half of September 1939, the Jewish population of Wadowice numbered about 1,400. Right after the occupation, the Germans torched and detonated the synagogue and a number of prayer houses. Germans, ethnic Germans (Volksdeutsche), and Poles plundered Jewish-owned property, apartments, and homes.

In the first half of October 1939, the entire area, including Wadowice, was annexed to the Third Reich as part of eastern Upper Silesia, and from this time onward, the Jews' freedom of movement was restricted, and they were no longer permitted to use the main streets. Jewish men and women alike were ordered

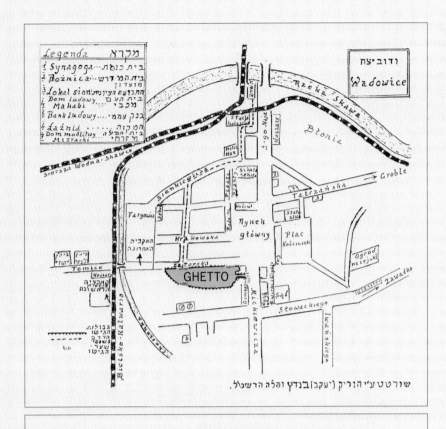

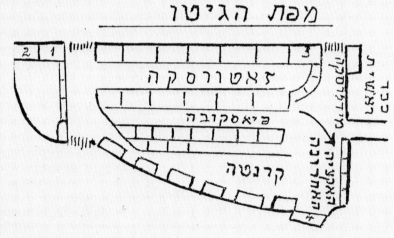

Wadowice plan and the ghetto plan, illustrated by Henrik (Yaacov) Bendetz and Fella Hershtal

(David Jakubowicz, *Sefer Zikaron Kehilot Wadowice, Andrychow, Kalwarja, Myslenice, Sucha*, Massada Publishing Ltd., Israel)

to wear a white Star-of-David armband and were recruited for forced labor. The ownership of Jewish shops and factories was transferred to "loyal Aryans", and Jews were required to remit ransom payments.

In November 1939, a Judenrat was established, headed by Reuven Sharfer, former chairman of the community council. When Sharfer grasped the nature of his role, he refused to obey Moshe Merin, the head of the Zentrale. Sharfer resigned from his position and was replaced as Judenrat head by Berish Wolf, a former Mizrachi leader. The reorganization of the Judenrat was carried out by Baruch Meirchek, who was a representative of Moshe Merin. The Zentrale sent members of its own Jewish Order Service to Wadowice to confront the efforts of Wadowice's Jewish Order Service to hinder the seizure of Jews for forced labor and the organization's failure to cooperate with the Zentrale. The Judenrat helped the needy with food, clothing, free medical treatment, and a monthly allowance. In 1940, the Wadowice Judenrat opened vocational courses to train Jews for various jobs, hoping to prevent abductions for forced labor outside the townlet.

In 1940, there were some 1,220 Jews in Wadowice. A local JSS chapter opened a public soup kitchen. Despite a prohibition on educational activity, secret study groups convened. In the summers of 1940 and 1941, the Judenrat organized summer camps for dozens of children in the village of Gorzen. In late 1940, about 100 Jewish men were sent to a labor camp in Gliwice and from there to the Ottmuth camp. In April 1941, more than fifty people were sent to the labor camp in Gogolin. These camps belonged to the Nazi Schmelt labor organization headed by Albrecht Shmelt. In 1941, there were some 1,400 Jews in Wadowice. In the spring of 1941, eight Jews were arrested for Communism and deported to the Auschwitz death camp, where they perished.

In early 1942, more than 1,000 Jews from the townlet and surrounding localities toiled in "workshops" in Wadowice. In June 1942, about 300 Jewish families from the area's localities were deported to the townlet as part of the liquidation of Zaglebie's Jewish communities.

On July 2, 1942, Gestapo and SS men from Sosnowiec*, representatives of the Schmelt organization, arrived in Wadowice accompanied by Moshe Merin and members of the local Judenrat. They ordered the Jews to vacate the factories and their apartments, which were then closed and sealed. A selection was carried out. A number of those considered fit for work were left in Wadowice to work in the townlet's sewing and rubber workshops; the others, apparently about 500 in number, were deported to the Belzec death camp.

The day after the operation, on July 3, 1942, a closed ghetto was established in the poorest quarter of Wadowice, mostly in wooden shacks designated for demolition. Overcrowding was severe and people were forced to sleep in shifts. The surviving members of the community were imprisoned in the ghetto, primarily those whose work was considered vital to the German economy. In addition, the last surviving Jews of the surrounding localities, including the Jews of Andrychow*, were transferred to the Wadowice ghetto, raising its population to about 1,400. In July 1942, Jews who had managed to hide during the operation attempted to steal into the ghetto. Many were caught and murdered by the Gestapo. Numerous ghetto Jews died of starvation and disease. A public soup kitchen was opened, as the act of cooking in the acutely overcrowded buildings was difficult. A clinic headed by Dr. Bater was also opened. Secret lessons were organized for dozens of children. Many people attempted to flee to Slovakia through the area of Wieliczka but were apprehended and murdered.

On May 10, 1943, altogether 100 young women were transferred from the ghetto to labor camps in Germany; several survived until the end of the war.

The ghetto was liquidated on August 10, 1943. Its inhabitants were rounded up and deported to Auschwitz, where they were murdered. Afterwards, a hunt was carried out for those still hiding in the ghetto and on the "Aryan" side of the townlet. Most of those in hiding were caught and murdered. It is estimated that ten Jews managed to save themselves by hiding in Wadowice itself.

WARKA

TOWNLET IN GRÓJEC COUNTY, WARSAW DISTRICT, POLAND

During the war: General Gouvernement, Warsaw District

Coordinates:
51°47' | 21°12'

In the early 1930s, about 2,200 Jews lived in Warka, representing roughly half of the townlet's population. Most earned their livelihood from small commerce and artisanship. They were supported economically by a Folksbank and charitable institutions. Chapters of Zionist parties, Agudath Israel, and the Bund were active in the townlet. Through to 1938, Jewish deputies held half of the seats on the Warka townlet council.

When the war broke out, many of the townlet's Jews fled to the area under Soviet control. On September 7, 1939, Warka was occupied by the Germans, who immediately began to seize Jews for forced labor. Ten Jewish men were sent to a labor camp near Lublin* and the townlet's Jews were compelled to pay a ransom to secure their release and return. Jewish property was plundered by both Germans and local residents.

In early 1940, a Judenrat was appointed in Warka; its function was to provide laborers for the Germans. The wealthy paid for their exemption from forced labor, but the majority of Warka's Jews were forced to perform very harsh labor. In the spring of 1940, a decree was issued requiring the all Jews above the age of twelve to wear a yellow badge.

In the fall of 1940, an open ghetto was established on a number of streets. The ghetto was severely overcrowded, and numerous families were forced to live in each house, which caused the spread of disease. To survive, most of the Jews bartered their remaining possessions to Polish farmers, who stole into the ghetto with food.

The Warka ghetto was liquidated on February 21, 1941, by the SS, Polish police, and Lithuanian and Ukrainian units. The Jews were rounded up in a square near the city hall and brought to the train station. They were deported to the Warsaw* ghetto, where they shared the fate of the other Jews of Warsaw: deportation to the Treblinka death camp.

WARKOWICZE

TOWNLET IN DUBNO COUNTY, VOLHYNIA DISTRICT, POLAND
(After World War II in the USSR/Ukraine; Ukrainian: **Varkovychy**; Russian: **Varkovichi**)

During the war: Reichskommissariat Ukraine

Coordinates:
50°28' | 25°58'

During the interwar years, there were about 880 Jews living in Warkowicze, a full 85 percent of the townlet's total population. Most engaged in crafts and petty trade, mainly in agricultural produce. They availed themselves of a Jewish merchants' association and a Jewish savings-and-loan association. The townlet had a private Jewish school that taught Hebrew among other subjects, a Beit Midrash, several *shtiblekh* (small prayer houses), a Talmud Torah, Hadarim, a public library, and a drama group.

During the era of Soviet rule in Warkowicze (1939–41), a Jewish kolkhoz was established on Jewish-owned land. When the Germans invaded the Soviet Union on June 22, 1941, some 5 percent of the Jews in Warkowicze set out for the east.

German forces entered Warkowicze on June 27, 1941. Two weeks later, the Germans murdered three Jews. A Judenrat and a Jewish Order Service were appointed. When the Germans demanded the community to turn over Jewish women as well as gold, one of the Judenrat leaders committed suicide.

The ghetto in Warkowicze was established behind a planked fence. Some twenty artisans and their families were housed outside of it. As it was not difficult to leave the ghetto, its inhabitants bartered with the local population. The ghetto inmates conducted educational activities and celebrated Jewish festivals surreptitiously. They performed forced labor, some of which was supervised by Germans from Organisation Todt (OT), who did not mistreat their workers. On September 25, 1942 (this date is an estimation), several of the OT Germans informed the ghetto inhabitants that liquidation was imminent. Two of the Germans entered the ghetto with cars and rescued many Jews. On September 29, 1942, Jews from the farming village of Ozierany were brought to the Warkowicze ghetto, which was then sealed.

The ghetto was liquidated on October 3, 1942. The Jews were trucked to the nearby forest and murdered. During the liquidation operation, the commander of the Jewish Order Service resisted and was immediately shot to death. Most escapees were murdered by Ukrainian policemen and peasants. About sixty Jews survived by finding shelter in Czech villages in the vicinity.

WARSAW

CAPITAL OF POLAND
(Polish: **Warszawa**; Yiddish: **Varshe**)

During the war: General Gouvernement, Warsaw District

Coordinates:
52°15' | 21°00'

Before the War: Poland's capital since 1596 and its largest city, Warsaw lies on both banks of the Vistula River. In the second half of the nineteenth century, Warsaw's Jewish community grew to the largest in Europe and the second largest in the world, after New York City. In 1910, Warsaw had more than 300,000 Jewish residents. Jewish political movements, including both Zionist and Orthodox movements as well as the Bund, were active in Warsaw. The city boasted a range of educational systems and a ramified Jewish economic infrastructure, including printing houses.

The Jews of Warsaw suffered great losses in World War I. The retreating Russian Army carried out pogroms against Jews, and they were exploited economically by German occupiers.

The Jewish population of Warsaw continued to grow during the interwar period, but their proportion relative to the city's total population fell: rising from 320,000 (42 percent) in 1918 to 378,000 (29 percent) on the eve of World War II. Nearly half of Warsaw's Jews earned their livelihood from industry and artisanship—most owned small factories and engaged in handicrafts—while another approximately 30 percent engaged in commerce and about 15 percent were members of the liberal professions.

Warsaw had a proliferation of Jewish, political, and cultural activities and attracted Jewish intellectuals from all over the world. The headquarters of the Jewish parties were located in the city, as were a range of welfare organizations, trade unions, and cultural, educational, and religious institutions. Most of the Jewish newspapers in Poland were published in Warsaw, also a major center for Jewish writers and artists. Its abundance of sports associations, student unions, youth movements, libraries, and Jewish theaters and clubs was a draw for many young people.

Despite the city's flourishing Jewish life, the Jewish community of Warsaw also faced numerous difficulties. Poverty rates increased owing to the global economic depression and Polish economic policies. Moreover, the Polish government and greater society displayed such antisemitism that attacks on Jews became the norm. Options for Jewish emigration from Poland were scant during this period.

German (Nazi) occupation: On September 1, 1939, Nazi Germany attacked Poland, and within days, Warsaw was under siege. The civilian population that remained in the city was targeted by bombings from the air and by cannon fire creating conflagrations that engulfed entire buildings, which collapsed on their residents. Although they shared the fate of the rest of the city, Warsaw's Jews were convinced that their community was a preferred target of the aerial attacks.

Warsaw ghetto map, reconstructed

(A. Czerniakow, *Warsaw Ghetto Diary*, Yad Vashem, Jerusalem 1968)

LEGEND

■ **"Sperrgebiet" – Jewish living area**, according to a German decree dated August 8, 1940

— **Ghetto boundaries on November 15, 1940** (establishment of ghetto)

- - - **Ghetto boundaries moved,** February-April 1941

— **Ghetto boundaries on July 22, 1942** (beginning of Great Deportation)

▨ **The remaining Ghetto area on April 19, 1943** (onset of uprising)

→ ← **Ghetto gates**

⊞⊞⊞ **Bridges**

⑤ **Main public institutions** (see partial list)

▫ **Battlegrounds during the uprising**

● **Fighting posts and bunkers of Jewish fighters during the uprising, April-May 1943**

A **The Central Ghetto** (after the Great Deportation)

B **The "Shops" area**

C **The Brush Shop**

D **The Többens Shop**

LIST OF PUBLIC INSTITUTIONS IN THE GHETTO

1. **Judenrat**
   Grzybowska 26/28; after the Great Deportation: Zamenhofa 19

2. **Jewish Order Service headquarters**
   Krochmalna 32, Ogrodowa 15/17; after the Great Deportation: Gęsia 4

3. **Jewish prison – "Gęsiowka"**
   Gęsia 24 (from June 10, 1941)

4. **Pawiac prison**
   Dzielna 24/26

5. **Law Courts**
   Leszno 53/55

6. **Labor Department - "Arbeitsamt"**
   Leszno 84

7. **The Great Synagogue**
   Tłomackie 7/9 (from June 1, 1941)

8. **Korczak Orphanage**
   Chłodna 33, Sienna 16 (from November 1941)

9. **"Oneg Shabbat" hidden archives**
   Nowolipki 68

10. **Deportations Headquarters – "Befehlstelle"**
    Żeliazna (from July 22, 1942)

11. **Deportations square – "Umschlagplatz"**
    Stawki 6/8/10

Warsaw surrendered to the German army on September 28, 1939, after nearly a month of battle and a siege that cost many civilian lives. About 360,000 Jews remained in the occupied city. German soldiers and police immediately set out terrorizing and abusing Jews, particularly those who were Orthodox in appearance or whose high social position was evidenced by their manner of dress. Jewish shops, businesses, and art collections were looted. Jewish apartments were confiscated, and Jewish property that was hidden in homes was unearthed by informer-guided Germans.

Upon their entry into the city, the Germans seized Jewish men and women for random forced labor, such as the removal of debris caused by the bombings. Jews were abused and humiliated as they worked. The day-to-day life of the Jewish community was largely paralyzed even prior to the publication of any official German anti-Jewish decrees.

In late October 1939, the military administration in Warsaw was replaced by a German civil administration. Throughout all the years of the war, Dr. Ludwig Fischer was governor of the Warsaw District, one of the four districts in the General Gouvernement. The SS, which did not view itself as subordinate to the civil administration, established a permanent headquarters in Warsaw during the same period. The SS acted independently in the city and generally communicated its demands directly to the Jewish community, without coordinating with the civil administration. Consequently, the Jews of Warsaw frequently found themselves planted in the middle of internal German power struggles. In rare cases, Jews managed to exploit the rivalry between the German authorities in their favor, but by and large, their subordination to the competing powers was detrimental to them.

On October 4, 1939, as an extension of the organization of the civil administration in Warsaw, the Germans ordered Adam Czerniakow to establish a twenty-four-member Judenrat and serve as its head. While Czerniakow, an educated man and an engineer by profession, had previously served as deputy head of the Jewish community in Warsaw, the Jewish public viewed him neither as a representative nor as a public figure. Most of the previous community leaders had fled from the city in early September 1939, including the community's head, Maurycy Mayzel.

The first Judenrat included key figures from the entire political spectrum of Jewish Warsaw. Fearing arrest for their pre-war activities, many public figures, including Judenrat members, took advantage of the limited opportunities to escape the city available within the first weeks of the German occupation. Their departure compounded the leadership vacuum in Warsaw's Jewish community, which now faced a dearth of renowned and accepted public figures.

The Judenrat was from its inception expected to fulfill German demands, which included the recruitment and payment of forced laborers. The Judenrat had not been provided with financial resources and had difficulty meeting the requisite expenses. A solution was devised, to release wealthy Jews from the work requirement and in exchange have them pay large sums

Left: **Warsaw, October 15, 1941**
Section of the ghetto wall on
Krochmalna Street (YV)

Right: **Warsaw, May 1941**
The wall built around the ghetto
streets. On the other side of the
wall, the Polish street is bustling
with life. (BA, 101I-134-0791-
29A. Photographer: Ludwig
Knobloch)

that went towards the community's needs. This arrangement created a class of regular workers, mostly the poor and refugees, who were assigned to forced labor on a daily basis. Furthermore, a number of people were exempt from the forced labor requirement or hired others for small sums to perform labor in their stead. Class divisions among Jews deepened, leading to further recriminations against the Judenrat.

Units of the German army and SS continued to randomly seize Jews from the street, underscoring the helplessness of the Judenrat. The Judenrat's failure to alleviate the Jewish community's plight triggered indignant accusations and weakened its already poor image in the eyes of Warsaw's Jewish community. In November 1939, the Germans published decrees that negatively impacted Jewish public life. One of the decrees involved the requirement to wear a white armband with a blue Star-of-David on the outer garment's right sleeve. Within several weeks, limitations were placed on the amount of money that Jewish families were permitted to hold in cash and bank accounts were frozen. Jewish businesses were confiscated and Jewish employees and members of the free professions were dismissed from their jobs without compensation or pension. The rental or leasing of Jewish property was prohibited. Within a short time, 95,000 of the approximately 175,000 Jewish breadwinners in Warsaw fell into poverty and were compelled to sell their possessions to survive.

In January 1940, it was announced that food would be distributed to the general civilian population by means of official ration cards. Shortly thereafter, differently colored cards marked with a blue Star-of-David were distributed to the Jews. The quantity of rations that the Jews received was not the same as that of the greater population, and continually diminished. Anti-Jewish decrees proliferated: in early 1940, Jews were forbidden to enter public parks; Jews (and later Christians, as well) were ordered to turn over all radio sets in their possession; and the use of public transportation by Jews was restricted. Any gathering of ten or more Jews without a permit from the authorities was forbidden, making it illegal and dangerous to worship in a *minyan* (prayer quorum of ten). From January to the spring of 1940, dozens of Jews were attacked by gangs of thugs and members of the Polish underworld, at the initiative of the Germans. Polish society expressed no concerted opposition to the assaults, to the great consternation of the Jews.

Warsaw, June 1941
Jews traveling by rickshaw on Leszno Street in the ghetto.
Photograph taken by German soldier W. George (YV)

From the outset of the war, Jewish refugees from all over Poland thronged to Warsaw, especially from the western areas annexed to the Third Reich; the number of refugees was estimated at about 90,000 prior to the establishment of the Warsaw ghetto. The local branch of the JSS was the only legally functioning Jewish institution aside from the Judenrat, and in addition to its lawful welfare activities and sponsorship of existing organizations such as CENTOS and TOZ, it ran an extensive illegal social welfare system. Owing to the JSS's lack of funds, its activities were largely supported by money provided by the JDC, an American organization recognized by the Germans until the United States entered the war in December 1941.

The welfare activities initially involved caring for refugees and casualties of the military campaign. They were run by public leaders and the heads of the JDC, including Itzhak Giterman, David Guzik, and Emanuel Ringelblum. In time, as it became clear that additional members of the Jewish community were likewise in need of support, the activities of the welfare agencies were expanded. Members of the intelligentsia and public activists were employed by the welfare system, giving rise to the criticism that the organizations had hired intellectuals lacking in any organizational ability.

The educational and cultural work carried out at the public soup kitchens, kindergartens, and clubs that were established provided the youth movements an arena in which to reorganize. The welfare institutions availed themselves of existing organizations, including the more than 2,000 housing committees that had been formed in the city before the establishment of the ghetto. The welfare institutions leveraged Jewish self-help in the city, organizing assistance for underprivileged tenants. Later, the less densely crowded buildings were instructed to support "shelter points" for refugees (established in public buildings, such as schools, synagogues, and social and cultural institutions) or houses that were in especially poor condition. The housing committees represented their tenants before the Judenrat and on occasion challenged its leadership. However, as hardship and distress mounted, the activities of the JSS and the housing committees diminished.

Ghetto setup, institutions, and internal life: The first initiative to concentrate the Jews of Warsaw in a ghetto was proposed by the SS in November 1939. The Judenrat was given three days to move tens of thousands of Jews into specific

Warsaw
Stall selling kitchenware on a ghetto street (YV)

streets. As the SS had issued the order without the knowledge of the city's military commander, however, the commander canceled the order. It was a rare achievement for the Judenrat, which in this instance had managed to exploit the divisions between the German army and the SS. In February 1940, attorney Waldemar Schön, the director of Population Evacuation and Resettlement in the Regional Office, was instructed to design and establish the Warsaw ghetto, but the initiative did not come to fruition because of other, more wide-reaching plans to either concentrate all Jews in the Lublin region or to deport them to Madagascar. Nevertheless, the Germans began to take real steps to separate out the Jews as early as 1940. Signs displayed at the perimeters of Jewish streets warned against entering "a restricted area contaminated with contagious diseases," and a number of streetcar lines that passed through the Jewish area were rerouted. In March 1940, the building of walls at the boundaries of the "contaminated area" had begun, the funding of which was imposed on the Judenrat. In the summer of 1940, the curfew was moved up to seven o'clock in the evening for those Jews who still lived outside the area.

On October 12, 1940, Yom Kippur eve, the Germans ordered the establishment of a ghetto in the heart of the Jewish quarter in north Warsaw, and gave Jews less than three weeks—until October 31, 1940 (a date that was later extended to November 15)—to move in. The absence of clear information as to the placement of the ghetto boundaries complicated the Jews' transition into its confines. Most moved their belongings into the ghetto in improvised wheelbarrows or on their backs and were compelled to leave behind a large proportion of their possessions. Several people managed to deposit their possessions with Polish friends. When the ghetto was sealed on November 16, 1940, however, its inhabitants discovered that with a few rare exceptions, they were forbidden to leave its grounds. Thus, any remaining business and personal ties between Jews and Poles were decisively terminated.

The Warsaw ghetto was encircled by a three-meter-high wall topped with barbed wire and broken glass. The ghetto initially had twenty-two gates, but in time, the number was reduced to four. The area that was fenced in on November 16, 1940, was too small to hold the entire Jewish population: about 380,000 Jews were packed into an area of less than 3.5 square kilometers; in other words, about 30 percent of Warsaw's population was concentrated into about 2.4 percent of the city's territory. The ghetto held fewer than 1,700 buildings, of which only 1,360 were residences, and under 14,000 apartments. According to German figures, an average of six to seven people inhabited each room in the Warsaw ghetto.

The Warsaw ghetto had two main sections: the northern part, known as the Large Ghetto, and the southern part, the Small Ghetto. A number of apartment blocks connected the two parts of the ghetto, but following a series of changes in the boundaries of the ghetto, and more notably after the size of the ghetto was reduced in December 1941, the Large Ghetto was cut off from the small one. The wooden bridge built between the two sections became a bottleneck where crossing Jews often became targets of German abuse and Poles' derision. The housing shortage was exacerbated by the reduction in the size of the ghetto and the arrival of more Jewish inhabitants. In March 1941, the population of the ghetto reached its all-time high of more than 460,000; by the summer of 1941, the population had fallen to 450,000 and by the end of the year, to 415,000. By the summer of 1942, the number of Jews in the ghetto had fallen to about 380,000, mainly as a result of death from starvation and contagious diseases.

There were Jews who viewed the establishment of the ghetto as being in their interests. They imagined that physical separation would protect them from the Germans and the hostility of the Polish population, and that forced enclo-

Warsaw, June 1941
Jews displaying their wares
for sale on a ghetto street.
*Photograph taken by German
soldier W. George* (YV)

sure would intensify the sense of mutual responsibility among Jews. The Jewish population soon realized, however, that the ghetto, far from serving as a place of refuge, would in fact endanger their very survival.

The ghetto Jews' primary concerns were related to the most basic existential hardships: hunger, cold, and poor sanitary conditions inevitably led to the outbreak of epidemic typhus and to death. In November 1940, the month in which the ghetto was sealed, close to 500 people died; in January 1941, nearly 900 people perished in the ghetto; in April 1941, more than 2,000 people died; in June 1941, close to 4,300 people perished; and in August 1941, the month featuring the highest death toll in the ghetto, more than 5,500 people died. From late summer 1941 until April 1942, the monthly death toll stood at between 4,000 and 5,000 people, and then fell significantly in May 1942. Altogether, squalid living conditions in the ghetto brought on the deaths of some 80,000 people.

On behalf of the civil administration, Waldemar Schoene, who had designed the ghetto, was the first to be placed in charge of the "Jewish residential quarter" (the Germans' designation of the ghetto). In May 1941, German attorney Heinz Auerswald was appointed ghetto commissar. He exacerbated certain conditions in the ghetto while alleviating others. For example, he decisively disconnected the ghetto from the Polish side of the city by adjusting the ghetto's boundaries, all the while encouraging economic activity within the ghetto and supporting Jewish employment outside of it. Throughout his term as commissar, until early 1943, Auerswald struggled to enforce his authority. However SS and police officers gradually acquired strength so that by the summer of 1942, they had gained full control of the ghetto.

The first SS and police commanders of the Warsaw district were Paul Morder and Arpad Wiegand. Ferdynand von Sammern-Frankenegg was appointed to carry out the planned deportation of Warsaw's Jews in the summer of 1942; he was replaced in April 1943, by Juergen Stroop.

The Judenrat was charged with moving Jews into the ghetto, managing daily life, and maintaining public order, and was also ordered to administer spheres not previously under the purview of the Jewish community, such as a police force (the Jewish Order Service), a legal system, and the maintenance of the power grid and

Warsaw, September 1941
Starvation in the ghetto.
Photograph taken by German soldier H. Joest (Yad Vashem, Courtesy of Schwarberg Guenter)

sewage system. At the height of its activities, the Judenrat of Warsaw employed some 6,000 Jews, and was responsible for economic, social assistance, health, burial, and employment departments. The Judenrat engaged in welfare activities, established clinics and hospitals, and strove to maintain a reasonable level of sanitation in the ghetto; however, a lack of resources to promote hygiene rendered their efforts futile. The Warsaw Judenrat's mission was untenable: it was required, without access to the necessary infrastructure or funding, to create a functioning community system for a needy population.

The Warsaw Jewish community's criticism of the Judenrat stemmed not only from its objective difficulties, but also from the way in which it operated and principles that its members adopted. Among the points of contention, the Judenrat sent the poorest and weakest elements of the ghetto to the labor camps, a policy that deepened social disparities. In distributing the burden of taxes, the Judenrat did not factor in the limited means of the lower socio-economic classes; the Jews of Warsaw were required to pay regular, uniform sums that were not contingent on their relative wealth, for the running the ghetto. Moreover, Czerniakow awarded numerous key positions in the Judenrat to professionals belonging to the assimilated intelligentsia, apparently reflecting his alienation from the experiences of Jewish life and the distress of the ghetto

Criticism directed at the ghetto leadership was especially harsh with respect to the Jewish Order Service and its head, Jozef Szerynski, a converted Jew. Although the Jewish Order Service was a department of the Judenrat, over time it gained enormous power and a certain measure of independence through its wide-ranging functions and direct ties with the Germans and the Polish police. In early November 1940, young, healthy, and educated Jews with a military record were called upon to volunteer for the Jewish Order Service. A public committee was established in the ghetto to screen the applicants. At the height of its activities, the Jewish Order Service had some 2,000 members. The desire to escape inactivity, expectation of eventual remuneration (Jewish Order Service employees were not promised wages), and the hope for immunity from deportation to labor camps that was guaranteed to members of the Jewish Order Service motivated many to apply for positions. Others joined the Jewish Police out of a sincere desire to contribute to the regulation of Jewish life in the ghetto. The main functions of the Jewish Order Service, however, were to execute the orders that the Judenrat received from the Germans (such as the collection of valuables and the payment of ransoms) and to maintain order in the ghetto. In time, its responsibilities were expanded. Members were expected to direct traffic and prevent crowds from gathering, to enforce cleanliness in the streets, to collect the taxes levied on the Jewish public, and to run the Jewish prison set up for "offenders" in the ghetto. It rapidly became apparent that the Jewish Order Service was a vehicle for implementing German policies, and many of those who had joined the organization for ideological reasons, left. Their positions were by and large filled by people of dubious character that lacked any sense of public service, leading to a downgrade in the moral standing of the Jewish Order Service.

An equally corrupt body in the Warsaw ghetto was the Office of the War on High Interest and Speculation, which became known, with its offices at 13 Leszno Street, as "The 13." In December 1940, a refugee from the Lodz* ghetto named Abraham Gancwajch established The 13 with the goal of supervising legitimate commerce. In truth, however, its members, headed by Gancwajch, were agents of the SD, the German Security Police. Gancwajch's ambition was to replace Czerniakow as head of the Judenrat, or to take over some of his areas of responsibility. Indeed through its ties to the SS, The 13 managed to assume control over several of the ghetto institutions. To create the impression that he was concerned for social welfare, Gancwajch initiated cultural activities, provided financial support for rabbis and public figures, and organized a first-aid institution in the ghetto. Despite Gancwajch's efforts, however, most ghetto inhabitants held a pejorative view of The 13 as dangerous, and feared all contact with the organization. In July 1941, apparently as the result of an internal power struggle among the Germans, The 13 was dismantled and most of its members were absorbed into the ranks of the Jewish Order Service.

The ghetto walls severed the Jews of Warsaw from their surroundings and limited their access to sources of information available to the general population. The Germans did not cut the ghetto's few telephone lines, installed mostly in authorized offices, but the Jews nevertheless felt isolated. Orders and decrees were transmitted to Jews by means of public notice boards in the ghetto streets and over loudspeakers. In the first three months of the ghetto's existence, three streetcar routes passed through its streets, but in February 1941, the streetcars were replaced with a special line marked with a Star-of-David, the only one of its kind in the ghetto. Within several months, Moryc Kohn and Zelig Heller, refugees from Lodz with questionable ties to the Germans, received a permit to operate vehicles harnessed to horses as another official means of public transportation. During the same period, an industry of human-pulled rickshaw carriages developed in the ghetto.

In the early months of its existence, the Warsaw ghetto suffered from a complete cessation of financial activities. Hundreds of thousands of Jews were cut off from their sources of livelihood, while alternate jobs had not yet been created in the ghetto. In December 1940, the Germans established the Transfer Bureau (*Transfer-stelle*), designed to regulate economic ties between the ghetto and the Aryan side

Warsaw
Starvation (YV)

of the city. However, the first person placed in charge of the institution, Aleksander Palfinger, undermined all independent economic activity on the part of Germans, Poles, or Jews, and thwarted most attempts by the Judenrat to create jobs in the ghetto. In May 1941, Palfinger was replaced by Max Bischof, who encouraged the Jews to obtain work in factories outside the ghetto (*placowka*). He also brought about the establishment of a number of workshops ("shops") and promoted production inside the ghetto, which attracted German entrepreneurs seeking to exploit the ghetto's cheap professional labor force. Products manufactured in the shops were delivered outside the ghetto via the transfer bureau, and payment was transferred through the Judenrat's supply department.

Initially, few Jews sought employment in the German factories. Those who worked outside the ghetto received no wages but a small meal, while the shop workers received a meager salary that amounted to less than the price of a half loaf of bread. People who were not hired by the official factories were often employed in clandestine workshops established without formal authorization in the ghetto by German and Polish businessmen, and especially by Jewish entrepreneurs. The employees of the workshops were generally offered higher wages and better treatment. In December 1941, about 65,000 people were employed in factories located both within and outside of the ghetto. Their meager wages did not entirely stave off hunger but did enable them to survive severe living conditions and provide for themselves and their families, while also giving them some means to hold onto reality. The vast majority of the ghetto's Jews lived in destitution and a constant state of existential distress; they struggled to survive through their savings or by selling the few possessions they still owned. As the amount of property in Jewish hands diminished, the number of poverty-stricken people rose, along with hunger and mortality rates. A small group of Jews in the ghetto—accounting for less than 5 percent of the ghetto's population—did not endure starvation and in several cases lived a life of luxury and dissipation. These were the ghetto wealthy—people who had managed to maintain the ownership of property possessed prior to the war, who held senior positions on the Judenrat, and who profited financially during the war.

The Judenrat's social help department and self-help institutions mobilized to provide assistance to the needy. The Judenrat mainly supported people sent to labor camps, employees of the ghetto factories, and orphans. For its part, the JSS focused on helping the refugees that flooded the ghetto, supporting the unemployed intellectual elite, and operating activities for children. The two institutions attempted to curb the high death toll by providing food and combating epidemics. At the height of their activities, the ghetto had more than 100 public soup kitchens, including kosher kitchens, kitchens affiliated with political organizations and trade unions (such as journalists and writers), and kitchens for children. Efforts to organize educational activities for children failed owing to dire conditions in the ghetto.

Until June 1941, the tens of thousands of refugees who had thronged to the city even prior to the establishment of the ghetto were joined by more than 60,000 additional deportees, arriving primarily from western Poland and provincial towns in the Warsaw district. The housing shortage that existed in the ghetto even before the arrival of these refugees forced many into the more than 100 "shelter points" under appalling conditions. The JSS mobilized associations composed of former residents of the deportees' native cities and towns to work with the refugees, striving, often in vain, to alleviate the economic hardship and profound sense of alienation the refugees faced. When the United States entered the war in December 1941, the transfer of funds from America was impeded, and it became difficult for the JSS to function. The crisis prompted the Judenrat to intensify the activities of its self-help department, which was however chronically ill-equipped to provide for the necessities of the needy ghetto population. Tens of thousands of unemployed Jews wandered throughout the ghetto aimlessly, and its streets soon filled with beggars. People lay on the pavement together with their starving children, appealing to the mercy of passersby. The mass starvation and collapse of all accepted public norms led to increasing cases in which hungry Jews attempted to grab parcels from passersby in search of food. As time passed, the number of destitute people dying of starvation grew.

Extreme living conditions compelled people to turn to "illegal" occupations, particularly smuggling. All forms of smuggling, especially of food, had existed from the early days of the Warsaw ghetto and persisted despite the presence of guards posted at the gates and along the wall of the ghetto. According to Czerniakow's estimation, about 80 percent of the food consumed in the ghetto was obtained illegally. Numerous Jews, mostly women and children, slipped outside the ghetto in order to bring back provisions for their families. Jews who worked outside the ghetto also engaged in petty smuggling; those caught in body searches conducted at the ghetto gates were severely punished. Jews (some of whom had belonged to the criminal underground before the war) also smuggled large quantities of food into the ghetto with the help of Polish smugglers. Hundreds of kilograms of food were smuggled in through and over the walls of the ghetto, through holes drilled into the walls of buildings located on the periphery of the ghetto, and through drainage pipes. Members of the Jewish Order Service, who turned a blind eye to the smuggling, and the smugglers themselves collected huge profits and became the ghetto wealthy. Many Jews felt that the profits came at the expense of the general public, which was starving to death. The Jewish Order Service and the smugglers were criticized for driving up food prices on the black market and for electing to smuggle luxury items into the ghetto.

In late 1941, the German authorities stepped up their efforts to combat smuggling. On October 15, 1941, the governor of the General Gouvernement, Hans Frank, announced that any Jew caught outside the ghetto would be executed. At the same time, Auerswald once again reduced the size of the ghetto and moved its boundaries to further impede smuggling. The number of Jews who were killed for smuggling increased significantly: in late 1941 and early 1942, dozens of

Warsaw, spring 1941
Women's purse factory on
Leszno Street in the ghetto (YV)

Jews were executed. Smuggling continued notwithstanding the challenges and punishment; it was run as a joint business between Jews on one side of the wall and the German and Polish police on the other.

The situation of the Jews in the Warsaw ghetto deteriorated further following the German invasion of the Soviet Union in June 1941. On December 24, 1941, as winter temperatures fell below zero, the "fur decree" was issued: all ghetto Jews were given one week to turn over not only fur coats and blankets, but all pieces of fur in their possession. Moreover, while over 11,000 young Jews had been sent to labor camps in the summer of 1941, the Germans, most often SS members, periodically raided the ghetto to randomly seize workers. Thus in early 1942, the number of men in the Warsaw ghetto, in particular men between the ages twenty to forty-nine, fell to about 70,000, while more than 107,000 women lived in the ghetto. The youths remaining in the ghetto who were not employed in a safe job attempted to hide, and the economic burden fell mainly on women and children, causing an upheaval in the traditional roles of the Jewish family. Although very few families remained intact, for many people the family continued to function in the ghetto as the basic living unit and to serve as a source of strength for its members. In other cases, extreme living conditions caused the family fabric to unravel. The food shortage decimated some families, and overcrowded living conditions aggravated tensions, exposing previously contained personal difficulties. Numerous abandoned children wandered the streets: several were orphans, others had left home on their own accord, and yet others took advantage of their parents' hours of absence from the home to wander the streets. Within a short period of time, Jewish gangs of ruffian youths formed.

The German prohibition issued in the early days of the occupation against schooling for Jewish children rendered the Judenrat's task of addressing these challenges especially difficult. The decree allowed the Judenrat to open a few high school vocational training courses, such as in architecture and graphics, which provided training to hundreds of youths. Under these circumstances, most of the education in the ghetto was conducted illegally. Parents with means hired private teachers for their children, and political movements and welfare institutions opened underground classrooms; a number of university-level courses were opened in the ghetto. In late 1941, the Germans permitted schools to operate in the ghetto; however, these institutions were attended by about 6,700 of the more than 50,000 children in the elementary school age group. Nineteen elementary schools belonging to the various movements and denominations were opened; yet, for most of the ghetto children, schooling was a luxury.

Youth Movements: In the early days of the war most of the veteran members of the youth movements left Warsaw; thus, in the initial period of the German occupation, it fell mainly to women and youths to renew these organizations' activities. Within several months, the veteran leadership of the youth movements returned to occupied Warsaw out of a sense of mission and commitment to their movements and to Jewish society. Among the most prominent returnees were Josef Kaplan and Mordechai Anielewicz of Hashomer Hatzair, Yitzhak Zuckerman (Antek) and Tsyvia Lubetkin of the Dror movement, and Eliezer Geller of Gordonia. The ties were quickly restored between the youth movement leaders and the balance of the public leaders in the Ghetto. The leadership of the various parties understood that the unique conditions of life under the occupation made cooperative work essential; thus, a representative body of the various political movements and youth movements was created to serve on a public advisory council alongside the JSS. Among its members were Maurycy Orzech of the Bund; Shakhne Sagan of Po'alei Zion Left; Yosef Sak of Po'alei Zion (Socialist Zionists); Menachem Kirszenbaum of the General Zionists; Aleksander Frydman of Agudath Israel; and David Wdowinski of the Revisionists. At a later stage, they were joined by the Mizrachi representative, Yitzhak Nissenbaum, and PPR representative Josef Lewartowski. Within a short time, they decided on their collective direction and objectives, which initially were centered on welfare works. Political life began to develop; social-welfare issues were debated in the public soup kitchens and political positions examined; many youths mobilized to occupy the ghetto children's time and educate them on subjects relating to their respective ideological paths.

The youth movements accepted the determinations of the political parties in the Warsaw ghetto and accorded them supreme authority. The movements soon developed into a regional leadership for their members living under the German occupation in the General Gouvernement. Male and female couriers maintained contact with movement members of different communities, and members from all over Poland participated in joint activities, including seminars and pioneer training facilities (Hachshara). In addition to teaching survival techniques, the political movements emphasized the need to advance the ideological awareness and foster the intellect of the younger Jewish generation. The underground newspapers published in the ghetto became the isolated ghetto residents' only sources of reliable information on the events of the outside world.

Religious and cultural Activities: A lively religious life was maintained in Warsaw, despite the danger posed by a religious lifestyle from the earliest days of the occupation: a number of religious commandments, such as public prayer, had been expressly prohibited. Most observant Jews endeavored to find private and public means of upholding a religious lifestyle. For example, while many people prayed in solitude on weekdays, public services were held on holidays that were likewise attended by non-observant Jews. In the spring of 1941, the prohibition against public prayer was canceled, and dozens of synagogues opened throughout the ghetto. In order to bypass the prohibition of the kosher slaughter of animals for meat, a ritual slaughterer butchered kosher meat outside the ghetto that was in turn smuggled into the ghetto. The lack of food, however, caused many Jews to abandon their observance of the *kashruth* laws. Traditional religious garb, while not explicitly forbidden, made ultra-Orthodox Jews a target of German abuse, and consequently, a number of Jews stopped wearing traditional garments and shaved off their beards. Others chose to maintain their traditional Jewish appearance throughout the years of the ghetto's existence. Alongside the

Warsaw, spring 1940
Synagogue that served to shelter refugees in the ghetto (YV)

Left: **Warsaw, 1942**
Jews waiting in line to receive a food ration at public soup kitchen in the getto. *Photograph from Ringelblum archive.* (AR-ŻIH)

Right: **Warsaw, May 1941**
Training of members of the Jewish Order Service in the ghetto. *Photograph taken by German soldier serving in propaganda detachment* (YV)

observant ghetto Jews who strove to maintain their religious lifestyle despite the imposed constraints, there were many, including youths from religious homes, who lost their faith and abandoned their observant way of life.

The rabbis and religious leaders who remained in Warsaw endeavored to meet the spiritual and practical needs of their followers. The rabbi of Piaseczno*, Rabbi Klonimus Kelmish Szapiro, sustained his ultra-Orthodox community in the ghetto, and other rabbis kept Torah study alive. A rabbinical council headed by Rabbi Aleksander Zyshe Frydman was established alongside the Judenrat and served as its religious department; it was in charge of official religious life in the ghetto. Prior to the holidays, the rabbis mobilized to obtain food products for the needy, and before Passover, they decreed special religious dispensations to ease hunger. In the wake of the rising death toll in the ghetto in late 1941, an appeal was issued to preserve hygiene. When in the summer of 1942, the religious department of the Judenrat proposed appointing Sabbath inspectors in the ghetto, a broad spectrum of the ghetto's nonobservant population firmly and acrimoniously rejected the proposal.

Christian religious activities were also held in the ghetto. About 2,000 Jews who had converted to Christianity but were defined as Jews by the Nazis were deported into the Warsaw ghetto in early 1941. Two ghetto churches served as their community centers. With the support of Christian welfare organizations, public soup kitchens were opened, loan funds were established, and an educational system operated for the converted Jews. The community of converted Jews in the Warsaw ghetto lived separately from the Jewish public, and some of its members harbored antisemitic views.

Extensive cultural activities, mostly clandestine, were held in the Warsaw ghetto. The Germans permitted Jews to open cafés and theaters; however, these institutions largely served the ghetto's nouveau riche population. Most of the cultural activities were linked to the existing underground political bodies. *Yikor* (*Yidishe Kultur Organizatsye*—an organization for the dissemination of Yiddish culture) held literary evenings and events to mark the jubilees of known Jewish artists; *Tkumah*, an organization of Hebrew-language devotees, organized performances in Hebrew; and various institutions held concerts and performances by cantors and others. Jewish writers, directors, and poets continued to practice their crafts during the war. Secret libraries were opened all over the ghetto. These cultural offerings supplied the public with relatively inexpensive entertainment and a partial livelihood for large numbers of artists. The activities were also the target of public criticism, however, as ghetto inhabitants argued that cultural events should not be held while so many people were dying.

The clandestine archive: The *Oneg Shabbat* archive was a unique project in the Warsaw ghetto, established and operated at the initiative of Emanuel Ringelblum with the aim of documenting Jewish life under German occupation. In addition to collecting documents, the archivists encouraged various sectors of Jewish society to keep records of their life in the ghetto. When the first news of the Final Solution arrived, the archive mobilized to collect information on the murder of Jews that was published for the Jews in the ghetto and passed on to the free world. Many of the documents that were collected in the archive and found after the war serve as an invaluable testimony to Jewish life under the Nazi regime.

Before the Deportations: In the fall of 1941, news began to filter into the ghetto regarding the mass murder of Jews in eastern Poland; in January 1942, rumors concerning the extermination of Jews of the Lodz District reached the ghetto, as did news in late March, of the murder of Jews of the Lublin District. The youth movements asserted that the Germans had launched a plan to exterminate all Jews and that consequently, there was no alternative but to organize armed resistance. In March 1942, the leaders of the Jewish community in Warsaw convened. Yitzhak Zuckerman, the representative of the youth movements, attempted to convince the leaders of the need to establish a centralized defense organization. His proposal was rejected, not only because of the impossibility of verifying and grasping the full scope of the news (and with it the conclusions drawn by the youths), but also for fear that such an organization might trigger German retribution and harm any chances of the Jewish population's survival. The Bund maintained that their ideology barred them from accepting any Jewish organization separate from the Polish ones. In April 1942, notwithstanding the public leadership's objections, the Communists established an "anti-fascist bloc" that also included the leftist Zionist movements. Efforts to remove young armed Jews from the ghetto to the forests in an organized fashion were unsuccessful. Following a number of arrests among the Communists and the danger of additional arrests, the bloc disbanded.

On the night that came to be known as the "Night of Blood" or "Bartholomew's Night," April 17, 1942, German forces entered the ghetto and executed fifty-two Jews according to a prepared list, including underground activists, known German agents, and food manufacturers in the ghetto. Czerniakow claimed that the Germans informed him that the massacre was in punishment for the underground press, and he requested that it be discontinued. However, those who disseminated the underground newspapers rejected the German explanation. They argued that the German actions were consistent with a pattern that preceded the deportation of Jews from the ghetto and that its purpose was to increase terror among Jews and eliminate the forces in the ghetto that were capable of carrying out an armed uprising.

Youth movements and political organizations attempted to expand their activities beyond the ghetto and establish official contact with the Polish underground. However, these ties were limited to the personal level. Although Warsaw was the center of Polish underground activities, its members were not inclined to create ties with the Jewish leadership in the ghetto, and they invited no Jewish representative into their ranks. Consequently, the Jewish political organizations concentrated on spreading the news about the murder of Jews throughout Poland and encouraging information from the front. Rumors of Jewish extermination, the now-routine

Warsaw

Shop window in the ghetto: "Sale of square and round *matzot,* under the supervision of the Warsaw Rabbinate." *Photograph from Ringelblum archive* (AR-ŻIH)

Germans nocturnal raids of the ghetto, and mounting German terrorization caused deep fear among the ghetto's Jews. Following rumors of an impending liquidation operation in the ghetto, Adam Czerniakow appealed to various German parties to determine whether there was any truth to the reports. In light of the Germans' firm denials, Czerniakow published an announcement declaring the liquidation rumors baseless. The deportation of Warsaw's Jews began a few days later.

Murder operations: The great deportation: On July 21, 1942, a number of Judenrat members were arrested and taken hostage. An official announcement was published in the ghetto regarding the evacuation of Warsaw's Jews to the east, with the exception of a number of sectors, including employees of the Judenrat, public institutions, and German factories; members of the Jewish Order Service; and those fit to work. The following day, on July 22, 1942, the "great deportation" began, during which the majority of Warsaw's Jews were sent to the Treblinka death camp and murdered. The prisoners of the Jewish jail, refugees, and street beggars were the first to be rounded up in the *Umschlagplatz*—the "loading square"—which until then had served as the *Transferstelle* (transfer office). The Jews were loaded onto cargo trains and removed to an unknown destination. The way in which the deportation was organized and conducted, coupled with the official announcement led Jews to believe that the Germans planned to deport some 70,000 unemployed and starving Jews from the ghetto, while the rest of the Jews would be permitted to remain.

When Czerniakow realized on July 23, 1942, that the deportations also included children, he committed suicide. That same day, public leaders and underground representatives met for an emergency meeting. Members of the youth movements and Bund representatives led the demand for organized public resistance to the deportations. However, the majority of those present were wary of or opposed this strategy. Several people argued that such action would endanger the entire ghetto and that the Germans only planned to deport a small proportion of the ghetto's inhabitants; others declared that they would rely on God's mercy.

Czerniakow's suicide severely undermined the Judenrat's standing and increased panic among Jews. Czerniakow was replaced by his deputy, Marek Lichtenbaum, who yielded to German orders and recruited the Jewish Order Service to carry out the deportations. Szerynski, the commander of the Jewish Order Service, had been arrested in May 1942 for black marketeering in furs. His deputy, attorney Jakub Lejkin, was now in charge of the members of the Jewish Order Service, who were required to supply a daily quota of Jews for deportation in order to preserve their own families' immunity from deportation.

As employment in German factories had initially guaranteed protection from deportation for the worker and his family, masses of Jews flocked to the doors of the official factories. However, when the factories refused to accept new workers, dozens of improvised factories opened in the ghetto, some of which received temporary German authorization. Political organizations and ideological circles strove to find their members organized asylum with work managers who shared their ideologies. As examples of this type of arrangement, numerous rabbis hid in the shop of Rabbi Abraham Hendel; public activists and members of the Hashomer Hatzair youth movement received asylum in the shop of Aleksander Landau; while most members of the Zionist movements Dror and Gordonia, left the ghetto during the time of the deportations.

In defiance of the objection of the representatives of the Jewish public to act against the deportation, the representatives of the youth movements Hashomer Hatzair, Dror, and *Akiva* met on July 28, 1942, a few days after the beginning of the mass murder operation, and established the Jewish Fighting Organization

(*ŻOB*). The Jewish National Committee (*Żydowski Komitet Narodowy – ŻKN*) was later established and served as a leading public body. The first task of the *ZOB* was to inform the Jewish public that the deportation transported Jews to the Treblinka death camp, and certain death. The flyers distributed by the *ZOB* were received with hostility by most of Warsaw's Jews, who viewed them as a German provocation intended to create a pretext for the complete liquidation of the ghetto.

A new hardship was introduced in the first week of the deportation: security around the ghetto's boundaries was tightened, leading to a cessation in all smuggling into the ghetto, which placed numerous Jews in danger of imminent starvation. On July 29, the Germans issued an order stating that all those who agreed to report voluntarily for deportation would receive three kilograms of bread and one kilogram of jam. Thousands of people thronged to the *Umschlagplatz*, until the number of people designated for deportation exceeded the amount of space in the train cars. A number of Jews waited for days, without food or water, for the train to Treblinka.

On July 31, 1942, SS forces and members of the auxiliary forces of "Aktion Reinhard" under the command of Hermann Hoefle joined in the implementation of the deportation. Brutality reached extreme levels. The SS, German police, and their Ukrainian and Latvian helpers, entered the alleys of the ghetto and seized people from the streets and their homes, with no regard for the residents' documents or permits. Within a short time, Jewish public street-life in the Warsaw ghetto ceased to exist. In early August, the immunity of the employees of public institutions was revoked, and numerous public activists were deported from the ghetto. The 200 children in Janusz Korczak's orphanage were also taken to the *Umschlagplatz*. As with other educators, the staff of the orphanage accompanied the children to the trains, led by the "old doctor," as Korczak was known, who refused offers from Polish friends to be saved.

On August 10, 1942, the Germans ordered the evacuation of the Small Ghetto, restoring its area to the Polish side of the city. Tens of thousands of Jews were forced to wander the streets in constant danger, in an attempt to find a place to hide in an area that was also under threat of deportation. During this period the number of suicides in the ghetto, a previously rare phenomenon among Warsaw's Jews, soared.

On August 15, the forces of "Aktion Reinhard" began to deport the Jews of Warsaw County, and their presence in the Warsaw ghetto declined. However, the few soldiers who remained systematically combed the ghetto. They entered

Warsaw, March 11, 1942
Judenrat chairman Adam Czerniaków (center), next to the Gęsia prison, with a group of released prisoners. On his left, a girl he had rescued from a group of smugglers that were apprehended and shot. *Photograph from Ringelblum archive* (AR-ŻIH)

Warsaw
Smuggling food into the ghetto.
Photograph from Ringelblum archive (AR-ŻIH)

homes, searched through hiding places, and began to carry out roundups in the "shops," as well. Anyone not working in the shops was deported, including family members of the workers. In many cases, an entire improvised shop was brought to the *Umschlagplatz*. A few survivors who fled from the death camp, as well as Jews who jumped from the trains, returned to the ghetto and told of their experiences. An underground publication was also circulated based on the testimony of Zalman Frydrych, a Bundist who had been sent in early August to discover where the trains carrying the deportees were headed and bring back news of their fate. During this period, the Jews of Warsaw learned what fate awaited them at Treblinka, and the acute danger posed by deportation.

This awareness led to increased underground activity: the *ZOB* dispatched Arie Wilner to establish contact with the Polish military underground, the Armia Krajowa. However, most of the people that Wilner attempted to contact kept their distance. He received weapons only from the Communists. On August 20, 1942, Izrael Kanal, a member of the *ZOB*, attempted to kill Szerynski, who had been released from prison to help manage the deportation; Szerynski was wounded in the attack—the underground's first important initiative. But on September 3, the incipient resistance movement received a severe blow that cut its activities short. Josef Kaplan and Shmuel Breslaw of the underground's leadership were murdered by the Germans, who also apprehended a young girl carrying the underground's few arms. Following these events, the younger members of the underground proposed an initiative to commit collective suicide in defiance of the Germans. Several of the older representatives thwarted the scheme, arguing that the underground should instead organize a final, thoroughly planned struggle.

In early September 1942, the German forces returned to the ghetto and initiated the final stage of the "great deportation." On September 5, an order was published requiring all ghetto Jews to assemble the following day within a defined area of several streets. The shop managers and the Judenrat were allocated approximately 35,000 "work permits" to distribute among the ghetto's more than 120,000 residents. Only a few of those who managed to prove that they were employed in German factories succeeded in obtaining a permit. For a week's time, from September 6 to September 12, a cruel selection was carried out in the designated streets, which later became known as the "cauldron," followed by a deportation operation to Treblinka. The great deportation ended with a number of murder operations, the last of which was carried out among the members of the Jewish Order Service and their families.

From July 22 (Tisha B'Av) to September 21, 1942 (Yom Kippur), more than 265,000 Jews were transported from the Warsaw ghetto to Treblinka. Another approximately 11,000 Jews were sent to labor camps, and about 10,000 people perished inside the ghetto. About 8,000 ghetto inhabitants fled to the Aryan side of Warsaw. Approximately 90 percent of the men and women living in the Warsaw ghetto were murdered during the great deportation; among the children and elderly, 99 percent were killed.

The post-deportation ghetto (September 1942–April 1943): The post-deportation ghetto was dramatically altered, not only in its human composition but also in its borders. The Small Ghetto and the southern part of the Large Ghetto were restored to the Aryan part of the city, while three islands were created in the part that remained: the Central Ghetto, the area of the shops, and the Brush Shop (a factory that had previously manufactured brushes). To the approximately 35,000 people who had managed to prove that they were employed in German factories inside and outside the ghetto and who were permitted to remain in the ghetto, were added another approximately 20,000 "wild" Jews, that is, people who were illegally hiding inside the ghetto. The Germans published strict orders

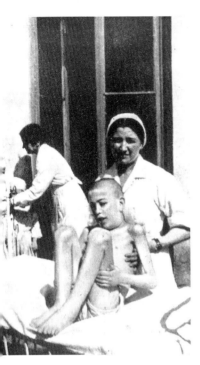

Warsaw
Boy receiving medical care in
the ghetto hospital. *Photograph
from Ringelblum archive* (AR-ŻIH)

forbidding anyone to leave during work hours, encircling the shops with walls. The authority of the Judenrat was significantly reduced, and any violation of a German order meant immediate execution.

The Warsaw ghetto's identity was transformed, as it now more closely resembled a labor camp. Residents worked seven days a week in the shops, without remuneration. The workers were expected to subsist on the paltry food obtained through ration cards that they were granted. For their part, the "wild" Jews—nearly one-third of the ghetto population—received no ration cards altogether. A parallel system of bakeries and food shops was soon established, accepting as currency the few valuables that remained, one of the most prized being poison.

The Germans continued to terrorize Jews. Hundreds of Jews were seized and shot to death in the streets, and others were murdered at their place of work. In early November 1942, the Germans ordered the establishment of a shelter for abandoned children in the ghetto, with the claim that "every nation must tend to its children." They also called upon Jews to open new shops, theaters, and cafés. These orders expanded the Jews' range of activity in the shops, and several people did indeed establish centers to care for children and mutual-aid funds for the ill. A form of patriotic allegiance began to arise surrounding the shops and Jewish labor *placowka's*, and alternative social frameworks were constructed to replace those that had been lost in the deportations.

The sense of individual helplessness coupled with the routine German brutality led to new phenomena among the Jewish populace, including drunkenness, sexual promiscuity, and theft. Many blamed themselves for their inability to protect their loved ones. Under these conditions, increasingly harsh criticism was leveled at the Jewish Order Service during the deportation, along with complaints that the Jewish public had not vociferously enough opposed German actions.

Underground and uprising: The underground, whose members had witnessed the brutality of the large-scale deportation, began to collapse. Mordechai Anielewicz, who was in Zaglebie in the summer of 1942 on a mission for the underground, returned to the ghetto after the deportations and reunified the shattered ranks of the underground. Under his leadership, another attempt was made to establish contact with the "Aryan" side. This time, Wilner managed to obtain *AK (Armia Krajowa)* recognition of the *ZOB*, resulting in the transfer of a small number of weapons—about fifty handguns and fifty hand grenades; the chief contribution of the *AK* was in raising the morale of the movement. The *ZOB* unified many of the youths that had grown up in the Zionist-socialist youth movements and in the Bund. An additional underground movement was established after the great deportation, the Jewish Fighting Union, (*Żydowski Związek Wojskowy—ŻZW*) of the Revisionist movement. The *ZZW* managed to obtain a significant cache of weapons through its ties with Poles. In October and November 1942, the underground groups in the ghetto warned the public of the fate of the deportees to Treblinka. They organized in preparation for future armed action. As a first step, the groups carried out more frequent executions of Jews viewed as acting against the interests of the Jewish population of Warsaw during the deportations, including Jakub Lejkin and other senior Judenrat members. The death sentences issued by the Jewish undergrounds were publicized throughout the ghetto.

On January 9, 1943, Heinrich Himmler arrived in Warsaw. He was displeased at the size of the ghetto population, which stood at more than 50,000 Jews (many illegal) at the time of his visit, and demanded that the population be reduced immediately. Large German forces consequently entered the ghetto on January 18, 1943, in order to deport some 8,000 "wild" Jews. While the Jews were taken by surprise at the deportation they responded swiftly: tens of thousands of Jews, including those with permits, went into hiding, and the Germans'

Warsaw, September 1941
An employee of the burial society in the ghetto pulling a wagon with bodies for burial. *Photograph taken by German soldier H. Joest* (YV, courtesy of Schwarberg Guenter)

orders demanding that Jews assemble to have their papers examined were not obeyed. This was the first time the Germans themselves were required to enter ghetto apartments in order to round up Jews.

The members of the underground were also caught unawares and had difficulty deciding on a coordinated action, but they, too, responded quickly. A group of fighters, members of Hashomer Hatzair under the command of Mordechai Anielewicz, took their place among a convoy of Jews being led to the *Umschlagplatz*; at a predetermined signal, they began to shoot at the Germans with the few pistols in their possession. All the fighters, with the exception of Anielewicz, were killed by the Germans within minutes, but a few Germans were hit and the convoy of deportees dispersed. A short time later, yet another act of armed resistance occurred: when German forces entered an apartment to force its residents into the streets, they were shot at by a number of underground members of the Dror movement in hiding, who then escaped through the rooftops.

German forces remained in the ghetto until January 22, 1943. During this time, about 5,000 people were deported, and another approximately 1,700 were shot in the streets. The Jewish public in the Warsaw ghetto, who were convinced that the Germans' aim was to renew the deportations and ultimately liquidate the ghetto, viewed the January deportation as a German failure, secured by the Jews' refusal to report as demanded. In the wake of the January deportation, the German decided to evacuate the shop employees before the final liquidation of the ghetto and appointed German industrialist Walter Casper Toebbens to discreetly transfer the skilled workers to a labor camp in the area of Lublin. However, Toebbens' appeals to the employees were rejected with utter distrust, among other reasons because of the underground's publications that warned of yet another German ruse. During this period, the Judenrat and Jewish Order Service altogether lost their authority in the ghetto, and for the first time, the underground functioned as an alternative Jewish leadership.

To finance the underground's activities, especially the purchase of arms, the *ZOB* and the *ZZW* began to levy taxes on the wealthy shop owners. This led to tension between the two undergrounds, whose ideological differences prevented them from uniting. Nevertheless, they communicated with one another and began to coordinate their activities.

Warsaw, September 1941
Mass grave within the Warsaw
Jewish cemetery. *Photograph
taken by German soldier H. Joest*
(YV, courtesy of Schwarberg
Guenter)

The failure of the January deportation combined with the German army defeat at Stalingrad and the Soviet bombings of Warsaw, led to a renewal of hope—if the ghetto inhabitants could delay the deportations by even a few months, the remainder of Warsaw's Jews might survive the war. The assurance of impending and inevitable death that had prevailed in the ghetto since the deportations had begun to falter, and all Jews began looking for ways to escape. The few people with financial means and connections with Poles moved to the "Aryan" side of the city. However, this was not an option for the majority of the Jews, who instead created hiding places within the ghetto. Unlike the temporary hiding places of the days of the deportations, the Jews now built well-equipped bunkers that could contain dozens or even hundreds of people for several months. They stocked the bunkers with hundreds of kilograms of dried food, while some of the bunkers were hooked up to the water system, electric grid, and municipal sewer system. Jews also tried to ensure the presence of a medical staff member in each of the hiding places. In a number of bunkers, arms were stored and tunnels leading to the Aryan side were dug. In the months that preceded the uprising, a veritable underground city was created, and nearly every single one of the 40,000 Jews who remained in the ghetto had an assigned bunker.

An opposing view arose among the members of the underground, who associated the halting of the deportation operation with the armed activities of the *ZOB* and did not believe that there was any chance of survival. They acted out of the belief that the Jews of Warsaw were lost and as such should fight to the last person. Consequently, they refrained from preparing bunkers or modes of retreat or escape from the ghetto. Thus while one segment of the ghetto population busied themselves with preparing hiding places, the members of the underground movements purchased arms and organized a resistance movement, in the hope that resistance would serve as an act of mass protest that would reverberate around the world. The January uprising, which later became known as the "small uprising," convinced the *ZOB* members that during deportation, they should not act as a single force. The ghetto was therefore divided up into separate sectors under Anielewicz's command: Marek Edelman was placed in charge of the area of the Brush Factory; Eliezer Geller was in command of the Shop Area; and Izrael Kanal was placed in command of the Central Ghetto. Yitzhak Zuckerman was sent to the "Aryan" side to renew the ties with the Polish underground that were severely undermined after Wilner was caught by the Gestapo. The small number of arms Wilner had obtained from the Poles before he was caught constituted too limited a supply for the *ZOB*: each of the approximately 500 fighters was provided with only one personal weapon—a handgun with about ten bullets, while each sector had possession of a single rifle. Later, the group received one submachine gun. The members of the underground began to fashion their own improvised weapons, such as grenades and Molotov cocktails. Conclusions drawn from the events of January suggested that the attack of Germans in an open area was unadvisable; the *ZOB* should instead confront the enemy within the labyrinth of ghetto buildings. Twenty-two groups organized according to movement affiliation were stationed in shared apartments from which the various sectors of the ghetto could be observed.

The *ZZW* took on entirely different measures. While firmly established on the ideological ground of the Revisionist movement, it took into its ranks people who disagreed with its views, including Communists. It was headed by Pawel Frenkel, a young member of Betar, and among its 250 members were people who had served in the Polish army before the war. Their military experience helped them to obtain more effective weapons than the *ZOB*. In coordination with the *ZOB*, most of the *ZZW* forces were concentrated in the northeastern part of the ghetto, turning Muranowski Square, where they were holed up, into an assault

compound. The commanders of the *ZZW* planned an onslaught of gunfire against the Germans, and at the end of the battle to escape the ghetto through a tunnel in order to continue the fighting as partisans.

The revolt: In early February 1943, Himmler ordered the final liquidation of the Jewish community of Warsaw. On April 19, 1943, on the eve of the first night of Passover, the ghetto was surrounded by massive German forces, and SS soldiers entered the ghetto with the intention of capturing the remaining Jews of Warsaw. The Jews responded with broad-based popular resistance and launched what would later become known as the Warsaw Ghetto Uprising.

The uprising was considered popular in nature owing not only to the fighting of the underground, but to the tens of thousands of Jews holed up in their bunkers. Thousands of German soldiers and policemen armed with tanks, canons, and with combat experience, who were regularly relieved of duty to regain their strength, faced about 750 mostly teenage defenders, armed for the most part with pistols, and tens of thousands of starving Jews holed up in bunkers. For twenty-seven days, the Jews of the ghetto withstood the far superior German forces and made it very difficult for them to carry out their mission.

Colonel Ferdinand von Sammern-Frankenegg, the SS and police commander of the Warsaw District, decided to start the deportation in the Central Ghetto, where there were relatively few workers. When his forces penetrated the ghetto on the morning of April 19, 1943, he discovered deserted streets. The Jews of the ghetto refused to obey German orders and the Jewish undergrounds attacked the German columns. The *ZOB* fired at them with their guns and tossed homemade hand grenades. The *ZZW* twice managed to set fire to one of the tanks brought into the ghetto. One of the *ZZW*'s positions facing the "Aryan" side featured a waving blue and white flag alongside a red and white Polish flag. One Jewish fighter was killed, and the Germans had numerous casualties. In the evening, the Germans withdrew from the ghetto after having apprehended only a few hundred Jews. The undergrounds and the Jews of the ghetto viewed the resistance as an enormous achievement and success, and the members of the underground were regarded as heroes.

The resistance mounted by the Jews and the intensity of the fighting took the German command by surprise. Von Sammern-Frankenegg was replaced by SS General Juergen Stroop, who had experience fighting partisans. Based on the experience of the first day, Stroop decided to put down the Jewish resistance in the Central Ghetto using a large military force, while concurrently accelerating the

Warsaw, 1942–1943
Jews rounded up at the Umschlagplatz prior to their deportation (YV)

evacuation of the working force from the ghetto factories. However, the fighting in the Central Ghetto, especially in Muranowski Square which was defended by the *ZZW*, continued. When the Germans approached the area of the brush "shop" on the morning of the second day, *ZOB* fighters detonated a mine and fired at the Germans from the windows of the buildings. For their part, ghetto inhabitants, including factory workers, did not report for an orderly evacuation. They instead remained holed up in the bunkers, despite their rapidly deteriorating conditions. On the second day of the uprising, electricity, gas, and water in the ghetto were cut off. Far more people were crammed into most of the hiding places than were originally planned for, and the ventilation systems had difficulty carrying the excess load. The extent of the Jewish entrenchment and the Germans' inability to deport thousands of Jews as planned became a serious problem for the Germans. In the first three days of the uprising, the German forces managed to seize only 6,000 Jews, the vast majority of whom were employees of the factories in the Central Ghetto who believed that their skills would spare their lives. To advance the deportation and protect his men from gunfire, Stroop decided to halt the street battles and fight Jews with fire.

On April 23, 1943, the Germans began to systematically set fire to the ghetto buildings. The raging flames succeeded where the trained German soldiers had failed and forced those hiding inside the buildings out into the streets; fighters were compelled to abandon their positions, and many lost their lives. The members of the *ZOB* moved from one bunker to the next and attempted to attack the Germans at night. The ghetto residents hid the fighters in the bunkers, enabling them to collect their strength before their next foray. The *ZZW* forces, for their part, left the ghetto following their fierce street battles. They moved their fighters through a tunnel to the "Aryan" side, but within a few days, their hiding place was discovered through the help of informants, and all were killed in battle with the Germans.

Buildings that were set aflame became death traps. The Germans searched with dogs for ventilation openings and used tear gas and grenades to force Jews out of hiding. Many were shot on sight, while others were cruelly abused and tortured.

On May 8, 1943, the Germans laid siege to the bunker where the commanders of the *ZOB* were concentrated, located at 18 Mila Street. The bunker's five openings were sealed, the main entrance was broken through, and poisonous gas was pumped in. Led by Anielewicz and Wilner, who several weeks earlier had been returned to the ghetto wounded, about 100 fighters refused to obey the German call to emerge from hiding, preferring to take their own lives. The *ZOB* fighters who were not in the Mila 18 bunker escaped from the burning ghetto, owing to the courageous actions of a young Jewish fighter, Symcha Ratajzer, known as Kazik, who led dozens of fighters out through the sewers and on to the forests around Warsaw.

The fires finally vanquished those who were in hiding, and the Jewish resistance force was weakened. On May 16, 1943, Stroop blew up the large synagogue of Warsaw and declared the large-scale operation over. In the triumphant report that Stroop submitted to his superiors, he boasted, "The Jewish quarter in Warsaw is no more."

According to the Stroop report, 50,065 Jews were caught in the ghetto during the uprising, of whom about 14,000 were summarily shot or sent to Treblinka. He reported that more than 5,000 others perished in the burning of the ghetto. These numbers appear to be greatly exaggerated, their purpose being to glorify Stroop's name and justify the lengthy time his forces needed to suppress the Jewish uprising. It may be assumed that some 30,000 out of a total of about 40,000 Jews who were in the ghetto on the eve of the uprising were sent to camps—a minority to Treblinka and the majority to Majdanek, Poniatow, and Trawniki. Another approximately 10,000 Jews were killed during the uprising itself, in mass executions or large fires. Although there is no consensus among Stroop's various reports regarding the number of German losses, it appears that they did not exceed sixteen killed and eighty-five wounded, the number that he officially reported, most of whom were struck down in the first days of the fighting. Stroop's strategy of keeping face-to-face battles to a minimum by burning down the ghetto, and of stripping the bunker survivors (thus uncovering concealed weapons), impeded an effectual Jewish attack.

The Warsaw ghetto revolt constituted the first urban uprising in occupied Europe and the largest act of resistance by Jews during the Holocaust. News of the uprising reverberated throughout occupied Poland and the entire world, during the war. To this day, for both Jews and non-Jews alike, the uprising symbolizes desperate courage and the triumph of the Jewish human spirit.

A few hundred Jews apparently continued to live among the ruins of the ghetto even after the official liquidation of the Warsaw ghetto, but owing to the untenable living conditions and the German presence in the area, only a small number of the "people of the ruins," as they were known, survived for long. The tens of thousands of Jews deported from Warsaw to camps in the area of Lublin worked under severe conditions for many months. Most were murdered in early November 1943, during the *Erntefest* or Operation Harvest Festival. Several thousand deportees who had been sent to Auschwitz earlier or to labor camps in western Poland, were temporarily spared. Most perished at a later stage of the war as a result of hard labor, selections, and death marches.

About 20,000 Jews, many of whom had previously lived in the ghetto, remained on the "Aryan" side of Warsaw after the liquidation of the ghetto. People of Jewish appearance remained in hiding, while others mingled with the Polish population under false identities. These Jews were helped by the *Zegota*, a Jewish-Polish underground organization established under the sponsorship of the Polish underground and the Polish government in exile. The *Zegota* offered thousands of Jews, including many children, financial help and false Aryan papers. In addition to the *Zegota*, tens of thousands of Poles risked their lives and those of their families to help Jews. Antisemitic sentiments and greed led many other Poles to hand Jews over to the authorities, and numerous Poles tracked anyone whose appearance was suspect.

The Jews who lived among the Poles endured the heavy burdens of being constantly on guard and hiding their Jewish identity. Consequently, when Jews discovered in mid-1943 that that the Germans had begun to round up Jews of neutral (especially South American) citizenship in order to exchange them for German civilians, thousands abandoned their hiding places and reported to the Germans. They were put up by the Gestapo in Hotel Polski in Warsaw, and realized too late that they had been lured into a trap. Several hundred Jews were in fact exchanged for German civilians from the Land of Israel, while thousands of Jews who had purchased expensive false papers were transferred within a short time to camps in Germany and France, and from there to Auschwitz.

In early 1944, Jewish prisoners from Greece, Hungary, and Italy were brought to Warsaw to demolish the remaining streets in the ghetto. These Jews, together with the thousands of Jews hiding in Polish Warsaw and the "people of the ruins," found themselves in the midst of yet another predicament in the summer of 1944, when on August 1, 1944, the Polish underground launched an uprising to liberate the capital. The Polish uprising eventually turned into a national tragedy: more than 23,000 fighters were killed, along with more than 150,000 civilians. Among the dead were numerous Jews, including several who had taken an active role in the fighting. The Polish Warsaw Uprising was brutally suppressed by the Germans, while soldiers of the Red Army stood by. Following a direct order from Hitler, Warsaw was razed to the ground, its buildings torched and blown up, and its residents driven out. The German strategy left no chance of survival for Jews in hiding; many abandoned their hiding places and were murdered. Others remained hiding in cellars and soon perished.

The destroyed city of Warsaw was liberated on January 17, 1945. Over 80 percent of the city's buildings had been destroyed and all of its residents driven out. The loss of life was even greater. In all, approximately 685,000 of Warsaw's inhabitants were murdered, including 370,000 Jews. Hundreds of Warsaw's Jews survived the Polish uprising, and fewer than 2,000 returned from the camps.

Havi Dreifuss (Ben-Sasson)

WARTA

(Yiddish: **Dvart**)

TOWNLET IN SIERADZ COUNTY, ŁÓDŹ DISTRICT, POLAND

During the war: Wartheland

Coordinates:
51°42' | 18°38'

The Jewish presence in Warta can be traced back to the sixteenth century, making it one of the first Jewish localities in the area.

During the interwar period, about 2,000 Jews lived in Warta, one-half of the townlet's population. They earned their livelihood primarily through petty trade, crafts, and fruit orchards that they leased in nearby villages and farms. Jewish political and social life in Warta was animated by Zionist parties and Agudath Israel. The townlet had one of the largest Jewish psychiatric hospitals in Poland, run by the Hevra Kadisha.

When World War II began, the inhabitants of Warta fled to nearby villages, but returned to their homes once the townlet was occupied. In the early days of the occupation, the Germans rounded up Jews in the marketplace, subjected them to beatings, and shaved off men's beards. Within a few weeks, the Germans ordered a Judenrat established under a man named London and gave it the task of recruiting forced-labor groups and collecting punitive taxes.

In late 1939, the Jews were ordered to leave the townlet, which belonged to an area that the Germans had annexed, and were advised that they would be transferred to the Lublin area. The first group of intended deportees was assembled by the Judenrat. They waited all night at the train station but were eventually sent home, and the deportation was cancelled.

In February 1940, an unfenced ghetto was established near the synagogue. Several Polish families continued to live in the area. The ghetto perimeter was guarded by members of the Jewish Order Service who did not prevent Jews from exiting or Poles from entering the ghetto. A number of Jewish artisans could therefore continue to make a living. The German authorities allowed them to practice their trades provided they attended to the Germans' needs first. Artisans who worked for the Germans were exempt from transports to labor camps.

The Judenrat intervened on behalf of 250 Jewish tailors, obtaining orders from the Wehrmacht through the mayor of Warta; a portion of this income was used to revitalize the townlet. The mayor, who treated the Jews well, also hired many young Jews for various kinds of farm labor.

In January 1941, the Germans began to transport Jews to labor camps in the Poznan area. The Judenrat and family members sent parcels of food and clothing to the camp inmates, but the Germans took punitive action after uncovering an attempt to send larger quantities than permitted.

On May 5 1942 (*Lag Ba'Omer*), about ten Jews were publicly hanged in the ghetto, including the Judenrat chairman, London; the leader of the General Zionists, Shmuel Yerozolimski; and Agudath Israel chairman, Motel Rotstein. Members of the Jewish Order Service were ordered to execute the condemned men.

By the summer of 1942, some 2,400 Jews lived in the ghetto. On July 27, the Germans held another public hanging, murdering thirteen Jews.

The liquidation of the Warta ghetto began on August 24, 1942. The Jews reported to the local athletics field and were taken to a nearby convent and church, where they were held for several days. Several Jews were murdered on the spot and buried in a mass grave. On the third day of the operation, Hans Biebow, head of the Lodz* ghetto administration, conducted a selection and had 400 Jews taken to the Lodz ghetto for forced labor. The rest were sent to the Chelmno death camp, where they were murdered.

WASILISZKI

TOWNLET IN SZCZUCZYN COUNTY, NOWOGRÓDEK DISTRICT, POLAND
(After World War II in the USSR/Belarus; Belarussian, Russian: **Vasilishki**)

During the war: Bezirk Białystok

Coordinates:
53°47' | 24°51'

When World War II broke out, about 1,800 Jews lived in Wasiliszki, representing the majority of the townlet's population. Most earned their livelihood from commerce and artisanship and were occasionally assisted by the JDC and other Jewish aid societies. In the interwar period, Wasiliszki was the site of lively Jewish political activity. The townlet also had a number of traditional religious and other institutions, such as a Tarbut Hebrew school, a library, and youth movements. After the Red Army occupied Wasiliszki in the second half of September 1939, Jewish parties were abolished, privately owned shops were nationalized or closed, and cooperatives were formed. The schools taught in Yiddish according to a Soviet curriculum.

On June 25, 1941, the Germans occupied Wasiliszki. The following day, eight Jews were handed over to the Germans by the local police and were executed. The Jews of the townlet were required to wear a yellow badge, their freedom of movement was restricted, and their property was confiscated.

In July 1941, at German orders, a ten-member Judenrat headed by Herman Sandik was established and ordered to recruit forced laborers for the Germans.

In November 1941, the Jews of Wasiliszki were moved into a ghetto, and were joined by Jews from other localities. Overcrowding was severe and living conditions were harsh. The Germans periodically ordered the Jews to submit ransom payments. SS soldiers from Szczuczyn* periodically entered the ghetto to abuse and murder Jews.

On May 10, 1942, the Jews were rounded up in the synagogue courtyard, and a selection was carried out, under the supervision of Herman Hanweg, the governor (Gebietskommissar) of Lida*, and Yezhievski, the chief of the local Belarussian police. During a period of twenty-four hours, 2,150 Jews were led in groups to the Jewish cemetery, where they were shot to death. About 180 young men and those with required professions, together with their families, were separated out and put up in a number of buildings along a single narrow street in the ghetto. During the operation, about thirty young men managed to escape to the forest, where they later joined various partisan units.

The day after the operation, the Germans called upon the Jews to emerge from their hiding places, promising that they would be sent to work. The approximately 130 Jews who responded were also murdered.

On May 12, 1942, two days after the operation, the surviving Jews were ordered to clean the abandoned ghetto buildings and collect all remaining belongings. By the beginning of August 1942, these Jews were sent in three groups to the Szczuczyn ghetto. Several were transferred from there to a labor camp of the Todt organization in Lida.

WASILKÓW

TOWNLET IN BIAŁYSTOK COUNTY, BIAŁYSTOK DISTRICT, POLAND

During the war: Bezirk Białystok

Coordinates:
53°12' | 23°13'

When World War II broke out, 950 Jews lived in Wasilkow, representing approximately one-quarter of the townlet's population. They engaged mainly in artisanship and commerce and were employed as hired workers. Wasilkow boasted chapters of Jewish organizations and youth movements, including Zionist parties and the Bund, as well as a Yiddish school and a library.

On September 13, 1939, Wasilkow was occupied by the Germans, who immediately set about plundering Jewish property and terrorizing Jews in the streets of the townlet. A few days later, Wasilkow was handed over to Soviet rule, in accordance with the Molotov-Ribbentrop Pact. Shops in the townlet were nationalized and cooperatives were formed. During this period, Jewish refugees from western Poland thronged to Wasilkow and the Jewish population of the townlet rose to 1,200.

On June 27, 1941, Wasilkow was once again occupied by the Germans. Without delay, the Jews were required to wear a yellow badge, and the Jewish men were recruited for forced labor. In January 1942, the Jewish area of Wasilkow was turned into an open ghetto. The Jews were packed into a small number of buildings under very harsh conditions. The residents of the ghetto also suffered from periodic looting and attacks by local police, and later from harsh forced labor and murders, which were carried out at the direct orders of the Germans.

On November 2, 1942, the Jews of the Wasilkow ghetto were rounded up in the central square of the ghetto and led to an abandoned barracks, which served as a round-up site for the Jews of Bialystok County. They were deported on November 19, 1942 to the Treblinka death camp.

WAWER

TOWNLET IN THE WARSAW COUNTY, WARSAW DISTRICT, POLAND

During the war: General Gouvernement, Warsaw District

Coordinates:
52°14' | 21°09'

In the interwar period, most of Wawer's Jews engaged in commerce and artisanship. A few hundred Jewish inhabitants were active in the Revisionist movement.

On September 15, 1939, the Germans entered the townlet, which had a population of about 3,000. The Jews were required to remit high ransom payments and were forbidden to board trains. A Judenrat headed by Menachem Kastenberg was established as well as a seven-member Jewish Order Service. As of December 15, 1939, the Jews were required to wear a distinctive badge and were seized for forced labor in Milosna, where the German officer Mueller was known for his cruel acts of terror and murder of Jews. On December 27, 1939, a total of 107 inhabitants of Wawer (ninety-seven Poles and ten Jews) were executed in retribution for the killing of two German soldiers.

In the spring or in December of 1940 (sources vary regarding the date), a ghetto was established for Wawer's Jews in the village of Czaplowizna, located on the eastern banks of the Vistula river. Some 2,000 Jews were concentrated in the ghetto, which was established in the Rozycka quarter, in a number of demolished buildings. The Jews were ordered to fence in and renovate their premises as well as install heating and windows. The ghetto's residents were employed as woodcutters. A shortage of water in the ghetto and sparingly distributed food rations prompted smuggling from the Polish side. As the sanitary conditions worsened, disease and mortality surged. The overcrowding and harsh economic conditions compelled people of means to leave, with only the poor staying behind. In January 1941, the situation in the ghetto deteriorated and urgent social aid was required for 612 people.

The ghetto was liquidated on March 26, 1942, when its 950 inhabitants were deported to Warsaw*.

WĄWOLNICA

TOWNLET IN PUŁAWY COUNTY, LUBLIN DISTRICT, POLAND

During the war: General Gouvernement, Lublin District

Coordinates:
51°17' | 22°10'

During the interwar period there were some 1,100 Jews in Wawolnica, about one-third of the townlet's population. Most were petty merchants and artisans. Chapters of Zionist youth movements and parties, and of Agudath Israel, provided educational, culture, and welfare services. Children attended a traditional Heder or Polish schools.

When World War II began, Jewish refugees from nearby towns poured into Wawolnica; mostly from Kurow*, which had been bombarded.

The Germans occupied Wawolnica in the middle of September 1939. At the end of December 1939, Jews who had been evacuated from Pulawy* arrived in the townlet. By early 1940, the Jewish population of Wawolnica had climbed to about 2,000, more than half of them refugees. They were sent out to forced labor under German and Polish overseers.

The Wawolnica Judenrat was established in early 1941. The council, headed by N. Rosenfeld, provided the Germans with forced laborers and set up a soup kitchen with assistance from the JDC in Warsaw*. In the winter of 1941/42, the Jews of Wawolnica were ordered to surrender their furs to the Germans. Contact between Jews and non-Jews was restricted.

The Jews of Wawolnica were ghettoized in February 1942. On March 22, SS men from Lublin* murdered 120 Jews, including members of the Judenrat, in reprisal for the murder of a German in the townlet. Jews hiding in Polish homes were murdered on their hosts' doorsteps.

The Wawolnica ghetto was liquidated on March 31, 1942. Most of the inhabitants were deported to the Belzec death camp. A group of men was transferred to the Opole* ghetto. In May 1942, they were sent on to the Trawniki and Poniatow labor camps in the Lublin area.

WĘGRÓW

COUNTY SEAT, LUBLIN DISTRICT, POLAND

During the war: General Gouvernement, Warsaw District

Coordinates:
52°24' | 22°01'

When World War II broke out, about 5,200 Jews lived in Wegrow, representing more than half of the town's population. Most engaged in small-scale commerce and artisanship, especially in the garment and food industries, while a few were large-scale merchants and industrialists. Wegrow boasted Zionist parties, Agudath Israel, and the Bund, as well as literature and drama classes, and a sports club. A variety of Jewish schools operated in the community: a traditional Heder, a Talmud Torah and a Yeshiva, as well as a Hebrew Tarbut school and a Beit Yaakov school.

The Germans occupied Wegrow on September 10, 1939. By that time, numerous Jews—young people and families—had fled to the area that was later annexed to the Soviet Union. In the early days of the occupation, Jews were seized for forced labor and a few were murdered, including the community's rabbi, Rabbi Morgenstein. Large, extortionate "contributions" were exacted.

In late 1939, the Germans appointed a twelve-member Judenrat, which was given the task of collecting ransom payments and recruiting forced laborers. Mordechai Ziman, the most recent head of the community, was appointed to head the Judenrat. A Jewish Order Service was also established. In 1940, the Judenrat opened a public soup kitchen in Wegrow.

In December 1940, the town's Jews were transferred to an open ghetto. Periodically, large groups of Jewish refugees were brought to the ghetto from Zelechow* and Lukow* in the Lublin District, from the area of Warsaw, Lodz, and various other localities. Forced laborers were sent from the ghetto to work in Wegrow and its environs; in the camp in the village of Klimonty, which was near Mordy*; and in the camp in Ostrow Mazowiecka. In January 1941, the Judenrat opened a school in the ghetto.

In the summer of 1942, the Germans sealed off the ghetto, with its approximately 8,300 residents. Hundreds of Jews perished from disease.

On September 20, 1942, Yom Kippur eve, about 8,000 of Wegrow's Jews were deported to the Treblinka death camp by SS soldiers, Polish policemen, and Ukrainian auxiliary forces. Many young people who tried to escape were murdered in the forest or in Wegrow's Jewish cemetery. Most of the Jews who were in hiding were handed over to the Germans by Polish collaborators and murdered in the cemetery.

The Jews that the Germans allowed to remain in the ghetto, mainly the members of the Judenrat, the Jewish Order Service, and their families, were employed collecting the belongings of the deportees and cleaning up the ghetto.

In late 1942 or early 1943, the Germans reestablished a ghetto in Wegrow, in which they concentrated between 200 and 300 Jews from the area who had managed to hide during the deportations or who practiced required professions. In May 1943, all were shot by the Germans.

WERBA

TOWNLET IN DUBNO COUNTY, VOLHYNIA DISTRICT, POLAND
(After World War II in the USSR/Ukraine; Ukrainian, Russian: **Verba**)

During the war: Reichskommissariat Ukraine

Coordinates: 50°17' | 25°37'

During the interwar years, there were about 300 Jews in Werba, more than half of the population of the townlet. They owned two flour mills, two alcohol distilleries, a sawmill, and a brick factory.

The Soviets took control of Werba in September 1939. The Germans occupied the townlet on June 24, 1941, but Ukrainians ran the municipal government until early July and conscripted Jews for forced labor. A German officer murdered several Jews.

On May 20, 1942, two ghettos were established: a small ghetto for skilled workers and their families and a large ghetto for the balance. Ten days later, the large ghetto was liquidated and 285 Jews were murdered. Jews who escaped or had gone into hiding moved into the small ghetto, which had a population of eighty-two. This ghetto was liquidated in the late summer or early fall of 1942.

WIDAWA

TOWNLET IN ŁASK COUNTY, ŁÓDŹ DISTRICT, POLAND

During the war: Wartheland

Coordinates: 51°26' | 18°57'

On the eve of World War II, some 730 Jews lived in Widawa, numbering one-third of the townlet's population. Several Zionist organizations and Agudath Israel were active in the community.

At the beginning of the occupation, the last rabbi of Widawa, Avraham Mordechai Maroko, was murdered; he was burned alive embracing a Torah scroll. During the first months of the war, most of the Jews left Widawa for Belchatow*, Zdunska Wola*, and Zelow*, while refugees from other locations fled to Widawa. The Widawa ghetto was not sealed. It housed approximately 100 Jewish families until it was entirely liquidated in 1942. On December 14, 1941, twenty-five Jewish families were deported from Widawa to Belchatow. The others were apparently sent to the Chelmno death camp in the summer of 1942, where they were murdered.

WIDZE

TOWNLET IN BRASŁAW COUNTY, VILNA DISTRICT, POLAND

(After World War II in the USSR/Belarus; Belarussian, Russian: **Vidzy**)

During the war: Reichskommissariat Ostland

Coordinates: 55°24' | 26°38'

About 1,100 Jews lived in Widze on the eve of World War II, representing roughly half of the townlet's population. Most earned their livelihood from commerce. Various Jewish parties and youth movements were active in Widze, including Zionist parties, the Bund, and the Communist party. The community had Jewish educational and cultural institutions, including a Yiddish school and a Jewish library. On September 21–22, 1939, the Red Army occupied Widze. During this period, Jewish refugees thronged to the townlet from the areas of Poland occupied by the Germans. Following the Soviet occupation, Widze was placed under Soviet rule, and privately owned shops were nationalized or closed.

After the Germans invaded the Soviet Union on June 22, 1941, a police force consisting of ultranationalist Lithuanians and Poles took over the townlet. For several days they looted the Jews' property and terrorized and abused the Jewish population. On June 27, 1941, Widze was occupied by the Germans and the abuse of the Jews worsened. In the first few days of the occupation, a local ultranationalist unit authorized by the Germans to serve as a local police force murdered either approximately 85 or 200 Jews (sources vary on the figure) outside of the townlet, among them the rabbi of Widze, Rabbi Efraim Yehuda Wein. The Jews were ordered to wear a yellow badge and their freedom of movement was restricted. At German orders, a Judenrat was established, headed by Lipe Levin, and a Jewish Order Service was set up, headed by Berl Basin of Dzisna*. They were placed in charge of collecting ransom payments for the Germans and recruiting forced laborers, some of whom were sent to distant labor camps.

In November 1941, a small ghetto was established in Widze for about 200 Jews who were artisans and were considered fit for work. The rest of the Jews were deported to the Opsa* and Glebokie* ghettos. The Widze ghetto was fenced in, and guarded by Germans and Belarussians. In March 1942, the Germans began to concentrate Jewish workers from a number of localities in the Widze ghetto, raising its population to about 2,000. Several of the workers were sent on to various labor camps. In the spring of 1942, epidemic typhus broke out in the ghetto, and a makeshift hospital was set up that operated with the help of a local Christian doctor. An underground organization headed by Noakh Svirski was active in the ghetto.

In the summer of 1942, the Germans transferred some 1,300 Jews to the Swieciany* ghetto, leaving about 50 Jewish workers in the Widze ghetto. On the eve of the evacuation to Swieciany, a group of young Jews escaped to the Koziany forests and joined the partisan units.

WIELICZKA

TOWNLET IN CRACOW COUNTY, CRACOW DISTRICT, POLAND

During the war: General Gouvernement, Cracow District

Coordinates: 49°59' | 20°04'

About 1,100 Jews lived in Wieliczka after World War I, representing roughly 15 percent of the townlet's population. They earned their livelihood from industry, predominantly in the sectors of food and garments, and a number also owned factories, chiefly in the salt, food, and leather industries. The Jews of Wieliczka were aided by trade and craft associations, a commercial bank, a free-loan society, and traditional welfare and charity organizations. The local chapter of CENTOS cared for needy children. Tarbut, *Takhkemoni*, and Yavne Hebrew schools, as well as a Talmud Torah under the supervision of Agudath Israel, provided Jewish children with their education. The community also boasted a drama circle and Hebrew courses, two Jewish libraries and a sports union as well as Zionist parties and youth movements, dozens of whose members participated in pioneering training facilities.

In 1918 and 1919, a great deal of Jewish-owned property was plundered and eleven Jews were injured, some quite seriously, in pogroms carried out by peasants. In 1933, an Anti-Nazi Youth Front was established in Wieliczka, with members from all the Jewish parties. Among other activities, the organization collected money for Jewish refugees from Germany.

On the eve of the German occupation, about 300 Jewish families lived in Wieliczka. In the early days of September 1939, most of the Jews left the townlet. The Gestapo arrived there on September 12, 1939, and murdered thirty-two Jewish men in a nearby forest. Following the killings, Jewish men fled from the townlet or hid inside it. In the fall of 1939, a great deal of property was stolen and a number of people were seized for forced labor. The Jews were ordered to wear a white Star-of-David armband and to bow before all Germans.

In late 1939, Bronislawa Friedman was appointed to head the Judenrat, which was initially made up exclusively of women. The Judenrat paid ransoms to the Germans and recruited Jews for forced labor (only women were recruited, as no men were left in the townlet). In time, the men began to return and were assigned to forced labor. A number paid the Judenrat a fee to be exempted from work. A Jewish Order Service was also established.

In 1940/41, thousands of Jewish refugees arrived in Wieliczka, mainly from Cracow*. Many were members of the intelligentsia, and at this stage, a number of men were added to the ranks of the Judenrat. Also at this time, young Jews were sent to the labor camp in Pustkow, and they were provided with food and clothing by the Judenrat.

In May 1941, a ghetto with a population of about 7,000 was established in Wieliczka. In late 1941, a chapter of the JSS was active in the townlet. In 1942, an attorney, Dr. Ludwig Steinberg, was appointed to head the Judenrat. It established a workshop that employed about 700 Jews; they manufactured products used by the Wehrmacht, among other items. With the help of the JSS center in Cracow, the Judenrat instituted a clinic and two public soup kitchens, and in February 1942, the local JSS chapter assisted some 1,200 people.

On August 20–22, 1942, Jews from surrounding localities were deported to Wieliczka. The roads from the townlet were blocked. In order to divert the Jews' attention from the impending operation, a Jewish hospital was inaugurated in the townlet on August 24.

On August 25, 1942, a Polish police unit and about 300 members of a German operative unit encircled the townlet. On August 26, eleven Jews were murdered in Wieliczka; 113 patients were removed from the Jewish hospital and executed in the Kozie Gorki forest. About forty doctors and nurses were murdered in the Judenrat building after convening a meeting to protest the treatment of patients. That same day, the Jews were ordered to pay another ransom in food products and cash. Hundreds of young Jews who feared the impending liquidation made arrangements to leave with their families for various labor camps, including camps in Prokocim and Plaszow.

In the evening, the Jews were ordered to gather the following morning near the Bogucice train station. On August 27, 1942, between 8,000 and 9,000 Jews were deported to the Belzec death camp. About 700 elderly people were taken by truck to Kozie Gorki and murdered.

One hundred and twenty-eight artisans and their families, about 280 people in all, remained in Wieliczka, along with about 600 young Jews. On August 28, 1942, the artisans and their families were sent to nearby Skawina*, where a liquidation operation was in process. Until August 29, the Germans continued to hunt down and murder Jews they found hiding in Wieliczka.

On August 30–31, 1942, the 600 youths were sent to the Plaszow and Rozwadow camps, near Stalowa Wola.

WIELOPOLE SKRZYŃSKIE

TOWNLET IN ROPCZYCE COUNTY, CRACOW DISTRICT, POLAND

During the war: General Gouvernement, Cracow District

Coordinates:
49°57' | 21°37'

When World War II broke out, about 550 Jews lived in Wielopole Skrzynskie, representing approximately half of the townlet's population. Most earned their livelihood from small-scale commerce and artisanship, especially in the garment industry. Zionist organizations were active in the community.

When the Germans occupied Wielopole Skrzynskie in early September 1939, dozens of young Jews fled from the townlet to the east. A number of the fugitives reached eastern Galicia, while others were exiled to the Soviet Union in the summer of 1940.

The Jews of the townlet were required to pay a monetary ransom and perform forced labor. Their freedom of movement was restricted. Contact was terminated between Jewish artisans and peddlers and those who lived in the surrounding localities, where they earned their livelihood.

In 1940, a public soup kitchen supported by JSS was established, and material help was given to the needy. In late 1940 and 1941, dozens of Wielopole Skrzynskie's Jews were abducted and sent to the labor camp in Pustkow. The Debica* Gestapo plundered Jewish property in the townlet with impunity.

In the spring of 1942, the Jews were forbidden to live in certain areas in the townlet and were forced to move into a number of narrow streets. The ghetto was not closed, but its inhabitants' freedom of movement was severely restricted.

On June 26, 1942, the Jewish inhabitants of Wielopole Skrzynskie were deported to the ghetto in Ropczyce*. About fifty patients and elderly people were murdered on site.

WIELUŃ

COUNTY SEAT, ŁÓDŹ DISTRICT, POLAND

During the war: Wartheland

Coordinates:
51°13' | 18°33'

Approximately 4,200 Jews lived in Wielun on the eve of the war. Most were artisans who maintained a trade association of their own. Several Jewish townspeople worked in transport and built a bus line between Wielun and Lodz*. The community established mutual-aid institutions, some of which received municipal funding. Jewish schools included Hadarim, a Mizrachi girls' high school, a Beit Yaakov girls' school, and primary schools. The Jewish library also served as a cultural center.

At the end of the 1930s, the antisemitic climate in Wielun intensified with stone-throwing incidents and the threat of pogroms.

On September 1, 1939, the first day of World War II, Wielun was heavily bombarded and many residents were killed. Following the German occupation of the town later that month, Jewish refugees arrived and were lodged in the Beit Midrash. In November 1939, several hundred Jews and Poles—most of them members of the intelligentsia—were arrested in the town and sent to the Radogoszcz prison near Lodz. The Germans also conducted a series of executions. Many Jews were conscripted for forced labor; one of their tasks was to build a swimming pool for the Germans using tombstones from the Jewish cemetery, which the Germans had destroyed.

In 1940, most of the 4,000 Jews in Wielun were concentrated in an area that while unfenced, was designated as a ghetto; there were Jews who continued to live outside its perimeters. The Jews enjoyed relative freedom of movement in the town, making it easier for them to obtain food. A Judenrat was established in

Wielun, 1942
Public hanging of nine Jews accused of forbidden kosher slaughter, in front of all of the ghetto's inhabitants (YV)

Wielun under a man named Lipshitz. Most residents worked outside the ghetto, and Jews were frequently assigned to service in labor camps in Germany.

The isolation of the Jews of Wielun became more acute in the spring of 1941; by then, all of the town's Polish residents had been deported, with Germans settling in their homes. The situation deteriorated further in early 1942. On January 6, the Germans selected ten ghetto inhabitants at random and hanged them publicly.

The deportation of the Jews of Wielun began in April 1942, when 2,000 Jews were sent from the ghetto to an unknown destination. The chairman of the Judenrat, Lipshitz, was murdered about two months later. As the final liquidation of the ghetto drew near, Jews from the nearby town of Praszka* were brought in. The liquidation took place on August 22–23, 1942, under the command of Gestapo officers Alfred Grossmann, Albert Richter, and others. It began with the murder of patients at the hospital. The rest of the Jews were ordered to report to the town square, and from there were taken to the local church and held for four days. Afterwards, members of the Lodz ghetto administration, under the command of Hans Biebow, conducted a selection for forced labor. Those whom Biebow did not select were murdered in Chelmno.

WIERUSZÓW

TOWNLET IN WIELUŃ COUNTY, ŁÓDŹ DISTRICT, POLAND

During the war: Wartheland

Coordinates:
51°17' | 18°10'

During the 1930s, about 2,400 Jews lived in Wieruszow. Most were petty merchants and artisans who belonged to Jewish associations affiliated with their trades. Zionist parties, the Communists, and Agudath Israel were all active in the community. There was a Beit Yaakov girls' school and a Yeshiva named Sfatei Tsedek. Zionist youth organizations held evening classes in Hebrew.

Many Jews left Wieruszow when the war broke out, but some returned after the townlet was occupied, bringing the Jewish population to 1,700. German occupiers murdered several dozen Jews on September 2–3, 1939, and began a campaign of dispossession. In early November 1939, many members of the Jewish and Polish intelligentsia, including officers of the community, were arrested and sent to the prison in Radogoszcz, near Lodz*. A Judenrat headed by Yosel Jedvab was appointed, and charged with preparing lists of the population and supplying people for forced labor. Punitive taxes were imposed.

In the spring of 1941, the Germans began to deport Jews to labor camps in the Poznan area using the lists drawn up by the Judenrat. The population of Jewish men in the townlet dropped considerably owing to deportations and escapes. The last large deportation to the camps in the Poznan area took place in the spring of 1942.

The Wieruszow ghetto was established in 1941 in a sealed and severely cramped area surrounded by barbed wire. The Judenrat established a Jewish Order Service to guard the ghetto and prevent escapes. Only Jews equipped with special skills useful to the Germans were allowed to live on the Polish side of the townlet. Some ghetto inhabitants were employed outside the ghetto and were thus able to obtain food illegally. Those who remained in the ghetto suffered from malnutrition. Congestion in the ghetto increased steadily both from new arrivals—refugees and deportees—and the reduction of the ghetto area to make room for "Aryan" Germans who were brought to the townlet. The ghetto population stood at about 2,000.

The Wieruszow ghetto was liquidated on August 21–23, 1942, by German police and an SS unit, aided by local Germans and Latvian collaborators. At the beginning of the operation, healthy males were seized and sent to labor camps in the Poznan area. The following day, the remaining inhabitants of the ghetto were concentrated in a church outside of it and at the Jewish ritual bath. A selection was performed: the Germans killed 107 Jews and took a few men and women to the Lodz ghetto. The Jews who remained were later trucked to Chelmno, where they were murdered.

WIERZBNIK-STARACHOWICE

COUNTY SEAT, KIELCE DISTRICT, POLAND

During the war: General Gouvernement, Radom District

Coordinates:
51°03' | 21°05'

In the interwar period, the distance between the two parts of the townlet, Wierzbnik and Starachowice, was two to three kilometers. About 2,200 Jews lived in Wierzbnik, representing more than one-third of the townlet's population. The Jews earned their livelihood from small-scale commerce, peddling, and artisanship as well as from involvement in the wood and metal industries. The townlet had three Jewish banks, a free-loan society, and the traditional charity institutions.

Most of the Zionist parties and youth movements, as well as the Bund, had active chapters in the town. Wierzbnik-Starachowice had a Tarbut elementary school, a Beit Yaakov school for girls, three Jewish public libraries, and two sports unions, one Zionist and the other, Bundist.

The Germans occupied Wierzbnik-Starachowice on September 9, 1939, and immediately instigated a regime of forced labor and persecution. They burned down the synagogue. In the first months of the war, about 500 Jewish refugees from Lodz* arrived in the townlet, in addition to hundreds from Pomerania, in western Poland. In October 1939, the Germans began to operate an ammunition factory that had been established in Starachowice in 1935 by the Poles but now belonged to the Reichswerke Hermann Goering firm.

On November 23, 1939, a Judenrat was established, headed by Minzberg. Its members were composed of the previous community council, along with a fifteen-member Jewish Order Service. The employment bureau was headed by a Jewish man named Tentser. The Judenrat was subordinate to the SIPO command in Radom* under the command of Hans Sultau. The Judenrat was ordered to collect ransom money and provide 300 to 400 forced laborers every day.

In early 1940, hundreds of Jews were arrested and held for one month in the Radom jail. During this period, the townlet's Jews were ordered to wear a white armband emblazoned with a blue Star-of-David.

On April 2, 1940, the Jews of Wierzbnik-Starachowice were transferred to a closed ghetto surrounded by a number of alleys in the area of the Wierzbnik marketplace. Severe overcrowding and a meager food supply forced many to sell their personal possessions to survive. The Jews were placed under curfew from nine o'clock at night until five o'clock the following morning and were permitted to leave the ghetto only with a special permit. The Judenrat maintained a public soup kitchen in the ghetto, supported by funds from the JSS in Cracow*. In 1940, some 7,000 people worked in the various factories operated by the Germans in Starachowice, among them about 300 Jews. By May 1941, the Jewish population in the ghetto stood at approximately 3,600.

When in 1942, the deportations from the Radom District began, the ghetto was inundated with Jewish refugees who hoped to save themselves from deportation by working in Starachowice's factories. About 2,000 Jews were employed in the factories at the time.

The Wierzbnik-Starachowice ghetto was liquidated on October 27, 1942, when some 2,000 Jews were brutally driven out and deported to the Treblinka death camp. Most of those who remained were sent to two labor camps, Strelnica and Majowka, which were newly established in the area. About twelve Jews discovered in hiding were murdered during the operation, while approximately thirty Jews were left behind to collect the deportees' belongings.

WIŚLICA

TOWNLET IN PIŃCZÓW COUNTY, KIELCE DISTRICT, POLAND

During the war: General Gouvernement, Radom District

Coordinates:
50°21' | 20°41'

Shortly before World War II, about 1,400 Jews lived in Wislica. Most earned a living from commerce and industry; many had merchandise warehouses, and hundreds worked in plaster and sock factories. The community boasted a Jewish saving-and-loan association and traditional charitable and welfare institutions as well as branches of Zionist political parties and Agudath Israel. Many Jews in Wislica, particularly the youths, left the townlet during the interwar period in search of a better living.

When World War II began, many Jewish townspeople fled to the Soviet-controlled zone in the east of Poland, where a number of people remained until the end of the war. On September 8, 1939, the Germans occupied Wislica and began to conscript Jews for forced labor. The synagogue was torched. In October, the Germans took ten hostages and ordered the community to pay a ransom for their release. Shortly afterwards, they established a Judenrat, many of whose members were former officials in the community; Yosef Flaum was appointed as chairman. The Germans instituted a requirement on December 1, 1939, that Jews wear a yellow star, subsequently replaced by a white armband with a blue Star-of-David.

In 1940, an influx of Jewish refugees from Warsaw*, Lodz*, Plock*, Radom*, and other locations in Poland boosted the Jewish population of Wislica to about 2,200 people. A relief committee and a soup kitchen were established to ease their plight. Smuggling enabled many Jews to survive trying conditions.

The Wislica ghetto was established in May 1941. During the summer, the Germans instructed the Judenrat to establish a Jewish Order Service. In the winter of 1941/42, the Jews were ordered to surrender their furs. Many died while performing forced labor outside of the townlet owing to exceedingly strenuous working conditions and severe cold. Epidemic typhus also claimed many casualties as refugees relentlessly poured in, even during mid-winter. During the epidemic, a Jewish hospital was set up with a staff of two doctors. The Germans dispossessed the ghetto population and demanded that men remove their beards.

On October 3, 1942, German gendarmes and Polish policemen surrounded the townlet and forced the Jews to gather in the market square. That day, 2,200 Jewish townspeople were removed in wagons to Pinczow* and on to Jedrzejow*. Many escaped during the roundup, and about 200 fled during the deportation.

WIŚNIOWIEC

TOWNLET IN KRZEMIENIEC COUNTY, VOLHYNIA DISTRICT, POLAND
(After World War II in the USSR/Ukraine; Ukrainian: **Vyshnivets'**; Russian: **Vishnevets**)

During the war:
Reichskommissariat Ukraine

Coordinates:
49°54' | 25°45'

During the interwar years, there were about 3,000 Jews living in Wisniowiec, more than half of the townlet's total population. They engaged in crafts, trade (mainly in agricultural produce), and petty industry (chiefly in clothing and food). Jews also owned flour mills and manufactured edible oil. They ran a Jewish "people's bank" and mutual-aid organizations. Wisniowiec boasted a private school where Yiddish and a little Hebrew were taught, a Hebrew-language Tarbut kindergarten and primary school, a Talmud Torah, and a Yeshiva. Only the Tarbut school, however, continued to operate after the 1920s. Zionist youth movements that were active in Wisniowiec also ran a Hebrew library and culture and sports groups.

The Soviets took control of Wisniowiec in September 1939 and exiled Zionist activists and affluent Jews to Siberia.

The Germans occupied Wisniowiec on July 2, 1941. Local Ukrainians plundered Jewish property and attacked Jews. Thirty-five hostages were killed, and by the end of the month hundreds of Jews had been murdered.

On September 4, 1941, a total of 146 Jews were murdered in Wisniowiec. On March 16, 1942, a sealed ghetto was established and placed under Ukrainian police guard. Jews from nearby Wyszogrodek and villages in the vicinity were brought to the ghetto, raising its population to roughly 3,500. Dozens of Jews starved to death. A Judenrat was established, chaired by a German-speaking refugee from Lodz*.

The ghetto was liquidated in August 1942. On August 8, Ukrainian policemen fired on the ghetto, killing dozens of inhabitants. On August 11, altogether 2,669 Jews, mostly women and children, were murdered outside the townlet. The manhunt for and murder of fugitives continued until August 22. A few of the young Jews who escaped from Wisniowiec reached the ghettos of Zborow* and Zbaraz* in Galicia.

WISZNICE

TOWNLET IN WŁODAWA COUNTY, LUBLIN DISTRICT, POLAND

During the war: General Gouvernement, Lublin District

Coordinates:
51°48' | 23°13'

During the interwar period, there were approximately 1,100 Jews in Wisznice, more than half the population of the townlet. Most were petty merchants and artisans, chiefly in the clothing industry. Zionist parties, the Bund, and Agudath Israel (which was dominated by Gerrer Hasidim) were active there.

The Germans occupied Wisznice in early October 1939. Before the end of that year, Jews were required to wear a yellow badge; it was later replaced by a white Star-of-David armband. The community was also forced to remit large ransoms. Most wealthy Jews fled to other cities and towns. The Wisznice Judenrat was appointed in November 1939 and the ghetto was established in late 1940.

Jewish refugees from Mlawa* reached Wisznice in December 1940. The overcrowding was so great that the Germans allowed some Jews to live outside the ghetto. On March 16, 1941, Jewish refugees from Cracow* were brought to the ghetto. On January 23–29, 1941, under the orders of the German Lublin District governor, Kalmar, 150 Jews from nearby localities were deported to Wisznice. About 20 of them died of starvation and cold on the day of their arrival. Epidemic typhus spread through the ghetto.

In late September 1942, about 1,000 Jews were deported from Wisznice to the Miedzyrzec Podlaski* ghetto. In an uprising that broke out during the deportation, young Jews who had secretly obtained weapons attacked the German gendarmes who oversaw the roundup. There were casualties on both sides, and many Jews managed to escape. Some of the escapees were caught in German manhunts.

Wisznice, 1942
Group of Jews near the entry gate to the ghetto. Inscription on the sign: "Jewish quarter, entry to non-Jews forbidden." (YV)

On October 27, 1942, Jews from Wisznice who had reached the Miedzyrzec Podlaski ghetto were deported to the Treblinka death camp, along with Jews in the vicinity.

The last Jews in Wisznice, some 120 people, were murdered on November 17, 1942.

WISZNIEW

TOWNLET IN WOŁOŻYN COUNTY, NOWOGRÓDEK DISTRICT, POLAND
(After World War II in the USSR/Belarus; Belarussian: **Vishneu**; Russian: **Vishnevo**)

During the war:
Reichskommissariat Ostland

Coordinates:
54°08' | 26°14'

About 930 Jews lived in Wiszniew in the interwar period, representing approximately 80 percent of the townlet's population. Most earned their livelihood from artisanship, commerce, small industry, woodworking, and peddling. Jewish parties were active in Wiszniew, including the Zionist movements and the Bund. The townlet also had Jewish educational, religious, and cultural institutions, including study halls and a Tarbut Hebrew school.

In September 1939, after World War II broke out, Jewish refugees thronged to Wiszniew from the German-occupied areas of Poland. The Red Army entered Wiszniew on September 17, 1939, and following Soviet occupation, privately owned shops were nationalized or closed and cooperatives were formed. The schools were converted to Soviet schools, and all political activity other than that of the Communist party was outlawed. The Germans occupied Wiszniew on June 27, 1941, and the German Wehrmacht, which controlled the area, immediately set up a local police force. The force turned over to the Germans all of the people who had held public positions during the Soviet period, including a number of Jews, and shot them to death. The Jews of Wiszniew were then rounded up; following a night of cruel terrorization and abuse, the women and children were sent home. The men were sent every day for the subsequent three weeks to perform forced labor. In late July 1941, the Germans appointed a Judenrat headed by Gedalia Podrzhebski. A few days later, an SS unit that set up camp in the townlet shot and murdered thirty-eight of its young Jews, with the help of the local police. This act was carried out despite the Judenrat head's pleas and offers of bribes.

In September 1941, the Judenrat was given two hours' notice to evacuate the Jews from their homes. They were moved, over 1,000 in number, to a ghetto situated in a narrow street near the synagogue. Although the ghetto was fenced in and guards were stationed to watch over it, Jews nevertheless risked their lives to go to nearby villages where they were able to obtain small quantities of food.

Growing numbers of Jews were seized for forced labor. Eighty men were sent to the Krasne labor camp, while others were sent to perform hard labor in the area of Wiszniew, among them children aged twelve, women, and young girls. The inhabitants of the ghetto maintained contact with Jews from other townlets through letters carried by non-Jewish couriers, and thus learned of the operations carried out in other places.

On the night of September 22, 1942, the Germans encircled the ghetto and with the help of the local police shot the elderly and ill in their dwellings. The rest of the Wiszniew ghetto's Jews were led first to the synagogue courtyard and then, a few hours later, in the direction of the village of Wistowice; they were shot to death along the way. More than 1,000 of the Wiszniew ghetto's Jews perished that day. Only a small number managed to escape during the operation; several joined the Chapayev Soviet partisan unit that was active in the Naliboki forests.

WŁOCŁAWEK

COUNTY SEAT, WARSAW DISTRICT, POLAND

During the war: Wartheland

Coordinates:
52°39' | 19°05'

In the early 1930s, there were about 10,200 Jews living in Wloclawek, representing roughly 20 percent of the town's population. They earned their livelihood mainly from commerce and artisanship, while several owned factories. Wloclawek had a community council with twelve members; various Zionist parties and youth movements held ongoing activities. The Jewish community had welfare institutions and a hospital. Jewish schools included a high school, elementary schools, and Yeshivot. Wloclawek also had public libraries.

On September 14, 1939, the Germans occupied Wloclawek and immediately began to plunder Jewish-owned property and terrorize and abuse Jewish inhabitants. On September 24, 1939, SS men burned down synagogues as well as the prayer house of the Gerrer Hasidim. The Germans accused the Jews of setting the fires and took 800 Jews hostage, demanding a ransom of 100,000 zlotys from the Jewish community of Wloclawek for their release. Several days later, another 200,000 zlotys was demanded, and one week later, yet another 250,000 zlotys. The German administration in Wloclawek was headed by Hans Kramer together with his deputy, Max Dunkhorst, a Nazi agent who had worked as a teacher in the Jewish high school.

On September 25, 1939, the Jews were ordered to wear a yellow badge and report for forced labor. Many of the city's Jews left for Warsaw*, Kutno*, and other localities. Young Jews left for areas under Soviet control.

In late 1939, Wloclawek was annexed to the Third Reich, and the Germans changed its name to Leslau. On December 1, 1939, thousands of the town's Jews were deported to Orzechow; on December 15, to Wloszczowa* and Zamosc*; and on February 15, 1940, to Tarnow*. Most of the deportees perished in the extermination camps.

Following these transports, some 4,000 Jews remained in Wloclawek. In late October 1940, a ghetto was established in a neglected area of the town, and its Polish residents were replaced with Jews. On November 9, 1940, the ghetto was encircled by a barbed-wire fence and SS guards were placed in charge of watching the ghetto. The Judenrat was given the task of maintaining internal order. Early on, non-Jews were permitted to enter the ghetto. Within a short time,

Left: **Wloclawek**
Entrance to the ghetto.
Inscription on the sign: "Jewish living area, entrance forbidden."
(YV)

Right: **Wloclawek, April 27, 1942**
Deportation of last Jews remaining in the ghetto to the Chelmno death camp (YV)

starvation in the ghetto rose. A public soup kitchen was organized for the poor and hungry. Young people organized cultural activities.

On June 26, 1941, the Jews were assigned to forced labor, mainly in the Poznan District. On September 26 and October 31, 1941, altogether 920 Jews, mostly children, women, and the elderly, were deported from Wloclawek to the Lodz* ghetto.

On November 6, 1941, the ghetto was completely sealed off. Jews risked their lives in attempts to obtain food from Poles. Those caught smuggling food were summarily shot. Expert tailors and shoemakers worked for German companies outside the ghetto. The main cultural activities in the ghetto were concentrated in a building near the cemetery that had previously served to purify the dead prior to burial; the building also housed a public soup kitchen and served as a site for political meetings. In the spring of 1942, the Germans began to liquidate the ghetto. On April 24, 1942, about 400 men were sent to labor camps in Kobylepole and other places in the Poznan District, where many perished. The ghetto was finally liquidated on April 27, 1942, when children, women, and elderly people were loaded onto trucks and transported to the Chelmno death camp.

WŁODAWA

COUNTY SEAT, LUBLIN DISTRICT, POLAND

During the war: General Gouvernement, Lublin District

Coordinates:
51°48' | 23°13'

Before World War II, there were about 6,500 Jews in Wlodawa, about two-thirds of the town's population. Most were petty merchants and artisans, chiefly tailors and shoemakers. Some owned factories, print shops, and even farms close to the town. There were two Jewish savings-and-loan associations, a free-loan society, and a chapter of TOZ. The Bund, Agudath Israel (comprised mostly of Gerrer Hasidim) and various Zionist parties were active in the town. The parties ran youth movements, libraries, and sports associations. The town also had a chapter of the ORT school system, a Tarbut Hebrew-language primary school, and two Agudath Israel schools.

The Germans occupied Wlodawa on September 18, 1939. Many young people fled eastward across the Bug River. The Jews were segregated from the other townspeople and, several weeks later, were ordered to wear a white armband with the letter *J* on it. The letter was later replaced by a yellow Star-of-David affixed to their clothing. Their movements were restricted, and the community was forced to remit a steep ransom.

By early 1940, all Jewish businesses had been expropriated. On April 29, 1940, a twelve-member Judenrat headed by Sommer was established. A sixty-member Jewish Order Service was set up. The Judenrat was made responsible for conscripting Jews for forced labor.

On January 17, 1941, the Jews of Wlodawa were moved into a ghetto where the Judenrat opened a soup kitchen and an orphanage. The Germans designated Wlodawa as a regional center for Jews in the area and removed Jews from nearby towns and villages into its ghetto. In March 1941, from all over Poland 1,014 deportees were brought to the ghetto, where lethal epidemics erupted. In early 1942, forty young people from Wlodawa and others from nearby towns were sent to Sobibor to build the death camp there. In March–April 1942, brought to the ghetto were 800 Jews from Mielec* and 1,000 deportees from Vienna.

The first operations took place on May 23–24, 1942. Ukrainian policemen, SS men, and a company of German gendarmes, aided by the Jewish Order Service, deported some 1,300 Jews from the Wlodawa ghetto to Sobibor in freight cars. The first to be deported were the refugees from Vienna, the orphanage children, the ill, the disabled, and the poor. Dozens of Jews were murdered on the spot. After the operation, Jews from Siedliszcze and other places were brought to Wlodawa. On October 24–25 and November 6–7, 1942, the remaining 5,400 Jews in the Wlodawa ghetto (both locals and refugees) were deported to Sobibor. Before and during every roundup a few Jewish individuals and families managed to hide or escape to the forests.

After the November operation, Friedrich Wilhelm Krueger, SS and Police Chief in the General Gouvernement, announced the re-establishment of the Wlodawa ghetto, promising that the Jews would now be safe. Some 500 Jews who had remained in the area returned to the ghetto and worked at the Wlodawa labor camp.

In late April 1943, the rebuilt ghetto was liquidated, and its inhabitants were sent to Sobibor. A few who escaped joined partisans of the Armia Ludowa (Polish People's Army) who operated in the area.

Wlodawa, 1942
Rachel Ejber with her niece and cousin in the ghetto street. Fajge Rajs in Rachel's arms, Hore Rajs next to them (USHMM, courtesy of Rachel Ejber Birnbaum)

WŁODZIMIERZ WOŁYŃSKI
(Ludmir)

COUNTY SEAT, VOLHYNIA DISTRICT, POLAND
(After World War II in the USSR/Ukraine; Ukrainian: **Volodymyr Volyns'kyi**; Russian: **Vladimir Volynskiy**)

During the war:
Reichskommissariat Ukraine

Coordinates:
50°51' | 24°20'

During the interwar years, there were about 10,500 Jews living in Wlodzimierz Wolynski, 40 percent of the town's population. They engaged in manufacturing and trade and owned, among other businesses, a sawmill, soap and candle factories, and flour mills. Many Jewish merchants, particularly those trading in agricultural produce, shipped their wares to central Poland and exported to foreign countries. Quite a number of Jews were artisans. The town had a Jewish savings-and-loan association and self-help organizations that received assistance from the JDC, as well as branches of TOZ and ORT. Chapters of Zionist political parties and youth movements, the Bund, and Agudath Israel were all active in the community. Jewish educational institutions in Wlodzimierz Wolynski included a kindergarten, a primary school, and a Tarbut agricultural high school, all of which taught in Hebrew, as well as a Talmud Torah and Yeshiva, a private Jewish high school, and ORT vocational schools. The community had a Jewish library, a sports association, and briefly published two weekly journals in Yiddish.

The Soviets took control of Wlodzimierz Wolynski on September 17, 1939. During the occupation, Jewish political parties and institutions were dismantled and economic enterprises were nationalized.

The Germans occupied Wlodzimierz Wolynski on June 23, 1941, at once abducting Jews for forced labor. On July 5, the 150 Jews who were kidnapped and disappeared were apparently murdered by the "South" Police Battalion. On July 7, a Judenrat was established in Wlodzimierz Wolynski under Rabbi Yaakov David Morgenstern, and a Jewish Order Service was set up under S. Kudish.

When Rabbi Morgenstern died several weeks later, a lawyer named Weiler took over as head of the Judenrat. When Weiler was abducted for forced labor in late August 1941, a dentist named Baradach was appointed in his stead. From late July 1941 to February 1942, more than 2,000 Jews were kidnapped, several under the pretext of forced labor, and murdered by Germans and Ukrainian police.

On April 13, 1942, all remaining Jews in Wlodzimierz Wolynski were concentrated in a ghetto, together with Jews from nearby localities. In May 1942, the ghetto was partitioned. About 14,000 skilled workers were housed in an area known as the "living ghetto," and the balance, some 4,000 in number, was placed in the area termed the "dead ghetto." The ghetto had a soup kitchen and hospital. Jews were assigned to manufacturing and farm labor, and the ghetto contained needlework and shoemaking workshops.

In August 1942, about 1,000 Jews were sent to an area near the village of Piatyden to dig trenches.

On September 1, 1942, the ghetto was surrounded by Germans and Ukrainians who launched a murder operation. The first killed were the 4,000 "unskilled" inhabitants of the ghetto, but by September 15 most skilled workers had also been murdered at the pits near Piatyden. Those who survived joined the people who emerged from hiding, and their numbers totaled 4,000. The ghetto was reestablished to hold these survivors. A man named Kudish was installed at the head of the Judenrat in the new ghetto, although most Jews objected to his modus operandi. The ghetto's Jews were released from the yellow badge requirement, and their main occupation was to sort Jewish property.

Most inhabitants of the reestablished ghetto were murdered on November 13, 1942, leaving just over 500 skilled workers. About 300 escapees and fugitives who tried to join the ghetto were murdered. The last Jews in Wlodzimierz Wolynski, including Kudish, were murdered on December 13, 1943.

There were several attempts to organize an uprising. According to one (dubious) report, a group of seventy-six Jewish officers in the Red Army who were in a POW camp near the town instigated an uprising with the help of the Jews of the Wlodzimierz Wolynski ghetto. They fashioned knives out of broken helmets but were discovered and executed.

Young Jews from the ghetto acquired weapons and attempted unsuccessfully to establish contact with Armia Krajova Polish partisans. A group left the ghetto in April 1943, and all but one died in combat.

WŁODZIMIERZEC

TOWNLET IN SARNY COUNTY, VOLHYNIA DISTRICT, POLAND
(After World War II in the USSR/Ukraine; Ukrainian: **Volodymyrets'**; Russian: **Vladimirets**)

During the war: Reichskommissariat Ukraine

Coordinates: 51°25' | 26°08'

During the interwar years, Wlodzimierzec had a Jewish population of 1,200, almost half of its total population. The townlet's Jews engaged in petty trade and crafts; some owned small food-processing plants. Jewish relief agencies operated with assistance from the JDC. Zionist parties and youth movements were active, and several Jews belonged to the underground Communist Party. Children were educated by private tutors who provided instruction in Hebrew and Jewish subjects, and, for a short time, a school that taught in Hebrew. The community also enjoyed the services of a Jewish library. After a great fire in 1934, many of Wlodzimierzec's Jews moved to large cities or left Poland for foreign destinations, including the Land of Israel.

The Soviets took control of Wlodzimierzec in September 1939, and nationalized private businesses. In late 1939, a Soviet Yiddish-language school was established in the townlet.

On June 26, 1941, a total of 500 young Jewish and non-Jewish men were conscripted for service in a Soviet battalion in Sarny*. The Germans captured the unit and murdered all of its Jewish members.

The Soviets left Wlodzimierzec on June 29, 1941, and the Germans moved in four days later. During the interim, Ukrainians murdered two Jews and dispossessed many others.

After they occupied Wlodzimierzec on July 3, 1941, the Germans compelled the Jews to establish a Judenrat under Yakov Eisenberg, to wear a Star-of-David armband, to remit ransoms in goods and cash, and to perform forced labor in and near the townlet.

In April 1942, an open ghetto was established in Wlodzimierzec. Its population, including Jews from villages in the vicinity, totaled about 3,000. A soup kitchen was established in the ghetto.

Before the ghetto was liquidated, a group of young Jews approached the Judenrat with their proposed strategy of setting the ghetto on fire; the Judenrat rejected the plan. Ukrainian officials offered to rescue the head of the Judenrat along with his family but he declined, saying that he wished to die with his community.

The ghetto was liquidated in late August 1942. One source documents that on August 28, the Jews of Wlodzimierzec were rounded up, removed from the townlet, and shot to death. According to another source, on August 26 the townlet's inhabitants were brought to Sarny, where they were executed together with the county's Jews on August 27–28. Hundreds escaped during the roundup and the march, but many were captured and murdered in the following days, including the community's rabbi. Several Ukrainian Baptists and Polish villagers assisted those who were not captured. Young escapees joined the Soviet and Polish-Soviet partisans.

WŁOSZCZOWA

COUNTY SEAT, KIELCE DISTRICT, POLAND

During the war: General Gouvernement, Radom District

Coordinates:
50°52' | 19°58'

Before World War II, about 2,700 Jews lived in Wloszczowa, accounting for approximately half of the townlet's population. Their main sources of livelihood were petty trade and skilled crafts. The community boasted three savings-and-loan associations, a free-loan fund, assorted caregiving and welfare societies, and several Jewish schools and sports groups. Political institutions active in the community included chapters of Zionist and pioneering parties, the Bund, and Agudath Israel.

The Germans occupied Wloszczowa in the first week of September 1939. Immediately they required Jewish residents to wear a Star-of-David armband, compelled the community to pay ransoms, restricted Jews' freedom of movement, and abducted Jews for forced labor. Thousands of refugees from nearby localities flowed into the townlet. In late September and early October 1939, the Germans transferred about 300 Jews from Szczekociny* to Wloszczowa. Hundreds of deportees from Lodz* and about 200 Jews from Poznan arrived later that year.

The Wloszczowa Judenrat was evidently established during the first weeks of the occupation. Most of its membership was drawn from the most recent community committee, and the chairman of the Judenrat, Landau, had chaired the community. A Jewish Order Service was set up as well.

Epidemic typhus broke out among the refugees in late 1939. Within a few days, by order of the German authorities, a hospital was established. Later, a clinic was set up as well.

During 1940, the JDC office in Warsaw* sent relief until the Warsaw ghetto was established. TOZ assisted with medicines. In 1941/42, the JSS also contributed to the community. The Judenrat welfare department started up a soup kitchen that provided hundreds of meals each day. In February 1940, a group of 440 Jews arrived from Wloclawek*.

The Wloszczowa ghetto was established on July 10, 1940, in a small slum quarter. Some 4,000 Jews were crowded into the already severely overpopulated

Wloszczowa, 1940
Jews waiting in the office of the Judenrat's social-welfare department (ŻIH)

ghetto. During the summer of 1940, hundreds of Jewish townspeople were sent to labor camps outside of the townlet. The Jewish Order Service was held responsible for this mobilization; the Germans abducted a member of the Service for every worker that failed to report. In February 1942, all able-bodied Jews in Wloszczowa were mobilized for labor in the townlet or in camps outside of it.

In April 1942, there were 4,277 Jews in and around Wloszczowa, including 1,654 refugees. In the summer of 1942, more than 150 Jews were sent to the Skarzysko-Kamienna labor camp. In September, some 600 Jews from surrounding villages were deported to Wloszczowa.

The Wloszczowa ghetto was liquidated on October 3, 1942, when the Germans deported about 5,000 Jews to Treblinka. Left behind and concentrated in a small labor camp were 180 Jews, primarily men, responsible for cleaning up the ghetto. On December 14, 1942, these remaining inhabitants were shot to death by German police.

WODZISŁAW

TOWNLET IN JĘDRZEJÓW COUNTY, KIELCE DISTRICT, POLAND

During the war: General Gouvernement, Radom District

Coordinates:
50°32' | 20°12'

At the outbreak of World War II, about 2,400 Jews lived in Wodzislaw, representing approximately one-third of the townlet's population. They earned their livelihood from petty commerce, peddling, and small-scale artisanship. Wodzislaw had chapters of Zionist parties and Agudath Israel, and a Jewish library. Most of the community's children studied in a state public school, a Hebrew school, and a Jewish school for girls.

On September 4, 1939, the Germans occupied Wodzislaw and immediately began to seize Jews for forced labor. In October 1939, the Germans appointed a Judenrat with twelve members, most of whom were previously involved in community affairs. The Judenrat recruited forced laborers in accordance with German demands.

In late 1939 and early 1940, the Germans confiscated Jewish-owned shops. In late 1940, the Jews' homes were seized as well. Refugees arrived in Wodzislaw during 1940 from Ciechocinek, Lodz*, and the Poznan region.

In June 1940, a ghetto comprising 200 buildings was established in the poorest neighborhood of Wodzislaw. The Jews of Jedrzejow* and Cracow* were deported to the ghetto, and its population grew to 4,000. On June 13, 1941, German police shot fifty Jews to death.

The Jews learned of an impending operation to be carried out sometime between September 16 and 25, and most prepared places to hide inside the ghetto. A group of young people fled to nearby localities. On Yom Kippur eve, September 20, 1942, SS soldiers and Polish policemen deported most of the inhabitants of the ghetto that were apprehended to the Treblinka death camp.

The remaining Jews of Wodzislaw were caught by November 1942, and nearly all were deported to Treblinka. About 300 were sent to the Sandomierz labor camp. The ghetto was torched and burned to the ground.

WOJSŁAWICE

TOWNLET IN CHEŁM COUNTY, LUBLIN DISTRICT, POLAND

During the war: General Gouvernement, Lublin District

Coordinates:
50°55' | 23°33'

During the interwar period, there were some 900 Jews in Wojslawice, about half the population of the townlet. Most were merchants and artisans. The community had self-help societies, free-loan funds, and vocational training courses. Zionist parties were active in Wojslawice and there was a chapter of Agudath Israel. There were Hadarim, Batei Midrash, and a Beit Yaakov school. Hebrew was taught in evening classes.

The Germans occupied Wojslawice on September 11, 1939, and immediately began abducting Jews for forced labor. Almost 100 of the inductees perished in the first few weeks. At the end of 1939, the Germans seized Jewish businesses, ordered the Jews to wear white armbands with a blue Star-of-David, appointed a five-member Judenrat headed by Einhorn, and instructed the newly established council to collect a ransom from the community. The Judenrat tried to help Jewish townspeople who were deported to remote labor camps by supplying them with food, clothing, and medicine.

Subsequently, a sealed ghetto was established in Wojslawice. At the end of 1941, the Germans deported Jews from nearby villages to the ghetto. In early 1942, fifty to sixty elderly people were deported from it to Wlodawa*, where they were added to a transport to the Sobibor death camp.

In October 1942, a total of 1,200 Jews, including Rabbi Yaakov Yitzhak Tsytrinbaum, were deported from the Wojslawice ghetto to Sobibor and, possibly, to other extermination camps. Jews who failed to report to the assembly point were rounded up and shot. Several Jews from Wojslawice reached the Chelm* ghetto, while others escaped to the forests and tried to join the partisans or find shelter among Poles. Most of the latter were murdered by the Poles or handed over to the Germans.

WOLANÓW

TOWNLET IN RADOM COUNTY, KIELCE DISTRICT, POLAND

During the war: General Gouvernement, Radom District

Coordinates:
51°23' | 20°58'

After World War I, there were about 350 Jews in Wolanow, more than half of the townlet's population. Many were food merchants; a smaller number were peddlers or skilled craftsmen. In the 1930s, Zionists were active in the community.

On September 5, 1939, the Germans entered Wolanow on their way to Radom*. On September 13, 1939, in the middle of Rosh Hashanah services, and for several days subsequent, the Germans, aided by Poles, seized Jews for forced labor and committed several murders.

In late 1939, a Judenrat was established in the townlet, headed by Moshe Barenholtz. A labor camp was set up there in 1940.

In the spring of 1941, dozens of Jewish families that had been expelled from Przytyk reached Wolanow, raising the Jewish population of the townlet to about 500 people. The Germans dissolved the first Judenrat and appointed Yaakov Berkovitz, a man in his twenties, to chair a new one.

In July 1941, the Jews of Wolanow were removed to a ghetto established in an open area, where they were authorized to build shacks for their housing needs.

In July 1942, the Germans deported most of the ghetto inhabitants to the ghetto in Szydlowiec*. Several dozen skilled and unskilled workers as well as the head of the Judenrat, Berkovitz, were left behind in Wolanow and joined the Jewish workers at the labor camp next to the townlet.

In September 1942, most of the women and children in the labor camp were deported to Treblinka. The camp was liquidated in August 1943.

WOLBROM

TOWNLET IN OLKUSZ COUNTY, KIELCE DISTRICT, POLAND

During the war: General Gouvernement, Cracow District

Coordinates:
50°24' | 19°46'

About 4,500 Jews lived in Wolbrom in the interwar period, representing more than half of the townlet's population. Most earned their livelihood from trade in agricultural produce, small artisanship, and industry. Their economic activity was aided by trade unions, a Jewish cooperative bank, and a free-loan society assisted by the JDC. Chapters of Zionist parties, Agudath Israel, and the Bund were active in Wolbrom. The townlet had libraries and a drama circle. Wolbrom's Jewish children attended traditional Hadarim and a Talmud Torah, and a state elementary school; a number of the girls attended a Beit Yaakov school.

About 5,000 Jews were living in Wolbrom when the Germans occupied the townlet on September 5, 1939. Young Jews fled to nearby localities and to the areas under Soviet control, but most returned to the townlet after several weeks. One of the first German decrees was to send the Jewish men to Zawiercie, where they worked at dismantling military posts and in a cement factory. In the first weeks following the occupation, the Jews of Wolbrom were placed under curfew and ordered to wear a white armband with a blue Star-of-David. Groups of Jews were assigned daily to forced labor. In September 1939, a Judenrat was appointed in Wolbrom, headed by Yekhiel Engelrad, who was deported a short time later to Auschwitz. Engelrad was succeeded by Moshe Aharon Volchinski, who served in that capacity until the Jewish community of Wolbrom was liquidated.

Wolbrom's proximity to a border-crossing accounted for the influx of numerous Jewish refugees that arrived in the townlet in late 1939 and early 1940 from nearby towns that had been annexed to the Third Reich. In the latter part of 1940, about 3,000 Jews deported from Cracow* arrived in Wolbrom. In October 1940, the Judenrat opened a public soup kitchen that distributed hundreds of meals daily. In 1941, a chapter of the JSS that contributed to funding the kitchen was established in Wolbrom.

In 1940/41, all of the children were vaccinated against smallpox by the Judenrat's public health department. In March 1941, a Jewish Order Service was established. In July 1941, at least 720 Jewish men were deported to various labor camps, including the Pustkow and Plaszow camps.

In late 1941 or in the spring of 1942 (testimonies vary regarding the date), a ghetto was established. Jewish shops and all furs owned by Jews were confiscated. Overcrowding in the ghetto was severe, and inhabitants suffered from an acute food shortage. In 1941/42 (according to various sources), a new gendarmerie commander who had arrived in Wolbrom, named Eduard Baumgarten, murdered dozens of Jews in the townlet.

In May 1942, hundreds of men were transferred from Wolbrom to labor camps near Cracow. In the latter part of that month, after the Jews of Cracow had been deported for extermination, the Germans arrested Jews of Wolbrom who had escaped from the labor camps and attempted to return to Wolbrom. They were taken to an unknown destination and murdered. In August 1942, about 200 Jews were brought to Wolbrom from smaller nearby localities.

The Wolbrom ghetto was liquidated in September 1942. On September 4, hundreds of Ukrainian and German policemen and Polish auxiliary forces surrounded the ghetto. On September 5, the elderly and ill Jews were rounded up in the Jewish cemetery, where they were murdered by German policemen, and the rest of Wolbrom's Jews were collected near the train station. The following day, 6,000 to 7,000 people in this group were deported to the Belzec death camp. Gendarmerie commander Baumgarten supervised the deportation.

On September 11, 1942, some 2,000 to 2,500 Jews who were being held in an open field were assigned to work in labor camps in Stalowa Wola, Rzeszow, Przemysl, and other camps, while others were brought to the Cracow ghetto. A number of the laborers escaped and returned to Wolbrom, where they were murdered by the Germans in late September 1942.

After the September 1942 operation, about 150 Jews remained in Wolbrom, among them members of the Judenrat and the Jewish Order Service and their families as well as Jews who had come out of hiding. They were put to work collecting and sorting the murdered Jews' belongings. Most of these remaining Jews were sent to Belzec following a final liquidation operation carried out on November 3, 1942. On the eve of the liquidation, a small number of Jews managed to escape to Bedzin* and Sosnowiec* or join the Polish underground.

WOŁKOWYSK

COUNTY SEAT, BIAŁYSTOK DISTRICT, POLAND
(After World War II in the USSR/Belarus; Belarussian: **Vaukavysk**; Russian: **Volkovysk**)

During the war: Bezirk Białystok

Coordinates:
53°10' | 24°28'

When World War II broke out, about 8,000 Jews lived in Wolkowysk, representing approximately one-third of the town's population. Most earned their livelihood from commerce, peddling, and artisanship. The Jewish community maintained cooperative savings and loan associations and local welfare organizations as well as a pharmacy, hospital, and Jewish orphanage. Jewish political organizations and youth movements, including Zionist parties, the Bund, and Agudath Israel held a range of activities. Wolkowysk also boasted Jewish educational, religious, and cultural institutions, including a Yeshiva and a Jewish theater troupe.

After the Red Army occupied Wolkowysk on September 18, 1939, privately owned shops and businesses were nationalized or closed, cooperatives were opened, Yiddish became the language of instruction in schools, and Jewish parties and organizations were abolished. During this period, Jewish refugees inundated the town, arriving from German-occupied areas of Poland.

On June 28, 1941, the Germans occupied Wolkowysk, following heavy bombing that destroyed the Jewish quarter; they immediately set about murdering Jews. Jewish Communist activists were handed over to the Germans and executed. The Jews were required to wear a yellow badge and to mark their homes, their freedom of movement was restricted, and they were seized for forced labor. At German orders a Judenrat was established, headed by Dr. Yitzhak Weinberg, along with a Jewish Order Service headed by M. Khantov.

In the spring of 1942, a group of young Jews made contact with a Soviet partisan unit in the nearby forest. Several youths managed to escape and joined the partisans. On October 14, 1942, twenty-seven Jewish doctors from Wolkowysk were executed in the forest near Izabelin after they were caught providing medical treatment to partisans. Among the doctors was the Judenrat head, Dr. Weinberg. He was replaced by his deputy, Noakh Fuks.

In the autumn of 1942, a fenced-in ghetto was set up along two narrow streets, concentrating the Jews of Wolkowysk together with Jews from surrounding localities; the ghetto was severly overcrowded.

On November 2, 1942, the Jews were moved to a bunker camp outside the town, where some 20,000 Jews from the entire area were concentrated. All elderly and ill Jews who had difficulty walking were executed in Wolkowysk. Conditions in the camp were harsh, and the mortality rate was high. Most of the Jews were deported within a few weeks to the Treblinka death camp; the rest worked in the camp until they, too, were deported on January 26, 1943, to Auschwitz-Birkenau.

WOŁOMIN-SOSNOWKA

TOWNLET IN RADZYMIN COUNTY, WARSAW DISTRICT, POLAND

During the war: General Gouvernement, Warsaw District

Coordinates:
52°21' | 21°15'

About 3,080 Jews lived in Wolomin in the interwar period, representing approximately half of the townlet's population. Although the townlet's Jews earned their livelihood mainly from commerce and artisanship, several toiled as laborers while others were factory owners. During this period, the social and cultural organization and activities of Jewish Wolomin gained momentum, especially the Zionist parties and youth movements. Religious and educational institutions in the townlet included Hadarim, a Talmud Torah, and an elementary school.

On September 13, 1939, Wolomin was occupied by the German army. The Germans began immediately to plunder Jewish-owned property and terrorize the Jews. A number of Jews were seized for forced labor. In late 1939, the Jews were ordered to wear a yellow badge. Many of Wolomin's Jews fled to eastern Poland, which was under Soviet control. In November 1939, a Judenrat was established at German orders, headed by Yaakov Blumberg.

In November 1940, the Germans issued a decree ordering the establishment of a ghetto and a Jewish Order Service. The Jews were commanded to move to the village Sosnowka, where the ghetto was established. It contained two quarters. The members of the Judenrat, Jewish Order Service, and the affluent Jews resided in the more prestigious neighborhood. The second neighborhood was designated for the townlet's poorer Jews, who lived in seventy-six buildings that were exceedingly small and mostly wooden. At first, about 2,800 Jews lived in the ghetto, including some 600 refugees from the surrounding localities and various other places. Later, additional refugees arrived in the ghetto, which was open, enabling its inhabitants to barter with the local population.

A public soup kitchen was established in the ghetto, providing about 1,000 of Wolomin's Jews with hot meals. Also established were an orphanage for some sixty children, a sanitary department, a bread bakery, and a hospital run by Dr. Reznik and Dr. Fraik. Jews were employed in daily forced labor in the train station and on Polish farms. Hundreds of young Jews were sent to perform forced labor in Lipnik, Izabelin, and Wilanow, and another approximately 3,000 worked in the labor camp located on the estate of Graf Potocki.

In February 1941, the number of people imprisoned in the ghetto reached about 3,000, and living conditions grew steadily worse. In the spring of 1941, the ghetto was closed and encircled with a barbed-wire fence, and a number of Jews were murdered during attempts to smuggle in food. In several cases, the Judenrat was required to pay a ransom in order to free the smugglers. In the summer of 1942, news reached the ghetto regarding the deportation of the Jews of Warsaw* to the Treblinka death camp, and rumors spread regarding the impending liquidation of the Wolomin ghetto. Jews began to flee en masse from the ghetto, and those who were caught paid with their lives.

In early October 1942, the orphanage was liquidated, and the children were executed outside the village. The Wolomin ghetto itself was liquidated on October 4, 1942, when its inhabitants were deported to Radzymin*, and later to Treblinka, together with the local Jews.

WOŁOŻYN

**COUNTY SEAT,
NOWOGRÓDEK DISTRICT,
POLAND**
(After World War II in the USSR/Belarus; Belarussian: **Valozhyn**; Russian: **Volozhin**)

During the war:
Reichskommissariat Ostland

Coordinates:
54°05' | 26°32'

About 1,500 Jews were living in Wolozyn when World War II broke out, representing one-quarter of the townlet's population. They earned their livelihood mainly from commerce and artisanship; Jews also owned a number of large enterprises, including two hotels. The Wolozyn Jewish community was famous for its rabbis and for the Etz Chaim Yeshiva, which was founded in the early nineteenth century by Rabbi Chaim, a student of the Vilna Gaon, Rabbi Elyahu Ben Shlomo. The Yeshiva was also highly reputed outside of Poland. One of its most celebrated students was the poet Chaim Nachman Bialik. During the interwar period, various Jewish parties and youth movements were active in Wolozyn. The townlet also boasted a range of Jewish educational and cultural institutions, including a Tarbut Hebrew school and a Jewish library.

After the Soviets occupied Wolozyn on September 17, 1939, Jewish parties were abolished, privately owned shops were nationalized or closed, and cooperatives were formed. The schools taught in Yiddish according to a Soviet curriculum. Jewish refugees thronged to the townlet from German-occupied areas of Poland.

The Germans occupied Wolozyn on June 26, 1941, and twenty-five Jews were murdered the very same day. The local police force was manned by antisemites and subordinated to SS command. Stanislaw Turski, an activist of the antisemitic Endencja party, was appointed the new mayor. The following day, Turski ordered the execution of eight members of the Jewish intelligentsia. About two weeks after the occupation of the townlet, at German orders, a twelve-member Judenrat was established, headed by Yaakov Garber. The Jews were ordered to wear a yellow badge, became subject to numerous restrictions, and were seized for forced labor.

In August 1941, a fenced-in ghetto was established. The Jews of Wolozyn and of other localities—a total of about 3,500 people—were concentrated in fifty to sixty buildings under conditions of extreme overcrowding. Polish police guarded the gates of the ghetto, while the approximately thirty members of the Jewish Order Service maintained order within. Overcrowding, hunger, and poor sanitary conditions led to the outbreak of contagious diseases.

On November 4, 1941, the inhabitants of the ghetto were rounded up in the Wolozyn cinema house, and a number of Jewish men, including the head of the Judenrat, Yaakov Garber, were arrested and then shot to death outside of the townlet. After this operation, the Germans reduced the size of the ghetto, appointed a new Judenrat head, and ordered the Jews to pay a ransom. The murders and terrorization of Jews continued. In March 1942, SS men entered an apartment in the ghetto where prayers were being held and shot the worshippers.

On May 10, 1942, a German SIPO force under the command of Untersturmfuehrer Grabe, with the assistance of the local police force, encircled the ghetto. The Jews were rounded up in a single street and led to a large smithy, as the German and local force sat opposite for a meal; as they ate they periodically turned around and shot at the smithy. The Jews were held for an entire day without food or water, then separated into groups of men, women, and children and shot to death in a building near the Jewish cemetery. The Germans then set fire to the building containing the bodies.

A small number of Jews managed to escape or hide at the beginning of the operation, but most were caught during manhunts. About 1,500 Jews were murdered during this operation.

Some time after the May 1942 operation, the Germans decided to round up the remaining Jews from the area and invited the Jews hiding in the forests to return to the ghetto. A few hundred Jews responded to the call and were put up in the ghetto. Most were shot in an operation carried out on August 29, 1942, while several dozen youths once again fled to the forest. A number of Jews with required professions and their families remained in the ghetto until their murder in August 1943.

WORNIANY

TOWNLET IN VILNA COUNTY, VILNA DISTRICT, POLAND
(After World War II in the USSR/Belarus; Belarussian: **Varnyany**; Russian: **Vornyany**)

During the war: Reichskommissariat Ostland

Coordinates: 54°73' | 26°01'

In the interwar period, about 240 Jews lived in Worniany, representing more than two-thirds of the townlet's population. Most earned their livelihood from small commerce, shopkeeping, and artisanship. Worniany was occupied by the Soviets in the second half of September 1939.

Following the German invasion of the Soviet Union on June 22, 1941, the Soviets withdrew from Worniany, and for several days the townlet was free from command. During this period, pogroms were carried out against Jews, and one Jew was murdered, but a local police force eventually restored quiet.

When the Germans entered Worniany in late June 1941, they confiscated Jewish property. Jews were also terrorized and abused, and seized for forced labor.

In the autumn of 1941, the Jews of Worniany were concentrated in a fenced-in ghetto located along four narrow streets. A Judenrat was established, with Hershel Magid appointed as its head. After some time, Jewish refugees from a number of localities in Lithuania were brought to the Worniany ghetto. On October 18, 1941, the Germans rounded up all of the ghetto's inhabitants and arrested the local rabbi, Rabbi Mikhael Yitzhak Sova, and his son Avraham Sova, along with another fifteen young men. A bribe was paid to the Germans, who exchanged the rabbi and his son for two young men. The seventeen young men were shot, but several survivors managed to climb out of the pit. Following additional acts of terror and abuse, Hershel Magid, who feared for his life, appealed to the Germans; in return for a bribe, he received a permit to join workers in the forests. He was replaced by Yudel Weinstein. Youths who worked in the forests often bartered for food. In May 1942, men, women, and children above the age of twelve years worked outside the ghetto, leaving mostly the elderly, the ill, and the children inside the ghetto.

In April 1942, the townlet was annexed to the Reichskommissariat Ostland as part of the Vilna-land County. At the orders of the county commander Horst Wulff, the ghettos located within a fifty-kilometer-wide strip were liquidated, and their inhabitants were transferred into four central ghettos: Oszmiana*, Swieciany*, Soly*, and Michaliszki*. In August 1942, the Jews of the Worniany ghetto were deported to the Michaliszki ghetto, where they shared the fate of the local Jews.

WORONÓW

TOWNLET IN LIDA COUNTY, NOWOGRÓÓDEK DISTRICT, POLAND
(After World War II in the USSR/Belarus; Belarussian: **Voranava**; Russian: **Voronovo**)

During the war: Reichskommissariat Ostland

Coordinates: 54°08' | 25°19'

About 1,000 Jews were living in Woronow when World War II broke out, representing the majority of the townlet's population. Most earned their livelihood from artisanship and commerce. Various Jewish parties and youth movements were active in Woronow, including Zionist parties and the Bund. A number of Jews were members of the Communist party. The Jewish community also boasted a variety of educational and cultural institutions, including a public library and a *Torah Veda'at* Hebrew school.

The Red Army occupied Woronow in the second half of September 1939. During the Soviet occupation (1939–41) the Jewish parties were abolished, privately owned shops were nationalized or closed, and cooperatives were formed. The schools taught in Yiddish according to a Soviet curriculum.

On June 23, 1941, Woronow was occupied by the Germans. Decrees and restrictions were immediately imposed on the Jews. They were required to wear a yellow badge. A Judenrat was appointed whose main function was to recruit forced laborers for the Germans.

The Woronow ghetto was apparently established in July 1941. Forced labor and abuse continued unabated. During the time the Jews were in the ghetto, three mass executions of Jews were carried out by SS officer Werner and his assistants. In late 1941, the Germans arrested about 250 Jews based on lists of people who had fled from Vilna* to Woronow following an operation in their city; they were murdered by the Germans in the Zamkowy forest. In January 1942, Jews from a number of surrounding localities were brought to the Woronow ghetto, raising its population to about 3,000.

On May 11, 1942, a large-scale operation was carried out in the ghetto. German and Lithuanian forces that had entered Woronow several days earlier rounded up the Jews and confiscated their remaining valuables. They separated out between 600 and 700 people with required professions. The balance of the Jews, who according to German sources numbered 1,834 people, was shot to death outside of Woronow. Those who attempted to resist or who lagged behind were shot along the way.

The professionals were held for twelve days in abandoned houses in the ghetto. A few escaped and reached the partisans, while the rest were transferred on May 23, 1943 to the Lida* ghetto, and deported on in September 1943 to the Majdanek extermination camp.

WYŚMIERZYCE

TOWNLET IN THE RADOM COUNTY, KIELCE DISTRICT, POLAND

During the war: General Gouvernement, Radom District

Coordinates: 51°37' | 20°50'

In the interwar period, about 100 Jews lived in Wysmierzyce out of a total population of approximately 1,400. A Zionist association was established, whose members participated in Zionist activity in nearby Przytyk and Radom*.

When World War II broke out, Jewish refugees arrived in Wysmierzyce from western Poland and Radom. In the spring of 1941, they were joined by deportees from Przytyk, driving up the Jewish population of the townlet to about 500. In the early years of the occupation, the Jews continued to live in their own homes and work for a living. However, overcrowding led to epidemic typhus and a rise in the death toll.

The Wysmierzyce ghetto was established in the spring of 1942, in a large courtyard. The refugees who remained homeless lived in ditches that they dug in the ground. The inhabitants of the ghetto did not work and suffered increasingly from starvation.

In July 1942, with little warning, the Jews were ordered to evacuate the Wysmierzyce ghetto and were transferred to the Bialobrzegi* ghetto. In August 1942, they were deported together with the Jews of the Bialobrzegi ghetto to the Treblinka death camp.

WYSOCK

TOWNLET IN SARNY COUNTY, VOLHYNIA DISTRICT, POLAND
(After World War II in the USSR/Ukraine; Ukrainian: **Vysots'k**; Russian: **Vysotsk**)

During the war:
Reichskommissariat Ukraine

Coordinates:
51°44' | 26°39'

After World War I there were about 900 Jews living in Wysock, one-third of the total population. Their numbers evidently increased during the interwar period. The Jews of Wysock engaged in petty trade, peddling, crafts, and agriculture. The JDC provided the community with food and subsidized public kitchens. Until the late 1920s, a Talmud Torah and a Hebrew-language Tarbut school educated the Jewish children in Wysock. The Jewish community also had a Hebrew library and a drama group. Zionist parties and the Bund were active in Wysock, as were Jewish Communists, who operated underground. About 150 Jews from Wysock participated in Zionist training communes and later moved to the Land of Israel.

During the Soviet occupation (1939–41), the townlet became connected to the electrical system, its roads were paved, and new factories and offices were opened that offered Jews employment.

In early July 1941, many Jews left Wysock as the Soviet authorities evacuated the townlet, but only 100 survived until the war's end. The Ukrainians established an administration and an auxiliary police force in Wysock.

The Germans occupied the townlet on July 17, 1941. Soon afterwards they established a twelve-member Judenrat. The Jews were forced to remit a large ransom, were dispossessed of furs and large quantities of property, were required to wear a white armband with the word *Jude*, and were conscripted for forced labor. In late September 1941, the armband was replaced by a yellow badge.

The ghetto of Wysock, sealed in a high barbed-wire enclosure, was established on July 20, 1942. Its inhabitants comprised about 1,200 Jews from Wysock, roughly 170 from Horodek, and some 150 from villages in the vicinity—approximately 1,500 in all. Epidemics soon broke out in the ghetto, most commonly typhus.

The ghetto was liquidated on September 9, 1942. German police and gendarmes, commanded by SIPO-SD officers and assisted by Ukrainian auxiliary police, led the Jews to trenches some distance from the townlet, where they were murdered. About fifty Jews had escaped from the ghetto the previous evening, and additional Jews attempted to escape by swimming across the Horyn River during the murder operation. About 100 Jews managed to reach to the opposite bank, while others drowned or were shot in the water. The escapees went into hiding in the forests, where they were assisted by rural Poles, or joined Soviet partisan units.

WYSOKIE LITEWSKIE

TOWNLET IN BRZEŚĆ ON THE BUGIEM COUNTY, POLESYE DISTRICT, POLAND
(After World War II in the USSR/Belarus; Belarussian: **Vysokae**; Russian: **Vysokoe**)

During the war:
Reichskommissariat Ukraine

Coordinates:
52°22' | 23°22'

During the interwar period, about 2,000 Jews lived in Wysokie Litewskie, accounting for approximately 80 percent of the townlet's population. A number of the Jewish inhabitants engaged in trade and food manufacturing, while others were unionized trade workers. Zionist parties and the Bund were active in the townlet, and the community ran two Jewish schools and an orphanage.

The Germans occupied Wysokie Litewskie on June 22, 1941, and established a sealed ghetto. Groups of young Jews obtained arms and prepared to escape to the forests. When the ghetto was liquidated on November 2, 1942, many of the youths (some of whom were armed) fled to them.

WYSOKIE MAZOWIECKIE

COUNTY SEAT, BIAŁYSTOK DISTRICT, POLAND

During the war: Bezirk Białystok

Coordinates:
52°55 | 22°31'

About 1,900 Jews lived in Wysokie Mazowieckie in the interwar period, representing approximately 60 percent of the townlet's population. They earned their livelihood from small commerce and artisanship and were assisted by a cooperative bank and a merchants' bank. The community had the traditional charitable institutions. Jewish schools included an elementary school, a Talmud Torah, and a Yeshiva. Nearly all of the major Jewish parties and youth movements were represented in the townlet.

Units of the German army entered Wysokie Mazowieckie on September 10, 1939. The Germans began immediately to abuse and terrorize the Jews and set fire to houses in the townlet. On September 12, all of the townlet's men—about 1,000 Jews and Poles—were concentrated in a Catholic church. Two days later, several of the men were transferred to a labor camp in Zambrow*, while about 800 were sent to the Stahlbach camp in eastern Prussia.

On September 19, 1939, the townlet's Jews were ordered to head eastward to the area under Soviet control. On September 26, 1939, in accordance with the Molotov-Ribbentrop Pact, Wysokie Mazowieckie was handed over to Soviet control which lasted for one-and-a-half years. The Jewish prisoners in the labor camps were released and allowed to return to the townlet. In early 1941, about 1,100 Jews lived there. Many of the younger generation were recruited into the Red Army.

On June 23, 1941, Wysokie Mazowieckie was reoccupied by the Germans. Looting, forced labor, abuse, and murder became daily occurrences. In the early days of the German reoccupation, two Jews accused of Communism were executed. The townlet was set ablaze, and Jewish men were driven out to the surrounding villages and localities. In July 1941, a Judenrat with thirteen members was established, headed by Shmuel Zakimovich. At about the same time, Jews were ordered to wear a yellow badge.

On August 10, 1941, a ghetto was established along three streets in Wysokie Mazowieckie. The Christians whose houses happened to be inside the area of the ghetto were evicted and given Jewish homes. The ghetto was encircled with a barbed-wire fence; Polish guards were stationed at the entrance and Jewish policemen maintained order inside the ghetto.

Soon afterwards, hundreds of Jews evicted from their homes in surrounding localities were packed into the ghetto, and by the fall of 1941, its population stood at about 2,000 people.

The Judenrat supplied the Germans with 250 people each day to pave roads and cut down trees. The Jewish artisans worked in the villages around the townlet. Many youngsters had to work in the farms in exchange for food. A black market soon flourished between the ghetto inhabitants and the population of the "Arian" side.

In the fall of 1941, the situation in the ghetto deteriorated; smuggling of food products into the ghetto became extremely dangerous; incidents of destitution, starvation, and disease escalated. The head of the Judenrat, Alter Zeik, and his daughter Dr. Golda Zeik did their best to care for the ill and hungry. Hundreds of hot meals were distributed to the poor.

The liquidation of the ghetto began in early November 1942. A few days earlier, rumors had spread regarding the impending liquidation, prompting many Jews to flee. On November 2, 1942, German and Polish police encircled the ghetto. When large numbers of Jews gathered in the street, the head of the Judenrat attempted to calm them by assuring them that the transport was destined for Zambrow. Polish and German police rounded up the ill and murdered them in fields near the townlet. Three hundred wagons had been collected from farmers in the vicinity, and Jews were deported, without any possessions, from the ghetto and the surrounding localities. They were transferred to the transit camp in Zambrow, where the conditions were very harsh. When this camp was liquidated in January 1943, the Jews were transported to Auschwitz.

WYSZOGRÓD

TOWNLET IN PLOCK COUNTY, WARSAW DISTRICT, POLAND

During the war: Bezirk Zichenau

Coordinates: 52°23' | 20°12'

Before the war, about 2,700 to 2,800 Jews lived in Wyszogrod. They earned their livelihood from commerce and artisanship; several owned factories. A cooperative bank provided the Jews of the townlet with loans, and traditional welfare institutions did what they could to ease the hardships of the poor. The community had a variety of Zionist parties and youth movements. Its educational institutions included public schools, traditional Hadarim, and a Talmud Torah.

On September 3, 1939, the Jews of Wyszogrod fled from the German bombings, and the townlet was nearly emptied of Jews. Wyszogrod's mayor, Leib Gamakh, organized a civil guard to protect their property.

On September 9, 1939, Wyszogrod was occupied by the German army. On the second day of the occupation, Jews were seized for forced labor. After Warsaw* surrendered on September 27, 1939, most of Wyszogrod's Jews returned home. In October 1939, Wyszogrod was included in the Bezirk Zichenau and annexed to the Third Reich. A Judenrat was established in the early days of the occupation; it supplied the Germans with forced laborers. Wyszogrod also had a Jewish Order Service.

The Jews were ordered to wear a yellow badge. In December 1939, they were ordered to dismantle the townlet's synagogue building with their own hands, and in 1940, numerous other Jewish community buildings, both public and private, were destroyed, as was the Jewish cemetery.

In 1940, an open Jewish quarter was established in which about 2,500 Jews resided. On August 13 of that year, 120 Jews from Wyszogrod were designated for transfer to the labor camp established in Bielsk; after the Judenrat refused to draw up a list of workers, the Germans compiled their own list, which included a number of Judenrat members.

In 1941, the chairman of the Judenrat was Yitzhak Boll. On March 6, 1941, the Jews of Wyszogrod were rounded up in the marketplace. Following a selection, about 700 people were sent to the transit camp in Dzialdowo, including the rabbi of Wyszogrod, Rabbi Naftali Spivak. On March 12, 1941, they were transferred from the transit camp to Kielce*, and then to Slupia Nowa, where they were kept under extremely harsh conditions.

About 400 Jews returned to Wyszogrod. After the deportation, the ghetto was reduced in size, and on August 2, 1941, it was encircled by a barbed-wire fence and sealed.

In July 1941, between 120 and 180 Jews were taken to an unknown place by the Germans. In the summer of 1941, about seventy of Wyszogrod's Jews were put to work building a defense rampart, paving roads, and working in fields.

On November 29, 1941, the Jewish community of Wyszogrod was completely liquidated. About 600 of Wyszogrod's Jews were sent to Czerwinsk*. Some 1,200 were transferred to the Nowy Dwor* ghetto; from there, all were transported to Auschwitz in late 1942. According to a different testimony, the Jews of Wyszogrod who were sent to Czerwinsk were also eventually transferred to Nowy Dwor.

WYŻWA

TOWNLET IN KOWEL COUNTY, VOLHYNIA DISTRICT, POLAND
(After World War II in the USSR/Ukraine; Ukrainian, Russian: **Vyzhva**)

During the war:
Reichskommissariat Ukraine

Coordinates:
51°24' | 24°25'

During the interwar years, there were about 400 Jews living in Wyzwa, one-fifth of the total population. Most were artisans who lived in new parts of the townlet near the railroad station. Three Jews owned flour mills, and others were shoemakers, tailors, carpenters, or blacksmiths. A few were peddlers and petty merchants.

There is no information regarding the Jews of Wyzwa during the Soviet occupation (September 1939–June 1941).

The Germans occupied Wyzwa on June 27, 1941. The Ukrainian administration and police force that were established in the townlet began to dispossess Jews and, in a few cases, to murder them. Jews were ordered to wear an armband with a blue Star-of-David. Their livestock and many of their basic possessions were confiscated. They were placed under curfew from between seven o'clock in the evening and seven in the morning, and many were taken away for forced labor.

On August 5, 1941, on the road to Maciejow* 260 Jewish inhabitants of Wyzwa were murdered. In the summer of 1942, the townlet's remaining Jews and those in the villages in the vicinity were gathered in an open ghetto. In late August of that year, all were murdered. Shortly before the liquidation, ghetto residents set many buildings on fire. Dozens of Jews escaped but only a few survived.

Yalta, Crimea, Russia, USSR

"Our life in the ghetto was unbearable; the living envied the dead. A number of people starved to death in the ghetto. The relatives of the deceased would say their goodbyes on the spot and the people in charge would bury him in ten minutes. One evening, a Polizei threw a rock into a room on the third floor of the building. A woman was sitting nursing her baby in the room. The rock hit the infant and killed him on the spot. No one could understand why the rock had been thrown. The baby's mother lost her mind. The Polizei who entered the room explained that the rock had been thrown because the room had not been camouflaged sufficiently."

Testimony of Meltsina-Perlova Margarita Abramovna, Yad Vashem Archives O.33/6026 [Russian].

YALTA

COUNTY SEAT, CRIMEAN AUTONOMOUS REPUBLIC, RUSSIAN FEDERATION, USSR

During the war: Military Administration Area

Coordinates:
44°30' | 34°10'

On the eve of World War II, Yalta had a Jewish population of 2,060, nearly 6 percent of its total population. They were employed in several Jewish kolkhozes established in the area during the 1920s.

The Germans occupied Yalta on November 8, 1941. Many Jewish townspeople had been evacuated or had managed to escape to the east beforehand. On December 5, the remaining Jews were concentrated in a ghetto established in former Soviet barracks located on the outskirts of town.

The conditions in the ghetto were very harsh. Due to the extreme conditions, several residents died of starvation. Dr. Kozirinski was appointed as head of the Judenrat. The Jews were forbidden use of town streets after two o'clock in the afternoon and were subjected to various other restrictions. Escape attempts evidently failed. The inhabitants suffered gravely from hunger and the depredations of German soldiers in Sonderkommando 11a.

The liquidation of the Yalta ghetto began on December 17, 1941. That day, all men were led out to a nearby botanical garden, shot to death, and then buried in a mass grave. The following day, about 1,500 women, children, and elderly people were taken by truck to a hillside and murdered.

YALTUSHKOV
(Ukrainian: **Yaltushkiv**)

TOWN IN BAR COUNTRY, VINNITSA DISTRICT, UKRAINE, USSR

During the war:
Reichskommissariat Ukraine

Coordinates:
48°59' | 27°30'

In the early twentieth century, about 1,200 Jews lived in Yaltushkov, representing approximately one-third of the local population. During the Russian Civil War (1918–20), about fifty of the town's Jews were murdered in pogroms carried out by soldiers of the Ukrainian army with the participation of local farmers. In the 1930s, most of the town's Jews were artisans, and a number had become factory workers. Many artisans organized into cooperatives, while others turned to agriculture. The town had both a Jewish Ethnic Soviet and a Yiddish-language school. On the eve of the German invasion of the Soviet Union, some 1,200 Jews lived in the town, representing roughly 10 percent of the total population.

Very few of the town's Jews managed to flee to the east in the wake of the German invasion of the Soviet Union. The Germans occupied Yaltushkov on July

15, 1941, and at once began to attack and abuse the Jews. Jewish inhabitants were seized for forced labor, repairing roads and bridges and toiling on farms. In several cases, groups of Jewish forced laborers did not return from their work and were never heard from again.

On December 20, 1941, the Jews were ordered to move into a ghetto located near the market. Jews from nearby localities were also concentrated in the Yaltushkov ghetto, which was encircled by a high barbed-wire fence. The death toll was high owing to overcrowding, hunger, and disease. The German commander of the town occasionally visited the town on horseback and randomly shot into the windows of Jewish homes and at Jews in his path on the street. Ukrainian policemen also abused and assaulted Jews.

On August 19, 1942, all of the ghetto's Jews were rounded up; those who did not report were shot to death. A selection was carried out to separate the Jewish men and women considered fit to work from the children, elderly, and infirm. The following day, on August 20, 1942, about 450 Jews were taken to pits readied in advance near the train station, ordered to strip, and shot.

Following the murder operation, groups of young men and women were transferred from the ghetto to labor camps in the villages of Guli and Yakushintsy. The Yaltushkov ghetto was liquidated on October 15, 1942, in an operation in which 1,194 Jews were executed.

YAMPOL
(Ukrainian: **Yampil'**)

COUNTY SEAT, VINNITSA DISTRICT, UKRAINE, USSR

During the war: Transnistria (under Romanian control)

Coordinates:
48°15' | 28°17'

During the Russian Revolution (1917), and later during the civil war in Russia (1918–20), the Jews of Yampol were targeted in a series of pogroms. Many of the town's Jews earned their livelihood from the manufacture of sugar and tobacco and had begun to form cooperatives in the early 1920s. Yampol had two Yiddish-language schools, one of which was a vocational agricultural school. Under Soviet rule, most of the synagogues were dismantled. On the eve of the German occupation, about 1,700 Jews lived in Yampol.

The Germans occupied Yampol on July 17, 1941. Few Jews managed to flee beforehand. In late July and August 1941, about fifty Jews were murdered by Einsatzkommando 10A, and on September 1, 1941, Yampol was annexed to Transnistria, which was under Romanian rule. The town became a transit point through which Jewish deportees from Romania were transferred to Transnistria. Although the authorities did not allow these deportees to remain in Yampol, about 500 professionals settled in the town in November–December 1941. In late October and early November 1941, a group of Jews that included children was transferred from Yampol to a camp in Trostyanchik. Several Jews perished there, while others were sent later to the camp in Pechera. The professionals and their families who managed to survive the camp returned to Yampol following the town's liberation.

In the fall of 1941, a ghetto was established in the center of the town, in an area inhabited by Jews prior to the war. Its inhabitants were required to wear a yellow Star-of-David badge. Jews, among them women and fourteen-year-old children, were assigned to various kinds of forced labor. One year later, the Jews were evacuated from this area and transferred to a new ghetto that was encircled by a barbed-wire fence. The Jews were permitted to leave the ghetto once daily to shop and collect water.

During the initial period of the ghetto's existence, the Romanian authorities treated the Jews fairly. Professionals were given the opportunity to work under tolerable conditions, and acts of violence were strictly forbidden. The spread of epidemic typhus in the ghetto was largely prevented by adequate medical practices and the admission of Jewish patients to the general hospital, which employed Jewish doctors.

Yampol, October–November 1941
Jews deported from Romania-Bessarabia and northern Bukovina on their way to Transnistria (CDEC)

The establishment of a military administration in Yampol changed matters for the worse. Gendarmes periodically entered the ghetto and carried out impromptu roll calls. The new Romanian commander, Dionisie Fotino, ordered that all Jews who violated orders be executed; he personally participated in the killings. In November 1942, Fotino deported a large number of local Jews to Cariera de Piatra. Most were murdered there, although a few managed to escape. In January 1943, another seventy-two Jews were murdered in Cariera de Piatra.

At the orders of the gendarmes, a Jewish council was appointed in the ghetto to supply manpower for work. One year later, after the council received financial assistance from the aid committee in Bucharest, a public soup kitchen was established in the ghetto. It had a single small synagogue, in which Jews worshipped on the Sabbath and holidays. Additional prayer quorums gathered in private homes. Marriage ceremonies were also held in the ghetto.

In September 1943, there were 156 Jews from Bessarabia and 348 Jews from Bukovina living in Yampol. Towards mid-March 1944, the Jews fearing the arrival of Germans, who were approaching the town as the Romanians retreated, fled the Yampol ghetto and hid with farmers in a nearby village.

Yampol was liberated on March 17, 1944.

YANOV

(Ukrainian: **Yaniv**)

TOWN IN KALINOVKA COUNTY, VINNITSA DISTRICT, UKRAINE, USSR

During the war:
Reichskommissariat Ukraine

Coordinates:
49°29' | 28°21'

In the early twentieth century, about 2,000 Jews lived in Yanov, representing roughly 37 percent of the local population. In July 1919, during the Russian Civil War (1918–20), Ukrainians carried out pogroms, killing about 300 of the town's Jews. In the mid-1920s, about 1,900 Jews lived in Yanov, representing approximately one-quarter of the town's population.

During the period of Soviet rule, most of the Jewish artisans in the town were organized into cooperatives, and in the 1930s, two Jewish kolkhozes were established near the town. Yanov had both a Jewish Ethnic Soviet and a Jewish school that offered instruction in Yiddish.

The Germans occupied Yanov on July 27, 1941. On the first day the occupation, the Germans murdered a few Jews, including the chairman of the Jewish Ethnic Soviet, Shteingard. The Jews were ordered to mark the letter J (for *Jude*) on the front of their homes and to wear marks of shame on their clothing. The men were recruited to perform forced labor.

In March 1942, the Jews were ordered to pay a ransom. That same month, they were also ordered to vacate their homes in the center of the town and to move to a special area in it, which in fact became a ghetto.

On May 30, 1942, near the town, 815 of the ghetto's Jews were executed. During the massacre, there were cases of individual resistance, including attacks on the murderers. In mid-June 1942, a second operation was carried out in the ghetto, in which about 200 Jews were killed near the Jewish cemetery. The last inhabitants of the ghetto were likewise murdered in the cemetery in the course of the following two weeks.

YANOVICHI

(Yiddish: **Yanovitsh**;
Belarussian: **Yanavichy**)

TOWNLET IN SURAZH COUNTY, VITEBSK DISTRICT, BELARUS, USSR

During the war: Military Administration Area

Coordinates:
55°17' | 30°42'

In the early twentieth century, about 1,700 Jews lived in Yanovichi, constituting roughly half of the local population. During the era of Soviet rule, many Jews practiced artisan trades, some in cooperatives. Others became white-collar workers at state-owned institutions, and a few turned to farming. The townlet had a Jewish Ethnic Council and a government school that operated in Yiddish; both were closed in the late 1930s. Due to urbanization and industrialization, the number of Jews in Yanovichi dropped to some 700 by 1939. In 1939–40, Jewish refugees from Poland settled in the townlet.

On July 9, 1941, Jewish refugees who had escaped from Vitebsk* reached Yanovichi, prompting a number of local Jews to attempt to flee to the east. Only a few reached the Soviet interior. Some Jewish men were inducted into the Red Army.

Yanovichi was occupied on July 12, 1941. In early August, the Germans registered the Jews, and in the middle of the month ordered them to wear a yellow mark on their chests. A Jewish Council was appointed under Dr. Efim Abramovich Lifshits, who was fluent in German. In a number of operations conducted between the end of July and mid-August, members of Einsatzkommando 9 arrested more than 200 Jewish men, whom they led to the nearby village and murdered. On August 25, 1941, the remaining Jews in the townlet—children, women, the elderly, and only seven men—were concentrated in a ghetto that was established on one street and surrounded by barbed wire. A road leading to the Russian cemetery crossed the ghetto, with gates at both ends. Non-Jewish residents were allowed to use this road but were absolutely forbidden to enter Jewish homes. Once in a while, the Jewish residents mingled among the passers-by and managed to slip out of the ghetto.

The appalling conditions in the ghetto inspired a revival of religious observance. Jews fasted and prayed for the abducted men to return home. Food supplies were paltry, but the inhabitants were able to barter possessions for food and grow vegetables on plots in the ghetto. Nevertheless, malnutrition and congestion spurred the rapid spreading of diseases. Lifshits's concerns about potential epidemic typhus outbreaks evidently hastened the decision to liquidate the ghetto. On September 10, 1941, members of the SS murdered the inhabitants ranging from about 1,000 to 1,600 in number (sources vary regarding the figure) in an anti-tank trench close to the nearby village of Zaytsevo.

YANUSHPOL

(Ukrainian: **Yanushpil'**)

COUNTY SEAT, ZHITOMIR DISTRICT, UKRAINE, USSR

During the war:
Reichskommissariat Ostland

Coordinates:
49°51' | 28°13'

During the civil war in Russia (1918–20), the Ukrainian army and the Red Army carried out a number of pogroms in Yanushpol, in the course of which dozens of Jews were killed. The Jews fled from the town, returning only once the Soviet regime had established itself. In the mid-1920s, about 1,400 Jews lived in Yanushpol, representing approximately one-fifth of the local population. In the 1920s and 1930s, Soviet policies coupled with the urbanization and industrialization that they fostered led to a decline in the town's Jewish population. In the late 1920s, private shops disappeared from the town, and most of the Jews were white-collar workers or engaged in artisanship or industry, mostly in the town's sugar factory. Yanushpol had a Yiddish school that was closed in the mid-1930s. The local synagogue had already been closed in 1929, in the wake of Soviet anti-religious policies. On the eve of the German occupation, about 700 Jews lived in the town.

The Germans occupied Yanushpol on July 3, 1941. A short time later, thirty-two Jews accused of being Soviet agents were murdered outside the sugar factory. Along with Jews of the surrounding localities, the Jews of Yanushpol were concentrated in a single street, which was turned into a ghetto, and they were required to wear a yellow Star-of-David badge. The Jews were seized for work in the sugar factory and for forced labor such as repairing roads, clearing snow, and performing assorted manual jobs. Ukrainian and German policemen robbed the Jewish population. In the winter of 1941/42, the Jews in the ghetto suffered considerably from hunger and cold. The Yanushpol Jews learned from refugees from the Lyubar* and Chudnov* ghettos about the murder of their local Jews, but their attempts to flee failed. On about May 20, 1942, approximately eighty men were sent to the Berdichev labor camp, where they were murdered in July 1942, together with the other inmates of the camp.

The Yanushpol ghetto was liquidated on May 28 or 29, 1942, when the Jews were led to a nearby grove, murdered, and buried in a pit dug beforehand.

YARUGA

TOWNLET IN MOGILEV-PODOLSKIY COUNTY, VINNITSA DISTRICT, UKRAINE, USSR

During the war: Transnistria (under Romanian control)

Coordinates:
48°20' | 28°03'

In the early 1920s, fewer than 1,000 Jews lived in Yaruga, a townlet located on the banks of the Dniester River, on the Ukraine-Bessarabia border; they represented about half of the townlet's population. Some 150 families belonged to a local Jewish kolkhoz. Yaruga had a Jewish Ethnic Soviet and a Jewish school, both of which operated in Yiddish.

After the German invasion of the Soviet Union, some of Yaruga's Jews were recruited into the Red Army. Others attempted to flee into the Soviet hinterland but were forced to return to the townlet owing to the swift advance of the German army. The Germans occupied Yaruga on July 18–19, 1941. One week later, all the Jews there were concentrated on a single street on the outskirts of the townlet. Near the townlet, on July 28, 1941, SS men murdered about 100 Jews deported from Bessarabia and Bukovina who had been brought to Yaruga by the Romanians.

In early September 1941, Yaruga was annexed to Transnistria, which was handed over to Romanian rule. In early October 1941, there were about 370 Jews in the townlet's Jewish quarter. As of the early months of the occupation, the Jews were required to wear a yellow patch on the chest and back, and their valuables were confiscated. The Jewish manager of the kolkhoz was appointed "Jewish elder," and the Jews continued to work on the farm that had previously been a kolkhoz.

In October–November 1941, the Romanians transferred about 500 Jewish deportees from Bukovina and Bessarabia to Yaruga. The townlet did not have its own Romanian commander or gendarmerie. The Romanians entrusted the Ukrainian police with guard duty, and they treated the Jews fairly. The police commander, Fedor Krievski, secretly supported the partisans. Krievski successfully arranged accommodations for the deportees in the Jewish homes.

At Krievski's initiative, the Jews were permitted to return to their former homes; the ghetto now included the entire quarter housing the majority of the Jewish population. A council was established in the ghetto, headed by Wieder, a ritual slaughterer and deportee from Bukovina. He was murdered in the spring of 1942, after he was caught outside the ghetto without a permit.

A Jewish self-defense force was set up following a first clash with farmers from Bessarabia, who crossed the river and raided the ghetto. Later, the inhabitants of the ghetto and the farmers from across the river began to cooperate in order to smuggle merchandise from Bessarabia to Transnistria. These smuggling efforts improved the economic condition of the ghetto's inhabitants, many of whom earned a living selling the contraband merchandise. Other Jews earned money by working for Ukrainian farmers, and women knitted. When an SS unit arrived to supervise the border area, Ukrainians hid ghetto residents in their homes. The ghetto had a hospital with sixteen beds and a public soup kitchen.

Many youths were transferred from the ghetto to labor camps in the area. According to official Romanian government figures, there were 369 local Jews and 416 deportees in Yaruga in January 1943. In September 1943, there were 478 deportees there. More than 100 of Yaruga's Jews perished during the occupation.

Yaruga was liberated on March 20, 1944.

YENAKIYEVO

(Ukrainian: **Yenakiyeve**; before 1937 and since 1943: **Ordzhonikidze**)

COUNTY SEAT, STALINO (SINCE 1961: DONETSK) DISTRICT, UKRAINE, USSR

During the war: Military Administration Area

Coordinates
48°40' | 38°20'

On the eve of the German invasion of the Soviet Union, 3,300 Jews lived in Yenakiyevo, approximately 4 percent of the city's population. Many held blue- and white-collar jobs at state-owned industrial plants; a few farmed on nearby Jewish kolkhozes. The city had a Yiddish-language government school.

After the German invasion of the Soviet Union, most Jews in Yenakiyevo managed to evacuate or flee to the east. The Germans occupied the city on November 1, 1941. By the end of that month, the Jews in the city were ordered to participate in a German military census and to wear armbands and white Stars of David on the front and back of their clothing. Soldiers and police periodically looted Jewish homes.

Jews' freedom of movement was restricted, and the able-bodied were conscripted for forced labor. A Jewish Council was established.

In February 1942, a ghetto consisting of four huts was established in the Krasnyi Gorodok quarter, and held the 750 Jews who had remained in Yenakiyevo. They were forbidden to leave, to have any contact with the general population, or to bring in food. Mortality rates soon rose.

In April 1942, Sonderkommando 4b sent approximately 500 Jews from the ghetto to a coal mine in the Gorlovka county, where they died a slow death. The eighteen Jewish families left behind in the ghetto were murdered in September 1942.

YEZERISHCHE

(Belarussian: **Yezyaryshcha**)

MEKHOV COUNTY SEAT, VITEBSK DISTRICT, BELARUS, USSR

During the war: Military Administration Area

Coordinates:
55°30' | 29°58'

Shortly before the German invasion of the Soviet Union, there were about eighty Jews in Yezerishche, most of them adults. The Germans occupied the town on July 17, 1941, and almost immediately imposed ransoms on the Jews. Some time later, they ghettoized the Jewish townspeople in two buildings near the railroad station, together with Jewish refugees from Poland. After a while, the ghetto was fenced in with barbed wire, and Jews were required to wear a yellow-armband. Food supplies in the ghetto were inadequate, but inhabitants were allotted several hours a day to go out and find food.

The ghetto was liquidated in late November or early December 1941, when SS men helped by local police murdered Yezerishche's Jewish inhabitants in nearby Ostrovki.

Z

Żyrardów, Poland

"February 1941

In the winter of 1940, an order was issued to settle the Jews in the ghetto. The Jewish population was forced to crowd into apartments in an unprecedented fashion. The Jews were given 24 hours to leave the streets not allocated for the ghetto area, although the non-Jews were permitted to remain in their apartments located inside the ghetto. The people were crammed into tiny apartments with considerable difficulty, because everyone wanted to bring in their belongings and there wasn't enough room. Belongings were consequently left in the courtyards, abandoned to thieves. And as if that were not enough, another 900 new refugees were sent here from Sochaczew, during the worst of the cold weather."

Oneg Shabbat Archive, Yad Vashem Archives, M.10/AR.1-947.

ZABŁUDÓW

TOWNLET IN BIAŁYSTOK COUNTY, BIAŁYSTOK DISTRICT, POLAND

During the war: Bezirk Białystok

Coordinates: 53°01' | 23°21'

About 2,000 Jews lived in Zabludow when World War II broke out, representing roughly two-thirds of the townlet's population. Most earned their livelihood from small commerce and artisanship. Zionist parties and youth movements were active in Zabludow, as was the Bund, and the townlet boasted Jewish educational, religious, and cultural institutions, including a Talmud Torah, a Hebrew school, and a Jewish library.

In early September 1939, the Germans occupied and held Zabludow for a number of days. In the second half of September 1939, the townlet was handed over to Soviet control in accordance with the Molotov-Ribbentrop Pact. Under Soviet rule, Jewish parties were abolished, privately owned shops were nationalized or closed, and cooperatives were formed. The schools taught in Yiddish according to a Soviet curriculum. Numerous refugees from the areas of Poland occupied by the Germans thronged to the townlet during this period.

The Germans reoccupied the townlet on June 27, 1941, and immediately set fire to Zabludow's ancient synagogue and various other buildings. The Jews, including Rabbi Yokhanan Mirski, were subject to acts of abuse and terrorization. During the early days of the occupation, many Jews fled from Zabludow to Bialystok* and other townlets. Those who remained in Zabludow crowded into the few homes left standing following the heavy bombardments. From that time forward, the Jews were required to wear a yellow badge, their freedom of movement was restricted, a portion of their property was confiscated, and they were seized for forced labor.

In January 1942, the Jews of Zabludow were concentrated in a ghetto located in the buildings of an abandoned factory. At German orders, a Judenrat was established, headed by Shimon Wissotzky. Overcrowding and hunger led to the outbreak of contagious diseases. In March 1942, many of the Jews were transferred to the Pruzana* ghetto, and the area of the ghetto in Zabludow was reduced in size.

From October 1942 onward, the ghetto was guarded more strictly. The youths who were in constant contact with the underground in the Bialystok ghetto responded by preparing escape plans and hiding places. On November 2, 1942, the Jews of the ghetto were taken in wagons to Bialystok, where Jews from the entire county were concentrated, and on November 21, 1942, they were deported to the Treblinka death camp. Most of those in hiding or who had escaped were caught and executed.

ŻABNO

TOWNLET IN TARNÓW COUNTY, CRACOW DISTRICT, POLAND

During the war: General Gouvernement, Cracow District

Coordinates: 50°08' | 20°54'

About 350 Jews lived in Zabno during the interwar period, representing approximately one-third of the townlet's population. They earned their livelihood from artisanship and small commerce, and were aided by a free-loan society. The community had a Jewish school and library, and offered Hebrew courses. Zionist parties and youth movements were active in Zabno.

The Germans occupied Zabno in the first half of September 1939. Although a number of Jews fled to the east, most returned some time later.

A Judenrat and Jewish Order Service were apparently established in 1940. The Judenrat recruited Jews for forced labor on estates in the area. On March 10, 1942, a number of Jews were murdered in the townlet.

In May 1942, a ghetto was established in Zabno, and the Jewish population of the townlet reached about 600, apparently also including refugees. The Judenrat established a public soup kitchen and was aided by a chapter of JSS that was opened in the townlet. In July 1942, after operations were carried out in the area, some 100 Jews from nearby localities were transferred to Zabno.

On September 10–18, 1942, the Jews of Zabno were deported to the Belzec death camp. About forty members of the Judenrat and Jewish Order Service along with their families remained in Zabno. On September 27, 1942, these Jews fled to the surrounding localities. The following day, the Gestapo set out in pursuit and most likely apprehended a number of the fugitives.

ŽAGARĖ
(Yiddish: **Zhager**)

TOWNLET IN ŠIAULIAI COUNTY, LITHUANIA

During the war: Reichskommissariat Ostland

Coordinates: 56°21' | 23°15'

On the eve of the war, about 1,000 Jews lived in Zagare, representing approximately 18 percent of the townlet's population. They earned their livelihood from artisanship, farming, and commerce. The townlet's Jewish schools and religious institutions included a school, Hadarim, a Talmud Torah, a Yeshiva, and four synagogues.

After Lithuania was annexed to the Soviet Union in 1940, all of the Zionist organizations and parties in Zagare were disbanded, and numerous businesses were nationalized. On June 14, 1941, a number of the townlet's Jews were exiled to Siberia.

On June 25, 1941, Zagare was occupied by the Germans with the assistance of local Lithuanians. Hundreds of Jews were imprisoned in the townlet's synagogue and severely abused. Dozens were shot to death.

In early July 1941, all of Zagare's Jews were concentrated in a single neighborhood that was declared a ghetto. Many Jews from nearby townlets were also concentrated there, and its population grew to more than 7,000.

The Jews of Zagare were required to carry out arduous forced labor. They suffered severe humiliation at the hands of Lithuanians and Latvians, who periodically rampaged through the ghetto.

On October 2, 1941, all of the townlet's Jews were summoned to the marketplace, where the German commander announced that they were being transferred to a new place of work. During the commander's speech, armed Lithuanians charged the marketplace, and at a signal from the Germans, gunned down the assembled Jews with automatic weapons. There were a few cases of resistance during the murder operation, and many Jews attempted to escape. Those who survived, including most of those who fled and were caught, were brought under armed guard to the Naryshkin park, where they were shot to death and buried. Children and babies had their heads smashed against trees; many were hurled into pits while still alive. Few Jews survived the murder operation.

ZAGÓRÓW

TOWNLET IN KONIN COUNTY, ŁÓDŹ DISTRICT, POLAND

During the war: Wartheland

Coordinates:
52°10' | 17°54'

There were 630 Jews in Zagorow on the eve of World War II. Most traded in agricultural produce or were petty artisans. The antisemitic climate of the 1930s led to hardship for the Jews of the townlet. During the annual fair in February 1936, Jews were attacked and injured by local peasants.

After the Germans occupied Zagorow on September 6, 1939, Jews were conscripted for forced labor, made to pay various fines, and ordered to wear white armbands. Dwellings were expropriated and property was looted. In February 1940, a group of Jews was sent out for forced labor.

The Zagorow ghetto was established in the spring of 1940. By early 1941, it housed about 2,000 people: 500 locals and 1,500 deportees from Kleczew, Konin, Slupca, Slesin, and Golina.

Late in the summer of 1941, about 450 men were sent from the ghetto to the salt mines at Inowroclaw for forced labor. The transports continued until October 1941, when the remaining Jews in the ghetto were taken to the forests near Kazimierz Biskupi, where they were murdered.

ZAKHARINO

TOWNLET IN KHISLAVICHI COUNTY, SMOLENSK DISTRICT, RUSSIAN FEDERATION, USSR

During the war: Military Administration Area

Coordinates:
54°59' | 32°04'

In the mid-1920s, about 550 Jews lived in Zakharino, representing over 90 percent of the townlet's total population. Although most Jewish inhabitants were farmers, several also earned their livelihood as petty merchants and artisans. Zakharino boasted a Yiddish elementary school and a drama group.

Zakharino was occupied by the Germans on August 1, 1941, and the plunder of Jewish property, humiliations, and murder of Jews began immediately. The townlet had a Judenrat.

The ghetto in Zakharino was established in October 1941, and about 300 Jews were moved into its grounds. The ghetto was liquidated in May 1942, when all of its inhabitants were shot to death.

ZAKLICZYN

TOWNLET IN BRZESKO COUNTY, CRACOW DISTRICT, POLAND

During the war: General Gouvernement, Cracow District

Coordinates:
49°52' | 20°49'

About 300 Jews lived in Zakliczyn during the interwar period, representing approximately one-quarter of the townlet's population. Most earned their livelihood from small-scale commerce and peddling. They were aided by a free-loan society supported by the JDC and a welfare society. A number of community members belonged to a Zionist association.

After the Germans occupied the townlet in September 1939, Jewish men and women were seized for forced labor. A number were recruited for work on farms in the area. The Jews were forbidden to obtain food in the nearby villages, and their freedom of movement was restricted. In 1941, Jews deported from other localities in the area were transferred to Zakliczyn. A JSS chapter in the townlet opened a public soup kitchen. In late 1941, the heads of the Jewish community, with the help of JSS, initiated a workshop. In an attempt to prevent the seizure of young Jews for labor camps, the workshop employed laborers, mainly in the garment industry and related fields.

In July 1942, a ghetto was established in Zakliczyn. Many deportees from Cracow*, Katowice, and Tarnow* were concentrated in the ghetto, raising its population to about 1,500. Hunger and disease spread due to extreme overcrowding. A number of the inhabitants continued to work in the ghetto workshops, while other groups worked outside the townlet.

In mid-September 1942, most of the ghetto inhabitants were deported via the Gromnik train station to the Belzec death camp; seventy-five Jews were shot to death during the transfer. A few dozen Jews, survivors of the Zakliczyn community, were put to work collecting the deportees' belongings. Others were employed in a number of factories in the townlet and its environs. Five of these Jews were shot to death on January 1, 1943, while the rest were murdered in April 1943.

ZALAEGERSZEG

COUNTY SEAT IN ZALA COUNTY, HUNGARY

Coordinates:
46°50' | 16°51'

The last national census conducted prior to the German occupation, taken in January 1941, recorded 873 Jewish inhabitants in Zalaegerszeg, roughly 6 percent of the total population. Most were merchants and artisans, while a few were factory owners and landowners. The Neolog Jewish community in the town ran a Jewish elementary school and a Talmud Torah. During the period of the White Terror following World War I, members of the "detachments"—semi-military units—murdered ten local Jews.

From 1938, the Hungarian government introduced a series of anti-Jewish laws as part of its anti-Jewish policy. The local authorities revoked the licenses of the artisans and state employees, and the majority of the Jews who practiced in the free professions were fired.

In 1941, Jewish men were drafted into the Hungarian army for forced labor service. Most died on the eastern front, in the Ukraine. Others were transported to the infamous copper mines of Bor in Serbia.

Immediately after the German army occupied Hungary on March 19, 1944, ten left-wing Jews were arrested in Zalaegerszeg; they were never seen again.

The Hungarian administration remained intact and operational after the German occupation. The ghettoization and deportation of the Jews were carried out on the basis of the decrees and orders of the Hungarian national and local authorities. In preparation for the ghettoization, on April 28, 1944, the mayor, Dr. Istvan Tamassy, ordered the president of the Jewish Council, Imre Berger, to submit a list of all of Zalaegerszeg's Jews.

On May 4, 1944, the Hungarian sub-prefect of Zala County, Laszlo Hunyadi, ordered the establishment of a ghetto in Zalaegerszeg for the Jews living in the town and the county-districts of Zalaegerszeg, Nova, and Lenti. The decree assured the Jews freedom of worship; each person was also allowed to bring along fifty kilograms of luggage. Hunyadi ordered the immediate establishment of a maternity home, an old-age home, a general hospital, and a hospital for infectious diseases in the ghetto.

A Jewish Council had already been established in Zalaegerszeg in March, directly after German troops entered the town and the Jewish community was dissolved. The president of the ghetto's Jewish Council was Miksa Fekete (ac-

Left: Zalaegerszeg
Jews wearing the yellow badge at the entrance to the ghetto. Inscription on the sign: "Jewish quarter. No entry to Christians." (YV)

Right: Zalaegerszeg
Jews in improvised living quarters in the ghetto (YV)

cording to other sources, the president of the Jewish Council was the last serving president of the Jewish community, Dr. Imre Berger, a lawyer).

The Zalaegerszeg ghetto was adjacent to the Gypsy neighborhood. On May 13, 1944, the assistant parson from Zalaegerszeg, Mihaly Sarlos, petitioned the mayor to house Jewish converts to Christianity in a separate block of the ghetto, to protect them from the incessant harassment of the other Jews. The ghetto was divided into two parts and consisted of designated houses along ten streets. The Jews were lodged in 162 apartments in the ghetto in severely overcrowded conditions; Jews from neighboring settlements were added to the already over-crowded ghetto. On May 31, 1944, altogether 1,221 Jews (375 families) lived in the ghetto. Until June 26, 1944, four people perished there.

A school and a hospital were set up in the ghetto, as was a Jewish Order Service. Teams were formed by the Jewish Council to operate the postal service and to address such difficulties as obtaining food supplies.

In June 1944, all men who were fit to work were drafted into the Hungarian Army for forced labor, thus escaping deportation to Auschwitz with the other ghetto inhabitants. Hungarian gendarmes searching for hidden valuables cruelly interrogated and tortured children, women, and the elderly.

In the second half of June 1944, Jews from other Zala County ghettos were transferred to the ghetto of Zalaegerszeg, which became one of the entrainment centers of Zala County. The Jews from the ghetto of Sumeg* were brought in on June 20, 1944, followed by the inhabitants of the ghettos of Tapolca* and Keszthely*. Ultimately, the Zalaegerszeg ghetto contained 3,209 inhabitants: about 900 local Jews and the balance, Jews from Zala County.

Some 3,000 Jews were deported to Auschwitz on July 5, 1944. The remaining Jews were transferred to Sarvar* (Vas County) and deported on to Auschwitz on July 6, 1944.

ZALASZENTGRÓT

TOWNLET IN ZALA COUNTY, HUNGARY

Coordinates:
46°57' | 17°05'

The last national census conducted prior to the German occupation, taken in January 1941, recorded 151 Jewish inhabitants in Zalaszentgrot, approximately 6 percent of the total population. Most were merchants, three were factory owners and one was a landowner. The town's Jewish community was Neolog. In 1941, Jewish men were drafted into the Hungarian army for forced labor service.

The German army occupied Hungary on March 19, 1944. On March 21, 1944, German units entered Zalaszentgrot. Soon thereafter, Jews were forbidden to leave their homes other than for two hours in the morning to purchase provisions.

The Hungarian administration remained intact and operational after the German occupation. The ghettoization and deportation of the Jews were carried out on the basis of the decrees and orders of the Hungarian national and local authorities. On May 4, 1944, the Hungarian sub-prefect of Zala County, Laszlo Hunyadi, ordered the establishment of a ghetto in Zalaszentgrot for the Jews living in the locality and in the county-districts of Zalaszentgrót, Nagykanizsa, Letenye and Pacsa. The decree assured the Jews freedom of worship; each person was allowed to bring along fifty kilograms of luggage. Hunyadi also ordered the immediate establishment of a maternity home, an old-age home, a general hospital, and a hospital for infectious diseases. A five-member Jewish Council headed by a "Jew-leader" [zsidovezeto] was formed in the ghetto.

The Zalaszentgrot ghetto was established on May 25, 1944, with about 400 people. They were joined by an additional 100 Jews on the following day.

The inhabitants of the Zalaszentgrot ghetto were apparently transferred by the end of June in carts to Zalaegerszeg*, one of the entrainment centers of Zala County, and were deported on to Auschwitz on July 5, 1944.

ZAMBRÓW

(Yiddish: **Zembrove**)

TOWNLET IN ŁOMŻA COUNTY, BIAŁYSTOK DISTRICT, POLAND

During the war: Bezirk Zichenau

Coordinates:
52°59' | 22°15'

About 3,200 Jews lived in Zambrow in the interwar period, representing approximately half of the local population. They earned their livelihood from artisanship and commerce. The community's institutions included two Batei Midrash, a cemetery, a synagogue, a Yeshiva, traditional Hadarim, schools, and traditional charity organizations. During the interwar period the activities of the Zionist parties and youth movements gained momentum.

The German army entered Zambrow a few days after the war broke out. For ten days, the Germans remained in the townlet, plundering as much Jewish property as they could manage to, until their withdrawal in accordance with the Molotov-Ribbentrop Pact. The Soviets appointed a Jew named Fishman as mayor of the townlet. During the Soviet rule, cooperatives were organized and factories nationalized.

The Germans reoccupied Zambrow a few days after the war broke out between Germany and the Soviet Union. The Germans immediately ordered the Jews to wear a Star-of-David armband and set about plundering Jewish property and seizing Jews for forced labor. At German orders, a Judenrat headed by Gershon Serberovich was appointed, responsible for paying the fines the Germans imposed on the community and supplying forced laborers. The Jews were employed repairing and fitting sewer and water pipes, loading and unloading transports, and cleaning the streets. As the first Judenrat did not fulfill the Germans' demands, it was replaced by a new ten-member Judenrat headed by Gliksman. The Jewish Order Service was headed by Eli Hirsh Shiniak.

In August 1941, one week after the appointment of the new Judenrat, a ghetto was established in Zambrow in an area covering only two streets. The ghetto was encircled by a barbed-wire fence and some 2,000 Jews were concentrated into its grounds. An operation was carried out the same day. The Jews were ordered to gather in the market square. Following a selection, about 800 of the fittest people, together with some of the most distinguished members of the community, including Rabbi Regenshburg, were removed to the Glebokie forest and shot.

In early September 1941, a second operation was carried out, and a selection was again performed. Jews considered unfit, including elderly people and pregnant women, were led to a forest near Rutki-Kossaki and shot.

Those who remained in the ghetto continued to be recruited for forced labor, and their wages were handed over to the Judenrat. Jews were ordered to wear a yellow badge when leaving for work. Although the ghetto suffered from a severe shortage of food, inhabitants were able obtain agricultural produce from farmers through bartering.

The liquidation of the ghetto was launched on November 2, 1942. The ghetto was encircled by German police, who were assisted by a Polish fire brigade under the command of Slizewski. The Jews of Zambrow were transferred to a transit and collection camp in the area of the old Russian army camps, where 14,000 to 17,000 Jews from the Bialystok and Bielsk Counties were concentrated. A number of Jews managed to escape along the way, and several found asylum in the forests and in farmers' shacks. Most were handed over to the Germans or turned themselves in.

Gliksman continued to head the Judenrat in the transit camp as well. The camp was encircled by a barbed-wire fence, and a deep water channel ran through its middle. The Jews of Zambrow did not perform forced labor outside the camp. The conditions in the camp were very harsh. Abuse and disease took many lives, and the medical staff, Drs. Grinwald and Friedman and head nurse Masha Slovik, demonstrated great self-sacrifice in their work. A plan to carry out an uprising in the camp with the help of the Polish underground was not executed.

Prior to the liquidation of the camp, between 500 and 800 ill people were murdered and buried. In mid-January 1943, all of the remaining Jews in the camp were deported to Auschwitz.

ZAMOŚĆ

COUNTY SEAT, LUBLIN DISTRICT, POLAND

During the war: General Gouvernement, Lublin District

Coordinates:
50°43' | 23°15'

During the interwar years, there were approximately 10,300 Jews in Zamosc, almost half the city's population. In pogroms in 1918 and 1920, Ukrainian and Polish soldiers murdered seven Jews and injured dozens. In the years after World War I, hundreds of young Jews from Zamosc emigrated in search of a brighter economic future.

The Jews of Zamosc worked in petty manufacturing (mostly in the clothing, footwear, and furniture industries) as well as in commerce and services, chiefly transport. Hundreds of artisans and merchants were organized in a large number of Jewish trade associations.

Zionist parties and youth movements, Agudath Israel, and the Bund functioned in Zamosc, and Communist activists operated covertly. The community had a free-loan fund assisted for a short time by the JDC, traditional welfare societies, an orphanage, an old-age home, a well-equipped hospital, and a clinic.

The town had a range of Jewish schools: kindergartens, a Hebrew-speaking Tarbut school, a Hebrew-speaking Yavne school (until 1923), the Yiddish-speaking I. L. Peretz Primary School, and a Polish-speaking Jewish high school. The community boasted drama and literature clubs, several libraries, and three sports clubs. Several Jewish journals were published in the town. For children from indigent families, TOZ established a home and offered summer camps.

On September 4, 1939, after the Germans invaded Poland, Jewish refugees from Kalisz*, the Kielce area, Czestochowa*, and other localities in western Poland passed through Zamosc on their way to the Soviet zone in eastern Poland. On September 9 and 12, 1939, German bombardments killed some 500 Jews in Zamosc and prompted many to flee to nearby villages and forests.

The Germans occupied Zamosc on September 14, 1939. Jews who returned from nearby villages after the bombardments discovered that Germans and Poles

Zamosc
The Jews of the ghetto are led through the city streets prior to their deportation to the Belzec death camp. (YV)

had looted their homes and shops. On September 26, in accordance with the Molotov-Ribbentrop Pact, the Germans left the city and the Soviets moved in. The Soviets retreated a week later, joined by a group of Jewish townspeople. For a week, there was no administration in the city. During that time, many Poles attacked Jews, accusing them of collaboration with the Soviets.

The Germans returned to Zamosc on October 7, 1939, and found about 5,000 Jews in the town. They immediately abducted Jews for forced labor, abused them in various ways, and looted their property. Three of those abducted did not return.

In early December 1939, the Gestapo established a Judenrat in Zamosc, composed of twelve public figures. The Judenrat was ordered to conscript 500–600 forced laborers every day and to remit occasional steep ransoms.

In the middle of December 1939, some 500 deportees from Wloclawek* and Kolo* were brought to Zamosc. About 150 of them, elderly and children, were sent to Szczebrzeszyn*, twenty kilometers away. Nineteen of them attempted to return to Zamosc but were murdered in nearby Janowce. The Judenrat set up a relief committee for the refugees, actually a chapter of the JSS in Cracow*. The committee established a soup kitchen that distributed hot meals for a nominal price to all comers and free of charge to the most destitute. The kitchen operated until the ghetto was liquidated in the autumn of 1942. The committee also helped to establish a school that functioned until April 1942. The JDC in Warsaw* provided a monthly financial subvention and, in advance of Passover 1940, a shipment of food.

In late 1939 or early 1940, the Germans ordered all Jews to wear a white armband with a yellow Star-of-David and forbade them to leave the city or to use motor vehicles.

In January 1940, the Judenrat was expanded to twenty-four members. Shortly afterwards, the original chairman, Ben-Zion Lubliner, was replaced by the attorney Mechislav (Memek) Gurfinkel. Azriel Sheps, who had headed the Judenrat labor department, was on good terms with the German responsible for Jewish forced labor, Paul Wagner. Sheps allowed Jews to avoid the labor requirement by making daily payments to the Judenrat, which used the money to pay the laborers' wages.

From June 1940, the Germans sent out hundreds of Jews in groups to labor camps in the Lublin area. Five hundred Jews were sent to the Wysokie camp, and hundreds more were sent to Bialobrzegi*, Kawalar, Izbica and Belzec. Some were murdered in the camps by SS men. The Judenrat sent food and clothing parcels to the laborers in Belzec but was not allowed to send food to the 350 Jews at the Kawalar camp. In return for hefty bribes, some Jews at Kawalar were allowed to sleep at home and by November 1940, the Jews of Zamosc who worked in Belzec were released.

In 1941, a large labor camp was established in Izbica, and 1,500–2,000 Jews from Zamosc and the area were sent there. A smaller labor camp for the Luftwaffe construction administration was also set up near Zamosc.

In early April 1941, an open ghetto was established in Zamosc, and the Polish mayor, Karol Foss, ordered the Jews to move there by May 1 on pain of deportation to Komarow*. Only a few Jews were allowed to continue living outside the ghetto. Some 7,000 Jews were packed into it, joining several Polish families who refused to leave. Although the ghetto was unfenced, inhabitants could leave only at designated times. Poles were allowed to enter it freely, which eased things somewhat.

The ghetto had a post office that the Germans authorized until June 1941, when they invaded the Soviet Union. At the end of that year, a Jewish Order Service was set up, composed of 10 young men who had served in the Polish army. In the winter of 1941/42, epidemic typhus broke out. In response, the Judenrat established a pharmacy as well as a hospital, directed by Dr. Frydhofer.

In the spring of 1942, thousands of Jews from the Protectorate of Bohemia-Moravia and Germany were deported to the ghetto. The Jewish Order Service was doubled in size.

On April 11, 1942, some 3,000 Jews from Zamosc were sent to the Belzec death camp by German gendarmes and SS troops, under the command of Gestapo chief Bruno Meyers and his assistant, SS officer Gotthard Schubert. About 250 people—the elderly, the ill, and those who had been in hiding—were murdered on the spot.

On April 30, 1942, the remaining 2,000 Jews in the ghetto were joined by 2,100 from the former Czechoslovakia, who had been brought there via Izbica, and a group of deportees from Dortmund and other parts of Westphalia, Germany. Many of them had practiced liberal professions; a few doctors found employment in the Jewish hospital.

During this time, members of the Jewish Order Service betrayed eighteen Jews to the Germans, who murdered them outside the ghetto. The "Old People's Aktion" began on May 17, 1942, and ten days later the Gestapo deported some 1,500 Jews, including a large number of elderly to the Belzec death camp, with assistance from the Judenrat and the Order Service. Some of the old people were murdered at the train station. On August 11, 1942, while the men were at work, 500 Jews (mostly women and children from the former Czechoslovakia and Germany) were deported to Belzec by German gendarmes and SS forces. After the deportation, the ghetto boundaries were contracted, and Jews working for the Wehrmacht in Zamosc and the vicinity were permitted to spend their nights at home. In early September 1942, another 400 Jews were deported from the Zamosc ghetto to Belzec.

The final liquidation of the ghetto began on October 16, 1942. About fifty Judenrat employees and other Jews who had worked for the Gestapo were murdered in the marketplace, where the ghetto residents had been rounded up. Some 4,000 Jews were deported on foot to Izbica, twenty-one kilometers away. About 100 Jews were shot en route; the rest were held in Izbica in the open air. Between October 19 and November 2, 1942, they were deported to Belzec and Sobibor in three transports.

Some 300 Jews were left behind in the Zamosc ghetto to gather up the deportees' property; they were murdered in March 1943. In early May 1943, the Germans liquidated most of the labor camps in the Zamosc area. About 1,000 laborers, most of them from Zamosc, were deported to the Majdanek death camp.

ZAPYŠKIS
(Yiddish: **Sapizishok**)

TOWNLET IN KAUNAS COUNTY, LITHUANIA

During the war:
Reichskommissariat Ostland

Coordinates:
54°55' | 23°40'

During the interwar period, about 300 Jews lived in Zapyskis, representing approximately half of the townlet's population. They earned their livelihood from the lumber craft, artisanship, and sailing barges. The community enjoyed traditional Jewish religious, educational, and welfare institutions as well as Zionist activity and sports in the local Maccabi chapter.

In June 1940, after Lithuania was annexed to the Soviet Union, a number of the shops in Zapyskis were nationalized, the Hebrew school was closed, and Zionist activity was outlawed.

After the entry of the Germans into Zapyskis in late June 1941, the local Lithuanians robbed Jewish-owned property and abused Jewish inhabitants.

The deportation of the Jews from their homes to the ghetto began on August 7, 1941. One week later, forty Jewish men were removed from the ghetto and murdered by Lithuanian policemen near the Jewish cemetery. On September 4, 1941, the rest of the inhabitants of the ghetto were taken to the banks of the Nemunas River, where they were killed. According to the Karl Jaeger report, 47 Jewish men, 118 Jewish women, and 13 Jewish children were murdered.

ŻARKI

TOWNLET IN ZAWIERCIE COUNTY, KIELCE DISTRICT, POLAND

During the war: General Gouvernement, Radom District

Coordinates: 50°38' | 19°23'

When World War II broke out, about 3,500 Jews lived in Zarki, representing more than half of the townlet's population. Most earned their livelihood from petty commerce, workshops and small-scale garment industry, construction and food factories. They received financial aid from the JDC, Jewish banks, and charity institutions. The community's Zionist party chapters and youth movements established clubs that hosted cultural and educational activities. Agudath Israel was also active in Zarki and had its own youth movement. The townlet also boasted a pioneer training facility and a Hebrew library.

Zarki was occupied by the Germans on September 2, 1939. Two days later, ninety of the townlet's Jews were murdered. The Jews were required to display the word *Jude* on their homes, were forbidden to maintain commercial ties with non-Jews, and were compelled to make large ransom payments. All Jews over the age of sixteen years were recruited for forced labor.

The Jewish inhabitants of Zarki were transferred into an open ghetto on an unknown date. On September 30, 1940, the Germans appointed a Judenrat and Jewish Order Service, both headed by Yisrael Bornshtein.

During the winter of 1940/41, about 250 Jewish refugees were brought to Zarki from Plock*. The Judenrat opened a public soup kitchen for the needy. In late 1941, many inhabitants perished in an epidemic typhus outbreak in the townlet. A small hospital was established.

In the summer of 1942, the members of Hashomer Hatzair established a small training farm near Zarki, and the Judenrat established an orphanage. Jews arrived in the ghetto from Wolbrom* and Kielce*, the survivors of deportations to death camps. Seven of these refugees were handed over to the Germans and murdered.

On October 1, 1942, the Jews learned that the Germans were planning a deportation operation. The chairman of the Judenrat warned the Jews, urging them to act to save themselves. He himself decided to remain in Zarki to help the members of the community. Many Jews fled to the forests or to other localities, including Pilica.

On October 6, 1942, the remaining approximately 800 Jews were rounded up and forced to run to the Zloty Potok train station. They were deported to the Treblinka death camp. Twenty-three Jews found hiding were murdered during the searches, and others were killed during the run. Thirty Jews were left behind in Zarki to collect the deportees' belongings.

Most of those who fled and hid were caught by early 1943, and transferred to ghettos reestablished in Pilica, Czestochowa*, and Piotrkow Trybunalski*. They were in turn deported in groups to death camps.

ŻARNÓW

TOWNLET IN OPOCZNO COUNTY, KIELCE DISTRICT, POLAND

During the war: General Gouvernement, Radom District

Coordinates: 51°15' | 20°11'

Shortly before World War II, Zarnow had a Jewish population of about 1,500. Most of the townlet's Jews were petty merchants and artisans, working as tailors and shoemakers. Several Zionist parties and Agudath Israel were active in Zarnow.

After the Germans occupied the townlet, its Jewish inhabitants were forced to wear Star-of-David armbands, forbidden to go beyond the townlet limits, and charged punitive taxes. The German authorities appointed Abraham Weinberg to chair the Judenrat, which was responsible for supplying forced laborers.

The Zarnow ghetto was unfenced, and there were Jews who continued to live outside of its confines. Jews left the ghetto to buy food in nearby villages, although they risked lives in doing so. In addition to the local population, some 1,600 Jewish refugees settled in Zarnow under the direst of conditions. A few Jews made a living by selling their property, while others did factory work, occasionally at plants that they had once owned. Some Jewish shop owners turned their establishments over to Poles, and they shared in the revenue.

In May 1942, the leaders of the Judenrat, headed by Chairman Weinberg, were murdered. Hillel Zakhariash was appointed in Weinberg's place.

Before the ghetto was liquidated in October 1942, the German authorities brought in about 2,500 Jews from the vicinity and crammed them into Jewish homes. On the day of the liquidation, all the Jews were ordered to assemble in the square. Those who stayed home—the ill, the frail, and children—were shot wherever found. The Germans selected fifty Jews to remain in Zarnow. All others were taken to nearby Opoczno* and deported the following day, along with Jews from Opoczno, to Treblinka. The fifty Jews who remained in the ghetto buried the dead and gathered up their belongings. Over time, they were joined by some 100 Jews who had survived in hiding. The last of them were transferred to Ujazd* in December 1942 or January 1943.

ZAŚKIEWICZE

TOWNLET IN MOŁODECZNO COUNTY, VILNA DISTRICT, POLAND
(After World War II in the USSR/Belarus; Belarussian: **Zaskavichy**; Russian: **Zaskevichi**)

During the war:
Reichskommissariat Ostland

Coordinates:
54°24' | 26°37'

About 200 Jews lived in Zaskiewicze in the interwar period, representing the majority of the townlet's population. Zaskiewicze's decimation in World War I left its inhabitants penniless. Aid from YEKOPO and the JDC enabled the renewal of economic activity in the townlet, and most of Zaskiewicze's Jews resumed their work as peddlers, shopkeepers, and artisans.

The Red Army occupied Zaskiewicze on September 17, 1939. Privately owned shops were nationalized or closed, and cooperatives were formed.

Upon occupying the townlet in late June 1941, the Germans immediately began to abuse and terrorize the Jews. The Jews' freedom of movement was restricted, and they were required to wear a yellow badge and perform forced labor.

After some time, a ghetto was established in Zaskiewicze and a Judenrat was appointed, given the task of recruiting forced laborers. The ghetto was liquidated in June 1942. According to one testimony, its inhabitants were rounded up and shot to death in a forest near the townlet; according to another, they were evacuated to the Smorgonie* ghetto where they shared the fate of the local Jews.

ZASLAVL

(Belarussian: **Zaslauye**)

COUNTY SEAT, MINSK DISTRICT, BELARUS, USSR

During the war:
Reichskommissariat Ostland

Coordinates:
54°00' | 27°17'

Shortly before the German invasion of the Soviet Union, there were about 250 Jews in Zaslavl, roughly 9 percent of the population. During the era of Soviet rule, Jewish wage earners were farmers and white-collar workers. The townlet had a Yiddish-speaking government school.

The Germans occupied Zaslavl on June 28, 1941. In late July, the Jews were ordered to wear armbands and a round badge on their chests. Some were sent to forced labor.

In September 1941, all Jews in the townlet were concentrated in a ghetto that the Germans established in a building previously used by the Soviet border police. They were joined by families from neighboring villages. The ghetto was guarded and enclosed with barbed wire; inhabitants were forbidden to leave except to perform forced labor. On September 26, 1941, the Germans burned twelve male Jews alive and the following day murdered another eight men from the ghetto. On September 29, some 100 Jews were murdered in Dryniny Forest near the townlet. The ghetto was liquidated on October 29, 1941, when the Germans murdered its remaining population—thirty-five young women—in a forest near the Zelenaya railroad station.

ZASTAVNA

TOWN IN CERNAUTI COUNTY, BUKOVINA, ROMANIA

Coordinates:
48°31' | 25°51'

About 650 Jews lived in Zastavna in the interwar period, representing approximately one-eighth of the town's population. They earned their livelihood from farming, flour milling, the wheat trade, and various kinds of small commerce. Zastavna had a Talmud Torah and a Hebrew-language school as well as a Jewish school that was likewise attended by Christian pupils. Until 1940, the community had a chapter of the Zionist Organization, the Jewish Romanian party, and WIZO. A Betar pioneer training facility in the town produced sixty to seventy graduates each year.

In June 1940, Zastavna was annexed to the Soviet Union together with all of northern Bukovina. The Soviets exiled wealthy Jewish families to Siberia, along with Zionist activists and their families. Some of the Zionist activists were sentenced to hard labor. The Jewish community's institutions were shut down. Jewish businesses were closed, and their merchandise confiscated.

In June 1941, the German and Romanian armies occupied Zastavna. The Jews were concentrated in a closed ghetto. At the beginning of the war against the Soviet Union, German and Romanian soldiers murdered nearly all of the Jews in the localities in the vicinity of Zastavna; few Jews succeeded in escaping to the Zastavna ghetto.

Jewish men were assigned to forced labor, hostages were seized, ghetto inhabitants were required to wear a yellow badge and their freedom of movement was restricted.

On October 13–14, 1941, the Jews of the Zastavna ghetto were deported to Transnistria. Many died during the march to Edineti, Bessarabia. In Transnistria, Zastavna's Jews were dispersed among a number of different ghettos and camps: Obodovka*, Bershad*, Tulchin*, and Yampol*. Roughly 10 percent of the deportees survived.

ZAWICHOST

TOWNLET IN SANDOMIERZ COUNTY, KIELCE DISTRICT, POLAND

During the war: General Gouvernement, Radom District

Coordinates:
50°48' | 21°51'

During the interwar years, there were approximately 1,500 Jews in Zawichost, more than one-third of the townlet's population. Most were petty merchants and artisans; some were large-scale grain merchants. Zawichost had chapters of Zionist parties, Agudath Israel, and the Bund. Children attended a traditional Heder, a Polish school, and a Yiddish-speaking CYSHO school.

On September 9, 1939, Zawichost was occupied by the Germans, who began abducting Jews for forced labor, ordered them to wear a white Star-of-David armband, and forbade them to walk on sidewalks and interact with non-Jews. In early 1940, a Judenrat was established. The Germans ordered it to remit a ransom and to conscript forced laborers.

After the German invasion of the Soviet Union in June 1941, the military government left the townlet, and German gendarmes, SS forces, and Polish police took over. From time to time, large groups of refugees were brought to the townlet, and young Jews were deported to labor camps.

The Zawichost ghetto was established in August 1942, and some 5,000 Jews were concentrated in it.

The ghetto was liquidated on October 29, 1942, when SS men, German gendarmes, and Polish police deported its inhabitants to the Belzec death camp. The elderly, the ill, and the children among the Jewish population were murdered in the townlet. After the operation, dozens of Jews from Zawichost still remained in labor camps and hiding places in and around the townlet. Some were murdered, and others joined the Armia Ludowa (Polish People's Army) partisans.

ZAWIERCIE

COUNTY SEAT, KIELCE DISTRICT, POLAND

During the war: Ost-Oberschlesien

Coordinates:
50°30' | 19°26'

On the eve of World War II, about 7,000 Jews lived in Zawiercie, representing roughly one-quarter of the city's population. They engaged mainly in commerce and artisanship, while several worked in the garment and metal industries. A print shop owned by Jews played a major role in the city's cultural life. Institutions providing assistance included associations for small-scale merchants and artisans, two banks, a free-loan society, and charitable societies. Various Zionist parties and Agudath Israel were active in Zawiercie during the interwar period. The city had a range of Jewish schools, including traditional Hadarim, a Talmud Torah, a Yeshiva, and a Tarbut school and kindergarten. In 1926, the leader of the Jewish community, A. Bornstein, was elected mayor of the city.

In 1919 and in 1921, a number of Jews were murdered in pogroms in the city, and most of Zawiercie's Jews were injured and sustained property damage.

The Germans entered Zawiercie on September 4, 1939, and immediately began to seize Jews for forced labor and to abuse Jewish inhabitants in various ways. On September 27, 1939, the Germans exacted large, extortionate "contributions."

In early 1940, all Jewish-owned businesses were confiscated. On January 5, 1940, a ten-zloty fine was levied for every Jew in the city. In April 1940, altogether 600 Jewish refugees were brought to the city from the Cieszyn area.

In September 1941, a ghetto was established in Zawiercie, and a Judenrat was appointed, charged with supplying the Germans with forced laborers. During the winter of 1940/41, the Jews were ordered to turn over all their valuables, furniture, and furs. On July 22, 1941, the Germans murdered seven Jews accused of being Communists. The Jewish population of Zawiercie in 1941 stood at approximately 5,500.

In May or August 1942, an operation was carried out in which about 2,000 of the ghetto's inhabitants were deported to Auschwitz by SS and Gestapo soldiers and German gendarmes, with the help of Polish policemen. Following the operation, a factory that made uniforms for the German air force was established in Zawiercie; by early 1943, the number of its Jewish employees had reached about 2,500.

In late 1942, an underground headed by Berl Shwartz and made up of members of the Hashomer Hatzair became active in Zawiercie. Mordechai Anielewicz of Warsaw* visited the members of the underground. The group smuggled Jewish

Zawiercie
The Jews of the ghetto are led to the train station prior to their deportation to Auschwitz. (YV)

families across the border from Poland to Slovakia. A number of the would-be escapees were caught and murdered.

In August 1943, the ghetto was liquidated when 6,000 to 7,000 Jews from Zawiercie were deported to Auschwitz by the SS, the Gestapo, and German gendarmes, assisted by Polish policemen. The members of the Judenrat were murdered in the city prior to the deportation. The deportation of about 500 workers who remained in the uniform factory as vital workers was postponed. The ghetto's liquidation was completed when this last group was finally deported to Auschwitz on October 18, 1943.

ZBARAŻ

COUNTY SEAT, TARNOPOL DISTRICT, POLAND

(After World War II in the USSR/Ukraine; Ukrainian, Russian: **Zbarazh**)

During the war: General Gouvernement, Galicia District

Coordinates:
49°40' | 25°47'

Close to 3,000 Jews lived in Zbaraz in the interwar period, representing approximately one-third of the town's population. They worked in industrial plants and also engaged in commerce and artisanship. The town had two Jewish banks and maintained a ramified network of social help. Various youth movements and Jewish parties, a Hebrew school, a range of Jewish cultural institutions, and a Jewish sports union all operated within the community.

When World War II broke out, hundreds of Jewish refugees from western Poland arrived in Zbaraz, where they found haven with the local Jewish community. The town's Jewish population rose to about 5,000. Zbaraz was occupied by the Soviets in the second half of September 1939, and under Soviet rule, the Jewish community's institutions were disbanded and private commerce was abolished. Many of the Jewish refugees who had arrived in the town were exiled by the Soviets into the Soviet interior.

On July 2–4, 1941, after the Red Army withdrew but before the Germans entered Zbaraz, local Ukrainians carried out pogroms, killing more than forty Jews. The Germans entered Zbaraz on July 6, 1941, and a few days later, at their orders, a Judenrat was established that was headed by Grinfeld, a Jewish refugee from western Poland who by and large obeyed German orders. According to one source, Ber Alterman served as head of the Judenrat.

On October 6, 1941, German commando soldiers murdered seventy-two men from Zbaraz, most of whom were members of the intelligentsia. In the winter of 1941/42 and the spring of 1942, Jewish men were transferred to labor camps located in the area. In June 1942, about 600 elderly and ill Jews were murdered on the way to Tarnopol*.

On August 31, 1942, altogether 560 Jews were deported from the ghetto to the Belzec death camp. A few weeks after this operation, a ghetto was established in Zbaraz, in which the Germans concentrated Jews from other localities in the area, as well. It was an open ghetto, but departure was restricted and food was difficult to obtain. On September 30, 1942, another approximately 260 Jews were deported. In early October 1942, a group of Jews was murdered in the town. On October 20–22, 1942, another operation was carried out, after which approximately 1,000 Jews were deported to Belzec, and a group of men was sent to the Janowska camp on the outskirts of Lwow*. Another approximately 1,000 Jews were deported to Belzec on November 8–9, 1942. Several of the people on the transport who managed to jump off the train returned to the ghetto. In December 1942, there were about 2,000 Jews in the ghetto.

In the winter of 1942/43, many of the people living in the ghetto died of hunger and disease. During this period, rescue efforts and attempts to find places to hide were stepped up, in the face of numerous difficulties. On April 9–10, 1943, more than 1,000 Jews from Zbaraz were murdered near the town.

On June 8, 1943, about 550 Jews were murdered, and on June 19, 1943, the ghetto's last 150 Jews were murdered near the town. These final operations were carried out by a German police unit under the command of Hermann Mueller and Friedrich Hildebrand.

ZBORÓW

COUNTY SEAT, TARNOPOL DISTRICT, POLAND

(After World War II in the USSR/Ukraine; Ukrainian: **Zboriv**; Russian: **Zborov**)

During the war: General Gouvernement, Galicia District

Coordinates:
49°40' | 25°09'

In 1931, about 1,900 Jews lived in Zborow. Most earned their livelihood from commerce, while others engaged in different forms of artisanship, wagon driving, and the liberal professions. The townlet had a supplementary Hebrew school and a kindergarten as well as schools for boys and girls run by Agudath Israel. Among the cultural institutions were a Jewish library, a drama circle, and a Maccabi sports club. The community had chapters of the various Zionist parties and Agudath Israel.

Zborow was occupied by the Red Army in the second half of September 1939. Under Soviet rule, Jewish factories and businesses were nationalized, private commerce was discontinued, and the various parties were disbanded. On the eve of Zborow's occupation by the Germans in July 1941, small groups of Jews managed to escape to the east together with the withdrawing Soviet forces.

Zborow was occupied by the Germans on July 4, 1941. That same day, members of Einsatzkommando B4, with the help of Ukrainians, rounded up and executed either about 600 or more than 800 local Jews (sources vary regarding the figure). In July 1941, a Judenrat headed by Yaakov Fuks was established in Zborow on German orders. The Judenrat's main duty was to recruit forced laborers daily. The Judenrat also established a public soup kitchen. On October 16, 1941, about 200 Jewish members of the intelligentsia were murdered by a commando unit of the German ORPO, under the command of Edmund Schoene.

In the summer of 1942, two labor camps were established in Zborow, one "open" and the other "closed", in which Jewish skilled workers from Zborow and its environs were concentrated. On August 29, 1942, a mass operation was carried out in the townlet, and about 1,300 people were deported to the Belzec death camp.

After the operation, numerous Jews from nearby localities were moved into Zborow, and in the fall of 1942, all were concentrated under conditions of extreme overcrowding in a ghetto encircled by a barbed-wire fence, located on two streets near the river. Severe epidemic typhus soon broke out in the ghetto. In December 1942, its population numbered about 3,000.

On April 4 or April 9, 1943 (sources vary regarding the date), an operation was carried out in Zborow. Germans and Ukrainians encircled the ghetto, and about 2,300 Jews were arrested. After being forced to dig pits, they were shot by a German police unit under the command of Hermann Mueller. After the operation, the survivors of the Zborow Jewish community attempted to organize hiding places and bunkers.

During this period, a Jewish underground was active in the ghetto under the leadership of Levi Remer. Its members collected weapons and maintained contact with the partisans.

The last operation in the ghetto was carried out on June 5, 1943. Germans and Ukrainians encircled the ghetto and began to comb through its homes. The members of the underground called upon the Jews to flee and opened fire on the Germans, causing them to retreat from the ghetto. The Germans set fire to the houses in which the underground fighters were holed up, and, after putting down the focal points of the resistance, completed the liquidation of the ghetto.

On June 15, 1943, the Germans liquidated the "open" labor camp; they began to liquidate the "closed" camp on June 23. As they were taken to the pits to be shot, several of the prisoners resisted the Germans and attempted escaping to the forests. In response, the Germans locked up the remaining 600 prisoners in wooden barracks that they set on fire.

ZDOŁBUNÓW

COUNTY SEAT, VOLHYNIA DISTRICT, POLAND
(After World War II in the USSR/ Ukraine; Ukrainian: **Zdolbuniv**; Russian: **Zdolbunov**)

During the war: Reichskommissariat Ukraine

Coordinates: 50°31' | 26°15'

Zdolbunow
Public hanging of Yaakov Diner in the marketplace in front of the inhabitants of the ghetto and members of the Jewish Order Service, for disobeying German police orders (YV)

During the interwar years, there were about 1,300 Jews in Zdolbunow, roughly one-fifth of the townlet's population. They engaged mainly commerce and artisanship. A Jewish savings-and-loan association operated in the townlet with support from the JDC. A Hebrew-language Tarbut school educated the community's children.

After the Soviets took control of the townlet in September 1939, private businesses were nationalized and the Jewish school adopted Yiddish as its language of instruction.

The Germans occupied Zdolbunow on June 30, 1941. The Jews were ordered to establish a Judenrat, wear a Star-of-David armband, and perform forced labor. On August 7, 1941, using lists prepared by local Ukrainians, an Einsatzkommando squad (evidently 4a) murdered 380 Jewish men, including most members of the Judenrat. After this operation, a new Judenrat was established under Simcha Shleifstein.

A German named Hermann Friedrich Graebe arrived in Zdolbunow in October 1941 and collectively employed some 3,000 Jews from Zdolbunow, Ostrog*, and Mizocz* in forced labor at construction sites and in his offices. Some of the workers from Zdolbunow were housed in the Rowne* ghetto.

The ghetto in Zdolbunow was established in May 1942. On July 13, 1942, the day the Rowne ghetto was liquidated, Graebe gathered approximately 140 Jewish forced laborers who had been working in Rowne and returned them to the Zdolbunow ghetto. He furnished thirty-five of these workers with "Aryan" papers and transferred them to Poltava, Ukraine, where he established a fictitious branch of his company, thereby enabling them to survive.

In August 1942, Ukrainian police murdered ten of Zdolbunow's Jews.

The Zdolbunow ghetto was liquidated on October 14, 1942. Its inhabitants were taken to trenches outside of the townlet and murdered. Several Jews set their homes ablaze, and dozens exploited the smokescreen to escape to the forests. A number of them joined up with Soviet partisan units, but others encountered Ukrainian units and were murdered.

ZDUŃSKA WOLA

TOWN IN SIERADZ COUNTY, ŁÓDŹ DISTRICT, POLAND

During the war: Wartheland

Coordinates: 51°36' | 18°56'

On the eve of World War II, there were almost 10,000 Jews in Zdunska Wola, accounting for more than one-third of the town's population. During the interwar period, most of the town's Jews worked or traded in textiles. Jewish merchants and manufacturers had their own organizations, and had access to Jewish savings-and-loan associations. The community had primary schools, a Tarbut school, and a Talmud Torah. Political life was dominated by Agudath Israel, but Zionist parties and the Bund were also active, organizing evening studies for secondary school students. Drama groups and sports clubs operated in the community as well.

Some 2,000 Jews left Zdunska Wola during the first months of the war, with a few returning once the fighting stopped. Three Jews were murdered on the day the town was occupied. The following day, the great synagogue was destroyed and the remains of the building were put to use as a stable. The

Zdunska Wola, May 22, 1942
On Shavuot eve, ten Jews are hanged in the marketplace in front of all the inhabitants of the ghetto. A poem by poet Itzhak Katzenelson depicted the final moments of Shlomo Zelichovsky, who was one of the executed. (YV)

Germans appointed a man named Jakobson as head of the Judenrat. After he fled the town in late 1939, Dr. Yaakov Lemberg was appointed his successor. Lemberg managed to persuade the Germans to cancel their plan to deport 400 Jewish families from Zdunska Wola.

Between March and May 1940, a ghetto was established in a small area on the outskirts of the town. Jews were ordered to move to the ghetto within three days and were allowed to bring hand luggage only. Between 8,000 and 9,000 Jews were packed into the ghetto and were joined over the course of the next two years by Jewish refugees. The first German governor of the ghetto was Oskar Fercho; in the summer of 1941, he was succeeded by Wilhelm Bittel.

The ghetto was unsealed during its first six months; the only sign of its existence was a street-corner post displaying a Star-of-David. Jews were allowed to leave the ghetto between ten o'clock in the morning and noon, and those employed by the Germans could remain outside all day long. Non-Jews were allowed into the ghetto and would occasionally exploit the opportunity to loot Jewish property. In September 1940, a wood- and barbed-wire fence was erected around the Zdunska Wola ghetto. There was a German police station inside it. A Judenrat comprised of public figures was appointed along with a twenty-member Jewish Order Service under the command of Aharon Pik.

During 1941, factories and workshops in the ghetto produced goods for the Wehrmacht. The work provided the Jews with income, extra food rations, and protection from deportation to labor camps. Jews also performed farm labor and built houses for the Germans. At Dr. Lemberg's initiative, a 1.12-hectare farm was established in the ghetto in the spring of 1940 to provide produce and goats' milk for children. The farm also served as a pioneering training facility, accommodating thirty young men and twenty young women who were members of Zionist youth movements. At the end of their workday, the youths studied Hebrew and Jewish history. The training farm operated until the ghetto was liquidated.

As public worship was prohibited, Jews held holiday services in private dwellings. Wedding ceremonies were conducted secretly by a cantor named Yankel. Three members of the Judenrat sat as a magistrate's court to try civil cases, while criminal cases were heard by the Germans.

Jews were periodically sent from the ghetto to labor camps: in June–July 1941, a group of about 1,000 Jews was sent to camps in the Poznan area. In late 1941, Dr. Lemberg learned from Polish railway workers that the Jews of the Wartheland were being killed at Chelmno.

As the liquidation of the ghetto approached, the Germans instigated a process of intimidation that included public hangings of Jews. The first incident of this kind took place on March 3, 1942 (Purim), when ten Jews were murdered. Ten more Jews were hanged on May 21 (Shavuot) and shortly thereafter, thirty Jews were abducted from the ghetto.

The liquidation of the Zdunska Wola Jews began on August 24, 1942, and lasted for three days. Hans Biebow, head of the Lodz* ghetto administration, visited with his entourage to conduct a selection. First, hospital patients were shot dead. Then, all ghetto inhabitants were ordered to report to a town square, where an initial selection took place. Hundreds of Germans meanwhile raided the ghetto's apartments and shot whomever they found. Afterwards, the Germans forced all Jews to run to the Jewish cemetery, where they were held for two days, without food or water. More selections were performed, as candidates for forced labor in the Lodz ghetto were separated out. In one selection, women seized for forced labor resisted parting from their children. The Germans responded by shooting indiscriminately into the crowd of parents. The operation ended with 8,594 people taken to the Chelmno death center and 1,169 to the Lodz ghetto.

During the liquidation the Germans offered Dr. Lemberg an opportunity to conduct the selection, and Biebow even proposed that the two collaborate in the Lodz ghetto. When Lemberg refused, he was placed aboard a railroad car. Before the train set out for Lodz, he was removed from the car and shot in the cemetery.

ZDZIĘCIOŁ/ŻETL
(Yiddish: **Zhetl**)

TOWNLET IN NOWOGRÓDEK COUNTY, NOWOGRÓDEK DISTRICT, POLAND

(After World War II in the USSR/Belarus; Belarussian: **Dzyatlava**; Russian: **Dyatlovo**)

During the war: Reichskommissariat Ostland

Coordinates: 53°28' | 25°24

About 3,500 Jews lived in Zdzieciol when World War II broke out, representing roughly three-quarters of the townlet's population. Most earned their livelihood from commerce, artisanship, and the liberal professions, and were supported by the JDC and local Jewish welfare organizations. Jewish political organizations were active in Zdzieciol, including Zionist parties, Agudath Israel, and the Bund, and were involved in the development of Jewish culture and education in the townlet. The Jewish community maintained a Yiddish school, a Hebrew school, and a library. In 1933 and 1936, Zdzieciol was struck by a number of large fires that burned down about half of the townlet's buildings, including Jewish institutions.

The Red Army occupied Zdzieciol on September 18, 1939. Soon afterwards Jewish parties were abolished, privately owned shops were nationalized or closed, and cooperatives were formed. The schools taught in Yiddish according to a Soviet curriculum.

On June 30, 1941, the Germans occupied Zdzieciol, and thirty-seven Jewish men were immediately murdered. From July 14, 1941, onward, the Jews of Zdzieciol were required to wear a yellow badge, and their freedom of movement was restricted. On July 15, 1941, the Germans rounded up all Jewish men aged sixteen to sixty, and separated out 120 of the community leaders, whom they imprisoned in Nowogrodek* and murdered the following day. In the autumn of 1941, additional anti-Jewish decrees were issued, including the confiscation of property and the recruitment of Jews for forced labor.

In September 1941, Zdzieciol's Jews were transferred to a ghetto established in the townlet's market area and encircled by a barbed-wire fence; about 1,500 Jews from surrounding localities were moved into the ghetto as well. A Jewish Order Service was established at German orders, along with a Judenrat headed by Alter Dvoretski, an attorney and Zionist activist. By the spring of 1942, the population of the ghetto had risen to about 6,000, but many perished from rampant epidemic typhus.

In the winter of 1941/42, about sixty young members of Po'alei Zion and Hashomer Hatzair established an underground in the Zdzieciol ghetto. It operated in small cells under the leadership of Judenrat head Alter Dvoretski, who helped acquire arms and prepare fighting plans. He even managed to install ten underground members into the Jewish Order Service. In the spring of 1942, a nineteen-year-old member of the underground named Shalom Piolon went to meet a Russian contact, who betrayed him and handed him over to the Germans. The following day, Dvoretski and a number of additional underground members fled. They attempted to convince the Russian partisans that were active in the area to attack Zdzieciol and smuggle Jews out to the forest, but the partisans refused and eventually murdered Dvoretski and another underground member named Moshe Pozdunski.

On April 30, 1942, a large-scale operation was carried out in the ghetto. The Jews were rounded up in the old cemetery, where a selection was carried out in which youths and professionals were separated out. The Germans shot some 1,200 Jews to death near the village of Kurpiesze. After the operation, more than 1,500 Jews remained in the ghetto. Gradually, a few hundred youths managed to flee to the forests.

The Zdzieciol ghetto was liquidated in a three-day-long operation that began on August 6, 1942. The ghetto was suddenly encircled, and the Jews were rounded up in and around the synagogue and led to the cemetery, where they were shot to death. After combing through the ghetto, the Germans found about 200 Jews in hiding. A number of them were shot, and the rest were sent to the Nowogrodek ghetto. During the operation, about forty young Jews escaped with their commander, Hirsh Kaplinski, to the Lipczany forests, where they established a partisan company. Its membership eventually grew to about 200, and it became renowned for its daring operations.

ŻELECHÓW

CITY IN GARWOLIN COUNTY, LUBLIN DISTRICT, POLAND

During the war: General Gouvernement, Warsaw District

Coordinates:
51°49' | 21°54'

About 5,500 Jews lived in Zelechow in the interwar period, representing roughly half of the town's population. They earned their livelihood from small-scale industry; sugar, alcoholic beverage, and soda factories; and petty commerce. They were aided by the JDC, an association of Jewish merchants, a free-loan society, and traditional Jewish mutual-aid and welfare institutions. Zionist parties, Agudath Israel, and the Bund were active in Zelechow. A private Heder, a community Talmud Torah, and a Beit Yaakov school provided the community's children with a Jewish education.

On September 8–9, 1939, hundreds of Jews arrived in Zelechow from Garwolin, which had been bombarded. On September 12, German forces entered Zelechow and began to beat Jews and burn their houses. Chaim Felhandler, a member of the town council, perished in a fire set in the town's synagogue. After a few days, the Germans deported numerous Jews from Zelechow to Ostrow Mazowiecka, murdering many people along the way.

In the wake of a border dispute between Germany and the Soviet Union, the Germans withdrew from Zelechow for a few days, but returned on October 4, 1939.

In November 1939, hundreds of Jewish refugees arrived in Zelechow from the townlets of Garwolin, Sobolew*, Deblin-Irena*, Wloclawek*, and from smaller villages in the area. A Judenrat was established, headed by Yisrael Mordechai Angel, who was replaced a short time later by Shalom Finkelstein. The Germans

Zelechow, 1941
The Jews of the ghetto participate in a "Black Canopy" ceremony held in the cemetery in the wake of an outbreak of epidemic typhus in the ghetto. (GFH)

ordered the Judenrat to collect a large ransom payment and commanded Jewish inhabitants to wear Star-of-David armbands.

From December 1939 onward, the Germans demanded that the Judenrat supply forced laborers, whom they sent in groups of 150 people to Jarczew and to Germany, and from 1941, to Wilga, which was not far from Garwolin. During the summer of 1940, Jewish-owned property was seized, and Jews were compelled to pay for the right to live in their homes. In July and August 1940, about 1,200 Jewish refugees from Warsaw*, Maciejowice*, and other localities arrived in Zelechow.

In October 1940, an open ghetto was established in Zelechow, along with a Jewish Order Service under the command of Sharfherts. In spring 1941, epidemic typhus broke out in it. The Judenrat opened a public kitchen, a hospital, and a bathhouse with the help of JSS and the JDC.

In June 1941, once fighting between Germany and the Soviet Union broke out, Jews were forbidden to leave their homes other than for work. By December 1941, a number of Jews who had traded with Polish farmers or attempted to smuggle in food were executed. A fire brigade was established; its fifty members were exempted from the forced labor requirement and were permitted to leave the ghetto and obtain food from Polish farmers.

In October 1941, the Zelechow ghetto was sealed. Additional refugees continued to inundate the ghetto from Warsaw, Lodz*, Garwolin, Laskarzew*, and various other localities; by late 1941, about 13,000 Jews lived in the ghetto.

In the summer of 1942, a Jewish underground organized in the ghetto under the leadership of Yosef Melinkovski. The underground established contact with Soviet partisans who were active in the area, extending the group assistance.

In the summer of 1942, the Judenrat sent about 500 Jews to labor camps in Wilga and in the Minsk Mazowiecki area. In late summer of 1942, the head of the Judenrat, Shalom Finkelstein, was executed along with brothers Shlomo and David Goldstein, who had been active in the community dating from before the war.

On September 30, 1942, the Jews of Zelechow were deported to the Treblinka death camp by SS guards and a Ukrainian auxiliary unit. About 1,100 elderly and ill Jews and those caught hiding were summarily killed. During the ghetto's liqui-

Zelechow, 1942
Jews receiving a food ration in a public soup kitchen established in the ghetto with the assistance of the JSS, the Jewish self-help organization (YV)

dation, the members of the underground escaped to the forests and continued to act as a partisan unit in cooperation with a Soviet unit. A number of Jews who escaped from the trains also joined the partisans who were active in the area.

About fifty members of the Jewish Order Service and the fire brigade remained in the ghetto to bury the bodies of those killed in the operation and collect the residual belongings. Afterwards, most were sent to the labor camp in Wilga, and on to a labor camp in the area of Sobolew, where the majority perished.

Twenty-five artisans who remained in the ghetto were murdered on February 28, 1943.

ZELÓW

TOWNLET IN ŁASK COUNTY, ŁÓDŹ DISTRICT, POLAND

During the war: Wartheland

Coordinates:
51°28' | 19°14'

In the early 1920s, there were about 1,800 Jews living in Zelow, accounting for approximately one-third of the townlet's population. Agudath Israel ran the community, to which several Zionist parties were introduced in the early 1930s.

The Germans occupied Zelow on September 6, 1939. A Judenrat was established during the first weeks of the occupation, headed by Naftali Meier, a local Zionist activist, and his deputy, Mandel. The commander of the Jewish Order Service was Yosel Frenkel.

Many Jews left the townlet during the early months of the occupation, however a large influx of refugees boosted the Jewish population to 4,500 by December 1940, and to between 6,000 and 7,000 by March 1941.

The ghetto in Zelow was not initially fenced and inhabitants continued to buy food at reasonable prices. There were Jews who earned a living by smuggling goods, chiefly textiles, between the Wartheland and the General Gouvernement. Several were caught and sent to Lodz* for trial. Workshops that produced goods for Germans were established in the ghetto. Jewish artisans also continued to ply their trades to meet local demand, despite German prohibitions. Food for Jews in Zelow was supplied by the German wholesaler Karl Leib, whose company was later sued by the German authorities for its excessive generosity in doling out rations. The Jews in Zelow led a relatively comfortable ghetto existence, as

Zelow
A group of Jews from the ghetto seized for forced labor in a factory in the town, photographed with German soldiers and administrative officials (GFH)

evidenced by testimonies recounting the participation by two Jews in a soccer match with the local Hitlerjugend in the summer of 1940.

The Jews of Zelow were, however, by no means exempt from many of the standard hardships of ghetto life. They were intermittently abducted for forced labor, and 400 men were sent to a labor camp in Poznan district in 1940. In the spring of 1942, the county governor, Johannes Berger, ordered the public hanging of ten ghetto inhabitants. Deportations ahead of the liquidation of the ghetto began several weeks later. On June 13, 1942, ninety-six Jews from Zelow were deported to the Lodz ghetto, while an indeterminate number of others were sent to the Chelmno extermination center. In another operation during August 1942, hundreds of Jews were deported from Zelow to Lodz and, almost certainly, to Chelmno.

The final liquidation of the ghetto took place on September 14, 1942. The inhabitants were concentrated in a factory and a church. Forty-one were transferred to Lodz, while the others were transported to the Chelmno death camp or murdered on the spot. A number of Jews were sheltered by local Poles, and several individuals managed to survive.

ZELWA

TOWNLET IN WOŁKOWYSK COUNTY, BIAŁYSTOK DISTRICT, POLAND
(After World War II in the USSR/Belarus; Belarussian, Russian: **Zelva**).

During the war: Bezirk Białystok

Coordinates:
53°09' | 24°29'

About 1,300 Jews lived in Zelwa when World War II broke out, representing approximately 60 percent of the townlet's population. They earned their livelihood mainly from industry, commerce, and artisanship. Jewish political organizations and youth movements were active in Zelwa, including Zionist parties, the Bund, and a Communist underground. The parties also undertook extensive educational and cultural work. Zelwa boasted a Tarbut Hebrew school, a *Tachkemoni* religious Hebrew school, and Jewish libraries. The townlet also had a variety of mutual-aid societies.

After the Red Army occupied Zelwa in the second half of September 1939, Jewish parties were abolished, privately owned shops were nationalized or closed, and cooperatives were formed. The schools taught in Yiddish according to a Soviet curriculum.

The Germans occupied Zelwa on July 1, 1941; a Judenrat was established soon afterward, headed by Abe Pupko. Jewish men were rounded up, and about forty to fifty of them, mainly from among the intelligentsia, were shot to death outside the townlet. The Jews of Zelwa suffered from an acute shortage of food, were required to wear a yellow badge, and were seized for forced labor. Seven

Jewish butchers who disobeyed German orders and traded with non-Jews were hanged; following this execution, the head of the Judenrat committed suicide.

A few weeks later, a ghetto was established in a number of run-down buildings. Living conditions were extremely harsh and mortality rates were high. Young Jews tried to flee to the forests, but most were caught or handed over to the Germans.

On November 2, 1942, SS members from Wolkowysk* encircled the ghetto and rounded up its Jews in the marketplace. From there, they were sent in train cars to a transit camp near Wolkowysk and then deported on November 26, 1942, to the Treblinka death camp.

ŽEMAIČIŲ NAUMIESTIS
(Yiddish: **Nayshtot-Tavrig** / **Nayshtot-Sugint**)

TOWNLET IN TAURAGĖ COUNTY, LITHUANIA

During the war:
Reichskommissariat Ostland

Coordinates:
55°22' | 21°42'

After World War I, about 650 Jews lived in Zemaiciu Naumiestis, representing roughly one-third of the townlet's population. They earned their livelihood from commerce and artisanship. The community had traditional Jewish religious, educational, and welfare institutions as well as a Jewish Folksbank. The children studied in a Hebrew school and a Heder. All of the Zionist parties were active in the townlet.

After Zemaiciu Naumiestis was annexed to the Soviet Union in 1940, most of its shops and factories were nationalized, the Hebrew schools were closed, and Zionist activities in the townlet were discontinued.

By the eve of the German occupation, about 120 Jewish families remained in Zemaiciu Naumiestis. On June 22, 1941, the German army entered the townlet. In the first weeks of the war, Jewish inhabitants were assigned to forced labor.

In early July 1941, the Jews were concentrated in a ghetto consisting of a number of homes in a neglected neighborhood. On July 19, 1941, the Jewish men who were deemed fit for work were separated from the ill and the elderly. They were brought to a labor camp in Heydekrug, some fifteen kilometers from the townlet. That same day, all elderly Jewish residents of Zemaiciu Naumiestis and Vainutas were murdered in a ravine near Siaudviciai. The women who remained in the ghetto worked for the farmers in the area until September 25, 1941, when they, too, were murdered in Siaudviciai.

ZEMBIN

TOWNLET IN BORISOV COUNTY, MINSK DISTRICT, BELARUS, USSR

During the war: Military Administration Area

Coordinates:
54°22' | 28°13'

In the mid-1920s, there were about 800 Jews in Zembin, accounting for half of the local population. During the era of Soviet rule, many practiced artisan trades, some in cooperatives, while others turned to farming at kolkhozes set up near the townlet. The townlet had a school that taught in Yiddish.

The Germans occupied Zembin in early July 1941. Their arrival was so sudden that nearly no one managed to escape to the east, save a few young men who had been inducted into the Red Army. A week later, the Germans ordered the Jews to wear a yellow "badge of shame" on the front and back of their clothing and restricted their relations with the rest of the local population.

A few days after the occupation began, all Jews in the townlet were concentrated near the Jewish cemetery on a street from which all non-Jews had been evicted. The area became a ghetto enclosed in barbed wire. Its inhabitants were put to forced labor and charged ransoms.

The ghetto was liquidated on August 18, 1941, when SS forces, in cooperation with Belarussian police, murdered all the inhabitants in a location near the townlet. The lives of two children from a mixed family, who were in the ghetto with their mother, were spared, as they declared that their father was not Jewish.

ZHABOKRICH

TOWNLET IN KRYZHOPOL COUNTY, VINNITSA DISTRICT, UKRAINE, USSR

During the war: Transnistria (under Romanian control)

Coordinates: 48°23' | 28°59'

In the mid-1920s, there were about 900 Jews in Zhabokrich, representing approximately 20 percent of the townlet's population. Most of Zhabokrich's Jews earned their livelihood from artisanship and commerce. During the civil war in Russia (1918–20), the Jews suffered from attacks by farmers and Ukrainian soldiers, prompting many of the Jews to leave the townlet. In the late 1920s, many Jews organized in artisans' cooperatives and a Jewish kolkhoz was established. The townlet had a Jewish Ethnic Soviet and a Jewish school, both of which operated in Yiddish.

After the German invasion of the Soviet Union on June 22, 1941, a number of Zhabokrich's Jews were recruited into the Red Army, while others were evacuated or fled into the Soviet hinterland. Concurrently, refugees from other localities in the Vinnitsa District and western Ukraine arrived in the townlet. The Germans occupied Zhabokrich on July 20, 1941, and as early as July 27–29, they murdered 435 Jews, of whom at least 230 were local residents. Jewish residences were looted.

On September 1, 1941, Zhabokrich was annexed to Transnistria, which was under Romanian control. Deportees from Bessarabia and Bukovina moved into the homes of the murdered Jews, joining the approximately 200 Jews who hid during the murders.

The area of Jewish homes was declared a ghetto and encircled by a barbed-wire fence, and the Jews were forbidden to leave its grounds. The ghetto residents suffered from overcrowding, hunger, and cold, and epidemic typhus spread, causing many deaths. Jews were assigned to forced labor, occasionally in distant places. At the orders of the Romanian gendarmerie, a Judenrat was established in Zhabokrich, headed by two deportees, Ziess and Anchel, and a local Jew named Toyvle Bogner. A Jewish Order Service was established as well. The ghetto residents, including women, were subject to improper behavior on the part of the Judenrat heads. One of the Judenrat leaders was executed by partisans for his inappropriate conduct.

According to figures from September 1, 1943, altogether 245 Jewish deportees lived in Zhabokrich (175 from Bukovina and seventy from Bessarabia). There are no population figures for the local Jews. An attempt to exterminate the entire ghetto population in the spring of 1944 was thwarted when partisans spread rumors that the Red Army was approaching the townlet.

Zhabokrich was liberated in mid-March, 1944.

ZHITOMIR
(Ukrainian: **Zhytomyr**)

DISTRICT SEAT, UKRAINE, USSR

During the war: Reichskommissariat Ukraine, USSR

Coordinates: 50°15' | 28°40'

Zhitomir was an important Jewish center in the nineteenth century. In 1837, a famous Hebrew-language printing house moved to the city from Slavuta*; in 1845, Zhitomir and Vilna* were the only two centers in Russia with the permission to publish Hebrew books. In 1848, the authorities opened a rabbinical seminary in Zhitomir, whose graduates eventually formed an important part of the Russian-Jewish intelligentsia. The authorities closed the seminary in 1885. From 1864 to 1882, the author Mendele Mokher Seforim (Shalom Jacob Abramowitsch) lived and worked in the city. On the eve of World War I, Zhitomir had a Jewish population of about 40,000.

During the Russian Civil War (1918–20), the community was targeted by several pogroms. In the course of two pogroms (conducted in January and March 1919) alone, Simon Petliura's army destroyed Jewish property and killed more than 400 Jews. Under Polish rule (May–June 1920) there were also incidents of abuse and several dozen executions of Jewish inhabitants. During the interwar

Zhitomir, August 7, 1941
About 400 Jewish men are rounded up in the city square and forced to watch the hanging of two Jews, Wolf Kieper and Mojsch Kogan. After the execution, all of the assembled men were murdered by the Einsatzgruppe. (YV)

period there were 30,000 Jews in Zhitomir; on the eve of the German invasion they comprised one-third of the city's population.

The introduction of Soviet rule in the summer of 1920 transformed Jewish life. In the 1920s and 1930s, private enterprise dwindled and was eventually eliminated altogether. Thousands of Jews joined trade unions, while artisans formed cooperatives. Zionist youth-movement and party activity waned and was ultimately outlawed. From January 1925 onward, the city had Jewish government schools and a state court of law that all operated in Yiddish. Teachers' colleges trained hundreds of young Jews to work in Yiddish-language government schools that operated throughout the Ukraine. Although prohibited, Hadarim continued to function, and a small Yeshiva was founded.

The Germans occupied Zhitomir on July 9, 1941. Most of the city's Jews were either evacuated at the order of the retreating Soviet authorities, fled, or dispersed to nearby localities before the Germans arrived. The invading forces were accompanied by a unit of Sonderkommando 4a, which set about murdering people. On July 15, 1941, approximately 100 Jews from Zhitomir were shot; by the end of the month some 360 had been murdered. In August 1941, several operations were conducted in the city: 402 Jews were shot to death and two hanged on August 7; another 266 were shot on August 17. A census conducted on September 5, 1941, counted 40,131 residents in Zhitomir, of whom 4,079 were Jews.

Following the census, the Germans ghettoized the Jews on three streets in the poorest quarter of the city. In the ensuing days, Jews from nearby localities were brought into the ghetto. Inhabitants were obliged to wear a Star-of-David armband. Jews were forbidden to bring furniture into the ghetto while a minimum of other goods, including food, was permissible. They were initially allowed to leave the ghetto during daytime hours to purchase provisions, but within a few days the ghetto was sealed and surrounded with barbed wire. The local authorities appointed a Jewish resident of the city as head of the Jews. Food rations for ghetto inhabitants were half of those allotted to Ukrainians. Overcrowding and starvation in the ghetto led to epidemics that claimed many lives. Jews were removed for harsh labor in city. Rumors spread among the Jews that they were to be deported to Odessa* and on to Palestine.

On September 18, 1941, Ukrainian police surrounded the ghetto. The following day, Sonderkommando 4a murdered 3,145 Jews in Bogun Forest. In October, the same unit murdered 1,500 Jews near the Vidumka estate. Concurrently, the Nazis removed thirty-five disabled Jews from the city's home for the handicapped and fifty children from the municipal orphanage, murdering all. After the liquidation operation, 237 skilled workers were left behind in a large building in the city to serve the Wehrmacht. On August 19, 1942, they, too, were murdered.

ZHLOBIN
(Yiddish: **Zlobin**)

COUNTY SEAT, GOMEL OBLAST, BELARUS, USSR

During the war: Military Administration Area

Coordinates:
52°54' | 30°03'

In the late 1930s, there were about 3,700 Jews in Zhlobin, roughly one-fifth of the local population. During the era of Soviet rule, many Jews practiced artisan trades, some in cooperatives. A few turned to farming at kolkhozes that had been set up in the vicinity. The town had a Yiddish-language government school.

The Germans first occupied Zhlobin on July 3, 1941. The Red Army managed to liberate the town on July 13, 1941, but the Germans reoccupied it on August 14. Apparently, much of the Jewish population had time to flee to the Soviet interior before the reoccupation. Under German rule, Jews were not allowed to shop for food in public places, speak with the locals, or walk on main streets.

The two ghettos in Zhlobin were liquidated on April 12, 1942, when their approximately 1,200 inhabitants were murdered near the neighboring village of Lebedevka.

ZHMERINKA
(Ukrainian: **Zhmerynka**)

COUNTY SEAT, VINNITSA DISTRICT, UKRAINE, USSR

During the war: Transnistria (under Romanian control)

Coordinates:
49°02' | 28°06'

On the eve of the German invasion of the Soviet Union, there were 4,630 Jews living in Zhmerinka, representing less than 20 percent of the town's population. During the Soviet period, most of Zhmerinka's Jews engaged in artisanship, and, in the 1920s, in commerce as well. A small number were farmers or clerks. In response to growing industrialization and urbanization and the harsh economic climate that prevailed in the town, many of the younger generation left Zhmerinka. The town had a Yiddish-language school.

In the wake of the German invasion of the Soviet Union, the greater part of the town's population, including most of its Jews, managed to escape into the Soviet interior, as Zhmerinka was located on a railroad route. The Germans occupied the town on July 17, 1941, and set about looting Jewish property and murdering Jews. According to the figures of the German administration, there were about 600 Jews living in Zhmerinka in late August 1941. In the second half of August 1941, the Germans began to concentrate the town's Jews near the market in a quarter vacated of its non-Jewish residents; the area gradually transformed into a ghetto of sorts.

On September 1, 1941, Zhmerinka was annexed to Transnistria, which was under Romanian control. Hundreds of Jewish refugees thronged to the Zhmerinka ghetto from the German occupation zone, and by early October 1941, the population had grown to some 1,200 Jews. In October 1941, about 500 Jewish deportees from Bukovina and Bessarabia were brought to the ghetto, and concurrently, Ukrainian Jews likewise arrived. In early November 1941, the ghetto was encircled by a barbed-wire fence.

The ghetto was extremely overcrowded, and the Jews were forbidden to leave its grounds under pain of death. Hunger was widespread. Ghetto inhabitants occasionally bartered possessions for food and received vegetables from the Ukrai-

Zhmerinka
Students and teachers in a ghetto school active in 1942–1943. Some 250 children attended the school, where they studied Jewish and general subjects. (YV)

nians. A community council was established in the ghetto in the first months of the occupation. Yosef Yukelis was appointed head of the council, and Ochakovskii was appointed to head the Jewish Order Service. After the arrival of the deportees from Romania, a Romanian department was established in the council, headed by attorney Adolf Herschman from Czernowitz*, who spoke both Romanian and German. Later, Herschman was appointed head of the ghetto, while Yukelis stayed on as a member of the Jewish council. Herschman, who received the title of "Ghetto President", ran ghetto affairs with an iron hand; he demanded discipline and punished those who disobeyed his orders. He appointed a local Jew, Matvei Belikovetskii, to head the Jewish Order Service. With the consent of Pretor Ionesco, the head of the Romanian administration in Zhmerinka, the Jewish Order Service was awarded the responsibility of guarding the ghetto, and neither Ukrainians seeking to carry out pogroms against the Jews nor German police were permitted to enter the ghetto boundaries.

The Jewish council in Zhmerinka organized labor groups to supply the Romanian and German authorities with forced labor. Those recruited were employed doing cleaning and construction work under harsh conditions, and many fell ill or froze to death. For his part, Herschman expended every effort to guarantee the safe return of the workers to the ghetto. Meanwhile, the ghetto council established leather tanning and bookbinding workshops with tax money collected from the Jews. The products manufactured in the workshops were sold outside the ghetto; the proceeds were handed over to the Romanians and distributed among the workshop foremen, the council, and the Jewish workers. Children were occasionally ordered to work, especially in harvesting agricultural produce.

The Jewish council also established sanitary and transportation departments and operated a public soup kitchen, a bathhouse, and a hospital, which managed to prevent the spread of epidemic typhus in the ghetto. In the years 1942–43, a Russian-language school operated in the ghetto. About 250 children studied Jewish and general subjects (with the exception of history and geography, which the Romanians considered political topics), as well as the German and Romanian languages. Most of the children's parents paid tuition, while the council subsidized the payment for the poor and orphans. The ghetto also boasted a kindergarten and traditional Heder as well as a club that put on theater plays in Yiddish once a week. Daily public services were held in a synagogue, and three shops and a café were opened.

The ghetto council was constrained to see to the continual absorption of Jews who had fled from ghettos in the German occupation zone. German policemen once visited the ghetto and demanded that the escapees be handed over. Herschman intervened, ordering the Jewish policemen to defy the command by force and notifying the Germans that he would hand the fugitives over only at Antonescu's orders. The Germans relented. In August 1942, the Germans exploited Herschman's absence to enter the ghetto and retrieve Jews who had escaped from the Brailov* ghetto. Herschman immediately returned to the ghetto and convinced the Germans to leave behind the escapees' children. However, 286 Jews were returned to the Brailov ghetto and murdered in its liquidation on August 25, 1942. After the deportation of the Brailov Jews, Herschman agreed to accept into the ghetto only wealthy deportees or professionals from among the Ukrainian Jews from the German occupation zone. He also attempted to remove to other localities a number of the Jewish refugees who were living in the ghetto. In anticipation of the future liquidation of the ghetto, Herschman ordered the digging of tunnels leading to nearby forests. In March 1943, a delegation of the Jewish aid committee in Bucharest visited Zhmerinka. At that time, there were 3,274 Jews in the ghetto, including 2,700 from Ukraine.

A Jewish underground headed by teacher Arkadi (Aharon) Gefter was active in the ghetto and maintained ties with Soviet partisans. The group collected arms and intelligence information from the town's train station, which it passed on to the partisans. False papers were produced in the ghetto that, among other applications, occasionally secured the release partisans from jail. The underground also had a secret radio receiver that printed out news dispatches broadcast on Radio Moscow that were then distributed among the Jews in the ghetto. In July 1943, the members of the ghetto underground were arrested and murdered in Tiraspol*.

In late 1943, Herschman was dismissed from his position by the Romanian gendarmerie commander following complaints by ghetto inhabitants of his high-handed style of government.

As the German-Soviet front drew closer to the area of Zhmerinka in February–March 1944, many of the ghetto's inhabitants fled to nearby localities, fearing the actions of the retreating Germans. The town exchanged hands a number of times. The Jews assisted units of the Red Army by transferring ammunition and securing the train station in which the Germans were holed up.

Zhmerinka was liberated on March 20, 1944.

ZHORNISHCHE
(Ukrainian: **Zhornyshche**)

TOWNLET IN ILYINTSY COUNTY, VINNITSA DISTRICT, UKRAINE, USSR

During the war:
Reichskommissariat Ukraine

Coordinates:
49°04' | 29°05'

In the mid-1920s, Zhornishche had a Jewish population of 1,000. When the Soviets took power, the Jews' economic and social lives were transformed. Private enterprise was abolished, former merchants found work in municipal and state-owned institutions, and artisans formed cooperatives. The townlet had a government school that taught in Yiddish.

After the German invasion of the Soviet Union, a number of Jewish townspeople fled to the Soviet interior. The Germans occupied Zhornishche on July 16, 1941, and in August 1941, thirteen Jews were murdered there.

In September 1941, a ghetto was established in Zhornishche holding over 500 Jews. Jewish refugees from Vinnitsa were likewise concentrated in the ghetto. The ghetto was liquidated on May 27, 1942, when all its inhabitants were transferred to Ilyintsy* and murdered along with other Jews from the vicinity.

ZHURAVICHI
(Yiddish: **Zhuravitsh**;
Belarussian: **Zhuravichy**)

COUNTY SEAT, GOMEL DISTRICT, BELARUS, USSR

During the war: Military Administration Area

Coordinates:
53°15' | 30°33'

In the early twentieth century, there were about 1,600 Jews in Zhuravichi, roughly 60 percent of the population. During the era of Soviet rule, Jewish artisans continued to practice their trades, and many organized in cooperatives. Others became white- or blue-collar workers; a few turned to farming. The townlet had a Yiddish school. Urbanization and industrialization in the Soviet Union prompted many Jews to leave the townlet; by the end of the 1930s, there were about 650 Jews left, one-quarter of the population.

After the Germans invaded the Soviet Union on June 22, 1941, many Jewish townspeople were inducted into the Red Army. The Germans occupied Zhuravichi on August 14, 1941. Some time later, they ordered the Jews to wear a yellow Star-of-David on the front and back of their clothing. The Jews were concentrated in a ghetto near the townlet and were forbidden to leave except to perform forced labor. In early December 1941, the Germans murdered seventy-two male Jews aged sixteen to sixty years near the villages of Novyi Krivsk and Staryi Krivsk.

The ghetto was liquidated on January 1, 1942, when the Germans, assisted by Belarussian police, murdered all 171 remaining Jews at nearby Starina ravine.

ZINKOV
(Ukrainian: **Zin'kiv**)

TOWN IN VINKOVTSY COUNTY, KAMENETS-PODOLSK DISTRICT, UKRAINE, USSR

During the war:
Reichskommissariat Ukraine

Coordinates:
49°05' | 27°04'

At the beginning of the twentieth century there were about 3,700 Jews in Zinkov, more than one-third of the town's population. During the Soviet era, the town had a Jewish Ethnic Soviet and a Jewish government school that taught in Yiddish. Many Jewish artisans formed cooperatives, and several Jews established a kolkhoz near the town. By the eve of World War II, rapid urbanization and industrialization had reduced the Jewish population of the town to 2,200, one-third of the total.

When the Germans invaded the Soviet Union in June 1941, some townsmen were conscripted into the Red Army. Several hundred Jews managed to evacuate to eastern parts of the USSR. Twenty-six Jewish refugees from western Ukraine were killed in German bombardments of the town.

The Germans occupied Zinkov on July 10, 1941, and, aided and abetted by local Ukrainians, immediately began to dispossess, abuse, and murder Jewish inhabitants. In August 1941, the Ukrainian local authorities appointed several Jewish dignitaries to represent the community, including Yosef Bukhgalter, Khaim Foigelman, and Einekh Fukelman. They served as hostages in exchange for whom the community was to remit ransoms to the authorities. Jews over the age of ten were obligated to wear a yellow star and were forbidden to walk on sidewalks or draw water from the central well. The Jews' mortality rate escalated as overcrowding, starvation, and poor sanitation contributed to the spread of contagious diseases. Skilled workers were allowed to practice their trades but were required to pay for labor permits.

On May 9, 1942, near the village of Stanislavovka, the Germans murdered some 600 mostly ill and elderly Jews. On August 4, 1942, they deported 1,882 Jews from Zinkov and the vicinity to Dunayevtsy*, leaving behind about 200 skilled workers in a ghetto of sorts consisting of one building surrounded by barbed wire. These Jews were murdered one month later.

ZLATOPOL

(Ukrainian: **Zlatopil'**)

COUNTY SEAT, KIROVOGRAD DISTRICT, UKRAINE, USSR

During the war: Reichskommissariat Ukraine

Coordinates: 48°50' | 31°40'

In the early twentieth century, there were about 6,300 Jews in Zlatopol, nearly 80 percent of the town's population. On May 2, 1919, more than 100 Jews were murdered in a pogrom perpetrated by Ukrainian peasants. In the aftermath of the pogrom, a Jewish self-defense system was organized. In the early 1930s, several Jews in Zlatopol formed artisans' cooperatives, while others became white-collar, blue-collar, or farm workers. Industrialization and urbanization in the Soviet Union reduced Zlatopol's Jewish population to about 1,000 shortly before the German invasion in June 1941.

The Germans occupied Zlatopol on August 1, 1941. An indeterminate number of Jews managed to flee to the east prior to the German invasion. In November 1941, of the town's Jews 174 were gassed to death. In December 1941, Zlatopol's remaining Jews were concentrated in the orphanage, which was transformed into a ghetto of sorts. The building was fenced in with barbed wire and guarded by Ukrainian sentries. On February 2, 1942, altogether 202 ghetto inhabitants were gassed to death. In May 1942, another 183 were shot to death near the village of Listopadovo. In July 1942, fourteen Jews who were caught in the nearby forest were killed.

The ghetto was liquidated on September 30, 1942, when Zlatopol's remaining 100 Jews were murdered. During this operation, several youths organized resistance against the Germans and Ukrainians. The murder of Zlatopol's Jews was carried out by Einsatzkommando 12.

ZŁOCZÓW

COUNTY SEAT, TARNOPOL DISTRICT, POLAND

(After World War II in the USSR/Ukraine; Ukrainian: **Zolochiv**; Russian: **Zolochev**)

During the war: General Gouvernement, Galicia District

Coordinates: 49°48' | 24°54'

In the early 1930s, about 5,700 Jews lived in Zloczow, representing approximately half the town's population. They earned their livelihood from commerce, artisanship, small-scale industry, and the liberal professions. Zloczow had various Jewish political organizations, including Zionist parties and Agudath Israel. The General Zionist party dominated the community council, and its representatives were on the town council. The Jewish community maintained various Jewish welfare institutions, including a hospital, as well as culture and sports clubs and a number of schools.

In the second half of September 1939, Zloczow was occupied by the Red Army and handed over to Soviet control. The Jews' industrial and commercial activities were phased out and artisans were organized into cooperatives. Jewish community activity was halted, with the exception of the synagogues, which remained open. Jewish refugees from western Poland thronged to the town, several of whom were exiled to the Soviet Union in June 1940. In the spring of 1941, young Jews from Zloczow were conscripted into the Red Army. In late June 1941, dozens of the town's Jews were killed in a German bombing.

On July 2, 1941, the German army occupied Zloczow, and on July 4, the Ukrainians began to terrorize the Jews, with the active assistance of the Germans. During the following three days they murdered between 300 and 500 Jews (according to German sources) in the town's streets or in a nearby fortress. On July 7–8, the Germans murdered a number of Jews who had been active during the town's Soviet occupation, and on July 10, about 300 Jewish members of the intelligentsia were killed.

In mid-July 1941, a Judenrat was established, headed by the Zionist activist Sigmund Meiblum, who had served as deputy mayor of Zloczow. The Judenrat had twelve members, all academics. A Jewish Order Service under the command of D. Landsberg was also established. Severe restrictions were placed on the Jews'

Zloczow, April 1943
The Jews of Zloczow are led to shooting pits near the village of Jelichowice. (GFH)

freedom of movement, along with limitations on the purchase of food; property and valuables were confiscated and many Jews were recruited for forced labor.

Within a few weeks, many Jews began to suffer from starvation, and the Judenrat established a public soup kitchen and provided assistance to the needy. From November 1941 onward, hundreds of young Jews were sent from Zloczow to various labor camps in the area. The Judenrat was partially involved in selecting the laborers; they attempted to distribute the burden and help those imprisoned in the camps. At this stage, Jews who worked in food plants and bakeries were considered "vital" and were consequently protected (to a certain extent) from the labor camps. As a result, many people endeavored to obtain jobs in plants and bakeries. The German administrator Josef Mayer, who was responsible for agriculture and food in the area, extended a great deal of help the Jews of Zloczow and was recognized as a "Righteous Among the Nations" on behalf of Yad Vashem after the war.

In April 1942, about 6,000 Jews lived in Zloczow. In mid-August 1942, the members of the Judenrat, headed by Meiblum, were called into the offices of the German police in Tarnopol*. German police officer Hermann Mueller instructed the Judenrat members to draw up a list of 2,500 Jews "unfit for work." On August 28, 1942, an operation was launched in Zloczow. German and Ukrainian police, with the help of members of the Jewish Order Service, arrested Jews and searched for those in hiding. Jews who attempted escape were shot. By August 30, about 2,000 Jews, including hospital patients and a number of members of the medical staff, had been rounded up and brought to the local train station and deported to the Belzec death camp. On November 2–3, 1942, another operation was carried out and about 2,500 Jews, mainly children, women, and the elderly, were deported to Belzec.

On December 1, 1942, Zloczow saw the establishment of a ghetto in which the surviving Jews of the town were concentrated together with the surviving Jews of numerous localities in the area—in all either about 4,000 or between 7,500 and 9,000 (sources vary regarding the figure) people. Overcrowding was severe, and epidemic typhus soon spread throughout the ghetto, costing many lives.

The Jews searched for ways to save themselves. A few managed to escape to Romania using false Aryan papers, and many others prepared hiding places in the town and forests.

On April 2, 1943, German police units under the command of Erich Engels carried out an operation to liquidate the ghetto. German and Ukrainian police encircled and entered the ghetto, and rounded up all of its approximately 3,500 or 6,000 (sources vary regarding the figure) inhabitants in the marketplace. The Germans prepared a document indicating the necessity to liquidate the ghetto owing to the epidemic typhus outbreak, which he demanded that Meiblum, the Judenrat head, and council members Shutz and Kier sign. All three refused to sign and were summarily executed. The Jews were then loaded onto trucks that transported them to pits near the village of Jelichowice, located some four kilometers from Zloczow, where they were shot to death. In the coming days, the hunts for Jews hiding in the forests and on the Aryan side of the town persisted and groups of Jews who were apprehended were executed near Jelichowice, and afterwards in the Jewish cemetery.

A group of artisans remained in the ghetto. Several of the artisans formed two underground groups with the goal of acquiring arms and escaping to the forest to join the partisans. Most of the groups' members, however, were caught by the Germans and executed.

ZLYNKA

TOWNLET IN NOVOZYBKOV COUNTY, OREL DISTRICT, RUSSIAN FEDERATION, USSR

During the war: Military Administration Area

Coordinates:
52°24' | 31°45'

On the eve of World War II, about 450 Jews lived in Zlynka, representing roughly 5 percent of the local population. They engaged mainly in artisanship and commerce, and received assistance from Jewish organizations in the United States. Zlynka had an artisans' union, two-thirds of whose members were Jews. The Jewish children of the townlet studied in Russian schools, although the townlet had traditional Hadarim as well, during the 1920s.

Zlynka was occupied by the Germans on August 25, 1941. In early September, twenty-seven local Jews were incarcerated for one week in a windmill without food or water and then shot to death.

In September or October 1941, the 200 to 230 Jews who remained in Zlynka were concentrated in a ghetto of sorts established in a building formerly used as a machine and tractor station, located one kilometer east of Zlynka.

The ghetto was liquidated on February 15, 1942, when its inhabitants were murdered in nearby anti-tank trenches. Local policemen participated in the murders.

ŻMIGRÓD NOWY

TOWNLET IN JASŁO COUNTY, CRACOW DISTRICT, POLAND

During the war: General Gouvernement, Cracow District

Coordinates:
49°37' | 21°32'

About 800 Jews lived in Zmigrod Nowy during the interwar period, representing roughly 40 percent of the townlet's population. The community had active Zionist parties and youth movements that held Hebrew classes and ran a library.

In November 1918, pogroms were carried out against the Jews in the townlet. A great deal of Jewish property was plundered and several Jews were seriously injured.

After the German invasion in September 1939, a number of the townlet's Jews fled to the zone controlled by the Soviets. In the summer of 1940, most of these Jews were exiled to the Soviet Union.

The Germans restricted the freedom of movement of Zmigrod Nowy's Jewish inhabitants, ordered them to wear a badge, and periodically levied ransoms. They also required the Jews to perform forced labor. In late 1939, a Judenrat was established, headed by Hirsh Eisenberg. The Judenrat was responsible for recruiting forced laborers for the Germans.

In 1940, deportees from localities in the area were brought to Zmigrod Nowy, along with refugees from more distant places, including Lodz*. The Judenrat and JSS members ran a public soup kitchen and provided medical and material assistance. In the second half of 1940, abductions of Jews from Zmigrod Nowy to labor camps escalated. A number of the people seized toiled near the border with the Soviet Union.

In the first half of 1942, a ghetto was established in Zmigrod Nowy. Additional deportees from localities in the area were concentrated there, and its population grew to more than 2,000. The Judenrat attempted to secure jobs outside the ghetto so as to maintain contact with the outside world and to obtain permits for work in vital factories.

In early July 1942, the Judenrat was required to remit a ransom payment. On July 7, 1942, an operation was carried out. Following a selection, altogether 1,250 Jews were shot to death in a forest near the village of Halbow by German, Ukrainian, and Polish policemen. Judenrat head Eisenberg was also murdered over the claim that he failed to pay the ransom. Dozens of Jews fled to the forests, and a group of between seventy and eighty Jews wandered the area in search of refuge. Most were apprehended and murdered, others fell in battle with German and Polish police.

On August 15, 1942, a group of skilled workers was transferred to the Zaslaw labor camp in Sanok*, and another group was transferred to the Plaszow camp in Cracow*. In late summer 1942, the last surviving members of the Zmigrod Nowy community were deported to the Belzec death camp.

ŻÓŁKIEW

COUNTY SEAT, LWÓW DISTRICT, POLAND

(After World War II in the USSR/Ukraine; Ukrainian: **Zhovkva**; Russian: **Zholkva**)

During the war: General Gouvernement, Galicia District

Coordinates:
50°04' | 23°58'

In the 1930s, some 4,400 Jews lived in Zolkiew, representing roughly half of the townlet's population. They earned their livelihood from commerce and various forms of artisanship, and many were destitute. Zolkiew had a number of welfare organizations. Among the Jewish parties, the Zionists were especially dominant and organized the cultural activities in the townlet. Zolkiew also had a community of Belz Hasidism.

On September 18, 1939, Zolkiew was occupied by the Germans, and on September 24, the townlet was handed over to the Soviets. During this period, hundreds of Jewish refugees thronged to it from western Poland. Under the Soviets, private commerce was almost completely discontinued, most of the Jewish artisans were integrated into the cooperatives, and Jewish Communists became involved in the local administration of the townlet. In the spring of 1940, a number of "bourgeois" families were exiled from it, and in June 1940, hundreds of Jewish refugees were deported to the interior part of the Soviet Union. The Jews of Zolkiew established a council to aid and maintain a certain level of contact with those who had been exiled.

On June 28, 1941, the Germans occupied Zolkiew and burned down the great synagogue the following day. In July 1941, a Judenrat was established, headed by Fobins Rubinsfeld, as was a Jewish Order Service under the command of P. Chachkes. A number of anti-Jewish decrees were issued: Jewish inhabitants were compelled to wear a Star-of-David armband, they were forbidden to shop in the municipal market, their valuables were confiscated, they were required to pay fines to the Germans, and they were required to perform forced labor. Jews were evicted from their homes, which were used to house German officers. In August–

September, a number of Jews who sympathized with the Soviet regime were arrested, interrogated, tortured, and finally executed. In December 1941, the Jews were ordered to turn over all furs in their possession. In the winter of 1941/42, starvation and epidemic typhus became rampant in the Jewish community. Using its meager means, the Judenrat established a hospital and public soup kitchens and extended assistance to the needy, but this help only slightly alleviated the suffering. From late 1941 to early 1942, about thirty teachers secretly organized small school classes for the children of the community.

On March 15, 1942, German police units under the command of Helmut Tanzmann carried out an operation in Zolkiew. They deported to the Belzec death camp 700 ill and elderly Jews who were on a list of the unemployed that the Judenrat had been constrained to draw up. The Judenrat attempted to ascertain the fate of the deportees, as their transport was the first ever from the entire area to leave for the death camp; the Judenrat did determine what had happened to the deportees through investigations carried out among the local farmers. Some time later, SS men seized sixty Jews for the Lackie labor camp located near Zloczow*.

In the summer of 1942, the Judenrat and Jewish Order Service extended assistance to Jews deported from other localities who, after jumping off the death trains headed for Belzec, had arrived in Zolkiew. They offered the fugitives asylum, food, and medical care. Upon learning that the Germans were searching the hospital for the escapees, they were put up in private homes.

On November 22–23, 1942, the Germans carried out another operation in Zolkiew. More than 2,000 Jews, including residents of townlets and villages in the area, were rounded up in the courtyard of the local castle. Those assembled were subjected to prolonged abuse, culminating in the deaths of several dozen people and the deportation of the rest in trains to the Belzec death camp.

Many of the deported jumped from the train cars (several people came equipped with tools to assist in breaking out), but few individuals managed to return to Zolkiew. When the operation ended, the Jews of Zolkiew located the bodies of some 300 people. The deceased were collected from where they lay, in the streets, at the round up site, or where they had jumped from the train, and given a Jewish burial.

About one week after the operation, on December 1, 1942, the surviving members of the Zolkiew community were concentrated in a ghetto along with numerous Jews from other nearby localities. The ghetto was encircled by a barbed-wire fence and was guarded from without by Germans and Ukrainians and from within by the Jewish Order Service. The inhabitants were forbidden to leave its grounds. Poor sanitary conditions and severe overcrowding in the ghetto led to an outbreak of epidemic typhus that caused numerous deaths. Several Jews managed to escape from the ghetto through false "Aryan" documents or by finding a place to hide with Christian acquaintances. The majority prepared places of concealment and attempted to join the lists of workers considered essential to the German economy. On March 15, 1943, altogether 618 Jews considered fit for work were removed from the ghetto to the Janowska camp in the suburbs of Lwow*.

The ghetto was liquidated in two murder operations carried out on March 25 and April 6, 1943, by a Gestapo unit from Lwow under the command of Erich Engels, aided by the gendarmerie and Ukrainian police. A brutal search was carried out in the ghetto in which walls and floor tiles were smashed. About

150 men and women were sent to the Janowska labor camp, and another 60 skilled workers were left in Zolkiew. The rest of the Jews, about 3,500 in number (according to a single testimony), including the last remaining members of the Judenrat and the Jewish Order Service, were brought to a forest located about three kilometers from Zolkiew and shot to death. The skilled workers were concentrated outside the ghetto and assigned the task of sorting through the belongings of the murder victims and assorted other jobs, until most were murdered on July 10, 1943.

A considerable number of Jews continued to hide in the ruins of the ghetto, in the townlet, and in the surrounding forests, and the hunt for the fugitives continued until the liberation. Those who were caught were rounded up in groups and executed in the cemetery. Other groups were sent to the Janowska camp in the fall of 1943.

ŻOŁUDEK

TOWNLET IN SZCZUCZYN COUNTY, NOWOGRÓDEK DISTRICT, POLAND
(After World War II in the USSR/Belarus; Belarussian: **Zhaludok**; Russian: **Zheludok**)

During the war:
Reichskommissariat Ostland

Coordinates:
53°36' | 24°59'

About 1,800 Jews lived in Zoludek on the eve of World War II, representing approximately two-thirds of the townlet's population. Most earned their livelihood from commerce and artisanship. In the 1920s and 1930s, Jewish public activity became so developed in Zoludek that it was known as "Little Vilna." The Jewish and Zionist parties in the townlet, among them the Bund, ran youth movements and established study circles, lectures, and schools, including Hebrew and Yiddish schools.

Following the entry of the Soviet army into Zoludek on September 18, 1939, a Soviet system was instituted in the townlet: privately owned businesses were nationalized or closed and cooperatives were formed.

The Germans occupied Zoludek on June 27, 1941 and immediately set fire to entire streets, an act that they accused the Jews of Zoludek of committing. A short time later, between forty and fifty Jews were arrested and beaten to death outside of the townlet. As of early July 1941, the Jews of Zoludek were ordered to wear a yellow badge and were required to turn over all of their valuables to the Germans. A number of them were seized for forced labor, and in the summer of 1941, twenty-two forced laborers working on the Zoludek estate were murdered.

On October 7, 1941, at German orders, the Jews established a Judenrat headed by Mendel Galai. The Judenrat was charged with recruiting Jews for forced labor. In early October or in November 1941 (sources vary on the date), a ghetto was established on one of the few streets that was not destroyed in the fire. On November 2, Jews from the village of Orla* were transferred to Zoludek, further exacerbating the overcrowded conditions in the ghetto. On November 10, 1941, twenty-eight Jews were murdered. In early 1942, about 200 of Zoludek's Jews were apparently taken to the Skrzybowce labor camp and returned to Zoludek on the eve of the large-scale operation. On March 1, 1942, another thirty-two Jews were murdered.

On May 9, 1942, a liquidation operation was launched in the ghetto, and between 1,000 and 1,400 Jews were murdered in pits outside the townlet; a few Jews caught hiding were also murdered. A number of Jews fled during the operation and joined the various partisan units in the forests.

The Germans spared some eighty skilled workers who were transferred on May 21, 1942, to the Szczuczyn* ghetto; several workers were sent on to the Lida* ghetto.

ŻURAWNO

TOWNLET IN ŻYDACZÓW COUNTY, STANISŁAWÓW DISTRICT, POLAND
(After World War II in the USSR/Ukraine; Ukrainian: **Zhuravne**; Russian: **Zhuravno**)

During the war: General Gouvernement, Galicia District

Coordinates:
49°15' | 24°17'

In the 1930s, about 1,000 Jews lived in Zurawno, representing roughly half the townlet's population. The Zionist movement was influential in the community, and Zurawno had a number of chapters of Zionist youth movements. The community ran several welfare organizations, a supplementary Hebrew school, a Talmud Torah, and a Tarbut library.

In the second half of September 1939, Zurawno was handed over to Soviet control. The economic activity of the townlet was nationalized and Jewish parties were abolished.

On July 3, 1941, Zurawno was occupied by the Germans. A number of anti-Jewish decrees were issued, and Jews were seized for particularly harsh forced labor. In July, a Judenrat was established, as were a Jewish Order Service and an employment bureau to register and recruit Jews for forced labor. In the fall of 1941, the daily quota of forced laborers reached 200 Jews. In mid-August 1941, absorbed into the community were 150 Jews driven out from Wojnilow were brought to Zurawno. Hunger and epidemic typhus soon spread, causing the deaths of more than 150 Jews in the course of the 1941/42 winter season. On March 13, 1942, gangs of Ukrainians, encouraged by the Germans, carried out a pogrom against the Jews. After the pogrom, a group of Jews was transferred to Chodorow*; their fate is unknown. In mid-June 1942, dozens of young Jews were sent from Zurawno to the labor camp in Chodorow.

On September 4–5, 1942, an operation was conducted in the townlet, and about 500 Jews were deported to the Belzec death camp. After the deportation, the Jews who remained in Zurawno were concentrated in a ghetto. On September 25, 1942, the Germans announced the liquidation of the Zurawno ghetto and the transfer of all its inhabitants to Stryj*, but the payment of a large ransom mitigated the decree, so that on September 29, only a portion of the inhabitants were deported to Stryj, where they joined those deported to Belzec.

The Jews who remained in the Zurawno ghetto strove to secure jobs classified as "essential" to the Germans, largely in quarries, sawmills, and collecting scrap metal. A few Jews managed to find places to hide in the forest or with Christian acquaintances.

The Zurawno ghetto was gradually liquidated in a series of executions that continued from February 1943 through to the murder of the last group of Zurawno's Jews on June 5, 1943.

ZVENIGORODKA
(Yiddish: **Zvinogorodke**; Ukrainian: **Zvenyhorodka**)

COUNTY SEAT, KIEV DISTRICT, UKRAINE, USSR

During the war: Reichskommissariat Ukraine

Coordinates:
49°05' | 30°58'

In the early twentieth century, Zvenigorodka had a Jewish population of 6,400. A pogrom in 1918 claimed the lives of twenty-seven Jews and injured many others. Under Soviet rule, many Jewish artisans continued to practice their trades, with several forming cooperatives. A few Jews became farmers; a Jewish kolkhoz was created near the town. Zvenigorodka had Jewish government schools and a department of the court of law that operated in Yiddish. Industrialization and urbanization in the Soviet Union prompted many Jews to leave the town in the 1920s and 1930s; at the onset of World War II, some 2,000 remained.

The Germans occupied Zvenigorodka on July 29, 1941. A nearby railroad track enabled a number Jews to flee, while others were evacuated to the east before the Germans' arrival. On August 16, 1941, the Germans murdered a group of Jews in the town. During September they murdered approximately 100 Jewish men.

In October 1941, the remaining Jews in Zvenigorodka were concentrated in a ghetto together with Jews from nearby towns and villages. Although it was unfenced, the Jews were forbidden to leave and were required to wear armbands. A man named Lazurik was appointed head of the Jews. A clinic operated in the ghetto. On May 5, 1942, a large group of youths was sent from the ghetto to a labor camp in the village of Nemorozh. During the same month, several dozen Jews were brought to Zvenigorodka from the Olshana* ghetto.

The ghetto was apparently liquidated on July 14, 1942, when most of its inhabitants—some 1,500 people—were murdered near the town. The survivors were young people and adults, mostly skilled workers. They were sent to the labor camp at Nemorozh, where they worked in quarries, felled trees, and repaired roads under appalling conditions. The camp prisoners were shot to death on November 2, 1942.

ZWOLEŃ

TOWNLET IN KOZIENICE COUNTY, KIELCE DISTRICT, POLAND

During the war: General Gouvernement, Radom District

Coordinates:
51°21' | 21°36'

After World War I, there were approximately 3,800 Jews in Zwolen, about half the population of the townlet. Most were merchants and artisans. The townlet had a Jewish haulage cooperative that transported goods to Warsaw*. Many Jews in Zwolen belonged to Hasidic courts, but Zionist movements and the Bund were also active. The community had charitable societies and a Beit Yaakov girls' school.

The Germans entered Zwolen on September 8, 1939. By the end of that year, a Judenrat was established under a baker named Velvl Kirshenblat. The Judenrat registered Jews aged fourteen to sixty for forced labor. In early 1940, a steep ransom was imposed on the community, an open ghetto was established, and a six-member Jewish Order Service under the command of Mendel Weintraub was appointed.

Zwolen
Sign at the entrance to the ghetto: "Boundary of Jewish living area. Jews leaving the living area without permission will be punished with death. Signed–District commander."
(YV)

The Germans sealed the ghetto in February 1942. In August of that year, some 500 Jewish laborers were taken to the Skarzysko-Kamienna camp, and fifteen of them were murdered.

During the summer of 1942, some 4,000 Jews from the towns and villages of Pionki, Garbatka, Gniewoszow*, Sarnowa, and Kazanow were moved to the Zwolen ghetto, bringing its population to about 8,000.

On September 29, 1942, the ghetto was surrounded, and the Jews were ordered to assemble in the marketplace, whence they were deported to the Treblinka death camp. Many elderly and ill Jews were murdered on the spot, along with those who had been in hiding. Members of the Jewish Order Service buried them in the Jewish cemetery.

Approximately 200 Jews were left behind to gather up the victims' belongings. On November 30, 1942, some of them were murdered, and the others were taken to the Skarzysko-Kamienna camp by members of the German *Werkschutz* (factory guards).

ŻYCHLIN

TOWNLET IN KUTNO COUNTY, WARSAW DISTRICT, POLAND

During the war: Wartheland

Coordinates:
52°15' | 19°37'

Before World War II, there were between 2,600 and 2,800 Jews in Zychlin, totaling more than one-third of the townlet's population. Most were petty merchants and artisans. The community had a Yeshiva, a Beit Yaakov girls' school, a Tarbut school, and Szabasowka schools with Jewish staff. Agudath Israel and various Zionist parties were active in the townlet.

The Germans occupied Zychlin on September 17, 1939, seizing Jews for forced labor, restricting their movement, and looting their property. In November 1939, the Jews were ordered to wear a yellow band, which was later replaced by two stars worn on the back and front of their clothing. Jews were required to post a sign with the word "Jude" on their front doors. In April 1940, several members of the Polish and Jewish intelligentsia were arrested and sent to concentration camps in Germany.

The Zychlin ghetto was established on July 20, 1940. Alter Rosenberg, chair of the Jewish community prior to the war, was appointed chair of the Judenrat. A Jewish Order Service was formed and placed under the command of Yosef Oberman.

The ghetto initially housed about 3,000 Jews, including some 600 refugees from nearby towns. The population steadily increased. The ghetto was divided into two sections. The "large" ghetto was located on the right side of Narutowicza Street and was crammed with 1,800 people; residents were ordered to seal all windows facing the "Aryan" side of townlet. The "small" ghetto was located in a suburb; living conditions were appalling, as it was located in moist, marshy terrain with neither a sewage system nor a well. The plight of the refugees was especially grave: several lived in such places as a ruined brick factory, while many others had no shelter at all. The ghetto was apparently not fenced, and even though departure was officially forbidden, Jews and Poles maintained contact. Poles frequented the ghetto to order clothing and buy what remained of the Jews' property, while Jews visited villages in the vicinity to purchase food. Jewish labor groups that worked outside the ghetto smuggled in food.

The Judenrat opened a public kitchen that distributed soup daily, and set up a small hospital whose director, Dr. C. Vinogron, and two assistants fought epidemic typhus in the ghetto with what meager medical supplies were at their disposal. The Judenrat labor department, headed by Yehoshua Sieger, supplied the Germans with labor groups. Jews with means could buy their way out of the labor requirement. Transports to labor camps began in August 1941. The Judenrat or the commander of the Jewish Order Service drew up lists and rounded up the candidates for the transports. By the end of 1941, several hundred young

Zychlin
Burning of Jewish property after their owners' deportation to the Chelmno death camp. *Photographs from the personal album of a German Gestapo member* (Instytut Pamieci Narodoewj Warsaw)

people had been sent to camps in the Poznan area, while some sixty women had been assigned to an estate for field labor.

The situation in the Zychlin ghetto worsened when the Germans began to liquidate ghettos in Jewish localities in its vicinity. Postal contact with nearby villages was suspended. A few Jews who had escaped from Chelmno apparently reached the ghetto and revealed to its inhabitants what was taking place at the death camp. The German authorities cracked down on smuggling and searched the ghetto regularly. Jews caught outside the ghetto were executed.

In late February 1942, the Germans arrested and hanged Rosenberg and Oberman. In the following days, additional members of the Judenrat and Jewish Order Service were hanged in public along with family members, and about 200 Jews were murdered when the German police surrounded the ghetto. The purpose of this last operation was to intimidate the Jews in advance of deportation, much as the Germans did elsewhere in the Wartheland.

On March 3, 1942, both parts of the Zychlin ghetto were liquidated. Approximately 3,200 Jews were gathered in the marketplace, and from there were taken to Chelmno. Many of them, including those who tried to hide, were murdered during the deportation.

ŻYRARDÓW

TOWN IN BŁONIE COUNTY, WARSAW DISTRICT, POLAND

During the war: General Gouvernement, Warsaw District

Coordinates:
52°04' | 20°26'

About 2,700 Jews lived in Zyrardow in the interwar period, representing approximately 10 percent of the town's population. They earned their livelihood from small commerce and artisanship, especially in the garment and textile industries, while several provided services to vacationers in the town. The Jews of Zyrardow maintained charitable and welfare institutions, as well as artisans' associations, and were aided by two Jewish banks and a free-loan society. Hundreds of the community's children attended a state elementary school for Jews, as well as a Talmud Torah maintained by the community, a modern Heder, a private Hebrew school, a Mizrachi Yavne school, a Beit Yaakov school for girls, and a WIZO kindergarten. The town boasted a popular Jewish library that held thousands of volumes in Hebrew, Yiddish, and Polish, and hosted literature and drama circles.

Zyrardow also had Jewish sports clubs as well as Zionist parties and youth movements that ran a pioneer training facility, dozens of whose members immigrated to the Land of Israel. The Agudath Israel and Bund parties were also active in Zyrardow. Some of Zyrardow's Jews were members of the Polish Socialist Party (PPS) or the Polish Communist Party.

When World War II broke out, many of Zyrardow's Jews fled to Warsaw* and eastern Poland, while numerous Jewish refugees arrived in the town from other localities in central Poland.

Zyrardow was occupied by the Germans on September 12, 1939, and the plunder of Jewish shops began immediately, in cooperation with antisemitic Poles. After a few days, the Germans began to abduct Jews for forced labor. About 200 Jews were assigned to forced labor in Breslau for a short time. Refugees also began to throng to the town, mostly from Lodz*, and for about two weeks, they filled a sports field on the edge of the town.

The Jews were ordered to wear a white Star-of-David armband. A Judenrat was appointed, headed by Yaakov Baron. The Judenrat was required to fulfill German demands and take care of all community matters; among other initiatives, it established a public soup kitchen that distributed about 700 meals every day, along with provisions that arrived with the help of the JDC. A few months after the occupation, the wealthier Jews were required to transfer their homes to non-Jews (about 5,000 Volksdeutsche lived in Zyrardow) and move into smaller apartments or in with their relatives. Later, after the arrival of refugees from Kowal and Lubien, the Judenrat expropriated large Jewish-owned apartments—sometimes by force—to lodge the newcomers.

In April 1940, on Seder night, local Volksdeutche robbed the homes of Zyrardow's Jews. On May 3, 1940, the Jews were required to pay a ransom. On Yom Kippur eve, in October 1940, the Germans arrested and murdered a number of Jews, including Rabbi Yechiel-Meir Kremski.

On December 11, 1940, all of the town's approximately 5,000 Jews, of whom about 1,500 were refugees, were ordered to concentrate in a closed ghetto by December 15. Some 900 refugees from Sochaczew*, most of whom were very poor, were concurrently brought to Zyrardow.

In late January 1941, the Germans ordered the Jews of the Zyrardow ghetto to relocate to the Warsaw ghetto within forty-eight hours. Each Jew was permitted to bring along a maximum of twenty-five kilograms of possessions. On February 1 and 2, 1941, the Jews of the Zyrardow ghetto were deported to the Warsaw ghetto and shared the fate of its Jews. Some of the young Zionists of Zyrardow were active in the Warsaw underground militia and participated in the spring 1943 uprising.

Immediately after the deportation to Warsaw, the Jews of Sochaczew, Wiskitki, and Mszczonow* were moved into the Zyrardow ghetto. They remained for a number of days, and were then likewise deported to Warsaw.

APPENDIX

JUDENHÄUSER IN GERMANY

Based on excerpts from articles by Marlis Buchholz and Konrad Kwiet

The year 1938 saw a marked escalation in the German *Judenpolitik* (anti-Jewish policy), which had begun in 1933, when the Jews were expelled from the social and economic circles of German life. At a meeting on November 12, 1938, following the *Kristallnacht* pogrom, Hermann Göring raised the matter of further isolating Jews in ghettos. Responsible for the "Four-Year Plan," he regarded the creation of large-scale ghettos in German cities as unavoidable.[1] Reinhard Heydrich—soon to be appointed head of the Reichssicherheitshauptamt, the Reich Security Main Office (RSHA)—spoke out in the meeting explicitly against the establishment of ghettos. He stated:

> From the point of view of the police, I don't think a ghetto in the form of a completely segregated district where only Jews would live, can be put up. We could not control a ghetto where the Jews congregate amidst the whole Jewish people. It would remain the permanent hideout for criminals and also epidemics and the like. We don't want to let the Jew live in the same house with the German population; but today the German population, their blocks and houses, force the Jew to behave himself. The control of the Jew through the watchful eye of the whole population is better than having him by the thousands in a district where I cannot properly establish a control over his daily life through uniformed agents.

On April 30, 1939, "The Law Concerning Tenant Relations with Jews" (Gesetz über Mietverhältnisse mit Juden) sanctioned the confinement of Jews into *Judenhäuser* (Jew Houses). It laid the foundations for the administration of Jewish residence by local governmental authorities.[2]

The eviction of Jews from their apartments and homes and their concentration in Judenhäuser was part of the process through which the Jews of Germany were excluded from all areas of public life and dispossessed of their rights. The geographic separation between Jews and non-Jews also represented a transitory stage on the way to their deportation and murder. The buildings transformed into Judenhäuser had in almost all cases been previously owned by Jews and were residences in which Jews already lived.

Any and all protection for Jewish tenants was declared null and void. Jews could be evicted under the condition that alternative accommodation in Jewish-owned buildings was guaranteed. This requirement ensured that Jews put onto the street would not become a burden on the welfare services for the homeless. In many places, Jews were forced to meet the cost of improvements and repairs requested by the new tenant. Henceforth, Jews were permitted to sign leases only with other Jews, and Jewish landlords were obliged to accept Jews as tenants or subtenants "at the request of the local authorities." It was up to the municipalities to place several Jewish families in one *Judenhaus*, "forcibly, if necessary." One basic principle was reconfirmed: the selection of Judenhäuser was not to lead to the establishment of ghettos.

---

1 Translation of Nuremberg Doc PS 1816, Stenographic Report on Meeting, November 13, 1938, p. 36f.

2 RGBL I 1939, pp. 864–65 (= Reichsgesetzblatt) published in Susanne Willems, *Der entsiedelte Jude, Albert Speers Wohnungsmarktpolitk für den Berliner Hauptstadtbau* (Berlin, 2000), pp. 138–39.

The April law of 1939 prescribed the registration of all living spaces whether vacant or occupied, whether rented to Jews or to Germans. Furthermore, every eviction, renting or leasing, and change of residence required the permission of the authorities. Later, these housing records—together with the *Judenkarteien* (Jew card indices)—were to facilitate the "round ups" of the Jews for deportation.

The residents of Judenhäuser were repeatedly warned to follow official instructions. Precise records of rents and subletting fees had to be maintained. Inspections of "vacant areas" could only be undertaken with official authorization. House keys were to be kept in an agreed location, to allow inspectors access at any time.

Eviction and relocation, isolation and concentration of Jews were not uniformly carried out throughout Germany. Their execution was dependent on local residential needs and political atmosphere, the depth of antisemitic sentiments as well as the behavior of regional and local officials representing state, party and police. Moreover, the general housing crisis—intensified by Allied bombings and Nazi redevelopment projects—alongside the "lust" for material incentives speeded up the process of vacating and confiscating Jewish homes.

The various interests that motivated the removal of Jews from their apartments and homes can be explained against the background of the complex fabric of the relations among the different authorities in each area. Nevertheless, Judenhäuser were established from mid-1939 on. Following Heydrich's guidelines, they were dispersed throughout cities to prevent a "concentration" (or rather "ghettoization") in residential areas and streets.

The National Socialists drew Jewish communities into their re-housing program. As in other issues involved in the persecution—emigration, welfare, forced labor, distribution of food and other goods, stigmatization and deportation —officials of the Reichsvereinigung der Juden in Deutschland (Reich Association of Jews in Germany set up in 1939) were compelled to assist in conveying Nazi orders and in implementing the housing policy. In major cities special Housing Advisory Boards were set up to keep the records, to draw up lists, and to organize the relocation of homeless Jews into Judenhäuser.

Moving into Judenhäuser involved an adjustment to new heterogeneous communities, and survival in wretched physical and psychological conditions. Jews who had retained the privilege of temporary residence in their own apartments had to take in new housemates: unmarried or divorced individuals, married couples, or families with children. Often confined in one room within a crowded apartment under one roof, or herded together in halls, sharing joint kitchens, washing and toilet facilities, there was hardly any space left for movement, let alone privacy. Overcrowding and competition for shared facilities often gave rise to irritability and nervousness, tension, and conflicts among residents.

In September 1941—on the eve of mass deportations—the Gestapo had instructed local authorities, "The Jews are to be assigned only the dirtiest and worst accommodation, whilst current sanitary regulations must be observed. Care should also be taken that not all houses are adjacent (in view of) the ban on ghettoization. The Jewish living space thus vacated is to be made available to those of German blood, without causing expense to the Reich or local councils."[3]

---

3   Letter of Gestapo Düsseldorf to local council in Kleve, September 18, 1941, quoted from H.G. Adler, *Der verwaltete Mensch, Studien zur Deportation der Juden aus Deutschland*, Tübingen, 1974, p. 47.

In most places, poor hygienic and sanitary conditions prevailed and in time deteriorated, since the local councils saw no reason to maintain these temporary Jewish housing estates properly or to supply them with sufficient fuel, essential for heating and for the supply of warm water.

The acute infringement of the freedom to choose one's place of residence also related to the private domain, which was subject to a system of controls and tight supervision by the Nazi authorities. The home lost its meaning as a place of refuge from the discrimination, vilification, and humiliations of the public domain. Freedom of movement outside the home was also regulated and restricted by the authorities. Jews were permitted to leave their homes mainly to reach the forced-labor sites. They were subject to night curfews and restrictions on shopping hours, and in many cases, were forbidden to use public transportation.

In March 1942, six months after the National Socialists had imposed the yellow Star of David on every Jew over the age of six, a similar stigma was introduced to mark all Judenhäuser. A black star printed on white paper was to be displayed next to the entrance door or nameplates of residents. Heydrich was confident "that now there is no further possibility of concealment."[4] Confined within ghettos without walls, residents of Judenhäuser were preferred targets for members of the party or Gestapo officials. *Kontrollgänge*, inspections, or "spot checks" provided the perfect excuse for molestation, looting and ill treatment.

In preparation for the deportation of the Jews to the east, an interim situation, somewhere between the Judenhäuser and the ghettos, began to take partial shape in Germany: The Nazi authorities began to concentrate some of the Jews in camps and special neighborhoods. In March 1941, a hut camp was established in Milbertshofen, an industrial suburb of Munich. Similar camps were established in Dresden, Köln, Essen, and other places. Some were called *Judensiedlungen*, Jewish settlements. The Jews of Breslau were concentrated in three camps. Jews from North Hesse were brought to Kassel, housed in five collection points, classified as *Sammelunterkünfte* (collection lodgings) or *Sammellager* (collection camps).

On October 15, 1941, mass deportation of Jews from Germany to Eastern Europe began, first to the Lodz ghetto, then to the Minsk, Kovno, Riga, and Warsaw ghettos, and later, from autumn 1942, mainly to Auschwitz. Jews in Berlin were systematically "removed" from Jewish homes and Judenhäuser, then from collection camps.

Initially, Jews living in a so-called "privileged intermarriage" (*privilegierte Mischehe*) were not confined to Judenhäuser, a privilege granted to childless couples in which the husband was of "pure German blood" and the woman was Jewish, or mixed couples whose children were raised and educated as Christians. However, from 1942 on, in some places priviligierte Mischehen and their children, termed by the Nazis as *Mischlinge* (persons of "mixed blood") were also herded into Judenhäuser—occasionally called by locals *Mischehenhäuser*—houses for people of mixed blood. Once almost all German Jews had been deported by 1943, most Mischehen and Mischlinge remained and survived in Judenhäuser.

---

4   Express letter by Reinhard Heydrich, March 13, 1942, published in Konrad Kwiet, "Nach dem Pogrom," in Wolfgang Benz (ed.), *Die Juden in Deutschland* 1933–1945 (München, 1993), pp. 618–19.

LIST OF ADDITIONAL GHETTOS AND CAMPS IN TRANSNISTRIA

(Romanian Spelling)

BALTA DISTRICT

Balanovca, Balta, Berizovca, Berşad, Bondurofca, Britevca Verhovca, Buda, Cicelnic, Dardcefca, Dimidovca, Dordobefca, Lihosofca Nouă, Luhova, Mala Kiriuca, Manicovca, Obodofca Nouă, Obodofca Veche, Olgopol, Pavlovca, Pesceana, Rodugca, Săvrani, Sihulovca Veche, Şimulovca, Tatarovca, Toseagii, Ţibulevca, Ustea, Voitovca

BEREZOVKA DISTRICT

Balaiciuc, Dobra-Nadejdea, Donsca-Balca, Hulcialovca, Lisencovo, Marianovca, Mostovoi, Saharovca, Slivina, Sofiievca, Suha-Balca, Veselinovo, Vladislavca, Zavadovca, Zlatuostova

DUBOSSARY DISTRICT

Ciorna (5 ghettos)

GOLTA DISTRICT

Acmecetca, Bogdanovca, Bucov, Carlovca, Crivoie-Ozero, Domanevca, Frunze, Golta (one camp and two ghettos), Marinovca, Nicolaevca, Tridubi, Vazdovca

JUGASTRU DISTRICT

Bila, Cacicova, Cernovtzi, Cneaje, Cojniţa, Comargorod, Crijopol, Dahtalia, Elaneţ, Golova-Rusova, Gorişcovca, Hajbievca, Iampol, Ianculovca, Jabocrici, Marianovca, Meastcovca, Mirinovca, Mişcovca, Molocnea, Netribovca, Olşanca, Palanca, Petroşivca, Pietrosu, Pisarevca, Podlesovca, Ratuş, Socelevca, Techinovca, Tomaşpol, Trostineţ, Vapniarca, Verbca, Zicovca

MOGILEV DISTRICT

Balki, Bandesovca, Capusterna, Carişcov, Cazaciovca, Chianovca, Clocotnea, Conotcăuţi, Copaigorod, Coşarinţi, Coţmanov, Crasna, Crasnoe, Cucavca, Cuzminţi, Derebcin, Djurin, Gorai, Grabivţi, Gromivca, Halcinţi, Hrinovca, Iaruga, Iuzina, Ivascăuţi, Lozova, Lucincic, Lucineţi, Marinovca, Milinovca, Mogilev, Murafa, Nasicovca, Nasicovca, Nemerci, Olcidaevu de Sus, Ozarineţi, Pasivca, Penchifca, Plosca, Politanchi, Popivţi, Primoşaniţa, Romanki, Rudanschi, Slidii, Stanislavca, Stepanchi, Şargorod, Şmerinca, Tivriv, Tropova, Vindiceni, Vinoj, Volodievţi, Voroşilovca, Zatişcea

OCHACOV

Oceacov, Trihati, Varvarovka, Vugoda

ODESSA DISTRICT

Berezovca, Inchisoarea Centrala (Central prison), Slobodka, Vigoda

RYBNITSA DISTRICT

Birzula, Budei, Codima, Râbniţa

TIRASPOL DISTRICT

Tiraspol

TULCHIN DISTRICT

Bratslav (two German camps and one ghetto), Capustian, Capustiani, Cariera de Piatră, Cetvertinovca, Gordievka, Ladijin, Nestervarca, Oleaniţa, Pavlovca, Peciara, Rogozna, Seminca Kernasovca, Spicov, Trostiancic, Trostianeţ

GLOSSARY

Words in caps in text are cross-references to Glossary entries.

AELTESTENRAT
(German, **Council of Jewish Elders**)

Name the Germans used for the JUDENRAT (Jewish Council) in certain ghettos, such as Łódź (Litzmannstadt) and Terezin (Theresienstadt).

AELTESTER
(German, **Jewish Elder**)

Name the Germans used for the head of the JUDENRAT (Jewish Council) in certain ghettos.

AGUDATH ISRAEL
(**Union of Israel**)

Organization of Orthodox Jews founded in 1912 in Kattowitz, Poland. Seeking to preserve Orthodoxy by adherence to *halakha* (religious obligations of the Jewish faith) as the principle governing Jewish life and society. It was deemed necessary to present a viable counterforce to the advances made by assimilationist and Reform trends, as well as by Zionism, the BUND, and Autonomism in Jewry.

AKTION
(pl. Aktionen)

German term for operation involving violent roundup of Jews by the Nazis and their collaborators during the Holocaust, for forced labor, mass execution, or deportation to the death camps.

AKTION REINHARD

Code name for the Nazi operation to exterminate all Jews living in the General Gouvernement. Aktion Reinhard was named after Reinhard Heydrich, one of the main architects of the "Final Solution" in Europe. SS chief Heinrich Himmler appointed Odilo Globocnik (high SS and police chief of the Lublin district) to head up Aktion Reinhard. Three death camps were established to cope with this operation: BELZEC, SÓBIBOR, and TREBLINKA. By the time Aktion Reinhard concluded in early November 1943, it had claimed the lives of more than two million Jews from the General Gouvernement and thousands more from other occupied lands.

ARMIA KRAJOWA
(AK; Polish, **The Polish Territorial Army**)

Main underground military organization in occupied Poland, active throughout prewar Poland from the fall of 1939 until its disbandment in January 1945. The AK included the vast majority of Polish underground military organizations. In February 1942, a department for Jewish affairs was established within the AK. Its role was to collect information on the condition of the Jewish population. The department sent reports to the exiled Polish government, in London. Jewish requests to enlist in the organization were largely refused.

ARMIA LUDOWA
(AL, Gvardia Ludowa; Polish, **The People's Army** or **People's Guard**)

Polish armed resistance organization active in Nazi-occupied Poland. Armia Ludowa, established in spring 1942, was linked to the Polish Communist party, the Polish Workers Party (PPR).

ARROW CROSS PARTY

Pro-German radical right-wing and antisemitic party led by Ferenc Szálasi that ruled Hungary from October 15, 1944, to January 1945. Its emblem, the arrow cross, was an ancient symbol of the Magyar tribes who settled Hungary, thereby representing the racial purity of the Hungarians in much the same way that the Nazi swastika alluded to the racial purity of the Aryans. The Arrow Cross rule was short-lived and brutal. In fewer than three months, death squads killed thousands of Jews and anti-fascists Hungarians. Quickly-formed battalions raided the *Yellow Star Houses* inhabited by Jews in Budapest and combed the streets, hunting down vulnerable Jews, who when apprehended were taken to the banks of the Danube and shot.

AUSCHWITZ

Largest Nazi concentration and extermination camp, located near the Polish town of Oswiecim, thirty-seven miles west of Cracow. One-sixth of all Jews murdered in the Holocaust were gassed at Auschwitz. In April 1940, SS chief Heinrich Himmler ordered the establishment of a new concentration camp in Oswiecim. The first Polish political prisoners arrived in Auschwitz in June 1940. Auschwitz soon became known as the most brutal of the Nazi concentration camps. In March 1941, Himmler ordered the construction of Auschwitz II in nearby Birkenau, as an extermination camp. It contained the complex's gas chambers and crematoria. Its inmates were subjected to the worst and most inhuman conditions. A third section, Auschwitz III, was built in nearby Monowitz, and consisted of a forced labor camp called Buna-Monovitz and forty-five other forced labor sub-camps. On January 27, 1945, Soviet troops liberated Auschwitz. In all, over one million Jews were murdered in the Auschwitz camps.

(AUTONOMOUS) HELP COMMITTEE IN BUCHAREST

Committee headed by attorney Arnold Schwefelberg that was established in late January 1941, at the initiative of members of the Federation of United Romanian Jewish Communities, to help Romanian Jews under the rule of Ion Antonescu. In its early stages, it collected money and belongings for Jewish victims of the pogroms in Bucharest, and over time strove to alleviate the suffering among the approximately 40,000 Jews that were deported from Romanian towns and villages to detention camps throughout Romania. When the committee was no longer able to meet the Jews' ever-mounting needs following the German and Romanian invasion of the Soviet Union on June 22, 1941, and the subsequent deportation of the Jews to Transnistria, school children, teenagers, and volunteers joined in to help. In early 1943, a committee delegation visited a number of ghettos in Transnistria. When in late 1943, deportees began to return to Romania from Transnistria, the committee attended to orphans, distributed money, food, and clothing, and regulated train travel. After the fall of the Antonescu regime, the committee cared for tens of thousands of Jews. From early 1945 on, Communist Jews took control of the committee and its activities declined.

BATEI MIDRASH

see Beit Midrash

BEIT MIDRASH
(pl. Batei Midrash; Hebrew, House [of] Lecturing or House [of] Learning)

Center for religious learning, often part of a synagogue building or complex and generally used for prayers.

BEIT YAAKOV SCHOOL FOR GIRLS (Hebrew, **House of Yaakov**)

System of schools for Orthodox Jewish girls founded by Sara Schenirer in Cracow in 1917, functioned in Poland between the two World Wars. The schools were endorsed and partially funded by AGUDATH ISRAEL.

BEŁŻEC

First of three death camps established as part of AKTION REINHARD, the Nazi plan to exterminate the two million Jews in the GENERAL GOUVERNEMENT. Located about half a mile south of the Belzec railroad station in the Lublin district. The camp began its murderous functions in March 1942. By the time the camp ceased operations in January 1943, more than 600,000 people, mostly Jews and several hundred Gypsies, had been murdered at Belzec.

BETAR
(Hebrew, acronym for **Brit [Covenant] of Trumpeldor**)

Right-wing Zionist youth movement associated with the Zionist Revisionist party founded in 1923 in Riga, Latvia. Betar promoted modern Hebrew language and culture, and encouraged its members to learn methods of self-defense and to immigrate to the Land of Israel by both legal and illegal means. The movement fused Revisionist leader Vladimir Jabotinsky's militarism with the ideal of Zionist pioneering, as exemplified in the life and death of Joseph Trumpeldor.

BEZIRK BIAŁYSTOK
(Polish, **Białystock District**)

District of 32,000 square kilometers established by the Nazi regime in August 1941, after the area was occupied by the German army. Bialystok District extended from the border of eastern Prussia in the northwest to Polesie in the south, with the city of Białystok at its center. The district had a population of 1.13 million, of which 150,000 were Jews. Erich Koch, the Gauleiter (governor) of eastern Prussia and the Reichskommissar of Ukraine, was appointed governor of Bezirk Białystok District.

BEZIRK ZICHENAU
(Ciechanów; Polish, **Zichenau District**)

In accordance with an injunction that the Germans issued on October 8, 1939, administrative changes were introduced into the Warsaw district, a part of which was annexed to the Reich. In the northern and northwestern parts, Zichenau District was established and annexed to eastern Prussia under Gauleiter (governor) Erich Koch. Included in Zichenau District were the Ciechanowiec, Maków, Mława, Plóck, Płońsk, Przasnysz, and Sierpc counties as well as areas of the Pultusk, Sochaczew, and Warsaw counties.

BIKKUR HOLIM SOCIETY

Jewish communal organization aimed at providing medical care to needy patients. From the late eighteenth century, these societies supported the establishment of Jewish hospitals in central and Western Europe, and from the mid-nineteenth century, they were further responsible for the establishment of Jewish hospitals in Eastern Europe.

BUND
(Yiddish, **Algemeyner yiddisher arbeter-bund in Lite, Poyln, und Rusland; The General Jewish Workers' Union in Lithuania, Poland, and Russia**)

Jewish socialist party founded in Vilna in 1897. In interwar Poland, the Bund had an important political and cultural presence, with candidates running in local and national elections and sponsoring Yiddish periodicals, youth movements, secular Yiddish schools, and children's camps. In contrast to Zionists and other Jewish political movements that advocated Jewish emigration from Eastern Europe, the Bund championed a secular Jewish Diaspora nationalism, in which Yiddish language and socialist culture played a central role.

CENTOS
(Polish Society for the Care of Orphans)

Jewish organization set up in 1924 that operated in Poland during the interwar period. During the Nazi occupation, CENTOS became part of the JSS and was active in the ghettos of the GENERAL GOUVERNEMENT.

CENTRAL COUNCIL OF THE HUNGARIAN JEWS

Jewish Council established in Budapest on March 20, 1944, the second day of the German occupation of Hungary. The eight-member Council was headed by Samu Stern. Under orders from the German authorities, at the beginning of April 1944, the Central Council conducted a census of some 740 Jewish communities in Hungary, most likely to assess their assets and to facilitate the eventual deportation of the Jews.

The Jewish Council, initially entirely under the control of the Germans, was recognized by the Hungarian authorities at the beginning of May 1944, and became an integral part of the Hungarian administration. Renamed "The Provisional Executive Committee of the Alliance of the Jews of Hungary," it now consisted of nine members. The Jewish Council was again reorganized in the summer of 1944, and once again after the Szálasi takeover (October 1944). Its president during the ARROW CROSS era was Lajos Stöckler.

The Jewish Council was in contact with both the Germans and Hungarian government circles. Responsible for internal order in the ghettos in Budapest, it strove to prevent the deportation of the Jews. The Council continued to operate until January 21, 1945, even after the large ghetto in Budapest was liberated on January 18, 1945.

CHABAD/HABAD

Major trend in the HASIDIC movement established in Eastern Europe in the second half of the eighteenth century. Its founder Rabbi Shneur Zalman of Liadi authored the *Tanya*, Habad's foundational text. Habad stresses the leadership of the *Zaddik* (equivalent to the "*rebbe*" in other Hasidic trends) as mainly spiritual.

CHELMNO
(German, **Kulmhof**)

Extermination camp located near the Polish village of Chelmno, seventy kilometers southwest of Łódź. Chelmno was the first Nazi camp in which gassing was used to exterminate Jews on a large scale. It was created to serve as the extermination center for the Jews in the Łódź ghetto as well as those from the WARTHELAND region. The first group of prisoners arrived at Chelmno on December 7, 1941, and the first exterminations with gas vans began the following day. The camp's victims included Jews as well as 5,000 Roma gypsies who had been imprisoned in the Łódź Ghetto, groups of Poles, Soviet prisoners of war, and eighty-eight children from the Czech village of Lidice. In March 1943, the Nazis stopped deportations to Chelmno, but reopened the camp in April 1944. On January 17, 1945, as Soviet troops drew near, the Nazis began evacuating Chelmno. In all, some 320,000 people were murdered at Chelmno.

CHEVRA KADISHA
(Burial Society)

Jewish community society that looks after the needs of the dying and the requirements of the dead. The Chevra Kadisha carried great weight in Jewish communities. In addition to matters of burial, it dealt with the financial matters of the community and managed a large budget.

"CONTRIBUTION"

In many ghettos, the Germans demanded ransom payments in exchange for certain dispensations, such as exemptions from forced labor and deportations to labor or death camps, and the release of prisoners. "Contributions" were generally paid in vain, at most gaining a postponement.

COOPERATIVES

Agricultural and industrial cooperative bodies established in the Soviet Union to purchase raw materials, as well as manufacture and sell goods. The cooperatives developed in the 1920s and 1930s based on economic principles, namely the collection of seed money and earning of profits through cooperative activity. From a legal standpoint, the industrial cooperatives were not set up on a national level, but in many countries, especially Ukraine and Belarus, the agricultural cooperatives were established as Jewish from the outset, and were often named in Yiddish after Jewish Soviet revolutionaries and politicians.

CYSHO
(Yiddish, **The Central Yiddish School Organization**)

Network of secular Jewish schools of all trends established in 1921, in the interwar period in Poland. It identified with socialist parties, mainly the BUND and PO'ALEI ZION-Left. Yiddish was the language of instruction in the CYSHO schools.

DROR
(Hebrew, **Freedom**)

Socialist-Zionist youth movement established in Russia in 1911, under the name *Freiheit* (Freedom). After the Bolshevik revolution, its center was moved to Warsaw. In 1925, Freiheit joined the PO'ALEI ZION party and became its youth movement. In 1938, Freiheit united with the youth movement of the HEHALUTZ and was renamed Dror. During the Nazi occupation, Dror was active in the ghettos in education and was among the leading movements in the ghetto undergrounds as well as in the Warsaw ghetto uprising.

EAM
(Ethniko Apeleftherotiko Metopo; Greek, **National Liberation Front**)

Main movement of Greek anti-Nazi resistance, founded in September 1941. Its driving force was the Communist Party but it succeeded in attracting many non-Communists as well. In February 1942, EAM's central Committee decided to form a military corps, called the Greek People's Liberation Army (ELAS), that would first operate in the mountains of central Greece.

ENDECS /ENDECJA
(Narodowa Demokracja, ND; Polish, **National Democratic Party**)

Popular name for a right-wing party in Poland founded at the end of the nineteenth century and particularly active from the end of World War I to the end of World War II. It comprised landlords, reactionary middle-class, and intelligentsia and advocated virulently antisemitic policies within the framework of an extremist nationalistic ideology formulated by Roman Dmowski.

EINSATZGRUPPEN
(Einsatzgruppen des Sicherheitsdienst und der Sicherheitspolizei; German, **Action Groups**)

Special units of the SS set up by the Nazis in 1938 before they annexed Austria. The most infamous Einsatzgruppen were formed before the invasion of the Soviet Union in June 1941. The task of the Einsatzgruppen in Eastern Europe was to terrorize the local population and murder those whom the SS deemed undesirable and who were considered upholders of the ideological infrastructure of the Soviet Union: political commissars, members of the Communist party, and above all, Jews. The overwhelming majority of the commanders of these units held graduate degrees and were deeply committed to building the Nazi utopia of a racially and ideologically pure society without Jews. It is estimated that along with their collaborators, the Einsatzgruppen murdered over 1.25 million Jews and hundreds of thousands of others, among them Soviet prisoners of war, gypsies, and Communist officials.

On the eve of the invasion of the Soviet Union in 1941, the Einsatzgruppen were reorganized into four main divisions (A, B, C, and D), each with a number of subunits known as Einsatzkommandos or SONDERKOMMANDOS. Einsatzgruppe A, the largest group—with about 1,000 men—was linked to Army Group North. They operated in the Baltic states (Lithuania, Latvia, and Estonia) and the area between their eastern borders and Leningrad. Einsatzgruppe B, a group of 655 men linked to Army Group Center, operated in Belarus and the Smolensk district, east of Moscow. Einsatzgruppe C, a group of 700 men linked to Army Group South, covered northern and central Ukraine. Einsatzgruppe D, with 600 men linked to the Eleventh Army, operated in southern Ukraine, the Crimea, and Ciscaucasia.

FERENCYZY REPORTS

After the German occupation of Hungary on March 19, 1944, gendarme Lieuten-ant Colonel László Ferenczy was appointed liaison officer between Eichmann's Special Task commando and the Hungarian policing forces by Gábor Faragho, the superintendent of the gendarmerie in the Ministry of Defense. Ferenczy person-ally supervised the deportation process and prepared reports according to zones of deportation that tallied the deported Jews. His last report was dated July 9, 1944, and was addressed to the Ministry of Interior, "From the beginning of the resettlement transportations on May 14, 1944, until today, altogether 434,351 persons belonging to the Jewish race have left the country on 147 trains. Apart from the capital, Budapest, the Jewish population has already moved out of the entire territory of the country."

FOLKSBANK

Network of Jewish banks in Lithuania in the interwar period.

FOLKSPARTEI
(Yiddish, **People's Party**)

Name of a number of Jewish political parties in various Eastern-European coun-tries in 1906–39, based on the ideology of Autonomism. In Poland, the People's Party was active in the interwar period. These parties were inspired by the ideas of historian Simon Dubnow, who believed that the Jewish-secular community, operating autonomously and according to democratic principles, should lie at the foundation of Jewish national existence. The language of instruction in the schools run by the parties, either Yiddish or the local language, was to be de-cided in accordance with the local conditions and parents' inclination, but the spirit and goals of the institutions were to be Jewish in nature.

FREE-LOAN SOCIETY
(Hebrew, **Gemach,** an acronym for *gemilut hesed* or charity)

The free-loan society was a nonprofit organization that provided interest-free loans to the needy for the purchase of various items. It enabled Jews to seek help discreetly and without shame, based on the verse in the Ethics of the Fathers, "On three things is the world sustained: on the Torah, on the Temple service, and on charity."

GENDARMERIE

Public security force in Hungary, subordinate to both the Ministry of Interior and the Ministry of Defense. The gendarmerie was notorious for its iron discipline, blind obedience, and cruelty. Following the German army's occupation of Hungary on March 19, 1944, the policing duties of ghettoization and deportation (rounding up and "escorting" Jews to the ghettos and the train centers, guarding Jews while accompanying them to the deportation trains, forcing Jews into cattle cars, etc.) were generally carried out by policemen in towns and cities and by the gendarmerie in smaller localities in the provinces. Frequently, however, gendarmes participated in the operations in towns and cities as well. During the deportations, the authori-ties usually employed units from other parts of the country, to prevent the Jews from exploiting any ties to local gendarmes members.

GENERAL GOUVERNEMENT
(GG)

Following the German and Soviet invasions of Poland in the fall of 1939, Poland was divided into three sections. The western section was incorporated into the German Reich, the eastern section was taken over by the Soviet Union, and the remaining part became known as the General Gouvernement, an administrative region with its capital in Cracow under the direction of the veteran Nazi Hans Frank. This section included four districts: Warsaw, Radom, Cracow, and Lublin. Ultimately, it became the dumping ground for most of the Jews in Nazi-dominated Europe, with Poland's six death camps either located within or adjacent to its territory.

GESTAPO
(German Secret State Police)

During the Nazi regime, the Gestapo was the main instrument of state terror. It was deeply involved in the persecution and murder of the Jews.

GORDONIA

Zionist youth movement established in 1924 in Galicia, Poland, based on the ideology of A. D. Gordon. The aims of the movement were to revive the Jewish homeland in the Land of Israel and Jewish culture in the Hebrew language, a humanistic education, and Jewish labor. The movement quickly spread throughout Poland, as well as Romania, the United States, and other countries. On the eve of World War II, the movement had 40,000 young members.

HABRICHA
(Hebrew, **Escape**)

Underground organization established in 1944–1945 by Holocaust survivors in Eastern Europe, whose goal was to transfer Jews through Bricha routes from camps in Eastern Europe to the shores of the Mediterranean and the Black Sea, to the Land of Israel. The number of Jews. who left Eastern Europe in 1944–48 is estimated at altogether 250,000 (about ninety percent left through Bricha, and most immigrated to Israel).

HACHSHARA

Zionist pioneering training farms that prepared members of the Zionist youth movements, mostly of socialist tendencies, for kibbutz life.

HADARIM

see Heder

HANO'AR HATZIYYONI
(Hebrew, **The Zionist Youth**)

Zionist secular youth movement established at the beginning of the 1920s. The non-socialist movement spread to central and Eastern Europe. In response to waves of antisemitism, the movement's leaders decided in 1926 to express Judaism, Zionism, and *Hagshama Atzmit* (Heb. "personal fulfillment") by settling in the Land of Israel. The veteran pioneers of Hano'ar Hatziyyoni made *aliya* (emigrated to the Land of Israel) in 1930 and established a branch of the movement.

HASHOMER HATZAIR

One of the largest Zionist youth movements, founded in Galicia in 1916, combined Socialism with Zionism and held up kibbutz life as an ideal. Its graduates founded many kibbutzim. Hashomer Hatzair is still active and has branches throughout the world.

HASIDISM

Popular religious movement founded by the mystic Israel Ba'al Shem Tov in the 1740s in Ukraine. In Hasidic thought, prayer, joyousness, and mysticism are central elements. According to Hasidism, the "*rebbe*" is a leader and religious authority, fulfilling the role of intermediary between his followers and God. In time, in a number of east-European localities, diverse Hasidic dynasties flourished (Belz, Carlin-Stolin, etc.), each centered on a charismatic leader.

HASKALA
(Hebrew, **Enlightenment**);
Maskilim (proponents of
Enlightenment among Jews)

The Enlightenment movement began within Jewish European society in the 1770s. Haskalah was rooted in the general Enlightenment movement in Europe of the eighteenth century. The movement contributed toward acculturation in language, dress, and manners by deploring Jewish feelings of alienation in the *galut* (diaspora) and fostering loyalty toward the modern state. The Maskilim also advocated productivity through learning crafts and agriculture. The movement spread towards Eastern Europe in the nineteenth century.

HAUPTSTURMFÜHRER

German rank for captain.

HAVATZELET
(Hebrew, **The Lily**)

Hebrew periodical published in 1863–1864, edited by Israel Back, then later in 1870–1911 by Israel Dov Frumkin. Both belonged to the HASIDIC movement.

HEDER
(pl. Hadarim; Hebrew, **Room**)

Common name for a religious elementary school, teaching Judaism. It was generally housed in a room in the private house of the *melamed*, or teacher. No secular studies were taught; subjects included reading in the prayer book, the Pentateuch, and Jewish Law. Most young Jewish boys attended the Heder, usually beginning at the age of four or five.

HEHALUTZ
(Hebrew, **The Pioneer**)

World organization of Jewish youth, which trained its members for pioneering work and self-defense in the Land of Israel. Before World War II, the movement had close to 100,000 members.

HOVEVEI ZION/HIBBAT ZION
(Hebrew, **Lovers of Zion/Love of Zion**)

Movement of Zionist associations that came into being in 1882, as a direct reaction to the widespread pogroms in Russia in 1881, for the purpose of encouraging Jewish settlement and achieving a Jewish national revival in the Land of Israel.

IRON GUARD
(Romanian, **Garda de Fier**)

Romanian ultra-nationalist and radically antisemitic movement active in the interwar period, founded in 1927 by Corneliu Codreanu as *The Legion of the Archangel Michael*, whose members were also known as the *Legionaries*. When Ion Antonescu became Romania's leader in September 1940, the Iron Guard became part of the government and immediately launched a wave of terror against Romania's Jews in hopes of removing them from Romanian life. They passed racist laws and revitalized their ties with the Nazis and the fascist government in Italy. In January 1941, the Iron Guard attempted a coup during which a great deal of Jewish property was set on fire and 123 Jews were murdered in Bucharest. The coup failed, however, and the Iron Guard lost its standing.

THE JAEGER REPORT

Karl Jaeger, the commander of the SD and Security Police in Lithuania who was responsible for the annihilation of Lithuania's Jews, reported in early December 1941 that no Jews were left in Lithuania except those in three ghettos: Siauliai, Kaunas, and Vilna. Three months later, Jaeger produced another report that included the number of people killed by his unit: 136,421 Jews; 1,064 Communists; 653 mentally ill people; and 134 others. Of these victims, 55,556 were women and 34,464 were children.

JEWISH ANTIFASCIST COMMITTEE
(Russian, **Evreiskii Antifashistskii Komitet**)

Soviet Jewish organization that operated in the Soviet Union from 1942 to 1948. In April 1942, the Soviet government founded several antifascist committees, of which the Jewish Antifascist Committee was the only to represent a national group. The committee's goal was to call on the Jews of the world, mainly American Jewry, to join the struggle against Nazi Germany. The committee was also one of the first institutions to document the atrocities of the Holocaust and the activities of the Jewish resistance. It worked with the Soviet Government Commission for the Investigation of Nazi Crimes, and put together a major work called the Black Book of Soviet Jewry, which documented the crimes committed by the Nazis in the Soviet Union.

The committee was dissolved by the Soviet authorities in November 1948; most of its leaders, among them the actor Shlomo Michoels, were killed by Stalin during his anti-Jewish purges.

JEWISH COLONIZATION ASSOCIATION
(JCA)

Philanthropic association founded in London by Baron Maurice de Hirsch in 1891 to assist Jews in depressed economic circumstances or countries of persecutions to emigrate and settle elsewhere in productive employment. Under the JCA's auspices, colonies were founded for Jewish settlement in Argentina.

JEWISH COMMITTEE/ COUNCIL

see Judenrat

JEWISH ETHNIC SOVIET

Jewish councils established in the Soviet Union from the mid-1920s to 1938–1939, when they were disbanded. The council meetings and documentation work were conducted in Yiddish.

JEWISH FIGHTING ORGANIZATION
(Polish, **Zydowska Organizacja Bojowa, ŻOB**; Yiddish, **Yiddishe Kamf Organizatsye**)

Jewish organization established in the Warsaw ghetto on July 28, 1942, to resist deportations and murder of Jews in the death camps. Its members were initially drawn from the ranks of the pioneering youth movements HASHOMER HATZAIR, DROR, and Akiva, and from October 1942, additional youth movements joined ŻOB, including the BUND and GORDONIA. Mordechai Anielewicz was the commander of the expanded ŻOB. One of the ŻOB's first acts was to purge the Warsaw ghetto of the elements that collaborated with the Germans in carrying out operations in the ghetto. In January 1943, they resisted Nazi attempts to round up Jews in the ghetto's streets to be deported to TREBLINKA. In April 1943, ŻOB members initiated the Warsaw ghetto uprising until the ghetto's total destruction.

JEWISH ORDER SERVICE
(German, **Ordnungsdienst**)

Jewish police units (also called, mostly unofficially, "Jewish police") set up on German orders within German-occupied areas. The JUDENRAETE in Eastern Europe were commanded to organize these units, frequently as a prerequisite to the establishment of ghettos in their area. The duties of the Jewish Order Service included collecting ransom payments, personal possessions, and taxes from their fellow Jews; gathering Jews for forced labor quotas; guarding the ghetto; and accompanying labor crews that worked outside the ghetto. Early on, Jewish policemen also carried out public welfare duties, such as distributing food rations and aid to the poor and overseeing sanitary conditions. Over time, the units were strongly affected by the mass deportations to extermination camps. Many of the police officers quit the force, rather than participate in the rounding up of their fellow Jews; others held their posts, following German orders to the very end.

THE JOINT
(**American Jewish Joint Distribution Committee**, Joint, JDC)

American Jewish institution established in 1914, soon after the outbreak of World War I, to provide aid to Jews in Europe and Palestine in the form of food, clothing, medication, and funds. The JDC helped Jews to escape during the Holocaust era and remained active after World War II.

JSS
(Juedische Soziale Selbsthilfe; Yiddish, **Jewish Social Self-Help**)

Official mutual-aid organization (referred to as *Żydowska Samopomoc Społeczna* in Polish documents) that provided monetary funds, medication, clothing, and food to Jews in the GENERAL GOUVERNEMENT under the Nazi rule. Headed by Michael Weichert at its center in Cracow, the JSS was part of an umbrella organization of general social services offered to Poles, Jews, and Ukrainians.

JUDENRAT
(pl. **Judenraete**; German, **Jewish Council**)

Jewish leadership organization commonly known as a Judenrat (Jewish Council) or an AELTESTENRAT (Council of Elders) established by the Germans in the countries they controlled. Their objective was to create a vehicle to control the Jews, isolate them from the outside world, and implement various decrees. The German authorities generally packed the councils with recognized pre-war Jewish leaders and respected public figures. The councils were often tragically torn between their desire to meet the Jews' needs and the harsh demands of the Germans. While not every Jewish administrative body under the Nazis was called a "Jewish Council" or was similarly constituted, "Judenrat" is nonetheless often used as a generic term for all such bodies.

JUDENREIN
(German, **"Cleansed of Jews"**)

Nazi term designating the status of a locality where all the Jews had either been deported or executed.

KARAITES

Jewish sect that came into being at the beginning of the eighth century, whose doctrine promotes the belief that all religious precepts derive directly from the Bible, and consequent denial of the talmudic-rabbinical tradition. In contrast to most of the Jews under Nazi occupation in Eastern Europe during World War II, the Karaites were not eliminated, because the Germans stipulated that they did not belong to the Jewish religious and racial community.

KASZTNER TRAIN

Name given to a train that left Hungary in late June 1944 with 1,684 Jews on board, following negotiations between senior Nazi leaders and delegates of the Hungarian Zionist movement, led by Rudolf (Rezso) Israel Kasztner. Kasztner and other Jewish leaders drew up a list of Jews to be released, including leading wealthy Jews, Zionists, rabbis, Jews from different religious communities, and Kasztner's own family and friends. After being detained in Bergen-Belsen, the passengers of the "Kasztner train" left on December 6, 1944, and reached safety in Switzerland.

KNESSET

Israel's legislature and House of Representatives, named after the assembly of elders during the time of Persian rule: the Great Knesset. The Knesset has 120 members, who are elected by the Israeli people and who choose the Israeli government.

KOLKHOZ
(kollektivnoe khozyaĭstvo; Russian, **collective economy**)

Russian term for a Soviet collective farm. The kolkhoz member was paid a share of the farm's products and profits, according to the number of days worked. In addition, the kolkhoz was required to sell its crops to the State, which fixed grain prices.

KOMSOMOL
(Kommunisticheskiy Soyuz Molodiozhi; Russian, **Communist Union of Youth**)

Established on October 29, 1918, Komsomol served as the youth wing of the Communist Party of the Soviet Union (CPSU).

KRIPO
(Kriminalpolizei; German, criminal police)

Division of the RSHA. In most cases, Kripo dealt with non-political crimes, while the GESTAPO handled political matters. On occasion, Kripo assisted the Gestapo in its operations against Jews and other political opponents.

KULTUR LIGUE
(Yiddish, Culture League)

Institution first established in Kiev in 1917, with the aim of fostering modern secular Yiddish culture (theater, literature, art, and scholarship). Local branches soon took root throughout Europe and the Americas. The main branch of the Kultur Ligue moved to Warsaw in 1921.

LAG B'OMER

Minor Jewish holiday that falls on the 18th day of the Hebrew month of Iyar (April–May), which corresponds to the 33rd day of the Omer (the period between PESACH and SHAVUOT). Lag B'Omer marks, according to Jewish tradition, the interruption of a plague that took the life of 24,000 of Rabbi Akiva's students. On that date, therefore, all of the prohibitions in effect during the Omer (to have one's hair cut, hold a wedding, etc.) are lifted.

LWY
(Polish, The Lions)

Jewish independent partisan unit active in Opoczno (Kielce district, Poland).

MACCABI

Worldwide Zionist sports association named after the Maccabees, who fought the Helenized Syrian government that had occupied Judea in the second century BCE.

In the modern era, Maccabi is an umbrella organization for all Jewish sports associations that was founded by Max Nordau in 1921, as part of the Zionist movement. Maccabi advocates physical education as a basis for the nation's spiritual power and the fostering of Jewish nationalism among Jews everywhere. The association later provided assistance to the State of Israel. On the eve of World War II, Maccabi members numbered more than 200,000 in thirty-eight countries.

MAJDANEK

Concentration, forced labor, prisoner, and internment camp located five kilometers south of Lublin. The camp's official purpose was to destroy enemies of the Third Reich, help carry out the extermination of the Jews, and take part in the deportation and "resettlement" of the Poles living in the Zamosc region of the GENERAL GOUVERNEMENT. Majdanek operated from September 1941 until its liberation by the RED ARMY in July 1944. In all, some 90,000 people were murdered in Majdanek, mostly Jews.

MIKVAH/MIKVEH
(pl. Mikva'ot/Mikves; Hebrew, Ritual bath)

In Orthodox Judaism, full immersion in a ritual bath is required for the individual to regain purity. Sources of impurity include contact with a corpse, childbirth, menstruation, venereal disease, and seminal issue. Together with the synagogue and religious school, the mikveh has from ancient times been a fundamental institution of Jewish community life.

MOLOTOV-RIBBENTROP PACT

Nazi-Soviet Pact entered into between Nazi Germany and the Soviet Union on August 23, 1939, by German Foreign Minister Joachim von Ribbentrop and Soviet Foreign Minister Viacheslav Molotov. The parties signed two agreements: the first dealt with economic relations, while the second was a non-aggression pact. The treaty also included a secret clause concerning the division of various territories. The Baltic states (Estonia, Lithuania, and Latvia) and Bessarabia were to be part of the Soviet sphere, while Lithuania's claim to Vilna and its environs was recognized by the Germans. Poland was to be divided between the two countries. One week after the agreement was signed, Germany invaded Poland. The Soviet Union took over the eastern part of the country, including western Belarus and western Ukraine, while Germany occupied the rest. In 1940, the Soviets annexed the Baltic states, Bessarabia, and northern Bucovina. The pact was nullified by the Germans when they invaded the Soviet Union in June 1941.

NEOLOGY, NEOLOGS

Hungarian branch of German "Reform Judaism." Many aligned themselves with the movement in the second half of the nineteenth century, when Hungarian Jewish communities were required to declare their religious orientation. In the interwar period, the movement became mainstream among Budapest's Jews as well as within Hungarian Jewry in general.

NSZ
(Narodowe Sily Zbrojne;
Polish, **National Armed Forces**)

Nationalistic and antisemitic Polish underground military organization established in 1942 that fought mainly Polish leftist underground, Soviet, and Jewish partisan groups. In 1944, the NSZ joined the AK.

OBERGRUPPENFÜHRER

German rank for major-general.

OBERSTURMFÜHRER

German rank for first lieutenant.

ONEG SHABBAT ARCHIVE
(Hebrew, **The Joy of the Sabbath**)

Archive in the Warsaw ghetto, founded by a group bearing that name and run by historian Emanuel Ringelblum from October 1939 through April 1943. The archive was given the name *Oneg Shabbat* because the archive staff held its secret meetings on the Sabbath. The group included historians, writers, rabbis, and social workers and was dedicated to chronicling life in the ghetto through documents and testimonies, essays, diaries, drawings, etc. After the massive deportation of the Warsaw ghetto's Jews in the summer of 1942, the archivists began sealing the contents of the *Oneg Shabbat* Archives in metal containers and hiding them in various places in the ghetto. The first group of documents was discovered in September 1946, and the second group in December 1950. The third group has never been found.

OPEN GHETTO

Ghetto with no physical barrier separating its Jewish inhabitants from the local population, which Jews were nevertheless forbidden to leave.

ORDNUNGSPOLIZEI
(ORPO; German, **Order Police**)

Reorganized German police force formed in 1936, based on orders from SS chief Heinrich Himmler. The new Order Police was a merger of the conventional police (SCHUPO) and the police that functioned in rural areas (GENDARMERIE). Many ORPO units also assisted in the persecution of the Jews, including deportations to extermination camps and shooting massacres. They were notorious for their cruelty.

ORGANISATION SCHMELT

A system of forced labor camps for the Jewish population of eastern Upper Silesia, established in 1940 and run by the commander of the Breslau police, Albrecht Schmelt. The labor camps were also organized in Lower Silesia and the Sudetenland. Throughout Organisation Schmelt's existence, 160 camps are known to have been active and by early 1943, it employed more than 50,000 Jewish forced laborers.

ORT
(Russian, **The Society for the Encouragement of Handicrafts**)

Established by Jews in Russia at the end of the nineteenth century, ORT set up Jewish vocational schools throughout the world. During the period of Nazi occupation, ORT was active in the General Gouvernement, as one of the social-welfare organizations that made up the JSS.

OUN
(The Organization of Ukrainian Nationalists)

Ultranationalist and antisemitic Ukrainian movement formed in 1929, under the leadership of Yevhen Konovalets. The movement was inspired by Italian Fascism and German National-Socialism, and viewed the communist Soviet Union as the prime enemy of the Ukrainian people. The movement's headquarters was moved to Berlin, where it received funding and support from the German government. In 1940, the movement divided into two factions, with the activist majority headed by Stepan Bandera. During the German invasion of the Soviet Union, OUN members formed two Ukrainian battalions within the German army, acted as interpreters, and attacked retreating Soviet troops. Following the German invasion of Lwów, OUN members proclaimed the establishment of a national Ukrainian government. However, the Nazis quickly foiled their plans by arresting the members of the provisional government. The OUN hoped to establish an independent Ukrainian state after the war, but the group was destroyed by the Soviet police in the 1950s.

OZE
(Russian, **Jewish Health Society**; French, OSE [Oeuvre de Secour aux Enfants])

Organization that promoted child care, health, and hygiene, founded by Jews in Russia in 1912. The OZE headquarters moved to France in 1919.

PALE OF SETTLEMENT

Territorial unit marking the boundaries of the only area where Jews were permitted to live, according to the laws of Czarist Russia. Its boundaries were first defined in 1791 and shifted over time, but essentially included the western areas of the empire conquered from the Poles and Ottomans. The Pale of Settlement was intended to prevent the Jews from immigrating to Russia. Certain czars allowed a minute fraction of Jews to live outside the Pale of Settlement. The Pale of Settlement was abolished in February 1917.

PARTISANS

Fighters active in areas occupied by the Germans, employing mostly guerilla tactics. During World War II, anti-Nazi partisans operated mainly in Eastern Europe and the Balkan states but there was also partisan activity in Yugoslavia, Greece, Slovakia, and Western European countries such as France (*maquis*) and Italy.

PESACH
(Passover)

Jewish holiday that begins on the 15th day of the Hebrew month of Nissan (March–April) and lasts seven days in Israel and eight days outside Israel. One of the three Jewish pilgrims festivals, Passover commemorates the Exodus of the Jews from Egyptian slavery. The holiday also bears an agricultural significance: as a spring festival, it is celebrated at the beginning of the barley harvest.

PETLYURA, SYMON
(1879–1926)

Leader of the Ukrainian national movement during the Russian Civil War. During the pogroms that were carried out against the Jews in Ukraine with the retreat of Petlyura's forces before the Red Army, in the winter of 1919, tens of thousands of Jews were murdered. From 1924, Petlyura was a political émigré in Paris, where he was assassinated in 1926 by a Jew, Shalom Schwarzbard.

PO'ALEI AGUDATH ISRAEL PARTY

Founded in 1922 in Poland as the workers' organization of AGUDATH ISRAEL, primarily to protect the rights of religious Jewish workers by seeking to implement Biblical ideals of social justice in Jewish life. The movement spread to other countries in Eastern Europe.

PO'ALEI ZION
(Hebrew, **Workers of Zion**)

Movement that sought to combine political Zionism with the class struggle of the Jewish proletariat and the realization of Socialism. Several groups named Po'alei Zion merged in 1907, to form the World Union of Po'alei Zion. In 1920, the movement split into Po'alei Zion Right and Po'alei Zion Left, over differences relating to international Socialism and Communism and Zionist political activities.

POLISH "BLUE POLICE"
(Polish, **Granatowa policja**)

Paramilitary force created by the Germans in the General Gouvernement, as a police force to keep law and order. The Polish population called it the "blue police" after the color of its uniforms. In 1943, 16,000 policemen served on the force, which was disbanded by the Polish Committee of National Liberation in August 1944.

PPR
(Polska Partia Robotnicza; Polish, **Polish Workers' Party**)

Communist party reestablished in Poland in 1942. The armed Polish resistance movement ARMIA LUDOWA operated under its auspices.

REBBE

see Hasidism

RED ARMY

Army of the Soviet Union. In June 1945, its name was changed to the Soviet Army.

REFORMED HEDER

Religious Jewish elementary school operating along the lines of the traditional HEDER but considerably modernized.

REICHSKOMMISSARIAT

Name given to various German occupation zones in Europe. In the Soviet Union, the occupied territories were transferred from a military to a civil administration on September 1, 1941, and were divided into two administrations: Reichskommissariat Ostland and Reichskommissariat Ukraine. Ostland covered the Baltic states (Lithuania, Latvia, and Estonia) and parts of Western Belorussia. The Jews living in the Reichskommissariat Ostland were exterminated by the mobile killing units of EINSATZGRUPPEN A (in the Baltic states) and B (in Belorussia), along with members of the SIPO, SD, and local collaborators. All of Ostland was liberated by the RED ARMY during the summer of 1944.

Hitler transferred the Soviet districts of Volhynia, Rovno, and Kamenets-Podolsk to the authority of Reichskommissariat Ukraine in August 1941. Einsatzgruppen C and D, two of the mobile killing units, were active in both the Reichskommissariat Ukraine and in the part of Ukraine that was controlled by the German military administration.

RESTGHETTO

Ghettos that the Germans reestablished in certain locations, inside ghettos whose Jewish inhabitants had already been liquidated. The reestablished ghetto served to lure the last surviving Jews in the area out of hiding. The Germans typically spread false rumors regarding the function of the reestablished ghetto (for example, that it was transformed into a labor camp, or a place to gather Jews who would then be exchanged for German prisoners of war). Almost all of the

Jews that turned themselves in or were rounded up into reestablished ghettos were ultimately murdered.

ROSH HASHANAH
(Hebrew, **New Year**)

Jewish New Year falls on the 1st and 2nd day of the Hebrew month of Tishrei (September–October). It marks the beginning of the annual Ten Days of Penitence, which culminate on YOM KIPPUR.

RSHA
(Reichssicherheitshauptamt; German, **Reich Security Main Office**)

Served as the central office handling the Nazis' political and ideological enemies. The RSHA was established in September 1939, combining the Security Service (SD) and the Security Police (SIPO), which included the GESTAPO and the Criminal Police (KRIPO). Under the leadership of Reinhard Heydrich, the RSHA grew exponentially, becoming the Nazis' most ubiquitous terror organization.

Department IV in the RSHA was the Gestapo. Its subsection IV B-4 was the Jewish Affairs Department. Headed by Adolf Eichmann, from late 1941, this section implemented the "Final Solution," including the deportation of European Jews to ghettos, forced labor camps, and extermination camps.

THE RUSSIAN CIVIL WAR

Armed conflict from 1918 to 1920, played out between the Bolsheviks and their opponents in Russia. The hostilities ended with the victory of the Bolsheviks and the consolidation of the Communist Soviet Union. During the civil war, numerous pogroms were carried out, killing hundreds of thousands Jews in more than 700 Jewish towns and villages in Ukraine and in certain areas in Russia and Belarus.

SA
(Sturmabteilung; German, **Storm Troopers**)

Nazi paramilitary organization. The SA, also known as the "Brown Shirts" for the color of its uniforms, was founded in 1922 to guard Nazi party meetings. In time, it grew into the foremost grassroots organization of the Nazi party. Its frequent public demonstrations and brawls with Nazi opponents thrust the SA into public prominence. On June 30, 1934, wary of a challenge to his power, Hitler had the SA leadership (including its head Ernst Röhm) purged in the "Night of the Long Knives." Subsequently, the SA continued to function but with its standing significantly diminished.

SCHUPO
(Schutzpolizei; German, **Protection Police**)

Branch of the ORPO, was responsible for standard police duties within municipal cities and townships with populations greater than 2,000. Prior to 1934, Protection Police units were organized as separate authorities in each province or state within Weimar Germany. In January 1934, the National-Socialist government began to reorganize all police authorities in Germany by placing them under direct national (Reich) control. Adolf Hitler appointed Heinrich Himmler as commander in chief of all police organizations in Germany. Thus began the association and close working relationship of the German Order Police and the SS.

SD
(Sicherheitsdienst des Reichsfuehrers-SS)

Security Service of the SS, set up in 1931 to provide intelligence to the SS. The organization, which became part of the RSHA in 1939, was commanded by Reinhard Heydrich from 1932. During various reorganizations of the SS, the SD essentially incorporated the GESTAPO, and the lines separating their activities remained blurred. The SD, in cooperation with the SIPO, were integrated in the EINSATZGRUPPEN forces operating in occupied east Europe.

SELEKTION
(pl. **Selektionen**; German, **Selection**)

Term used by the Nazis to denote the sorting of ghetto residents, deportees, or prisoners into two groups: those who were designated for forced labor, and those who were to be killed.

SHAVUOT
(Hebrew, **Weeks**)

Festival celebrated on the 6th day of the Hebrew month of Sivan (May-June). This feast, one of three pilgrim festivals to Jerusalem, marked the end of the barley and beginning of the wheat harvest. Shavuot traditionally commemorates the giving of the Tablets of the Law on Mount Sinai.

"SHOPS"

Workshops in the ghettos, usually established by German entrepreneurs. Among the firms active in the Warsaw ghetto were Walther Toebbens, Schultz, Roehrich, Hoffmann, and Schilling, producers of textiles, armaments, and other manufactured goods. The brush-makers' area of the ghetto was a major center of manufacture.

SHTIBL
(pl. **Shtiblech**)

Yiddish term used by Hasidic Jews for their own type of synagogue, combining the functions of a prayer, study, and social center.

SIMHAT TORAH
(Hebrew, **Rejoicing of the Law**)

Joyful festival observed when the annual cycle of the Pentateuch reading in the synagogue is completed and begins anew. It ends the SUCCOT holiday, on the 22nd day of the Hebrew month of Tishrei (September–October).

SÓBIBOR

Second of three death camps created by the Nazis as part of AKTION REINHARD, the Nazi plan to exterminate the Jews from the GENERAL GOUVERNEMENT. The camp was established in March 1942 and was located in the Lublin district of Poland, near the village of Sóbibor. It was shut down in October 1943, after a prisoner uprising. About 250,000 Jews were killed at Sóbibor.

SONDERKOMMANDO
(German, **special force or commando**)

Originally, referred to a German SS unit that carried out special tasks or missions dedicated to the goal of killing Jews, as sub-units of the EINSATZGRUPPEN, or as a unit in Chelmno death camp. The term Sonderkommando was also assigned to units of prisoners selected by the Germans in the Nazi death camps who were forced to facilitate the murder process and dispose of the victims' bodies in the gas chambers and crematoria.

SONDERKOMMANDO ARAIS

Latvian auxiliary force, headed by Viktor Arais, which aided the German SD. This volunteer unit established by the Germans in the early days of July 1941 had on average 200–250 members, peaking with about 1,000 members in 1943. The commando actively participated in the mass murder of the Jews of Latvia, Lithuania, Belarus, Ukraine, and Poland. The members of the unit traveled in blue buses, and thus the operations they participated in were also known as "blue-bus operations." In all, the unit murdered some 30,000 Jews.

SS
(Schutzstaffeln; German, **Protection Squads**)

Originally organized as Hitler's personal bodyguard, the SS was transformed into the "racially pure" elite guard of the Third Reich as well as its main tool of terror and destruction, under the command of Heinrich Himmler. The SS was distinguished by a black cap with a death's-skull emblem, and later by their entirely black uniforms. Racial ideology and mythology was institutionalized in the SS; after Hitler's rise to power, the SS took control of the concentration camps and later implemented the "Final Solution," which aimed to annihilate the European Jewry.

STAROSTA
(Russian, **Head**)

Term used in areas of the Soviet Union to refer to village heads. In a number of ghettos in the Soviet Union, it was applied to the JUDENRAT head.

STATUS QUO ANTE TREND

Hungarian congregations that remained unaffiliated after the split of Jewish communities in 1869, that is, adhering neither to NEOLOGY nor Orthodoxy (hence "Status Quo Ante" as their full nomenclature).

SUCCOT

Jewish holiday that begins on the 15th day of the Hebrew month of Tishrei (September–October) and lasts seven days in Israel and eight days outside Israel. Succot commemorates the makeshift shelters that served as dwellings for the Jews in the desert after the Exodus from Egypt.

SZABASÓWKAS

Polish state schools for Jewish children with Polish instructions held on Sundays instead of Saturdays, the Jewish Sabbath. These schools aimed to advance the Polonization of the Jewish children.

TALMUD TORAH
(Hebrew, **Study of Torah**)

Name given to community schools, especially in Eastern Europe. The Talmud Torah, unlike the HEDER, had various classes, each taught by its own master. It was often funded by the community.

TARBUT
(Hebrew, **Culture**)

Organization dedicated to Hebrew culture and education. Tarbut was founded in Russia at the beginning of the twentieth century and was active throughout Eastern Europe. During the interwar period, a network of schools was set up by Tarbut in Poland and Lithuania. Students studied Hebrew and were encouraged to support Zionism. In 1935, about 38,000 students attended 270 Tarbut schools.

TISHA B'AV

Jewish day of atonement, mourning, and fasting on the 9th day of the Hebrew month of Av (July–August) to commemorate the destruction of the First Temple by the Babylonians (586 BCE) and the Second Temple by the Roman legions of Titus (70 CE) in ancient Jerusalem, the expulsion from Spain (1492), as well as other calamities that befell the Jews throughout history.

TODT ORGANIZATION

Large civil and military engineering concern in Nazi Germany named for its founder, Dr. Fritz Todt. Employed millions of forced laborers, many from concentration and prisoner-of-war camps, to build roads and fortifications.

TOZ
(Towarzystwo Ochrony Zdrowia Ludności Żydowskiej; Polish, **The Society to Safeguard the Health of the Jewish Population**)

Founded in 1917, and affiliated with OZE. The organization promoted preventive medicine and sponsored over 400 hospitals and clinics in some fifty towns. After Poland was occupied by Germany, TOZ became part of the JSS, and in this context, extended medical aid to Jews throughout the occupied areas. In 1942, the German occupation authorities closed the society down.

TRANSNISTRIA

Artificial geographic term created during World War II. Refers to a region in Ukraine between the Bug River to the east and the Dniester to the west, and between the shore of the Black Sea to the south and a line north of the city of Mogilev-Podolskiy. It was granted by Hitler to Romania for the country's support in the campaign against the Soviet Union. After the Romanians occupied

Transnistria, they expelled hundreds of thousands Jews who lived in Bessarabia, Bukovina, and the Dorohoi region to be murdered and confined in dozens of ghettos and camps, such as Bogdanovka, Domanevka, and Akhmetchetka.

TREBLINKA

Last of three death camps established by the Nazis in July 1942, as part of AKTION REINHARD, to exterminate the Jews from the GENERAL GOUVERNEMENT. It was located near the train station of Malkinia in the northeastern part of the General Gouvernment and was active until the prisoner uprising in August 1943. In all, some 870,000 Jews were murdered in the gas chambers at Treblinka.

TZE'IREI ZION
(Hebrew, **Youth of Zion**)

Zionist youth movement founded in Russia and Galicia in 1905. Aligned with the World Zionist Organization, it absorbed scores of youth groups. In the wake of the Russian Revolution, its activities were curtailed in the Soviet Union, and within a few years, the remaining groups outside the Soviet Union had merged with other Zionist youth movements.

TSUKUNFT
(Yiddish, **Future**)

Youth wing of the BUND in interwar Poland, founded in 1919. Led by young adults, Tsukunft addressed problems specific to young workers, especially unemployment and long workdays. Its members organized lectures, libraries, dramatic clubs, choirs, conferences, and summer camps. Membership in Tsukunft numbered 15,000 on the eve of World War II.

TZE'IREI HAMIZRACHI
(Hebrew, **Youth of Hamizrachi**)

Religious-Zionist organization established in Łódź, Poland, in 1917, by religious youth who did not find their place in the existing Zionist youth organizations. The movement espoused Torah values, work, and immigration to the Land of Israel.

UPA
(Ukrainska Povstanska Armyia)

Military wing of the Organization of Ukrainian Nationalists (OUN). During World War II, the UPA fought both Soviet troops and Polish resistance fighters in an effort to achieve Ukrainian independence; along the way they murdered thousands of Polish civilians.

VOLKSDEUTSCHE

Nazi term for ethnic Germans living outside Germany and Austria before the outbreak of World War II. Volksdeutsche residing in the territories conquered by the Nazis were identified on lists and were granted a status equal to that of Germans born in Germany. Many were complicit in Nazi crimes on various levels.

WAFFEN SS

Military branch of the SS. Fought alongside the WEHRMACHT in World War II and was subordinate to SS leader Heinrich Himmler.

WARTHELAND, WARTHEGAU

Territory established by the Germans in October 1939, in the part of Poland that was incorporated into the Reich, namely the pre-war Poznan district and parts of the Bydgoszcz, Łódź, Pomerania, and Warsaw districts. Two large cities, Łódź and Kalisz, were part of the Wartheland. At the beginning of World War II, 4,922,000 people lived in the area, including 385,000 Jews and 325,000 Germans. The Warthegau was run by Arthur Greiser, who intended to turn the region into a model of racial purity. Within weeks, the Germans had taken over all the high posts in the business, political, and economic administration of the region.

From early 1940 to late 1941, the Jews were herded into 173 ghettos and forced labor camps. Beginning in December 1941 through the war years, most of the 385,000 Jews living in the Warthegau were exterminated.

WEHRMACHT

Official name of the German armed forces from 1935 until 1945.

WHITE TERROR

Anti-revolutionary and antisemitic wave of terror that swept through Hungary a few months after the Communist regime of Bela Kun was toppled, in August 1919. During the months of the White Terror, more than 1,500 people—among them Jews—were murdered, and tens of thousands of others were detained in concentration camps or forced to leave Hungary as refuges or political émigrés.

WIZO
(Women's International Zionist Organization)

Established in London in 1920, with a focus on community and family welfare, WIZO was active throughout Europe between the world wars and continues to operate all over the world.

YAVNE SCHOOLS

Network of religious Jewish schools with a Zionist orientation, sponsored by the Mizrachi party in Lithuania and Poland. In 1938, its 235 schools were attended by over 23,000 children.

YEKOPO
(Russian, **The Jewish Relief Committee for War Victims**)

Founded in Russia in 1915, to aid Jews who escaped or had been expelled from the western regions of the Russian Empire during World War I.

YESHIVA
(pl. Yeshivot)

Institution dedicated to advanced rabbinic study. Its curriculum consists almost entirely of the study of Talmudic texts with an all-male student body of teenagers and adults. Yeshivot are not institutions for professional training.

YEVSEKTSIA
(Russian, **Yevreyskaya sektsiya**)

Official section of the Communist party in Soviet Russia, established in 1918 to disseminate the values of Communism among Yiddish speakers, boost productivity among the Jews, and develop Soviet culture and education in Yiddish. The Yevsektsia opposed Zionism and Hebrew culture, and also spearheaded an emphatically anti-religious Soviet policy against Judaism. The section was closed down along with other national sections in 1930.

YOM KIPPUR
(Day of Atonement)

Jewish holiday of atonement, fasting, confession, and prayer on the 10th day of the Hebrew month of Tishrei (September–October). It is the holiest and most solemn day in the Jewish religious calendar, marking the climax of the Ten Days of Penitence, which begin on the New Year, ROSH HASHANA.

ZECHE

Craftsmen and artisans' trade union whose membership was open to Christians only.

ZENTRALE DER JUEDISCHEN AELTESTENRATE IN OSTOBERSCHLESIEN
(German, **Center for the Jewish Elders Council in Upper Silesia**)

Central JUDENRAT of Upper Silesia, established in January 1940, based in Sosnowiec and headed by Moshe Merin. From 1940 to 1943, the Zentrale dominated some forty-five communities with approximately 100,000 Jews. At its peak, the Zentrale had approximately 1,200 employees in its legal, social-welfare, health, supply, education, financial, administrative, and statistics departments and its archive.

SELECTED BIBLIOGRAPHY

GENERAL REFERENCE WORKS AND HISTORIES

Memorial books collection, Yad Vashem Library.

Encyclopedia of Jewish Communities (Pinkas Hakehilot), Jerusalem: Yad Vashem, 1976–2005, in Hebrew.

Spector, Shmuel, ed., *The Encyclopedia of Jewish Life Before and During the Holocaust*. New York: New York University Press, 2001.

GENERAL BOOKS

Arad, Yitzhak. *Belzec, Sobibor, Treblinka: The Operation Reinhard Extermination Camps*. Bloomington: Indiana University Press, 1987.

Bankier, David, and Israel Gutman, eds. *Nazi Europe and the Final Solution*. Jerusalem: Yad Vashem, 2003.

Bartov, Omer, ed. *The Holocaust, Origins, Implementation, Aftermath*. New York: Routledge, 2000.

Bergen, Doris L. *War and Genocide: A Concise History of the Holocaust*. Lanham, MD: Rowman and Littlefield, 2003.

Berenbaum, Michael, ed. *The Holocaust and History: The Known, the Unknown, the Disputed, and the Reexamined*. Bloomington: Indiana University Press, 1998.

Browning, Christopher. *Nazi Policy, Jewish Workers, German Killers*. Cambridge: Cambridge University Press, 2000.

———. *The origins of the Final Solution, The evolution of Nazi Jewish policy, September 1939–March 1942*. London: Heinemann, 2004.

———, et al. *Ghettos 1939–1945. New Research and Perspectives on Definition, Daily Life, and Survival*. Washington, D.C.: United States Holocaust Memorial Museum/Center for Advanced Holocaust Studies, 2005.

Cole, Tim. *Holocaust City, The Making of a Jewish Ghetto*. New York and London: Routledge, 2003.

Dawidowicz, Lucy. *The War Against the Jews, 1933–1945*. New York: Holt, Rinehart and Winston, 1975.

Dwork, Deborah, and Robert Jan van Pelt. *Holocaust: A History*. New York: W.W. Norton, 2002.

Friedman, Philip. "The Jewish Ghettos of the Nazi Era," in *Roads to Extinction, Essays on the Holocaust*. New York and Philadelphia: Jewish Publication Society, 1980, pp. 59–87.

Gilbert, Martin. *The Holocaust, A History of the Jews in Europe during the Second World War*. New York: Holt, Rinehart and Winston, 1985.

Goetz, Aly, and Susanne Heim. *Architects of Annihilation: Auschwitz and the Logic of Destruction*. London: Weidenfeld and Nicolson, 2002.

Gutman, Israel, editor in chief. *The Encyclopedia of the Holocaust*. New York: Macmillan, 1990.

Hilberg, Raul. *The Destruction of the European Jews*. Chicago: Quadrangle Books, 1961 (definitive edition, New York: Holmes and Meier, 1985).

Laqueur, Walter, ed. *The Holocaust Encyclopedia*. New Haven: Yale University Press, 2001.

Marrus, Michael. *The Holocaust in History*, Hanover, NH: University Press of New England, 1987.

McKale, Donald M. *Hitler's Shadow War: The Holocaust and World War II*. New York: Cooper Square Press, 2002.

Rhodes, Richard. *Masters of Death: The SS-Einsatzgruppen and the Invention of the Holocaust*. New York: Knopf, 2002.

Sterling, Eric J., ed., *Life in the Ghettos During the Holocaust*, Syracuse, NY: Syracuse University Press, 2005.

Wistrich, Robert S. *Hitler and the Holocaust*. New York: The Modern Library, 2001.

Yahil, Leni. *The Holocaust: The Fate of European Jewry.* New York: Oxford University Press, 1990.

FORMER U.S.S.R: RUSSIA, UKRAINE, BELARUS, LITHUANIA, LATVIA, ESTONIA

Altman, Ilya. *Victims of Hatred: Holocaust in the USSR 1941–1945.* Moscow, 2002 (in Russian).

Altshuler, Mordechai. *Soviet Jewry on the Eve of the Holocaust, A Social and Demographic Profile.* Jerusalem: Hebrew University Center for Research of East-European Jewry, 1998.

———. "The Unique Features of the Holocaust in the Soviet Union," in Yaacov Ro'i, *Jews and Jewish life in Russia and the Soviet Union.* Ilford: F. Cass, 1995, pp. 171–188.

Arad, Yitzhak. *Ghetto in Flames: The Struggle and Destruction of the Jews of Vilna in the Holocaust.* Jerusalem: Yad Vashem, 1980.

Arad, Yitzhak, *History of the Holocaust—Soviet Union and the Annexed Territories,* Jerusalem: Yad Vashem, 2004 (in Hebrew).

Arad, Y., S. Krakowski, S. Spector, eds. *The Einsatzgruppen Reports.* New York: Holocaust Library, 1989.

Bauer, Yehuda. "Jewish Baranowicze in the Holocaust," in *Yad Vashem Studies* 31, 2003, pp. 95–151.

Chernoglazova, Raisa, ed. *The Tragedy of Byelorussia's Jews. Collection of materials and documents.* Minsk, 1997.

Chiari, Bernhard. *Alltag hinter der Front, Besatzung, Kollaboration und Widerstand in Weissrussland 1941–1944.* Duesseldorf: Droste, 1998.

Cholawski, Shalom. *The Jews of Bielorussia during World War II.* Amsterdam: Harwood Academic Publishers, 1998.

———. *Soldiers from the Ghetto.* San Diego, London: A.S. Barnes, 1980.

Dean, Martin. *Collaboration in the Holocaust, Crimes of the Local Police in Belorussia and the Ukraine.* New York: St. Martins Press, 2000.

Deletant, Dennis. "Ghetto Experience in Golta, Transnistria, 1942–1944," in *Holocaust and Genocide Studies* 18/1 (Spring 2004): 1–26.

Dieckmann, Christoph. "Das Ghetto und das Konzentrationslager in Kaunas 1941–1944," in Ulrich Herbert, Karin Orth und Christoph Dieckmann, *Die nationalsozialistischen Konzentrationslager – Entwickelung und Struktur.* Band I, Göttingen: Wallstein, 1998, pp. 442–43.

Dobroszycki, Lucjan, and Jeffrey S. Gurock, eds. *The Holocaust in the Soviet Union, Studies and Sources on the Destruction of the Jews in the Nazi-occupied Territories of the USSR, 1941-1945.* Armonk: M. E. Sharpe, 1993.

Dubson, Vadim, "Ghettos in the Occupied Territories of the Russian Federation (1941–1942)," in *Bulletin of the Jewish University* 21, no. 3 (2000): 157–84 (in Russian).

———. "On the Problem of the Evacuation of Soviet Jews in 1941" (New Archival Sources), in *Jews in Eastern Europe* 40, no. 3 (1999): 37–56.

Dworzecki, Mark (Meir). *Jerusalem of Lithuania in Rebellion and the Holocaust.* Tel Aviv: Mifleget Po'alei Israel, 1951 (in Hebrew).

Ehrenburg, Ilya, and Vasily Grossman. *The Black Book.* New York: Holocaust Library, 1981.

Einat, A. "Internal Life in the Vilna Ghetto," Ph.D. diss., Hebrew University of Jerusalem, 2006 (in Hebrew).

Fatal-Knaani, Tikva. "The Jews of Pinsk, 1939–1943, Through the Prism of New Documentation," in *Yad Vashem Studies* 29 (2001), pp. 148–82.

Feferman, Kiril. *The Holocaust in the Crimea and the Caucusus,* Jerusalem, 2007 (in Hebrew).

Gerlach, Christian, and Morde Kalkulierte. *Die deutsche wirtschafts–und Vernichtungspolitik in Weissrussland 1941 bis 1944.* Hamburg: Hamburg Edition, 1999.

Gitelman, Zvi, ed. *Bitter Legacy Confronting the Holocaust in the USSR.* Bloomington: Indiana University press, 1997.

Ioffe, Emanuil, Galina Knatko, and Viacheslav Selemenov. *The Holocaust in Byelorussia, 1941–1942.* Minsk, 2002 (in Russian).

Jews in Crimea—A Historical View. Simferopol-Jerusalem, 1997 (in Russian).

Kruglov, Alexander. "Extermination of Jews in Smolensk and Briansk Areas in 1941–1943," in *Bulletin of Jewish University in Moscow* 7, no. 3 (1994): 193–220 (in Russian).

Kruk H. *The Last Days of the Jerusalem of Lithuania; Chronicles from the Vilna Ghetto and the Camps, 1939-1944.* New Haven: Yale University Press, 2002.

Levin, Dov. *Baltic Jews under the Soviets, 1940–1946.* Jerusalem: Yad Vashem, 1994.

————. *Fighting Back, Lithuanian Jewry's Armed Resistance to the Nazis.* New York: Holmes and Meier, 1985.

————. *The Lesser of Two Evils, Eastern European Jewry under Soviet Rule.* Philadelphia: Jewish Publication Society, 1995.

Ofer, Dalia. "Life in the Ghettos of Transnistria," *Yad Vashem Studies* 25 (1996), pp. 175–207 (in Hebrew).

Romanovskii, Daniel, "The Number of Jews Who Perished in the Industrial Cities of Eastern Byelorussia at the Beginning of the German Occupation (June–December 1941)," in *Bulletin of Jewish University*, Moscow-Jerusalem 22 (2000): 151–72 (in Russian).

Rozenblat, Evgeniy, and Irina Yelenskaya, *The Jews of Pinsk*, 1939–1944. Brest, 1997 (in Russian).

Ryvkin, Mikhail, and Arkady Shulman. *The Chronicle of the Tragedy of the Vitebsk Ghetto.* Vitebsk, 2004 (in Russian).

Shachan, Avigdor. *Burning Ice: The Ghettos of Transnistria.* Tel Aviv: Beit Lohamei haGetta'ot, 1988 (in Hebrew).

Shenderovich, M., and A. Litin, *The Destruction of the Towns in Mogilev Area.* Mogilev, 2005.

Smilovitskii, Leonid. *The Catastrophe of Byelorussia's Jews, 1941–1944.* Tel Aviv, 2000 (in Russian).

Sterling, Eric J. *Life in the Ghettos During the Holocaust.* Syracuse: Syracuse University Press, 2005.

Tory, Avraham. *Surviving the Holocaust: The Kovno Ghetto Diary.* Cambridge, MA: Harvard University Press, 1990.

Trunk, Isaiah. *Judenrat, The Jewish Councils in Eastern Europe under Nazi Occupation.* New York: Macmillan, 1972.

Vesterman, M. *Fragments of the Jewish History of Riga, A Brief Guide-Book with a Map For a Walking Tour.* Riga: Museum and Documentation Centre of the Latvian Society of Jewish Culture, 1991.

Zabarko, Boris, ed. *Holocaust in the Ukraine.* London: Vallentine Mitchell, 2005.

Zhits, Dan, *The History Minsk Ghetto in Light of New Documentation,* Ramat Gan: Bar-Ilan University, 2000 (in Hebrew).

CZECHOSLOVAKIA

Bondy, Ruth. *"Elder of Jews", Jacob Edelstein of Theresienstadt.* New York: Grove Press, 1989.

Karny, M., V. Blodig, and M. Karna, eds. *Theresienstadt in der "Endlosung der Judenfrag".* Prague: Theresren staedfer Initiative, 1992.

Redlich, Egon. *The Terezin Diary of Gonda Redlich.* Lexington, KY: University Press of Kentucky, 1992.

Rothkirchen, Livia. *The Jews of Bohemia and Moravia Facing the Holocaust.* Jerusalem: Yad Vashem, 2005.

GREECE

Hondros, J. L. *Occupation & Resistance, The Greek Agony 1941–1944*. New York: Pella, 1983.

Mazower, M. *Inside Hitler's Greece, The Experience of Occupation 1941–1944*, New Haven, London: Yale University Press, 1993.

———. *Salonica, City of Ghosts, Christians, Muslims and Jews, 1430–1950*. New York: Knopf, 2000.

Raphael, Shmuel, *On the Path to the Netherworld, the Greek Jews in the Holocaust,* Tel Aviv: The Institute for the Study of Salonikan Jewry and the Organization of Survivors of Extermination Camps among Jews of Greek Origin in Israel, 1988 (in Hebrew).

Recanati, D. A., ed., *Remembering Salonika, The Greatness and Destruction of the Jerusalem of the Balkans*, 2 vols. Tel Aviv: The Committee for the Saloniki Community, 1972–1986 (in Hebrew).

HUNGARY

Braham, Randolph L. *The Politics of Genocide: The Holocaust in Hungary.* New York: Columbia University Press (revised edition, 1994).

Cesarani, David, ed. *Genocide and Rescue, The Holocaust in Hungary 1944.* Oxford: Berg, 1997.

Cole, Tim, and Graham Smith. "Ghettoization and the Holocaust, Budapest 1944," in *Journal of Historical Geography* 21, no. 3 (1995): 300–16.

Katzburg, N. *Hungary and the Jews. Policy and Legislation 1920–1943.* Ramat Gan: Bar-Ilan University, 1981.

Moskovits, C. *Jesivdk Magyarorszdgon, Adalekok a zsido hitkdzsegek 1944. Aprilisi osszeirasanak torteneti er- teklesehez.* Budapest: Andreas Hess, 1999.

Stark, Tamas, *Hungarian Jews during the Holocaust and after the Second World War 1939–1949: A Statistical Review.* Boulder: East European Monographs, 2000.

Szita, S. *Verschleppt, verhungert, vernichtet. Die Deportation von ungarischen Juden auf das Gebiet des annektierten Osterreich 1944–1945.* Vienna: Eichbauer, 1999.

POLAND

Bender, Sara, *Facing Lurking Death: The Jews of Bialystok during World War II, 1939–1943.* Tel Aviv: Am Oved, 1997 (in Hebrew).

Burstyn-Berenstein, Tatiana, "Forced Transfers to the Warsaw Ghetto during the German Occupation (1941–1942)," *Bletter far Geschichte,* Warsaw: Jewish Historical Institute, 1948, pp. 124–65 (in Yiddish).

———, "The Deportations and Liquidation of the Jews in the Warsaw District," *Bletter far Geschichte*, Warsaw: Jewish Historical Institute, 1951/52, pp. 102–33 (in Yiddish).

Burstyn-Berenstein T., A. Eisenbach, and A. Rutkowski. "The Extermination of the Jews on Polish Lands. Warsaw." Warsaw: Warszawa zydowski Instytut historyczny polsce, 1957 (in Polish).

Czerniakow, Adam. *The Warsaw Diary of Adam Czerniakow.* New York: Stein and Day, 1979.

Eisenbach, A. *The German Policy of the Jews Extermination in 1939–1945, as a Characteristic of German Imperialism*. Warsaw: Warszawa zydowski Instytut historyczny polsce, 1953 (in Polish).

———. *The Question of Equal Rights for Jews in the Polish Kingdom*. Warsaw: Warszawa zydowski Instytut historyczny polsce, 1972 (in Polish).

Engelking B., and J. Leaciak. *The Non-Existent Warsaw Ghetto Guide*. Warszawa: Wydawn, IfiS, Pan, 2001 (in Polish).

Fatal-Knaani, Tikva. *This Is Not the Same Grodno*. Jerusalem: Yad Vashem, 2001 (in Hebrew).

Grynberg M. *The Jews in Ciechanow District 1939–1942*. Warszawa: P.W.N., 1984.

Gutman, Y. *The Jews of Warsaw, 1939–1943, Ghetto, Underground, Revolt,* Bloomington: Indiana University Press, 1982.

———, et al., eds. *The Jews of Poland between Two World Wars*. Hanover, NH, London: University Press of New England, 1989.

Kaplan, Chaim. Scroll of Agony, *The Warsaw Diary of Chaim Kaplan*. New York: Macmillan, 1965.

Krakowski, S. *Chełmno, A Small Village in Europe: The First Nazi Mass Extermination Camp*. Jerusalem: Yad Vashem, 2009.

———. *The War of the Doomed, Jewish Armed Resistance in Poland, 1942–1944*. New York: Holmes and Meier, 1984.

Peled (Margolin), *Y. Jewish Cracow 1939–1943, Resistance–Underground–Struggle*. Tel Aviv: Beit Lohamei haGetta'ot, 1993 (in Hebrew).

Perlis, R. *The Pioneering Youth Movements in Occupied Poland*. Kibbutz Lohamei haGetta'ot: Beit Lohamei haGetta'ot, 1987 (in Hebrew).

Pohl, *D. Von der "Judenpolitik" zum Judenmord: der Distrikt Lublin des Generagouvernements 1939–1944*. Münchner Studien zur neueren Geschichte (3), Frankfurt am Main: Larg, 1993.

Rilski, Henryk. "Mezritsh During the Nazi Occupation," in *Bletter far Geschichte*, Warsaw: Jewish Historical Institute, 1955, pp. 34–50 (in Yiddish).

Ringelblum, E. *Notes from the Warsaw Ghetto, The Journal of Emmanuel Ringelblum*. New York: Schocken Books, 1974, c.1958.

Ronen, Avihu, "The Jews of Zaglembie during the Holocaust," Ph.D. diss., Tel Aviv University, 1989 (in Hebrew).

Rutkowski, Adam. "The Jewish Population in the Radom District," in *Bletter far Geschichte*, Warsaw: Jewish Historical Institute, Warsaw, 1959, pp. 75–118 (in Yiddish).

Sandkühler, T. *"Endlösung" in Galizien – der Judenmord in Ostpolen und die Rettunginitiativen von Berthold Beitz, 1941–1944*. Bonn: Dietz, 1996.

Silberklang, David, "The Holocaust in the Lublin District of Poland." Ph.D. diss., Hebrew University of Jerusalem, 2003 (in Hebrew).

Spector, S. *The Holocaust of Volhynian Jews, 1941–1944*. Jerusalem: Yad Vashem, 1990.

Trunk, Isaiah. *Judenrat: The Jewish Councils in Eastern Europe under Nazi Occupation*. New York: Macmillan, 1972.

Unger, Michal, ed. *The Last Ghetto: Life in the Łódź Ghetto, 1940–1944*. Jerusalem: Yad Vashem, 1995.

Yones, Eliyahu, "The Jews of Lvov during the Holocaust 1941–1944," Ph.D. diss., Hebrew University of Jerusalem, 1994 (in Hebrew).

Zuckerman, Yitzhak. *A Surplus of Memory: Chronicle of the Warsaw Ghetto Uprising*. Berkeley: University of California Press, 1993.

ROMANIA

Ancel, Jean. *The History of the Holocaust: Romania*, 2 vols. Jerusalem: Yad Vashem, 2002 (in Hebrew).

———. *Transnistria*. Bucharest: Atlas, 1998.

Braham, R. *Romanian Nationalists and the Holocaust, The Political Exploitation of Unfounded Rescue Accounts*. New York: Columbia University, 1998.

———, ed. *The Tragedy of Romanian Jewry*. New York: Greenwood, 1994.

Butaaru, I. C. *The Silent Holocaust, Romania and Its Jews*. New York: Greenwood, 1992.

Carp, Matatias. *Holocaust in Romania, Facts and Documents on the Annihilation of Romania's Jews*, 1940–1944. Safety Harbor, FL: Simon, 2000.

Finkelstein, A. *Etre ou ne pas naître, Chronique de Holocauste en Roumanie*. Paris: Etoile de la Pensée, 1997.

Ioanid, Radu. *The Holocaust in Romania, The Destruction of Jews and Gypsies Under the Antonescu Regime, 1940–1944*. Chicago: Ivan R. Dee, 2000.

Safran, A. *Resisting the Storm, Romania, 1940–1947*. Jerusalem: Yad Vashem, 1987.

Siperco, A., ed. *Ecouri dintr-o epoca tulbure, Documente elvefiene 1940–1944*, Bucharest: Hasefer, 1998.

PHOTO SOURCES

Archiwum Państwowe w Lodzi, Poland (APL)

Beth Hatefutsoth Photo Archive, Tel Aviv, Israel (BH)

Bildarchiv Preussischer Kulturbesitz, Berlin, Germany (BPK)

Bundesarchiv, Koblenz, Germany (BA)

> Kutno, page 383: Bundesarchiv, 183-L25174, Photographer: Hugo Jaeger
>
> Salonika, page 683, down: Bundesarchiv, 101I-168-0895-07A, Photographer: Dick
>
> Warsaw, page 900, right: Bundesarchiv, 101I-134-0791-29A, Photographer: Ludwig Knobloch

Braunschweig, Westermann Unternehmensarchiv, Germany (WUB)

Deutsches Historisches Museum, Berlin, Germany (DHM)

Dokumentationsarchiv des Österreichischen Widerstands, Wien, Austria (DOEW)

Fondazione Centro Di Documentazione Ebraica Contemporanea, Milano (CDEC)

Gettyimages-imagebank, Tel Aviv, Israel (TimePix)

Ghetto Fighters' Museum, Photo Archives, Kibbutz Lohamei HaGetaot, Israel (GFH)

Hashomer Hatzair–Moreshet Archives, Kibbutz Givat Haviva, Israel (Moreshet)

Hessisches Staatsarchiv Darmstadt, Germany (HStA Darmstadt)

Hessisches Hauptstaatsarchiv Wiesbaden (HHStAW)

Imperial War Museum, London, United Kingdom (IWM)

Instytut Pamieci Narodoewj, Warsaw (IPN)

Jewish National & University Library, Jerusalem (JNUL)

Jüdisches Museum Frankfurt am Main, Germany (JMF)

Landesarchiv Nordrhein- Westfalen, Hauptstaatsarchiv Dusseldorf (LNWHD)

Landeshaupstadt Stadtarchiv Munchen, Germany (LStAM)

Lithuanian Photographic and Video Archives, Vilnius, Lithuania (LPVA)

Memorial Museum of Hungarian Speaking Jewry, Safed, Israel (MMHSJ)

Museum of the State of Belorussia (MSB)

Staatsanwalt beim Langdericht Hamburg (StLH)

Stadtarchiv Tübingen, Germany (StA Tübingen)

United States Holocaust Memorial Museum, Washington, D.C, U.S.A (USHMM)

Werkarchiv Westermann Braunschweig, Germany (WWBG)

Yad Vashem Holocaust Martyrs' and Heroes' Remembrance Authority Archives, Jerusalem, Israel (YV)

YIVO Institute for Jewish Research, New York, U.S.A (YIVO)

Żydowski Instytut Historyczny Instytut Naukowo-Badawczy, Warsaw, Poland (ŻIH)

MAPS

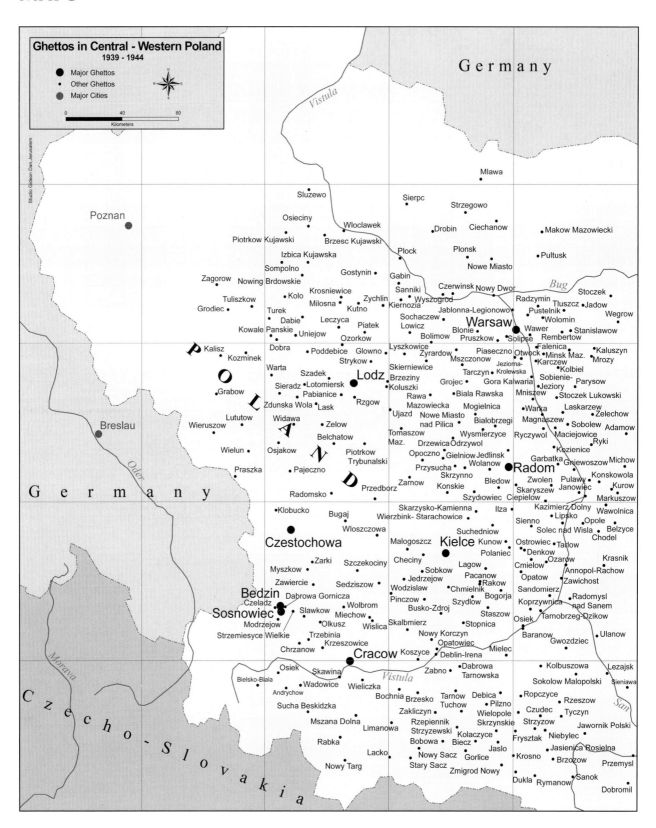

Ghettos in Central - Western Poland 1939–1944

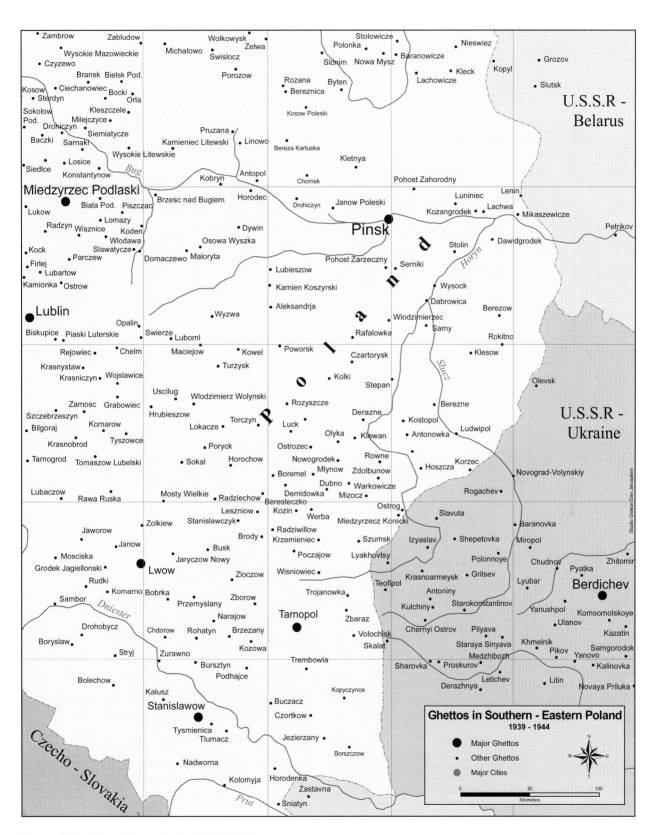

Ghettos in Southern - Eastern Poland 1939–1944

Ghettos in Northen Poland and the Baltic Countries 1939–1944

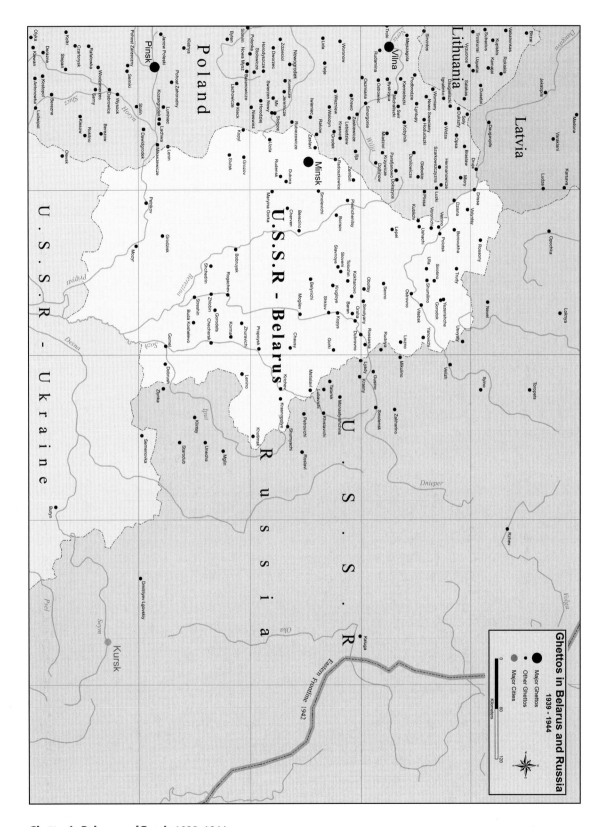

Ghettos in Belarus and Russia 1939–1944

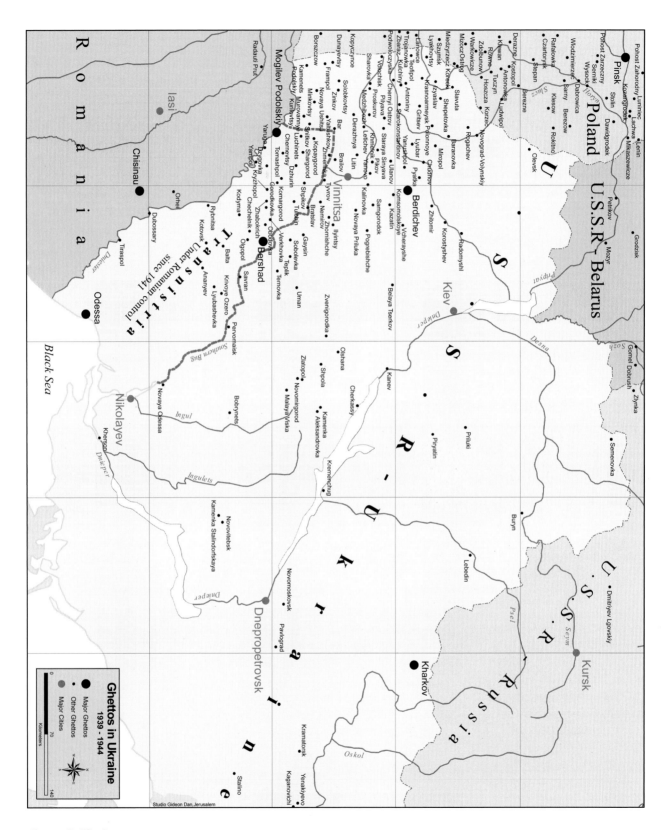

Ghettos in Ukraine 1939–1944

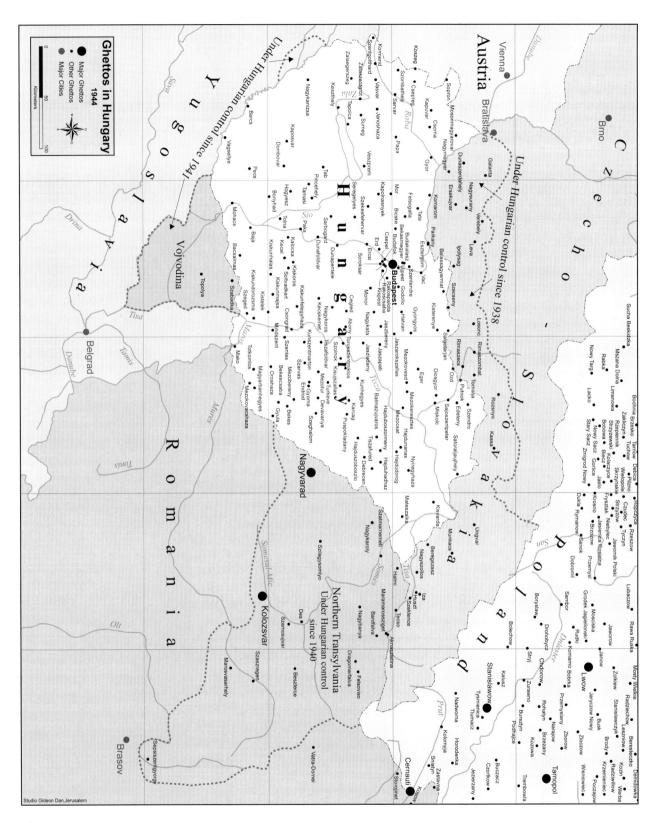

Ghettos in Hungary 1939 –1944

GHETTOS LOCATION

According to the administrative division to which they belonged
through most of the interwar period

CZECHOSLOVAKIA

Theresienstadt (Terezin)

GREECE

Salonika

HUNGARY

ABAÚJ-TORNA COUNTY

Kassa

BÁCS-BODROG COUNTY

Bácsalmács

Baja

Szabadka

Topolya

BARS-HONT COUNTY

Ipolyság

Léva

Verebély

BARANYA COUNTY

Mohács

Pécs

BÉKÉS COUNTY

Békés

Békéscsaba

Endrőd

Gyoma

Gyula

Mezőberény

Orosháza

Szarvas

Szeghalom

Tótkomlós

BEREG COUNTY

Beregszász

Munkács

BESZTERCE-NASZÓD COUNTY

Beszterce

BIHAR COUNTY

Nagyvárad

BORSOD COUNTY

Diósgyőr

Edelény

Mezőkeresztes

Mezőcsát

Mezőkővesd

Miskolc

Ózd

Sajószentpéter

Szendrő

Budapest

CSANÁD-ARAD-TORONTÁL COUNTY

Makó

Magyarbánhegyes

Mezőkovácsháza

CSONGRÁD COUNTY

Csongrád

Kiskundorozsma

Mindszent

Szeged

Szentes

ESZTERGOM COUNTY

Esztergom

Párkány

FEJÉR COUNTY

Bicske

Dunapentele

Ercsi

Érd

Kápolnásnyék

Mór

Sárbogárd

Seregélyes

Székesfehérvár

GÖMÖR AND KISHONT COUNTY

Putnok

Rimaszombat

Rimaszécs

Rozsnyó

Tornalja

GYŐR-MOSON COUNTY

Győr

Mosonmagyaróvár

HAJDÚ COUNTY

Balmazújváros

Debrecen

Hajdúböszörmény

Hajdúdorog

Hajdúhadház

Hajdúnánás

Hajdúszoboszló

Püspökladány

HÁROMSZÉK COUNTY

Sepsiszentgyörgy

HEVES COUNTY

Eger

Gyöngyös

Hatvan

Tiszafüred

JÁSZ-NAGYKUN-SZOLNOK COUNTY

Déványa

Jászapáti

Jászárokszállás

Jászberény

Jászladány

Karcag

Kisújszállás

Kunhegyes
Kunszentmárton
Mezőtúr
Szolnok
Tiszaföldvár
Törökszentmiklós
Túrkeve

KOLOZS COUNTY
Kolozsvár

KOMÁROM COUNTY
Dunaszerdahely
Felsőgalla
Komárom
Nagymegyer
Tata

MÁRAMAROS COUNTY
Aknaszlatina
Bárdfalva
Dragomérfalva
Felsővisó
Huszt
Iza
Máramarossziget
Szeklence
Técső

MAROS-TORDA COUNTY
Marosvásárhely
Szászrégen

NÓGRÁD COUNTY
Balassagyarmat
Kisterenye
Losonc
Salgótarján
Szécsény

PEST-PILIS-SOLT-KISKUN COUNTY
Abony
Békásmegyer
Budafok
Cegléd
Csepel
Gödöllő
Kalocsa
Kecskemét
Kecel
Kiskőrös

Kiskunhalas
Kiskunfélegyháza
Kiskunmajsa
Kistelek
Kispest
Monor
Nagykáta
Nagykőrös
Pestszenterzsébet
Pestszentlőrinc
Rákospalota
Rákoscsaba
Sashalom
Soltvadkert
Soroksár
Szentendre
Újpest
Vác

POZSONY-NYITRA COUNTY
Érsekújvár
Galánta
Nagysurány
Vágsellye

SOMOGY COUNTY
Barcs
Kaposvár
Tab

SOPRON COUNTY
Csepreg
Csorna
Kapuvár
Sopron

SZABOLCS COUNTY
Kisvárda
Nyíregyháza

SZATMÁR COUNTY
Mátészalka
Nagybánya
Nagykároly
Szatmárnémeti

SZILÁGY COUNTY
Szilágysomlyó

SZOLNOK-DOBOKA COUNTY
Dés
Szamosújvár

TOLNA COUNTY
Bonyhád
Dombóvár
Dunaföldvár
Hőgyész
Paks
Pincehely
Tamási
Tolna

UGOCSA COUNTY
Halmi
Nagyszőllős

UNG COUNTY
Ungvar

VAS COUNTY
Jánosháza
Körmend
Kőszeg
Muraszombat
Sárvár
Szentgotthárd
Szombathely
Vasvár

VESZPRÉM COUNTY
Pápa
Veszprém

ZALA COUNTY
Keszthely
Nagykanizsa
Sümeg
Tapolca
Zalaegerszeg
Zalaszentgrót

ZEMPLÉN COUNTY
Sátoraljaújhely

LATVIA

KURZEME DISTRICT
Liepāja
Ventspils

LATGALE DISTRICT
Balvi

Daugavpils
Kārsava
Ludza
Varaklāni
Viļaka

VIDZEME DISTRICT
Madona
Riga

ZEMGALE DISTRICT
Jēkabpils

LITHUANIA

ALYTUS COUNTY
Alytus
Butrimonys (Butrimoniai)
Merkinė

BIRŽAI COUNTY
Biržai
Pasvalys
Pumpėnai (Pampenai)
Vabalninkas

KAUNAS COUNTY
Jonava
Kaunas (Kovno)
Vandžiogala
Vilkija
Zapyškis

KAISIADORYS-TRAKAI COUNTY
Darsūniškis

KĖDAINIAI COUNTY
Ariogala
Cracės
Kėdainiai

KRETINGA COUNTY
Salantai

MAŽEIKIAI COUNTY
Viekšniai

PANEVĖŽYS COUNTY
Krekenava
Kupiškis
Panevėžys

Šeduva
Subačius
Troškūnai

RASEINIAI COUNTY
Kražiai
Raseiniai
Viduklė

ROKIŠKIS COUNTY
Kamajai
Rokiškis

ŠAKIAI COUNTY
Kudirkos Naumiestis
Šakiai

SEINIAI COUNTY
Lazdijai

SEINIAI–LAZDIJAI COUNTY
Rudamina

ŠIAULIAI COUNTY
Bazilionai
Joniškis
Kuršėnai
Radviliškis
Šiauliai
Tryškiai
Žagarė

TAURAGĖ COUNTY
Eržvilkas
Kvėdarna
Tauragė
Žemaičių Naumiestis

TELŠIAI COUNTY
Alsėdžiai
Telšiai

TRAKAI-KAISIADORYS COUNTY
Semeliškės

UKMERGĖ COUNTY
Širvintos
Ukmergė

UTENA COUNTY
Užpaliai
Vyžuonos

VILKAVIŠKIS COUNTY
Vilkaviškis
Virbalis

ZARASAI COUNTY
Dusetai/Dusetos
Salakas

POLAND

BIAŁYSTOK DISTRICT
Augustów
Białystok
Bielsk Podlaski
Boćki
Brańsk
Brzostowica Wielka
Ciechanowiec
Czyżewo
Dąbrowa Białostocka
Drohiczyn
Druskieniki
Grajewo
Gródek
Grodno
Indura
Janów
Jasionówka
Jedwabne
Jeziory
Kleszczele
Knyszyn
Krynki
Kuźnica
Łomża
Łunna
Marcinkańce
Michałowo
Milejczyce
Orla
Piaski
Porozów
Porzecze
Rajgród
Siemiatycze
Skidel
Sokółka
Sopoćkinie
Stawiski
Suchowola

Świsłocz
Szczuczyn
Wasilków
Wołkowysk
Wysokie Mazowieckie
Zabłudów
Zambrów
Zelwa

CRACOW DISTRICT
Andrychów
Biecz
Bielsko-Biała
Bobowa
Bochnia
Brzesko
Chrzanów
Cracow
Dąbrowa Tarnowska
Dębica
Gorlice
Jasło
Kołaczyce
Krzeszowice
Łącko
Limanowa
Mielec
Mszana Dolna
Nowy Sącz
Nowy Targ
Osiek
Pilzno
Rabka
Rzepiennik Strzyżewski
Rzeszow
Sędziszów
Skawina
Stary Sącz
Sucha Beskidzka
Tarnów
Trzebinia
Tuchów
Wadowice
Wieliczka
Wielopole Skrzyńskie
Żabno
Zakliczyn
Żmigród Nowy

KIELCE DISTRICT
Będzin

Białobrzegi
Bogorja
Busko-Zdrój
Chęciny
Chmielnik
Chmielów
Ciepielów
Czeladź
Częstochowa
Dąbrowa Górnicza
Denków
Drzewica
Garbatka
Gniewoszów
Iłża
Janowiec
Jedlińsk
Jędrzejów
Kielce
Kłobucko
Końskie
Koprzywnica
Koszyce
Kozienice
Kunów
Łagów
Lipsko
Magnuszew
Małogoszcz
Miechów
Modrzejów
Mniszew
Myszków
Nowy Korczyn
Olkusz
Odrzywół
Opatów
Opatowiec
Opoczno
Osiek
Ostrowiec Świętokrzyski
Ożarów
Pacanów
Pińczów
Połaniec
Przedbórz
Przysucha
Radom
Raków
Ryczywół
Sandomierz

Sienno
Skalbmierz
Skaryszew
Skarżysko-Kamienna
Sławków
Skrzynno
Sobków
Solec On The Vistula
Sosnowiec
Staszów
Stopnica
Strzemieszyce Wielkie
Suchedniów
Szczekociny
Szydłów
Szydłowiec
Tarłów
Wierzbnik-Starachowice
Wiślica
Włoszczowa
Wodzisław
Wolanów
Wolbrom
Wyśmierzyce
Żarki
Żarnów
Zawichost
Zawiercie
Zwoleń

ŁÓDŹ DISTRICT
Bełchatów
Brzeziny
Bugaj
Chocz
Dąbie
Dobra
Głowno
Grabów
Grodziec
Izbica Kujawska
Kalisz
Koło
Koluszki
Kowale Pańskie
Koźminek
Łask
Łęczyca
Łódź
Lutomiersk
Lututów

Nowiny Brdowskie
Osjaków
Ozorków
Pabianice
Pajęczno
Piątek
Piotrków Trybunalski
Poddębice
Praszka
Radomsko
Rzgów
Sieradz
Sompolno
Stryków
Szadek
Tomaszów Mazowiecki
Tuliszków
TurekV
Ujazd
Uniejów
Warta
Widawa
Wieluń
Wieruszów
Zagórów
Zduńska Wola
Zelów

LUBLIN DISTRICT

Adamów
Annopol-Rachów
Baczki
Bełżyce
Biała Podlaska
Biłgoraj
Biskupice
Chełm
Chodel
Dęblin-Irena
Firlej
Grabowiec
Hrubieszów
Kamionka
Kazimierz Dolny
Kock
Kodeń
Komarów
Końskowola
Konstantynów
Kosów
Kraśniczyn

Kraśnik
Krasnobród
Krasnystaw
Kurów
Łaskarzew
Łomazy
Łosice
Lubartów
Lublin
Łuków
Maciejowice
Markuszów
Michów
Międzyrzec Podlaski
Mordy
Opole
Ostrów
Parczew
Parysów
Piaski Luterskie
Piszczac
Puławy
Radzyń
Rejowiec
Ryki
Sarnaki
Siedlce
Sławatycze
Sobienie Jeziory
Sobolew
Sokołów Podlaski
Sterdyń
Stoczek
Stoczek Łukowski
Świerże
Szczebrzeszyn
Tarnogród
Tomaszów Lubelski
Tyszowce
Wąwolnica
Węgrów
Wisznice
Włodawa
Wojsławice
Zamość
Żelechów

LWÓW DISTRICT

Baranów
Bóbrka
Borysław

Brzozów
Chodorów
Czudec
Dobromil
Drohobycz
Dukla
Frysztak
Gielniów
Gródek Jagielloński
Janów
Jaryczów Nowy
Jasienica Rosielna
Jawornik Polski
Jaworów
Kolbuszowa
Komarno
Krosno
Leżajsk
Lubaczów
Lwów (Lemberg)
Mościska
Mosty Wielkie
Niebylec
Przemyśl
Radomyśl On The San
Rawa Ruska
Ropczyce
Rudki
Rymanów
Sambor
Sanok
Sieniawa
Sokal
Sokołów Małopolski
Strzyżów
Tarnobrzeg-Dzików
Tyczyn
Ulanów
Żółkiew

NOWOGRÓDEK DISTRICT

Baranowicze
Byteń
Dereczyn
Dworzec
Horodyszcze
Horodziej
Iwieniec
Iwje
Jeremicze
Kleck

Korelicze
Lachowicze
Lida
Lubcza
Mir
Nieśwież
Nowa Mysz
Nowogródek
Ostryna
Połonka
Raduń
Rubieżewicze
Słonim
Stołowicze
Stołpce
Świerżeń Nowy
Szczuczyn
Wasiliszki
Wiszniew
Wołożyn
Woronów
Zdzięcioł (Żetl)
Żołudek

POLESYE DISTRICT

Antopol
Bereza Kartuska
Brześć On The Bug
Chomsk
Dawidgródek
Domaczewo
Drohiczyn
Dywin
Horodec
Janów Poleski
Kamieniec Litewski
Kobryń
Kosów Poleski
Kożangródek
Łachwa
Lenin
Linowo
Łuniniec
Małoryta
Mikaszewicze
Pinsk
Pohost Zahorodny
Pohost Zarzeczny
Prużana
Różana
Stolin

Wysokie Litewskie

STANISŁAWÓW DISTRICT

Bolechów
Bursztyn
Gwoździec
Horodenka
Kałusz
Kołomyja
Kosów
Nadwórna
Rohatyn
Śniatyn
Stanisławów
Stryj
Tłumacz
Tyśmienica
Żurawno

TARNOPOL DISTRICT

Borszczów
Brody
Brzeżany
Buczacz
Busk
Czortków
Jezierzany
Kopyczyńce
Kozowa
Leszniów
Narajów
Podwołoczyska
Podhajce
Przemyślany
Radziechów
Skałat
Tarnopol
Trembowla
Zbaraż
Zborów
Złoczów

VILNA DISTRICT

Brasław
Bystrzyca
Daugieliszki
Dokszyce
Dołhinów
Druja
Dukszty
Duniłowicze

Dzisna
Głębokie
Gródek
Hermanowicze
Hoduciszki
Ignalino
Ilja
Kiemieliszki
Kobylnik
Krasne
Krewo
Krzywicze
Lebiedziew
Łużki
Łyntupy
Mejszagoła
Miadzioł
Michaliszki
Miory
Nowo Święciany
Opsa
Ostrowiec
Oszmiana
Parafjanowo
Plissa (Plisa)
Podbrodzie
Postawy
Radoszkowice
Raków
Smorgonie
Soły
Święciany
Świr
Szarkowszczyzna
Troki
Vilna (Vilnius)
Widze
Worniany
Zaśkiewicze

VOLHYNIA DISTRICT

Aleksandrja
Antonówka
Beresteczko
Berezów
Bereżnica
Berezne
Boremel
Czartorysk
Dąbrowica
Demidówka

Deraźne
Dubno
Horochów
Hoszcza
Kamień Koszyrski
Kiwerce
Klesów
Klewań
Kołki
Korzec
Kostopol
Kowel
Kozin
Krzemieniec
Łanowce
Łokacze
Lubieszów
Luboml
Łuck
Ludwipol
Maciejów
Międzyrzecz Korecki
Mizocz
Młynów
Ołyka
Opalin
Osowa Wyszka
Ostróg
Ostrożec
Poczajów
Powórsk
Poryck
Radziwiłłów
Rafałówka
Rokitno
Równe
Rożyszcze
Sarny
Serniki
Stepań
Szack
Szumsk
Torczyn
Trojanówka
Tuczyn
Turzysk
Uściług
Warkowicze
Werba
Wiśniowiec
Włodzimierz Wołyński

Włodzimierzec
Wysock
Wyżwa
Zdołbunów

WARSAW DISTRICT
Biała Rawska
Błedów
Błonie
Bolimów
Brześć Kujawski
Ciechanów
Czerwińsk
Drobin
Falenica-Miedzeszyn
Gąbin
Góra Kalwaria
Gostynin
Grodzisk
Grójec
Jabłonna-Legionow
Jadów
Jeziorna Królewska
Kałuszyn
Karczew
Kiernozia
Kolbiel
Krośniewice
Kutno
Łowicz
Łyszkowice
Maków Mazowiecki
Miłosna
Mińsk Mazowiecki
Mława
Mogielnica
Mrozy
Mszczonów
Nowe Miasto
Nowe Miasto On The Pilicą
Nowy Dwór
Osięciny
Otwock
Piaseczno
Piotrków Kujawski
Płock
Płońsk
Pruszków
Pultusk
Pustelnik

Radzymin
Rawa Mazowiecka
Rembertów
Sanniki
Sierpc
Skierniewice
Służewo
Sochaczew
Solipse
Stanisławów
Strzegowo
Tarczyn
Tłuszcz
Warka
Warsaw
Wawer
Włocławek
Wołomin-Sosnowka
Wyszogród
Żychlin
Żyrardów

ROMANIA

BESSARABIA
Chişinău (Kishinev)
Orhei

BUKOVINA
Czernowitz (Cernăuţi)
Rădăuţi
Storojineţi
Vatra-Dornei
Zastavna

USSR

BELARUS

GOMEL DISTRICT
Buda Koshelevo
Chechersk
Dobrush
Gomel
Gorodets
Korma
Rechitsa
Rogachev
Streshin
Zhlobin
Zhuravichi

MINSK DISTRICT
Borisov
Cherven
Dukora
Grozov (Grozovo)
Kopyl
Maryina Gorka
Minsk
Pleshchanitsy (Pleshchenitsy)
Rudensk
Slutsk
Smolevichi
Uzda
Zaslavl
Zembin

MOGILEV DISTRICT
Belynichi
Berezino
Bobruysk
Chausy
Gorki
Khotimsk
Krasnopolye
Krichev
Krugloye
Lenino
Mogilev
Mstislavl
Propoysk
Shklov

POLESYE DISTRICT
Mozyr
Petrikov
Shchedrin

VITEBSK DISTRICT
Baran
Borovukha I
Drissa
Dubrovno
Gorodok
Kokhanovo
Kopys
Kublichi
Lepel
Liozno
Lyady
Oboltsy
Orsha

Ostrovno
Polotsk
Rossasna
Rossony
Senno
Shumilino
Sirotino
Slavnoye
Sloveni (Slaveni)
Smolyany
Tolochin
Trudy
Ulla
Ushachi
Vetrino
Vitebsk
Volyntsy
Voronichi
Yanovichi
Yezerishche

RUSSIAN FEDERATION

CRIMEAN AUTONOMOUS REPUBLIC
Dzhankoy
Yalta

KALININ DISTRICT
Loknya
Nevel
Opochka
Pustoshka
Rzhev
Sebezh
Toropets

KURSK DISTRICT
Dmitriyev Lgovskiy

LENINGRAD DISTRICT
Pskov
Staraya Russa

OREL DISTRICT
Kletnya
Klintsy
Mglin
Starodub
Unecha
Zlynka

SMOLENSK DISTRICT
Gusino
Ilyino
Khislavichi
Krasny
Lubavichi
Mikulino
Monastyrshchina
Petrovichi
Pochinok
Roslavl
Rudnya
Shumyachi
Smolensk
Tatarsk
Usvyaty
Velizh
Zakharino

STAVROPOL DISTRICT
Mikoyanshakhar

TULA DISTRICT
Kaluga

UKRAINE

CHERNIGOV DISTRICT
Priluki
Semenovka

DNEPROPETROVSK DISTRICT
Kamenka Stalindorfskaya
Novomoskovsk
Novovitebsk
Pavlograd

KAMENETS-PODOLSK DISTRICT
Antoniny
Chernyi Ostrov
Derazhnya
Dunayevtsy
Frampol
Gritsev
Izyaslav
Kamenets-Podolsk
Kulchiny
Letichev
Lyakhovtsy
Medzhibozh
Minkovtsy

Novaya Ushitsa
Pilyava
Polonnoye
Proskurov
Sharovka
Shepetovka
Slavuta
Solobkovtsy
Starokonstantinov
Staraya Sinyava
Teofipol
Volochisk
Zinkov

KHARKOV DISTRICT
Kharkov

KIEV DISTRICT
Belaya Tserkov
Cherkassy
Kanev
Olshana
Shpola
Uman
Zvenigorodka

KIROVOGRAD DISTRICT
Aleksandrovka
Bobrynets
Kamenka
Malaya Viska
Novomirgorod
Zlatopol

THE MOLDAVIAN AUTONOMOUS REPUBLIC
Ananyev
Balta
Dubossary
Kodyma
Kotovsk
Rybnitsa
Tiraspol

NIKOLAEV DISTRICT
Kherson
Novaya Odessa

ODESSA DISTRICT
Krivoye Ozero

Lyubashevka
Odessa
Pervomaisk
Savran

POLTAVA DISTRICT
Kremenchug
Piryatin

STALINO DISTRICT
Kramatorsk
Stalino
Yenakiyevo

SUMY DISTRICT
Lebedin

VINNITSA DISTRICT
Bar
Bershad
Brailov
Bratslav
Chechelnik
Chernevtsy
Dzhurin
Dzygovka
Gaysin
Ilyintsy (Lintsy)
Kalinovka
Kazatin
Khmelnik
Komargorod
Komsomolskoye
Kopaygorod
Kryzhopol
Litin
Luchinets
Mogilev-Podolskiy
Murovannye Kurilovtsy
Myastkovka
Nemirov
Novaya Priluka
Obodovka
Olgopol
• Pikov
Pogrebishche
Samgorodok
Shargorod
Shpikov
Snitkov
Sobolevka

Stanislavchik
Teplik
Ternovka
Tomashpol
Tsibulevka
Tulchin
Tyvrov
Ulanov
Verkhovka
Yaltushkov
Yampol
Yanov
Yaruga
Zhabokrich
Zhmerinka
Zhornishche

VOROSHILOVGRAD DISTRICT
Kaganovichi

ZHITOMIR DISTRICT
Baranovka
Berdichev
Chudnov
Korostyshev
Krasnoarmeysk
Lyubar
Miropol
Novograd-Volynskiy
Olevsk
Pyatka
Radomyshl
Rogachev
Vcherayshe
Yanushpol
Zhitomir

INDEX

The editorial board decided not to place accent marks on names of places listed in the index. Country names are listed as entries only for those where no ghettos existed. Forests and valleys that served as killing sites are included; mountains, seas, and rivers are not.

N